Water Transport in Brick, Stone and Concrete

Water Transport in Brick, Stone and Concrete

Third Edition

Christopher Hall

William D. Hoff

CRC Press
Taylor & Francis Group
Boca Raton London New York

CRC Press is an imprint of the
Taylor & Francis Group, an **informa** business

Third edition published 2022
by CRC Press
2 Park Square, Milton Park, Abingdon, Oxon, OX14 4RN

and by CRC Press
6000 Broken Sound Parkway NW, Suite 300, Boca Raton, FL 33487-2742

© 2022 Christopher Hall and William D. Hoff

First edition published by Taylor & Francis, 2002
Second edition published by Taylor & Francis Group, LLC 2012

CRC Press is an imprint of Informa UK Limited

British Library Cataloguing-in-Publication Data

Names: Hall, Christopher (Materials scientist), author. | Hoff, William D., author.
Title: Water transport in brick, stone and concrete / Christopher Hall, William D. Hoff.
Description: Third edition. | Boca Raton : CRC Press, 2022. | Includes bibliographical references and index.
Identifiers: LCCN 2021001519 (print) | LCCN 2021001520 (ebook) | ISBN 9780367371265 (hardback) | ISBN 9781032033983 (paperback) | ISBN 9780429352744 (ebook)
Subjects: LCSH: Building materials--Moisture. | Building materials--Permeability. | Masonry--Materials--Permeability. | Dampness in buildings.
Classification: LCC TA418.64 .H35 2022 (print) | LCC TA418.64 (ebook) | DDC 693.8/9--dc23
LC record available at https://lccn.loc.gov/2021001519
LC ebook record available at https://lccn.loc.gov/2021001520

ISBN: 978-0-367-37126-5 (hbk)
ISBN: 978-0-429-35274-4 (ebk)
ISBN: 978-1-032-03398-3 (pbk)

Contents

List of Figures

List of Tables

Acknowledgements

We wish to thank the Engineering and Physical Sciences Research Council (and its predecessors) for research grants over many years; this support has made possible much of the research described in this book. We thank UMIST, the University of Edinburgh and Schlumberger Cambridge Research; and also Princeton University for its hospitality to Christopher Hall in 1998. We are grateful to the Universities of Nottingham, Cambridge, Birmingham and London (Birkbeck College) for access to specialist facilities; and to Paul Barnes and to Hans-Wolf Reinhardt for involving us in productive collaborations. We are indebted to many friends and colleagues: to Gerry Meeten, Ken Letherman and Jane Blackford for reading and improving drafts of parts of the text; to Véronique Baroghel-Bouny, Muhammed Basheer, Jim Beaudoin, Luigia Binda, Mark Bomberg, Michele Dondi, Göran Fagerlund, Doug Hooton, Poul Lade, David Lockington, Adrian Long, John McCarter, Leo Pel, Staf Roels, George Scherer, Folker Wittmann and Konrad Zehnder for supplying papers, data, information or advice; to Jesper Arfvidsson, Harold Brocken, Filip Descamps, Bruno Gérard, Leo Pel and Massimo Sosoro for copies of theses; to Jane Blackford and Francis Clegg for SEM images; and to Sarah Taylor for several figures. We are especially indebted to Moira Wilson for reading the whole manuscript.

For the Second Edition

We thank the University of Edinburgh and the University of Manchester; and the UK Engineering and Physical Sciences Research Council, the European Commission, The Royal Society and the Leverhulme Trust for research support. Christopher Hall is grateful to Andrew and Christine Putnis for their hospitality at the Institute of Mineralogy at the University of Münster in 2010. We are indebted to the following for their help in preparing the new edition by providing advice, information, publications and illustrations: Dale Bentz, Delia D'Agostino, Andrea Hamilton, Doug Hooton,

Hamlin Jennings, Leo Pel, Staf Roels, George Scherer, Heather Viles and Moira Wilson.

For the Third Edition

We thank the University of Edinburgh and the University of Manchester; and the UK Natural Environment Research Council and the UK Arts and Humanities Research Council for research support. We are indebted to David Benavente, Tobit Curteis, Rick Davis, Amanda Goode, Andrea Hamilton, Ioannis Ioannou, Gloria Lo, Victoria Pugsley, Maurice Rogers, Jason Weiss, Moira Wilson and Hong Zhang for their kindness in providing advice, comments, information, data, publications, illustrations and materials.

Preface to the Third Edition

The third edition takes account of technical and research publications that have appeared since 2010. Their large number shows the extent of world-wide activity on topics that we cover in this book.

We have made changes to the organization of the book by reversing the order of Chapters 5 and 6, and splitting the long Chapter 8 into two. The reconstructed Chapter 9 also contains new material on driving rain. There is new text on many other topics throughout. New and recalculated data have been added to the Appendices where appropriate.

We have resisted a tempting suggestion to include topics such as leaching and salt crystallization. These processes are essentially chemical, and seem to us to require (and to deserve) a book in their own right.

We state once more our view that continuum descriptions of flow provide the indispensable basis for understanding water transport in building construction and at the supporting laboratory scale. We recognize that this approach should be informed by microscopic and network perspectives, but problems of scale are perhaps less acute in applications in building physics than in hydrology, geology and reservoir engineering.

We express again our gratitude to those who have worked with us for their essential contributions: to all those we thanked previously, and in recent years also Cleopatra Charalambous, Delia D'Agostino, Chi Feng, Isobel Griffin, Vincent Hare, Gloria Lo, Heather Viles and Chunsheng Zhou. We thank particularly Andrea Hamilton for her invaluable and continuing collaboration on many of the topics in this book.

Christopher Hall
William Hoff
Edinburgh, Cambridge and Manchester
September 2020

Preface to the Second Edition

In revising the first edition, we have incorporated some new analyses of important topics in water transport, included many references to new publications (also several to older work previously overlooked), and corrected a few errors.

The purpose of the book is unchanged. We believe that a continuum analysis of water transport in brick, stone and concrete materials is the best available basis for understanding deterioration in built structures. It provides also at least some of the principles for rational building construction.

Perhaps surprisingly, the material that we have expanded the most is that on evaporation in Chapters 7 and 8. The evaporation physics of course is unaltered, but we now show how to couple capillary absorption and evaporation into a model that can be widely applied. In the first edition, this analysis was sketched only in a note. Since 2007, the coupled model has been fully developed. This model deals also with the influences of varying microclimate. It is now becoming obvious that moisture dynamics in building structures is driven overwhelmingly and universally by evaporation. Porous building materials and the structures made from them are continuously (and almost invisibly) engaged in water exchange with their immediate environment. The water transfers at building surfaces largely drive the internal capillary migration of water. These internal flows are the main cause of chemical alteration within materials, and they lead inexorably to alteration and deterioration on the long timescales that apply to buildings.

We express our gratitude again to those who have worked with us for their invaluable contributions: to all those we thanked previously, and in recent years Ceren Ince, Nick Collier, Armin Ellis, Kostas Kyritsis, Victoria Pugsley, and Shaun Savage. We thank particularly Andrea Hamilton for her fine contributions, both experimental and numerical.

Christopher Hall
William Hoff
Edinburgh and Manchester
February 2011

Preface to the First Edition

If there is a science of building, the interplay of water and materials must be one of its themes. There are many processes in building construction and performance that are mediated by water, including of course processes of degradation and decay. Many of the important inorganic building materials, such as brick, stone, tile, plaster, mortar and concrete, are porous and permeable and absorb and transmit water more or less freely. In use, these materials respond to the moisture around them, absorbing water as vapour or liquid, redistributing it within the fabric and in the end breathing it back into the air. There is a delicate and dynamic relation between material and surroundings, which is apparent in good building and architecture.

This book is about a theory of water and its movement in building materials and structures. We use 'theory' in the scientific sense of a framework of ideas, put into physical concepts, quantities and methods of measurement; expressed in mathematical terms for precision and manipulation; and built on observations and experimental tests. The theory we set out has been developed over many years by many people. It drew originally on work carried out by physicists working on the movement of water in soils and there is of course an affinity between building and the land. The relations between buildings and their environments have the same slow and seasonal rhythms; the forms of buildings are the product of climate and landscape; many building materials come from the ground and owe their properties to the character of natural clays, sands and rocks. Perhaps this is why the science of water movement in soils adapts so easily to the water-related phenomena in building structures. However we draw on technical advances and methods in other fields, especially petroleum and chemical engineering, where processes of liquid transfer in porous media are also important; and of course on the results of many years of research in building and civil engineering.

Good theory should be able to explain effects and phenomena not yet explored. Therefore we make no apology for concentrating on the principles and fundamentals of water transport. On the whole, we have not discussed at length the consequences and effects of wetness although we have often noted them. We have aimed above all at coherence because it is lacking in the building physics literature of water transfer and its consequences. We emphasize the engineering scale rather than the microscopic scale, since our aim is to describe water transfer as a continuum process. The microscale is not wholly neglected, but it is not the subject of this book.

We take this opportunity to thank all those who have worked with us over many years for their innumerable contributions: especially but not only Bob Gummerson, Mark Nixon, Mahzad Skeldon, Thanos Kalimeris, Kam Ming Tse, Steve I'Anson, Andrew Platten, Bill Prout, Beom-Gi Yoon, Margaret Carter, Sarah Taylor, Kim Green, Julia Shannahan, Bernard McKay, Ioannis Ioannou, and above all Moira Wilson, who has been an outstanding collaborator. We have been fortunate to work with several fine experimentalists, and in the experimental sciences there is no substitute for experiment.

Christopher Hall
William Hoff
Edinburgh, Cambridge and Manchester
February 2002

1 Porous materials

This book is about the dynamics of water movement in building materials and structures. Our subjects are brick, stone and concrete. We talk of the *absorption* of water when we want to emphasize the entry of water into materials and building elements, *migration* when we are concerned with its movement within the fabric and *desorption* for the loss of water from materials and structures to surroundings.[1]* These processes occur because porosity is the rule in the main classes of building materials. Porous materials are almost invariably permeable and both liquid water and water vapour can penetrate into the pores and permeate through them. The porosity and the mineralogical constitution of inorganic building materials are usually such that liquid water is absorbed spontaneously through the action of capillary forces, and once absorbed migrates freely in response to these same capillary forces. These forces drive the movement of other liquids such as salt solutions and nonaqueous (organic) solvents. Desorption occurs most commonly by *evaporation*.

1.1 DESCRIBING THE POROSITY

The porosity of many materials is visible to the eye: some materials – sands and soils – are granular, and it is easy to imagine the porosity as the connected space between the individual particles. Sedimentary rocks like sandstones and limestones are formed by the consolidation and cementation of sand or calcareous grains in slow geochemical processes. The original particles are joined at points of contact but part of the original intergranular porosity remains. The structure of the rock may be altered gradually by the diagenetic effects of compaction, dissolution and recrystallization. New mineral material forms within the original framework of particles, but equally the surfaces of grains may dissolve or etch or roughen to produce an intricate geometry [637]. Chemical effects are responsible also for binding the particles in cements, concretes and plasters, although the timescale on which they

*Notes are located at the end of each chapter.

work is much shorter. Here again, the microstructure that we see is the result both of removing and of reforming material [111]. In the case of fired-clay ceramics such as brick and tile, the particles of the green clay dehydrate, transform to produce new minerals [340] and then coalesce by the high temperature sintering of partly molten material, a process that also leaves a considerable residual porosity. Raising the firing temperature allows pores to merge and coarsen [1235, 105, 353, 1051, 285]. Other kinds of porosity, often visible to the eye as fissures, arise from the way in which the clay is folded and pressed or extruded as the bricks and tiles are formed [792]. The sizes and shapes of the individual grains and the nature and arrangement of the cementation determine the texture of the material in the hand. The full complexity and character of the porosity can only be appreciated through microscopic examination and by precise measurements. Figures 1.1, 1.2 and 1.3 show microstructures of typical specimens of stone, brick and cement-based materials. We see that each material has a distinct appearance and form, but we also see that in all cases the pore system is irregular, sometimes folded and twisted, and certainly not readily described as having any simple shape or organization. The surfaces of pores and particles are often rough, and there are angular contacts that create crevices and interstices on the most minute scale.

In all cases we see pore features having a wide range of sizes (and still larger and smaller sizes would be found in images of different magnification). In these pictures, there are pores that have widths and lengths ranging from below 1μm to 0.1 mm or more. These features no doubt arise because all these materials are formed by compacting, cementing and sintering particles whose original dimensions were in that size range and the pore space has at least a vestigial relation to the original packing geometry. It is for the same reason that the porosity of these inorganic materials rarely exceeds about 0.35 (in other words the voids comprise 35 per cent of the total volume). A random pile of particles of the same size pack to give a minimum porosity of about 0.36; even slight cementing of the particles reduces this somewhat. If there is a range of particle sizes, the packing density is higher because small particles insert themselves between larger ones.[2] It is therefore difficult to produce a solid material from a granular precursor with a porosity greater than about 0.35. In sedimentary rocks, the grains become cemented about their points of contact by precipitation of secondary minerals. In bricks, the clay and sand particles partially fuse during firing, producing a reduction in overall porosity that is reflected directly in the overall shrinkage of each brick, which may be as much as 10 per cent in length. In cements [1013] and plasters [1116] on the other hand at least part of the ultimate porosity arises from the evaporation of uncombined water during curing. Low porosity cement-based materials can therefore be made by ensuring that the amount of water added to the wet mix is not much more than is needed for complete chemical hydration [675]. As a rule, traditional ceramic and stone

Figure 1.1 The porosity of building materials: I, Clashach sandstone. (a) Coarse structure in a fracture surface, showing the packing of grains, mainly quartz with some potassium feldspar, 0.2–0.5 mm in diameter. (b) Polished surface, displaying the angular pore spaces between grains; quartz grains are mid-grey, feldspar lighter grey and porosity black. Scale bars 200 μm. Back scattered electron micrographs by Francis Clegg.

materials used in practical construction have porosities which fall throughout the range from about 0.3 to close to zero (as, for example, in some engineering bricks, tile ceramics, marbles and granites).

Anhydrous cement as used in the construction industry is composed of particles with a wide particle size distribution. The median diameter is usually around 10–20 μm, but there are much larger particles up to 100 μm and also fine material around 1 μm and less. Dry cement is therefore a mechanical assembly of separate and relatively coarse particles. We shall discuss the

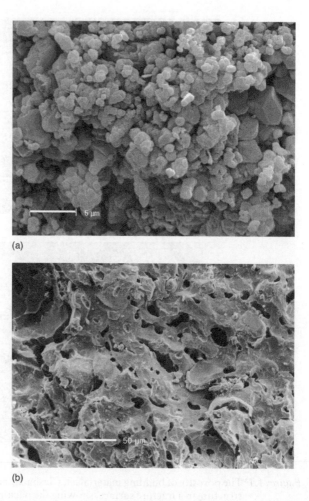

(a)

(b)

Figure 1.2 The porosity of building materials: II, limestone and brick. (a) Lépine limestone, packing of fine calcite grains. Scale bar 5 μm. Scanning electron microscope [SEM] image by Jane Blackford. (b) Fired-clay brick ceramic (UK fletton brick, Oxford clay), fracture surface. Scale bar 50 μm. SEM image by Mahzad Skeldon.

water retention properties of wet slurries in some detail in Chapter 8. The wide particle size distribution means that rather high volume fractions of solids can be achieved in such wet mixes.

The pore structure of fully hydrated cement is radically different from, say, that of a limestone or a sandstone. In these sedimentary stones, the diagenetic cementation of individual grains does not generally destroy the identity of the original mineral grains. In the course of the hydration of a cement most

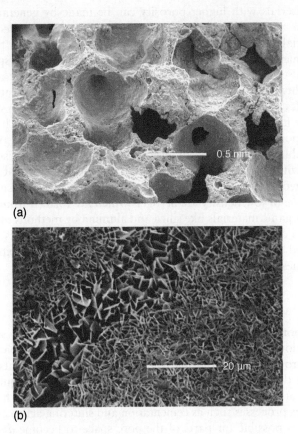

Figure 1.3 The porosity of building materials: III, cement materials. (a) Low
magnification view of the coarse structure of a fracture surface
of autoclaved aerated concrete (bulk density 450 kg/m^3) showing aeration pores. Scale bar 0.5 mm. (b) High magnification view
of microstructure of AAC material shown in (a): linear mesopore,
filled with highly crystalline tobermorite, running between regions
of microporosity. Scale bar 20 μm. Both SEM images by Andrea
Hamilton, reproduced from [621] with permission.

of the original anhydrous material is transformed by a series of complex
chemical reactions into new solid material [322, 648, 202, 19]. Hydration
produces a new pore structure and at the same time consumes much of the
water present in the wet mix, binding this into chemical compounds. Some
of the water is unambiguously chemically combined in solid minerals such
as portlandite, ettringite, or tobermorite (see Figure 1.3b). Other parts of
the water however are bound more or less strongly within noncrystalline or
poorly crystalline material, commonly known as *cement gel*.

Materials with higher porosity can be made by generating gas bubbles within a paste before curing or during firing. These *aerated* or *foamed* materials have microstructures strikingly different from those of sintered or cemented materials, with conspicuous large, roughly spherical aeration voids: see Figure 1.3a. Autoclaved aerated concrete [AAC] and several kinds of lightweight aggregates are formed in this way. To create a stable foam, bubbles must resist the tendency to coalesce. If they remain stable during curing or firing, then the microscale structure is dominated by isolated pores. Incorporating fibres is another good route to materials of high porosity: assemblages of fibres easily become entangled and give rise to bulky materials with low packing densities (like fur and down in nature). Glass fibre, rock wool and asbestos are inorganic examples of such substances. At the extreme of low density are aerogels which are formed from dilute solutions of inorganic materials like silica and alumina by methods of drying that preserve a delicate reticulated solid structure of linked strands. Aerogels can be formed that consist of 99 per cent air or more and have extraordinarily low densities as a result [173].

1.1.1   Connected and disconnected porosity

In a porous medium such as a sand pack, formed from solid particles, it is obvious that all the porosity is *connected*. A nanoscopic ant could wander throughout the void space and eventually visit all points within it.[3] This means that all pore space is available for flow of gas or liquid and is in communication with the environment in which the material finds itself. However, as processes such as cementation and sintering act to reduce the porosity, it is possible for parts of the pore space to become *disconnected*. Disconnections can be of several kinds, but most important for our purposes here is to recognize that some of the pore space may be entirely *closed*, isolated from the rest of the porosity and the surroundings and never to be visited by an ant. Such closed porosity does not contribute to the transport of gases and liquids. It may or may not be counted in the measured porosity: that depends on how the porosity is determined. Pores that arise from gas bubbles dispersed within a precursor paste or generated within a melt are commonly isolated and disconnected from neighbouring pores.[4]

For transport of liquids and gases, only the part of the total porosity which is connected to the boundaries or surfaces is of importance. We call this the *open* porosity to mark the distinction between it and the closed porosity.[5] Closed porosity can be hard to detect and is often counted as part of the solid matrix (where it thus contributes to the solid density).

The analysis of connectivity in porous materials (both of the solid components and of the pore space) is fundamental to the general understanding of their physical properties. Of particular power are *percolation* concepts [415, 1195, 1102, 458, 1237, 606] that show how the properties of porous media depend on the connections between voids, cavities, interstices and fissures that make up the total porosity. Porosity that percolates is connected so that it spans a sample of any length. This means that there is at least one continuous path through the material. If we consider a group of materials of similar structure (say stones or ceramics) we find that as the porosity decreases a point is reached where a percolation path no longer exists. We have already described a simple random granular material made up of spherical particles of equal size. In this porous material, the pores that are formed by the spaces between the touching grains are interconnected. All these pores form part of a single infinite *cluster* of linked porosity. Since the cluster is infinite it spans a region of any size and in particular extends to its surface or boundary. If we now reduce the porosity of this material by crushing the particles together (or equally well if we fuse the particles by sintering), we progressively reduce the size of the pores and eventually the connections between adjacent pores are closed off. Roberts and Schwartz [1068] were the first to describe how this happens in an analysis of the percolation behaviour of their *grain consolidation model*. They showed that for a simple sphere-pack solid which consolidates uniformly the percolation threshold occurs at a critical volume-fraction porosity f_p of about 0.035. Experiments on several different porous materials confirm this. For example, densification of calcite by compression [1372] shows a percolation threshold at $f = 0.04$; and for sintered glass beads [1334], f_p is about 0.03. The existence of a percolation threshold reflects the fact that with decreasing porosity the pores become increasingly isolated and it is more and more improbable that they are connected. At $f < f_p$, there is no cluster that spans a sample, effectively no infinite cluster. The value of f_p of course depends on the nature of the pore space geometry and the way in which for a particular class of materials the pores shrink during consolidation [1141].[6] However, it is a general result of percolation theory that for $f > f_p$ the probability that an individual pore belongs to an infinite percolating cluster increases as $(f - f_p)^\mu$ where μ is a universal critical exponent ≈ 0.40.

We see therefore that the traditional operational and industrial distinction between open and closed porosity in porous construction materials corresponds to the distinction in percolation theory between pores in finite (nonpercolating) and infinite (percolating) clusters. Below the percolation threshold, there can be only closed porosity. Above it, there may be both open and closed porosity, but the proportion of open porosity increases as the total porosity rises.[7]

1.1.2 Defining the porosity

The simplest question we can ask about a porous material is: how much porosity is there? The porosity (or more explicitly *the volume-fraction porosity*), for which we use the symbol f, is defined as the ratio of the volume of the pore space/bulk volume of the material. The porosity f so defined therefore can take values in the range 0 to 1 and is a pure number. For granular materials and suspensions, another quantity is often used: the void ratio e which is defined as volume of pore space/volume of solids.[8] It is easy to see that $f = e/(e + 1)$. When $f = 0$, $e = 0$; when $f = 1$, $e = \infty$. When $e = 1$, $f = 0.5$.

The porosity and void ratio can also be expressed as ratios of densities. We define the bulk density ρ_b as the solid mass/bulk volume, and the solid, matrix or grain density ρ_s as the solid mass/solid volume.[9] In these definitions, the solid mass is often taken to be the weight in air. Then,

$$f = \frac{(\rho_s - \rho_b)}{\rho_s} \tag{1.1}$$

and

$$e = \frac{(\rho_s - \rho_b)}{\rho_b}. \tag{1.2}$$

In some cases, it is useful to make a clear distinction between the open and closed porosity which we denote f_o and f_c. Clearly $f = f_o + f_c$ by definition. Sometimes measured and reported values are of the total porosity f; more often, the quantity implied is the open porosity f_o.

As we have defined it the porosity is clearly a volume average; our definition says nothing about the size of the volume over which we take our average. It is obviously possible to define the porosity as a local quantity, by letting the averaging volume become very small. For many purposes, we shall be happy to take the porosity as the average over the whole volume of a sample or specimen. For example, we may measure the porosity of whole bricks or of 100 mm concrete cubes. If we measure the porosity of each of a batch of bricks, then we shall find differences between the members of the batch. We should suspect that we should also find differences if we took one such brick, cut it into pieces and measured the porosity of each piece. Particularly, we should expect differences between the surface and the interior of clay bricks or concrete products, since these have different firing or curing histories. We must therefore be careful in defining the sampled volume, and if necessary we should state quite explicitly the volume over which the average is taken. There is nothing in principle to prevent the porosity being defined at a point, although on the scale of the pore structure itself this porosity will jump between the values 0 and 1, depending on whether the point is located inside a pore or inside the solid matrix. If we repeat this measurement at many points taken at random and average the answers, we obtain a good estimate of the total porosity. This is the basis of a stereological procedure for measuring the porosity, in which we take a surface cut through the material and count points (either taken at random or more commonly on a grid). The same result is obtained if we place a line across the surface and measure the ratio of the sum of the chord lengths in pores to the total length of the line. These stereological methods provide powerful ways to measure porosity which we discuss further below. They fall within the domain of image analysis.

1.2 MEASURING THE POROSITY

Commonly used methods of measuring the porosity involve penetration of liquid or gas into the pore system (liquid saturation or gas pycnometry). They therefore determine the open porosity. Direct imaging of the pores (stereology and image analysis) and methods that depend on attenuation of radiation count all pores and provide estimates of the total porosity. The total porosity may also be found from independent measurements of the bulk and solid density.

1.2.1 Liquid saturation methods

The most widely used liquid saturation techniques are gravimetric, based on weighing the material in a dry and a saturated state. If we weigh a specimen of bulk volume V_b in both water-saturated and dry states (weights w_s and w_d), then the volume-fraction porosity

$$f = \frac{w_s - w_d}{V_b \rho_w}, \qquad (1.3)$$

where ρ_w is the density of water. f so determined is obviously the open porosity. This procedure is simple in principle but so important in the study of porous construction materials that we shall discuss it carefully. Good results depend on achieving accurate estimates of the quantities w_s and V_b.

In the brick industry, the measurement of porosity has been carried out for many years both for routine quality control and for the purposes of laboratory research. Many test procedures have been published, for example [1062, 1063]. Some are compared in [1316]. The measurement is usually made on whole bricks (sometimes half bricks) and the brick under test is first dried in an air oven at 105 °C. The dried brick is allowed to cool and is then placed in a chamber which is connected to a vacuum pump. The chamber is evacuated by pumping for a prescribed period (typically 5 h) and is then filled with water to cover the sample. The chamber is then returned to atmospheric pressure and the sample left to soak for some hours. The dry weight, the saturated weight and the bulk volume of the sample are used to calculate the open volume-fraction porosity f_o. In practice, the results are often reported as water absorption by weight, $WA = (w_s - w_d)/w_d$ (often as a percentage). WA cannot be directly compared with f unless the bulk density ρ_b is also reported which is often not the case. If it is, then $WA = f\rho_w/\rho_b$.[10]

The procedure we have described is generally known as the *vacuum saturation* method. In a widely used alternative, which avoids the need for a vacuum pump, the sample (a whole brick or perhaps several) is placed in a large container of water, which is brought to boiling point and held there for several hours (see for example the early work of McBurney [801, 802] and ASTM methods [50, 51, 52, 54]). The sample is left to cool under water and then weighed. The rationale is that during heating to boiling air originally within the pores expands and is flushed from the pore system by water vapour and steam generated within the sample. On cooling no permanent gases remain within the pore structure and water is drawn into the open porosity by the combined action of capillary forces and the external atmospheric pressure. The saturated weight may be used to calculate f_o or WA, just as in the vacuum saturation method.

These two procedures are strikingly dissimilar. Comparisons tend to show differences between the results of vacuum saturation and boiling methods applied to the same materials: Table 1.1. However, these differences are not always easy to understand. Peake and Ford [931] found that slightly higher

Table 1.1 Selected results from a round-robin test of British bricks using 5 h boil and vacuum saturation methods. Values given are fractional water absorptions by weight obtained in replicate tests in two laboratories [931]

Brick material	Water absorption WA	
	5 h Boil	Vacuum saturation
Wire-cut Etruria marl solid	0.043	0.011
	0.035	0.010
Hand-made Devonian	0.122	0.123
	0.119	0.119
Wire-cut Keuper	0.303	0.315
	0.306	0.309
Lower Oxford semi-dry pressed	0.256	0.255
	0.254	0.251

values were often obtained by vacuum saturation but for bricks of low porosity the results from a 5 h boiling test were systematically and considerably higher. These authors also showed that for bricks of low porosity the vacuum saturation increased with time of immersion. Wilson *et al.* [1316], using a longer immersion time, presented comparisons for several brick and stone materials which showed that the vacuum saturations were usually higher and in no case lower than the results obtained by the boiling method. There is a similar comparison for concrete which reached similar conclusions [1101]. Yet other results [931] provide cautionary evidence of variations found in a round-robin testing between laboratories. There is a remarkably large spread of values in bricks of low porosity.

These procedures pose several experimental questions.

1 *What is the dry state?* Since we are determining the porosity from the volume of liquid required to saturate the pore space, it is essential that there is no liquid in it initially. We therefore require that the material is well and truly dried, using a procedure such as oven drying to constant weight at a defined temperature. In fact, most porous materials contain small amounts of water under almost any procedure, and making the drying conditions progressively more severe will generally produce step-wise reductions in weight. The long established practice of drying brick ceramic to constant weight at 105 °C in an air oven cannot necessarily be applied to other materials. In particular gypsum and portland cement-based materials are subject to mineral dehydration at temperatures well below this. For cement-based materials, other drying procedures have been developed in which the sample is brought to equilibrium with an atmosphere of controlled water vapour pressure and the use of heat is avoided.[11]

2 *Have we achieved saturation?* The differences between the results obtained by different methods suggest that complete liquid saturation is not easy to achieve and not always attained. For large samples (and especially samples of low porosity and small pore size) the times needed for the saturating liquid to penetrate may be surprisingly long. Likewise the time for air to be removed in the boiling or vacuum pumping stage needs also to be assessed. Given sufficient time for these two processes to occur, the two methods can give estimates of the open porosity which are in close agreement. However, pumping, boiling and immersion times required may be as much as 10 h or more and depend strongly on the size of the sample and the nature of its porosity [1026, 931]. For research purposes, we recommend that suitable pumping and immersion times are established for the particular materials in hand.

3 *How is the bulk volume or bulk density determined?* There are three main methods of determining the bulk volume of a porous material. The first, which is applicable only to rigid materials of regular shape, is by direct measurement of dimensions. For materials that can be cut or cast as cylinders or prisms, this method is easy and for some techni-cal purposes adequate.[12] A second method, which may be used also for irregular specimens, is to apply Archimedes' principle to calculate the volume from the weight of the fully saturated sample suspended in the saturating liquid, normally water. Here $V_b = (w_s - w_A)/\rho_w$ where w_s is the saturated weight in air and w_A is the weight of the saturated sample when immersed in the saturating liquid of density ρ_w. w_A is sometimes called the Archimedes weight. (An alternative and often easier procedure [602] is to measure the gain in weight of the container of immersion liq-uid when a fully saturated sample is suspended in it, as this weight gain equals $w_s - w_A = \rho_w V_b$). The Archimedes method is widely used in technical testing of ceramics, rocks and concrete [351]. A third method,

applicable also to irregular materials, is to immerse the sample in mercury and measure the volume (or mass) of mercury which is displaced (another procedure in which we exploit the inability of mercury to enter the pores of a mineral material).[13] This may be done by direct measurement of volumes or also via Archimedes' principle from the change in weight of a mercury filled container when the sample is immersed in it. These pycnometric methods are described in numerous standards [59, 28] and are capable of giving research results of high quality when carefully applied.[14]

4   *Other sources of error.* In a remarkable but rarely cited paper published in 1921, Washburn and Footitt [1300] reported their investigations of the errors in water absorption methods applied to fired-clay brick ceramic. They recognized the importance of ensuring that the initial dry state and the water contact time are carefully defined. They also showed continuing small increases in the mass of brick ceramic on prolonged boiling which they attributed to chemical alteration of the material by rehydration[15] (see Figure 1.4).

Nonaqueous liquids

In using liquid saturation to determine porosity, we imagine that the liquid passively occupies the open porosity; that it is an inert probe of the pore

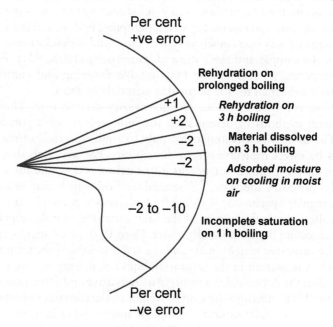

Figure 1.4 Washburn and Footitt's analysis of errors in the measurement of liquid saturation by boiling [1300].

space and does not alter the pore structure in any way, and in particular it does not cause the material to swell. Water is most commonly used, although for many materials water may be unsuitable because of strong interactions with the dry solid. This may be the case for cement-based materials (particularly at early age) and for gypsum and lime plasters. For concrete, procedures have been developed that use various nonaqueous fluids: for example xylene [721] and tetrachloroethene [379, 1004, 192].

Archimedes buoyancy method

Of the various combinations of measurements which may be used to calculate the porosity f from Eqn 1.3, the Archimedes method is the most widely used for brick, stone and concrete. Here three separate measurements are made on the test specimen, all by weighing: the dry weight w_d, the saturated weight (in air) w_s and the Archimedes weight w_A, the weight of the saturated specimen fully immersed in the saturating liquid, usually water.[16] Then from the Archimedes buoyancy relation $V_b = (w_s - w_A)/\rho_w$ and Eqn 1.3 we have

$$f = \frac{w_s - w_d}{w_s - w_A}. \tag{1.4}$$

The bulk density ρ_b and the solid density ρ_s are also be obtained directly, since

$$\rho_b = \frac{w_d \rho_w}{w_s - w_A}, \tag{1.5}$$

and

$$\rho_s = \frac{w_d \rho_w}{w_d - w_A}. \tag{1.6}$$

We note that since the density of the saturating liquid varies with temperature, it is necessary in accurate work to control and measure the temperature if Eqns 1.5 and 1.6 are to be used. For a full analysis of errors and uncertainties in the Archimedes method, see [490, 491].

It also follows from Eqns 1.5 and 1.6 that

$$f = 1 - \rho_b/\rho_s. \tag{1.7}$$

This simple relation (which we have seen already as Eqn 1.1) is exact for a single specimen. It shows that of the three quantities f, ρ_b and ρ_s, only two are independent. Given values of any two, the third is fixed. In practice, porosity tests by the Archimedes method routinely report f, sometimes ρ_b, but rarely the solid density ρ_s. Standard test protocols such as [1062] do not mention the calculation of ρ_s, although as we discuss later this quantity is useful and revealing [490, 491].

Nongravimetric methods

In principle, any quantitative method of estimating the amount of water (or other liquid) in a saturated specimen can be used to obtain the quantity w_s in Eqn 1.3. In practice, direct weighing is generally the method of choice: there is no other common laboratory procedure which can compete with weighing in accuracy. Low-field (benchtop) nuclear magnetic resonance [NMR] instruments provide such information, and are used in some settings, notably in the analysis of rock cores [853, 846], and of foods [1259]. More important for brick, stone and concrete is another technique which measures the volume rather than weight of the liquid in the specimen at saturation, and which we now describe.

Mercury intrusion porosimetry

Mercury intrusion porosimetry [MIP] is a liquid saturation technique that provides an estimate of the pore volume of a small specimen [1329, 551, 1303]. As mercury does not absorb spontaneously into porous solids such as brick and stone it must be forced into the pores under pressure. To do this requires elaborate equipment and this would not be a method of choice for measuring porosity were it not for the fact that MIP provides other information at the same time. (We shall have more to say about this later in the chapter.) Sample size is typically 1–5 cm^3. The method is widely used in many technical fields; its use for soils and rocks is the subject of ASTM [59] and ISO [630] standard test methods. The large hydrostatic pressures applied to the sample (sometimes as great as 4000 bar) may damage the material and alter the pore structure. Such effects have been described in hardened cement paste [893]. Robert [1067] has compared the porosities by MIP and by vacuum saturation of five diverse sedimentary rocks (Table 1.2). There is good agreement over a wide range of porosity.

1.2.2 Helium pycnometry

Helium pycnometry is an established method of determining the solid density, and hence the porosity [28], although employed in construction materials laboratories much less than elsewhere.[17] Helium gas is used as a probe of the open porosity. The amount of gas entering the pore system is calculated from pressure measurements. The solid volume of the sample is measured by expanding a volume of helium into a chamber of known volume containing the sample (Figure 1.5). Knowing the sample weight, the solid density is determined. If the bulk density is known, the porosity is then calculated from Eqn 1.7. Alternatively, the volume of the pore space is estimated by measuring the change in pressure which occurs when a known volume of helium gas expands into the sample. Helium is chosen for its low viscosity and minimal tendency to adsorb on mineral surfaces. Its *PVT* characteristics are well described by the ideal gas law, which simplifies calculations.

Table 1.2 Sedimentary rocks: Comparison of volume-fraction porosity by mercury intrusion porosimetry and vacuum saturation with water [1067]

	Porosity *f*	
	MIP	*Vacuum saturation*
Sandstones		
Fontainebleau	0.123	0.117
grès à meules	0.202	0.210
Limestones		
Mons chalk	0.405	0.407
tuffeau	0.451	0.460
Vuillecin	0.113	0.115

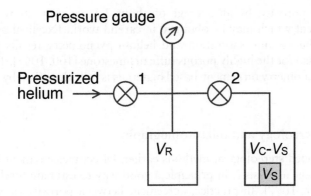

Figure 1.5 Schematic of the principle of operation of the two-chamber helium pycnometer. First, valves 1 and 2 are open and the apparatus is filled with gas. With valve 1 closed and valve 2 open, the initial pressure is measured. Valve 2 is then closed and helium (pressure $\approx$ 10 bar) admitted to the reference chamber volume V_R. Valve 1 is closed. The pressure is noted and then valve 2 is opened to allow the gas to expand into the sample chamber of known (empty) volume V_C. The pressure is again noted and application of Boyle's Law enables the sample solid volume V_S to be determined.

The design of the helium pycnometer (or Boyle's law porosimeter [28]) is discussed in detail by Tamari [1215]. These methods applied to sandstones are comprehensively reported by Luffel and Howard [765]. In Table 1.3, we show a comparison of porosities measured by helium pycnometry and vacuum water saturations for several sandstones and limestones. These results, in which the helium porosity is generally slightly higher than the vacuum

Table 1.3 Sandstones and limestones: Comparison of volume-fraction porosity by helium pycnometry and vacuum saturation with water [385]

	Porosity *f*	
	Helium pycnometry	*Vacuum saturation*
Sandstones		
Clashach	0.132	0.127
Berea	0.185	0.181
Ohio	0.148	0.141
Limestones		
Estaillades	0.327	0.324
Ketton	0.251	0.252
Richemont	0.313	0.303

saturation porosity, by an average of about 2.5 per cent, show the kind of agreement which may be obtained in careful work. Excellent agreement between the vacuum saturation and helium pycnometry results has been reported also for the highly porous tuffeau limestone [100, 1067]. The use of helium pycnometry on cement-based materials is fully described by Aligizaki [19].

1.2.3   Stereology and microtomography

We mentioned stereological methods earlier. Direct measurement by quantitative image analysis is in principle a good way to estimate total porosity [1254, 359, 1097]. In practice, agreement between porosity estimated by image analysis and other methods is often disappointingly poor [1032, 3, 1078, 260]. One general reason for this is that it is difficult to detect pores of widely different sizes in images of fixed magnification: the method has limited dynamic range. For this reason, it is perhaps most useful for estimating subsets of the total porosity which have relatively narrow size distribution, for example air voids [1184, 53]. As a manual method it is laborious; its precision depends on the number of points or traverses sampled. Automated digital image analysis reduces the labour but may increase the error which comes from misidentification or misclassification. The analysis is normally carried out on a cut surface, and both small and large areas can be analyzed to give porosity estimates for correspondingly small or large volumes. Microscopic stereology (which can be applied to electron micrograph images just as well as to images from the light microscope) is perhaps the only method for estimating local porosity on a sub-millimeter scale. We note that routine stereological methods do not distinguish between open and closed porosity and therefore provide estimates of total porosity.

X-ray computed microtomography (*micro-XCT*) offers potential for direct three-dimensional imaging of the pore space in building materials, although at present the method is unable routinely to resolve components of the porosity smaller than 5–10 μm [115, 258, 260, 1100]. Synchrotron X-ray instruments achieve significantly higher resolution (for example, [1025]).

1.2.4   X-ray and gamma-ray attenuation

The intensity of penetrating radiation is reduced in passing though materials to an extent which depends on the composition and the path length. Figure 1.6 shows the attenuation of high energy X-rays in passing through a number of substances commonly found in the matrix of porous construction materials. We show here the *stopping distance* as a function of X-ray photon energy. The attenuation of X-rays can be represented by $I = I_0 \exp(-\alpha\rho_b L)$ where I and I_0 are the transmitted and incident intensities, α is the mass-attenuation coefficient of the material [599], ρ_b the bulk density and L the path length. The stopping distance $L_e = 1/\alpha\rho_s$ is the thickness of solid (zero porosity) material which reduces the intensity by a factor e^{-1}. In the photon energy range up to about 100 keV, attenuation falls rapidly with increasing photon energy and increases strongly with atomic number, but is subject to discontinuous changes at energies characteristic of each element. X-rays with energies in the range 30–150 keV are able to pass through several centimetres of materials such as stone, brick and cement. Steel attenuates X-rays much more strongly while there is considerably less absorption in passing through water. Since the attenuation depends directly on the total amount

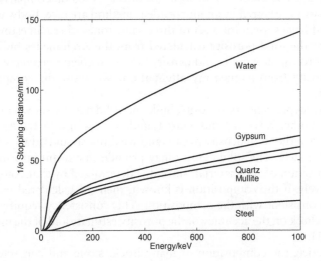

Figure 1.6 1/e Stopping distances of hard X-rays and gamma rays in minerals, steel and water.

of material through which the radiation passes, we can determine the bulk density (and hence the porosity) of a material by measuring the incident and transmitted X-ray intensity [66, 408, 535]. Calibration can be carried out using standard samples of the same composition and known porosity and thickness or by means of calculations based on the elemental composition of the material.

Gamma radiation, with still higher photon energies, say from 50 keV to 10 MeV and greater, has similar penetrating power. At these energies, attenuation is dominated by incoherent Compton scattering. The mass-attenuation coefficients of the elements vary only weakly with photon energy and vary much less with atomic number. Radioactive isotope sources such as caesium-137, which emits gamma rays at 662 keV, are the basis of practical devices for measuring porosity [708, 150].

Similar principles underlie the use of neutron attenuation [998], although the variation of neutron attenuation from element to element is entirely unlike that of X-rays. In particular hydrogen, which is a rather weak absorber of X-rays, is a strong scatterer of thermal neutrons. Neutron attenuation is therefore particularly well-suited to the detection of water and we therefore discuss this method more fully in Chapter 2 as a method of measuring and mapping water contents.

1.2.5   Usefulness of the solid density

For materials whose solid density is known or can be estimated reliably from the composition, the bulk density provides a means of finding the total porosity using Eqn 1.7. Good demonstrations of this based on comparisons with total porosity measured by an independent method are rare. Bodwadkar and Reis [150] have shown for a set of three sandstones, three limestones and a chalk that the total porosity calculated from the Archimedes bulk density and the directly measured solid density are in excellent agreement with the total porosity from gamma-ray attenuation. We show the comparison in Table 1.4.

The interdependence of porosity, bulk and solid density shown by Eqn 1.7 is useful in other ways. If f and ρ_b are found, for example by the Archimedes method, then the solid density ρ_s can (and we think should) always be calculated [490, 491]. The solid density may provide significant information on the composition of the material, since it is determined by that composition. Alternatively, if the composition is known, then the calculated value of ρ_s must be consistent with the composition. This consistency requirement is a valuable check on the accuracy of the porosity estimate and of the underlying data [491].

In practice, the composition of many brick, stone and concrete materials is often known, at least approximately. In some cases, both the identity and the volume fraction of the main constituents have been either found by

Table 1.4 Total porosity: comparison of total volume-fraction porosity *f* from solid and bulk density by Archimedes' method and from gamma-ray attenuation [150]

	Total porosity *f*	
	Archimedes' method	*Gamma-ray attenuation*
Sandstone A	0.168	0.166
Sandstone B	0.141	0.149
Sandstone C	0.217	0.203
Limestone A	0.300	0.300
Limestone B	0.195	0.200
Limestone C	0.158	0.160
Austin chalk	0.190	0.190

direct analysis (for example by X-ray diffraction [XRD]), or inferred from comparison with similar materials. In mortars and concretes, the mix ratio is often known, as is the mineralogy of the sand and aggregate. If so, we can calculate the *composite mineral density* [CMD], ρ_{CM}, of the material. A specimen of solid volume V_s consists of mineral components *i*, each of volume V_{si}, so that

$$\rho_{CM} = \Sigma v_i \rho_i, \tag{1.8}$$

where $v_i = V_{si}/V_s$ is the solid volume fraction of the component *i*, and ρ_i its mineral density [491]. It follows immediately from Eqn 1.7 that for materials of that composition

$$\rho_b = \rho_{CM}(1 - f) \tag{1.9}$$

exactly. For groups of materials of similar composition, this simple linear relation should describe the relationship between porosity and bulk density, at least approximately.

We list the solid densities of some common minerals in Table 1.5.

Limestones provide a straightforward illustration of the link between porosity and bulk density, since most quarry limestones are composed predominantly of the mineral calcite. In Figure 1.7 we show the porosity–bulk density relation for a large number of calcitic limestones. The mineral density of calcite is 2709 kg/m^3, and the intercept of the regression line is close to this value, as is the reciprocal of the slope, in agreement with Eqn 1.9. Any porosity test on a calcitic limestone which yields an outlier value of the solid density should be checked either for experimental error or for an unusual mineral content. Figure 1.7 shows that the porosity of a calcitic limestone can usually be estimated reliably from its bulk density alone. Of course, a minority of building limestones are dolomitic rather than calcitic, and these form a distinct group with a higher solid density.

Table 1.5 Some mineral solid densities [491, 1070, 861, 73]

Mineral	Solid density (kg/m^3)
Calcite	2709
Dolomite	2866
Quartz	2648
Orthoclase	≈ 2590
Anorthite	2760
Mullite	3010–3130
Wollastonite	2909
Diopside	3277
Siderite	3944
Hematite	5275
Goethite	4269
Illite	≈ 2750
Kaolinite	≈ 2645
Portlandite	2246
Gypsum	2305
Ettringite	1778
Tricalcium silicate	3120–3180
Calcium silicate hydrate C–S–H	2650–2720
Tobermorite 11Å	2511
Tobermorite 14Å	2228

There is rather greater compositional variation in sandstones, but even so the solid density of sandstone materials [1160, 490] lies in a narrow range centred on the mineral density of quartz, 2650 kg/m^3. Brick materials show yet greater diversity, but even for these and other fired-clay ceramics the range of solid density is sufficiently small to make it worthwhile to check the consistency of the result of a porosity measurement. Figure 1.8 shows the porosity–bulk density relation for a number of production bricks (see also [490]). While there is considerable scatter, a strong trend is clear. In individual cases, it is possible to reconcile the solid density with the calculated density through the CMD. Here we are not justified *a priori* in assuming a common value of the solid density. Nonetheless the whole dataset is well represented by a straight line of the form of Eqn 1.1 and this allows us to estimate an apparent solid density of about 2680 kg/m^3 for all these bricks as a group. The chemical composition of brick is variable but brick ceramic is composed of quartz and silicate, aluminosilicate and calc-silicate minerals such as feldspars, pyroxenes, gehlenite, wollastonite, together with some glassy material and minor oxides such as hematite and mullite [959, 151, 339, 478, 325, 283, 284, 340, 92, 457]. Typical brick ceramic compositions have solid densities of about 2600–2800 kg/m^3 based on the densities of the individual minerals. If we do know the mineral composition of an individual brick ceramic, it should then be possible to reconcile the measured solid density and the CMD. For example, an archaeological

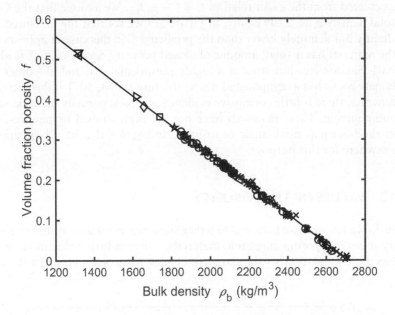

Figure 1.7 Porosity versus bulk density for 133 calcitic limestones: data from [491, 336, 1265, 1074, 306, 259, 302, 1048, 71, 1264, 1267, 1067, 846, 101]. The straight line is $f = 1 - \rho_b/\rho_{CM}$ with $\rho_{CM} = \rho_s = 2709$ kg/m^3, the solid density of mineral calcite.

brick material with a composition found from XRD and XRF analyses had a CMD of 2760 kg/m^3 [530], the same as that obtained by the Archimedes buoyancy method [515]. In this case, the relatively high solid density can be traced to the balance between the intermediate-density feldspar anorthite, the lower-density glass and the high-density hematite.

Estimates of porosities based on arguments from bulk and solid density have been developed most elaborately in relation to hydrated cements [1011, 644, 861]. However, for these materials there has been little or no analysis of the link between the solid density estimated from porosity and the composite mineral density.

Closed porosity

While the mineral composition exerts the dominant control on the solid density of brick, stone and concrete materials, there may in some cases be an influence also from closed porosity. We can illustrate this with the data of Roels [1074] on Savonnières stone, a high porosity calcitic limestone. Roels measured bulk density ρ_b and water absorption porosity f_o on 118 samples taken from a single large block of stone. In Figure 1.9 we show the relation between bulk density and open porosity. The solid line is the total porosity calculated from the exact relation $f = 1 - \rho_b/\rho_s$. We assume that the CMD solid density ρ_s is 2709 kg/m^3. In Figure 1.9 we see that the measured f_o is slightly but definitely lower than the predicted f. In this case, it appears that the material has a small amount of closed porosity, such that f_c/f is about 0.01. Savonnières limestone is a highly porous material and like other carbonate rocks has a complicated microstructure [1074, 307]. Taken broadly, however, there is little conclusive evidence of closed porosity in brick, stone and concrete. These materials have not yet been studied by new research methods such as small-angle neutron scattering [69] that have been applied elsewhere for this purpose.

1.3   VALUES OF THE POROSITY

In Table 1.6 we have gathered together some representative values of porosity in several porous inorganic materials. There is little value in an encyclopedic compilation so the data are chosen to indicate typical values for

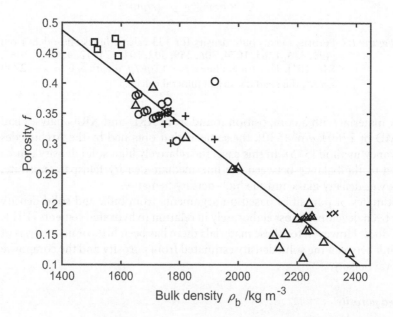

Figure 1.8 Porosity versus bulk density for fired clay brick. A study of 63 bricks manufactured in the United Kingdom [1026, 506]. Symbols □, O, ×, + denote groups of bricks of similar make or type. △ denotes a miscellaneous group of individual bricks of many different types, including several engineering bricks. The straight line is the least squares fit to the whole dataset, $f = 1.022 - 3.821 \times 10^{-4}\rho_b/(\text{kg m}^{-3})$.

Table 1.6 Selected porosity data on construction and similar materials by several methods (water saturation unless noted otherwise)

Material	Scale	Porosity f	Bulk density ρ_b/kg m^{-3}
Calcium silicate brick[a]	140 × 140 × 10 mm	0.359	1689
Dry-pressed clay brick[b]	25 × 15 mm dia cores	0.161–0.255	–
Extruded clay brick[b]	25 × 15 mm dia cores	0.070–0.279	–
Clay ceramic brick[c]	190 × 80 × 40 mm	0.238	2002
Shale brick[d]	40–80 × 25 mm dia cores	0.210–0.274	1665–1895
Sandstone[e]	38 mm dia plugs	0.045–0.141	–
Sandstone[f]	–	0.14–0.24	1950–2150
Sandstone[g]	25 mm dia plugs	0.152	–
Sandstone[h]	38 × 20 mm dia core	0.152	–
Limestone[i]	10 × 25 mm dia discs	0.245	2010
Limestone[j]	75 × 25 mm dia plugs	0.176	2240
Limestone[k]	50 × 50 × 100 mm	0.128–0.286	1930–2359
Quarry rocks[l]	50 × 38 mm dia cores	0.17–0.51	1605–2230
Dolostone[m]	500 mm^3 cubes	0.017–0.050	–
Marble[n]	50 mm^3 cubes	0.002–0.004	2680–2720
Aerated concrete[o]	–	0.822	449.5
Cement-sand mortar[p]	50 × 30 × 7 mm	0.167	2070
Hardened cement paste[q]	–	0.28	1764
Hardened cement paste[r]	60 × 10 mm dia plugs	0.200–0.339	1342–1785
Early-age cement paste[s]	1.5 g fragments	0.095–0.194	–
Hydrated calcium silicate[t]	100 × 100 × 80 mm	0.895	267.6

Notes
a Sand-lime brick, vacuum saturation with water, 3 h immersion, mean of 50 samples, standard deviation SD 0.013; solid density 2635 kg/m^3 [312].
b Canadian clay bricks (23 production brick types), mercury intrusion porosimetry [689, 690].
c Vacuum saturation measurements in four laboratories, SD 0.0047, solid density 2627 kg/m^3 [1077, 490].
d Five Scottish shale bricks, vacuum saturation with water, solid density 2230–2510 kg/m^3 [451].
e Sandstone core plugs, Travis Peak, Texas, comparative tests by three laboratories using helium pycnometry; mean of 18 samples [765, 28].
f Four German building sandstones (Baumberger, Obernkirchner, Rüthener, Sander), solid density 2500–2571 kg/m^3 [700]. For round-robin data on Baumberger and Sander stones with statistical analysis, see [536].
g Clashach sandstone, helium pycnometry, mean of three samples [385].
h Fontainebleau sandstone, helium pycnometry and vacuum saturation, ± 0.002 [67].
i Lépine limestone [663].
j Salem limestone, helium pycnometry [729].
k Seven French and English limestones, vacuum saturation, solid density 2697–2719 kg/m^3 [490]
l Four sandstones and four limestones, vacuum saturation compared with NMR relaxometry, solid density 2638–2702 kg/m^3 [846].
m Five Spanish building dolostones, vacuum saturation [106].
n Six Jordanian archaeological marbles, vacuum saturation, solid density 2720–2730 kg/m^3 [12].
o AAC: vacuum saturation measurements in four laboratories, SD 0.007, solid density 2529 kg/m^3 [1077, 621]; see also [289].
p 1:3 Cement:sand; mean of 26 samples, SD 0.002, solid density 2797 kg/m^3 [287].
q Fully hydrated cement paste: helium pycnometry and arguments based on densities [1013, 1011].
r Three CEM II/A-V cement pastes, w/c 0.30–0.60: porosity by helium pycnometry, compared with MIP, water absorption [1244].
s Total porosity by MIP and NMR relaxometry, evolution during hydration 1–28 d [860].
t Xonotlite insulation material, round-robin study, mean of 71 vacuum saturation measurements in four laboratories, SD 0.001, solid density 2542 kg/m^3 [1077, 526, 527].

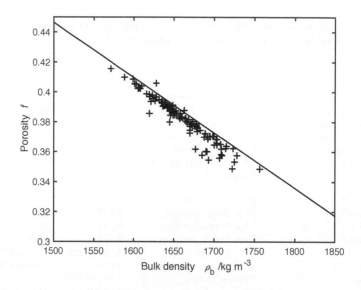

Figure 1.9 Porosity versus bulk density for Savonnières limestone [1073]. The data plotted are measurements on $14 \times 14 \times 14$ mm cubes of stone taken from a single slab $216 \times 180 \times 14$ mm cut perpendicular to the bedding plane. The straight line is $f = 1 - \rho_b/\rho_s$ with $\rho_s = 2710$ kg/m^3, the solid density of mineral calcite.

different materials and also to serve as examples of high quality porosity measurements made by the methods which were described earlier in this chapter. Most of the values are of open porosity f_o.

Other notable sources of data on porosity and bulk density include: Phillips on the physical properties of Canadian bricks [982] (and later statistical analysis by Mallidi [778, 779]); Butterworth on English bricks [207]; Dondi and collaborators on Italian brick [325, 326, 1037]; and Cultrone *et al.* on Spanish brick [283]. For stones, there is Honeyborne on French limestones [585], Leary on British limestones [722] and British sandstones [723], and Hart on British magnesian limestones [538] and British slates [539]. Less comprehensively, Dreesen and Dusar [331] provide useful information on some Belgian building stones; likewise we note Modestou *et al.* [849] on limestones from Cyprus, Siegesmund and collaborators [1161, 1205, 1204] on German stones, Yu and Oguchi on Japanese stones [1357], and Valdeon, Esbert and Grossi [1255] and Vázquez *et al.* [1267] on some Spanish stones. There are extensive statistical analyses of the published petrophysical properties of dimension stones from many localities by Mosch and Siegesmund [855, 854], and of building sandstones by Stück *et al.* [1202]. Some old but still useful information on porosity and density (and mechanical and thermal properties) can be found in International Critical Tables: on building stones (mostly American) [676], and on heavy-clay ceramics [1139]. Hirschwald

[565] provides early data on German stones, and Manger [780] tabulates the porosity and density of some 900 sedimentary rocks, mostly from American, British, German and Swiss sources. There is a general compilation of porosity data on building materials by Whiteley *et al.* [1309].

1.4 PROPERTIES OF THE POROSITY

1.4.1 Temperature dependence

At various points in this book we shall ask how the properties and processes we describe are affected by changes of temperature. Here we consider the porosity. If we measure a porosity f at one temperature T, what is its value at another temperature T'?

If we have a uniform porous material without internal stresses, then its thermal expansion or contraction is identical to that of the (zero porosity) substance which forms its solid matrix.[18] On changing the temperature, the external dimensions of the sample change by a factor $(1 + \alpha_t)(T - T')$ and so also do the dimensions of the pore space (α_t is the thermal expansivity of the matrix material). Therefore f, which is the ratio of the pore volume to the bulk volume, is exactly constant, independent of temperature.

This useful result is not strictly reliable for heterogeneous materials (for example concrete) in which changes of temperature may cause internal thermal stresses to develop as a result of differences in the thermal expansivity of different regions or components of the material. Such thermal stresses may be concentrated (in concrete for example at aggregate/paste interfaces) and may promote crack propagation, with a consequent increase in porosity. The effect on the porosity averaged over large volumes is unlikely to be great but the effect on local porosity may be appreciable.

More generally, it cannot be assumed that the porosity is unaffected by heating in any material subject to thermal dehydration or decomposition. This is particularly true of materials containing chemically bound water, such as gypsum and inorganic cements [1013, 1364]. Thermal cycling may produce progressive dehydration, accompanied by microstructural changes, and progressive changes in the porosity. Similarly changes in porosity may occur in the course of drying or freezing episodes.

1.4.2 Stress dependence

The stress dependence of the porosity is much more complicated than the temperature dependence. In general, compression of a porous material of any kind tends to reduce its volume-fraction porosity. For the simple case of a dry rigid porous material, like brick or stone or concrete, the change in pore volume ΔV_f on compression (produced, say, by applying a compressive load Δp) is similar to the overall change in volume ΔV. That is to

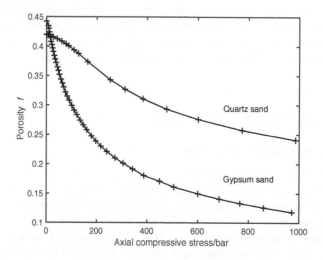

Figure 1.10 Change in the porosity f of hard quartz sand and soft gypsum sand during uniaxial compression [1339].

say, the porosity change accounts for most of the strain. In fact we have $\Delta f = f_0 - f = \Delta V_f/V = \alpha \Delta p/K$, where $K = V\Delta p/\Delta V$ is the bulk elastic modulus of the porous material and α is the Biot coefficient.[19] For sandstones and limestones having porosities of 0.1–0.3, α is typically about 0.8. However since K is around 10 GPa for such materials, the change in porosity is negligible for all but the most extreme loads (a 1000 bar hydrostatic compression gives a reduction of porosity of about one-tenth in Boise sandstone which has $f = 0.26$ at ambient pressure [366, 367]).

For granular materials, changes in porosity occur at much lower stresses. Powders (dry cement, soils, fillers) indeed show large changes in packing density (and hence porosity) when loaded lightly or even on tamping. In this case, the deformation is not elastic. It is a consolidation which comes about by reorganizing the arrangement of particles, and *all* the volume change occurs through porosity reduction. A logarithmic consolidation law is often used, linking the void ratio e to the applied pressure p, such that $e = f/(1 - f) = e_0 - C \ln p/p_0$, where C is a *compression index* and e_0 is the void ratio at some low initial pressure p_0. The kinds of porosity changes which can be found are illustrated in Figure 1.10, which contrasts the compression behaviour of hard and soft granular materials, quartz sand and gypsum sand (meaning here a coarse powder) [1339, 716].

The situation becomes much more complicated if the pores are filled with fluid which is able to exert hydrostatic fluid pressure p_f on the pore walls (or particles), either as a result of being externally pressurized or because the fluid is trapped in the pores and is pressurized by the deformation itself. In this case, the porosity change becomes a function of the effective stress

$p' = p - \alpha p_f$. These cases are treated in the theory of poroelasticity [317] in relation both to rock mechanics and to soil mechanics. However in only one circumstance is there no change in porosity on deformation, and that is when $p = p_f$.

1.4.3 Scale dependence

We have already noted from a practical point of view that if a material is structurally heterogeneous it is important in measuring the porosity to work on specimens which are large enough to comprise a representative portion of the whole material. This principle can be refined by consideration of statistical measures of the variance of composition with specimen size. This is rarely done but within certain testing traditions (soils, bricks, concrete for example) there are rules-of-thumb or recommended procedures which give guidance on the appropriate size and number of specimens.

However, at a rather deeper level, we should recognize that in porous materials of many kinds the porosity is not independent of length scale. Generally speaking, the materials with which we are concerned contain voids of many sizes, ranging from the submicroscopic to the macro-scale (vugs, cracks, wormholes). Clearly, a small sample of dimension l cannot show porosity arising from features of scale larger than l. Furthermore, there is a tendency to bias laboratory samples towards material which is uniform on the scale l, by rejecting specimens which are cracked or which have rough surfaces awkward to seal or measure. If in making a series of porosity measurements on specimens of increasing size, we include new types of voids while retaining all those sampled at smaller l, we reach the conclusion that f will tend to increase with sample size. Thus the selection of appropriate sample size for any type of material is a matter for judgment and objective experimentation.

Such scale-dependent porosity is a feature of *fractal* objects. There is now strong evidence [697] that many natural porous materials have fractal pore structures over several orders of magnitude in length scale. This is true of soils [1057, 1058, 957] and sedimentary rocks [698, 697, 1228, 10, 1036]. The pore structure of most sedimentary sandstones, limestones and shales is fractal from sizes about equal to the size of the individual grain (say 100 μm) to the lowest that can be measured (say 0.01 μm). Likewise, evidence is accumulating that in hydrated cements the texture of the fine-scale gel porosity in the size range 2–500 nm is fractal [22, 996, 19, 1226, 688]. A measure of the density as a function of the scale is itself one of the most direct ways of obtaining the fractal dimension [1058, 1103].

1.4.4 Formation factor

Consider the following experiment. We take a porous material in the form of a rectangular prism and we saturate it with a salt solution (say 1 per cent sodium chloride in water). We measure the electrical conductivity σ_0 of the salt solution and we measure also the electrical conductivity σ of the saturated prism. Next we resaturate the sample (by a suitable displacement process) with a sodium chloride solution of higher concentration. We again measure the conductivities of the solution and the prism. We acquire data at several more salt concentrations. We plot σ against σ_0 and find they are linear: the ratio σ_0/σ is known as the *formation factor F* of the material. Archie [37] found there was such a linear relation for different types of sandstones and then showed, for groups of similar materials such as sandstones or limestones, that the formation factor was determined by the (open) porosity f:

$$F = 1/f^m \tag{1.10}$$

where the exponent m is constant for groups of similar materials; m generally lies in the range 1.5–2.5 [211, 1049].

This deceptively simple relation, known as Archie's law, was presented as an empirical result but is now thought to embody a general and fundamental feature of the structure of porous media and is supported by theoretical arguments [1334, 358, 606]. It holds for most sedimentary rocks and some other granular materials. Attempts to show that Archie's law holds for hydrated cements have been inconclusive [888, 738]. The formation factor describes the connectivity of the pore structure and the Archie exponent m how this depends on the porosity. However both the porosity and the formation factor are dimensionless and F does not depend on the pore size. Thus we can regard it as a bulk property of the material, closely related to the porosity itself.

1.5   PORE SIZE AND ITS MEASUREMENT

Early in this chapter, we said that the simplest question we can ask about the porosity is: how much porosity is there? We have seen that even that question is not so simple. The next question we ask is: what are the sizes of the pores? This is a yet more complicated question (or set of questions) but one which cannot be entirely avoided in a book about fluid transport, even one which strongly emphasizes the continuum approach.

If we look again at the images of Figures 1.1, 1.2 and 1.3, we see immediately the difficulty of assigning a 'size' to the pores in these materials. In the case of the open porosity, which is our main interest, the pore system is by definition of unlimited *length*. The length of the tortuous path through the pores to get from A to B (in particular from one side of a block of material to another) may be much longer than the direct distance AB, but nevertheless is finite (Figure 1.11). This ratio is one measure of the *tortuosity* of the pore system [257, 421]. The tortuosity has nothing to do with the size of

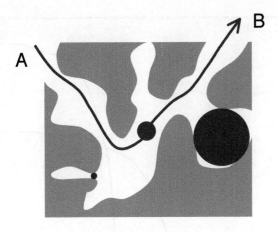

Figure 1.11 Cartoon of a porous material showing tortuosity of a path AB, and
test spheres for passage along AB and for the smallest throat and
the largest cavity.

the pores but entirely depends on the connectivity of the pore system. If we
shrink a porous material by a factor of, say, 10 (maintaining the structure
and of course the porosity constant), the tortuosity is unchanged. The tortuosity (which we denote τ) is in fact closely related to the formation factor F
and one experimental measure is that $\tau = fF$ where f is the porosity [1208].
Typical values of τ for rocks and ceramics lie in the range 2–6. Archie's law
tells us that at least for rocks $\tau = f^{1-m}$, so that the tortuosity tends (for
a group of similar materials) to increase as the porosity falls [421]. τ must
$\rightarrow 1$ as $f \rightarrow 1$, and is not defined below the percolation threshold f_p.[20]

In searching for a characteristic size for the open porosity, we must therefore look instead at measures of the *width* of pores. We might ask, for example, what is the largest object (say a sphere) which can pass through the pore
system? This is limited by the size of the narrow throats which exist within it.
Alternatively we might ask, what is the largest sphere which can be accommodated within the pore system? This of course is determined by the widest
parts of the pore system. In a geometrically regular porous medium, such as
a packing of single-size beads, these sizes are geometrically well-defined. If
we know either one of them we have a complete description of the scale of
the pore system. However, in random porous materials like bricks, stones
and concretes, this approach is inadequate and provides information only
on the extreme features of the pore geometry.

A more complete description of the pore system might be obtained by
using test spheres of many sizes and asking how many of each could be
accommodated within the pores. In practice, something similar is achieved
by the technique of mercury intrusion porosimetry [1329, 59, 777, 1303,
19, 630, 117] which we have mentioned earlier as a method for measuring

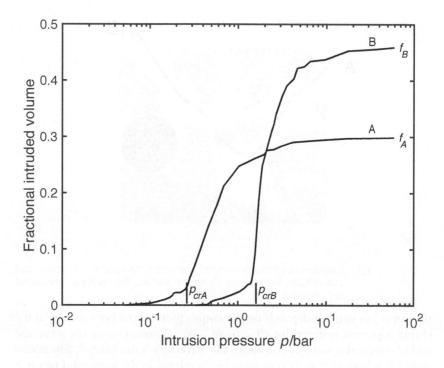

Figure 1.12 Mercury intrusion porosimetry: volume-pressure curves for two different Leicester clay brick ceramics A, B [1026]. p_{crA}, p_{crB} mark the critical pressures, which correspond to critical lengths $l_c = 2r(p_{cr})$ of 56 and 9.2 μm. $f_A = 0.30$, $f_B = 0.46$ indicate the MIP total porosities.

the open porosity. Since mercury does not absorb spontaneously into (*does not wet*) the pores of inorganic materials, it must be driven in by hydrostatic pressure. The pressure p needed for mercury to enter a pore is determined by the radius of curvature r of the mercury meniscus as it passes through the entry throat, so that $rp = 7.354$ μm bar.[21] As we ramp up the pressure, mercury is able to pass through smaller and smaller throats and into finer pores. We can therefore use the volume-pressure curve of any particular material as a description of the sizes present in its open porosity, as shown for two brick materials in Figure 1.12. If we re-express the pressure as a length by using the equation just given, then we obtain a 'pore size distribution.' However, we note that these lengths are simply transformations of the original pressure data and that the notional pore size distribution is just a way of expressing a geometrical property of the pore system [400], in particular one which emphasizes the radius of curvature of the entry throats. We are using mercury, a nonwetting fluid of low compressibility, as a probe of particular features of the pore structure. At the lowest intrusion pressures, MIP sees *accessible* pores with entry dimensions around 100 μm; at the highest pressures used, it detects pores around 2.5 nm. This range is well matched to the primary porosity of many inorganic constructional materials and it is pores in this range which play an important role in capillary transport and degradation processes.

The MIP pore size distribution falls far short of a complete description of the pore geometry and MIP pore sizes should not be interpreted too literally [323, 1078]. Even so, an MIP measurement does establish a characteristic length scale for the pore system. If we shrink a porous material by a factor of 10 in size, then the new MIP pore size distribution will likewise shift precisely by a factor of 10. The MIP volume-pressure curve tells us not so much about pore size distribution as about the percolation properties of the pore system [1102]. At each pressure, the intruded volume is a measure of how much of the pore system is accessible to a test sphere of a given radius. It is generally found that mercury intrusion curves have a roughly sigmoidal shape, reflecting the underlying size distribution and connectivity of pores. The point of inflection of the MIP volume-pressure curve marks the point at which mercury is able to penetrate from the surface layers of the sample into the interior (the 'breakthrough' pressure). This critical pressure p_{cr} therefore corresponds to the percolation threshold, and allows us to assign a characteristic length l_c to the pore system [668, 669]. This can be loosely regarded as the diameter of the largest test sphere which can percolate through the material (Figure 1.12).

We should note for completeness, although we shall not discuss it fully here, that there are several other techniques for probing the size distribution of the porosity. One of these exploits the tendency of condensible gases (such as nitrogen at low temperatures or water vapour) also to recognize the internal curvature of the pore system. Measuring the amount of gas which adsorbs and condenses within a porous material as a function of the gas pressure provides a pore size distribution [447, 631, 632], this time one which puts less emphasis on the size of the entry throats. These *gas adsorption* methods are widely used for materials with fine-scale porosity (nm to μm sizes): they provide useful information on hydrated cements [646, 1225, 19, 643, 1210]. Gas adsorption methods also provide information about the total surface area A_s of the accessible pore system since gas penetrating throughout the open porosity tends to adsorb on all accessible surfaces to form, at low pressures, an adsorbed film a single molecule thick. Making assumptions about the density of such monolayers allows the pore surface area to be estimated from measurements of weight gain or adsorbed gas volume [361, 1227]. The surface area is another property of the pore system which may be used to set a characteristic length which we call $\Lambda_A = V_p/A_s$, the ratio of the pore volume V_p to its surface area A_s, where both are expressed per unit of dry mass. As an example [515], for an English fired-clay brick of porosity f 0.219, bulk density ρ_b 2130 kg/m^3 and A_s 140 m^2/kg, and since $V_p = f/\rho_b$, we have $\Lambda_A = 0.73$ μm.

Information on pore structure may also be obtained from the scattering of neutrons [23, 1040] and X-rays [168]: the angular distribution of the scattered intensity is determined by the spatial distribution of pore/matrix interfaces. Like gas adsorption, these methods [1225, 1041] are sensitive to the fine-scale porosity in the range 10 nm–10 μm. Finally we mention that the freezing temperature of a liquid within the pore system is strongly influenced by the curvature of its interface with the solid matrix. A measurement of the distribution of freezing temperatures within the material is used to estimate pore sizes. This can be done using scanning calorimetry, and then the method is generally known as *thermoporometry* [188, 1210]. The same information can be efficiently (and more commonly) obtained using NMR relaxation methods, when the method is usually called *cryoporometry* [1198, 1200, 1199, 848, 961]. An alternative NMR method exploits the fact that the distribution of proton relaxation times from liquid water reflects the distribution of pore sizes. Such *NMR relaxometry* methods are widely used in characterizing rocks [845], and are proving valuable in research studies of cement pastes [861].

In a perfect world, different methods of measuring the same property would give the same results. But pore size distribution is a subtle and elusive property, especially in cementitious materials. For comprehensive analysis, see [19, 647, 35].

NOTES

1 The term *imbibition* is also now widely used to mean much the same as absorption, the word and its usage having spread from petrophysics into the broader field of porous media hydrodynamics. In biology, imbibition connotes a process in which water uptake is accompanied by swelling of the material, but there is no such connotation in the field of porous media physics and engineering. The loss of liquid water without evaporation is sometimes called *drainage*, especially in soil physics and petrophysics, while desorption by evaporation is widely described as *drying*.

2 The densest packings of equal sized spherical particles have a porosity $f = 1 - \pi/\sqrt{18}$, about 0.26. These are *regular* cubic or hexagonal arrangements (Kepler's conjecture); each sphere makes contact with 12 neighbours. The porosity of a randomly assembled sphere-pack is always greater than this but its exact value depends on how the units stick together. For not-very-sticky particles, f is in the region of 0.4 and each particle is in contact with 7 or 8 neighbours on average. For work on random packings of identical spheres and the effects of jamming, see [1238, 1186, 1239]. If the particles have different sizes, we can achieve higher packing densities. However, with just two sizes of particles, the lowest porosity we can attain is 0.14. In finely powdered materials such as plasters and cements, with a wide range of particle sizes, when loosely packed in air (as they would be in a sack), the porosity is found to be much higher, around 0.7. If these powders form clumps and aggregates the structure may have a fractal porosity, increasing as the distance over which it is measured increases [826]. The density of random packings of rods varies inversely with the aspect ratio of the rod [1312], so that extremely low packing densities are obtained with long rods. Porosities as high

as 0.9 are achieved in insulation materials composed mainly of long needles of the calcium silicate hydrate mineral xonotlite [526].

3 The ant is often met in the literature of porous media as a tireless explorer of networks and percolation clusters. It seems that all the modern ants of statistical physics descend from one put to work by de Gennes in 1976 [415].

4 Closed or poorly connected (almost closed) pores may be formed in other ways. In hydrated cements, *hollow shells* typically a few microns across are produced when individual cement grains slowly dissolve outwards through a hydrated rim [469]. In the dolostones described in [106] the clast particles are porous; as frequently are the ooid grains found in oolitic limestones such as Portland stone [342, 336]. In these cases, the internal porosity of the grains may be poorly connected to that of the matrix in which they are embedded.

5 The term *effective porosity* is also used, especially in petrophysics, for the open porosity.

6 The value of percolation threshold f_p varies greatly from one type of material to another. Thus the grain consolidation model appears to represent well the diagenesis of sandstones. However, the high temperature reactive sintering of industrial ceramics leads to a quite different evolution of the porosity. Work on porcelain tile ceramics [105, 791] shows that the maximum firing temperature has a strong influence. As this increases through the range 1180–1300 °C, the connectivity of the pores is rapidly destroyed. However considerable residual closed porosity exists (f_c 0.08–0.11) in the form of isolated, round pores. If a ceramic is made from calcareous clays, vitrification and the formation of closed porosity occurs at rather lower temperatures [1235, 1236].

7 Although there is no open porosity in the form of sample-spanning infinite clusters below the percolation threshold, there is generally a small amount of porosity below f_p near to and accessible from the surface of an experimental sample of material. Thus surface pores and some finite clusters are 'edge-connected' and may be open to fluid penetration in particular experimental techniques.

8 For suspensions and pastes, the volume fraction of solids, ϕ_s = volume of solids/bulk volume, is also a natural and widely used quantity to employ in describing the composition. ϕ_s is sometimes called the *solidosity* of the material. By definition, $\phi_s = 1 - f$ where f is the volume-fraction porosity and hence is related to the void ratio e by $\phi_s = 1/(e + 1)$.

9 The bulk density is sometimes called the apparent density; and the solid density is variously known also as the real, true or skeletal density.

10 Alternatively, if the solid density ρ_s is reported, then $WA = f\rho_w/[(1 - f)\rho_s]$. ρ_s is rarely measured but may sometimes be known from the composition of the material.

11 To avoid the adverse effects of heating on cement-based materials [270], drying by contact with an atmosphere of low water vapour pressure is often used in research studies, especially on cement pastes. In *D-drying* [279], the air is dehumidified by cooling with solid carbon dioxide, so that the vapour pressure of water is below 1 Pa. Other ways to achieve a low water activity and a controlled removal of water use solvents or sequences of solvents [1367, 1369]. It remains the case that for many practical purposes in testing gentle drying in air is common and satisfactory [221, 36].

12 Measuring the dimensions of the test specimen is a rapid and often excellent way to estimate the bulk volume V_b. However, it can be surprisingly difficult to cut an accurately rectangular block with flat faces, and if that is not achieved simple calculations of V_b may be in error. For such out-of-true specimens, there are more elaborate ways to calculate the volume by measuring the lengths of all edges and

some face diagonals [472], but the extra measurements and calculations nullify the apparent simplicity of the approach.

13 In place of mercury, a free-flowing dry powder may also be used [1289, 1358]. Powder pycnometry requires that the packing density of a powder is reproducible (see Note 2 above), and the accuracy of the method is not yet established.

14 For authoritative accounts of these and other pycnometric methods, see [299, 298]. For guidance on good practice in laboratory weighing, see [294].

15 The mention of *rehydration* by Washburn and Footitt [1300] is apparently the first clear recognition that fired-clay ceramics have a strong tendency to recombine chemically with environmental moisture. This slow continuing rehydration is the cause of long-term *moisture expansion* in bricks. More recently, the associated mass gain has been shown to follow a sub-diffusive kinetic law. We discuss this behaviour of fired-clay ceramics more fully in Chapter 8, p 276.

16 In using the Archimedes buoyancy method to obtain the bulk volume $V_b = (w_s - w_A)/\rho_w$ it is not necessary to use a vacuum-saturated sample but only one sufficiently wet that it does not absorb measurable additional liquid during the test. The sample can be prepared by a simple immersion. On the other hand, the sample used to measure the porosity from the quantity $w_s - w_d$ in Eqn 1.4 must be saturated. This is because the quantity $w_s - w_A$ is not sensitive to incomplete saturation, while quantities w_s and w_A are [491].

17 The method of gas expansion pycnometry was devised 100 years ago by Washburn and Bunting [1299] in the course of Washburn's classic study of porous ceramics, and applied to fired-clay materials. Air, hydrogen and helium were used and little or no difference was found between the results using the three gases. Washburn liked and recommended the method, and it is rapid and easy to use.

18 For experimental evidence that this is so, see Coble and Kingery [261].

19 The Biot coefficient α tells us how the overall volumetric strain is partitioned between the pore space and solid fabric. Strictly, $\alpha = 1 - K/K_s$ where K_s is the bulk elastic modulus of the solid material. When the porosity becomes very small, K approaches K_s and $\alpha \to 0$.

20 The notion of tortuosity as the penalty paid for taking a meandering path through a porous medium is clear enough. But the precise route through the maze is different for charged ions migrating in an electric field (as in measuring the formation factor), for liquids following streamlines in viscous flow, and for molecules diffusing kinetically. Each is longer than the strictly geometrical minimum path length. The electrical, hydraulic and diffusive modes of mass transport have all been used to derive information on tortuosity, but no unifying material property has emerged. Firm numerical values are also elusive, although NMR relaxation times now provide estimates of tortuosity from molecular diffusion rates in porous materials. For example from [1342] we have for limestones: Estaillades, porosity f 0.30, tortuosity τ 3.3; Ketton f 0.25, τ 3.1; Indiana f 0.17, τ 4.0; Portland f 0.16, τ 5.6.

21 This is the Washburn equation for a cylindrical capillary, using the recommended value of 140° for the contact angle of mercury [630] and 0.480 N/m for its surface tension. It was Washburn who first proposed the MIP method in 1921 [1297]. The contact angle for mercury in a porous material is rarely known with any certainty [432, 770, 860].

2   Water in porous materials

In *Walden*, Thoreau [1229] writes: 'When I came to build my chimney I studied masonry. .... I did not plaster till it was freezing weather. I was surprised to see how thirsty the bricks were which drank up all the moisture in my plaster before I had smoothed it, and how many pailfuls of water it takes to christen a new hearth.'

Why bricks are thirsty is the subject of this chapter. We consider why water (and other liquids) are absorbed spontaneously into porous materials and how we can describe in measurable physical quantities the state of water in such a material. We are concerned not only with completely wet materials, in which the entire open porosity is occupied by water (or other liquid), but also with materials in which water and air share the pore space at lower degrees of wetness.

We describe the former state as *saturated* and the latter as *unsaturated*.[1] Building materials in use are far more commonly unsaturated than saturated.

2.1   DEFINING THE WATER CONTENT

The *water content* is the term most commonly used to describe the concentration of water in a material. We define the volume-fraction water content θ of a porous material as the volume of water/bulk volume. This definition is the same as that generally used in soil physics [1086, 788] and is consistent with our definition of porosity f as a volume ratio. Like f, θ is a pure number. For inert materials, the water content at saturation $\theta_s = f_o$, the open porosity. Indeed, the (open) porosity may have been determined directly from the water content at saturation so that this is necessarily so.

These definitions are deceptively simple. The definition of the dry state is important for water content measurement just as it is for porosity. The principle is clear enough: the state $\theta = 0$ must be well-defined and ideally should correspond to the state in which the material has no water within it. However, many of the materials with which we are concerned keep a tenacious hold on some of the water they contain. For all materials, it is essential to adopt a clear operational definition of the nominal dry state $\theta = 0$. By operational, we mean that the state must be defined in terms of reproducible practical procedures: for example, by drying at $105\,^\circ$C in an air oven until the sample reaches constant weight; or by drying over solid carbon dioxide at $25\,^\circ$C.

In theoretical analysis, it is often tidier to use a *reduced* or *normalized* water content $\theta_r = (\theta - \theta_d)/(\theta_s - \theta_d)$. Here θ_s is the operational saturated state and θ_d is the operational dry state. Often $\theta_d = 0$ but in some cases it may be a minimum water content attained in a particular set of procedures. θ_r has values in the range 0 to 1. For many practical purposes, $\theta_r \approx \theta/f_o$.[2]

The water content may also be expressed on a mass or weight basis. In order to avoid any confusion, we use the subscript symbol m to denote quantities calculated from masses: thus the mass-fraction water content $\theta_m = $ mass of water/mass of dry material. θ_m and θ can only be interconverted if the appropriate densities are known since $\theta_m = \rho_w\theta/\rho_b$, and this is often a source of confusion and error in the technical literature. A mixed mass/volume basis is also occasionally used, especially in the brick industry.[3]

Of course, these simple relations hold only if there is no change in the dimensions of the pore framework when air is replaced by water. For many materials, this can be taken to be the case, although there are few materials for which it is exactly true (see later discussions of moisture expansion in brick ceramic and cementitious materials). For instance, in materials which contain soluble components, the reduced water content calculated as θ/f_o may be subject to slight error. In addition – and requiring more attention – there are a number of materials which swell markedly on absorption of water. For such swelling materials, the saturation water content is greater than the volume-fraction porosity measured with a nonswelling fluid (as for example in helium pycnometry). For swelling materials, the water content is commonly expressed as the *liquid ratio* or *moisture ratio* $\nu = $ volume of water/volume of dry solids [975, 155, 1174].[4] This is analogous to the use of the void ratio e for describing porosity and indeed $\nu = \theta(1 + e)$. In a swelling medium, e varies with water content and $e(\nu)$ is a material property. At saturation $e = \nu$.

It is also to be noted that the water content is usually calculated by measuring a weight rather than by measuring a volume directly. In calculating θ, it is assumed that the water within the material has the density of pure liquid water at the same temperature. This assumption is normally uncontentious, but may introduce slight errors in the case of materials containing soluble components (so that an aqueous solution, most commonly a salt solution, occupies the pores); or in fine-grained materials where most of the water is in close nanoscale proximity to mineral surfaces.[5]

2.2 MEASURING THE WATER CONTENT

Methods of measuring water content are numerous and vary greatly in accuracy, ease of use and reliability [1336, 921, 885]. We have grouped them loosely into *direct* and *indirect* methods. The direct methods are those in which the water content is estimated by removing the water from a sample of the material and then determining its amount by a weight or volume measurement or by chemical analysis. The indirect methods depend on the measurement of a physical property (such as the electrical resistivity) of the material which is known to change as the moisture content changes. The indirect methods require calibration. In general, direct methods are capable of higher accuracy and are used as the means of calibrating the indirect methods. Of the many techniques available, some are well suited to laboratory use; others can be used for field and survey purposes [8]. Methods vary considerably in the amount of material required or the volume over which the measurement is averaged. Techniques which can provide localized estimates of water content and therefore allow water content *distributions* to be mapped are of special interest, as are those that record changes of water content with time. Many of the methods used for determining water contents in soils are applicable to porous building materials [901, 1179, 788, 1211].

2.2.1 Direct methods

Gravimetric methods

Methods based on weighing are nearly always preferred in laboratory determinations of water content. Standard laboratory gravimetric balances allow weights to be determined to 1 part in 10^4 or better, so that small weight changes in bulk samples can be determined with considerable precision. Typical procedures consist of weighing material in the wet state and after drying in an air oven at 105 °C to constant weight to determine the weight change due to loss of water (see for example [626]). Such operations can be applied to samples ranging in size from 0.1 g to 5 kg or more.

Chemical analysis of water

Free water (that is, water which is not chemically combined) can be determined accurately by several standard analytical methods. Among the best known is the Karl Fischer method [847, 623] in which the sample is added to an iodine/sulphur trioxide reagent in dry methanol. Water reacts quantitatively to liberate iodide ion which is determined by titration. This method is widely used in routine technical analysis, for example of foodstuffs [1138] and soils [1028, 1362], but little used in the analysis of construction materials.

A less accurate chemical method exploits the reaction between calcium carbide and water to generate acetylene gas. This is the basis of a long established field test for water content in building materials, widely used especially in brickwork (see for example [874, 132, 1001]). The carbide reagent and the sample (usually a powder sample drilled from the structure under investigation) are combined in a sealed container and the amount of gas evolved is estimated from the rise in pressure.

2.2.2   Indirect methods

Almost every physical property of a porous material is altered by the presence of water in its pores. Even so, only a few properties have been successfully used as the basis of methods of water content measurement, either in the laboratory or on site.

Neutron radiography

As we noted in Chapter 1 a beam of thermal neutrons is strongly attenuated by hydrogen (mainly by scattering), and therefore by water and organic liquids such as hydrocarbons [950, 949]. However, the other elements which are present in common inorganic masonry materials are weak neutron absorbers and scatterers. Neutron radiography therefore provides a strong contrast between wet and dry regions of a partially saturated porous material and is a powerful research technique for measuring water content distributions nondestructively. Neutron radiography can be used to map water content distributions over the whole range of porous construction materials, as shown in early work [704, 300, 455, 1017, 942, 659, 576, 999, 1000]. The technique continues to be of value in well-conceived research studies, for example on drying [1157, 1155, 1274], transport through interfaces [1371], barrier properties [169], capillary imbibition [541, 820, 761, 1042, 762] and transport in fractures [1366]. Instrumentation and applications in cement-based materials are reviewed in [1365]. Most neutron radiography uses the powerful neutron sources available only at nuclear reactor and spallation facilities. Occasionally [576] smaller electron-accelerator sources have been employed, and there is renewed interest in these [1349]. Safety and cost militate against the use in building physics of the isotope sources that are established methods in hydrology and geophysical logging.[6]

The attenuation of a beam of neutrons passing through a material of thickness L is described by the equation $I = I_0 \exp(-\alpha \rho_b L)$, where I_0 is the incident intensity and α is the mass-attenuation coefficient of the material. We have already shown the X-ray and gamma ray stopping distances of solid materials and water in Figure 1.6. For comparison, the $1/e$ stopping distances $L_e = 1/\alpha \rho_b$ for thermal neutrons for these same substances are (in mm): water 1.86, calcite 1450, quartz 2500, mullite 1400 and steel

45.6. Hydrated materials attenuate strongly because of the presence of chemically combined water: so L_e for gypsum is 3.83 mm, for tobermorite (as an indication of hydrated Portland cement) is 3.56 mm and portlandite 3.40 mm. Organic materials including hydrocarbons and other nonaqueous liquids also attenuate strongly (L_e for *n*-hexane is 1.93 mm).[7] Traditionally photographic techniques are used for neutron detection. Neutrons are first captured in either a dysprosium or gadolinium metal foil which generates radioactivity that decays via β^- or γ emission. The pattern of radioactivity can then be transferred to a photographic film which in turn can be analyzed using a microdensitometer. More recent developments in neutron detection include image-plate and scintillator/camera systems that provide a rapid read-out of transmitted neutrons over the field of view [869, 870, 1366].

Gamma ray and X-ray methods

Gamma-ray attenuation techniques have been developed to measure water contents and to detect density variations in porous solids. We have already noted in Chapter 1 that the attenuation coefficients for gamma rays vary little with atomic number. Because of this it is necessary to undertake careful calibration experiments to determine the relative contributions of the different materials to the attenuation of the gamma ray beam. The standard attenuation equation may be written in the form

$$I = I_0 \exp(-\alpha \rho_b L) \tag{2.1}$$

and

$$\ln I = \ln I_0 - \Sigma A_i \tag{2.2}$$

where $A_i = \alpha_i \rho_i L_i$ for each material (solid, water, specimen holder) in the beam. In measuring water contents in porous media it is a straightforward matter to determine the term for water by measuring the attenuation produced by a tube filled with water, correcting in turn for the attenuation produced by the empty tube. It is also advisable to carry out measurements on standard specimens of known water contents (as determined gravimetrically) to produce accurate calibration curves. In addition, in accurate work the homogeneity of the dry material must be checked by measuring the beam attenuation through different parts of the solid. Gamma-ray attenuation has been widely used for laboratory measurements of water content distributions in porous media [878, 879, 880, 708, 311, 312]. Good spatial resolution of water distribution is possible by using appropriate collimation of the beam. The technique has been applied to measure hydraulic diffusivities of construction materials in a similar way to NMR, neutron radiography and positron emission tomography.

Microfocus X-ray methods are also used in a two-dimensional projection geometry with excellent results [1075, 1082, 1077, 224, 1076, 1118]. X-ray computerized tomography (XCT) techniques provide fully three-dimensional information on water distributions, although with limited contrast [857, 1095]. High penetration and high resolution can be achieved by using the intense energetic X-rays available at synchrotron radiation sources (for example [1154]), especially if two X-ray energies are available [408].

Nuclear magnetic resonance

NMR methods allow liquid water to be detected and with careful calibration to be determined quantitatively. Numerous NMR techniques are now applied in the physical, biological and medical sciences for analysis of molecular structure and chemical composition and for imaging. In the last decade NMR has become established also as a primary method of geophysical investigation by means of borehole instrumentation. In simple NMR measurements, data are obtained on the magnitude of the bulk magnetization due to protons in the liquid state. In moist porous materials, the measured magnetization is due solely to liquid water and the magnitude of the magnetization is a direct measure of the amount of water per unit volume of material. In principle NMR methods can be used to estimate the water content of small laboratory samples but in this mode has little advantage over direct methods and is little used. In addition, most NMR systems provide data on the relaxation time of the proton magnetization: this property is controlled largely by the surface/volume ratio of the pore structure, is a good estimator of a characteristic length scale of the porosity and hence of the permeability. There is increasing interest in NMR methods in cement materials science (see for example [1166, 688]).

The laboratory measurement of water content *distributions* in building materials, including stones, plaster and mortar, was among the first non-biological applications of NMR imaging some 40 years ago [466]. Today, magnetic resonance imaging (MRI) is well-established as one of the best research methods for water content mapping in laboratory specimens of building materials [123, 1166, 1079, 1331, 941] and also soils [29, 30, 798]. There are numerous applications to water absorption [936, 687, 229, 937, 152, 670, 153, 700, 939, 671, 154, 108, 731, 1187], to the absorption of hydrocarbons and other nonaqueous liquids [518, 1092], to drying [946, 943, 124, 177, 121, 122, 948, 835], and to migration through interfaces [183, 184, 960]. Similar methods may be used to obtain information on the spatial distribution of porosity [784] and to detect fractures and voids [384, 783].

Positron emission tomography

PET is a radioactive tracer technique that can be used to image distributions of a dosed liquid within porous media. A radioisotope is used which undergoes a form of beta decay with emission of a positron. The positron rapidly annihilates by combining with an electron (its antiparticle) and energy is released as a pair of 511 keV gamma rays which are emitted back-to-back, 180° apart, to conserve momentum. Simultaneous detection of these gamma rays on opposite sides of the imaging system defines a line passing through the point of emission. By counting the number of such events along each line of sight we obtain a tomographic image of the tracer distribution. Two- or three-dimensional imaging is possible by different arrangements of gamma ray detectors around the specimen. The gamma rays are strongly penetrating (see Figure 1.6) so that tracking tracer solutions within laboratory specimens of porous construction materials several cm thick is feasible.

Several positron-emitting tracers are available, having half-lives ranging from minutes to days or years. The tracer selected must of course have a half-life appropriate to the timescale of process which is being studied. In experiments to monitor unsaturated water flow in brick ceramic and lime-stone [578] a ^{64}Cu tracer (half life 12.7 h) was complexed with EDTA to create a chemically inert species soluble in water. Some tracers tend to adsorb on solid surfaces rather than move with the migrating water and trials need to be undertaken to check for adsorption effects. The method provides an alternative to NMR imaging, particularly in those materials with short NMR relaxation times. A comparison of X-ray and PET methods to track water absorption into a sandstone [430] has shown some inconsistencies, possibly associated with the adsorption of the PET tracer.

Electrical resistance measurements

When they are dry, brick, stone and concrete have very high electrical resistance. The presence of water in their pores reduces this resistance if there is sufficient water to provide a continuous percolating path between the measuring electrodes. The more water that is present the lower the resistance. In principle a water content versus resistance calibration can be established. An obvious problem which follows from our discussion of the formation factor in Chapter 1 is that the bulk resistance depends on the conductivity of the pore water which in turn is sensitive to the type and concentration of any ionic salts dissolved in it.

Nevertheless, the development of electrical resistance methods to monitor water contents in concretes has received much attention and the techniques have proved capable of providing valuable data on water and ion movement processes [1310, 812, 992, 809, 805, 814, 815], in both the laboratory and the field. It has been recognized that direct current measurements of resistance are contaminated by polarization effects and chemical reactions at the electrodes between which the resistance is measured. This has led to the use of alternating current measurement of electrical impedance. There are two components of the AC electrical response of a water-containing solid. These are a resistive component determined by the conductivity of the pore liquid

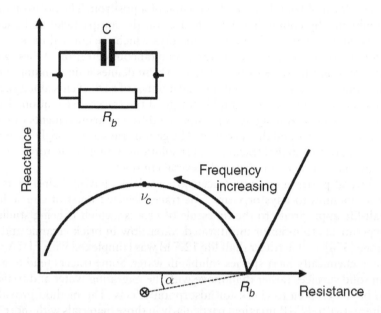

Figure 2.1 Electrical impedance of an unsaturated porous material as a function of frequency.

and a capacitive component related to polarization mechanisms operating within the system.

The total resistance is essentially determined by the ionic conduction through continuous water-filled capillary pores. Capacitive effects can arise through ionic charges in closed pores or in branch pores sealed at one end producing interfacial polarization. At the simplest level we can represent the AC electrical response of a porous solid as a resistor and capacitor in parallel [246, 815], as we show in Figure 2.1.

The complex impedance response of this system takes the form of a semi-circular arc, the centre of which is displaced below the resistance axis. Many examples of experimentally determined plots of this type are seen in the literature (for example [810]). The low frequency intercept of the arc with the resistance axis gives the ionic resistance of the bulk solid R_b. The low frequency linear spur in the complex impedance response is part of the response from the electrode-specimen interface. The maximum of the arc is associated with a particular frequency ν_c, characteristic of the material. This frequency and the depression angle α may be interpreted in terms of the pore sizes within the solid [813, 806, 796]. We can envisage that the smaller the pore size the greater will be the reduction in mobility of ions contained within the pore water. As the frequency of the electrical field increases ions within finer pores are less able to follow the field alterations and are as a consequence unable to contribute to the capacitive response. Therefore, there is a decrease in characteristic frequency with a decrease in pore diameter.

In laboratory studies using AC impedance spectroscopy, stainless steel electrodes are usually cast within the solid specimens of mortars or concretes. Clearly the technique can be applied to *in situ* monitoring of concrete structures provided an appropriate electrode system is incorporated in the concrete. The technique has provided useful data on the movement of water and ionic solutions into concretes (by determining R_b). As with simple DC measurements of resistance, the AC impedance of a saturated or unsaturated porous solid is strongly influenced by the ionic composition of the pore water. The capillary pores of cement contain predominantly sodium Na^+, potassium K^+ and hydroxide OH^- ions, the proportions of which change as hydration proceeds. After about one month the conductivity of the pore water attains a steady value. Impedance spectra of saturated specimens can be interpreted to provide information on pore sizes and pore surface textures.

The movement of water and ionic solutions into cement-based materials can be monitored by determining the bulk resistance R_b at various locations in the concrete as a function of time. The resistance falls as the amount of pore solution increases. Large changes in resistance are associated with the ingress of, for example, chloride ions into the pore solution. The power of the technique in this application is shown by the work of McCarter *et al.* [807] on concrete, in which profiles of resistance against time at fixed locations are used to detect chloride ion migration during water absorption.

2.2.3   Field methods

Sound practical guidance on the measurement of moisture content in building materials and structures is provided by Massari and Massari [795]. There are reviews of methods for building survey [984] and building conservation [991, 8].

Gravimetric analysis of solids provides the most accurate method of measuring water contents in the field. At the simplest level this involves taking samples of the appropriate material from the building fabric, weighing these samples accurately, oven drying them at an appropriate temperature and then re-weighing [1109]. Even these procedures are not entirely straightforward. Normally the samples are in powdered form drilled from the material being tested. The act of drilling generates heat and may cause some loss of water. In a careful analysis of the drilling method Newman [874] has shown that accurate data can be obtained using this technique. It is essential to use good masonry drills and to avoid prolonged drilling and overheating. The drying of brick and stone materials is conveniently carried out at 105 °C. In the case of gypsum plasters lower temperature drying ($\approx$40 °C) is necessary to avoid loss of water of crystallization [626]. With cementitious materials it is also advisable to dry at somewhat lower temperatures ($\approx$60 °C).

As we discuss later in Chapter 9, the selection of which materials to test in dampness surveying is also critical. Generally in a masonry wall the masonry units, rather than the mortar or plaster, should be tested. In many cases it is most convenient to take drillings from the brick, stone or block material. Sometimes when surveying is part of major renovation work it is possible to remove a masonry unit from the structure and weigh and dry this to produce an accurate measure of water content.

A chemical alternative to the gravimetric method, which avoids the problems of weighing and drying and which gives accurate data, is the use of a portable carbide moisture meter. This exploits the reaction between calcium carbide and water to produce acetylene gas mentioned previously. The carbide reagent and the sample (usually powder drillings) are combined in a sealed container and the gas generated produces a rise in pressure in the container. The commercial equipment is calibrated to provide the pressure data in the form of water content for a standard weight of sample. Apart from providing accurate data the whole process has the advantage of being carried out in the field thus providing results within a few minutes of sampling. Binda [132] has published a comparison of results obtained using the gravimetric method and a carbide moisture meter.

A disadvantage of the gravimetric and carbide methods of water content measurement is that some disruptive sampling is necessary. This has encouraged the use of nondestructive methods of moisture content determination. In building surveying a widely used nondestructive method relies on direct current electrical resistance measurements between two points in a porous solid. Typically the measuring probe consists of two pins at fixed separation that are pressed into contact with the surface of the material. Sometimes longer pins are used which are inserted into holes drilled into the fabric. Instruments to make such measurements were first developed to monitor moisture contents in timber where their performance is generally satisfactory, because the composition of pore solutions in untreated timber does not vary much. These methods have serious shortcomings when used on brick ceramic because this material can contain large amounts of soluble salts which, as we have mentioned, increase the conductivity of the pore water, often strongly. Appreciable quantities of soluble salts may also be present in stone and plaster as a result of water migration in the building fabric. In general when using DC conductivity meters in surveying it is essential to recognize that a high conductivity cannot be taken as conclusive evidence of a high water content. On this basis we may regard DC electrical resistance meters as useful for detecting the presence of water rather than for quantifying the amount of water within a masonry material. Electrical resistance meters, while convenient to use, give results that must be interpreted with caution. They cannot be relied upon to give accurate quantitative data on moisture contents of masonry.[8]

The use of arrays of electrodes is a powerful way of assessing the moisture state of larger structures. These *earth resistivity tomography* methods originally developed for soils have been applied successfully to stone masonry walls by Sass and Viles [1112, 1113, 1114]. The electrode arrays provide information on the distribution of resistivity from which moisture distributions may be mapped.

A more elaborate technique [129, 1059] to measure the electrical conductivity in masonry uses a transmitter coil operating in the range 10–15 kHz. A receiver coil is located a short distance (≈ 1 m) away from the transmitter coil and this senses the secondary magnetic field generated by the small eddy currents induced in the structure by the time-varying magnetic field produced by the transmitting coil. The secondary field depends not only on such factors as inter-coil spacing and operating frequency but also on the conductivity of the masonry materials. Commercial equipment and software are designed to provide maps of conductivity distributions in building and civil engineering structures. Depending on the frequency used, conductivity measurements can be made to depths up to 6 m. The mapping of conductivity is normally undertaken over a considerable area (typically at least 3 m × 3 m) to give a large scale view of moisture content profiles within the structure being surveyed. As with other conductivity measurements the soluble salt content of any masonry structure has a strong influence on the results. Accordingly any conductivity data need to be calibrated by comparison with drillings or other samples which have been subjected to gravimetric analysis.

An important field method to determine the water content of soils depends on the direct measurement of the dielectric constant. In *time domain reflectometry* [887], the dielectric constant in the vicinity of a probe (typically a stainless steel rod, say 0.2 m long) is estimated from the time taken for a high frequency GHz electromagnetic pulse to travel along the probe and for the reflected pulse to return. The propagation velocity varies as $\kappa^{-1/2}$, where κ is the dielectric constant of the medium in which the probe is embedded. Water has a much larger dielectric constant than any of the mineral or other solid components, so κ varies strongly with the liquid water content of the medium. Unlike the conductivity, the dielectric constant of water is little affected by the presence of dissolved salts. This method of making local water content measurements has only recently received attention in measuring water contents in brick, stone and concrete [929, 985, 236, 1348, 850, 9]. There are signs of increasing use of TDR for field monitoring of built structures [1348, 235, 1275].

Massive masonry structures may also be surveyed by using radar. The technique has been developed mainly to locate physical defects and voids in structures but it also enables moisture content distributions to be identified [710, 1147, 7]. The principle is to apply an electromagnetic impulse as a half sine wave via an antenna having an appropriate central frequency. In between pulsing at 50 kHz the antenna switches to receiving mode. The electromagnetic pulse is partially transmitted and partially reflected at each boundary between materials having different dielectric properties. As well as changes in structural materials, discrete zones of dampness and regions containing higher levels of soluble salts are also identified using this technique. Impulse radar has been used to identify capillary rise in masonry [131, 1060]. As we show in Chapter 9, capillary rise (rising damp) is characterized by a sharp transition from saturation to dryness at the height of capillary rise equilibrium. Sharp transitions in water content are readily seen using radar but the technique is not appropriate for identifying gradual changes in moisture content.

Changes of water content also alter the thermal diffusivity of porous materials, and the *thermal probe* method has been developed for the measurement of moisture in soils [1218]. The instrumentation is uncomplicated. Its application to building materials has been described [295, 1347, 296, 1348].

Of the several research methods we have described, only NMR has been developed as a field method. It is not yet widely used but so called *single-sided* NMR devices have been described which can detect moisture when brought into contact with a building surface [1332, 1331, 1002, 220, 1024].

Visible signs of dampness are always noted in general surveying and it is clear from our discussion of changes in appearance on wetting and drying (in Section 2.8 below) that there is a sound scientific basis for this. However, appreciable water may be present in materials visually indistinguishable from fully dry specimens. We must also remember that visible signs of dampness are seen on the surface of the material and the solid below the surface may or may not be equally affected. We have more to say on these matters in Chapter 9.

2.3   HOW THE WATER IS HELD IN A POROUS MATERIAL

2.3.1   Capillary forces and wetting

It is the tendency of liquids to spread spontaneously over solid surfaces that drives capillary absorption. Wetting occurs whenever replacing the dry solid/air surface with a solid/liquid interface reduces the energy of the system [900, 416, 338, 417, 1033, 162]. This is often the case, although not for every liquid on every surface.[9] All materials, solids and liquids, have characteristic surface energies, which reflect the fact that the atoms and molecules which form the surface are in a less energetically favourable (less stable) location than in the interior. Therefore to create more surface costs energy. A consequence of this is that the surface is in tension. The notion of a surface tension, which goes back to Thomas Young, and the notion of a surface or interfacial energy are essentially one and the same. A liquid drop, in the absence of other forces acting on it, will form a sphere because this is the shape of minimum surface area. The surface is in tension and acts like a stretched skin. The pressure of the liquid forming the drop is greater than the ambient pressure by an amount Δp. In this simple case, we can see that to create extra surface area $dA = 8\pi r\, dr$ requires energy $\sigma\, dA$ where σ is the surface tension, and to change the size of the drop requires work $= \Delta p\, dV = \Delta p.4\pi r^2 dr$. Equating these gives us $\Delta p = 2\sigma/r$: the equilibrium excess pressure inside the drop depends on the radius and the surface tension of the liquid. This is the law of Young-Laplace.[10] For a spherical droplet, the centre of curvature lies within the liquid and the excess pressure is positive. We give values of surface tension for water in Appendix B and for some salt solutions in Appendix C. For water at 25 °C, $\Delta p/$atm $= 1.421 \times 10^{-6}/(r/m)$, so that the pressure drop across a surface whose radius of curvature is 100 μm is 0.0142 atm and that across a surface whose curvature is 1 μm is 1.42 atm.

Solids also have surface tensions or surface energies, though these are harder to measure and have less obvious consequences, because of the rigidity of the solid. When a liquid comes into contact with a solid surface, we have to consider three surface (strictly, interfacial) energies: σ_{SA}, the surface energy of the solid in contact with air; σ_{LA} that of the liquid in air; and σ_{SL}, that of the solid in contact with liquid (and equally of liquid in contact with solid). If $\sigma_{SA} - \sigma_{SL} > \sigma_{LA}$ then it pays for the liquid to spread over the solid surface, because the gain in replacing solid/air surface with solid/liquid interface more than compensates for the associated cost of creating additional liquid/air surface. This is the case of *complete wetting*. The quantity $\sigma_{SA} - (\sigma_{SL} + \sigma_{LA})$ is sometimes called the spreading parameter S. It represents the energy change in spreading a liquid film over a solid surface. For complete wetting, $S \geq 0$, unlimited spreading is energetically favourable and occurs spontaneously.[11]

On the other hand, if the quantity $\sigma_{SA} - \sigma_{SL} < \sigma_{LA}$, then $-\sigma_{LA} < S < 0$. In that case, the liquid does not spread without limit on a plane surface but forms a stable droplet at the edge of which the liquid surface and the solid surface meet at a well-defined *contact angle* γ [416, 332]. This the case of *partial wetting*. In this state, the resolved parts of the three surface tensions acting in the plane of the solid surface are balanced at equilibrium. The algebraic sum of the three terms, $\sigma_{SA} - \sigma_{SL} - \sigma_{LA} \cos\gamma$ is called the Young stress, Figure 2.2. For a small droplet for which we can neglect the flattening effect of gravity the liquid surface is part of a sphere. In partial wetting the liquid spreads only until it establishes an equilibrium contact line at which the Young stress is zero. Since $\cos\gamma_e = (\sigma_{SA} - \sigma_{SL})/\sigma_{LA} = 1 + S/\sigma_{LV}$, the equilibrium contact angle γ_e lies between 0 and $\pi/2$.[12]

When liquids spread on curved surfaces, such as water does when it is absorbed by capillarity into materials with connected pores such as brick, stone and concrete, the local equilibrium condition remains the same. At equilibrium, the Young stress is zero. An elementary case is that of capillarity in a cylindrical tube of radius r. If the interfacial energies are such that the contact angle is zero and the liquid completely wets the interior surface of the tube, the equilibrium meniscus has *negative* curvature r, so that the

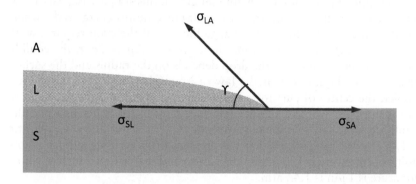

Figure 2.2 Young stress: surface forces at the contact line of a partially wetting liquid on a solid surface.

pressure in the liquid at the meniscus is *lower* than the external air pressure by an amount $\Delta p = 2\sigma_{LA}/r$. At capillary rise equilibrium in a vertical or inclined capillary tube in contact with a liquid reservoir at ambient pressure, the pressure deficit arising from meniscus curvature is balanced by the hydrostatic pressure of the liquid column. In particular these are equal at the entrance to the tube and consequently there is no flow. The equilibrium height of rise above the reservoir $z_e = 2\sigma_{LA}/\rho_L gr$ where ρ_L is the liquid density.[13] For water at $25\,°C$, $z_e/m = 14.72 \times 10^{-6}/(r/m)$: water rises to a height of $14.72\,m$ in a tube of $1\,\mu m$ radius and $0.147\,m$ in one of $100\,\mu m$ radius.

The analysis is only slightly changed if we have partial wetting with a finite contact angle $\gamma \neq 0$. Then we replace σ_{LA} by $\sigma_{LA} \cos \gamma$ throughout. For a fixed tube radius r, the curvature of the meniscus falls as γ increases and the pressure deficit is correspondingly smaller. Even so, the equilibrium height of rise $z_e > 0$ provided that $\gamma < \pi/2$. On the other hand, if $\gamma \geq \pi/2$, $z_e < 0$, and the liquid does not rise into the tube. Instead, the capillary forces act against the entry of liquid into the tube. We note that for all cases where $z_e > 0$, the gauge pressure at the meniscus $p' = p - p_0 = -\Delta p$ is negative. Indeed for $\Delta p > p_0$, the liquid at the meniscus is in a state of absolute hydrostatic tension.

In capillary absorption of a liquid into a porous material, the shape of the water/air interface [380] is of course much more complex than the simple spherical surface found in a cylindrical tube. Nevertheless surface wetting leads always to the formation of a curved capillary meniscus between liquid and air when liquid is contained within a pore. We can expect that *at equilibrium* the shape of the air–liquid interface is such that the Young stress is zero everywhere. This requires that the air–liquid interface always meets the pore surface at the appropriate contact angle and that the meniscus curvature is likewise constant everywhere.[14] For wetting and partial wetting with contact angle $\gamma < \pi/2$ the curvature is always negative (that is, the local centre of curvature lies outside the liquid phase) and therefore the pressure p in the liquid phase is lower than the ambient pressure p_0. Thus there is a negative gauge pressure in the liquid phase.

A negative gauge pressure is often described as equivalent to a tension and this term is frequently used in describing the state of a liquid in a porous medium. It is this tension that causes a wetting liquid to be drawn into a pore from an external source of bulk water (a 'free-water reservoir'). By extension, similar tensions across many menisci cause a wetting liquid to be spontaneously absorbed into a porous solid. This leads us to the concept of *suction*, a term which is widely used in a qualitative and descriptive way in the construction industry to denote the absorption or retention of water by a porous material. We see that the suction depends upon the pore sizes in the solid.

2.3.2 The Kelvin equation in capillary systems

An important consequence of the pressure change across a curved interface is that the vapour pressure is altered. The vapour pressure p of any liquid or solid phase increases as the pressure p of the condensed phase with which the vapour is in equilibrium rises. Thus small droplets like those formed when water is sprayed into the air and which have positive curvature have *higher* vapour pressures than bulk water under the same conditions. On the other hand the vapour pressure at an air/water interface in a porous material which is wetted by water is *less* than that of bulk water at the same temperature. Here the curvature is negative, the hydrostatic pressure in the liquid is lower than the external pressure and the vapour pressure is reduced.

Thermodynamic arguments [1167] lead to the Kelvin equation which describes the variation of vapour pressure with curvature r:

$$\ln \frac{p_L}{p_{L0}} = -\frac{2\sigma_{LA} M_L}{r \rho_L RT}. \tag{2.3}$$

Here p_{L0} is the vapour pressure of the bulk liquid phase (zero curvature) and M_L is the molar mass of the liquid. For water at $25\,°C$, $\ln(p_w/p_{w0}) = -1.0493 \times 10^{-9}/(r/m)$. Values of liquid pressure difference Δp and the vapour pressure p_w for several values of meniscus curvature are given in Table 2.1. The Kelvin equation is well supported experimentally [381]. It should be noted that significant reduction in vapour pressure occurs only when r is well below $1\,\mu m$.

2.3.3 Capillary forces and suction in unsaturated materials

If a wetting liquid is brought into contact with a porous material, it spreads within the open porosity under the action of the Young stress [242]. If the

Table 2.1 Properties of an air–water interface with negative curvature at
25 °C: difference in gauge pressure Δp across the interface; and
relative vapour pressure p_w/p_{w0} where p_{w0} is the vapour pressure
of bulk water

Radius of curvature r/μm	Pressure difference Δp/bar	Relative vapour pressure p_w/p_{w0}
0.01	−144.0	0.900
0.03	−48.0	0.966
0.1	−14.4	0.990
0.3	−4.80	0.997
1.0	−1.44	0.999
3.0	−0.48	1.000

amount of liquid available is less than is required to saturate the material,
the system reaches an equilibrium state in which the meniscus curvature has
a constant value throughout and in which the menisci meet solid surfaces at
the appropriate contact angle. Were this not true, pressure differences would
exist from place to place. Even liquid regions which are disconnected from
each other come to a common state since vapour diffusion occurs to transfer
liquid by local processes of vaporization and condensation, thus equalizing
the vapour pressure throughout. At equilibrium in an unsaturated porous
material, the liquid phase is thus at a definite pressure p which is less than
the ambient pressure p_0; and at a definite vapour pressure p_L which is less
than the saturated vapour pressure of the liquid p_{L0}.

If different amounts of wetting liquid – let us say water – are present in
different specimens of the same material, the equilibrium distributions are
necessarily different. At low water contents, the water adopts configurations
with high curvature of the air–water interface, for example by occupying the
smallest pores and throats and by encircling points of contact between particles. Fluid flows between all configurations to equalize the hydrostatic pressure of the liquid phase throughout. At higher water contents, water adopts
configurations of decreasing curvature, and correspondingly smaller Young-
Laplace pressure drop and higher Kelvin vapour pressure. We see therefore
that the gauge pressure $\Delta p = p - p_0$ of the pore liquid is a strong function
of the water content θ. We have thus established one of the fundamental
elements of the physics of unsaturated porous media.

We call the quantity Δp the *capillary pressure*, and denote it p_c. For porous
materials and liquids which wet or partially wet them, $p_c \leq 0$. The pos-
itive quantity $|p_c|$ is sometimes called the capillary tension. In the case of
water we call the relation $p_c(\theta)$ the *water characteristic* or *water retention
function* of the material [1250]. In pore systems as intricate as those which
exist in materials such as brick, stone and concrete, it is not imaginable that

the *microscopic* configurations of water menisci at each water content are unique. Repeated wetting of a material to achieve the same bulk water content yields innumerable variations in microscopic distribution. In spite of this, we find that in bringing a dry material to a particular water content θ, $p_c(\theta)$ is a well-defined function and a reproducible property of the material. We call this curve $p_c(\theta)$ the *capillary wetting curve* or more fully *the wetting branch* of the water characteristic. On the other hand, we also find that if we bring the same material to the same final water content by withdrawing water from an initially saturated specimen, then $p_c(\theta)$ lies on a distinctly different curve. This is the *capillary drying curve* or *drying branch*. The water characteristic therefore shows strong hysteresis, a feature found generally in capillary porous materials and notably in soils.

A definition of capillary suction

We see therefore that the equilibrium state of the water in an unsaturated porous material is characterized by its capillary pressure function $p_c(\theta)$. We may regard this as defining the capillary suction property of any porous material. It is of course defined in relation to a stated wetting liquid – which for brick, stone and concrete is invariably water.

At first sight, this definition is somewhat surprising because it shows that the suction depends not only on the material, but also on the water content θ. This is consistent with everyday experience. When saturated, materials exert no suction. The suction exerted by any and every material is at its greatest when the material is dry and diminishes as the water content rises. When we talk descriptively of a 'high' suction material, we mean that the material has a large negative capillary pressure at low water contents in the air-dry state. Such a material absorbs water from an external water reservoir, just as water rises into a fine capillary tube. However, our definition of suction tells us only about the stress within the water and not about the amount of water that the material can absorb. The suction is an intensive property. The *capacity* of the material depends of course on the porosity rather than the suction. Finally, we see that our definition of capillary suction tells us that suction has the dimension of pressure and has unit Pa, atm or bar.[15]

We note that the capillary pressure may also be interpreted as the work required to transfer unit volume of liquid from the porous material *at fixed water content* to an external reservoir. The work is performed against the capillary forces acting on the liquid. Capillary rise equilibrium in a simple cylindrical capillary can similarly be analyzed in terms of work. Transferring a unit volume of water from the meniscus of a liquid at equilibrium in a vertical capillary tube at elevation z_e to an external reservoir at the same elevation requires energy Δp. Transferring this in turn to the water reservoir recovers gravitational energy $\rho g z_e$. These are equal, so $z_e = -\Delta p/\rho g$, as we have already established.

As this suggests, we can also define for a capillary-porous material a quantity $\Psi_c = p_c/\rho_L g$ which we call the capillary potential or the Buckingham potential [195]. Ψ_c has dimension [L].[16] In fact in capillary systems with only a single liquid phase, the quantity Ψ_c, the capillary potential, is more commonly used than p_c. The quantity Ψ_c relates to the energy of unit weight of liquid, rather than of unit volume as p_c. It should be noted that for wetting liquids, $\Psi_c \leq 0$, although the sign convention is not consistently observed in the literature.

Dependence on liquid properties and temperature

In unsaturated capillary systems, we assume the liquid phase occupies an equilibrium configuration of constant surface curvature throughout the pore space at each θ. The capillary pressure p_c is assumed to be controlled by the Young-Laplace equation and so equals $2\sigma_L/r_c$ where σ_L is the air–liquid surface tension, and r_c the meniscus radius of curvature. The corresponding capillary pressure potential $\Psi_c = p_c/\rho_L g = 2\sigma_L/r_c\rho_L$.

We consider two liquids with different surface tensions *both of which completely wet the porous material*. We assume also that at the same volumetric liquid content θ the meniscus curvature r_c is the same for both liquids. Then

$$\frac{\Psi_{c1}}{\Psi_{c2}} = \frac{\sigma_1\rho_2}{\sigma_2\rho_1}. \tag{2.4}$$

Thus the capillary potential $\sim \sigma_L/\rho_L$, while the capillary pressure $p_c \sim \sigma_L$. The direct evidence for these scalings is sparse, but it is an economic assumption and reasonable given that completely-wetting liquids all have zero contact angle and therefore the meniscus configurations may be expected to be similar. To generalize Eqn 2.4 to the case of the general contact angle γ is more adventurous: tentatively we expect for any θ that $p_c \sim \sigma \cos \gamma$ and $\Psi_c \sim \sigma \cos \gamma/\rho_L$. The scaling provides also the temperature variation of the capillary pressure and capillary potential for a single liquid. We see that it depends mainly on the variation of surface tension with temperature. For water (see Appendix B for data), we expect that the magnitude of the capillary pressure should decrease by about 6.1 per cent between 5–35 °C, while the capillary potential decreases by about 5.5 per cent. There are few if any direct tests of this in brick, stone and concrete, although it is broadly if not exactly supported for capillary water by tests on soils [658]. In any case, the variation is rather small and can often be neglected.

Vapour pressure as a master variable

We have assumed that the capillary pressure is controlled by the Young-Laplace law. Unfortunately we cannot directly measure the meniscus curvature in porous materials such as brick, stone and concrete. However, the

Kelvin equation provides a proxy, since it tells us that the vapour pressure p_L (which we can measure) is exactly related to the curvature. Since $p_c = 2\sigma_L/r$ and $\Psi_c = p_c/\rho_L g$, we have from Eqn 2.3

$$\ln \frac{p_L}{p_{L0}} = \frac{g\Psi_c M_L}{RT}. \tag{2.5}$$

This important equation links the capillary potential Ψ_c and the vapour pressure of an unsaturated porous medium [341, 886].

It is therefore useful to consider the vapour pressure as a master variable in determining the state of liquids in unsaturated porous media. This allows us to extend our mechanical definition of capillary potential to include not only liquid but also vapour states. Two materials are in capillary equilibrium if their capillary potentials are equal or, equivalently, if their vapour pressures are equal. An unsaturated porous medium is in equilibrium with an atmosphere in which the partial vapour pressure of the liquid phase equals p_L.

The liquid of paramount interest is water, and so we write p_w to denote the partial water vapour pressure. It is useful here to show how the capillary potential Ψ_c and the water vapour pressure p_w are related for water. From Eqn 2.5 we have $\Psi_c = RT/(gM_w) \ln(p_w/p_{w0})$, so that at 25 °C $\Psi_c/m = 1.4032 \times 10^4 \ln(p_w/p_{w0})$, where of course $p_w/p_{w0} = (RH/100)$.

2.4   HYDRAULIC POTENTIAL

So far, we have given a purely mechanical account of the forces acting on water and other liquids in unsaturated porous materials. We have assumed that the origin of these forces lies entirely in capillary phenomena: that is, that we are dealing with pure capillarity, described by the Young-Laplace and Kelvin equations and in which the liquid phase is described by its bulk properties such as density and surface tension.

For many materials, and among these many brick and stone materials, this is an excellent assumption. It is likewise good for many soils, although it is not adequate for all materials. In some cases strong chemical forces come into play at the pore surface between solid and liquid during sorption and which contribute to the binding of water to the matrix of a porous material. These effects are particularly evident in porous materials with large surface areas and fine pores, and also at low water contents.[17] We wish therefore to generalize the definition of the capillary potential to include these other forces along with the capillary forces. In fact we can abandon all reference to the Kelvin equation and meniscus curvature. Instead we can set up a definition based on the energy of water sorbed within a porous material, the energy now including contributions from both capillary and other physicochemical effects. This provides a powerful general definition of the state of a liquid within a porous medium. The liquid of greatest interest is water and the thermodynamic analysis leads us to a definition of the general *hydraulic potential* Ψ.[18]

2.4.1   Defining the hydraulic potential

We wish to describe the state of water in an unsaturated medium by reference to its energy relative to that of an external water reservoir, which acts as a reference state [473]. The thermodynamic criteria of phase equilibrium are expressed in terms of the Gibbs function G. Usually in chemical thermodynamics we use *molar* quantities, expressing extensive variables per unit amount, that is per mole. For a pure phase, the molar Gibbs function G_m is called the *chemical potential* μ. We take therefore as a reference state liquid water at temperature $T^{\ominus}$ and total pressure $p^{\ominus}$, having chemical potential $\mu^{\ominus}$. In order to take account of gravitational effects we also define a zero of gravitational potential at the horizontal plane $z = 0$, z positive upwards. Thus

$$\mu(T^{\ominus}, p^{\ominus}, z) = \mu(T^{\ominus}, p^{\ominus}, z = 0) + Mgz \tag{2.6}$$

where M is the molar mass of water (see Appendix B). Water sorbed into a porous solid has a lower (more negative) chemical potential than the bulk phase. The chemical potential of the sorbed water, which we denote μ', depends on the water content θ, so that

$$\mu' = \mu'(T, p, z, \theta). \tag{2.7}$$

The gravitational term depends simply on z so that we can write

$$\mu' = \mu'(T, p, \theta) + Mgz. \tag{2.8}$$

The free energy of the sorbed water can be determined experimentally from vapour pressure measurements. The chemical potential of water vapour at vapour pressure p_w is

$$\mu_g(T, p) = \mu_g^{\ominus} + RT \ln \frac{p_w}{p^{\ominus}} + Bp_w \tag{2.9}$$

where B is the second virial coefficient, $\mu_g^{\ominus}$ the standard molar Gibbs function and $p^{\ominus}$ a standard pressure. (The effect of the term Bp_w is very small unless p_w is large and will be neglected in what follows.) When bulk liquid and vapour phases are at equilibrium

$$\mu = \mu_g \tag{2.10}$$

and

$$p_w = p_{w0} \tag{2.11}$$

where p_{w0} denotes the saturated vapour pressure at T and p (p_{w0} is almost independent of p). Thus

$$\mu = \mu_g^{\ominus} + RT \ln \frac{p_{w0}}{p^{\ominus}}. \tag{2.12}$$

If the vapour pressure in the vapour phase in contact with the sorbed water is p_w, then

$$\mu' = \mu_g^{\ominus} + RT \ln \frac{p_w}{p^{\ominus}}. \tag{2.13}$$

Therefore the difference

$$\Delta \mu(\theta) = \mu' - \mu = RT \ln \frac{p_w}{p_{w0}} \tag{2.14}$$

represents the molar change in Gibbs function accompanying the transfer of water from bulk liquid to porous material at constant temperature, total pressure, gravitational potential and moisture content. It follows that $\Delta \mu$ is a differential molar Gibbs function of sorption. The quantity $-\Delta \mu / Mg$, the Gibbs function of sorption *of unit volume* is known as the *total potential* Φ. The nongravitational part of Φ is usually separated so that

$$-\Delta \mu / Mg = \Phi = \Psi + z. \tag{2.15}$$

The quantity Ψ is the hydraulic potential that we seek, a generalized form the capillary potential Ψ_c.

Equilibrium between water in a porous material and bulk water

The condition that an unsaturated porous material and a free water reservoir are at equilibrium is that they are at the same total potential. There are several ways in which such an equilibrium can be established and these are shown in Figure 2.3. Some of these are the basis of methods of measuring the hydraulic potential property of materials [886].

Let us consider first the case shown in Figure 2.3a. This shows that a porous material in contact either directly or through the gas phase with liquid water at the same T, p and the *same gravitational potential* reaches thermodynamic equilibrium ($\Delta \mu = 0$) only when $p_w = p_{w0}$, a condition met only when the porous material is saturated ($\theta_r = 1$).

Of greater interest are the two cases shown in Figures 2.3b, c. There can be sorption equilibrium at water contents less than saturation ($\theta < \theta_s$) if the sorbed water is at a higher hydrostatic or gravitational potential than the bulk water in the reservoir. Raising the hydrostatic pressure in the sorbed

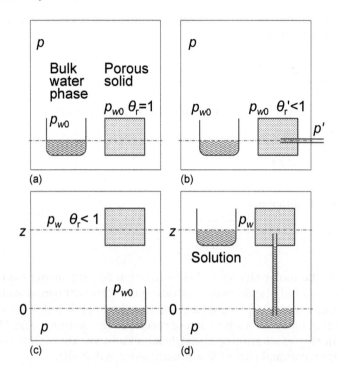

Figure 2.3 Thermodynamic basis of hydraulic potential: equilibrium between sorbed water and bulk water. All systems are closed and isothermal. (a) Porous solid and water reservoir at the same elevation and pressure; (b) change of hydrostatic pressure of pore water; (c), (d) change of water reservoir elevation and salt solution reservoir.

water from $p^\ominus$ to p increases the vapour pressure (at constant θ) from p_w to p'_w so that

$$\frac{p'_w}{p_w} = \exp\left[\frac{V_m^\ominus (p - p^\ominus)}{RT}\right] \tag{2.16}$$

where $V_m^\ominus$ is the molar volume of liquid water at $T^\ominus$ and $p^\ominus$ and compressibility is neglected. As a consequence water distils from the porous material to the bulk phase to re-establish equilibrium, and the water content of the porous material θ falls to a new equilibrium value θ' such that

$$p_w(\theta = \theta') = p_{w0}. \tag{2.17}$$

Table 2.2 shows how the vapour pressure of liquid water increases with hydrostatic pressure.

Table 2.2 The dependence on hydrostatic pressure p of the chemical potential and vapour pressure of liquid water at 25 °C [473]. $\Delta\mu = \mu(p) - \mu^{\ominus}(p^{\ominus})$ where $p^{\ominus} = 1$ atm; $p_{w0} = 3.169$ kPa; $\mu^{\ominus} = -237.19$ kJ/mol

p/MPa	p/atm	$\Delta\mu$/J mol^{-1}	p_w/p_{w0}	p/kPa
0.2	1.97	1.783	1.001	3.172
1	9.87	16.24	1.007	3.191
10	98.7	178.9	1.075	3.406
100	987	1805	2.071	6.562

Table 2.3 The variation of chemical potential $\Delta\mu$ and relative vapour pressure $p_w(z)/p_w(z=0)$ of liquid water at 25 °C with the elevation z above the liquid surface [473]. $\Delta\mu = \mu(z) - \mu^{\ominus}(z=0)$ where $p^{\ominus} = 1$ atm and $\mu^{\ominus} = -237.19$ kJ/mol

z/m	$\Delta\mu$/J mol^{-1}	p_w/p_{w0}
1	−0.1767	0.9999
10	−1.767	0.9993
100	−17.67	0.9929
1000	−176.7	0.9312

Alternatively, an equilibrium can be established at $\theta < \theta_s$ if the porous material is at a higher elevation than the bulk water reservoir. Figure 2.3c shows such an arrangement. The vapour pressure of water due to the free water surface at $z = 0$ decreases with elevation according to the equation

$$\frac{p_w(z)}{p_{w0}} = \exp\left[\frac{-Mgz}{RT}\right]. \tag{2.18}$$

Table 2.3 shows this variation of vapour pressure with elevation above a free water reservoir. When a saturated porous material with initial vapour pressure p_{L0} is introduced at height z above the reservoir, its vapour pressure is greater than that of the reservoir which is at lower elevation $z = 0$. Consequently water distils from the porous material to the reservoir and the water content falls until the vapour pressure of the pore water $p_L(\theta)$ equals $p_{L0}(z)$. Equilibrium would of course be achieved extremely slowly by such a process. In experimental devices, the porous material and the reservoir may be linked by a hanging water column and redistribution occurs rapidly by outflow of pore water as z is increased, as depicted in Figure 2.3d.[19]

Finally we note that a porous material can also attain hydraulic equilibrium with a reservoir at the same elevation if the reservoir contains a salt solution rather than pure water. Dissolved salts and other solutes invariably lower the vapour pressure of water (see Appendix C). Water distils between the porous material and the salt solution until the vapour pressures of solution and unsaturated porous material are equal.[20]

2.4.2   Equations for the hydraulic potential

Given the paucity of good data on hydraulic potentials of building materials, it is not surprising that there has been little effort to establish equations to represent Ψ as a function of water content θ. However, such equations are needed for modelling of water transfer and greatly assist the comparison of data. The situation is different in soil physics, where how best to represent *water retention* data has been examined much more thoroughly [1263, 844, 1089, 957, 605]. The great mass of data has been found, broadly speaking, to be well represented by power-law relationships of various kinds. Thus Brooks and Corey [186] found that Ψ data on a number of soils and two sandstones were well represented by straight lines on log-log plots. They proposed a simple two parameter representation of the data

$$\theta_r = (\alpha\Psi)^{-\lambda} \quad (\alpha\Psi > 1)$$
$$\theta_r = 1 \quad (\alpha\Psi \leq 1) \tag{2.19}$$

with α and λ as fitting constants and properties of the material. λ is a number which characterizes the pore size distribution (Brooks and Corey called it the *pore size distribution index*) and $\alpha = \Psi_c^{-1}$ where Ψ_c is the capillary potential corresponding to the maximum pore size. The *Brooks–Corey equation* is commonly expressed, as here, in terms of the reduced water content θ_r, and so hidden in it are two other parameters θ_s and θ_d, the wet and dry water contents. In building materials, we usually have independent information on these (for example as the saturated and the oven-dry water contents) and they are not therefore to be regarded as free parameters. The Brooks–Corey equation frequently does not capture entirely the characteristics of the data, especially towards saturation, where the discontinuity at $\alpha\Psi = 1$ is awkward. A more widely used equation is that of *van Genuchten* [1261] which changes the functional form and introduces another parameter (though as we shall see does not always use it):

$$\theta_r = \left[\frac{1}{1 + (\alpha|\Psi|)^n}\right]^m . \tag{2.20}$$

This equation[21] varies smoothly over the entire range $0 \leq \theta_r \leq 1$. We note that $1/\alpha$ is the value of the hydraulic potential Ψ at $\theta_r = 2^{-m}$. In Figure 2.4 we show data on the hydraulic potential of a clay brick [463] fitted to Eqn 2.20. In fact the van Genuchten equation is often used in a constrained form in which $m = 1 - 1/n$. This simplifies considerably some mathematical results which are derived from it. We show this form in Figure 2.4. We shall use the constrained form of the van Genuchten equation to represent

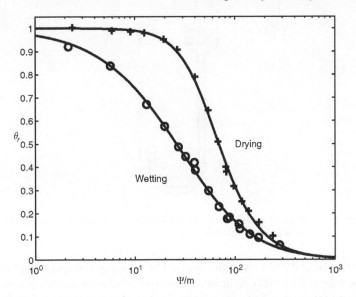

Figure 2.4 Hydraulic potential of common clay brick ceramic, showing absorption and desorption (wetting and drying) curves; points are experimental data of Gummerson [463]; solid lines are fits to the van
Genuchten equation: $\alpha = 0.0193$ m^{-1}, $n = 2.60$ (drying); and $\alpha =$
0.0863 m^{-1}, $n = 1.80$ (wetting).

capillary potential data elsewhere in this book, without implying that this
is necessarily the only or the best equation for materials such as concrete,
stone and brick.[22]

In some cases, the underlying pore size distribution may be bimodal, and
then the water retention curves can be represented as the weighted sum of
two van Genuchten terms [1375, 228]. Such is the case for some oolitic
limestones such as Portland [1083] and Savonnières [1074, 1078], and even
some fired-clay bricks [994].

2.5 MEASURING THE HYDRAULIC POTENTIAL

A complete determination of the hydraulic potential of any porous solid
requires the measurement of both drying and wetting curves over the full
range of water contents from dry to saturation. Direct methods of measurement involve the use of either suction or pressure or vapour pressure
(humidity) to control the desorption or absorption of water.

Hanging column method

Hanging columns of water (or in some cases mercury) have long been used
in soil science to provide suction forces to measure the water retaining

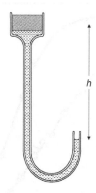

Figure 2.5 A rigid specimen of a porous material supporting a hanging column of water of length h.

properties of soils (for example [62]). The hanging column technique can also be adapted to make hydraulic potential measurements on porous construction materials, albeit over a limited range of water content. Unlike soils, construction materials are rigid solids and this allows the use of a simple experimental system as shown schematically in Figure 2.5.

Desorption measurements are made by starting with an initially saturated specimen and determining its water content as the length h of the hanging column is increased from zero. Absorption measurements are made by determining the water content of an initially dry specimen as the length h is reduced from its maximum value. To establish an equilibrium water content at any value of h commonly takes some days or even several weeks for a clay brick or stone specimen. The water content of the specimen is determined by weighing. In practice it is convenient to use a specimen ≈ 20 mm in diameter and ≈ 10 mm in thickness. The hanging column is typically ≈ 8 mm in diameter.

The hanging column method has only a limited value in obtaining hydraulic potential data for construction materials. In practice the maximum value of the length h is about 3 m. When greater lengths are used air comes out of solution at the reduced pressure and breaks the water column. We have seen that the forces of suction associated with the fine pores in brick, stone and cementitious materials are much greater than those that can be produced by a hanging column of this length. Therefore the method can only be used to measure small parts of the wetting and drying curves at water contents close to complete saturation, say 0–0.03 MPa hydraulic potential.

Pressure membrane method

The principle of this method is to balance the negative pressures under the menisci in the pores of the solid with an applied gas (air or nitrogen) pressure

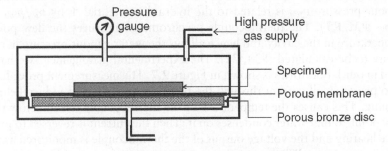

Figure 2.6 Schematic of the pressure membrane apparatus. The upper part of the pressure cell is filled with high pressure gas (usually nitrogen). The specimen is in hydraulic contact with the porous membrane which in turn is in hydraulic contact with the porous bronze disc. There is free water in contact with the lower surface of the disc.

[1053, 1054, 1055, 1056, 281, 269, 57, 58, 625, 62, 56]. Sufficiently large gas pressures can be used to overcome the suction forces associated with the finest capillaries in many if not all brick and stone materials. For such materials, it is therefore possible to determine hydraulic potential data for the full range of water contents between dry and saturated states using this technique [157, 158, 159, 360, 160, 638, 700, 639, 179, 536, 640]. The apparatus is shown schematically in Figure 2.6. For cementitious materials, the method is generally appropriate for determining the water retention curve at the higher end of the water content range only [652, 653]. A full water retention curve can be obtained by combining data from pressure membrane and sorption methods.

The drying data are obtained by starting with an initially saturated specimen and determining the equilibrium water contents as the pressure is increased from zero. The wetting data are obtained starting at a high pressure with an initially dry specimen. Careful application of this technique gives accurate and reproducible results. As with the hanging column it may take days or weeks for the specimen to attain an equilibrium water content at any fixed value of pressure. The water content is determined by removing the specimen from the pressure cell and weighing it. In order to achieve hydraulic equilibrium in a reasonable time it is an advantage to use relatively thin specimens. The typical size of the specimen is ≈20 mm in diameter and ≈2 mm in thickness. A useful check of the accuracy of the experimental procedures is that different specimens of the same material ought to give results which all lie on the same hydraulic potential curves.

Thermocouple psychrometer method

The hydraulic potential can be determined indirectly by measuring the water vapour pressure inside a cavity within a specimen of the porous medium. The ratio of the water vapour pressure p_w in the cavity to the saturated water vapour pressure p_{w0} is related to the hydraulic potential Ψ by $p_w/p_{w0} = \exp(-\Psi M/RT)$. The thermocouple psychrometer measures the dew point temperature in the cavity and hence allows the water vapour pressure in the cavity to be calculated [834, 32]. The experimental arrangement we have used in our laboratories is shown in Figure 2.7. The measurement procedure is to pass a small current through the thermocouple so as to induce Peltier cooling. This causes the temperature of the thermocouple to fall below the dew point so that water condenses on it. Then the current is reversed to produce heating and the voltage output of the thermocouple is monitored as its temperature rises. When water begins to evaporate from the thermocouple its temperature remains constant, before rising again when evaporation is complete. The constant temperature during evaporation is the dew point.

In principle the thermocouple psychrometer can be used to measure the hydraulic potential over a wide range of water contents for both wetting and drying. However, analyzing the data for a typical brick ceramic (Figure 2.4) we find that even if the water content is 20 per cent of saturation p_w/p_{w0} will only have fallen to 0.986. Great care is needed if useful data are to be obtained and the practical range of hydraulic potential is only about 0.2–7 MPa [468, 467, 375]. It is essential that the temperature of the specimen is maintained at a fixed value with small tolerances, since small changes in dew point temperature have to be measured with confidence. Also it is difficult to produce specimens to measure the wetting curve of the water characteristic. As with the pressure method described in the previous section lengthy times are needed to reach equilibrium.

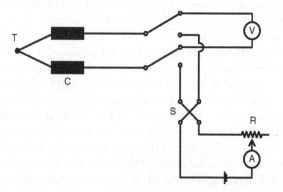

Figure 2.7 The circuit for a thermocouple psychrometer. T is the thermocouple (chromel/constantan 25 μm diameter), C are copper heat sinks, S is a reversing switch, R is a variable resistance set to give a constant current (typically ≈3 mA) through the circuit.

Sorption at constant humidity

We have seen that the vapour pressure of water in an unsaturated porous material is a direct measure of its hydraulic potential Ψ. If a porous material is placed in an environment of controlled humidity, it takes up or releases water until its vapour pressure p_w becomes equal to that of its environment. The water content of the material at equilibrium can then be determined, for example by weighing. The $\theta(p_w/p_{w0})$ curve is commonly called a *sorption isotherm*. It is often measured in both adsorption and desorption directions, and frequently at a number of temperatures.[23] Because Ψ varies as $\ln p_w$, the method provides information only on large negative values of Ψ. Saturated salt solutions can used to provide stable, known vapour pressures in the test enclosure (see [446, 63, 1003] for vapour pressure data on a number of salts for use in humidistats). This method is well-established and has been widely used for determining the water sorption characteristics of materials such as hydrated cements and concretes which have strong affinity for water (for example [471, 891, 534, 80, 725, 726, 78, 79]). Practical procedures have been standardized for building materials: see for example [627]. Saturated salt solutions are available for only a few humidities. Samples are often slow to reach equilibrium, and the procedure is laborious. Much more accurate sorption data are provided by instruments in which a sensitive microbalance records the mass of a sample exposed to an air stream[24] having a controlled and programmable humidity [651, 930]. Figure 2.8 shows a sorption isotherm of fired-clay brick obtained with such a *dynamic vapour sorption* instrument.

In this typical brick material the change in volume-fraction water content θ on raising the humidity from 10 to 80 per cent is only about 0.0012 (0.12 per cent). This low sorption capacity reflects both the low surface area and coarse pore structure of most fired-clay ceramics and their chemical inertness towards water. The sorption capacity of cement-based materials is generally much larger [1013, 1338, 79, 398]. These materials have large surface areas, some nanoscale porosity and a strong chemical affinity for water. Data on building stones are scarce [386, 1160, 776], but sorption capacities are low unless they contain clays. Materials selected and designed to provide humidity control or *moisture buffering* of indoor spaces (p 107) have high sorption capacities [1071, 1080], often achieved by incorporating clays or organic fibres into inorganic matrices.

Equations for sorption isotherms

Many equations have been developed in surface science to describe the sorption behaviour of porous and particulate materials. One such is the Guggenheim-Anderson-de Boer [GAB] function[25]

$$\frac{\theta}{\theta_1} = \frac{c_G k_G x}{(1 - k_G x)[1 + (c_G - 1)k_G x]},$$
(2.21)

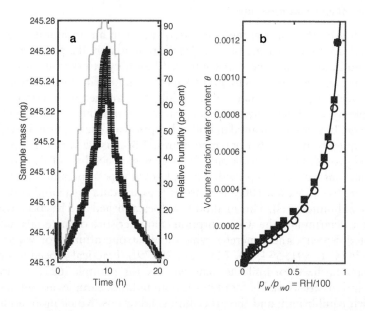

Figure 2.8 Water-vapour sorption isotherm of an English fired-clay brick ceramic (f 0.22) at 25 °C [1317]. (a) Raw mass data (in black, left axis) from 38 programmed humidity steps (in grey, right axis); (b) The sorption isotherm $\theta(p_w/p_{w0})$ derived from (a); the solid line is the Guggenheim-Anderson-de Boer isotherm function [1233] fitted to the mean of the adsorption ○ and desorption ■ branches.

where we write the independent variable $p_w/p_{w0} = x$ for clarity. Here θ_1 is the water content at monolayer coverage (p 31), and c_G and $k_G \leq 1$ are parameters of the model. The GAB function, which we see in Figure 2.8, has been used occasionally for brick, stone and concrete [1338, 930], but routinely for food and pharmaceuticals [1234] and increasingly for soils [44]. Generally, the GAB function models data well in the p_w/p_{w0} range up to about 0.8, that is to say $|\Psi| > 3 \times 10^3$ m.

More commonly, sorption data are fitted to the van Genuchten function, Eqn 2.20, an equation developed for the primary purpose of representing capillary-water retention data extending to much smaller values of $|\Psi|$. Examples are given in Table 2.4. We show in Figure 2.9 vapour sorption data for a cement-sand mortar, to which we have fitted both GAB and van Genuchten functions. The GAB function describes the isotherm well over most of the p_w/p_{w0} but fails in the capillary range at high RH/100, above about 0.9. On the other hand the van Genuchten function fits the sorption curve well throughout the capillary range and most of the adsorption range as well, failing only in the monolayer adsorption region, say RH/100 < 0.15. It should be noted that the sorption uptake of water by this cement mortar

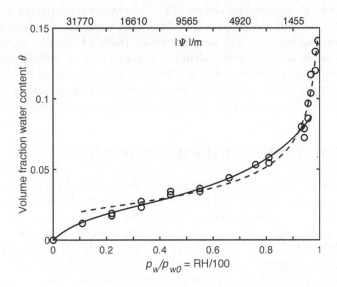

Figure 2.9 Water-vapour sorption isotherm $\theta(p_w/p_{w0})$ of a cement-sand mortar (f 0.16) at $20\,^{\circ}\text{C}$ [287]. Experimental data (points) are fitted to the Guggenheim-Anderson-de Boer isotherm (solid line) and the van Genuchten function (dashed line). Some corresponding values of hydraulic potential Ψ are shown.

is greater by a factor of about one hundred than the uptake by brick ceramic shown in Figure 2.8.

Site methods

Little effort has been devoted to the direct *in situ* measurement of hydraulic potential in structures. This is surprising since the hydraulic potential is a fundamental measure of 'wetness,' reflecting the availability of water rather than its amount. However, the hydraulic potential within a material may be estimated easily from the Kelvin equation by measuring the humidity within a small sealed cavity in a porous material. Several methods are available, including the use of small humidity sensors based on electrical capacitance. These are sealed into cylindrical holes cast or drilled into the structure. This method has been extensively used by Parrott to investigate drying in concrete [919, 920, 922, 925]. Another simple method is to use a second porous material as a sensor. A small plug of gypsum or absorbent paper sealed into the cavity takes up water until its hydraulic potential is the same as that of the walls of the cavity. Gypsum blocks are inaccurate and slow to respond to changes in water content [248]. On the other hand, filter papers are widely used in soil physics for this purpose [20, 522, 237, 440, 301, 785] and there is an ASTM standard procedure [61]. Laboratory filter papers have reproducible and uniform properties and the calibration relation between water content and humidity can be easily found [829, 1173]. The papers from a field test are removed and sealed; the water content of each is measured by weighing before and after drying. The hydraulic potential of the structure at each test position is found from the calibration water retention curve of the filter paper. However, the method is little used in construction monitoring.

2.6   VALUES OF THE HYDRAULIC POTENTIAL

We mention here some useful sources of data on the hydraulic or capillary potential of brick, stone and concrete. Various methods are used. Frequently, the data do not cover the entire water content range; and often only a wetting curve or a drying curve is reported, not both. For clay brick: [463, 663, 225, 227, 994, 1120, 375]; for stone: [1083, 663, 700, 702, 1074, 1078, 100]; for hardened cementitious materials: [11, 663, 287, 1117, 81, 80, 725, 542, 706, 726, 78, 79, 1090, 65, 1016]; for wet mortars: [556].

A few values of van Genuchten parameters are given in Table 2.4. Good quality datasets on brick, stone and concrete are in short supply. The reason is that the measurements are difficult and laborious. Nonetheless, the lack of reference-quality data hinders the modelling of water transport in building materials and structures. The situation compares unfavorably with that in soil physics and hydrology, where abundant data are available (for example [230, 728]).

2.7   CAPILLARY CONDENSATION AND HYGROSCOPICITY

We have seen that a dry porous material exposed to an atmosphere containing water vapour at partial pressure p_w will take up water until its water content θ is such that $\Psi(\theta) = (RT/M_w g) \ln(p_w/p_{w0})$, where p_{w0} is the saturated vapour pressure at the same temperature. This is basis of the usual method of determining sorption isotherms, as we have just described. In the capillary régime, the transfer of water from the atmosphere to the porous material involves a phase change from vapour to liquid. The phase change occurs by nucleation of liquid water droplets and films on solid surfaces in the smallest pores of the material. This process is called *capillary condensation*. Once initiated by nucleation, water vapour continues to diffuse into the pores and condense on existing menisci until the internal and external water vapour pressures come into balance and equilibrium is reached. In finer-pored materials, adsorption may come into play also. The equilibrium water content may be appreciable even in what are considered to be quite dry atmospheres [288]. Some materials may reveal their moisture contents by

Table 2.4 Water retention properties of selected materials: van Genuchten parameters

Material	θ_d	θ_s	α m^{-1}	n
Clay brick, *wetting*[a]	0	0.163	0.0863	1.80
drying[a]	0	0.163	0.0193	2.60
Lépine limestone, *wetting*[b]	0	0.245	0.144	1.77
drying[b]	0	0.245	0.088	1.88
Baumberger sandstone[c]	0	0.187	0.0296	1.51
Sander sandstone[c]	0	0.177	0.450	1.20
Cement paste, ordinary, w/c 0.34[d]	0	0.303	2.60×10^{-4}	1.86
Cement paste, HP, w/c 0.19[e]	0	0.204	1.02×10^{-4}	2.04
Cement paste *as cast*[f]	0	0.398	1.13×10^{-4}	2.27
carbonated[f]	0	0.293	6.56×10^{-4}	1.52
Cement mortar, w/c 0.5[g]	0	0.155	4.59×10^{-3}	1.41
Cement mortar, w/c 0.32 [h]	0	0.290	2.6×10^{-4}	1.60
Concrete, ordinary, w/c 0.48[i]	0	0.122	5.25×10^{-4}	1.78
Concrete, HP, w/c 0.26[j]	0	0.082	2.08×10^{-4}	1.94
Concrete, w/c 0.47[k]	0	0.106	1.66×10^{-4}	2.14
Concrete, w/c 0.62 *wetting*[l]	0	0.137	6.8×10^{-3}	1.38
drying[l]	0	0.137	1.11×10^{-3}	1.49
Concrete, w/c 0.55, *wetting*[m]	0	0.131	1.39×10^{-3}	1.63
drying[m]	0	0.131	9.29×10^{-4}	1.53
Concrete, w/c 0.40, *wetting*[n]	0	0.127	1.18×10^{-3}	1.61
drying[n]	0	0.127	3.42×10^{-4}	1.75
Clay[o]	0.07	0.38	0.8	1.09
Clay loam[o]	0.10	0.41	1.9	1.31
Loam[o]	0.08	0.43	3.6	1.56
Sandy loam[o]	0.07	0.41	7.5	1.89
Sand[o]	0.05	0.43	14.5	2.68

Notes
Parameters α, n as in Eqn 2.20.
a Pressure membrane [462].
b Pressure membrane [663].
c Pressure membrane desorption [536].
d Hardened cement paste, vapour desorption [80].
e Hardened cement paste, with silica fume and superplasticizer; vapour desorption [80].
f Hardened cement paste, CEM III/A (OPC 0.39, slag 0.61), water/binder 0.40; vapour desorption [65].
g Sand/cement 3.0, 20 °C, vapour sorption [287].
h Sand/cement 1.6, age 180 d, vapour sorption [1013].
i Ordinary quality concrete, aggregate/cement 5.48, sand/aggregate 0.62 (all by weight); vapour desorption [80].
j High performance concrete, aggregate/cement 4.55, sand/aggregate 0.51 (all by weight), with silica fume and superplasticizer; vapour desorption [80].
k Concrete for radioactive waste storage, CEM I, limestone aggregate/cement 3.0, sand/aggregate 0.66 (all by weight), with superplasticizer; controlled humidity desorption [1016].
l Aggregate/cement ratio 6.28; vapour sorption/desorption [725].
m Aggregate/cement ratio 5.33; vapour sorption/desorption [725].
n Aggregate/cement ratio 3.79; vapour sorption/desorption [725].
o Selected soils for comparison [230].

changes in appearance or properties and appear to have an unusual propensity to take up moisture from the atmosphere. Seaweed and hair and nylon all change their mechanical properties as humidity changes and are used in simple instruments for measuring humidity. These materials are described as *hygroscopic*. All porous materials show capillary condensation to some degree: hygroscopic materials as a class have a marked tendency to do so because of their large negative hydraulic potentials. As a consequence they take up water from air under normal conditions of humidity. Typically, they also reveal their water contents readily through changes in material properties.

Some materials contain highly soluble components (for example efflorescent salts in certain bricks and stones). The presence of these salts can greatly increase the amount of water that is absorbed under humid conditions. The process is quite separate from capillary condensation and does not depend in any way on porosity. In this case, the diffusion of water vapour to the salt surface depends on the vapour pressure of water in equilibrium with a saturated solution. If the solubility of the salt is high, this equilibrium vapour pressure may be low. When exposed to an atmosphere having a higher vapour pressure, the vapour pressure gradient leads to diffusion into the porous material and condensation of water on to the film of saturated salt solution distributed within it. Water will continue to condense in the material until all the salt is dissolved and thereafter until the concentration of salt solution has fallen to the point where its vapour pressure is in balance with that of the external atmosphere. Salts whose saturated aqueous solutions have low water vapour pressures and readily take up moisture to become covered with films of solution when exposed to the air are known as *deliquescent*. Deliquescence is seen most commonly on brick masonry subject to efflorescence [1361].

2.8   CHANGES OF APPEARANCE ON WETTING AND DRYING

Coloured porous materials are darker when wet than when dry. Thin materials (paper and textiles for example) become less opaque and more translucent when wet. Thus we have Brooks and Corey [186] carefully describing some rocks used in permeability tests: 'One of these, Berea sandstone, was cut perpendicular to the bedding planes. In the dry state and in the fully saturated state the stratification was not visible. After saturating the material completely with liquid and then desaturating to a value of S [reduced water content] of about 0.80 to 0.90, the strata became plainly visible. At this average saturation, the finer-textured strata were still fully saturated and darker than the partially desaturated coarser-textured strata. The finer and coarser strata alternate in position, in a more or less regular pattern, the individual strata being about 1/8 inch thick.'

These general observations are explained by the physics of diffuse light scattering [411, 174]. Beyond its undoubted scientific interest, there are practical reasons for developing this topic briefly here. The water movement research literature contains numerous references to observations of features such as 'wetted zones' and 'visual wet fronts' in experimental studies. Some test methods rely on tracking the movement of a visual wet front as a primary quantitative datum. Expert survey methods include visual assessment of dampness which depends on visual cues, not least variations in depth of colour and opacity.

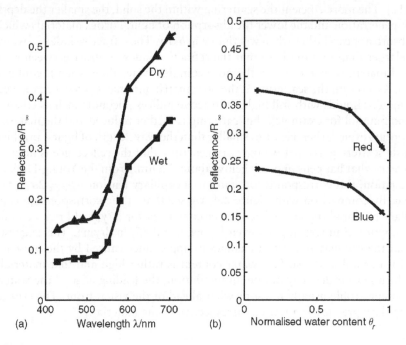

Figure 2.10 Diffuse reflectance of brick ceramic. (a) Comparison of wet and dry material at different wavelengths of visible light. (b) Dependence of R_∞ of the brick surface on water content for red and blue light [472].

We show in Figure 2.10 how the photometric *reflectance* of a brick ceramic surface depends on its water content. We see that as expected the reflectance is lower when wet than dry (meaning that the surface returns less light to the eye and appears darker). However, the relation is rather nonlinear; most of the change in reflectance occurs at the wet end. The reflection of light from an optically heterogeneous material occurs by diffuse scattering at refractive index discontinuities at and below the material surface. If the solid is an intense absorber, the depth of penetration is small and light is reflected only from a thin layer close to the surface. The efficiency of scattering depends on the variation of refractive index and the size of the inhomogeneities in relation to the wavelength of light. Light absorption also occurs and the total absorption (and hence the depth of colour) depends on the length of the optical path within the various coloured phases present. The diffuse reflectance R_∞ of a thick sample is related to absorption and scattering by

$$\left(\frac{1 - R_\infty}{2R_\infty}\right)^2 = \frac{8\Sigma_a}{3\Sigma_s} \tag{2.22}$$

where Σ_a and Σ_s are the light absorption and scattering coefficients [174, 412]. The more efficient the scattering within the solid, the smaller the depth of penetration and the lower the absorption of light. Porous materials which absorb appear darker when wet than when dry. The refractive index of water is larger than that of air so that the refractive index contrast between pore and matrix is smaller when the pore contains water than when it contains air. As a result, the scattering at the pore/matrix interfaces is reduced on wetting. For liquids with still higher refractive indices (alcohols such as ethanol and butanol for example), the scattering is further reduced and the material appears even darker. Features smaller than the wavelength of light λ produce little scattering, so that we may say generally that the reflectance is insensitive to what happens in pores below about $0.5\ \mu m$. From the Young-Laplace equation, this corresponds for water to a capillary tension $-p_c = 2\sigma/\lambda \approx 3$ bar. By comparison with Figure 2.4, we see that at the corresponding capillary potential the normalized water content θ_r for a typical brick ceramic is about 0.5 in wetting and even higher, say 0.85, in drying. This suggests that the eye may not detect changes in appearance caused by the presence of water unless the surface water content is rather high and that materials which appear dry may not be. In imbibition, the leading edge of the water-content profile usually lies somewhat ahead of the visual front. The critical capillary pressure is a few bar, irrespective of the material.

2.9   THE MOISTURE STATE

We began this chapter by asking why bricks are thirsty. That question has been answered by a full discussion of wetting energetics and of the hydraulic potential. At the outset we also pointed to the important distinction between a saturated and an unsaturated material. To understand that difference we need to know both water content and porosity. Hydraulic potential and water content are therefore two important measures of the *moisture state* of a material. But beyond that the moisture state is a broader term useful for describing the overall condition of a material in relation to the water within it. It includes not only quantitative but also qualitative attributes. We can examine the signal it produces in an NMR instrument or its response to an electrical probe, or even just see if it looks wet. The moisture state of the material so defined may then provide clues to many properties and much about performance and behaviour.

NOTES

1 The unsaturated state is also sometimes called 'partially saturated,' an awkward alternative. We consistently use the term *saturated* to mean that the open porosity is completely occupied by a single liquid, avoiding the use of phrases such as 'completely' or 'fully' saturated.

2 A normalized water content θ_r can be defined in the interval between any upper and lower water contents θ_1 and θ_0. Commonly but not invariably these are the appropriately defined saturated and dry states, so that $\theta_1 = \theta_s$ and $\theta_0 = \theta_d$. The quantity θ/f_o is the same as the *water saturation* of petrophysics [148].

3 Also in some hygrothermal models in building physics, where w denotes 'the mass of water in the open pores divided by the volume of dry material' (meaning divided by the bulk volume V_b), and is called the *moisture content* [254, 352] or more explicitly in [624] the *moisture content mass by volume*. Then $w = \rho_w\theta$.

4 A trap for the unwary. Sometimes the moisture ratio is defined on a mass basis. Thus in [254], the moisture ratio, denoted u, is defined as the mass of water/mass of dry solids (and so is the same as our θ_m). Conversions are straightforward: $\theta = (1 - f)v = (1 - f)\rho_s u/\rho_w$. In terms of void ratio e, $\theta = v/(1 + e)$ and $\theta_r = u\rho_s/e$.

5 These effects are only small. As an example of the effects of dissolved salts, consider a brick containing 2 per cent by weight of efflorescent salts, let us say predominantly in the form of highly soluble potassium sulphate. The solubility of potassium sulphate at 25 °C is about 0.120 kg/kg water (see Appendix C). The solubility of the salt is such that at all water contents the liquid phase is a saturated potassium sulphate solution (density 1086 kg/m^3) rather than pure water. An estimate of θ from weight measurements will be correspondingly in error. The estimate of $\theta_r = \theta/f$ may be somewhat better as a result of compensating errors. The question of the true density of water in close proximity of mineral surfaces is also a subject which has been actively debated for many decades. In the research literature of construction materials, this was first comprehensively investigated by Powers and Brownyard in the course of their huge study of the physical properties of hardened cement paste [1013]. In hydrated cement paste, the strongly bound water (graphically described as 'compressed' water) has a density as high as 1220 kg/m^3. Similar considerations arise in the case of clay-water systems. In nanoporous silica there is now clear evidence [409] for strong modification of water structure within about 0.6 nm of the surface.

6 Neutrons are present in cosmic rays at the ground surface, and are strongly scattered and absorbed by water in the vadose zone. This is the basis of new methods of monitoring soil water at field-scale [33], methods which may have future application in monitoring built infrastructure.

7 The neutron mass-attenuation coefficients were calculated at a neutron wavelength of 0.154 nm (thermal neutron energy 37.5 meV) using NIST data on absorption and incoherent scattering [1143].

8 There are theoretical reasons [604, 358] for expecting that the way the electrical conductivity σ of a porous material varies with water content θ is closely related to Archie's law. Thus $\sigma(\theta) = \sigma_0(\theta - \theta_c)^\mu$, where θ_c is a the water content at the percolation threshold and μ is an Archie's law exponent. This relation may be useful for guiding calibration in electrical resistance methods of water content measurement.

9 An example of nonwetting is the behaviour of mercury on brick, stone and concrete, mentioned in Chapter 1, p 29 in our discussion of porosimetry.

10 Laplace contributed the inverse dependence of pressure on radius, based on analysis and observations (by others) of the rise of wetting liquids in tubes. Thomas Young, however, introduced the concept of surface tension as a material property. It is perverse that Young and Laplace, whose relations were highly acrimonious, should be hyphenated in perpetuity in this fundamental law of capillarity [127, 128].

11 An important difference between spreading on an extended open surface and imbibition into a porous material (or even a single capillary) concerns the liquid-air interface. When a wetting film forms on an open surface, the liquid-air interface is greatly enlarged. The liquid-air surface tension σ_{LA} therefore appears in the spreading parameter S (p 47). In sharp contrast, in imbibition little or no new liquid-air interface is created. The energetics now depends only on replacing solid-air interface with solid-liquid interface. Instead of S, the figure of merit is the *imbibition parameter* $I = \sigma_{SA} - \sigma_{SL}$. Imbibition occurs when $I \geq 0$. However, in imbibition the meniscus mechanics remains much the same as for surface spreading. The liquid-air surface tension σ_{LA} contributes to the Young stress that acts at the contact line, either as it moves or as it finds equilibrium. Since for spontaneous imbibition $I = \sigma_{LA} \cos \gamma \geq 0$, then γ lies between 0 and $\pi/2$. We can therefore have spontaneous imbibition with a nonzero contact angle γ.

12 The equilibrium condition that the Young stress is zero is known as the Young-Dupré equation. We denote the equilibrium contact angle γ_e. When a partially-wetting liquid spreads across a surface, the contact line moves under the action of the nonzero Young stress. The dynamic contact angle γ differs somewhat from γ_e [416, 162].

13 The quantity $(\sigma_{LA}/\rho_L g)^{1/2}$, dimension [L], is called the capillary length and denoted λ_c. For water at $25\,°C$ it has the value 2.71 mm. The capillary length appears in the analysis of phenomena that involve both surface tension and gravity forces: for example (among many), λ_c sets an upper limit on the size of raindrops [691].

14 Many materials, including many bricks, stones and concretes, are composed of several minerals. If some of these minerals are partially rather than completely wetted by water, there may be some variation in the local contact angle over the pore surface. Even so, the Young stress is zero throughout at equilibrium.

15 Practical pressure units are the bar and the atmosphere. 1 atm = 101 325 Pa exactly = 760 torr exactly; 1 bar = 100 000 Pa exactly. 1 mm Hg = $10^{-3}\rho_m g$ = 133.322 Pa, where ρ_m is the density of mercury (Hg) = 13.5951×10^3 kg m^{-3}. Hence 1 atm = 760.0021 mm Hg = 10.3629 m water at $25\,°C$.

16 The terminology used to describe the energetics of the moisture state is confused. Usages in soil physics, petrophysics and building physics are often at variance. Of course, these fields have developed independently and have different preoccupations. Petrophysics deals mainly with viscous flow and capillarity, which it formulates in terms of *capillary pressure*, with wettability prominent, and with important hydrostatic and external applied pressures. In hydrology and soil physics, unsaturated flow is a matter largely of coupled water-air transport, with significant gravitational influences. Capillarity is dominant in the vadose zone. The moisture state is usually expressed in terms of pressure potentials of dimension [L], with contributions to the *total potential* from capillarity, adsorption, osmosis and elevation (gravity). The term *capillary potential* is now abandoned in favour of the less prescriptive *matric potential*. This term was introduced by Richards more than 60 years ago [406] but has never become established outside soil physics. It is more or less equivalent to the *hydraulic potential*, the

term we use in this book. In building and civil engineering, the terminology is also confused. Attempts to standardize vocabulary, definitions and notation are inconsistent [624, 254, 352], and take little account of practice in other fields. The hydraulic potential is generally described as *suction*, and the water retention function as a *suction curve*, sometimes also as a *moisture retention curve* or as a *moisture-storage function* [702, 352, 375]. Terminology in building physics is dominated by practice in hygrothermal HAM modelling, while that used in concrete technology is at least partly influenced by practice in soil mechanics.

17 The effects which we include here arise from strong molecular interactions which often occur between mineral surfaces and the sorbed liquid. The forces are largely confined to the molecular layer in direct contact with the surface. The term *adsorption* is used to denote the formation of such a layer in which strong noncapillary forces act: see for example [447, 1227]. The general term *sorption* includes the binding of substances by a porous medium under the action of forces of all kinds. The rigorous definition of the hydraulic potential in a porous medium in which capillary, chemical and osmotic forces are acting is controversial [97, 886].

18 We use the term *hydraulic potential* to mean the nongravitational part of the total potential for any liquid in a porous material.

19 The hydrostatic pressure of the pore water in Figure 2.3d is less than $p^\ominus$ by an amount $Mgz/V_m^\ominus$. This reduction in pressure diminishes the vapour pressure of the pore water by exactly the same amount as the increase in elevation diminishes the vapour pressure of the reservoir. Thus equilibrium is maintained through the vapour phase also.

20 The equilibrium we describe between a salt solution and a porous medium assumes that there is transfer of water by vapour diffusion only and that flow of water and solution is prevented.

21 The inverted form is $\Psi = \alpha^{-1}(\theta_r^{-1/m} - 1)^{1/n}$. This form is used by Baroghel-Bouny for cementitious materials [80, 81].

22 The parametric fitting of hydraulic potential (and hydraulic conductivity) data for soils is the subject of a thoroughgoing analysis by van Genuchten *et al.* [1262], which also describes the RETC code for fitting experimental data to various forms of the van Genuchten equation and conductivity equations.

23 Sorption isotherms generally describe the hydraulic potential of materials at low θ_r, outside or at least mostly outside the capillary régime. The temperature dependence of Ψ is not controlled solely by σ/ρ but at least partly by stronger chemical forces. The temperature dependence of the vapour pressure p_w of sorbed water *at constant water content* θ is given by $(\partial p_w/\partial T)_\theta = \Delta H_{ad}/TV_m^\ominus$. Then to a good approximation $[\partial \ln p_w/\partial(1/T)]_\theta = \Delta H_{ad}/R$. Here ΔH_{ad} is the *isosteric enthalpy of adsorption*.

24 An air-stream apparatus was used by Powers and Brownyard [1013] in their early and comprehensive study of water-vapour sorption in cement pastes and mortars.

25 The GAB function is also known as the Brunauer-Skalny-Bodor function. With $k_G = 1$ the GAB function reduces to the Brunauer-Emmett-Teller [BET] function, used almost universally in estimating the surface area of porous materials from sorption data [1227] (see p 31). The water-vapour sorption isotherm functions developed in surface science and the water retention functions developed in soil physics have not yet been brought together in a unified way. Recent attempts [1249, 1094, 1292, 1093] to combine capillary and adsorption régimes in soil physics are extensions of the van Genuchten equation and do not incorporate established sorption-isotherm models such as the GAB function. On the other hand, Bažant has argued [1338, 93, 876] that multilayer adsorption is severely

hindered in nanoporous cements, and has proposed modifications of the BET function to cover the capillary range to saturation [875]. These modifications share some features of the GAB model, but do not incorporate the van Genuchten function.

3   Flow in porous materials

Most of the common inorganic construction materials have open porosity. They take up water according to their exposure to rain, groundwater, condensation and humid air, and release it in response to the drying effects of the atmosphere. We have seen in Chapter 2 how capillary forces act to hold water and other liquids within these materials. We have given the *equilibrium* relations between water content and such environmental quantities as humidity and pressure potential. Now in this chapter, we set out the principles which govern the *movement* of water in these materials and show how transport in both saturated and unsaturated materials can be described.

For many years, the treatment of water transport in porous construction materials was preoccupied with two main topics: the transport of liquid water in saturated materials, and the transport of water vapour in relatively dry materials. Little attention was directed to the transport of water in unsaturated materials across the entire range of water contents. The central place of *unsaturated flow* is now more widely recognized [473, 504, 463, 482]. It is certainly true that construction materials are rarely saturated in use and that unsaturated flow is the main mode of mass transfer in building materials during construction and throughout their often long lifetimes. Even if materials or building elements are *locally* saturated from time to time (for example on façades exposed to driving rain or at the base of walls), they are almost never saturated throughout and water migrates from the saturated regions to unsaturated regions and ultimately back to the environment. Here we shall deal with both saturated and unsaturated flow, integrating the two into a single general framework.

Following the original work of Henry Darcy, mathematical descriptions of liquid flow in porous media are based on Darcy's law. This states that the volumetric flow rate Q of liquid through a specimen of porous material is proportional to the hydrostatic pressure difference Δp across the specimen, inversely proportional to the length L of the specimen, and proportional to its cross sectional area A. Darcy's law is expressed simply as $Q = kA\Delta p/L$.

The constant of proportionality defined by Darcy's law we shall call the Darcy permeability of the material. The quantity Q/A has dimension $[LT^{-1}]$ and is the flow rate, flux or Darcy velocity u, so that Darcy's law is more commonly written as $u = k\Delta p/L$. It is clear that Darcy's law is a simple linear transport law and has exactly the same form as Ohm's law, Fick's law and the heat conduction equation. Each of these laws defines a transport property, a *conductivity*, that relates to the flow process that each describes, and we might envisage a unifying theoretical framework which could have application to heat, diffusion and electrical current and to water flow. In fact valuable insights into water flow processes may be gained by comparing these with heat flow problems. Even so, we strike a note of caution in respect of this approach. Darcy's law as originally formulated applies to saturated flow. It is also widely applied to the analysis of unsaturated flow processes, but in these circumstances we replace the Darcy permeability by a generalized transport property, the capillary or hydraulic conductivity, which we usually denote as K. K is strongly dependent on the water content θ. As we shall show this severely limits the extent to which we can find analytical solutions to unsaturated flow problems and therefore also limits the extent to which solutions based on heat flow and other linear transport equations can be used.

In order to avoid ambiguity in definition, we use the term *permeability* when we discuss saturated flow processes and *hydraulic conductivity* or *capillary conductivity* when dealing with unsaturated flow. The permeability is, of course, exactly the same as the saturated hydraulic conductivity. Next we discuss the definition and measurement of permeability in more detail.

3.1   PERMEABILITY

If AB in Figure 3.1 is fully saturated with liquid, then imposing a difference in hydrostatic pressure $\Delta p = p_A - p_B$ between A and B leads to a steady Darcian flow $u = k\Delta p/L$. u is the (scalar) flow rate (dimension $[L\,T^{-1}]$). Darcy's law may be expressed locally as $\mathbf{u} = -k\nabla p$, with $\mathbf{u}$ the vector flow velocity. We do not assume that the Darcy permeability k is necessarily con-

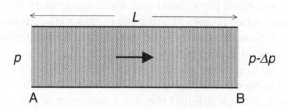

Figure 3.1 Simple Darcy flow through a liquid-saturated homogeneous medium under the action of a pressure gradient.

stant in time and indeed for water in concrete there is evidence that this is not always the case. We defer all discussion of such effects until Section 3.3.

The permeability k as defined in this equation has dimension $[M^{-1}L^3T]$. However, it is common (and as we have already done in section 2.3.3) to express hydrostatic and other pressures in terms of the pressure potential $P = p/\rho g$, where ρ is the liquid density (for example [975]). P has dimension $[L]$ and is entirely equivalent to the hydrostatic head. We then express Darcy's law as

$$\mathbf{u} = -K_s \nabla P \qquad (3.1)$$

where $K_s = k\rho g$. The quantity K_s is the conventional saturated permeability of the material, with dimension $[L\ T^{-1}]$.

We note that the permeability so defined depends both on the material and on the fluid. For permeation flows which are geometrically similar (in practice, Newtonian liquids in laminar flow in inert nonswelling media) the permeability k (and K_s also) varies inversely as the fluid viscosity η. We can therefore define an intrinsic permeability $k' = k\eta$ such that $\mathbf{u} = -(k'/\eta)\nabla p$, in which k' is a material property independent of the fluid used to measure it. k' has the dimension $[L^2]$. Both definitions of permeability are used in the concrete and cement materials literature, although K_s more widely than k'. The conversion between the two depends not only on the viscosity but also on the density of the fluid at the temperature of measurement since $k' = K_s \eta/\rho g$. For water at 25 °C, $k'/K_s = 9.103 \times 10^{-8}$ m s.

It follows from the definition of K_s that a series of measurements of K_s on a single material using different fluids should scale as ρ/η if the material is truly inert to the fluids. Failures of this scaling are an indication of specific interactions between the material and the test fluid.

We note that the variation of K_s (and similarly k) with temperature is controlled mainly by the change of viscosity, so that $dK_s/dT = -K_s(d\ln\eta/dT)$. For most liquids, the temperature coefficient of permeability is in the range +0.01 to +0.03 K_s/°C.

A further unit of permeability, the darcy, denoted D, is widely used in petroleum engineering and petrophysics. The darcy is a non-SI metric unit of intrinsic permeability k', equal to cm^2 cP/(atm s) where cP denotes the centipoise. Since the unit group cP/(atm s) is dimensionless and has the value 9.8692×10^{-9}, it follows that D $= 9.8692 \times 10^{-13}$ m^2. It is helpful to remember that $1\,D \approx 1\,\mu m^2$.

3.1.1 Gas-phase flows

Darcy's law describes also the flow of gases through permeable media [222]. The transport equation must however take account of the compressibility of the gas and this leads to some differences in the equations for liquid and gas flows. For incompressible liquids it makes little difference whether we consider mass or volume flow rates, but for gases it is mass that we must track, since this is constant in each volume element in steady processes whereas the volume is not. We write the Darcy equation in terms of mass flow $\rho u = -(\rho k'/\eta)\nabla p$. For gases, density increases with pressure according to the ideal gas law $\rho = pM/RT$, where M is the molar mass of the gas, R the gas constant and T the absolute temperature. Therefore

$$p u = -\frac{k'p}{\eta}\nabla p = -\frac{k'}{2\eta}\nabla p^2. \tag{3.2}$$

The gas viscosity is independent of pressure over a wide range and can be treated as a constant (for a particular gas at each temperature). For steady one-dimensional flow through a uniform porous material of length L, we obtain

$$u_2 = \frac{k'(p_1^2 - p_2^2)}{2\eta p_2 L} = \frac{k'\bar{p}\Delta p}{\eta p_2 L} \tag{3.3}$$

where u_2 is the volume flow velocity measured at pressure p_2 at the out-flow face, p_1 is the pressure at the inflow face, and $\bar{p}$ is the mean pressure $(p_1 + p_2)/2$. Alternatively, the equation used for incompressible liquids $u = -k\Delta p/L$ can be applied provided that u is defined as the volume outflow rate per unit area measured at the mean pressure.

Klinkenberg effect

In gas flow through permeable materials with small pores, the mean free path λ of the molecules (that is, the mean distance between kinetic collisions) may become comparable to the pore size. $\lambda = a\eta/p$ where $a = (\pi RT/2M)^{1/2}$. The viscous drag is no longer transferred completely to the pore walls and the flow behaves as though there were slippage at the gas-solid interface. In effect, the measured permeability k' becomes a function of pressure and Eqn 3.3 is replaced by the Klinkenberg equation

$$\frac{u_2 p_2 L}{\bar{p}\Delta p} = k' + \frac{\eta b}{\bar{p}}, \tag{3.4}$$

where b is a constant. The pressure-dependence of the apparent permeability, the Klinkenberg effect [680, 1337], is often evident in gas permeability measurements on construction materials [1308, 74, 2, 81, 1273]. The flow rate should be determined at a number of mean pressures and data extrapolated to zero mean free path, that is to $1/\bar{p} = 0$. For air at $25\,°C$, a has the value 370 m/s, so that $\lambda \approx 0.07\,\mu$m at 1 bar pressure.

We note that the mean free path of a gas varies as T, the absolute temperature. The gas viscosity also *increases* with temperature, varying as $T^{1/2}$.

3.2 MEASURING THE PERMEABILITY

We have defined the saturated permeability K_s in terms of Darcian flow through a liquid-saturated material under the action of a pressure gradient. Consistent with this definition, the most direct way to determine K_s is to measure the steady flow of liquid through a specimen of uniform cross-section with the specimen surfaces sealed parallel to the direction of flow.

There are two fundamental requirements that must be satisfied in the design of any permeameter which operates in this way. There is the need to measure accurately the quantity of liquid flowing through the specimen, and the need to ensure satisfactory surface sealing of the specimen to produce unidirectional flow. For materials which have relatively high permeability (typically certain coarse-grained granular solids like sands and soils) it is relatively straightforward to make permeability measurements using a simple constant-head permeameter of the type shown in Figure 3.2. For granular materials the sample of material is contained in a cylindrical tube. For rigid solids, typically in the form of a cylindrical core, the sides of the specimen are sealed, for example with epoxy resin. The flow rate is determined by weigh-

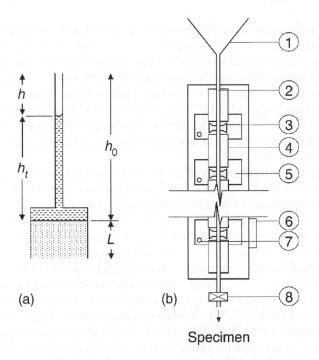

Figure 3.2 Simple permeameters [1322]. (a) Schematic of constant-head and falling-head instruments. (b) Automated falling-head permeameter: *1* reservoir; *2* permeameter tube; *3* emitter-detector pair; *4* acrylic cylinder; *5* circuitry; *6* PC connection; *7* LED; *8* permeameter tap.

ing the outflow, the hydrostatic head h_0 being kept constant. From Darcy's law $Q = K_s A h_0 / L$ where Q is the volumetric flow rate, A the cross-sectional area of the specimen and L its length. Preferably, measurements should be made for a range of values of h_0. The flow rate varies linearly with h_0 if flow is Darcian. It is useful to check this because Darcy's law is limited to low volume flow rates. At high flows the pressure gradient required to produce a given flow rate is higher than that predicted by Darcy's law by an amount proportional to the product of the liquid density and the square of the flow rate [383].[1]

An alternative to the constant head permeameter is the falling head perme- ameter in which the flow rate is measured under the action of a diminishing pressure head. Unlike the constant head permeameter the falling head per- meameter is an unsteady-state method: a schematic is shown in Figure 3.2. During the operation of this permeameter the level of water in the sight tube falls from an initial height h_0 at $t = 0$ to some height h_t at time t. Applying Darcy's law to this flow process we obtain

$$\ln \frac{h_0}{h_t} = -\frac{K_s A}{L A_s} t \qquad (3.5)$$

where A_s is the cross-sectional area of the liquid column in the sight tube. In its simplest form this equipment provides a single point measurement, the time taken for the meniscus in the liquid column to fall from h_0 to a single point h_t being determined. More generally the time taken for the meniscus to pass a series of marks on the sight tube enables a plot of $\ln(h_0/h_t)$ against t to be produced. Provided the flow is Darcian, this graph is a straight line from the gradient of which K_s can be estimated. It has been shown that an automated permeameter operating in this way can produce accurate and reproducible results [1322].

Although some rigid porous solids are sufficiently permeable to permit the use of constant head and falling head permeameters, most brick, stone and concrete materials are of relatively low permeability. To establish even small flow rates through such materials requires a relatively high pressure to drive the flow liquid through the material. This, in turn, demands efficient surface sealing of the specimens parallel to the direction of flow.

It is normally convenient to use cylindrical specimens and to establish axial flow by sealing the circumferential faces of the cylinder. Some permeameters operating in this way use an epoxy resin or epoxy mortar as the surface seal- ing compound [590, 133, 75] although the design of the equipment normally provides further circumferential support to prevent this seal breaking under the pressure of the flowing liquid. Various permeameters have been devel- oped [76, 546, 345, 346] in which surface sealing and high flow pressures are maintained by containing the test specimen in a triaxially pressurized cell. The Hassler cell, Figure 3.3, provides a convenient triaxial pressure

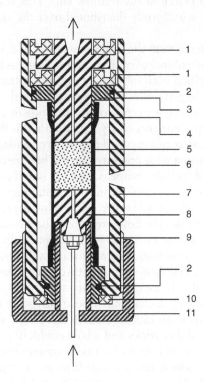

Figure 3.3 Hassler cell permeameter [444]: 1 Retaining ring; 2 nitrile rubber
O-ring seal and PTFE back-up ring; 3 sleeve carrier; 4 fixed platen;
5 nitrile rubber sleeve; 6 sample; 7 stainless steel case; 8 movable
platen; 9 platen carrier; 10 retaining ring; 11 end cap.

cell specimen holder designed to take cylindrical cores. Hassler cell permeameters have been much used in petroleum technology [28] and are now
being used for construction materials [1191, 444].

In the Hassler cell system the specimen is contained within a sleeve of
nitrile rubber which acts as a barrier between the liquid flowing through the
core and pressurized water or oil in the outer chamber of the cell. This pressurized water or oil provides a containing pressure to seal the nitrile sleeve
tightly against the surface of the specimen thus ensuring axial flow of liquid
through the specimen. Clearly the containing pressure must be higher than
the flow pressure, and in order to maintain the containing pressure constant
for long periods of time a pressure accumulator is often incorporated in the
outer chamber pressure circuit.

A movable platen at the inlet end of the Hassler cell enables specimens of
a range of lengths to be accommodated. A network of channels, consisting
of radial lines and concentric circles, is machined on to the faces both of this

platen and the fixed platen at the outflow end. This is necessary to ensure that the flow liquid is uniformly distributed over the circular cross section of the specimen.

In any permeameter system the simplest method of determining the liquid flow is to measure the volume of outflow liquid. Systems have been described [546, 345, 346] in which both inflow and outflow volumes are measured to provide a check on the reliability of the operation of the system.

An alternative approach is to control the flow rate to a constant value and to measure the flow pressure necessary to maintain this flow rate [444, 986]. Modern chromatography pumps are designed to provide accurate, pulse-free constant flow rates over a wide pressure range. They are capable of operating at high pressures and include compensation for liquid compressibility. Such pumps therefore provide an ideal means of maintaining a constant flow rate through a specimen held in a Hassler cell. Fitting a pressure transducer in the input flow line enables the flow pressure to be monitored continuously.

Some stone and concrete materials have exceptionally low permeabilities so that it is difficult to establish constant measurable flows at practical pressures using a simple axial flow geometry through a cylindrical specimen. It is however still possible to establish steady-state flows through such materials if the flow geometry is changed. Two steady-state methods have been developed in the petroleum industry which have been shown to be appropriate for low-permeability rocks and which could, in principle, be adopted for permeability measurements on high performance concretes.

The first method, which has a radial-flow geometry, uses a cylindrical specimen with a central bore. Flow is normally established between the outer circumferential face of the core and the central bore, although sometimes it may be appropriate for the flow to be in the reverse direction. Figure 3.4 is a schematic diagram showing the principle of operation of this equipment. Using this flow geometry the permeability is given by

$$K_s = \frac{Q}{G(P_1 - P_2)} \qquad (3.6)$$

where the geometrical factor G is given by $G = 2\pi L / \ln(r_2/r_1)$ in which L is the length of the specimen. Radial-flow devices have been described for cementitious materials for gas permeability [403] and for water permeability [655, 656].

The second steady-state method for low-permeability materials involves establishing transverse flow through a core held in a Hassler cell core holder. Liquid flows through a segment of the circumference along the full length of the specimen and the outflow is collected through an equal, diametrically opposite, element, Figure 3.5. In this case $K_s = QG_w/L(P_1-P_2)$ where G_w is a dimensionless geometrical factor which depends on the angle w subtended by the area of surface exposed to liquid. The full range of values of G_w is given in [28], but when w is $90°$, $G_w = 1$.

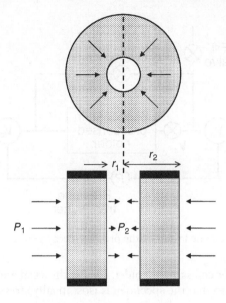

Figure 3.4 The principle of operation of the radial-flow permeameter.

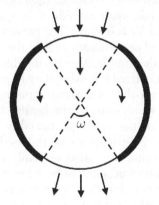

Figure 3.5 The principle of operation of the transverse-flow permeameter.

Steady-state flow devices, using radial or transverse-flow geometries are capable of measuring permeabilities two orders of magnitude smaller than may be achieved using an axial flow geometry. In addition to steady-state methods, pressure-decay techniques have also been developed in the oil industry for measurements on low-permeability rocks [1247, 597, 871, 1248, 740, 654, 28]. Clearly these methods may also be suitable for use on high performance concretes. A schematic diagram of a suitable pressure decay apparatus is shown in Figure 3.6. The specimen is contained in a

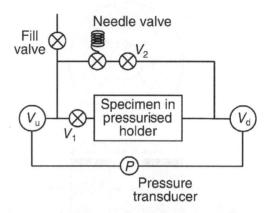

Figure 3.6 Schematic layout of the pressure-decay permeameter system.

pressurized Hassler cell sample holder. Ideally the axial and radial confining stresses are equal so that the specimen is isostatically stressed. The system is filled with liquid pressurized to an appropriate pore pressure. The fill valve is then closed and with valves V_1 and V_2 open the upstream and downstream volumes V_u and V_d are allowed to come to equilibrium. Then V_1 and V_2 are closed and the pressure in the upstream side of the system increased by means of the needle valve. Then V_1 is opened. The pressure difference established between the upstream and downstream ends of the specimen falls over time as liquid flows through the sample. Monitoring this pressure decay enables the permeability to be calculated following the API procedure [28]. The pressure decay technique is capable of measuring permeabilities four orders of magnitude smaller than steady-state methods using the axial flow geometry.

In any measurement of the liquid permeability of a porous solid it is essential first to saturate the specimen with the test liquid. With most stone and fired-clay ceramics water saturation is readily achieved by oven drying followed by vacuum saturation. Cement-based materials may also be oven dried and vacuum saturated, but the drying process can cause microstructural damage due to shrinkage of the cement paste. If it is necessary to use this procedure a gentle heating regime should be adopted (for example, 40 °C followed by 105 °C). Water saturation of most laboratory-made cementitious specimens can best be carried out by long-term curing under water immediately following the initial set of the fresh mix, with any remaining air in the pore structure of the solid being purged from the specimen during the stabilization of water flow in a constant flow permeameter. The effects of entrapped air on permeability measurement have been analyzed in detail by Scherer [1132].

Clearly the same vacuum saturation procedures can be used with nonaqueous liquids as with water. If a constant flow permeameter is used it is normally also possible to achieve saturation with a chosen liquid by passing a series of liquids through the specimen, each miscible with the previous liquid, so that the specimen is ultimately saturated with the appropriate liquid by a succession of miscible displacements.

In principle, therefore, it is possible to measure the liquid permeability of any saturated porous solid. We must recognize that there are often considerable practical difficulties in making accurate and reproducible measurements. Careful experimental technique, including close temperature control is important [28]. In addition the measurement process itself can affect the microstructure of the material and this, in turn, can change the permeability. Two aspects of measurement – the effective stress acting on the solid and the interactions between the flow liquid and the solid – are of critical importance.

3.2.1   Effect of compressive stress on permeability

It is well known in petroleum engineering that the permeability of rock decreases with increasing net stress. The net stress is defined as the difference between the confining stress and the mean pore pressure. When using a constant flow Hassler cell permeameter it is convenient to define the effective stress as the difference between the confining pressure and the pressure of the flow liquid at the input. Results on construction materials [419, 171, 444, 550, 16, 314, 315] are consistent with those reported by the oil industry [28] except that some of the former results have been obtained at relatively higher effective stress levels to give a clearer picture of the overall effect of stress on permeability. In general as the effective stress is increased from close to zero the permeability falls until it reaches a constant value at which further increase in stress causes no change in measured permeability. When the effective stress exceeds approximately 70 per cent of the ultimate failure stress of the solid, the permeability rises rapidly with further increase in effective stress. An explanation for these results is that as the effective stress, which acts in compression, is increased from zero microcracks will tend to be closed and the permeability reduced. At high stress levels microcracking damage begins to occur, thereby increasing the permeability. To obtain reliable measurements of the true permeability of a porous solid using this type of permeameter the confining pressure should therefore be set so that the effective stress lies in the range over which the measured permeability remains constant. Whatever the permeameter design, it is essential to control both the stress state and the flow conditions simultaneously, so that equipment is necessarily complex (as [313] for instance).

3.2.2   Comment on permeability test methods

Some test methods and results described in the literature are deficient because they are not based on a satisfactory theoretical description of the flow. In particular the attempts (such as [1288]) to obtain a liquid permeability from a single-sided geometry in which capillary forces contribute to the stress gradient are not generally supported by an analysis which takes account of these capillary forces. These methods have been used to obtain data on very low permeability concretes where it has not been possible with axial flow equipment to produce measurable flow through the specimens.

The simple analysis suggests that the advance of a liquid into a specimen is driven solely by the pressure head h. On this assumption, we obtain the distance x_1 by which the liquid advances in time t in terms of the permeability K_s from Darcy's law $f dx_1/dt = K_s h/x_1$. On integration we find the result

$$K_s = f x_1^2 / 2ht \tag{3.7}$$

for the permeability. We see that the flow rate $f dx_1/dt$ varies as $t^{-1/2}$. In fact in tests of this kind the flow may be driven as much by capillary forces as by the external hydrostatic head and capillary forces may often be dominant. Therefore the total pressure gradient acting on the fluid may be larger than h/x_1 and data which are based on Eqn 3.7 may overestimate K_s considerably. We discuss such flows further in Chapter 4, and also in Chapter 6 where single-sided tests (such as the CLAM test) are described.

3.2.3   Gas permeability measurements

In Section 3.1 above, we noted that gas phase flows through permeable media are also described by Darcy's law, as we noted in Section 3.1.1, but account must be taken of the compressibility of the gas and this leads to some differences in the equations for liquid and gas flows. The volumetric outflow rate is given by $kA\Delta p/L$, the volume being measured at the mean pressure. The gas viscosity is independent of pressure over a wide range and can be treated as a constant for a given gas at a defined temperature. Steady flows are described not by Laplace's equation in p but by $\nabla^2 p^2 = 0$. In the accurate analysis of gas flow data it is necessary to apply the Klinkenberg correction for gas slippage [680, 1121, 28, 167]. This correction is invariably applied to gas permeability measurements on rocks [60] and the permeability values on the same material using gas and water usually differ by less than a factor of two. The Klinkenberg correction has not routinely been applied to gas permeability measurements on concretes. As a consequence, the reported air and nitrogen permeabilities of these materials are higher than those measured with water. When the Klinkenberg correction has been applied the differences are smaller [1308, 74]. Close agreement between water and gas permeabilities is not to be expected for cement-based materials in view of their sensitivity to water. However, it has been shown that the Klinkenberg-corrected gas permeability and the liquid permeability measured with ethanol are in close agreement for a cement mortar [758].

All the accumulated evidence that cement-based material are subject to significant material change during the course of contact with water in permeability measurements has led many to favour the use of gas permeability methods [208, 1356, 6]. Several of the techniques described in Chapter 3 are also used for gas permeability measurements on rocks in the petroleum industry. For cements, the low pressure RILEM-Cembureau method is popular [685, 1064]. In this, oxygen or nitrogen gas is used, at an inlet pressure of up to 3 bar. Equipment has also been developed for use in the field to measure gas permeability *in situ* [927, 1240]. For concretes, a comparison of accurate permeability measurements using gas, water and a range of inert liquids is desirable.

3.2.4   Calculating the permeability from microstructural information

The difficulties of measuring permeability (or sometimes of obtaining suitable specimens on which to make measurements) have stimulated work to calculate the permeability directly from microstructural information. Given a complete description of the open pore structure it is in principle possible to compute numerically from the Navier-Stokes equation the pressure distribution of a saturating liquid flowing in response to appropriate boundary conditions. This approach was set out by Bentz and Martys [113]. The statistical properties of the pore space are estimated from a 2-D microstructure image, from which a 3-D microstructure is reconstructed. In fact, with powerful tomographic methods now available the 3-D microstructure can be determined directly. The application of these methods to cementitious materials has been described. A difficulty is to obtain microstructural information which fully captures the complexity of the pore structure and especially the nanoscale features present in cementitious materials. The most successful examples have been in high permeability materials [110, 1209] and in hydrothermal systems [712] where the high crystallinity removes the nanostructure associated with C–S–H gel.

3.3   PERMEABILITIES OF CONSTRUCTION MATERIALS

We collate some indicative values of permeability in Table 3.1. In this small group of unexceptional materials, the lowest and highest permeability differ by a factor of 10^7. This reflects the underlying dependence of the intrinsic permeability k' on l_c^2 where l_c is some characteristic length scale of the pore system (see Chapter 1). Of course these materials are not geometrically similar, but nonetheless the sensitivity of the permeability to the fine-grainedness of the porosity is apparent. Also apparent is the strong dependence of the permeability of cement-based materials on the water:cement ratio [1013, 1271].

3.3.1 Permeabilities of cement-based materials

We have given some examples of the permeability of cement-based materials in Table 3.1. The wide range of these values is notable, extending as it does over at least five orders of magnitude. This of course is hugely greater than the range of porosity and reflects the connectivity and the length scale of the percolating porosity, as embodied in the Katz-Thompson model.[2] In dense well-compacted cement-based materials, the pore space is extremely fine-grained. This is the case with hardened cement paste [1014, 1010] and high performance concretes made at low water-cement ratios. The wide range of permeabilities depending on free water content, water/cement ratios, curing and drying conditions is clear from the work of Dhir *et al.* [321], Mills [839, 840, 841, 842], Hooton [588] and Parrott [926] .

Measurement

For cementitious materials, measurement of permeability is an active research field [273, 274, 587, 764, 272, 763, 564, 699, 1046, 79, 1136], reported in a voluminous literature. As we have shown, there are many permeability test procedures although preferred, recommended and standard methods have not yet clearly emerged. That permeability is so widely investigated reflects the global interest in the durability of concrete which is rightly seen as being intimately associated with water migration and water-mediated chemical reactions. It is our view however that most water transport in cement-based materials occurs by means of *unsaturated* flow, for which it is necessary but not sufficient to know the saturated permeability.

Permeability measurements for cement-based materials need to take account of two main features of the materials: first, that the permeabilities of some cements and concretes are extremely low; and, second, that if liquid water is used as the permeating fluid the flow rate under constant pressure gradient may fall with time. In addition, the need to assess the permeability of concrete materials in use has stimulated a large technical effort on *in situ* test methods, many of which do not provide an estimate of the Darcy permeability as conventionally defined. We analyze the *in situ* tests in detail in Chapter 6. We now consider some aspects of permeability measurements on cementitious materials, giving most attention to their time dependence.

Low permeability concretes

A material with an intrinsic permeability of less than 10^{-17} m^2 requires high pressure equipment to generate measurable flows of water through a laboratory sample. A minimum sample length and diameter is necessary to satisfy the need for a test specimen representative of the bulk composition (this condition generally demands a much larger sample for concrete than for brick and stone). High pressure equipment was used by Glanville in early work

Table 3.1 Selected permeabilities of construction and similar materials by several methods

Material		Fluid	Water Permeability K_s/m s^{-1}	Intrinsic permeability k'/m^2
Limestones				
Estaillades[a]		Brine	2.7×10^{-6}	2.5×10^{-13}
Ketton[a]		Brine	2.1×10^{-5}	1.9×10^{-12}
Lépine[b]		Water	2.5×10^{-9}	2.3×10^{-16}
Portland[a]		Brine	1.8×10^{-7}	1.6×10^{-14}
St Maximin fine[c]		Water	2.5×10^{-6}	2.3×10^{-13}
Sandstones				
Berea[d]	*normal to bedding*	Water	1.1×10^{-7}	1.0×10^{-14}
	parallel to bedding	Water	9.7×10^{-7}	8.7×10^{-14}
Bentheimer[e]	*normal to bedding*	Brine	2.0×10^{-5}	1.3×10^{-12}
	parallel to bedding	Brine	3.8×10^{-5}	2.6×10^{-15}
Clashach[f]		Gas	3.3×10^{-6}	3.0×10^{-13}
Fontainebleau[e]	*normal to bedding*	Brine	3.6×10^{-8}	2.4×10^{-15}
	parallel to bedding	Brine	6.9×10^{-8}	4.7×10^{-15}
Fontainebleau[g]		Air	4.3×10^{-9} -4.5×10^{-5}	3.9×10^{-16} -4.1×10^{-12}
Fired-clay brick				
Brick ceramic[h]		Water	3.2×10^{-8}	2.9×10^{-15}
Brick ceramic[i]		Water	3.8×10^{-9}	3.5×10^{-16}
Brick ceramic[j]		Water	1.9×10^{-7}	1.8×10^{-14}
Brick ceramic[k]		Water	1.2×10^{-6}	1.1×10^{-13}
Brick ceramic[l]		Water	7.4×10^{-10}	6.7×10^{-17}
Brick ceramic[m]		Water	7.6×10^{-8}	6.9×10^{-15}
Cement-based and other materials				
Autoclaved aerated concrete[n]		Gas	3.1×10^{-7}	2.8×10^{-14}
Hardened cement paste w/c 0.5[o]		Water	4.6×10^{-12}	4.2×10^{-19}
Hardened cement paste w/c 0.6[o]		Water	3.1×10^{-11}	2.8×10^{-18}
Hardened cement paste w/c 0.7[o]		Water	1.7×10^{-10}	1.5×10^{-17}
Hardened cement paste w/c 0.8[o]		Water	5.6×10^{-10}	5.1×10^{-17}
Cement-sand mortar[p]		Water	1.5×10^{-9}	1.4×10^{-16}
High strength concrete, moist cured[q]		Water	7.7×10^{-13}	7.0×10^{-20}
High strength concrete, air cured[q]		Water	1.9×10^{-11}	1.7×10^{-18}
Gypsum plaster[r]		Water	8.0×10^{-8}	7.3×10^{-15}

Notes

a Means of six, Estaillades, f 0.278; Ketton, f 0.223; Portland, f 0.190; NaCl/KCl aqueous brine permeant, 20 °C [26]. b f 0.245 [663]. c f 0.39 [663]. d f 0.183, NaCl aqueous brine permeant, 25 °C [1115]. e Bentheimer, f 0.244; Fontainebleau f 0.058; NaCl aqueous brine permeant, 40 °C [291]. f Nitrogen gas permeability, water permeability estimated, f 0.145 [385]. g f 0.042–0.222; 69 outcrop cores [1049]. h Clay brick, f = 0.40 [575]. i English extruded production brick, f = 0.31 [663]. j American extruded shale brick, mean of eight, f = 0.125 [1206]. k American pressed clay brick, mean of ten, f = 0.298 [1206]. l Dresden hard-fired clay brick, f = 0.19 [994]. m Dresden traditional clay brick, f = 0.33 [994]. n Bulk density 390 kg/m^3, hydrogen gas permeability, water permeability estimated [635]. o Fully hydrated cement paste [1013]. p Cement:sand 1:3 by weight, w/c 0.75 [441, 444]. q Portland cement concrete *w/c* 0.45 [588]. r Plaster:sand:water 2:2:1 by weight, bulk density 1245 kg m^3 [441].

[423]. There may be some advantage in using radial-flow geometries. However, as we have noted, the vast experience of permeability measurement in petroleum engineering [165, 28, 291] has not yet been fully applied to cements and concrete materials. In particular, the pressure-decay methods which are widely used for low permeability rocks have yet to be exploited.

Several ingenious methods based on strain relaxation in beam bending [1124, 1127, 1270, 1271, 1272, 1129, 1256], in heating [1134, 1126, 13, 1128, 252] and on abrupt (stepwise) pressurization of an immersed specimen [456, 439, 1131, 438, 655, 657] have been developed and comprehensively analyzed by Scherer and his collaborators [1130, 1136, 1368], and applied to cement materials. These methods as a group are powerful and elegant; they largely avoid the problems of handling high pressure liquids; do not require samples to be dried; involve minimal flow through the specimen; and provide experimental values not only of permeability but also entailed properties such as the bulk modulus. They appear to be well suited to low permeability materials such as cement pastes and structural concrete, for which the relaxation times of conveniently-sized specimens are measured in minutes and hours.

Time-dependence of the permeability

The most distinctive and striking empirical feature of the permeability of concrete is its time-dependence. There are many reports which show that the rate of flow of water through concrete and other cement-based materials under a constant applied pressure gradient falls progressively with time, at least for the first few hours of a measurement run. The magnitude and the duration of the diminution of flow (which can be expressed as a nonconstancy of the Darcy permeability k') depend on many factors, but especially on the curing history and the wetting-drying history of the specimen. Nonconstancy of the permeability is known in other classes of porous materials, for example in viscoelastic gels [1122] and especially in certain types of sedimentary rocks, where it is often associated with the presence of swelling clays in the mineral composition. Rocks which exhibit such behaviour are described as *water sensitive*.[3] A simple confirmation that swelling clays (smectites such as montmorillonite) are the cause of water sensitivity is to compare permeability data using pure water and using concentrated salt solutions such as potassium chloride (see for example [732]). The salt inhibits the swelling and dispersion of clay particles and largely eliminates the water sensitivity observed in the flow.

The origin of water sensitivity in cement-based materials (which of course is not in any way associated with clays) has been examined in detail in a number of studies, notably those of Hearn [547, 548, 549, 551, 553]. Hearn made systematic comparisons of the permeability of various concrete mixes measured with water and with isopropyl alcohol, using a variety of curing and conditioning procedures, some of which involved drying and

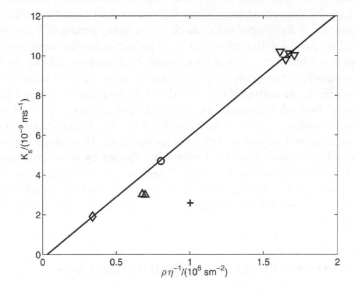

Figure 3.7 Saturated permeability K_s versus ρ/η for water (+) and nonaqueous liquids (*n*-decane O, *n*-heptane ∇, isopropyl alcohol ◇, ethanol △) for a 1:3 by weight Portland cement:sand mortar, 0.6 by weight water: cement, cured under water for 28 d, dried at 40 °C for 24 h and at 105 °C to constant weight. The solid line is the least squares fit to the heptane, decane and isopropyl alcohol data.

some of which did not. At the risk of over-simplifying complex findings, it appears that specimens which have been wet-cured and not subjected to drying before a measurement is made have a constant permeability. The intrinsic permeability is much the same whether water or isopropyl alcohol is used. Concretes which have been dried show a progressive decline in permeability measured with water over a number of hours (typically by a factor of 10), but with isopropyl alcohol the permeability changes little. Intrinsic permeabilities measured with isopropyl alcohol on dried samples match well with the early time values measured with water. Other reports (for example [441, 725, 1136]) demonstrate the same progressive decrease in the water permeability of cement-based materials.

As we have shown in Section 3.1, the permeability of a material measured with a series of liquids should scale as ρ/η where ρ is the density and η the viscosity of the test liquid. Taylor *et al.* [1221] have reported permeability values for a cement:sand mortar measured with several liquids, Figure 3.7. The permeability measured with nonaqueous liquids does show the expected scaling, suggesting that the pore structure of the mortar is unchanged. However, the water permeability is anomalously low. The specimens were dried before saturation with the flow liquid.

A qualitative explanation of this behaviour is that cement-based materials which have been dried undergo some microstructural alteration which may be thought of as distributed microcracking probably produced by shrinkage of the gel on partial dehydration [1370]. This increases the connectivity and of the pore system, as measured for example by a gas permeability measurement or equally a permeability measurement using an inert liquid such as a hydrocarbon. Rewetting the material before and during a water permeability test allows dehydrated material to rehydrate, a process which probably closes shrinkage cracks. It may also be that some migration of detached débris occurs, and in young concretes (particularly laboratory specimens) that unhydrated clinker material which is exposed by microcracking during drying hydrates for the first time. There is some evidence of this from environmental scanning electron microscopy [509] which we discuss further in connection with the sorptivity behaviour of cement-based materials in Chapter 4.

3.4   UNSATURATED FLOW: EXTENDED DARCY LAW

So far we have considered only flow in saturated porous media. However, as we emphasized in the introduction to this chapter, saturated flow is the exception rather than the rule in construction materials. A common example in civil construction is that shown in Figure 3.8 in which the material, say brick or stone or concrete, is dry at first and is later exposed to liquid (most commonly water) at A. Water is absorbed into the interior of AB through the face A by capillary forces arising from the contact of the pores of the material with the liquid phase. The flow is described locally by the so-called extended Darcy equation [1214]

$$\mathbf{u} = K(\theta)\mathbf{F} \tag{3.8}$$

where $\mathbf{F}$ is the capillary force and θ is the ratio of liquid volume to bulk vol-

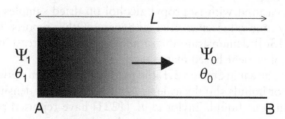

Figure 3.8 Flow through an unsaturated porous material under the action of a gradient of capillary potential Ψ or liquid content θ.

ume (volume-fraction saturation). F is identified with the negative gradient of the capillary potential Ψ, so that

$$\mathbf{u} = -K(\theta)\nabla\Psi. \tag{3.9}$$

Here Ψ (dimension [L]), defined to be coherent with the pressure potential P, is the capillary potential/unit weight of liquid. As we have shown in Chapter 2, Ψ is the energy required to transfer unit weight of liquid from the porous material to a reservoir of the same liquid at the same temperature and elevation. It can be visualized as the tension head measured by a suitable tensiometer. $K(\theta)$ is a generalized or unsaturated permeability but is conventionally described as a liquid conductivity, the term permeability being reserved for the value at saturation $K(\theta = \theta_s)$, here denoted K_s. Here, we shall use the term conductivity for $K(\theta)$, to be consistent with the terminology in soil physics and hydrology [155, 1086].[4] The dimensions and units are exactly as for permeability. $K(\theta)$ is a strong function of the fluid content θ. Equation 3.9 is commonly described as the *extended* Darcy equation and expresses the Buckingham unsaturated flow law [195, 975, 976, 1192].

Combining Eqn 3.9 with the continuity equation leads to the fundamental equation of unsaturated flow, the Richards equation [1052, 1192, 1193]

$$\frac{\partial\theta}{\partial t} = \nabla K(\theta)\nabla\Psi. \tag{3.10}$$

Clearly two material properties must be known in order for flow rates to be calculated. These are $K(\theta)$ and $\Psi(\theta)$. It is often more convenient to write Eqn 3.10 in terms of θ rather than Ψ. If we define a quantity $D = K(d\Psi/d\theta)$ then Eqn 3.10 becomes

$$\frac{\partial\theta}{\partial t} = \nabla D\nabla\theta. \tag{3.11}$$

We call D the capillary diffusivity (strictly, diffusivity function), with dimension $[L^2T^{-1}]$.[5] D depends both on the material and on the fluid: it describes the tendency of the material to transmit the fluid in question by capillarity. Most commonly, the fluid is water or other liquid and D is then called the hydraulic diffusivity.[6]

We note that the functions $D(\theta)$ and $D_r(\theta_r)$ differ, since

$$D_r(\theta_r) = K\frac{d\Psi}{d\theta_r} = (\theta_s - \theta_d)D(\theta) \tag{3.12}$$

where θ_s and θ_d are the water contents used to define the range of the reduced water content θ_r.

Dependence of transport properties on liquid properties

We note that as for K_s, so the functions K, D and Ψ depend both on the solid material and on the liquid. We assume that the material is microscopically unchanged by contact with different liquids. Then, like K_s, K scales as [$\sim$] ρ_L/η_L, where η_L is the liquid viscosity and ρ_L its density, Similarly $\Psi_c \sim \sigma_L\rho_L$, where σ_L is the surface tension, provided that Ψ is determined solely by capillarity and that each liquid has the same microscopic distribution at all liquid contents θ. It follows from the scaling of K and Ψ that D should scale as σ_L/η_L [462]. We can as a consequence define the intrinsic quantities $\mathcal{K} = K\eta_L/\rho_Lg$ and $\mathcal{D} = D\eta_L/\sigma_L$ with the same caution as expressed earlier: namely, that in the case of cement-based materials, there is evidence that water at least does produce microstructural modification to the materials and therefore the notion of an intrinsic material property independent of the fluid is idealized and may be misleading. However, the careful application of these scaling relations can be extremely useful in revealing the existence of such microstructural modifications.

The formulation of the theory of unsaturated flow in this way tends somewhat to neglect the gas-phase transport which accompanies that of the liquid phase. The theory as presented can be reconciled with a full two-phase theory in the limit that the gas-phase pressure is constant and equal to the external pressure [94, 96, 95, 148]. This pseudo-single-phase formulation has been pioneered by soil physicists and in this domain it has been highly successful. The assumptions have not been carefully investigated in relation to construction materials.

3.5   THE POTENTIAL–CONDUCTIVITY FORMULATION

The relationship between $K(\theta)$ and $\Psi(\theta)$ is defined by Eqn 3.9, which in one-dimensional form may be written

$$u_x = -K(\theta)\frac{\partial\Psi}{\partial x} \tag{3.13}$$

defining horizontal flow of liquid through an unsaturated porous solid. It is the gradient of liquid tension $\partial\Psi/\partial x$ which pulls liquid through the porous solid. In pressure terms it is the difference in pressure across the curved liquid/air interfaces in the solid that causes the flow. In saturated flow it is the difference in liquid pressure at inflow and outflow surfaces of the solid that produces flow.

However, we recall that Ψ is not a single-valued function of water content θ. At any given θ the value of Ψ depends upon whether that value of θ has been reached by drying the solid from saturation or by allowing the solid to absorb liquid from the dry state. The hysteresis in $\Psi(\theta)$ between wetting and drying implies that the conductivity $K(\theta)$ also is not a single-valued function of θ. From a microstructural viewpoint it might be expected that the conductivity would depend only on the amount of liquid in the system, and that K would as a consequence be a unique function of θ. The unsaturated conductivity must be determined by the distribution of liquid in the pore networks as well as by the total amount of liquid present. During drying water tends to be retained in larger pores with fine necks. In wetting the same amount of water tends to be distributed through a network of finer pores and thus providing better overall liquid conductivity through the system. On this basis the wetting conductivity is expected to be greater than the drying conductivity at any given water content. For practical reasons, as we shall show later, the variation of K with θ which is normally used is based on the water content being increased from an initial state of dryness. It is rare to find the $K(\theta)$ function determined from drying measurements although such data are needed to model accurately some practical problems in drying.

3.6   MEASURING THE CONDUCTIVITY

Direct measurement of the unsaturated hydraulic conductivity is experimentally difficult and in practice has been limited largely to unsaturated conductivity measurements on soils. To carry out a direct measurement it is necessary to establish steady flow through an unsaturated solid. The practical problem is to maintain the solid in the same state of unsaturation while supplying liquid at the inflow face. To do this it is necessary to apply a liquid tension gradient along the length of the specimen, and this may be achieved by applying a gas pressure. Procedures have been developed for doing this with soil samples. In comparatively low conductivity solids like most brick, stone and concrete materials the unsaturated flow rates are small and it is difficult to envisage making direct conductivity measurements using the type of apparatus used for soils.

Indirect estimates of unsaturated conductivity may be obtained from measurements of the diffusivity D and the hydraulic potential Ψ, both of these properties being relatively straightforward to measure.

3.6.1   Equations for the conductivity

Hydraulic conductivity data for brick, stone and concrete are sparse. Nonetheless representing the $K(\theta)$ function for modelling and data analysis deserves some attention. In soil physics, the most widely used model of $K(\theta)$ is the Mualem equation [858, 1261, 1262]. This is strictly a means of calculating K from data on the hydraulic potential Ψ based on a physical model of the unsaturated flow [244]. The Mualem equation takes various forms but used with the van Genuchten hydraulic potential function, Eqn 2.20, with $n = 1/(1 - m)$ it leads to the following function for $K(\theta)$:

$$K(\theta_r) = K_s \theta_r^l \left[1 - \left(1 - \theta_r^{1/m} \right)^m \right]^2 \tag{3.14}$$

where m is the van Genuchten parameter and l is a constant equal to about 0.5. The Mualem equation is now often used to represent the hydraulic conductivity of concrete [1117, 81, 725, 851, 706, 867, 78, 641, 727, 1183].

3.7   THE DIFFUSIVITY–WATER-CONTENT FORMULATION

We have defined $D(\theta)$ by the equation

$$D(\theta) = K(\theta)\frac{d\Psi}{d\theta}.$$ (3.15)

From Eqn 3.13 we may write

$$u_x = -D(\theta)\frac{d\theta}{dx}$$ (3.16)

for the horizontal capillary flow of liquid. This equation expresses $D(\theta)$ as defining liquid flow under the action of a liquid gradient. Although this gives a clear physical significance to D, this definition must be used with caution. The diffusivity is only the factor of proportionality for flow under a liquid gradient in a homogeneous material. We emphasize that it is the gradient $\nabla\Psi$ which causes liquid to move through an unsaturated porous medium. In a homogeneous material gradients in Ψ are produced by differences in liquid content, and equilibrium is established when Ψ (and therefore θ) is the same for all x. When two different unsaturated materials are in contact, the values of Ψ in the two materials must be equal at equilibrium. Because of the microstructural differences between the two materials the liquid contents at equal values of Ψ are different. So at equilibrium there is a nonzero liquid gradient but zero flow. A practical example of two different materials in hydraulic contact exists in the brick/mortar joint in a wall. At equilibrium in a damp wall there is no flow of water between brick and mortar, but the water content of each is different in order to maintain constancy in Ψ across the interface. A lack of understanding of this point can lead to erroneous recommendations in respect of surveying for dampness.

3.8   MEASURING THE DIFFUSIVITY

One dimensional horizontal flow of liquid is defined from Eqn 3.11 by

$$\frac{\partial\theta}{\partial t} = \frac{\partial}{\partial x}\left(D\frac{\partial\theta}{\partial x}\right).$$ (3.17)

If we consider first the case of the absorption of liquid under the action of a potential gradient, Eqn 3.17 is subject to the boundary conditions $\theta = \theta_s$ for $x = 0$, $t \geq 0$; $\theta = \theta_d$ for $x > 0$, $t = 0$. To obtain Eqn 3.17 in the form of an ordinary differential equation we let θ be given by $\theta = f(\phi)$ where ϕ is a function of x and t given by

$$\phi = xt^{-1/2}. \tag{3.18}$$

Equation 3.18 is the Boltzmann transformation and using this Eqn 3.17 may be written

$$-\frac{\phi}{2}\frac{d\theta}{d\phi} = \frac{d}{d\phi}D\frac{d\theta}{d\phi} \tag{3.19}$$

with $\theta = \theta_s$ at $\phi = 0$ and $\theta = \theta_d$ as $\phi \to \infty$. The solution of Eqn 3.17 is then

$$x(\theta, t) = \phi(\theta)t^{1/2}. \tag{3.20}$$

This is a central result in the application of unsaturated flow theory. It shows that as liquid is absorbed into a porous solid the liquid content versus distance profile advances as $t^{1/2}$ maintaining constant shape $\phi(\theta)$. At any time $t > 0$ the liquid content at a distance x from the inflow face is θ_x say and remains at θ_d at distances beyond the advancing liquid front.

Integrating Eqn 3.19 between the limits $\theta = \theta_d$ and $\theta = \theta_x$ and noting that $(d\theta/d\phi) = 0$ when $\theta = \theta_d$ we obtain on rearrangement

$$D(\theta_x) = \frac{1}{(d\theta/d\phi)_{\theta_x}}\left(-\frac{1}{2}\right)\int_{\theta_d}^{\theta_x}\phi d\theta. \tag{3.21}$$

Equation 3.21 is the basis for determining the hydraulic diffusivity function, first demonstrated for unsaturated flow in soils by Bruce and Klute [187] for soils. This is an application of Matano's method [799] of deriving concentration-dependent diffusivities from concentration profiles. The usual experimental procedure is to allow liquid to be absorbed into a bar of porous solid which is initially dry ($\theta_d = 0$) and to measure the liquid content versus distance profiles at various precise times after absorption commences. When the θ versus x profiles are replotted as θ versus $xt^{-1/2}$ (that is, θ versus ϕ), all the experimental data should fall on a single master curve. Dividing this curve into appropriate strips from $\theta = \theta_d$ to $\theta = \theta_x$, determining the area between θ_d and θ_x and measuring the gradient of the curve at $\theta = \theta_x$ enables the diffusivity corresponding to $\theta = \theta_x$ to be calculated from Eqn 3.21. The measurement of the gradient is the main source of error in data analysis, and the $\theta(x)$ profile is generally smoothed in some way. The optimal procedure for obtaining the diffusivity was investigated in the HAMSTAD project [226] and is also the subject of [741, 330].

Profiles may be determined gravimetrically or nondestructively. The gravimetric process is the simplest in terms of equipment, but several bars of material are needed to determine profiles after different absorption times. In the authors' laboratories the normal procedure with porous construction materials is to prepare bars of approximately 10 mm × 10 mm in cross section and of sufficient length that the absorbing liquid does not reach the end of the specimen during the time of the experiments. After the chosen time of absorption has elapsed the bars are immediately sectioned into 10 mm lengths by snapping the bars between blades mounted in a vice. The liquid content of each section is then determined by weighing, drying and then weighing dry.

Nondestructive methods of profile measurement have considerable advantages over the gravimetric method including generally a better spatial resolution. Techniques that have been used successfully to monitor water absorption into construction materials include NMR imaging [466, 229, 5, 937, 943, 938, 946, 940, 947], positron emission tomography [578], neutron radiography [942, 577, 576] and gamma-ray absorption [878, 1031, 312]. We show an early set of water content profiles for water absorption into a gypsum/lime plaster bar obtained by NMR imaging in Figure 3.9.

Figure 3.10 shows a $\theta(\phi)$ master curve for water absorption into a calcium silicate prism obtained using a microfocus X-ray method and obtained in the HAMSTAD study already mentioned [1077, 226]. The profiles are in the form $\phi(\theta_r)$, where θ_r is the water content and ϕ is the Boltzmann variable defined in Eqn 3.18. The dataset shown consists of 4353 $\phi(\theta_r)$ values, comprising a composite curve obtained by Boltzmann transformation of sixteen experimental water content profiles $\theta(x)$ measured at different elapsed times t. Since the individual profiles contributing to the composite master curve cannot be distinguished, we can assume that there is no statistically significant dependence on t in the composite data: in other words, the Boltzmann transformation is valid for this dataset. Values for $\phi = 0$ and $\theta = 0$ are not included. The diffusivity was obtained by Matano's method. The procedure is first to smooth the raw data, and then to use a cubic piecewise interpolation of the smoothed data to estimate $\phi(\theta_r)$ on a fine regular grid, from which we evaluate integral and gradient at each point. This procedure allows the diffusivity $D(\theta_r)$ to be calculated with the result shown in Figure 3.10b. Over most of the water content range D varies approximately exponentially with θ, but not exactly. Two technical matters deserve comment. First, even with sensitive water content measurement, the exact shape of the leading edge of the profile is uncertain. Nonetheless we undoubtedly see that ahead of the main steep wetting front there is a precursor zone. We may associate this with vapour transport at low water contents. It leads to an upturn in the calculated diffusivity at these same water contents [5]. Second, we note that at the absorption face there is a rapid change in moisture content. It appears that at the absorption face itself the water content is at or close to the total

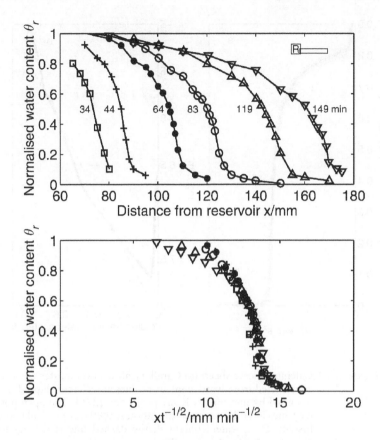

Figure 3.9 Water content profiles obtained by NMR during capillary absorption of water by a plaster bar [466]. Elapsed times t are shown. The bar ($235 \times 33 \times 33$ mm) was cast from a mix (1:2 by volume) of a commercial hydrated lime and a commercial retarded hemihydrate plaster (class B, type b2 gypsum building plaster). After setting and drying, all side faces were sealed with an epoxy coating. Inset sketch shows bar with attached reservoir R to supply water to the inflow face during the experiment. Signal amplitude is scaled to the range 0–1. Volume-fraction porosity f 0.45.

open porosity, but that immediately behind the absorption face there is a small but sharp fall in water content because of air trapping.

Although the wetting diffusivity is relatively straightforward to measure, the application of a similar theoretical analysis to the drying process imposes considerable experimental difficulties in the maintaining of appropriate boundary conditions. Essentially a solution of the type given by Eqn 3.20 for the drying process requires that drying is taking place from the end of a semi-infinite column of porous material and that at times $t > 0$ the

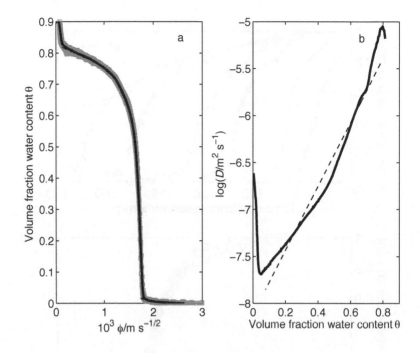

Figure 3.10 Calcium silicate sheet: (a) Capillary absorption master curve $\phi(\theta)$ constructed from water-content profiles at different elapsed times, obtained by microfocus X-ray projection [226]. The open porosity f measured by vacuum saturation is 0.895. (b) Calculated diffusivity D *vs* water content θ; the dashed line is the equation $D(\text{m}^2/\text{s}) = 7.64 \times 10^{-9} \exp(7.85\theta)$ fitted to data in the water content range 0.08–0.81.

drying end of the column must be maintained at constant liquid content (that is, $\theta = \theta_s$ for $x > 0$ at $t = 0$; $\theta = \theta_d$ for $x = 0$ at $t > 0$). The semi-infinite condition requires that the column be sufficiently long that during drying the end remote from the drying face remains at constant liquid content. If these conditions are satisfied then the liquid content versus distance profiles formed during drying maintain constant shape $\phi(\theta)$, and a drying diffusivity can be calculated just as for wetting [678].

In general the drying of bars of clay brick and stone materials proceeds in such a way that the boundary conditions cannot be satisfied in simple laboratory experiments. The diffusivities of these materials are such that flows during drying result in the liquid content remote from the drying face falling significantly over short times. Cementitious materials (mortars and concretes) tend to dry in a way that produces a sharp increase in liquid content a short distance from the drying face, and the specimen end remote from the drying face retains a reasonably constant liquid content. Some attempts have been made to obtain drying diffusivities of cementitious materials [997] but the results must be interpreted with caution.

An alternative to the profile measurement method of determining diffusivity has been proposed by Gardner [404]. This method uses a pressure membrane apparatus of the type used to determine hydraulic potential. A thin saturated specimen of thickness L is placed in the apparatus, a gas pressure increment ΔP applied and the cumulative outflow $Q(t)$ monitored. Using this technique

$$\ln\left[Q_0 - Q(t)\right] = \left[\ln\left(\frac{8Q_0}{\pi^2}\right)\right] - \left(\frac{\pi}{2L}\right)^2 Dt \qquad (3.22)$$

where Q_0 is the total outflow (strictly for $t = \infty$). A graph of $\ln[Q_0 - Q(t)]$ against time should be a straight line from the slope of which the quantity D can be calculated [679]. Here D is the diffusivity at the mean the water content during the outflow experiment.

The conductivity K can also be calculated from the outflow data from the equation

$$K = \frac{4B_1 Q_0 L^2 \rho g}{\pi^2 V \Delta P} \qquad (3.23)$$

where $B_1 = \pi^2 D/4L^2$ and V is the bulk volume of the sample. We note that the Gardner method involves drying of a pre-wetted specimen and the technique may therefore be considered as useful for measuring the drying diffusivity and the drying conductivity.

It is clear that the method of Bruce and Klute applied to the analysis of wetting profiles is the technique that is widely accepted as being most appropriate for determining the liquid diffusivities of construction materials. The measurement of D allows K to be calculated provided $\Psi(\theta)$ is known. It is relatively straightforward, although time-consuming, to measure $\Psi(\theta)$ for most construction materials, using the pressure membrane method and the calculation of $K(\theta)$ from $D(\theta)$ and $\Psi(\theta)$ is therefore the practical way of determining the unsaturated conductivity.

3.8.1   Equations for the diffusivity

Brutsaert diffusivity

The hydraulic diffusivities of several materials measured from wetting profiles [466] show that $\ln D$ is roughly proportional to θ. The diffusivity is therefore commonly represented by the equation

$$D(\theta) = D_0 \exp(B\theta) \approx D_0 \exp(B_r\theta_r) \qquad (3.24)$$

Table 3.2 Hydraulic diffusivities of building materials, represented by Eqn 3.24

Material	Diffusivity	
	$D_0/\ m^2\ s^{-1}$	$(\theta_s - \theta_d)B$
Lépine limestone[a]	6.3×10^{-9}	4.9
Cleris limestone[b]	3.2×10^{-9}	6.4
St Maximin fine limestone[c]	1.3×10^{-8}	5.6
Grès de Vosges sandstone[d]	2.4×10^{-9}	5.0
Clay brick ceramic, moulded[e]	3.4×10^{-9}	8.3
Clay brick ceramic, extruded[f]	2.2×10^{-9}	6.3
Sand-lime brick[g]	7.9×10^{-11}	8.4
1:5 cement:sand mortar[h]	9.5×10^{-10}	8.0
1:3:12 cement/lime/sand mortar[i]	8.2×10^{-9}	6.6
Calcium silicate board[j]	7.6×10^{-9}	7.0
Concrete, w/c 0.62[k]	1.5×10^{-10}	6.2
Concrete, w/c 0.55[l]	3.7×10^{-11}	7.2
Concrete, w/c 0.40[m]	1.3×10^{-11}	7.4

Sources and notes:
a [229], ρ_b 2080 kg/m^3, f 0.239, S 0.99 mm/min$^{1/2}$;
b [663], ρ_b 1890 kg/m^3, f 0.290;
c [663], ρ_b 1590 kg/m^3, f 0.390;
d [663], ρ_b 2040 kg/m^3, f 0.221;
e [936], ρ_b 1570 kg/m^3, f 0.41;
f [508], f 0.284, S 1.49 mm^2/min;
g [936], ρ_b 1617 kg/m^3, f 0.34;
h [936], ρ_b 1900 kg/m^3, f 0.23;
i [466, 475, 753], f 0.27;
j Data from [226], D_0 and B_r recalculated, ρ_b 267.6 kg/m^3, f 0.89, θ_1=0.81;
k [725], aggregate/cement ratio 6.28, f 0.145; S 0.12 mm/min$^{1/2}$;
l [725], aggregate/cement ratio 5.33, f 0.146; S 0.10 mm/min$^{1/2}$;
m [725], aggregate/cement ratio 3.79, f 0.148, S 0.057 mm/min$^{1/2}$.

where D_0, B and B_r are constants. From Eqn 3.12, we see that if $D(\theta)$ is an exponential function of θ, then $D(\theta_r)$ is likewise an exponential function of θ_r.[7] Both forms of exponential diffusivity appear in the literature. The exponential diffusivity is widely used in soil physics to model the diffusivity [190], and for construction materials is at least adequate for engineering calculations. No strong theoretical basis for the exponential diffusivity appears to have been advanced, although it has been linked to the Kelvin equation through the capillary potential [1294]. The available data (for example [466, 663, 936, 753]) suggest that $(\theta_s - \theta_d)B$ lies in the range 4–9. Some data are collected in Table 3.2.

The wetting diffusivity may also be represented by a power law form [753]:

$$D(\theta) = D_0 \theta^n \tag{3.25}$$

where n is a constant. The small amount of evidence available [753] suggests that the exponential model fits wetting profile data better than the power law model.

van Genuchten-Mualem diffusivity

The general diffusivity function obtained by combining the van Genuchten equation for the hydraulic potential with the Mualem equation for the hydraulic conductivity is extremely complicated [1262]. It is useful neither for numerical and analytical modelling nor for representing experimental data. However, there are several simpler approximate forms that have value in estimating $D(\theta_r)$ when the van Genuchten parameters are known. Combining the definition of the diffusivity D from Eqn 3.15 with Eqns 2.20, 3.14 we obtain the following diffusivity function valid for $m = 1 - 1/n$ and $l = 1/2$:

$$D(\theta_r) = C[(1 - \theta_r^{1/m})^{-m} + (1 - \theta_r^{1/m})^m - 2] \tag{3.26}$$

with $C = (1 - m)K_s\theta_r^{(1/2-1/m)}/[\alpha m(\theta_s - \theta_d)]$.

Comment on drying diffusivity

The diffusivity function determined from drying data generally shows more complicated behaviour [962, 937, 938], with a more or less well-defined minimum at some low water content, let us say θ_m. This minimum is identified with the percolation threshold for vapour diffusion. The drying diffusivity thus contains contributions from both liquid and vapour transport. Below θ_m, vapour transport is dominant. No equations have been proposed to model the entire diffusivity behaviour. The occurrence of vapour transport at low water contents is usually apparent in drying experiments because drying profiles have a low water content zone adjacent to the drying boundary (see Chapter 7). This zone presumably exists in front of an advancing wetting front but it is not detected in normal wetting profile measurements.

3.9 DIFFUSION IN THE GAS PHASE: VAPOUR TRANSPORT

In Sections 3.1.1 and 3.2.3 we have described convective transport of the gas phase in response to a gradient of total pressure; and noted that a Darcian gas permeability is the material property which determines the flow.

Let us suppose we have a permeable barrier separating two *different* gases A and B (or more generally two different multicomponent gas mixtures) which are at the same pressure. In this case, convection is zero but initially there is a concentration gradient of each component across the barrier and the kinetic tendency of the components to mix establishes fluxes of both A and B through the barrier.

These fluxes arise from the action of molecular diffusion, which promotes mixing just as it would if the barrier were absent. In the simplest case, the barrier serves only to reduce the rate of mixing which now has to occur through the maze of interconnected pores which make up the open porosity. The barrier impedes mass transfer by increasing the path lengths and by decreasing the effective area of contact of A and B.

The only case of real importance in building physics[8] is that in which we have air of different relative humidity on the two sides of the barrier (Figure 3.11a). In other words, A and B are binary mixtures of air and water vapour having different water vapour concentrations. Even if the total pressures P_A and P_B are equal, the existence of a water vapour concentration gradient drives water from higher relative humidity to lower. This water vapour flux can be described by Fick's linear law of diffusion

$$j_m = -D_w \frac{dc_w}{dx} \tag{3.27}$$

where c_w is the gas phase water concentration, j_m is the mass flux and D_w is a

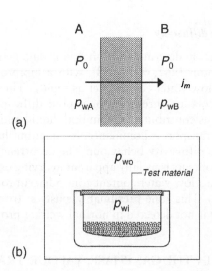

(a)

(b)

Figure 3.11 (a) Vapour transmission through a barrier: air of different relative humidity but equal total pressure is separated by a permeable barrier. (b) Standard cup method for measuring vapour permeability.

diffusivity with dimension $[L^2\, T^{-1}]$. So long as the water moves through the barrier solely by means of molecular diffusion in the gas phase, we can expect D_w (at any temperature) to have a constant value independent of c_w. In the same spirit, we can express c_w as a pressure: c_w equals the vapour density ρ_v, and assuming ideal behaviour the water vapour pressure $p_w = \rho_v RT/M$, where M is the molar mass of water, so that

$$j_m = -\frac{D_w M}{RT}\frac{dp_w}{dx} = -D_v\frac{dp_w}{dx}. \tag{3.28}$$

In building physics the lumped quantity $D_v = D_w M/(RT)$ is called the *water vapour permeability* [624] and denoted δ_p; it is not a permeability in the Darcian sense but rather a quantity proportional to a binary molecular diffusivity. The vapour permeability so defined is a property of the barrier material expressing the rate at which it can transmit water under the action of a gradient of water vapour pressure at constant total pressure. D_v has dimension $[T]$. The barrier effect is seen more vividly by comparing D_w with the diffusivity of water vapour in air itself D_{w0} (usually described as the 'diffusivity in stagnant air' to emphasize that all convection is suppressed). The quantity D_{w0}/D_w (or its equivalent D_{v0}/D_v) is sometimes called the *(water) vapour resistance factor* of the barrier material [624, 628], or elsewhere the *diffusion resistance factor* [352].

D_{w0} is a binary gas phase diffusivity but, recognizing that water is usually a minor constituent, the appropriate quantity is the *tracer* diffusivity, measured in the dilute limit in which water diffuses in a background of pure air. At 25 °C D_{w0} is 2.55×10^{-5} m^{2}s^{-1}, and D_{v0} is 1.85×10^{-10} s. We note that the requirement that the total pressures of A and B are equal means that the partial pressures of air (oxygen and nitrogen together) on the two sides of the barrier are unequal, so that a counterflux of air accompanies the flux of water vapour. Indeed the pressure gradient of air is equal and opposite to that of the diffusing water vapour. However, since the air is the predominant component, the fraction of air diffusing is small and the centre of mass of the air remains almost stationary. At 30 °C, the mass fraction of water vapour in the gas phase does not exceed 0.04 even at saturation.[9]

If water is indeed transmitted through the barrier material by molecular diffusion through the gas phase, then the vapour permeability is controlled by the physics of molecular diffusion [787]. In particular, diffusivity varies with absolute temperature T and total pressure P as T^n/P where n is around 2 (rather than 3/2 as in elementary kinetic theory), so that a similar temperature and pressure dependence is expected for D_w. Accordingly, D_v varies as T^{n-1}/P.[10]

3.9.1 Measurement of vapour transmission

Standard and widely used methods for measuring vapour transmission are mostly variants of the steady-state sealed cup experiment, which we show schematically in Figure 3.11b. A sample in some well-defined initial state is sealed over the open mouth of a cup containing a desiccant or saturated salt solution which maintains a constant relative humidity. The cup is then placed in an enclosure in which a second different relative humidity is imposed. By such an arrangement, the test sample experiences boundary conditions of constant water vapour concentration at A and B, and eventually the flow through the sample becomes steady. Periodic weighing of the cup/sample assembly allows the mass transfer rate to be determined. Under these conditions, $j_m = -D_v(p_{wB} - p_{wA})/L$ where p_{wA} and p_{wB} are the water vapour pressures and L is the sample thickness. Numerous reports of such methods exist, both for the purposes of research and for routine testing [365, 203, 394, 628]. The flux may be inwards or outwards according to the direction of the water vapour pressure gradient. If inwards, the arrangement is described as 'dry-cup'; if outwards, as 'wet-cup.' Galbraith [394] has reported results of round-robin tests and compared the test methods used in a number of national standards. Typical values of D_v at about 25 °C for dry gypsum plasterboard are around 0.2×10^{-10} s [393], suggesting a vapour resistance factor of about 10. For other inorganic porous materials (concrete, mortar and brick), D_v lies in the range 0.06–0.3×10^{-10} s [700, 707].

A comment on the mass transfer mechanism

The analysis of vapour transfer that we have given is idealized. It is not safe to assume that water is transferred exclusively by molecular vapour diffusion in cup tests (nor of course in moisture transfer in buildings) where the boundary conditions are expressed in terms of water vapour pressure or relative humidity [79]. The boundary conditions p_{wi} are equivalent to hydraulic potential boundary conditions Ψ_i and hence to water content boundary conditions θ_i. If these conditions are independent of time, then the steady flux established is described in unsaturated flow theory [473] by the equations:

$$\frac{d\theta}{dt} = -K\frac{d\Psi}{dx} = -D\frac{d\theta}{dx} = 0. \tag{3.29}$$

Fick's law requires that the flux depends only on the vapour pressure gradient and for any material scales as $\Delta p/L$, irrespective of the absolute values of the p_{wi} at the boundaries. This is not generally found in wet and dry cup measurements. In many materials [394] the water vapour permeability increases as the relative humidity to which the sample is exposed increases. This is because the water content of the material increases with increasing relative humidity in accordance with the hydraulic potential function. The presence of a gradient of liquid water content within the material introduces an efficient mechanism of water transfer which augments (and in some cases may even entirely replace) the vapour phase transfer by molecular diffusion. The hydraulic diffusivity of Eqn 3.29, provided it is appropriately measured,

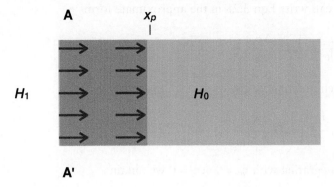

Figure 3.12 A thick slab of uniform material conditioned at humidity H_0 and subject to a step change to humidity H_1 at the surface AA'.

of course includes both liquid and vapour transfer. A single measurement of steady flux through the material is insufficient to determine $D(\theta)$, although a series of such measurements at a variety of different boundary conditions p_{wi} when combined with knowledge of the hydraulic potential curve can be used for this purpose [38, 40, 39].

3.9.2 Moisture buffering

In buildings prone to episodes of high humidity it is sometimes useful to line interior surfaces with materials which have both high water-vapour permeability and high adsorption capacity. Such materials extract water from humid air, and release it again when the humidity is lower. This is the essence of moisture buffering. We can use our analysis of vapour diffusion to understand something of the dynamics of buffering, for example in the simple slab of Figure 3.12.

We ask how the slab responds when the relative humidity at the surface at AA' is increased from H_0 to H_1 at time $t = 0$. We can apply Eqn 3.28 to describe the diffusion of water vapour from AA' into the interior of the slab. We recognize that almost all the water entering the material is adsorbed and immobilized, and also that the amount of water adsorbed rises steeply with humidity. Therefore for $t > 0$ the slab develops a zone of higher water content which moves slowly inwards from the surface. If the thickness of this zone is x_p (the 'penetration depth') then the cumulative mass of adsorbed water (per unit area of surface) is $i_m \approx x_p \rho_b \Delta \theta_m$, where $\Delta \theta_m$ is the change in θ_m (the mass-fraction water content) produced by increasing the humidity by $\Delta H = H_1 - H_0$. Information about $\theta_m(H)$ comes directly from the water-vapour sorption isotherm of the material (p 63), so that, let us say, $\rho_b \Delta \theta_m = a\Delta H$. Noting that $H = p_w/p_{w0}$, we have $i_m \approx x_p a \Delta p_w/p_{w0}$.

We can write Eqn 3.28 in the approximate form

$$\frac{\mathrm{d}i_m}{\mathrm{d}t} = j_m D_v \frac{\Delta p_w}{x_p}.$$

(3.30)

Then eliminating x_p gives

$$i_m \frac{\mathrm{d}i_m}{\mathrm{d}t} = a D_v \frac{(\Delta p_w)^2}{p_{w0}},$$

(3.31)

and integrating with $i_m = 0$ at $t = 0$ we obtain

$$i_m = 2^{1/2}\Delta p_w \left[\frac{a D_v}{p_{w0}}\right]^{1/2} \cdot t^{1/2} = 2^{1/2}\Delta p_w \mathsf{A} \cdot t^{1/2}.$$

(3.32)

Here the quantity $\mathsf{A} = (aD_v/p_{w0})^{1/2}$, with dimension $[\mathrm{L}^{-1}\,\mathrm{T}^{3/2}]$, is the same as the *moisture effusivity* used in the standard analysis of moisture buffering [1071, 1080].[11] The penetration depth at time t is $x_p \approx \mathsf{A}(p_{w0}/a)^{1/2} \cdot t^{1/2}$. The effect of the adsorption is to retard the diffusion process, roughly by a factor $(a + 1)$.

Test results on several materials [1071] confirm that the mass of water adsorbed following a step change in the imposed humidity generally increases as $t^{1/2}$. Figure 3.13 shows data [793] on a clay plaster. The sorption behaviour is reversible, and the adsorption and desorption rates are similar.

3.10   LIQUID–LIQUID MULTIPHASE FLOWS

The simultaneous flow of two different liquid phases in a porous material is a rather minor topic in building physics and civil engineering. Flows of this kind do arise in barrier structures for containing petroleum and industrial wastes and the barrier performance of concrete for such purposes has been the subject of several studies [64, 369, 1045, 1047, 477, 1188, 1189, 480, 1190] and a RILEM report [1046]. We consider several interesting cases involving unsaturated flow of two liquids in Chapter 4.

This represents the most complex of the systems to be considered. We distinguish between two cases: (1) that in which the two fluids are miscible in all proportions; and (2) the case where the two fluids are completely immiscible (no mutual solubility).

The case of miscible fluids is by far the simpler of the two. Closely related problems have been treated in other domains and we summarize the physics briefly here. The most important general result is that the displaced fluid is ultimately removed completely from the system. Therefore simultaneous occupation by the two fluids occurs only transiently. The displacement is

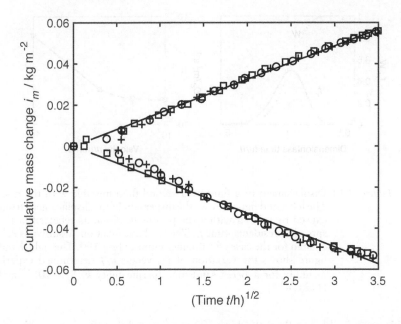

Figure 3.13 Change in mass of sorbed water in clay plaster, calculated from [793]: three adsorption/desorption cycles, surface condition alternating at 12 h intervals between 50 per cent and 75 per cent RH at 23 °C; i_m set to zero at each humidity change; $di_m/dt^{1/2} = \pm 0.016\,\text{kg}/(\text{m}^2\,\text{h}^{1/2})$. First cycle +; second cycle □; third cycle O.

described by a hydrodynamic dispersion equation, with the dispersion coefficient D_d a property of the porous medium but also a function of the flow rate [1087, 1084, 1085].

For immiscible liquids the situation is much more complex, since the contact surface between the two liquids introduces a capillarity stress due to the interfacial tension; and there may also be differences in the wettability of the pore surface to the two liquids. Furthermore, the general result is that the displaced phase is never totally removed even at long times and there is always a residual saturation of the displaced phase. This case has been most extensively treated in the petroleum engineering literature: see for example [786, 166].

3.11   MISCIBLE DISPLACEMENT AND HYDRODYNAMIC DISPERSION

We consider the case where the barrier is initially saturated with a fluid A and is then exposed to a fluid B with which A is completely miscible. Since the

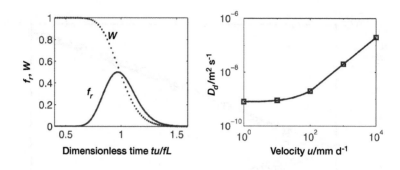

Figure 3.14 Displacement of a fluid by a second fluid miscible with the first. The left-hand figure shows the dispersion of the displacement front caused by mixing within the porous medium, as reflected in the spread of residence-time f_r. The washout function W shown is calculated for the case of a Brenner number Br = 100. The right-hand figure shows the variation of D_d versus u/f determined experimentally for a Berea sandstone (permeability k' 8 × 10^{-12} m^2) [1121, 477].

fluids are miscible, no fluid-fluid interfaces exist and therefore no capillarity phenomena come into play. In the absence of pressure gradients, molecular diffusion alone acts, causing a long-term slow mixing of the two fluids. This can be modelled using Fick's law and the appropriate liquid state binary diffusion coefficient D_l. This case does not appear to be of great interest in relation to barrier performance.

Of greater importance is the case where a hydrostatic head exists tending to force fluid B into the barrier, with displacement of A (Figure 3.14). At the beginning of the process pure fluid A flows across the outflow surface, followed at a well-defined time (the *breakthrough time* t_b) by the first detectable amounts of B. The ratio of B/A rises progressively until after sufficiently long time pure B is produced and all A has been flushed from the system.[12] The displacement process can be described by the *washout function* W (or by the derivative of $1 - W$ which is the residence-time density f_r of fluid A). In this case (B displacing A), $W = \theta_B/f$ measured as a function of time at the outflow face. This simple form of hydrodynamic dispersion [866] is described (in one dimension) by the equation

$$\frac{\partial \theta_B}{\partial t} = -\frac{u}{f}\frac{\partial \theta_B}{\partial x} + D_d\frac{\partial^2 \theta_B}{\partial x^2} \qquad (3.33)$$

where θ_B is the volume concentration of the displacing fluid and D_d is a (longitudinal) dispersion coefficient. For the case of a finite one-dimensional system of length L, the important dimensionless group is the Brenner number $\text{Br} = uL/fD_d$.

Experimentally it is found that D_d depends on both the flow rate u (strictly, u/f) and the pore structure of the medium through a Péclet number $\text{Pe} = ud/fD_l$, where d has dimension [L] and is a measure of pore size. When $\text{Pe} \ll 1$, D_d is roughly constant and equals D_l', the Fickian molecular diffusion coefficient in the porous material (as measured in simple immersion experiments, for example for several nonaqueous liquids on cements [370]). $D_l' \approx FD_l$, where F is the petrophysical formation factor [955, 399] already defined. At higher values of Pe, D_d becomes approximately proportional to Pe and therefore proportional to the flow rate u. For high flow rates, f_r is roughly gaussian and its width is a measure of the hydrodynamic dispersion accompanying the displacement process. However, it seems likely that most seepage flows through concrete and other construction materials correspond to low values of Péclet number and that the dispersion coefficient may be close to the apparent molecular diffusion coefficient.

No data have been traced for dispersion coefficients in brick, concrete and other construction materials. However, consistent behaviour is found for a wide range of porous materials including sedimentary rocks [338, 1085, 955] and there is no reason to expect that other construction materials will be an exception to the general pattern.

3.12 IMMISCIBLE DISPLACEMENT

In the literature of porous media, the term *immiscible displacement* generally refers to flow processes involving two liquid phases.

The case of displacement of one fluid in a porous medium by a second immiscible fluid has been fully studied as a central problem in petroleum reservoir engineering [786, 77, 148]. Both liquid–liquid and liquid–gas two-phase flows are considered. In all cases of two immiscible fluids, there are fluid–fluid interfaces throughout the system, which introduce a capillary pressure p_c between the two fluids which is directly related to the meniscus curvature and the interfacial tension. The curvature of the meniscus is determined by the contact angle made by the two liquids with the solid surface, that fluid with the acute contact angle being the wetting fluid. It is found experimentally that in a displacement process the displaced fluid is never completely removed, even at the longest times. This is because appreciable amounts of the displaced fluid become disconnected and trapped in pores throughout the medium. Once disconnected, such trapped fluid is not remobilized by continued flow. This result applies both to displacement of a nonwetting fluid by a wetting fluid (imbibition) and to displacement of a wetting fluid by a nonwetting fluid (drainage).

A limiting case is that in which there is no external pressure gradient. A wetting liquid spontaneously displaces a nonwetting (or less wetting) liquid

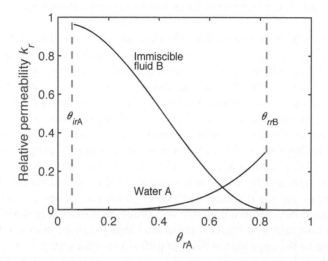

Figure 3.15 Relative permeability versus fractional saturation of A, θ_{rA}, for two immiscible fluids A and B: the data shown are for oil and water in a sandstone.

simply by the action of capillary forces [608, 77]. However, a nonwetting liquid cannot spontaneously displace a wetting liquid in the absence of a pressure gradient sufficient to overcome the capillary pressure (the so-called 'entry pressure'). The limiting saturations of displaced fluid are shown in Figure 3.15 in a schematic drainage/imbibition cycle, behaviour typical of oil/water displacement in a sandstone. The irreducible saturation of A (θ_{irA}) and the residual saturation of B (θ_{rrB}) are clearly shown. Between these two limiting saturations both fluids flow simultaneously. The two fluids separately obey an extended Darcy's law. The pressure in the two fluid phases differs at all points in the system by the capillary pressure, determined as already noted by the interfacial tension of the two fluids. A separate permeability k_i describes the relation between the flow velocity and pressure gradient in each fluid i. It is conventional to describe this as $k_{ri}k'$, where k_{ri} is the relative (fractional) permeability (between 0 and 1) for each fluid and k' the intrinsic permeability of the material. For two-phase flow it is invariably found that $k_{rA} + k_{rB} < 1$.

Buckley-Leverett theory

When the rate of displacement u is high, the influence of the capillary pressure diminishes in importance and the flow is dominated by viscous pressure losses. Under these circumstances, it is found that the displacement front becomes very steep (essentially a shock front). The evolution of the displacement is described (at least approximately) by Buckley-Leverett theory [196]. Buckley-Leverett theory applies at high values of the capillary number Ca $= \eta u / \sigma$.

3.13 TEST METHODS FOR TWO-PHASE FLOW PROPERTIES

Miscible fluids

The procedures developed for measuring dispersion coefficients in soils [788], chemical engineering operations (packed beds and other reactors) [866] and rocks [166] are applicable. All such methods in essence involve making a step-change in the composition of the fluid at the inlet and monitoring the breakthrough as a function of time in a series of experiments with the flow velocity u as an experimental variable. This is sufficient to determine the dispersion coefficient D_d and to estimate the dependence of D_d on Pe.

Immiscible fluids

Standard experimental methods for the measurement of relative permeability in rocks are described in [166, 338, 1038, 1121]. Most of these methods (for example the widely used Hassler method) involve establishing a steady and uniform partial saturation of the two fluids in a one-dimensional geometry. The steady flow velocity of each fluid is then measured under a fixed pressure drop. Measurements are repeated at a series of partial saturations. The same cell can also be used for determining the capillary pressure p_c.

3.14 AN HISTORICAL NOTE

The statement of a linear flow law for porous media is credited to Henry Darcy, who in 1856 measured rates of saturated flow through sand columns [388, 979]. For unsaturated flow, the seminal paper is that of Edgar Buckingham [195] in a Bulletin of the USDA who in 1907 stated the extension of the Darcy equation to the unsaturated state; and also set out the essential physics of the capillary potential (sometimes called the Buckingham potential), namely that the gradient of the capillary potential is the driving force for the unsaturated flow. While Buckingham emphasized the close parallel between unsaturated flow in porous media and heat flow and the conduction of electric current [1192], the differential equation of unsaturated flow was first written down by Lorenzo Richards [1052, 164] only in 1931, in the K-Ψ form. There was during that period considerable interest in experimental methods for characterizing the hydraulic properties of soils [405]. In 1951, Arnold Klute [681, 682] recast the Richards equation in the diffusivity form; and in 1955 John Philip [962] showed that for some simple one-dimensional cases, a relatively easily calculated solution could be obtained by a quasi-analytical procedure. Later around 1971 Jean-Yves Parlange [904, 905] gave a number of simpler approximate analytical solutions. In Melbourne in 1911 W. Heber Green and G. A. Ampt had published their simple sharp-front view of capillary absorption in soils [445], but this had little impact until resurrected by Ernest Childs [242] in the 1950s. Empirical and model-based expressions for the hydraulic properties (R. H. Brooks and A. T. Corey [186], M. van Genuchten [1261] and others) are frequently cited in the building materials research literature but more recent work in soil physics has had less influence.

In the construction field, Julius Hirschwald, a mineralogist in Berlin, launched the scientific study of hygral properties by his work on building stones [565], and influenced thereby the standardization of test methods for durability. We note equally the early and rigorous investigations of Edward Washburn [1296, 1298, 1299, 1300] on porosity measurement and the comprehensive study of the saturated permeability of concrete by William Glanville [423]. Green and Ampt were the first to state clearly the $t^{1/2}$ law of water absorption kinetics, but Washburn derived it again by analogy with his own well-known analysis of capillary rise in a cylindrical tube [1295]. There was no agreement on the $t^{1/2}$ law in building materials research until much later [464]. It was however stated by Edwin Madgwick [771, 772] and then once more by Treval Powers and Theodore Brownyard [1013] in their work on hydrated cement. They introduced the 'absorptivity' as the coefficient of proportionality, although they had no adopters for the term. That is an unimportant detail when set against the unmatched quality of their work on the physical properties of cements and mortars.

The first applications of unsaturated flow theory to construction materials are found in the writings of Bob Vos and E.Tammes [1283, 1277, 1285, 1278, 1279, 1284, 1286, 1287, 1281, 1282], who had had links with the soil physics school in the Netherlands; and of Sven Pihlajavaara [988] in Finland. The work of Aleksei Luikov [768], Otto Krischer [696] and W. F. Cammerer [215, 216, 217] had some influence at this time (see [410] for references to the German sources). This approach was taken up by Mark Bomberg [157, 158, 159, 160] in Lund who made the first systematic measurements of capillary potentials and unsaturated conductivities in materials like brick and concrete. This work in building physics was and continues to be motivated by interests in moisture in walls and is closely linked with engineering models of the thermal behaviour of buildings. Much research from the 1980s onwards has been driven by the durability of concrete and the conservation of historic buildings and structures.

NOTES

1 The conditions under which Darcy's law holds have been examined by many investigators. There is a succinct analysis by Rumer [1096], discussion by Philip [974, 975] and a review by Lage [717]. Darcy's law can be confidently applied to

slow creeping flow. As the flow rate increases, the effects of local accelerations along the flow path caused by the tortuous pore system manifest themselves as a deviation from the linear law, which is often described by the Forchheimer equation [383], $\nabla p = u/k + C\rho u^2$, where the constant C depends on the geometry of the pore system. At still higher flow rates, the flow may become locally turbulent. For the slow flows which we see in mass transfer phenomena in building elements, we need to know as a practical matter at what flow rates the quadratic term in the Forchheimer equation becomes apparent. We can express this transition in terms of the permeability Reynolds number $\mathrm{Re}_k = \rho u k'^{1/2}/\eta$. Experimental data suggest that deviations from Darcy's law are perceptible when Re_k is greater than about 0.1. To have a sense of the magnitudes, let us write the pressure gradient in terms of Re_k and the conventional permeability $K_s = k'\rho g/\eta$: so that $\nabla p = \mathrm{Re}_k (\eta \rho g^3 / K_s^3)^{1/2}$. For water with $\eta \rho \approx 1\ \mathrm{Pa}^2\,\mathrm{s}^3\,\mathrm{m}^{-2}$, and so with $\mathrm{Re}_k = 0.1$ we estimate that the maximum pressure gradient for Darcian flow $(\nabla p)_c \approx 3 K_s^{-3/2}$. For a sand column, with a permeability of 100 mm/min, this pressure gradient is about 30 bar/m, an unusually severe circumstance. Most materials of interest have much lower permeabilities and so the critical pressure gradients are correspondingly much higher. We conclude that the deviations from Darcy's law generally lie well outside our practical domain, both on site and in the laboratory. Weak deviations from Darcy's law arising from electrochemical effects have been reported by Swartzendruber in studies on salt solutions [1213].

2 The permeability is not an easy property to measure and there is a long trail of efforts to find ways to predict the permeability from other properties and in particular from microstructural parameters, not least in relation to cementitious materials [1069, 399, 645, 170, 401, 773, 552]. The Kozeny-Carman formula [222, 338] has been widely used and works well for certain classes of granular and tubiform porous materials, especially for groups of materials which are approximately geometrically similar. On the other hand, for many practical materials the permeability is dominated by the percolation network of highest conductivity and this feature may not be well captured by traditional measures of the length scale of the porosity. For sedimentary rocks, Katz and Thompson [668, 1103] argued that the intrinsic permeability scales as the quantity l_c^2/F where l_c is a percolation length which can be obtained directly from the inflection point of the mercury intrusion curve and F is the formation factor (both of which we mention briefly in Chapter 1). For sedimentary rocks, especially sandstones, Katz-Thompson permeabilities agree excellently with experimental values over a wide range, but for ceramics and cement-based materials the model has proved difficult to test [344, 247, 1251, 1136], not least because of problems of microcracking in sample preparation [1230].

3 Several building sandstones contain swelling clays and these cause mechanical deterioration as a result of cycles of expansion and shrinkage [650, 649]. The effect of these clays on the water permeability appears not have been investigated directly.

4 In petrophysics, the "relperm" convention is to formulate flow models in terms of the *relative permeability* function $k_r = K/K_s$ [148]. See also pp 111ff.

5 The quantity $d\theta/d\Psi$ is called the *differential water* (or *liquid*) *capacity* C_θ in soil physics [155]. In building physics the capacity is more usually defined in terms of water content w and fractional relative humidity $H = p_w/p_{w0}$ as $\xi = dw/dH$ and commonly called the *moisture (differential) capacity* [624]. The diffusivity $D(\theta) = K(\theta)/C_\theta$.

6 In building physics, it is common to write the Darcy equation in terms of the *mass* flow rate $\mathbf{u_m} = \mathbf{u}\rho_L$ and the pressure p, so that for a saturated material

$\mathbf{u_m} = k_{m,s}\nabla p$. The mass-flow permeability $k_{m,s}$ so defined has dimension [T]. From Eqn 3.1 we have $k_{m,s} = k\rho_L$ and $K_s = gk_{m,s}$. Correspondingly, the extended Darcy equation written in terms of $\mathbf{u_m}$ and capillary pressure p_c is $\mathbf{u_m} = -k_m\nabla p_c$. The quantity k_m is called the *moisture permeability* or *moisture conductivity* [624, 254, 560]. Of course k_m is a function of the liquid content. Water is invariably the liquid of interest, and k_m is the equivalent of the hydraulic conductivity function $K(\theta)$ defined in Eqn 3.9, with $k_m = K/g$. The mass-flow *moisture diffusivity* of [624] $D_w(w) = k_m(dp_c/dw)$, where $w = \theta\rho_L$, is the same as the hydraulic diffusivity $D(\theta)$.

7 The Brutsaert diffusivity function $D(\theta) = D_0\exp(B\theta)$ may be written $D = D_0'\exp(B_r\theta_r)$ where $B_r = B(\theta_s - \theta_d)$, $D_0' = D_0\exp(B\theta_d)$ and as usual $\theta_r = (\theta - \theta_d)/(\theta_s - \theta_d)$. If $\theta_d = 0$, $D_0' = D_0$. Note that by Eqn 3.12, $D_r(\theta_r) = (\theta_s - \theta_d)D_0\exp(B_r\theta_r)$. Note also that the value of the diffusivity function $D(\theta)$ at saturation is $D_1 = D_0\exp(B\theta_s) = D_0'\exp(B_r)$. Therefore we have $D(\theta) = D_1\exp[B_r(\theta_r - 1)]$.

8 The amount of attention devoted to water vapour transmission in building physics has been generous and perhaps excessive. The standard model of vapour diffusion promotes the view that the building element (usually a composite wall or roof construction) is an inert barrier which in an isothermal setting serves primarily to control the rate of water vapour transfer. In the presence of temperature gradients, we have also the possibility of reaching the dewpoint within the structure [1280]. This is the essence of Glaser's method of predicting interstitial condensation [424, 425, 426, 427], and the basis of an approach applied widely in many countries in the design of building enclosures. The method is powerful and easily understood but it does not embody other mechanisms of transferring water between vapour and sorbed states or processes of internal capillarity-driven water transport (for which of course it was not originally devised). Nonetheless its use has stimulated much important research on ways of using climatological data to define more or less realistic boundary conditions for heat and moisture transfer in buildings.

9 At the highest temperatures reached in building structures the dilute approximation is increasingly inaccurate. Thus at 60 °C the saturated vapour pressure of water is 20 kPa and the mass fraction of water in air at 100 per cent relative humidity is about 0.25. The density of dry air at this temperature is 1.0595 kg m^{-3} and that of water-saturated air is 0.98120 kg m^{-3}. However, the effect of relative humidity on the vapour diffusivity is completely negligible.

10 Analysis of the available data on the vapour diffusivity of water in air [797] confirms the earlier work of Schirmer [1137] and supports the use of the semi-empirical equation $D_w(T)/\mathrm{m^2s^{-1}} = 2.178 \times 10^{-5}(T/T_f)^{1.81}$ to describe the temperature dependence of the diffusivity at 1 atm (here T is the kelvin temperature (K) and T_f is the ice-point temperature 273.15 K). The precision of the exponent 1.81 is probably unwarranted. Some calculated values of D_w are given in Appendix B. Note that $D_v \sim D_w/T \sim T^{0.81}$.

11 This simple analysis treats the zone from the surface to the penetration depth x_p as being close to adsorption equilibrium at the imposed surface humidity condition H_1. It is an example of a Sharp Front [SF] model, in that the location of the penetration front is well-defined. We discuss many more SF examples in Chapter 4, starting on p 132, and in later chapters, mostly in relation to capillary liquid transport. It is appropriate to use an SF model here because of the strong localization of the sorbed water.

12 It is to be expected that miscible displacement of water by a nonaqueous liquid (such as an alcohol) should be accompanied by a severe desiccating effect [479]. In a mixture of a nonaqueous liquid and water the thermodynamic

activity of the water component falls to low values as the fraction of nonaqueous component rises and approaches 1. A low water activity of the liquid phase is equivalent to a low relative humidity and at mass transfer equilibrium brings the porous material to a high capillary water potential. It follows that if ethanol, for example, displaces water from a water-saturated concrete sample, there must be a severe tendency to dehydrate the cement paste at and behind the displacement front. The chemical stress imposed on the cement matrix may lead to changes in pore structure and to shrinkage. Some evidence of this form of dehydration came from Feldman [371] who measured strain in hardened cement paste samples during uptake of methanol and isopropyl alcohol. On the other hand, using isopropyl alcohol to remove water is put to advantage as a means of drying hydrated cement for various research purposes, such as microscopy. Carried out carefully it provides an excellent way of preserving the microstructure with little alteration [1369], and also of halting incomplete hydration reactions [1363]. The chemical stress accompanying miscible displacement is in sharp contrast to the situation in an immiscible displacement, where the thermodynamic properties of each liquid phase are unaffected by the presence of the other phase(s). In immiscible displacement of water by a nonaqueous liquid, the presence of the irreducible water content maintains a relatively high water activity.

4   Unsaturated flows

In Chapter 3, we have set out the main ideas of unsaturated flow theory and discussed in some detail the material properties associated with it. Now we take the first steps in applying the theory in various forms to situations of practical interest. We confine ourselves in this chapter to systems of one dimension, that is to say to unidirectional water transport processes. This allows us to present the essential arguments while avoiding the mathematical complications which arise in two- and three-dimensional problems.

We shall look at capillary absorption as an unsaturated flow process, described by the Richards equation. It will become clear that the number of cases for which we can obtain analytical solutions is extremely small. We shall also use a simpler approximate method of analysis, which we call Sharp Front [SF] theory, which is frequently useful as a means of describing unsaturated flows. Sharp Front theory offers us a route to simple approximate solutions of many important capillary flows of practical importance in construction: notably phenomena such as capillary rise, absorption into composite materials and absorption from circular and cylindrical cavities, all of which are discussed later in this book.

We also introduce a material property called the *sorptivity* that is of paramount value in understanding unsaturated flows of all kinds and in characterizing porous construction materials. The sorptivity is the property which expresses *the tendency of a material to absorb and transmit water and other liquids by capillarity*. Knowledge of the sorptivity is not a substitute for a complete specification of the hydraulic properties which we have defined in Chapter 3 but in the absence of full information it serves as a valuable guide to capillary behaviour. More particularly, it is a property which is rigorously defined in terms of the fundamental hydraulic properties, the diffusivity D, the conductivity K and the potential Ψ.

4.1   ONE-DIMENSIONAL WATER ABSORPTION

It is the Richards equation which provides the basis for our description of unsaturated flow in porous materials. We generally prefer to use this in the

Klute form [681], with the water content θ as the independent variable and the hydraulic diffusivity D as the controlling material property. Given a good knowledge of the diffusivity, then unsaturated flow processes can be represented by solutions to Eqn 4.1 subject to appropriate boundary conditions:

$$\frac{\partial \theta}{\partial t} = \nabla D \nabla \theta. \tag{4.1}$$

However, the strong dependence of D on water content presents difficulties in solving this equation.

Steady flow

For steady flow, the solution is easily obtained [473]. For the simple case of flow from a boundary at $x = 0$ maintained at water content $\theta = \theta_1$ to a boundary at $x = L$ with fixed water content $\theta = \theta_0$, we have $d\theta/dt = 0$ and hence

$$\frac{d}{dx} D \frac{d\theta}{dx} = 0. \tag{4.2}$$

We use the Kirchhoff transformation

$$\lambda(\theta) = \int_0^\theta D(\theta)d\theta \tag{4.3}$$

so that steady state solutions are given by Laplace's equation in the Kirchhoff potential λ.[1] For our one-dimensional case,

$$\frac{x}{L} = \frac{\lambda(1) - \lambda(\theta)}{\lambda(1)} = \frac{\int_\theta^1 D d\theta}{\int_0^1 D d\theta}. \tag{4.4}$$

The solution applies to any case in which a steady unsaturated flow is established between two reservoirs at different hydraulic potentials. This provides a model for several interesting practical cases, for example the movement of water through the interior of a composite wall where adjacent layers have constant but different water contents and hydraulic potentials, or the steady migration of water through a buried permeable pipe. In Figure 4.1 we show the steady water distribution through a material having a hydraulic diffusivity typical of many brick, stone and concrete materials. The strong dependence of diffusivity on water content is responsible for the increasing gradients in water content as we approach the drier face. The distribution differs sharply from the case of constant diffusivity.

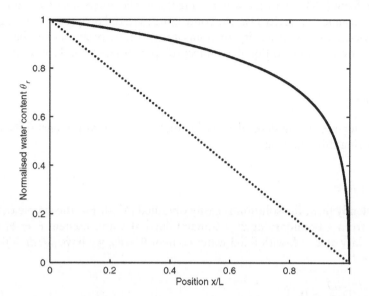

Figure 4.1 Steady-state water distribution in a porous barrier, thickness L with wet and dry faces. Solid line: exponential hydraulic diffusivity $D = D_0 \exp(B_r\theta_r)$ with $B_r = 6$; dotted line, constant diffusivity ($B_r = 0$).

Time-dependent solutions for the semi-infinite porous solid

The fully time-dependent one-dimensional case is of greater importance since it provides the foundation for understanding many practical phenomena and is also the basis of many experimental methods and test procedures. We consider the case of water absorption into a semi-infinite one-dimensional material which is initially dry ($\theta = \theta_d$) and subject to a free water boundary condition $\theta = \theta_s$ at $x = 0$, $t \geq 0$. We showed earlier that the cumulative water absorption i increases as $t^{1/2}$ but now we wish to calculate the entire water content distribution as a function of time for a material given a knowledge of its diffusivity property $D(\theta)$. An accurate quasi-analytical iterative method of solving the nonlinear diffusion equation was first developed and applied in soil physics by Philip [963, 964, 965, 974]. Parlange [904] gave another approximate method which provided adequate results without iteration. A better solution has been found by Parlange and his collaborators [917, 197]. This is obtained by a generalization of a method originally used by Heaslet and Alksne [554] to solve the restricted case of nonlinear diffusion in a material with a power law diffusivity. The extended Heaslet-Alksne method can be used whatever the form of the diffusivity function.[2] It has been applied to water absorption in concrete [753]. For the case of an exponential diffusivity $D = D_0 \exp(B_r\theta_r)$, which as we have seen provides a good representation of the hydraulic wetting diffusivity of brick, stone and concrete, the computation of the water distribution $\phi(\theta_r) = x(\theta_r)/t^{1/2}$ is particularly efficient. ϕ is obtained as the solution of Eqn 4.5

$$\frac{A}{2}\phi^2 + s\phi - 2D_0\left[\text{Ei}(B_r) - \text{Ei}(B_r\theta)\right] = 0 \tag{4.5}$$

where Ei is the exponential integral

$$\text{Ei}(x) = \int_{-\infty}^{x} \frac{\exp(t)}{t}dt, \tag{4.6}$$

and

$$s^2 = D_0\left[\left(\frac{2}{B_r} - \frac{1}{B_r^2}\right)\exp(B_r) - \frac{1}{B_r} + \frac{1}{B_r^2}\right] \tag{4.7}$$

and

$$A = \left[\frac{\exp(B_r)}{n} - 1 - \frac{1}{n}\right]\Big/\left[\exp(B_r) - 1\right]. \tag{4.8}$$

In Figure 4.2a, we show the calculated water content profiles for one-dimensional absorption into a semi-infinite initially dry medium using the extended Heaslet-Alksne method. In this example, we use the diffusivity of a clay brick ceramic, so that water content distribution is typical of brick masonry. The profile exhibits the characteristic steep gradients in the vicinity of the wetting front, and advances as $t^{1/2}$ maintaining constant shape, as the Boltzmann transformation requires. In Figure 4.2b we compare the calculated distribution $\phi(x)$ using the extended Heaslet-Alksne method with the accurate iterative method of Philip [963]. The curves are almost indistinguishable.

4.2 THE SORPTIVITY

In Section 3.8, we showed that the solution of the unsaturated flow equation

$$\frac{\partial\theta}{\partial t} = \frac{\partial}{\partial x}\left(D\frac{\partial\theta}{\partial x}\right) \tag{4.9}$$

subject to the boundary conditions $\theta = \theta_s$ for $x = 0, t \geq 0$; $\theta = \theta_d$ for $x > 0$, $t = 0$ is

$$x(\theta, t) = \phi(\theta)t^{1/2}. \tag{4.10}$$

Equation 4.10 shows that as water is absorbed horizontally into an initially

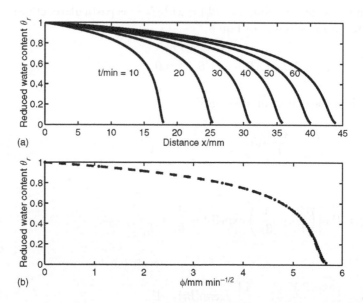

Figure 4.2 (a) Water content profiles $\theta_r(x)$ at a series of elapsed times t for capillary absorption into a porous medium having the diffusivity function $D/mm^2 \, min^{-1} = 0.13 \exp(-6.28\theta_r)$ measured for a wire-cut clay brick ceramic [508]. The material $x > 0$ has initial water content $\theta_r = 0$ and the free water boundary condition $\theta_r = 1$ is imposed at $x = 0$ and $t \geq 0$. The curves are calculated by extended Heaslet-Alksne method [917]. (b) Master curves $\phi(\theta_r)$ for the same material: comparison of the Heaslet-Alksne method (dashed line) with the iterative method of Philip [963] (dotted line).

dry porous solid all points on the advancing wetting profile advance as $t^{1/2}$. This has been confirmed experimentally for many inorganic construction materials, first by Gummerson *et al.* [466] for gypsum plasters, Portland limestone and a lime/sand/cement mortar, and subsequently for many other materials [229, 937, 700]. Typical profiles have been shown in Figure 3.9.

It is clear from Eqn 4.10 that the total amount of water absorbed in time t is given by

$$\int_{\theta_d}^{\theta_s} x d\theta = t^{1/2} \int_{\theta_d}^{\theta_s} \phi(\theta) d\theta = St^{1/2}. \tag{4.11}$$

Equation 4.11 defines the *sorptivity S*, a most important measurable property of a porous material [462] and one which we shall use frequently in the rest of this book. We present the sorptivity here as a quantity derived from unsaturated flow theory and which emerges from the application of the Richards equation to one-dimensional absorption into a semi-infinite material. Philip [966] first introduced the term in this way in the field of soil physics and hydrology. Unsaturated flow theory therefore provides theoretical support for $t^{1/2}$ laws of water absorption and penetration which were recognized by earlier investigators whose work was either empirical [838, 1301] or based on other theoretical models [771, 772, 1013].[3]

The significance of the sorptivity

Equation 4.10 shows that the sorptivity is the area under the ϕ–θ curve multiplied by the volume-fraction porosity f. Since ϕ is determined by $D(\theta) = -Kd\Psi/d\theta$, it follows that S is also determined by $D(\theta)$. It is for this reason that the sorptivity is such a useful and characteristic material property. The sorptivity, unlike the saturated permeability, is sensitive both to the conductivity and the suction characteristics of the material.[4]

The physical significance of the sorptivity is further clarified by the following subsidiary relations:

Inflow velocity. Since $i = St^{1/2}$

$$\frac{di}{dt} = u_0 = \frac{1}{2}St^{-1/2} \tag{4.12}$$

and

$$iu_0 = \frac{1}{2}S^2 = \text{constant.} \tag{4.13}$$

u_0 is the flow velocity at the inflow face ($x = 0$). u_0 sets the maximum rate of absorption of water by a porous solid, for example of rain by a masonry material (see Chapter 9).

Differential relation at the inflow face. For horizontal flow obeying the extended Darcy equation, we have

$$u_x = -K\frac{\partial\Psi}{\partial x}. \tag{4.14}$$

Thus $u_x = -fD(\theta)(\partial\theta/\partial x)$ where θ is the reduced water content. Combining this with Eqns 4.10 and 4.12 we obtain

$$S = -2fD_1\left(\frac{\partial\theta}{\partial\phi}\right)_{\phi=0} = -2fD_1\left(\frac{\partial\theta}{\partial x}\right)_{x=0} \cdot t^{1/2} \tag{4.15}$$

where D_1 is the diffusivity at $\theta = 1$ (normally saturation). The rate of flow across the inflow face diminishes as $t^{1/2}$ because the water content gradient at $x = 0$ decreases as $t^{1/2}$.

Advance of a wetting front. For many porous materials, the leading part of the advancing wetting profile is found to be steep, and may often be represented by a step function. On simple physical grounds the quantity $St^{1/2}/f$ provides an estimate of the distance of *penetration* at time t of the notional sharp front. Thus $S/f \approx B_w$, the *water penetration coefficient* in CIB terminology [253, 254] (or called B by ISO [624]).

Advance of the centre of mass of the absorbed water. We note that if the wetting profile advances as $t^{1/2}$ with constant shape $\phi(\theta)$ the centre of mass $\overline{x}(= \overline{\phi}t^{1/2})$ must also advance as $t^{1/2}$. On simple physical grounds $f\overline{\phi}/S$ cannot be less than 0.5, which is the limiting case of a step function wet front. The other limiting case may be taken as the constant diffusivity D for which $\theta = \mathrm{erfc}(\phi/D^{1/2})$. In this case, $f\overline{\phi}/S \approx 0.81$. For practical purposes for media with diffusivities which decrease continuously with water content $0.5 \leq f\overline{\phi}/S \leq 0.81$. The motion of the centre of mass can be observed simply but accurately by measuring the moment a bar of material pivoted about a point near the inflow face as water is absorbed [1352, 462]. This provides a direct means of obtaining some information about the shape of the water content profile during absorption. If it is assumed that the diffusivity is an exponential function, then the parameter B can be determined in this way.

It is also evident from the definition of the sorptivity that S depends on both the initial and final water contents. We discuss the variation of S with initial water content later in this chapter.

The intrinsic sorptivity

The capillary absorption of a liquid by a porous solid depends not only on the microstructure of the solid but also on three characteristic properties of the liquid which are its surface tension σ, viscosity η and density ρ. The intrinsic hydraulic properties which we briefly discussed in Section 3.4 are readily justified here.

The diffusivity defines flows which are entirely attributable to capillarity, such flows arising in response to gradients in Ψ. In turn Ψ depends on σ, the radius of curvature of the liquid meniscus within the pores and the liquid density ρ so that $\Psi\rho = 2\sigma/r$. Because r varies with θ for geometrical reasons, Ψ is also a function of θ. It follows that in any solid at any given liquid content the capillary potentials of two liquids A and B are related by

$$\frac{\Psi_A \rho_A}{\sigma_A} = \frac{\Psi_B \rho_b}{\sigma_B} = \Psi'. \tag{4.16}$$

Also, as discussed in Section 3.1, for any solid the permeability in respect of different Newtonian liquids varies with viscosity and density so that an intrinsic permeability $\mathcal{K} (= gk')$ is given by

$$\mathcal{K} = \frac{K\eta}{\rho}. \tag{4.17}$$

Since the diffusivity is given by

$$D = K\frac{\partial \Psi}{\partial \theta} \tag{4.18}$$

it follows that

$$D = \frac{\sigma}{\eta}\left(\mathcal{K}\frac{\partial \Psi'}{\partial \theta}\right) = \mathcal{D}\frac{\sigma}{\eta} \tag{4.19}$$

where $\mathcal{D}$ is an intrinsic diffusivity, independent of the properties of the liquid phase (and of temperature).

The solution of the unsaturated flow equation for $D = \mathcal{D}\sigma/\eta$ may be written in the form

$$x = \phi(\sigma t/\eta)^{1/2} \tag{4.20}$$

and thus

$$S = \left(\frac{\sigma}{\eta}\right)^{1/2} \mathbb{S} \tag{4.21}$$

where $\mathbb{S}$, the *intrinsic sorptivity*, depends only on θ. The intrinsic sorptivity is independent of the properties of the liquid (and therefore independent of temperature) and has dimension $[L^{1/2}]$.[5]

Equation 4.21 is an important result. It tells us that if we measure the sorptivity on a given material using a number of different test liquids, the sorptivity S should scale as $(\sigma/\eta)^{1/2}$. That this is so for one particular brick ceramic was demonstrated many years ago [462] using alcohols and hydrocarbons as well as water, and has since been confirmed for other fired clay materials [104]. We show the original data on a common clay brick material in Figure 4.3. The success of the scaling relation strongly suggests that these materials are completely wetted by all of these liquids (that is to say the contact angle is zero), that the materials are inert during the liquid absorption and that there are no microstructural changes. However, there are several reports of failures of the scaling in other materials which reveal that one at least of these assumptions is unjustified. We discuss the complex case of the 'sorptivity anomaly' in cementitious materials later in this chapter. A failure of the scaling in the sorptivity of some quarry limestones was first reported by Taylor [1219, 1220]. For five limestones (Brauvilliers, Jaumont, Lépine, Portland and Richemont), the sorptivities for the hydrocarbons *n*-heptane, *n*-decane and *n*-dodecane and methanol, ethanol and isopropyl alcohol conform to the scaling, but the water sorptivities are anomalously low. We show this in Figure 4.4a for three of these limestones: the sorptivities measured with the nonaqueous liquids scale accurately with $(\sigma/\eta)^{1/2}$. The slope of

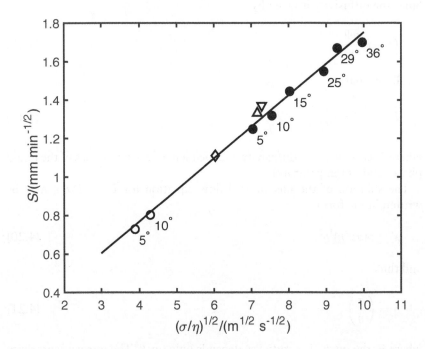

Figure 4.3 Capillary absorption of water and nonaqueous liquids by clay brick ceramic [462]. ● water, ○ ethanol, (temperature/°C as shown); ◇ methanol (13.5 °C); △ *n*-heptane (26 °C); ▽ ethyl acetate (24 °C). The measured sorptivity S is plotted against the quantity $(\sigma/\eta)^{1/2}$, where σ is the surface tension and η is the viscosity. For this material, the intrinsic sorptivity $\mathbb{S}$ is 2.1×10^{-5} m$^{1/2}$.

these lines is the intrinsic sorptivity $\mathbb{S}$. In Figure 4.4b, we normalize the measured sorptivity by $\mathbb{S}$ to collapse all imbibition data on to the line of equality. We then see that the water sorptivities, similarly normalized by $\mathbb{S}$, lie far below the line of equality. For these limestones, the sorptivities do not scale simply as $(\sigma/\eta)^{1/2}$. The deviation indicates partial wetting (lower than expected rates of capillary imbibition), with a wetting coefficient for water $\beta = S_w^2 \eta_w/(\mathbb{S}^2 \sigma_w) < 1$. Here the wetting coefficient β is formally equivalent $\cos \gamma$ where γ is a notional contact angle.[6] From these results, we can conclude that for the nonaqueous liquids the imbibition parameter $I \leq 0$, while for water $I > 0$. For these limestones, it seems that the water anomaly is caused by the fact that water does not completely wet the pore surface while the nonaqueous liquids do [622]. Later results [513] on other limestones confirm that quarry limestones invariably have water wetting coefficient $\beta < 1$. The range of β is at least 0.3–0.7 (corresponding to notional contact angles from 45° to 70°).

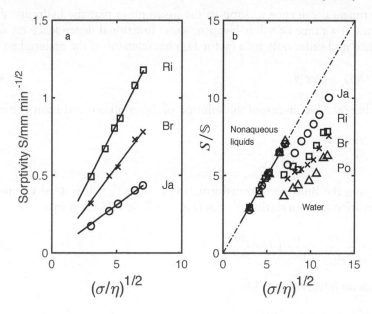

Figure 4.4 Capillary absorption of water and nonaqueous liquids by limestones [1219]. (a) Sorptivity of limestones measured with nonaqueous liquids *n*-heptane, *n*-decane, *n*-dodecane, isopropyl alcohol at temperatures in the range −4 to 62 °C: Br Brauvilliers, Ja Jaumont, Ri Richemont; (b) Normalized sorptivities $S/\mathbb{S}$ measured with nonaqueous liquids and with water; Po Portland.

Variation of the sorptivity with temperature

It follows from Eqn 4.21 that, neglecting any possible changes in contact angle, the change in S with temperature is controlled by the quantity $(\sigma/\eta)^{1/2}$. Generally the viscosity η falls more rapidly with increasing temperature than does the surface tension σ. Data for water are given in Appendix B. A change in temperature from 10 °C to 30 °C causes $(\sigma/\eta)^{1/2}$ for water, and hence the water sorptivity S, to increase by about 25 per cent.[7] The experimental data shown in Figure 4.3 demonstrate how the sorptivity of a common clay brick ceramic increases with temperature. The same dependence of S on $(\sigma/\eta)^{1/2}$ has been found in several other brick ceramics [666, 373], and in building stones [618]. That S varies with $(\sigma/\eta)^{1/2}$ provides indirect but strong evidence that σ controls the temperature variation of the capillary pressure p_c in these materials (see also p 52).

The sorptivity as a scaling parameter

We have seen that it is relatively straightforward to measure the sorptivity but measuring the diffusivity is rather more complex. However, there is experimental evidence to support the assumption that the hydraulic diffusivities of a range of solids have the same functional dependence on water content and differ only by a factor D_0 characteristic of the material so that

$$D(\theta) = D_0 F(\theta). \tag{4.22}$$

In Chapter 3 we discussed the solution of the nonlinear diffusion equation

$$\frac{\partial \theta}{\partial t} = \frac{\partial}{\partial x}\left(D\frac{\partial \theta}{\partial x}\right) \tag{4.23}$$

by using the Boltzmann transformation $\phi = xt^{-1/2}$. If instead we use the alternative transformation $\phi' = x(D_0 t)^{-1/2}$ Eqn 4.23 leads to

$$-\frac{\phi'}{2}\frac{d\theta}{d\phi'} = \frac{d}{d\phi'}\left(F(\theta)\frac{d\theta}{d\phi'}\right) \tag{4.24}$$

which on integration yields

$$\int_{\theta_d}^{\theta_s} \phi' = -2F(\theta)\frac{d\theta}{d\phi'}. \tag{4.25}$$

The cumulative absorption is then given by

$$\int_{\theta_d}^{\theta_s} x d\theta = t^{1/2}\int_{\theta_d}^{\theta_s} \phi' D_0^{1/2} d\theta = S t^{1/2}. \tag{4.26}$$

We therefore have for the sorptivity S

$$S = D_0^{1/2}\int_{\theta_d}^{\theta_s} \phi' d\theta. \tag{4.27}$$

This is a particularly useful result because it shows that the sorptivity varies as $D_0^{1/2}$. So by measuring the sorptivity of a material we can calculate D_0 and hence $D(\theta)$ from a knowledge of the sorptivity and diffusivity data of an appropriate reference material.

As we have discussed, data for building materials [466, 663, 753] suggest that the diffusivity is approximately an exponential function of water content and such a diffusivity function has frequently been suggested for soils [407]. Thus we can rewrite Eqn 4.22 as

$$D(\theta) = D_0 \exp(B\theta). \tag{4.28}$$

The effect of initial water content on the sorptivity

Usually when we determine the sorptivities of building materials we make measurements on specimens which are dry at the outset ($\theta_0 = \theta_d \approx 0$). However, our definition of the sorptivity makes it clear that whatever the initial water content, and provided it is uniform, the water absorption increases as $t^{1/2}$ and a sorptivity can be measured. It is therefore a matter of some importance to know how the sorptivity depends on the initial water content of the material [508]. It is evident that the sorptivity is reduced if the solid has a nonzero initial water content. We can calculate the variation of sorptivity with initial water content by determining $\phi(\theta)$ from Eqn 4.25. This can be done, for example using the iterative method of Philip, and leads to the theoretical curve drawn in Figure 4.5, which shows the variation of S/S_0 with reduced water content. Here S is the sorptivity at any given uniform initial water content and S_0 is the sorptivity of the initially dry material. Experimental data for brick plotted on the same figure confirm the validity of the analysis and show clearly that the sorptivity of brick ceramic falls with increasing initial water content.

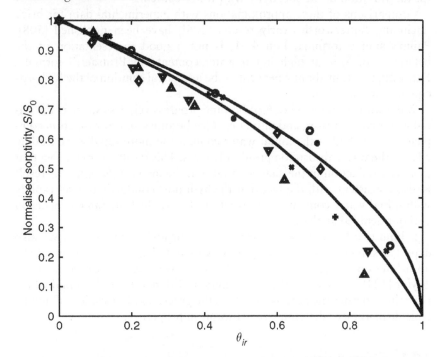

Figure 4.5 Variation of S/S_0 with initial reduced water content θ_{ir} for brick. Points are experimental data on several different brick materials [508]. Lower line: calculated from unsaturated flow theory for a typical brick material having exponential hydraulic diffusivity with $B = 6.3$; upper line: Philip's approximate formula, Eqn 4.31.

Approximate solutions of Eqn 4.25 have been proposed by Parlange [911], Brutsaert [189] and Lockington et al. [753].[8] Brutsaert showed that for the case of a material with an exponential hydraulic diffusivity of the form $D = D_0 \exp(B\theta)$ the sorptivity is given by

$$S = D_1[2B(\theta_1 - \theta_i)][1 + F(c)]^{1/2}/B \qquad (4.29)$$

where $c = B(\theta_1 - \theta_i)$, $D_1 = D_0 \exp(B\theta_1)$ and

$$F(c) = [\exp(-c)M(-0.5, 0.5, c)]/(2c - 1) \qquad (4.30)$$

in which $M(a, b, c)$ is the confluent hypergeometric function.

Philip [967] has also proposed the simple expression

$$\frac{S}{S_0} = (1 - \theta_{ir})^{1/2} \qquad (4.31)$$

for the variation of the sorptivity with water content.

Comparisons of these approximations with experimental data for brick (including Butterworth's early results [206]) have been published [508]. Philip's simple formula, Eqn 4.31, is not a good representation of the behaviour of S/S_0 at high initial water content but Brutsaert's formula, Eqn 4.29, is within about 2 per cent of the numerical solution of the Richards equation for $\theta_i \leq 0.9$.

Water absorption profiles $\theta(\phi)$ become progressively less steep as the initial water content rises, and ultimately $\theta(\phi)$ becomes an error function complement. The higher the initial water content the more rapidly the leading edge of the water absorption profile advances. This results from the fact that there is a reduction in the change in $D(\theta)$ in the interval (θ_s, θ_0). This result is also consistent with the fact that the hydraulic conductivity rises rapidly with initial water content. Butterworth [206] reached the same conclusion without detailed analysis.

If liquids other than water are used in sorptivity experiments we also expect a similar change in sorptivity with initial uniform content of the absorbing liquid. This has been confirmed in some careful experiments by Taylor [1219]. When the absorbing liquid is different from the liquid which partially saturates the porous solid then the processes of miscible and immiscible displacement determine the absorption properties.

4.2.1   Contact time

We generally assume that materials are stable on contact with an imbibed liquid and that their material properties do not alter during capillary absorption. This may often be true, or sufficiently so for practical purposes: for example for most liquids, and usually for brick and stone materials even with water. On the other hand, cement-based materials are often sensitive to contact with water. Microstructural alteration may produce changes in transport properties: these changes then need to be incorporated as explicit time-dependences in analysis of data and formulation of models.

Here, as a preliminary to later discussion, we introduce the concept of a *contact time*. We recognize that the alteration of any material property (such as porosity, conductivity or diffusivity) depends on the duration of contact with water. For example in a capillary absorption test alteration at any location is triggered only by the arrival of an advancing wet front. There may be a well-defined time $t = 0$ which marks the first contact of water with the inflow surface, but at this time the interior of the sample remains dry. If water arrives at interior position x at some time $t(x)$, then at any later time t' the material at x has been in contact with water for a total time $t_c = t' - t(x) < t'$. Necessarily $t_c \to 0$ as $x \to x_f$, where x_f is the location of the advancing wet front. The quantity $t_c(x)$ can be called the contact time. In an imbibition process (whether in a test specimen or in a component in service) the contact time measures the duration of direct contact between liquid and matrix. It is defined in relation to the matrix – and is the answer to the question: how long has this material *at this location* been wet?

There is a complementary question: how long has the water been in contact with the solid material? This arises for example if we wish to understand advection of dissolved substances driven by evaporation. The characteristic time for contact of water with solid is then the *residence time* (see p 110). Both contact time and residence time may vary from minutes to years in the great variety of laboratory and field situations in which capillary-driven flows occur.

4.3 THE DESORPTIVITY

In defining the sorptivity, we considered one-dimensional water absorption from a free water reservoir into a uniformly dry material. The boundary condition imposes a saturation water content θ_1 at $x = 0$ at $t = 0$. At this inflow surface, the hydraulic potential is then $\Psi = 0$. We can also envisage the analogous desorption process, where a condition of low water content, say θ_0 is imposed at the boundary of an initially saturated material ($\theta = \theta_1$ and $\Psi = 0$ throughout). This establishes an outflow at $x = 0$ where the hydraulic potential now has some large negative value $\Psi(\theta_0)$. For this case, the cumulative desorption i_d is given by

$$i_d = t^{1/2} \int_{\theta_1}^{\theta_0} \phi(\theta)d\theta = Rt^{1/2} \tag{4.32}$$

where R is the desorptivity [918] of the material. Like the sorptivity, the desorptivity has dimension $[\mathrm{LT}^{-1/2}]$. For reasons we discuss more fully in

Chapter 7 it is difficult to achieve the desorption boundary condition in experiments.

There is no simple relation between the sorptivity and the desorptivity because the underlying hydraulic property, the diffusivity, is hysteretic. Therefore water distributions in desorption are determined by the drying diffusivity while absorption distributions are controlled by the wetting diffusivity. This hysteresis has its origin mainly in the nature of the water retention curves. Approximate formulas which allow the desorptivity to be estimated if the drying diffusivity is known have been published by Lockington [749].

4.4   THE SHARP FRONT MODEL

The capillary diffusivity D of most porous materials varies so strongly with liquid content θ that the capillary absorption profiles are often very steep-fronted, as we have already seen. It is often justifiable and useful to represent the wetted region by a rectangular ('shock-front') profile. This is the Sharp Front [SF] approximation.[9] By using the SF model we can obtain comparatively simple mathematical descriptions of many wetting processes without resorting to numerical and computational methods. We shall use SF models in many places in the rest of this book. At the heart of the SF approach is the assumption that we can treat the wetted region has having a uniform and *constant* water content and that this is the saturation water content or at least some value close to it. By means of this assumption we reduce the unsaturated flow problem to an unconfined (free surface) saturated flow problem. The condition on the wetting front is that it has a well-defined and constant capillary potential Ψ_f. We mean by this that the total potential of the liquid phase at the front differs from the pressure potential just ahead of the front by an amount Ψ_f. Ψ_f therefore expresses the capillary force or capillary stress acting at the front. It is an assumption of the model that, for a particular liquid (let us say water) in a uniform material, Ψ_f is constant throughout the absorption process. We can think of Ψ_f as an *effective* capillary potential.

Thus we depict the absorption process as in Figure 4.6, where we have a bar of initially dry porous material of length L which is placed in contact with a water source at $x = 0$ at time $t = 0$. We show this as a horizontal flow so that there are no gravitational effects. The analysis applies also to vertical flows in circumstances where capillary forces are much stronger than gravitational forces, which can therefore be neglected (as is often the case in brick, stone and concrete). This therefore represents our simplest capillary rise (CR) model.

Water is absorbed spontaneously and a wet front located at $x_f = l(t)$ travels into the bar. We call the water content of the wetted region θ_e and the permeability of the material K_e, the e denoting effective quantities. It is useful to define also an effective porosity f_e which relates the total water

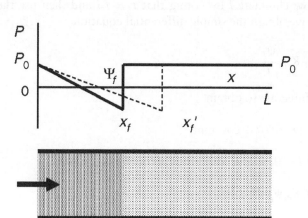

Figure 4.6 One-dimensional water absorption into a porous material: Sharp Front model.

content of the wetted region, in other words the cumulative absorbed volume I, to its volume V: that is, $f_e = I/V = i/l$, where i as usual is the cumulative absorption per unit area of inflow surface. Then of course $\theta_e = f_e$. As we shall discuss later the experimental evidence is that f_e is somewhat less than the porosity f, and can generally be taken to be equal to hf, where h is the fractional Hirschwald coefficient (page 162). The quantities K_e, θ_e and Ψ_f (are assumed to) remain constant throughout the absorption.

We now apply the simple form of Darcy's law, so that

$$u = -K_e \frac{d\Phi}{dx} = -K_e \frac{\Psi_f}{l}. \tag{4.33}$$

We can write the second equation because $\Phi = P_0$ at $x = 0$ and $\Phi = P_0 + \Psi_f$ at $x = x_f$, so that $d\Phi/dx = \Psi_f/l$. We note that since the water content θ_e of the wetted region is independent of position, we have

$$\frac{du}{dx} = -K_e \frac{d^2\Phi}{dx^2} = 0. \tag{4.34}$$

This means that $d^2\Phi/dx^2 = 0$. This is the one-dimensional form of Laplace's equation, which holds generally in SF problems. There are many analytical solutions to Laplace's equation in one, two and three dimensions, which is one of the main reasons why SF models of water absorption are so useful.

If we now eliminate l by noting that $i = f_e l$ and then use the relation $u = di/dt$, we obtain the simple differential equation

$$\frac{di}{dt} = -K_e f_e \frac{\Psi_f}{i} \tag{4.35}$$

which we integrate to obtain

$$i^2 = -2K_e f_e \Psi_f t + \text{constant}. \tag{4.36}$$

At $i = 0$ at $t = 0$, so the constant is zero, and we have

$$i = (2f_e K_e |\Psi_f|)^{1/2} t^{1/2} \tag{4.37}$$

for the cumulative inflow as a function of time t.[10] Remembering that unsaturated capillary potentials are negative quantities, we take the modulus of Ψ_f in Eqn 4.37. While we regard K_e and Ψ_f as model parameters, we can certainly identify their product with the measured sorptivity S since for this model

$$S = (2f_e K_e |\Psi_f|)^{1/2}. \tag{4.38}$$

We can use this model also to describe the case where there is a positive hydrostatic pressure at the inflow face, so that $\Phi = P_1$ at $x = 0$. Then the cumulative inflow is

$$i = \left[2f_e K_e (P_1 - P_0 + \Psi_f)\right]^{1/2} t^{1/2} = S' t^{1/2}. \tag{4.39}$$

The cumulative inflow from a pressurized reservoir therefore also increases as $t^{1/2}$ and at reservoir pressure P_1, the sorptivity $S' = [2f_e K_e (P_1 - P_0 + \Psi_f)]^{1/2}$. In terms of the standard sorptivity S, we have

$$(S'/S)^2 = (1 + (P_1 - P_0)/\Psi_f). \tag{4.40}$$

Mathematically, there is no reason to restrict this result to cases where $P_1 > P_0$. A tension head may equally exist at $x = 0$, but so long as $P_1 - P_0 < |\Psi_f|$ the material will absorb liquid at the rate given by Eqn 4.40. A full analysis of one-dimensional capillary absorption with pressure and tension heads based on Buckingham-Richards theory [969, 970, 908] confirms that i varies as $t^{1/2}$ as SF theory predicts. The SF results however assume a constant value of the effective permeability K_e of the wetted zone. This may be a good approximation for positive hydrostatic pressures P_1 but a poorer one for tension heads.

The system we have just described, that of the absorption of water into a one-dimensional porous medium of unlimited length (the *semi-infinite solid*),

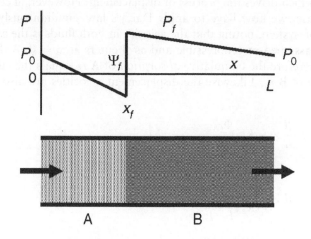

Figure 4.7 One-dimensional displacement of a liquid B by a wetting liquid A: Sharp Front model.

is the simplest of all, with a correspondingly simple mathematical basis. It is important both as an introduction to the SF model and also because it describes the common one-dimensional sorptivity test procedures. Before leaving this case, we note that if the specimen is of finite length L, then we may use the SF equation up to the point at which the wet front reaches the end of the specimen. The wet front has no advance knowledge that it will encounter a boundary at $x = L$ until the moment it does so.

That this is so is partly due to the fact that the air pressure ahead of the wet front has been assumed to be constant, that is to say the gauge pressure $P' = P_1 - P_0 = 0$. (We have also assumed that the air everywhere is at atmospheric pressure, but in fact the rate of absorption depends not on the absolute pressure but only on the gauge pressure P'.) Therefore the progress of the wet front is not affected by anything happening ahead of it. As a second example, we now look at the case where this is not so and in which the wet front displaces a second fluid which has a finite viscosity.

Immiscible displacement of one liquid by another

Figure 4.7 shows a porous material, porosity f, in the form of a bar of length L which is initially saturated with a liquid B which is then displaced by a second liquid A with which it does not mix. This is the case of immiscible displacement. The displacement will only proceed spontaneously if A is wetting and B is not. There is a capillary pressure at the A-B contact surface, strictly a difference in capillary pressure in the two phases, such that $\Psi_f = \Phi_{fA} - \Phi_{fB}$, the difference in total potentials Φ_A and Φ_B in the two phases at the displacement front. In the SF model, this capillary pressure is the SF potential which drives the process of displacement. However, in contrast to the first case, we now have to apply Darcy's law simultaneously to both parts of the system, noting that the velocity in both fluids is the same. The fluids are assumed incompressible and as B enters at $x = 0$, A departs at $x = L$. Therefore the cumulative *absorption* of A i_A equals the cumulative *desorption* of B i_B. Likewise the displacement velocities are also equal so that

$$\frac{di_A}{dt} = f_e \frac{dl}{dt} = -K_{eA} \frac{\Phi_{fA}}{l} \tag{4.41}$$

and

$$\frac{di_B}{dt} = f_e \frac{dl}{dt} = -K_{eB} \frac{\Phi_{fB}}{l - L}. \tag{4.42}$$

Therefore

$$K_{eA} \frac{\Phi_{fA}}{l} - K_{eB} \frac{\Phi_{fB}}{l - L} = 0. \tag{4.43}$$

If we write $\Phi_{fB} = \Phi_{fA} + \Psi_f$ we get

$$\Phi_{fA}^{-1} = \frac{K_{eA} - K_{eB}}{K_{eB} \Psi_f} - \frac{K_{eA} L}{K_{eB} \Psi_f l} = C - \frac{D}{l}, \tag{4.44}$$

where the quantities C and D involve only material properties.

If we now put this relation into the differential form of the Darcy equation (that is, we eliminate Φ_{fA} from Eqn 4.41) we obtain

$$\left(C - \frac{D}{l} \right) l \, dl = -\frac{K_{eA}}{f_e} dt \tag{4.45}$$

which on integration gives the general equation for the advance of the displacement front

$$\frac{1}{2} Cl^2 - Dl = -\frac{K_{eA}}{f_e} t, \tag{4.46}$$

or more explicitly

$$\frac{1}{2} \frac{K_{eA} - K_{eB}}{K_{eB} \Psi_f} l^2 - \frac{K_{eA} L l}{K_{eB} \Psi_f} = -\frac{K_{eA}}{f_e} t. \tag{4.47}$$

The main interest in this example is the influence of liquid viscosity on the displacement. Since the permeability is inversely proportional to the liquid viscosity we write $K_{eA}/K_{eB} = \eta_B/\eta_A = \chi$, so that

$$\frac{1}{2}(\chi - 1)l^2 - \chi Ll = -\frac{K_{eA}\Psi_f}{f_e}t. \qquad (4.48)$$

It is useful to divide by L^2 and write $X_f = l/L$ and $T = t/L^2$, so that we finally obtain a general equation for the displacement process:

$$\frac{1}{2}(1 - \chi)X_f^2 + \chi X_f = \zeta T \qquad (4.49)$$

where $\zeta = K_{eA}\Psi_f/f_e$.

We can now look at different cases in terms of χ. When the viscosities of the two liquids are equal, $\chi = 1$, the first term vanishes and $X_f = \zeta T$ or

$$\frac{dl}{dt} = \frac{u}{f_e} = \frac{K_e\Psi_f}{f_e L} \qquad (4.50)$$

where K_e is the common permeability. The displacement velocity is *constant* throughout the process, since the total resistance to flow remains constant from beginning to end. This is the middle curve shown in Figure 4.8.

When the displacing liquid has a much higher viscosity than the displaced liquid, $K_{eA} \ll K_{eB}$ and χ is small. As $\chi \to 0$, $X_f^2 \to 2\zeta T$. Hence

$$\frac{1}{2}\frac{l^2}{L^2} = \frac{K_{eA}\Psi_f}{f_e}\frac{t}{L^2}. \qquad (4.51)$$

L^2 cancels so that the solution is independent of the specimen length. Thus

$$l = \left(\frac{2K_{eA}|\Psi_f|}{f_e}\right)^{1/2} t^{1/2}. \qquad (4.52)$$

Putting $i = f_e l$ we obtain our previous expression for the SF sorptivity

$$i = (2f_e K_{eA}|\Psi_f|)^{1/2}t^{1/2} = St^{1/2}. \qquad (4.53)$$

The third case is that in which the displaced fluid has the higher viscosity. As $\chi \to \infty$, Eqn 4.49 becomes

$$-\frac{1}{2}\chi X_f^2 + \chi X_f = \zeta T. \qquad (4.54)$$

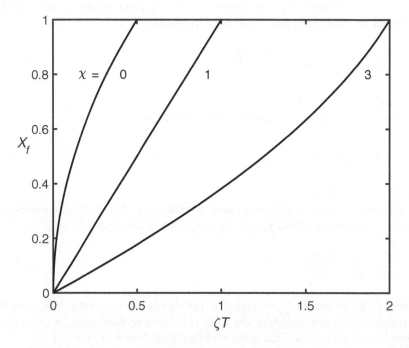

Figure 4.8 One-dimensional immiscible displacement: Sharp Front model. Eqn 4.49, $X_f(T)$, with different values of the parameter χ (0, 1, 3), reflecting the influence of the viscosities of the two liquids.

This is interesting as an example of an accelerating process.[11] The rate of displacement is

$$\frac{dX_f}{dt} = U = \frac{\zeta}{\chi(1 - X_f)}. \tag{4.55}$$

At early times, when $X_f \approx 0$, $U = \zeta/\chi = K_{eB}\Psi_f/f_e$. Thus the rate of displacement is controlled by K_{eB}, that is by the viscosity η_B of the displaced fluid. At late times, as $X_f \to 1$,

$$\frac{dX_f}{dt} \to \infty. \tag{4.56}$$

If we write $X_f = 1 - \epsilon$ with $\epsilon \ll 1$ then

$$-\frac{d\epsilon}{dt} = \frac{\zeta}{\chi\epsilon} \tag{4.57}$$

so that

$$\frac{1}{2}\epsilon^2 = \frac{\zeta}{\chi}(T_d - T) \tag{4.58}$$

where T_d is the time of complete displacement ($\epsilon = 0$). The last stages of displacement are therefore described by the equation

$$\frac{1}{2}(1 - X_f)^2 = \frac{\zeta}{\chi}(T_d - T). \tag{4.59}$$

This is an accelerating $t^{1/2}$ process, controlled by the length of the viscous fluid which remains to be displaced.

Finally we note that for complete displacement to occur, Ψ_f must always be negative, that is for all values of K_{eA}, K_{eB} and at all positions of l. Referring to Figure 4.7, it is obvious that this is necessary for the Darcy flow velocities to remain positive throughout in both liquids. If Ψ_f is negative, so also is Ψ_f^{-1}. Therefore from Eqn 4.44, we require that

$$\frac{K_{eA}L}{K_{eB}\Psi_f l} > \frac{K_{eA} - K_{eB}}{K_{eB}\Psi_f} \tag{4.60}$$

or

$$\left(\frac{L}{l} - 1\right) > -\frac{K_{eB}}{K_{eA}}. \tag{4.61}$$

This is always true because K_{eA} and K_{eB} are positive quantities and L/l is always ≥ 1.

Sequential imbibition of immiscible liquids

Next we consider the more complex problem of the successive imbibition of two different immiscible liquids into a porous medium [507]. In the previous example, the displacing liquid enters a porous material which is presaturated with a liquid with which it is immiscible. Now we allow the second liquid to be absorbed while the first liquid is still advancing, as in Figure 4.9. Capillary forces act on both the liquids.[12]

In our SF analysis of immiscible displacement, we worked in terms of a pressure potential P and used the conventional Darcy permeability K. Here, for the case of sequential imbibition we follow [507] and express Darcy's equation in terms of pressure p rather than pressure potential $P = p/\rho g$ (with liquid density ρ) to avoid a difficulty in defining the pressure potential at the interface between the two liquids. As a consequence, we use the Darcy

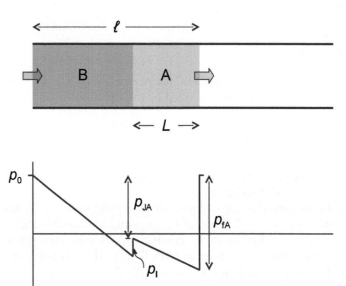

Figure 4.9 Schematic of unidirectional sequential imbibition of two liquids, A and B, into a porous material of unlimited length. In the Sharp Front model, the liquid phase pressure varies linearly within each liquid; for immiscible liquids, there is a pressure jump p_I at the interface between A and B. The values p_0, p_{fA} and p_{JA} are constant throughout the imbibition process.

permeability k rather than K. We also avoid the use of the intrinsic permeability $k' = k\eta$, dimension [L^2], as we do not wish to assume the simple scaling of flow rate with $1/\eta$, where η is the viscosity.

In SF models, the wetted region is assumed to have a constant liquid content close to saturation so that the wetted region has a rectangular liquid content versus distance profile. We assume that the wetting front capillary pressure p_f is constant throughout the absorption process and that the capillary pressure is zero throughout the wetted region at all times.

We apply Darcy's law separately to the two liquids. We label the leading liquid A, the trailing liquid B; and denote the time at which B first enters the porous medium the switchover time t_{so}. For $t \geq t_{so}$

$$u_A = -\frac{k_A(p_{fA} - p_{JA})}{L} \tag{4.62}$$

and

$$u_B = -\frac{k_B p_{JB}}{l - L}. \tag{4.63}$$

Since $p_{JB} = p_{JA} - p_I$, $l = i/f$ and $u_A = u_B = u$, say, then we have from Eqns 4.62 and 4.63

$$u = -fk_B(p_{fA} + p_I)/[i + fL(\frac{k_B}{k_A} - 1)]. \tag{4.64}$$

We define a quantity

$$j = i + fL(\frac{k_B}{k_A} - 1) \tag{4.65}$$

to obtain

$$u = \frac{di}{dt} = \frac{dj}{dt} = -\frac{fk_B(p_{fA} + p_I)}{j}. \tag{4.66}$$

We can now integrate Eqn 4.66 to obtain the SF equation for the absorption rate $j(t)$ for $t > t_{so}$

$$j^2 = -2fk_B(p_{fA} + p_I)t + f^2L^2\frac{k_B}{k_A}\left[\frac{k_B}{k_A} - \frac{p_{fA} + p_I}{p_{fA}}\right]. \tag{4.67}$$

We can further simplify Eqn 4.67 by noting that the sorptivity of the leading liquid A, $S_A = (2fk_A|p_{fA}|)^{1/2}$, so that

$$j^2 = S_A^2 r_k\left[(1 + r_p)t + (r_k - 1 - r_p)t_{so}\right], \tag{4.68}$$

where $r_k = k_B/k_A$ and $r_p = p_I/p_{fA}$. Equation 4.68 describes the complete evolution of the two-liquid imbibition process for all $t \geq t_{so}$.

Also, we can define a *hybrid sorptivity* $S_h = (2fk_B|p_{fA} + p_I|)^{1/2}$, so that Eqn 4.67 may be written

$$j^2 = S_h^2 t + f^2L^2\frac{k_B}{k_A}\left[\frac{k_B}{k_A} - \frac{p_{fA} + p_I}{p_{fA}}\right]. \tag{4.69}$$

At long times, as $t \to \infty$, $j = S_h t^{1/2}$, so that we revert to a simple $t^{1/2}$ law of capillary absorption. The hybrid sorptivity, S_h, is a remarkable property which describes a $t^{1/2}$ process in which the wetting front capillary tension is provided by liquid A but the viscous drag in the wetted region is provided by liquid B. We note the useful relation

$$S_h^2 = S_A^2 r_k(1 + r_p) \tag{4.70}$$

so that for materials with similar wettability properties S_h/S_A should be constant for sequential imbibitions of a given pair of liquids imbibed in the same order.

This analysis has been tested against experimental data on capillary absorption of *n*-decane and dimethylsulphoxide (DMSO) using concrete cylinders 150 mm length × 100 mm dia [507]. Capillary imbibition measurements were carried out by immersing an end face to a depth of 10 mm in the test liquid. The amount of liquid absorbed was measured from time to time by weighing. In different tests, the specimen was allowed to absorb the leading liquid for 1.5, 6 and 24 h. Capillary absorption data for the sequential imbibition of DMSO followed by *n*-decane are shown in Figure 4.10, where the cumulative absorption *i* is plotted against $t^{1/2}$. In all cases, the absorption of the leading liquid obeys the standard law $i = St^{1/2}$, but after t_{so} when the trailing liquid enters the concrete a complex curvature is found. At the end of the tests the imbibed liquids reached final penetration distances of about 70 mm after some 100 h. In Figure 4.10 the solid lines are the theoretical fits based on the SF model we have described. Broadly, the ability of the simple SF model to represent the complete sequential imbibition datasets from early to long times is impressive, given that there are

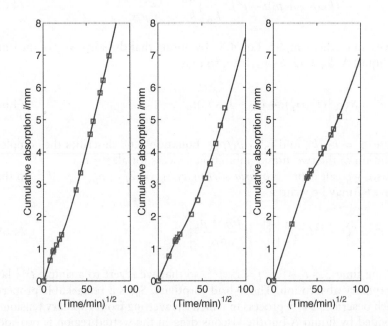

Figure 4.10 Experimental data for sequential imbibition of DMSO followed by *n*-decane into concrete, with switchover times t_{so} 1.5, 6, 24 h (from left to right). Solid lines are nonlinear least squares fits to Eqn 4.68 (see text).

only two disposable parameters (taking S_A as fixed by independent experiment). More generally, results [507] on a single well characterized concrete material show that the interfacial tension acting between the two liquids can oppose or assist imbibition, according to the sequence of liquids.

Imbibition with air confinement

We can ring further changes on the theme of one-dimensional absorption to analyze processes in which the fluid ahead of the wet front is confined[13] and not free to leave the specimen across an outflow surface. This is of little interest if fluid A is an incompressible liquid for then nothing happens.[14] However when A, the confined nonwetting fluid, is a gas (usually of course air) we have a common and important situation to which we shall return several times later. Often in such situations, displaced air is confined by other wet fronts, an example being absorption by a flat plate completely immersed in water. Here water absorption occurs simultaneously from both sides. Air driven by the wet front advancing from one side is confined by the wet front approaching from the other side and is compressed by the pincer action of the two. We now look at an SF description of imbibition with air confinement.

Figure 4.11 shows a porous material of porosity f_e in the form of a bar of length L which is sealed on all surfaces except the inflow surface at $x = 0$. (Mathematically this is exactly the same as the infinite plate of thickness L.) As usual, we define a constant wet front potential Ψ_f and a (barometric) pressure P_0 at the liquid reservoir at $x = 0$. Initially, the air pressure within the material P_a equals P_0. As the wet front moves forward, the volume

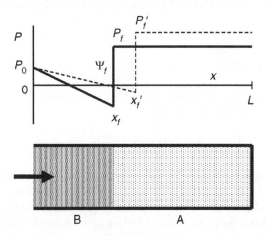

Figure 4.11 One-dimensional imbibition into a material sealed against the escape of the displaced air.

occupied by the fixed mass of air decreases and P_a rises. By Boyle's law, $P_a = P_0 L/(L - l)$ where $x = l$ is the position of the wet front. The advancing wet front feels increasing resistance as it compresses the air ahead of it. Eventually an equilibrium is established when $P' = P_a - P_0 = -\Psi_f$. At equilibrium the wetted length $x_\infty = L\Psi_f/(\Psi_f - P_0)$ and the ultimate cumulative absorption $i_\infty = f_e x_\infty$. Whatever the numerical values of the parameters, the wet front is destined never to reach the end of the bar. We can apply Darcy's law as usual to this case, noting that the pressure difference acting on the wetted region is now a function of l. Thus we have

$$u = -K_e \frac{\Psi_f + P_a - P_0}{l} = -K_e \frac{\Psi_f + P'}{l}. \tag{4.71}$$

Since $P' = P_0 l/(L - l)$ and $i = f_e l$, we obtain the differential equation

$$u = \frac{di}{dt} = -K_e f_e \frac{\Psi_f}{i} - K_e f_e \frac{P_0}{i_L - i}, \tag{4.72}$$

where $i_L = f_e L$ is the total pore volume of the sample.

Although describing a simple enough problem, this equation quickly becomes quite complicated, as the reader can check by integrating it. Therefore, we recast Eqn 4.72 in terms of dimensionless variables, a procedure we shall adopt again in other SF analyses. The ultimate absorption i_∞ imposes a natural length and so we define a space variable $X = i/i_\infty$. As usual in unsaturated flow problems, the sorptivity establishes a natural time scale, so we define a dimensionless time $T = S^2 t/i_\infty^2$. We expect that the quantity $\lambda = i_\infty/i_L$, which tells us how much of the sample is ultimately wetted, will also be parameter of interest. By expressing Eqn 4.72 in terms of X, T and λ, we obtain

$$\frac{dT}{dX} = \frac{2X(1 - \lambda X)}{1 - X}. \tag{4.73}$$

We now integrate this to obtain $X(T)$. After eliminating the constant of integration (using $X = 0$ at $T = 0$) we get

$$T = \lambda X^2 - 2(1 - \lambda)[X + \ln(1 - X)]. \tag{4.74}$$

This equation describes the entire absorption process and how it depends on the SF material parameters Ψ_f, K_e and f_e and the quantities L and P_0. The result expressed in terms of the variables X and T and the parameter λ also shows clearly how these quantities work in combination. Thus if we express the $i(t)$ behaviour in terms of X and T, then the solution depends only on the parameter λ, which as we have seen is equal to $i_\infty/i_L = \Psi_f/(\Psi_f - P_0)$.

At early times, we would expect the absorption to be insensitive to the presence of the air at all values of λ and indeed with $X \ll 1$ Eqn 4.74 reduces to $T = X^2$, so that $X = T^{1/2}$ and $i = St^{1/2}$, just as in the unsealed absorption case. We show $X(T^{1/2})$ in Figure 4.12. At later times, X falls below the $T^{1/2}$ line and eventually approaches the limiting value 1 (where $i = i_\infty$). The importance of the parameter λ is that it tells us how the presence of the air buffer retards the absorption at late times, say for $T \geq 1$. (We should caution that since the definition of T ($= S^2 t / i_\infty^2$) involves i_∞^2, large values of T correspond to comparatively short clock times t when λ is small).

We note also a particular significance of the final state of the system, in which all dependence on transport properties has disappeared and we have of course the simple equilibrium condition $|\Psi_f| = P'$. This illustrates a general law of capillary systems at equilibrium, namely that the total potential is everywhere constant. This particular case is of great interest however because it offers a means of measuring directly the material property Ψ_f which enters all SF models. As we have remarked before, the sorptivity $S = (2K_e f_e |\Psi_f|)^{1/2}$, so that S yields Ψ_f only if assumptions are made about the values of K_e and f_e. An experiment of the kind depicted in Figure 4.11 provides a direct and simple measure of the wet front capillary pressure from porosity and weight measurements alone. It is perhaps worth pointing out that the experiment is essentially a pycnometric one, identical in concept to

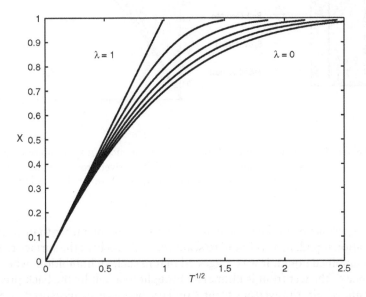

Figure 4.12 X versus $T^{1/2}$ for the Sharp Front model of capillary imbibition with air confinement. Curves show the influence of the parameter λ.

the methods already described for measuring the porosity. Here we use the total mass change on wetting to determine the final volume of a fixed mass of gas whose initial volume is known. Hence we determine its final gauge pressure P' which is equal to $-\Psi_f$. Alternatively stated, $-\Psi_f = \lambda P_0/(1 - \lambda)$.

Air confinement during imbibition has been studied experimentally in the case of clay brick [620]. The compression of air ahead of the advancing wetting front was measured directly with an embedded pressure sensor and the entire time-evolution of the imbibition was observed (Figure 4.13). The equilibrium gauge pressure of the confineded air provides a measure of the wetting front capillary pressure p_f. For the particular case of the high porosity commercial brick described in [620], this pressure was 0.11 MPa, equivalent to a hydraulic tension head of 11.5 m and to a Young-Laplace pore diameter of 2.6 μm. These measurements show that the imbibition kinetics are well described by the SF model. The final equilibrium mass gain provides an independent estimate of p_f. This is an important result, since it offers an experimentally simple method to obtain this quantity [665, 616].

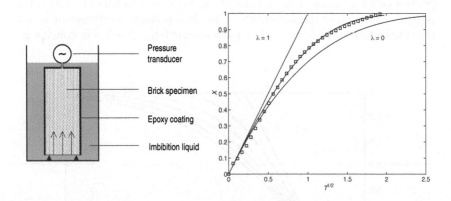

Figure 4.13 (a) Experimental arrangement for measuring imbibition kinetics with air confinement; (b) $X(T^{1/2})$ derived from experimental pressure data, showing best fit to Eqn 4.74 for $\lambda = 0.52$. Adapted from [620].

In experiments on the same material with n-heptane rather than water as imbibition liquid, p_f was found to scale approximately as the surface tension of the imbibed liquid. It was suggested that in such an imbibition, where the advance of the wet front is ultimately brought to a halt by the back pressure of confined air, the wetting front capillary pressure so measured is equal to the air pressure at which liquid phase continuity goes to zero. At that pressure, the unsaturated conductivity also vanishes. If this interpretation is correct, the wet front capillary pressure appears to be a fundamental percolation property of the material. An interesting side result is that any air trapped within the wetted region (behind the wet front) has the same pressure as the wet front capillary pressure.

Absorption by a porous sphere

A dry porous sphere which is totally immersed absorbs water over its entire surface and the air originally occupying the pore space is driven towards the centre. As a three-dimensional radially symmetrical absorption involving only a single space coordinate, the SF analysis is similar to that of the one-dimensional process just set out. This interesting problem has been discussed fully [1354] in connection with water uptake by soil aggregates, an important practical case where air is frequently confined. It is equally applicable to water absorption by sorptive coarse aggregate particles in concrete [441]. The result [1354] for a sphere of porosity f and radius a, using the same dimensionless variables as before, is that

$$T = \frac{6}{\lambda} \int_0^X \frac{(1 - \lambda X')^{2/3} - (1 - \lambda X')}{1 - X'} dX' \qquad (4.75)$$

where $X = i/i_\infty$ and $T = S^2 t/i_\infty^2$. i is the cumulative absorption per unit surface area, so that at complete saturation (no air trapping) $i_a = af/3$ and we define $\lambda = i_\infty/i_a$. Tests using gypsum plaster spheres of 25–50 mm radius show excellent agreement with SF theory for cumulative absorption kinetics [441]. Here ingenious experiments on hemispheres in which the plane surface is not immersed, and is either open to the atmosphere or sealed, allow absorption with and without air-confinement to be compared.

Absorption by a porous cylinder

Water absorption into a solid porous cylinder [485] is a useful practical case, also using only a single space coordinate. Cylindrical geometry is found in pipes, drains, arches and conduits, and in drill cores for testing. Here as in Figure 4.14a we analyze absorption of a liquid through the cylinder faces of a solid right cylinder of length L and radius R. In cylindrical coordinates, the cylinder axis is at $r = 0$, and the cylinder surface is at $r = R$. The plug, initially dry, is made of a uniform, isotropic material of volume-fraction porosity f. At time $t = 0$ it is placed in contact with water (or other liquid) so that liquid is freely available at atmospheric pressure at $r = R$ (the free-liquid reservoir condition). The top face is unsealed so that air can be displaced ahead of the advancing wet front. We satisfy the usual SF assumption that the air (the nonwetting phase) is at atmospheric pressure throughout.

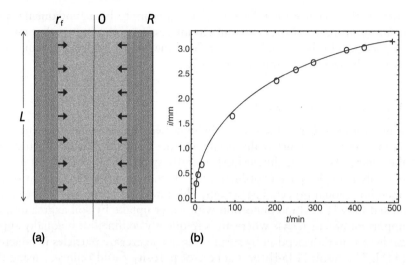

Figure 4.14 Radial liquid absorption through the lateral surface of a solid porous cylinder. (a) Inward flow of wetting front from cylinder surface. (b) Imbibition of isopropyl alcohol into a cylindrical plug of gypsum plaster [485], $R = 38.3$ mm, $L = 20.9$ mm. Test data (points) and fit (solid line) to Eqn 4.82; best-fit parameters $a = 494.0$ min, $b = 0.314$ mm^{-1}; estimated material property values $f_e = 0.166$, $S = 0.203$ mm/min$^{1/2}$. + marks the end of the absorption process at time $t = a$.

During capillary absorption, the wet front at $r = r_f$ moves radially inwards, and the volume of absorbed liquid $V = \pi f_e (R^2 - r_f^2) L$. The cumulative absorption per unit area of the inflow surface is therefore

$$i = \frac{f_e R}{2} [1 - (\frac{r_f}{R})^2],\tag{4.76}$$

so that

$$\frac{r_f}{R} = (1 - \frac{2i}{f_e R})^{1/2}.\tag{4.77}$$

The total potential $\Phi(r) = p/\rho g$ in the wetted region is obtained as a solution of Laplace's equation $\nabla^2 \Phi = 0$, with appropriate boundary conditions. In cylindrical coordinates, Laplace's equation becomes

$$\nabla^2 \Phi = \frac{1}{r} \frac{\partial}{\partial r} (r \frac{\partial \Phi}{\partial r}).\tag{4.78}$$

A first integration gives $d\Phi/dr = A/r$, and a second integration gives $\Phi = A \ln r + B$, with A and B constants. Subject to boundary conditions $\Phi = \Psi_f$

at r_f and $\Phi = 0$ at the inflow surface $r = R$, we have $A = \Psi_f / \ln(r_f/R)$. Hence at the inflow surface $R(\text{d}\Phi/\text{d}r)_{r=R} = \Psi_f / \ln(r_f/R)$. By Darcy's law, the inflow flux $v_0 = -K_e(\text{d}\Phi/\text{d}r)_{r=R} = \text{d}i/\text{d}t$ by mass balance. Therefore

$$\frac{\text{d}i}{\text{d}t} = \frac{|\Psi_f|K_e}{R} \frac{1}{\ln(r_f/R)} = \frac{2|\Psi_f|K_e}{R} \frac{1}{\ln(1 - 2i/f_e R)}. \tag{4.79}$$

We can use dimensionless variables $I = 2i/f_e R$ and $T = K_e|\Psi_f|t/(f_e R^2) = S^2 t/(2f_e^2 R^2)$ to simplify Eqn 4.79:

$$\frac{\text{d}T}{\text{d}I} = \frac{1}{2}\ln(-2I + 1). \tag{4.80}$$

Integrating this, with initial condition $I = 0$ at $T = 0$, gives the following general equation for absorption into a porous cylinder:

$$T = \frac{1}{4}[2I + (-2I + 1)\ln(-2I + 1)]. \tag{4.81}$$

The maximum value of I, $\max(I) = 1/2$ at $T = 1/4$. This occurs when the wet front reaches the cylinder axis, $r_f = 0$.

For data analysis, Eqn 4.81 is written as

$$t = a[bi + (-bi + 1)\ln(-bi + 1)], \quad 0 \le t \le a, \tag{4.82}$$

with $a = f_e^2 R^2 / 2S^2$ and $b = 2/f_e R$. The material properties can then be found from the best-fit parameters a and b by means of the relations $f_e = 2/bR$, and $S = (2/ab^2)^{1/2}$. Absorption is complete when $t = a$ and $i = 1/b$. An experimental test on imbibition of isopropyl alcohol into a gypsum plaster plug (Figure 4.14b) confirms the analysis.

Contact-time effects: material alteration

We cannot always assume that materials are unchanged by contact with an imbibed liquid. Such effects are rare with nonaqueous liquids, but they may occur with water. We therefore consider how such alteration may be incorporated into the SF model of capillary absorption [486]. This analysis makes use of the concept of contact time, introduced earlier in this chapter (p 131).

We start by noting an unexpectedly simple result for the mean contact time $\bar{t}_c$ for a material of sorptivity S and porosity f in which the cumulative imbibed volume $i = St^{1/2}$, and the position of the wet front $x = i/f$. Then at any time t

$$t_c(x) = t - (fx/S)^2 \tag{4.83}$$

and

$$\bar{t}_c(t) = \frac{f}{St^{1/2}} \int_0^{St^{1/2}/f} t_c(x)\,dx \tag{4.84}$$

so that $\bar{t}_c = 2t/3$ for all t. More generally, for a power-law imbibition $i = S't^n$, with constant exponent n, $\bar{t}_c/t = 1/(n+1)$, so that $\bar{t}_c/t \to 1$ as $n \to 0$.

Now we turn to the SF sorptivity, which depends on f, K and Ψ through Eqn 4.38. While all three of these properties may be changed by contact with water, it is reasonable to attribute any observed sorptivity anomalies to a time-variation of the permeability K, while the porosity f and Ψ_f remain constant. For illustration, we shall assume that the local permeability changes from an initial value K_0 to a final (long-term) value K_1 over a defined time, or at a defined rate. An exploratory option is to represent the time-variation in permeability as an exponential decrease from K_0 to K_1, with time constant τ. There is some support for this from data [758] on water flow through a cement mortar over a period of 15 days. The permeability decrease, by a factor of about 30, is roughly exponential, with a time constant of about 2 days.

The extent of the permeability decrease at any location depends on the contact time t_c, not on the elapsed time from the start of imbibition. Thus

$$K(x,t) = K_1 + (K_0 - K_1)\exp[-t_c(x,t)/\tau]. \tag{4.85}$$

Now we have from Eqns 4.35, 4.38, substituting $x_f = i/f_e$:

$$x_f \frac{dx_f}{dt} = \frac{S^2}{2f_e^2} = \frac{K_e(t_c)\Psi_f}{f_e}, \tag{4.86}$$

where $K_e(t_c)$ is the effective permeability of the wetted region between the inflow face at $x = 0$ and the advancing wet front at $x = x_f$. The permeability K_e here varies with contact time.

$$K_e(t_c) = \frac{1}{x_f} \int_0^{x_f} K(t_c)\,dx. \tag{4.87}$$

Equations 4.86, 4.87 then yield an integro-differential equation for the position of the wet front during imbibition:

$$x_f^2 \frac{dx_f}{dt} = \frac{\Psi_f}{f_e} \int_0^{x_f} K(t_c)\,dx \tag{4.88}$$

with initial condition $x_f = 0$ at $t = 0$.

Equation 4.88 can be solved numerically by means of an algorithm for the n-layer composite which we shall meet in Chapter 5. In the SF model, the hydraulic suction is provided by the capillary tension at the wet front, which is constant throughout the absorption since the contact time at the front is always zero. The hydraulic impedance is determined by the permeability distribution throughout the wetted region, which falls progressively from K_0 to K_1. This behaviour is shown in Figure 4.15. At early times, the imbibition corresponds to the higher value of permeability K_0 (and a higher sorptivity), and then decreases, reaching an eventual $i(t^{1/2})$ slope corresponding to

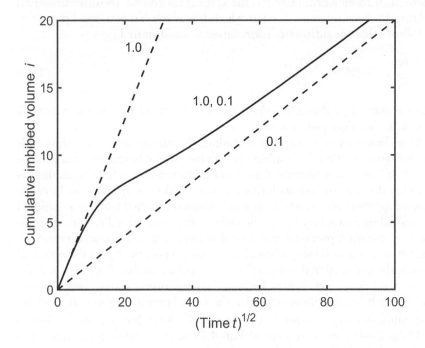

Figure 4.15 Imbibition kinetics: cumulative absorbed volume i vs $t^{1/2}$, where t is the elapsed time from the start of imbibition, for $f = 0.2$, $\Psi_f = 1$, $\tau = 100$ (in any consistent unit). Solid line: decreasing permeability, $K_0 = 1.0$, $K_1 = 0.1$; dotted lines: constant permeability, $K_0 = K_1 = 1.0$, and $K_0 = K_1 = 0.1$ as labelled.

K_1 (and a lower sorptivity) in a time about 5τ. An example of anomalous imbibition of this kind is shown in Figure 4.23 later in this chapter.

4.5 GRAVITATIONAL EFFECTS

In many cases in building materials, the strong capillary forces and the short distances over which migration occurs mean that we can neglect the effects of gravity on unsaturated flow. If the heights involved are much less than the variation in hydraulic potentials (let us say, if $\Delta z \ll \Delta \Psi / Mg$), then the assumption is justified. However this is not always so, and such examples arise in materials of inherently weak suction, in materials which are close to saturation and in situations where large heights may be involved. For this case, we generalize the fundamental equation of unsaturated flow Eqn 3.9 to include the effects of gravity by replacing the hydraulic potential Ψ by a total potential $\Phi = \Psi + z$ which thus depends on elevation. Problems involving flow between different levels are then accommodated easily within the theoretical framework. Here z is the vertical coordinate (positive upwards) relative to some reference level at which free water has zero total potential. It follows that the diffusivity formulation of unsaturated flow is

$$\frac{\partial \theta}{\partial t} = \nabla(D\nabla\theta) + \frac{dK}{d\theta}\frac{\partial \theta}{\partial z}. \tag{4.89}$$

We see that *for problems involving gravity effects* we need to know both D and K, rather than just D alone.

One-dimensional absorption including the effects of gravity thus calls for solutions to Eqn 4.89 subject to the free water boundary condition at $x = 0$. If flow is downwards, then water infiltrates and at long times there is a steady downward flow such that $v_\infty = K_s$. If flow is upwards we have the case of *capillary rise* in which an equilibrium is attained when gravitational forces balance capillary forces throughout the unsaturated region. At equilibrium, the total potential Φ is zero throughout the unsaturated region, so that $\Phi = \Psi + z = 0$ everywhere. As a consequence, the hydraulic potential equals the gravitational potential at every point, so that $\Psi(z) = -z$. If the water retention curve $\Psi(\theta)$ is known, the equilibrium water content distribution with height follows directly. The cumulative absorption at capillary rise equilibrium i_∞ is given by the integral $\int_0^\infty \theta dz$ which equals $\int_0^{\theta_1} \Psi d\theta$.

Philip [964] gave a solution of Eqn 4.89 in the form of a polynomial in $t^{1/2}$ which for infiltration[15] is

$$i = St^{1/2} + At + Bt^{3/2} + \cdots . \tag{4.90}$$

The coefficients $A, B \ldots$ are obtained by an extension of Philip's quasi-analytical method for simple absorption. For capillary rise, the solution is the same except for a change of sign in alternate terms of the polynomial, so that A becomes $-A$ and so on [972, 463]. Philip's solution is useful for representing the behaviour at early times when the sorptivity law of water absorption is subject to minor perturbing effects of gravity. However, the series solution fails to converge at times longer than about $(S/K_s)^2$ where K_s is the permeability. Approximate solution methods valid at all times have been developed [912, 752].

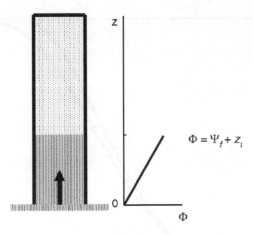

$$\Phi = \Psi_f + z_1$$

Figure 4.16 Capillary rise into a uniform porous material: Sharp Front model.

Sharp Front model: capillary rise with gravity effects

An SF model is easy to develop. Capillary rise is of much greater interest in building physics than is infiltration, so we consider this case (which we denote CRG), Figure 4.16. If we set $z = 0$ at the level of the inflow boundary, then we can solve the SF problem with the total potential $\Phi = \Psi + z$ having the value $\Phi_0 = 0$ at $z = 0$ and $\Phi_f = \Psi_f + z$ at the wet front. Then, from Eqn 4.33, we have for the absorption flow rate u and the cumulative absorption i

$$u = \frac{di}{dt} = -K_e \frac{\Phi_f - \Phi_0}{l} = K_e \left(\frac{f\Psi_f}{i} - 1 \right) \tag{4.91}$$

where we have used $i = fl$ to eliminate l, the wetted length. The sorptivity $S = (2fK_e|\Psi_f|)^{1/2}$ as usual. We also know that at capillary rise equilibrium $u = 0$ and from Eqn 4.91 the limiting value of the cumulative absorption

$$i_\infty = f|\Psi_f|. \tag{4.92}$$

Then we have the differential equation

$$\frac{di}{dt} = \frac{S^2}{2i_\infty} \left(\frac{i_\infty}{i} - 1 \right). \tag{4.93}$$

We define the dimensionless variables $I = i/i_\infty$ and $T = (S^2/2i_\infty^2)t$. Then by integrating Eqn 4.93 we obtain[16]

$$T = -\ln(1 - I) - I. \tag{4.94}$$

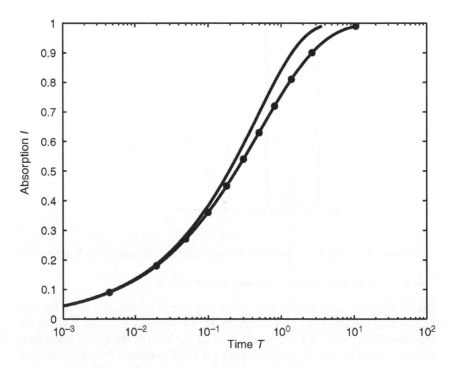

Figure 4.17 The approach to capillary rise equilibrium. The plain line shows
the dimensionless absorption $I(T)$ from Eqn 4.94 and the line •
Eqn 4.95.

We plot $I(T)$ in Figure 4.17. The importance of Eqn 4.94 is that it allows us
to estimate the timescale for attaining capillary rise equilibrium, given data
on S and i_∞. The quantity $2i_\infty^2/S^2$ is a measure of this timescale. When the
elapsed time $t_v = 2i_\infty^2/S^2$ (that is, when $T = 1$), the dimensionless absorption
$I = 0.841$.

We find that the times needed to approach capillary rise equilibrium estimated in this way are surprisingly long [463]. This reflects the high hydraulic
potentials of many common building materials and the correspondingly
large heights which are reached in capillary rise in the absence of any other
effects. We list a number of calculated values in Table 4.1.

It has been proposed [580] empirically that the approach to capillary rise
equilibrium in masonry materials can be represented by an exponential function which we can write in terms of our reduced variables I and T as

$$I = 1 - \exp(-2T^{1/2}). \tag{4.95}$$

We have plotted this also in Figure 4.17 for comparison with Eqn 4.94.
There is agreement at early times where both reduce to $I = T^{1/2}$, but Eqn

Pressure head: integrating saturated and unsaturated flow 155

Table 4.1 The timescale of approach to capillary rise equilibrium

Material	Water content i_∞ m	Sorptivity S mm min$^{-1/2}$	Time t_v y
Aerated concrete	2.40	0.54	75
Gypsum plaster	2.46	3.50	1.9
Clay brick	2.57	1.16	19

Note
The quantity i_∞ is calculated from the water retention curves, by integrating from $\Psi = 0$ to $\Psi = 10$ m [463].

4.95 does not represent well the approach to equilibrium in the later stages of capillary rise [499].[17]

Experimental tests

Capillary-rise equilibrium has not been observed experimentally in brick, stone and concrete because of the long timescales involved. Capillary forces in most of these materials are strong, and gravity effects in spontaneous imbibition are usually negligible on bench-scale specimens of height $H < 0.3$ m, say. The characteristic pore size r is such that for imbibition of water (density ρ_w and surface tension σ_w) the Bond number Bo $= \rho_w H r g / \sigma_w < 0.1$, indicating that capillary forces dominate at all but large heights of rise. Just a few experiments on glass-bead model systems [304, 718] have shown deviations from the SF CRG (or Lucas-Washburn) description. Observed heights of rise at late times exceeded prediction, and there was continuing slow movement of the wet front beyond the Lucas-Washburn limit. In the SF model the equilibrium condition at the stationary wet front is that there is no gradient of total potential, and the wet front is therefore located (Eqn 4.92) at height $h_\infty = |\Psi_f|$. To account for observations, it has been proposed [752] that the Lucas-Washburn model should be modified to allow for gradients of water content. This however eliminates the Sharp Front, and in essence reverts to a solution of the Richards equation, in which there is an equilibrium water-content distribution $\theta(z)_\infty = |\Psi(\theta)|$, but no well-defined equilibrium height of rise. Alternatively, the anomalous behaviour has been ascribed [1152, 1153, 898] to intermittent pinning of the wet front at pore throats, slowing the rate of advance at late times. In fact, there is no evidence yet of any deviations from Lucas-Washburn (or Darcy) behaviour in brick, stone and concrete materials.

4.6 PRESSURE HEAD: INTEGRATING SATURATED AND UNSATURATED FLOW

We have so far treated somewhat separately saturated flow and unsaturated flow. Saturated flow is described by Darcy's law and the entire region through which liquid flows has been considered to be saturated. Flow occurs in response to pressure differences at the surface of the saturated material and consequent pressure gradients acting within it. Unsaturated flow is described by the extended Darcy law and we have considered that the flow is driven entirely by gradients of capillary (or more generally hydraulic) potential within the material. It is true that in the SF model of unsaturated flow the wetted region is considered to be saturated but the forces acting on the fluid are associated with gradients of hydraulic potential. Capillary effects often dominate water transport in construction materials and building structures so that descriptions based on the Richards equation are appropriate. However, for sub-surface structures designed for fluid retention, the mixed case of transport involving both external pressure heads and capillary or matric forces can easily be envisaged. It is therefore desirable to have a unified description of saturated flow and unsaturated flow.

This is readily done since our definitions of saturated flow, Eqn 3.1, and unsaturated flow, Eqn 3.9, are closely similar. Both may be written as $\mathbf{u} = K\mathbf{F}$ (Eqn 3.8), providing the force $\mathbf{F}$ acting on the fluid is appropriately defined. We define a total potential $\Phi = \Psi + z + P$, where Ψ is the hydraulic potential, z the gravitational potential and P the pressure potential. We can then apply Eqn 3.10 (with Φ replacing Ψ) to mixed problems in which both saturated and unsaturated flows may be present. We note in passing that P almost invariably makes a positive (compressive) contribution to Φ while Ψ always makes a negative (tensile) contribution.

The solution of Eqn 4.1 for one-dimensional absorption into a semi-infinite porous solid with a positive hydrostatic head at the supply surface was first discussed by Philip [969]. We use Eqn 4.1 subject to the conditions

$$\theta = \theta_0, \quad t = 0, \quad x > 0, \tag{4.96}$$

$$\theta = \theta_1, \quad x = x_0, \quad t > 0, \tag{4.97}$$

with

$$x_0 = K_s h \Big/ \frac{d}{dt}\left(\int_{\theta_0}^{\theta_1} x\, d\theta\right). \tag{4.98}$$

The unsaturated flow equation is solved for the region $x > x_0$. The position of this moving boundary is defined by Eqn 4.98. This problem can be solved by a small modification [969] of the Philip method for capillary absorption [963, 965]. For analysis based on the extended Heaslet-Alksne method, see [913]. We should note that if the hydrostatic head h at the inflow boundary is negative, then we have a fully unsaturated problem with the concentration boundary condition $\theta = \theta_{\Psi=-h}$ at $x = 0$.

As an example we show in Figure 4.18 the water content penetration profiles $\phi(\theta_r)$ calculated for water absorption into a clay brick ceramic at applied

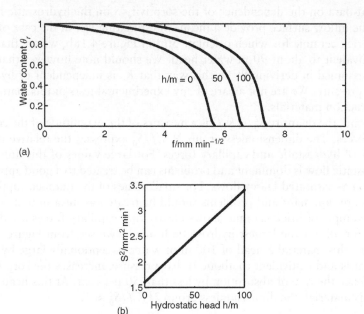

Figure 4.18 (a) Water absorption profiles under different hydrostatic heads: $\phi(\theta_r)$ calculated by Philip's method [969] using the diffusivity function $D/mm^2\ min^{-1} = 0.13\exp(6.28\theta_r)$ for a wire-cut clay brick ceramic [508] and a saturated permeability $K_s = 3 \times 10^{-5}$ mm/min. (b) The quadratic dependence of the sorptivity S on hydrostatic pressure h. In this case the standard sorptivity S_0 measured at $h = 0$ is 1.3 mm/min$^{1/2}$.

hydrostatic pressures between 0 and 100 m fluid head. The position of the saturation front is shown by ϕ_0.

Two notable features of the flow are illustrated by this example. First, the total inflow increases as $t^{1/2}$, just as for capillary absorption with zero hydrostatic head. Therefore a sorptivity $S(h) = i/t^{1/2}$ may always be defined which is a function of the material and the applied head h. We have already given a simple SF analysis of this case in Section 4.4 and from Eqn 4.40 we can write

$$S = [S_0^2 + 2hK_{ef}]^{1/2} \qquad (4.99)$$

to provide a formula for $S(h)$ which may be useful for engineering calculation. We note also from Eqn 4.40 that

$$\frac{S^2}{S_0^2} = 1 + \frac{h}{\Psi_f} \qquad (4.100)$$

so that data on the dependence of the sorptivity S on the hydrostatic head h at the inflow surface provide a means of estimating Ψ_f. In the case of the clay brick ceramic for which calculate $S(h)$ in Figure 4.18b, we see that Ψ_f is equivalent to about 90 m water head. We should note however that we have assumed in deriving Ψ_f in this way that K_e is independent of hydrostatic pressure. We are not aware of any experimental tests of this matter in construction materials.

Second, the quantity $S_0^2/(2K_ef)$ is a measure of the magnitude of the capillary forces. The dimensionless group $2hK_ef/S_0^2$ expresses the relative magnitude of hydrostatic and capillary forces. For large values of this number, hydrostatic flow is dominant and problems can be treated to a good approximation as saturated Darcy flows. For small values of the number, capillary forces are dominant and problems should be treated as unsaturated flows. The example of brick ceramic shows clearly that capillary forces are dominant for all but the largest hydrostatic heads.[18] We see from Figure 4.18 that for this material a head of 100 m of water, exceptionally large by any standards and equivalent to about 10 bar pressure, increases the sorptivity and hence the rate of absorption by less than 50 per cent. At this head and for this material, the dimensionless group $2hK_sf/S_0^2 \approx 1$.

4.7 MEASURING THE SORPTIVITY

The sorptivity as defined in Section 4.2 has emerged as one of the most important of the transport properties of a porous material. We now discuss in some detail how it may be measured.

4.7.1 Direct gravimetric method

The most straightforward laboratory method of determining the sorptivity of a porous solid is to monitor the increase in weight of a specimen of the material over time $\Delta w(t)$ during capillary absorption of liquid of density ρ [514, 477, 1079]. Several standards describe more or less equivalent procedures (for example, [350] for stone, [55] for concrete, and [629] for building materials in general). The test method is based on the Buckingham-Richards description of one-dimensional unsaturated flow into a semi-infinite material, with initial conditions $\theta_r = 0$ for all x at $t = 0$ and $\theta_r = 1$ at $x = 0$ and $t > 0$ (the free water reservoir boundary condition at $x = 0$). Our analysis shows that the cumulative absorption per unit of inflow surface area A is $i = \Delta w/\rho A = St^{1/2}$ *provided* that the material is homogeneous and that gravitational effects are negligible. The test method must realize all the features of the model. The specimen must be of constant cross-sectional area parallel to the absorbing face, most conveniently in the form of a rectangular or cylindrical prism. We have noted already that most brick, stone and concrete materials are sufficiently fine-pored that the effects of gravity on the

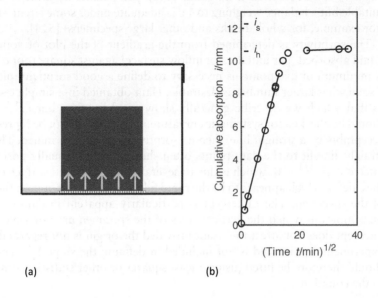

(a)   (b)

Figure 4.19 (a) A simple test arrangement for measuring the sorptivity of an inorganic porous material. (b) A typical experimental dataset obtained in a sorptivity test on a 50 mm cube of Bath limestone, absorbing water through a face area A 2.468×10^3 mm^2. The cumulative absorption $i = \Delta w/(A\rho_w)$ is plotted against the square root of the elapsed time $t^{1/2}$. The block dry weight is 255.46 g, test temperature 24.8 °C (water density $\rho_w = 997$ kg m^{-3}). The line through the early-time points is a least squares fit, giving an estimated sorptivity $S = 0.704$ mm/min$^{1/2}$. Here $i_h = 10.61$ mm and $i_{sat} = 12.27$ mm, so that the fractional Hirschwald coefficient h = 0.864.

short-term capillary rise process may be neglected. We can therefore conveniently measure the sorptivity in a simple vertical capillary rise experiment rather than in a necessarily more complicated horizontal configuration. A typical arrangement is shown in Figure 4.19. The specimen is placed on a porous pad or on rods or other suitable supports in a tray containing the test liquid (usually water) so that the entire lower surface of the specimen is in unrestricted contact with the liquid. In practice the depth of the liquid is normally such that the lower surface of the solid is a few mm below the liquid surface. If a large shallow tray is used, there is little change in the liquid level during the test. The specimen is weighed at intervals (for example at 1, 4, 9, 16 min…) to determine the quantity of liquid absorbed. Each weighing operation should be completed as quickly as possible (within 30s), and the clock should not be stopped while the weighing is carried out. Normal practice is to blot excess liquid from the absorbing surface with a damp absorbent paper or cloth before each weighing. A top pan balance accurate to 0.1 g is suitable but a balance weighing to 1 g is adequate under some circumstances (for example, for whole bricks and other large specimens) [514].

The sorptivity is determined from the gradient of the plot of volume of liquid absorbed (per unit area of inflow surface) against square root of time. A minimum of five points is necessary to define a good sorptivity plot and a somewhat larger number is desirable. Data obtained in a simple test such as that which we describe generally show good linearity but $i(t^{1/2})$ plots should be checked for systematic curvature. If the data cannot be represented acceptably by a straight line, then no sorptivity can be determined. The best straight line fit to the data points often shows a small (usually positive) i-intercept at $t^{1/2} = 0$, which is due to several minor edge and surface effects, the chief of which appears to be the rapid filling of surfaces pores on the sides of the specimen. The i-intercept is particularly apparent in data obtained on samples in which the vertical sides of the specimen are not sealed. The intercept does not affect the result provided the origin is not regarded as an experimental point and is not included in defining the slope S.[19] The data should therefore be fitted (using a least squares or other statistical criterion) to the equation

$$i = A_0 + St^{1/2} \tag{4.101}$$

where A_0 is a constant. A total time of a few hours is sufficient for most laboratory measurements of sorptivity, although data can be acquired over much longer times. We show in Figure 4.19 data obtained in a laboratory sorptivity test on a Bath limestone [472]. In Figure 4.20 we show a sorptivity plot for Lépine limestone [1219] which shows that the $t^{1/2}$ relationship applies until the wet front reaches the top of the absorbing specimen. The sorptivity has dimension $[LT^{-1/2}]$ and a convenient unit for construction materials is mm min$^{-1/2}$. Most brick and stone materials have sorptivity values in the range 0.5–3.0 mm min$^{-1/2}$ with the sorptivities of concrete materials being rather lower.

The sorptivity varies appreciably with temperature: for water, at 25 °C, the variation is about 1 per cent/K. The sorptivity should therefore be measured at a regulated temperature and both sample and test liquid should be given time to come to this temperature. For many purposes, the sorptivity S can be measured at the ambient laboratory temperature T, provided this is stable, and reported as the adjusted value S_0 at an appropriate standard temperature T_0 (such as 20 °C) using the established scaling $S_0 = S(\eta_T \sigma_0 / \eta_0 \sigma_T)^{1/2}$ where η is the viscosity and σ the surface tension of the test liquid [464, 1219]. Standards such as [350, 55, 629] do not pay sufficient attention to the temperature variation of the sorptivity either in measurement or in report.

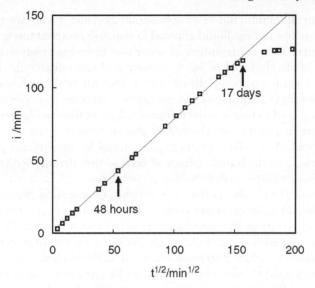

Figure 4.20 Long-term cumulative capillary absorption *i* versus $t^{1/2}$ for water into a Lépine limestone specimen 630 mm high [1219].

In accurate work, particularly with volatile nonaqueous liquids, it is wise to take some care to minimize evaporation from the material. This is sometimes done by sealing the sides of the test specimen, while leaving the top surface open to allow for the escape of displaced air. Equally effective for many materials (and usually more straightforward) is to carry out the test in a lidded tray or box. Sealing may be preferred for materials of high adsorption capacity, notably for cement-based materials.

It is essential that the absorbing specimen is uniformly dry or has a uniform initial liquid content if a well-defined sorptivity is to be determined. Normally materials are oven dried before measurements are made, but sometimes for research purposes it is necessary to achieve a uniform initial liquid content throughout the specimen [508]. Oven drying at 105 °C is suitable for brick ceramic and stone materials. Concrete and other cement-based materials may suffer some chemical alteration and damage to microstructure as a result of heating a 105 °C but drying at lower temperatures takes a considerable time. In our laboratories we have found that the values of sorptivity of specimens dried at 105 °C were essentially unchanged from those obtained by drying at 65 °C. However, with cement-based specimens it is best to dry initially at 40 °C before final drying at 105 °C. Gypsum-based materials may be severely dehydrated at temperatures above about 40 °C. When volatile nonaqueous liquids with lower boiling points are used in absorption experiments much lower drying temperatures may be used between tests.

If it is required to establish a uniform initial liquid content oven drying is followed by absorption of a known quantity of liquid. The specimen is then wrapped in aluminium foil or an appropriate polymer membrane to prevent evaporative loss and the liquid allowed to redistribute spontaneously within the specimen. The redistribution of water and of low viscosity nonaqueous liquids is relatively rapid in brick ceramic and stone materials. In typical brick-sized specimens liquid distribution is uniform within a few days. The timescale of the redistribution process can be confirmed by experiments similar to those used to measure the diffusivity. Bars of material (approximately 1 cm square in section) are allowed to absorb measured amounts of liquid from one end. After allowing appropriate times for redistribution the bars are sectioned and the liquid content of each section determined gravimetrically to check whether redistribution is complete.

Experience [1219] shows that it is difficult, or indeed in practice impossible, to obtain uniform water contents in cementitious specimens at low overall water contents by spontaneous capillary redistribution. This is probably associated with the continuing chemical interaction of water with the hydrated cement (which also results in an anomalously low water sorptivity in these materials).[20] Not only does this make laboratory measurements of the variation of sorptivity with water content difficult in these materials, but more significantly it means that obtaining uniformly dry specimens is difficult without oven drying preferably at 105 °C. Certainly drying at ambient temperatures – which is the best that can be achieved in concretes subject to *in situ* testing – is likely to result in a nonuniform water content which, in turn, will result in a departure from linearity in the i versus $t^{1/2}$ plots.

There are many reports of how the simple manual method we have described may be automated [673, 883, 789, 833, 263, 1099, 856, 995, 1269, 21, 1252], for example by suspending the specimen from a gravimetric balance so that a continuous record of the capillary uptake process is obtained. There are sources of error in some of these devices as a result of the upthrust arising from the partial submerging of the lower part of the specimen and from surface tension effects. They have proved valuable when the imbibition is rapid and the samples small [892].

Hirschwald coefficient

It has long been known that spontaneous capillary imbibition does not lead to complete filling of the open porosity. This was established for many materials over 100 years ago by Hirschwald,[21] who called the volume percentage of the filled porosity the *saturation coefficient*, for which we use the symbol H. It is more convenient to work with the fractional Hirschwald coefficient $h = H/100$. We can see this incomplete filling in a sorptivity test in Figure 4.19. When the wet front reaches the top surface of the test block, the quantity of water absorbed (which we call i_h) is well below the saturation value i_s, and $h = i_h/i_s$. In the case shown $h \approx 0.86$. The mean water content of the material in this moisture state is $\theta_h = hf$. Since for this limestone block $f = 0.245$, $\theta_h \approx 0.21$. It is novel, but may be useful, to call θ_h the

Hirschwald water content. It is also useful to designate the moisture state at the end of imbibition, with $\theta = \theta_h$, as the Hirschwald state.

The incomplete filling of the porosity during capillary imbibition occurs because the air present in the dry material is not completely displaced. Some of the air becomes isolated and compressed in parts of the pore network. Because this air is isolated it is largely trapped and immobile, and remains in place at the end of primary imbibition. We postpone a full discussion of air-trapping until Chapter 8. However it is timely here to note that the Hirschwald coefficient is sensitive to the size-distribution and connectivity of pores, and varies widely from material to material.[22] Some representative values are collected in Table 4.2. Data from different sources may not be strictly comparable if different test methods are used.

Capillary absorption in two- and three-dimensional geometries

In Chapter 6 we show that the sorptivity of a porous solid can also be esti-mated from analysis of data obtained in absorption processes which produce nonplanar wet fronts, that is in two- and three-dimensional geometries. The analysis of experimental data is based on SF models of water absorption. Such arrangements are found in several of the methods which have been proposed for *in situ* measurement of absorption properties. For these mea-surements, it is convenient to monitor the absorption of liquid either through a circular area on an extended surface or through a cylindrical hole drilled into the solid. In these cases the volume of liquid absorbed is usually mea-sured directly by monitoring the movement of a meniscus along a gradu-ated capillary. These methods are more complicated and less straightfor-ward to analyze than the direct one-dimensional water absorption test we have described and are almost never used for laboratory determination of the sorptivity. They are described more fully in Chapter 6.

4.7.2 Methods based on penetration distance

Some investigators have defined a sorptivity in terms of the distance that the absorbed liquid advances rather than the cumulative absorbed volume of liquid i. This has a practical justification because in many engineering sit-uations we are interested in the extent and rate of penetration of a wetting front into a construction element. In estimating the sorptivity, the technique originally proposed by Ho and Lewis [571] is to allow a specimen to take up liquid for a fixed period of time and after splitting the specimen to measure the penetration of the wet front inside the specimen. A sorptivity, let us call it S_x, is then defined as $x_{wf} t^{-1/2}$, where x_{wf} is the distance advanced by the wet front in time t. In the Buckingham-Richards description of capillary absorp-tion the position x_{wf} is undefined but in the SF model $x_{wf} = i/f$, where f is the porosity. By comparison with the standard definition of sorptivity we see that $S_x = S/f$. It is therefore necessary to know the porosity f if published

Table 4.2 Some selected values of the fractional Hirschwald coefficient

	Hirschwald coefficient h	Porosity f
Limestones		
Ancaster[a]	0.89	0.156
Bath[a]	0.85	0.245
Brézé tuffeau[b]	0.84	0.472
Clipsham[a]	0.80	0.212
Clunch[a]	0.78	0.326
Estaillades[c]	0.75	0.278
Ketton[a]	0.59	0.242
Portland[a]	0.73	0.212
Savonnières[d]	0.56	0.269
Savonnières[e]	0.59	0.315
Vilhonneur[b]	0.90	0.092
Sandstones		
Bentheim[f]	0.57	0.256
Grès à meules[d]	0.72	0.166
Pietra serena[d]	0.82	0.051
Sander[f]	0.79	0.170
Other		
Hydrated calcium silicate[g]	0.90	0.895
Fired-clay brick[g]	0.62	0.238
Fired-clay brick[h]	0.62	0.308
Fired-clay brick[i]	0.73	0.353
Fired-clay brick[j]	0.91	0.260

Notes
a [472]; b [1020]; c [26]; d [724]; e [354]; f [1203]; g [1077]; h [372]; i [1120]; j [210]; all h values from imbibition with water (c with brine), mostly recalculated from reported two-tangent w_{cap} values, except b, e (from S_{48} by total immersion), and c (estimated from CT images).

sorptivity data obtained by these two different methods are to be compared. Values of porosity for construction materials cover a wide range, but commonly lie between 0.1 and 0.3. Thus the quoted sorptivity values obtained from measurements of the advance of a wet front are between three and 10 times greater than those obtained by measuring the cumulative absorbed volume, *although the unit is identical*. This is a source of some confusion in the literature and the basis on which sorptivity values have been determined must be clearly stated. In general it is much easier and more accurate to measure the volume of liquid absorbed; and the absorbed volume may be measured at numerous elapsed times on a single specimen. Determining the actual position of the wet front is difficult, not least because the wet front becomes increasingly diffuse as the absorption process proceeds. Indeed appreciable liquid contents may exist beyond the visual wet front. When volatile nonaqueous liquids are used a visual determination of the position of the wet front is often difficult or impossible because the liquids evaporate rapidly. In these cases it has been shown that thermal imaging of the split surface can be used to reveal the distribution of absorbed liquid [1046]. It should be noted that the normal measurement of sorptivity from a measurement of the cumulative absorbed volume, coupled with a knowledge of the porosity (which is straightforward to measure), enables the distance of penetration of the wet front to be estimated.

4.7.3   Methods based on measurement of moisture distributions

In Chapter 2 we have discussed methods of measuring liquid (specifically water) content including the use of nuclear magnetic resonance imaging, positron emission tomography, neutron radiography, X-ray absorption and gamma-ray absorption. These techniques are particularly useful for measuring water content versus distance profiles as water advances into an initially dry porous solid as described more fully in Chapter 3. Normally the purpose of measuring these profiles is to enable the diffusivity to be determined. However, in a one-dimensional absorption process, the total volume of liquid absorbed can be estimated from the area under any such profile at a given time and this clearly provides a direct measure of the sorptivity.

Deviations from time$^{1/2}$ behaviour

Deviations from the linear behaviour described by Eqn 4.101 are not common but when found can usually be attributed to one of several causes [476, 477, 483]: (1) the material is not homogeneous (see Chapter 5); (2) the material is not dimensionally and/or microstructurally stable during absorption (most commonly found in cement-based materials, see Section 4.8.2); and (3) the effects of gravity on capillary rise absorption cannot be neglected. Here we discuss gravitational effects in sorptivity measurement.

Deviations from the theoretical $i = St^{1/2}$ equation for vertically upwards capillary absorption into a one-dimensional homogeneous semi-infinite material may occasionally be due to the fact the pore structure is such that gravity drainage is not negligible. This means that the water absorption approaches (or may reach) capillary rise equilibrium in the course of the sorptivity test. This was the proposed explanation in the case of tests on poorly compacted concretes [517]. The analysis of capillary rise in Section 4.5 shows that the cumulative absorption is described by the equation $i = St^{1/2} - b_1 t + b_2 t^{3/2} \dots$. If a deviation from linearity can be confidently ascribed to this effect and if it is such that it produces only slight curvature in the $i(t^{1/2})$ dataset, then S can be estimated by fitting data to the three parameter equation $i = A_0 + St^{1/2} - A_1 t$ rather than to Eqn 4.101.

Effects of this kind occur in materials with large pores. An interesting and important case is that of autoclaved aerated concrete AAC, the material whose microstructure is shown in Figure 1.3. Water absorption of AAC in a standard capillary rise sorptivity test initially deviates strongly from the standard $t^{1/2}$ law. This was first noted for AAC by Gummerson *et al.* [462]. The anomaly is a result of the unusual pore size distribution in AAC, and in particular of the presence of large aeration pores which contribute substantially to the total porosity but exert little capillary suction [1021, 1081]. The unusual AAC micro/macro-structure comprises a fine pored matrix of high suction within which are dispersed large aeration pores formed by foaming the wet slurry. The matrix is constructed of thin platelets of tobermorite. The platelets are of rather uniform thickness, not more than a few tens of nm; their widths however are typically 5–10 μm. The micropore structure is thus a network of sharp-edged box-like cells. This structure undoubtedly has high capillary suction. The aeration pores are roughly spherical cavities, originally created as bubbles in the wet mix. These pores are about 0.1–1 mm dia. The aeration pores although largely isolated from one another are interconnected through the microporous matrix. The pore size distribution thus comprises the matrix pores and the aeration pores, with characteristic pores sizes which differ by about three orders of magnitude.

An analysis of capillary rise water absorption in AAC has been developed [621]. This is based on the SF concepts described earlier in this chapter. The experimental imbibition data in Figure 4.21a show four well-defined stages: (1) an early time stage where i is linear in $t^{1/2}$, with slope S_e which defines the early-time sorptivity; (2) a transitional stage which deviates strongly from $t^{1/2}$ kinetics; (3) a late time stage where i is again linear in $t^{1/2}$ but with a slope S_m which is lower than in the early stage and which defines the matrix sorptivity; and (4) a terminal stage at which the wet front has more or less reached the end of the specimen and further absorption is much slower. This behaviour can be understood if we assume that the measured total absorption is made up of a contribution from the filling of the matrix porosity and a second contribution from the absorption into the aeration pores (Figure 4.21b). The matrix porosity is fine-scale, capillary forces are much greater than gravitational forces and capillary absorption may be expected to follow the standard law, Eqn 4.101. In contrast, the coarse aeration pores have weak capillary suction and do not conform to the standard $t^{1/2}$ sorptivity law. We assume that because of the low suction, capillary absorption into the aeration pores reaches capillary rise equilibrium rapidly (that is to say, within the timescale of the test). For the filling of these macropores we use the CRG model of Eqn 4.93. A simple procedure is described in [621] to separate macropore and micropore contributions to the total imbibition. Analysis shows that for a typical AAC material, the capillary rise into the aeration pores (Figure 4.21c) extends to heights of about 1–2 cm only before reaching gravitational equilibrium, as is entirely consistent with the pore size. The matrix suction is much larger and a normal matrix sorptivity S_m can be measured. Similar analysis can be applied to other materials with strongly bimodal pore size distributions, such as vuggy limestones [619, 617] and aerated gypsum [1187].

4.8 SORPTIVITIES OF CONSTRUCTION MATERIALS

The sorptivity is perhaps the most useful of the capillary transport properties, being both easily measured and rigorously defined in unsaturated flow theory. We gather some representative values in Table 4.3 to show the range of values found in construction materials. Once again there is little value in an encyclopedic collection. Unlike the permeability, the sorptivity does not have a large numerical range and a factor of 10 covers most common sorptive construction materials and a factor of 100 almost all. This is the result of the opposing influence of pore length scale on the permeability and the capillary potential which together determine the numerical value of the sorptivity. We can see the composite character of the sorptivity directly from the SF expression $S = (2f_e K_e |\Psi_f|)^{1/2}$. For geometrically similar materials having a pore structure of characteristic scale λ, K_e varies as λ^2 while Ψ_f varies as λ^{-1}.[23] The sorptivity should therefore scale roughly as $\lambda^{1/2}$, a

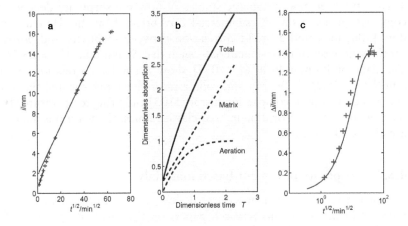

Figure 4.21 Capillary rise liquid absorption into AAC [621]. (a) Cumulative absorption i vs $t^{1/2}$: experimental points are marked by crosses. The matrix sorptivity S_m is defined by the main linear portion of the graph. (b) Schematic: contributions to total absorption i from matrix and aeration pores. (c) Estimated absorption into aeration pores: experimentally-derived points are marked with crosses and fitted to the SF capillary rise with gravity (CRG) model, Eqn 4.93. The quantity $\Delta i(t)$ is the contribution of the aeration pore filling to the observed total absorption.

weak dependence on pore size. Nonetheless, at constant porosity, fine pored materials are expected to have smaller sorptivities than coarse grained.[24] This prediction is difficult to test. Data on fifteen Italian clay brick types [1037] show that porosity and median pore size have the strongest influence on sorptivity, although the range of parameters tested is not large.

Construction materials commonly have different sorptivities for flow in different directions. Thus for a typical fired-clay wire-cut brick we reported [462] a sorptivity for absorption through the bed face of 1.49 mm/min$^{1/2}$, but 1.10 mm/min$^{1/2}$ through the header face and 0.95 mm/min$^{1/2}$ through the stretcher face. Similar anisotropy in sorptivity was found in extruded bricks [693]. Ince *et al.* [616] find in a pressed clay brick that the sorptivity through the bed face is about 40 per cent higher in sections cut close to the header faces than elsewhere. Roels [1074] has measured sorptivity for water absorption parallel and perpendicular to the bedding plane of Savonnières limestone, the values of which are given in Table 4.3. Marked anisotropy is likewise reported in Portland brownstone [1135].

In using values of sorptivity from Table 4.3 it must be remembered that S varies considerably with temperature (p 175).

4.8.1   Sorptivity and composition

There have been few systematic studies of how the sorptivity depends on composition. Data on 63 commercial clay bricks from the United Kingdom [506] indicated a broad correlation between sorptivity and porosity for the whole set of diverse materials, such that $S/\text{mm min}^{-1/2} = 23.7f^{2.6}$. The data of Raimondo *et al.* [1037] show a similar correlation, $S/\text{mm min}^{-1/2} = 25.2f^{2.3}$. Beltrán and collaborators have investigated the influence of composition, compaction history [103] and firing temperature [105] on capillary water absorption in fired-clay ceramics. Cementitious materials are discussed below.

4.8.2   Sorptivity of cement-based materials

The increasing interest in unsaturated flow in cement-based materials is reflected in the numerous research papers on the sorptivity property. For a review of early published work up to about 1989, see [475]; and for a brief survey of more recent work [1269]. The sorptivity is increasingly used in the specification of durability [572, 574, 567, 566]. A number of studies have examined the relation between the sorptivity and the composition, compaction and curing history of mortars and concrete [571, 514, 570, 572, 573, 517, 569, 349, 589, 782, 568]. In mature concretes, the sorptivity is markedly altered by carbonation [324]. The sorptivities of cement-stabilized rammed earths have been comprehensively measured [521, 519, 520].

Table 4.3 Water sorptivities of selected construction materials

Material	Bulk density ρ_b kg m^{-3}	Porosity f –	Sorptivity S mm min$^{-1/2}$	Note
Clay brick				
Pressed semi-dry	1727	0.357	1.32	a
Hand-moulded facing	1784	0.334	2.21	a
Extruded facing	1567	0.461	2.35	a
Soft-mud facing	1857	0.324	4.15	b
Extruded wire-cut	2003	0.238	1.24	c
Extruded wire-cut	1910	0.309	1.55	d
Engineering	2210	0.065	0.09	e
Limestones				
Ancaster	2305	0.150	0.53	f
Bath	2040	0.248	0.44	f
Cleris Charentenay	1890	0.290	1.49	g
Ketton	2055	0.242	3.24	f
Lépine	2080	0.239	1.00	h
Portland	2130	0.213	0.83	f
St Maximin fine	1590	0.390	4.60	g
Savonnières	1661	0.38		i
Parallel to bedding			0.66	
Normal to bedding			0.42	
Jordanian marbles	2713	0.003	0.005	j
Sandstones				
Baumberger sandstone	1980	0.23	0.34	k
Grès de Vosges	2225	0.169	0.09	f
Obernkirchner	2150	0.14	0.36	j
Rüthener	1950	0.24	2.33	k
Sander	2120	0.17	0.16	k
Gypsum/sand plaster				l
1 Water:0.45 Plaster	1390	0.42	1.62	m
1 Water:0.45 Plaster	1480	0.39	1.44	n
1 Water:0.45 Plaster	1590	0.35	1.31	o
1 Water:0.40 Plaster	1490	0.37	0.83	p
Mortars–typical values				q
1 cement: 3 lime: 10 sand	1760	0.364	1.94	r
1 cement: 2 lime: 8 sand	1860	0.346	1.38	s
1 cement: 0.5 lime: 4 sand	1990	0.273	0.56	t
Concretes–typical values				
1 cement:2 sand:4 aggregate				u
w/c 0.55	2526	0.10	0.19	
w/c 0.75	2233	0.13	0.29	
1 cement:2 sand: 4 aggregate				v
w/c 0.5	2310	0.113	0.25	
w/c 0.7	2260	0.139	0.29	
w/c 0.8	2270	0.141	0.35	
1 binder:2 sand:4 aggregate	2348	0.13	0.19	w
Other				
Hydrated calcium silicate	268	0.895	9.50	c

Notes
a [1026, 506]; b [472]; c [1077]; d [462]; e [1026]; f [472]; g [663]; h [229]; i [1074]; j [12], mean of six materials; k [700]; l [510], volume fraction sand α: m 0; n 0.077; o 0.17; p 0.047; q [514]; r w/c: 3.2; s 2.2; t 0.93; u [1219]; v [517]; w [1219], binder 65:35 GGBS:OPC, w/c 0.6.

Problems of measurement

We have emphasized that four conditions must be satisfied in order that the cumulative absorption i in a single-sided water absorption test increases as the square root of the elapsed time t. These are that: (1) the initial water content is uniform; (2) the flow within the material is strictly one-dimensional and water is freely available at the inflow face; (3) the material is homogeneous; (4) the material is unaltered stucturally and microstructurally by changes of water content. Conditions (1) and (2) are under the control of the experimentalist.[25] Meeting conditions (3) and (4) depends mainly on features of the test specimen and inherent properties of the test material. For brick and stone, these conditions are generally satisfied and as we have seen experimental data on capillary absorption routinely show $t^{1/2}$ behaviour so that the sorptivity is an experimentally well-defined material property. For brick and stone, gross inhomogeneities are not often encountered in laboratory samples. Sawn specimens of quarry stones are generally uniform, though frequently anisotropic in their water absorption properties [1074]. However, anisotropy related to the orientation of bedding planes in sedimentary rocks does not produce deviations from $t^{1/2}$ behaviour. Surface layers in brick may contribute to intercepts in i–$t^{1/2}$ plots but a sorptivity value may of course be determined. If there are constitutional changes in wetting and drying, their effects are not evident in the cumulative absorption. We know for example that Lépine limestone is dimensionally stable on wetting [1219], and that for numerous brick and stone materials the sorptivity has a value which does not change in repeated tests. We know furthermore that for brick materials the water sorptivity has the value expected from the intrinsic sorptivity $\mathbb{S}$ determined from tests using nonaqueous liquids [462]. For cement-based materials, these conditions deserve careful scrutiny. We know – not least from permeability measurements – that wetting may produce marked changes in the microstructure of cements. We are not justified *a priori* in assuming that condition (4) is met in water sorptivity tests. For concrete specimens, condition (3) may also not be met (whatever the test liquid).

We deal first with the problems which arise when the material is inhomogeneous. In concretes made with coarse aggregate it is essential that the sample is sufficiently large to be representative of the bulk. It may be inconvenient to work with large test specimens in which the inflow face has an area of, say, 0.01 m^2 or more, but this presents no real difficulties for laboratory samples. Recovering field samples of adequate size may sometimes be less easy. Test samples may also be nonuniform because they contain surface layers, most commonly as a result of segregation and bleeding after casting. Many field samples of mature concrete also have carbonated surfaces. Single-sided water absorption into such materials cannot be expected to exhibit linear $t^{1/2}$ behaviour because of variations in transport properties with depth. However, if these samples are treated as layered composites in the way we describe in Chapter 5, then well conducted water absorption experiments are a powerful means of mapping the *variation* of sorptivity with depth, which itself is often a property of importance.

Sorptivity anomaly in cementitious materials

As with permeability, it is the sensitivity of microstructure to the water content and the wetting history of the material which presents the greater challenge for experiment and interpretation. The experimental evidence is that for tests on materials in which conditions (1), (2), (3) and (4) are scrupulously satisfied, water absorption into cementitious materials is well described by the sorptivity law and i increases as $t^{1/2}$ in a well behaved way [475, 514, 517, 483]. Here the critical requirement is (4), as frequently cementitious materials are reactive under the conditions of the test.

Much has been learned from a comparison between absorption of water and nonaqueous liquids. We have shown in Section 4.2 that if water absorption is a pure capillarity-driven phenomenon the sorptivity S scales as $(\sigma/\eta)^{1/2}$ and that this scaling is found to hold for brick. Taylor [1219] has carried out a comprehensive comparison of absorption into cement-based materials which shows that both water and nonaqueous liquids obey the i–$t^{1/2}$ sorptivity law accurately. Similar data from Sosoro [1190] lead to the same conclusion. In addition, the nonaqueous liquids as a group show the expected dependence of S on $(\sigma/\eta)^{1/2}$, but water does not and is markedly deviant. This *sorptivity anomaly* [509] is shown in Figure 4.22. The results, which are fully confirmed by a later extensive study [1144] on a cement mortar, show that the water sorptivity of a variety of cement-based materials is typically half of what would be expected. In SF language, this is consistent with a reduction of effective permeability K_e on water absorption, a reduction which does not occur on wetting with nonaqueous liquids. An important item of supporting evidence comes from measurements of wetting strain during water absorption. Data on mortar bars show that the existence of wetting expansion which is synchronous with the water absorption in a test carried out over a few hours. The wetting expansion in the direction of capillary flow also increases as $t^{1/2}$. That the wetting expansion and the water absorption occur synchronously and that both follow $t^{1/2}$ kinetics suggests that on wetting the material rapidly adjusts to a stable value of K_e. Our simple SF model of sorptivity indicates a fourfold reduction in K_e is needed to halve the sorptivity. Microstructural evidence of alteration on wetting comes from ESEM observations which show rapid swelling and hydration on rewetting hydrated and dried cement paste. Sorptivity data appear therefore to support the view of water/cement interactions which we have already developed from the permeability data.[26]

Materials for liquid sorptivity and permeability measurements are conditioned differently however, and the flow tests are carried out on different timescales. Samples for water permeability testing are usually

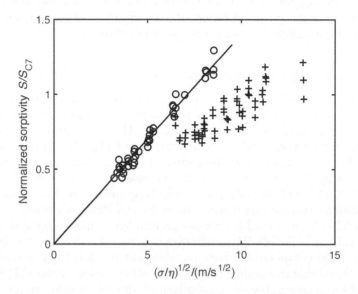

Figure 4.22 Sorptivity S of a variety of cement-based materials (mortars and concretes) plotted as the normalized sorptivity $S_n = S/S_{C7}$ where S_{C7} is the sorptivity measured with *n*-heptane at 20 °C for the same material. + Water sorptivities; ○ sorptivities measured with non-aqueous liquids [509].

pre-saturated, often for long times, so that any rapid microstructural adjustment to rewetting occurs well before testing begins. By definition, sorptivity tests are carried out on materials which are dry or at least in some well-defined unsaturated state. Early time water absorption data thus reflect the time-dependence of the hydraulic properties. Data from many sources show the existence of slow and gradual reductions in water permeability on a timescale of hours and days. It is interesting to ask if sorptivity data show the same feature. Data from Taylor [1219] show that this is the case. In Figure 4.23 we plot the water absorption into a cement mortar and compare this with absorption of the liquid hydrocarbon *n*-decane. This cementitious material has a stable sorptivity for the first few hours, but at longer times the cumulative absorption falls well below what would be expected. The hydrocarbon absorption shows no deviation from the sorptivity law throughout the 16 d test. Strikingly similar behaviour is found in hardened cement pastes tested with water and *n*-hexane [701].

There is therefore evidence that the anomalously low sorptivities and permeabilities of these materials can be attributed to their water reactivity. Some interesting results [1221] have been published which show that the differences in intrinsic sorptivity between nonaqueous liquids and water are much less when a 35:65 Portland cement/ground granulated

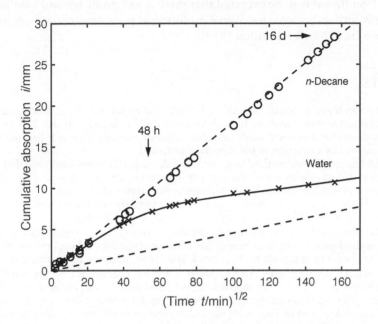

Figure 4.23 Long-term cumulative capillary absorption i versus $t^{1/2}$ for water and n-decane into a mortar, 1:2 Portland cement:sand by weight, 0.4 water:cement ratio by weight, cured under water for 28 d, dried at 40 °C for 24 h and at 105 °C to constant weight [1221]. Solid line is a fit to water data points using the time-dependent permeability model of Section 4.4, this chapter, with $S_0 = 0.16\,\text{mm min}^{-1/2}$, $K_0/K_1 = 12.4$, $\tau = 2090\,\text{min}$; dashed lines calculated for constant permeability, $S = 0.18\,\text{mm min}^{-1/2}$ (upper line), and $S = 0.045\,\text{mm min}^{-1/2}$ (lower line) [486].

blast furnace slag binder is used to replace Portland cement in mortar or concrete mixes. Moreover the long-term capillary absorption of water into mortar made with the blended cement does not depart from $t^{1/2}$ behaviour until after approximately 75 h of absorption. Evidently the rate of long-term reactivity is much slower than in pure Portland cement materials. These results on blended cements are consistent with concepts of cement microstructure. Jennings and Tennis [646] have proposed that there are two types of calcium silicate hydrate C-S-H gel. A physical basis for this model is that the two types of C-S-H gel have different densities, and that it is only the low density form which takes part in microscopic shrinkage and swelling of the hydrated material. In the case of blended cements Jennings suggests that as the pozzolan reacts the ratio of low- to high-density C-S-H gel decreases and is much lower than in ordinary Portland cement alone. Accordingly if there is less of the low-density

C-S-H gel then it is to be expected that there is less shrinkage and swelling. There is further evidence for a slow evolution of pore structure in hydrated cements from NMR relaxation [819].

NOTES

1 The Kirchhoff potential provides a further way to formulate the fundamental unsaturated flow equation. It has been argued [255, 38, 39, 40] that it is to be preferred for numerical work and that material property data can be usefully presented as a function of the Kirchhoff potential.

2 The Heaslet-Alksne method was originally developed for one-dimensional non-linear diffusion with a constant concentration boundary condition in a material with a power-law diffusivity. In addition to the extension to arbitrary diffusivity [917], there is also an extension to arbitrary boundary condition [916] with the inflow surface subject to time-dependent concentration or flux.

3 The empirical law of water absorption $\Delta m = \text{constant} \cdot t^{1/2}$ (where Δm is the measured gain in weight at time t) has been recognized for a long time for inorganic building materials such as brick and stone, and practical definitions of a material property are derived from it. Thus the quantity $A_w = \Delta m/(At^{1/2})$ (where A is the area of the inflow face) is known as the *water absorption coefficient* [253, 629] (sometimes [666] called the *capillary absorption coefficient* and denoted A_{cap}, and by ISO [624] the *water sorption coefficient A*). We can make the simple identification $A_w \equiv S\rho_w$, thus linking the empirical constant A_w with the sorptivity S which is rigorously defined in terms of unsaturated flow theory. Our definition of sorptivity (and other hydraulic properties) is consistent with the established terminology in soil physics [1086]. S is usually reported in unit $\text{mm/min}^{1/2}$, and A_w in unit $\text{kg/(m}^2\,\text{s}^{1/2})$, so that the interconversion involves the density: $S = (60^{1/2} \times 10^3/\rho_w)A_w$ where ρ_w is the density of water at the temperature of interest. Thus in these units $S = 7.463A_w$ at $5°C$ and $S = 7.7935A_w$ at $35°C$.

4 Since there is no general analytical solution for ϕ given $D(\theta)$, there is no anaytical expression for S in terms of D. However there are several useful approximations [748]. We have already given one in Eqn 4.7 for the case of an exponential diffusivity in which the quantity $s = (\theta_1 - \theta_0)S \approx fS$. Other useful formulae for the sorptivity have been proposed and discussed [711]. One that is simple and practical is $S^2 \approx f^2 \int_0^1 (1 + \theta_r)D_r d\theta_r$ [914].

5 We have noted that the sorptivity S is proportional to the quantity $(\sigma/\eta)^{1/2}$. The capillary water absorption law $i = St^{1/2}$ can be written in terms of the intrinsic sorptivity $\mathbb{S}$ as $i = \mathbb{S}(\sigma/\eta)^{1/2}t^{1/2}$ and this may then be compared with the well-known Washburn equation [1295, 338] for the motion of the meniscus in a simple cylindrical capillary of radius r, $x(t) = (\sigma rt/2\eta)^{1/2}$. Evidently the quantity $2(\mathbb{S}/f)^2$ can be interpreted as an effective or equivalent hydraulic pore radius for the pore system of the sorptive medium. For the case of brick ceramic for which data are shown in Figure 4.3 and for which the intrinsic sorptivity $\mathbb{S}$ is 2.2×10^{-5} $\text{m}^{1/2}$ and the porosity f is 0.31, this effective hydraulic radius is about 10 nm. This small value shows that the geometry of the pore space, its tortuosity and connectivity, are such that the capillary penetration of liquids is severely impeded.

6 The Young-Laplace equation for complete wetting is $\Psi = 2\sigma/r\rho g$ where Ψ is the capillary potential, r is the pore radius which is also the curvature of the liquid

surface, and σ the surface tension of the liquid. For partial wetting the radius of curvature of the liquid surface *at the same liquid content by volume* is increased by a factor $1/\beta$ where we define β as the wetting coefficient ($0 \le \beta \le 1$). Then the Young-Laplace equation becomes $\Psi = 2\beta\sigma/r\rho g$. Consequently the intrinsic sorptivity $\mathbb{S}$ which we have written in Eqn 4.21 for complete wetting should more generally be written as $\mathbb{S} = (\eta/\beta\sigma)^{1/2}S$. The data on several limestones [1219, 1220, 622, 513] indicate water-wetting coefficients lying between about 0.3–0.7. Capillary rise of liquids has been used similarly to investigate the wettability in packed powders [347, 1159]. Note that in earlier publications ([1220, 500, 622, 502]) we have called β the *wetting index*, but here we revert to the term wetting coefficient used elsewhere [1185, 1091], and to avoid confusion with the *wettability index* used in petrophysics [148].

7 To good accuracy and for all materials, at normal environmental temperatures, say 5–35 °C, the fractional change in sorptivity S is $+0.011$ per °C. An accurate interpolating equation [618] for the scaling factor at temperature T°C (0–50 °C) is $(\sigma/\eta)^{1/2} = 8.552(1 - 0.01121\Delta T - 3.233 \times 10^{-5}\Delta T^2 - 3.609 \times 10^{-8}\Delta T^3)\,\mathrm{m}^{1/2}/\mathrm{s}^{1/2}$, where $\Delta T = 20 - T$.

8 Lockington *et al.* [753] show that if $S \approx f[\int_0^1 (1 + \theta_r)Dd\theta_r]^{1/2}$ (see Note 4 above) then $S/S_0 \approx [\int_{\theta_i}^{\theta_1}(\theta + \theta_1 - 2\theta_i)Dd\theta / \int_0^{\theta_1}(\theta + \theta_1)Dd\theta]^{1/2}$.

9 The Sharp Front theory is essentially the Green-Ampt model of soil physics [445]: see for example [974, 788]. In earlier publications we have usually called this the Sharp Wet Front or SWF theory, but we use the term Sharp Front [SF] throughout this book because we also apply the theory in Chapter 8 to slurry compaction where the designation *wet front* is less appropriate.

10 Equation 4.37, written in terms of capillary pressure p_c and intrinsic permeability k', is known in petroleum engineering as Handy's equation [532].

11 This case is similar to that of *linear encroachment* described by Muskat [863]. In our case, the displacement is driven solely by the capillary pressure at the interface between the two fluids; in contrast Muskat analyses the case of displacement driven by an external pressure difference and ignores the role of the capillary pressure. In both cases, the rate of displacement accelerates if the displaced liquid is of higher viscosity than the displacing liquid.

12 This topic is closely allied to fundamental work on the capillary physics of pairs of immiscible liquids in tubes and other simple geometries [125, 126]. Experiment and theory show remarkable effects in the behaviour of such 'bislugs' and 'bidrops' caused by the asymmetry of the Young-Laplace forces. These have their counterpart in the capillarity-driven imbibition of immiscible liquids in porous media [507].

13 In earlier publications [500, 620, 502] we have used the term *air trapping* to describe this process, rather than *air confinement* as here. However, we now reserve the term air trapping for the rather different phenomenon in which air becomes isolated at the pore-scale during imbibition (see Section 4.7.1 of this chapter and also Section 8.1).

14 It is true that nothing happens in the SF model, but in real materials and real experiments it is observed that the wetting fluid does succeed in at least partially displacing the nonwetting fluid, which is caused to flow in the opposite direction. The nonwetting liquid A leaves the sample through the same boundary as B enters. This happens by local flow processes which are not captured in the SF model and are certainly not one-dimensional in nature.

15 Absorption is a broad term to describe the spontaneous entry of liquids into a porous material, under the action of capillary or other forces. More narrowly, the term is used in soil physics to describe the entry of a liquid into a soil or other

porous medium in a situation where gravitational forces are absent or constant or negligible, most commonly in a horizontal flow. In soil physics, the term *infiltration* is used to describe downward flow in systems in which gravity effects cannot be neglected. Such downward gravitational drainage is rarely met in brick, stone and concrete construction, while capillary rise against gravity is common.

16 Equation 4.94, first obtained by Philip [972] for the Green-Ampt soil, is the solution also to the Lucas-Washburn problem with gravity (see for example [794, 496]). Its inverse for $0 < I < 1$ is $I(T) = 1 + W[- \exp(-1 - T)]$, where W is the Lambert W function [82, 390].

17 The exponential equation 4.95 does not accurately describe simple capillary rise kinetics (the CR/CRG cases). However, we have shown [501] that in the case of capillary rise *with evaporation* (the CRE/CREG cases, Chapter 7) the approach to the steady-state is exponential.

18 We can now see why single-sided tests for estimating permeability are prone to error. Instead of using Eqn 3.7, we should rather make measurements of sorptivity S at several hydrostatic pressures (including zero head) and derive the permeability from Eqn 4.99.

19 The existence of intercepts in these plots points to a serious flaw in the procedures suggested in several recommended methods [194, 1063] of measuring the initial rate of suction, especially single point methods [1316]. It may be argued that the intercept does represent a real volume of liquid which has been taken up in the initial stages of absorption, but since this appears to arise largely from filling of surface pores, it is sample size dependent and is unlikely to correspond to practical circumstances.

20 The strong chemical interaction of water and cement is most apparent during primary curing when capillary water is used to feed the hydration reaction. In a concrete with low water/cement ratio, the amount of pore water and the vapour pressure may ultimately become small by *self-desiccation* [889].

21 Hirschwald's huge compilation of test results on building stones [565] showed definitively that incomplete filling of the porosity occurred both in partial and total immersion, and not sometimes but invariably. He was anticipated in the discovery of partial filling by Bloxam, who much earlier had noted the same behaviour in several Scottish sandstones [146, 147].

22 The Hirschwald coefficient h is now more widely used in petrophysics [1373] than in building physics, where it has been largely superseded by the *capillary moisture content*, denoted w_{cap} [558, 1077]. While the quantities h and w_{cap} are closely related, they may be measured by different procedures, making direct comparisons difficult. The Hirschwald coefficient (often just called the saturation coefficient or the saturation index) is often determined by a simple 48 h total immersion [1061], and denoted S_{48}. A 24 h test is sometimes used [1088]. On the other hand the capillary moisture content w_{cap} is usually found by the two-tangent method from sorptivity test data [374], as shown in Figure 4.19, and is reported as (mass of water)/(bulk volume of material), usually in unit kg/m^3. This unit is not ideal. Without the porosity f, w_{cap} provides no information about the amount of trapped air, usually the quantity of greatest interest. By contrast, h shows directly the fraction of the pore-space which is occupied by water at the end of primary imbibition. The volume fraction of the porosity occupied by trapped air, λ_a, then of course equals $1 - h$. The quantity λ_a is the same as the so-called residual nonwetting-phase saturation S_{nwr} in the terminology of petrophysics [148]. In our view there is merit in reporting the capillary moisture content as a fractional Hirschwald coefficient h.

23 Materials that show such scalings are known in soil physics as *Miller-similar* [836, 1194].

24 We can extend the scope of these scalings by considering materials of different porosity f_e, liquids of different surface tension σ_L, and varying wetting coefficient β. Then $\lambda \sim \sigma_L \beta / p_c$, and also $\lambda \sim (k'/f_e)^{1/2}$. The dimensionless quantity $p_c (k'/f_e)^{1/2}/(\sigma_L \beta)$ is therefore expected to be an invariant. In petroleum engineering, where the intrinsic permeability k' of reservoir rocks is often known, this quantity is the Leverett *J*-function [733, 148], used to scale (or compute) the capillary pressure. Two further relations follow from the λ scalings [492]. These concern the sorptivity: (1) the intrinsic sorptivity, from Eq 4.38, can be written $\mathbb{S} = (2 f_e k' \mathbb{p})^{1/2}$ where $\mathbb{p} = p_c/\sigma_L$ is a reduced (or normalized) hydraulic potential of dimension $[\mathrm{L}^{-1}]$; and (2) the intrinsic sorptivity $\mathbb{S} \sim (f_e^3 k')^{1/4}$ (where $\mathbb{S}$ has dimension $[\mathrm{L}^{1/2}]$). There is support for (2) from some exceptional data on a suite of Spanish building stones [107, 492].

25 Condition (1), the need for a uniform initial water content, appears to be more difficult to achieve in laboratory experiments on cements and concretes than on bricks and stones. There is evidence that water is slow to redistribute spontaneously to eliminate water content gradients and drying rates may be low. Protocols for conditioning test specimens have been proposed [925, 316, 36, 1341]. Condition (1) may be impossible to achieve in *in situ* field tests.

26 The water sensitivity of cementitious materials which is evident in both permeability and sorptivity properties (particularly on dried materials) carries an important message. It indicates that all water transport in cement-based materials is *reactive*, and that appropriate reactive transport models are required: see for example [238]. In addition to rehydration in dried cements, there is the leaching of soluble components, notably portlandite, with microstructural consequences.

5   Composite and nonuniform materials

It has been useful up to this point to deal with the fundamentals of water transfer in uniform and homogeneous materials. This has allowed us to concentrate on the physics of capillarity and unsaturated flow. However, building materials are often heterogeneous and building structures, unavoidably and almost by definition, are composite.

Many building materials are manufactured by blending mineral fillers with porous inorganic binders. Particularly important are those based on Portland cements: cement grouts, mortars and concretes. Mortars are produced by adding nonsorptive fillers (mainly sands) to cement pastes, concretes by adding coarse and usually nonsorptive mineral aggregates to mortars. The capillary properties of mortars and concretes are determined partly by the properties of the paste and partly by the additional porosity which may be incorporated during the admixing of the sand or aggregate. All such materials can be considered to be formed by adding *inclusions* to a homogeneous matrix: pudding with raisins.

Masonry is another form of composite structure, made by the repetitive assembly of units with one set of hydraulic properties, bonded with a mortar of different properties. Composite concrete structures may also be formed by sequential casting of mixes of different properties or by bonding precast elements. Even in plain concrete, the surface material often differs in properties from the interior, as a result of contact with formwork, enhanced drying or depletion of coarse aggregate. The thin, multiple coatings formed in plastering, rendering and screeding afford further examples. All these constructions can be regarded as composed of *layered* materials.

The question therefore arises: given that we can describe how water moves through the uniform component materials, can we predict how it will move through composite materials, whether layered or formed by random inclusions? Can we describe water movement in other kinds of nonuniform material?

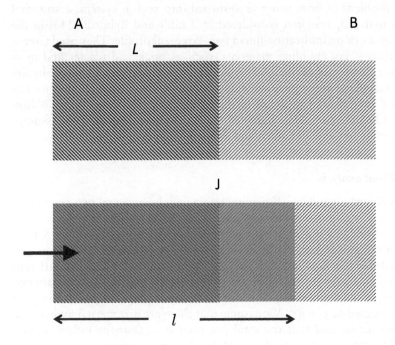

Figure 5.1 Water absorption into a two-layer composite A–B: layer A of length L, with junction at J; wet front at distance *l* from the inflow face moves from left to right.

5.1 LAYERED MATERIALS

We consider first the simple case of two materials in hydraulic contact, the *two-layer composite*. Our analysis is based in the main on Sharp Front [SF] theory. The results we derive can be usefully applied to several situations, including especially the case of thick components of materials such as concrete which may have surface layers whose properties differ from those of the bulk. We then extend the analysis to the case of many parallel layers, the *n*-layer composite. This allows us to obtain results for composite materials such as those made of layers having alternating properties (rather like masonry construction) and also materials whose hydraulic properties vary gradually with depth.

5.1.1 Two-layer composite

The simplest composite system which we can consider is that formed by placing two homogeneous bars in contact end-to-end, as shown in Figure 5.1. The analysis of one-dimensional flow in this composite bar also applies to flow processes normal to the plane of the two-layer composite slab.

The problem of how water is absorbed into such a system, a stratified porous material, was first considered by Childs and Bybordi [243] in the course of work on infiltration into a two-layer soil profile. They used Green-Ampt theory. For building materials, such as brick and plaster and mortars, the role of gravitational forces is usually secondary, as we have already noted. Capillary absorption of water in composite construction materials has been investigated in detail in the framework of SF theory by Wilson [1313, 1325, 1326, 1319, 1320, 579], the analysis starting from assumptions similar to those of Childs and Bybordi.

Sharp Front analysis

We can describe capillary absorption into a one-dimensional two-layer composite by a straightforward application of the SF model which we have applied already to homogeneous materials in Chapter 4. In Figure 5.1 we depict a composite bar, made up of a portion A of length L joined at J to a second portion B of indefinite length. We imagine A and B are different materials and have distinct moisture transport properties. Water is applied freely to the surface of A at $x = 0$ and during absorption the penetrating wet front is located at $x = l(t)$. We assume that there are no external hydrostatic pressures acting and that the total potential $\Phi = 0$ at the inflow surface $x = 0$ (the *free water reservoir* condition). So long as the wet front remains inside A, that is for $l < L$, the rate of absorption $u = \frac{1}{2}S_A t^{-1/2}$ where the sorptivity $S_A = (2K_A f_A |\Psi_{fA}|)^{1/2}$. Here Ψ_{fA} is the capillary potential at the wet front and K_A and f_A are permeability and porosity as usually defined in the SF model. The wet front reaches the junction J after a time t_J given by

$$i(l = L) = f_A L = S_A t_J^{1/2} \tag{5.1}$$

so that

$$t_J = \frac{f_A^2 L^2}{S_A^2}. \tag{5.2}$$

After it passes through the junction, the wet front advances into B. Applying the SF equation to flow in both parts separately gives

$$u = -\frac{K_A \Phi_J}{L} \tag{5.3}$$

and

$$u = -\frac{K_B (\Psi_{fB} - \Phi_J)}{l - L}, \tag{5.4}$$

where Φ_J is the hydraulic potential at the junction. Now for $l > L$, the cumulative absorption

$$i = f_A L + f_B(l - L) \tag{5.5}$$

so that on eliminating Φ_J and l, we have

$$u = -\frac{f_B K_B \Psi_{fB}}{i - f_A L + f_B K_B L / K_A}. \tag{5.6}$$

Since $u = di/dt$, this is the differential equation describing the motion of the wet front beyond the junction. We note that the denominator in Eqn 5.6 is a quantity which has the dimension of cumulative absorption. Denoting this by j, we obtain

$$u = \frac{di}{dt} = \frac{dj}{dt} = -\frac{f_B K_B \Psi_{fB}}{j}. \tag{5.7}$$

Integrating this leads to the principal result, an expression for $i(t)$

$$i - L(f_A - f_B K_B / K_A) = S_B \left[t + \frac{L^2}{2K_A^2} \left(\frac{f_B K_B}{\Psi_{fB}} - \frac{f_A K_A}{\Psi_{fA}} \right) \right]^{1/2}. \tag{5.8}$$

Since $S_A = (2f_A K_A |\Psi_{fA}|)^{1/2}$ and $S_B = (2f_B K_B |\Psi_{fB}|)^{1/2}$, we can write this in terms of the component sorptivities S_A and S_B

$$i - L(f_A - f_B K_B / K_A) = S_B \left[t + L^2 \left(\frac{f_B^2 K_B^2}{S_B^2 K_A^2} - \frac{f_A^2}{S_A^2} \right) \right]^{1/2}. \tag{5.9}$$

that is

$$i + LY = S_B (t + L^2 X)^{1/2}, \tag{5.10}$$

with

$$X = \left(\frac{f_B}{S_B} \right)^2 \left(\frac{K_B}{K_A} \right)^2 - \left(\frac{f_A}{S_A} \right)^2 \tag{5.11}$$

and

$$Y = f_B \frac{K_B}{K_A} - f_A. \tag{5.12}$$

We can write Eqn 5.10 even more succinctly as

$$j = S_B \tau^{1/2} \tag{5.13}$$

where

$$j = i + LY \tag{5.14}$$

and

$$\tau = t + L^2 X. \tag{5.15}$$

This is an important and perhaps rather unexpected result. Eqn 5.13 tells us that the cumulative water absorption as the wet front moves through the second part of a two-layer composite also follows a simple square root law, but in the variables j and τ rather than i and t [484]. The physical cause of this that the advance of the wet front through B is subject to a hydraulic impedance from the motion of the fluid through A. Notionally, this effect can be represented by replacing the length L of material A by an *equivalent length* $L_e = LK_B/K_A$ of material B. Thus the water absorption proceeds within B as though the entire composite were composed of a single material [1313]. There is however an offset in the time variable which is proportional to L^2 and depends in general on the material properties of both A and B. When the wet front is located at the junction, $l = L$ and $\tau = (f_B L_e/S_B)^2$. The equivalent length L_e depends on the contrast in permeability of the two materials, not on their sorptivities.

We can now summarize the SF relations describing the absorption of liquids into a two-layer composite. For $l < L$

$$i = S_A t^{1/2} \tag{5.16}$$

and

$$u = \frac{1}{2} S_A t^{-1/2}. \tag{5.17}$$

For $l > L$

$$j = S_B \tau^{1/2} \tag{5.18}$$

and

$$u = \frac{1}{2} S_B \tau^{-1/2}. \tag{5.19}$$

These equations describe the absorption of water into a two-layer composite in terms of the hydraulic properties f, S and K of the individual components A and B.[1]

To them we can add two useful subsidiary results. First, the wetted length of part B of the composite at time t is

$$l_B = l - L = \frac{S_B}{f_B}\tau^{1/2} - L_e. \tag{5.20}$$

Second, the time for the wet front to travel from the junction a distance l_B into B is

$$\Delta t_B = \frac{f_B^2 l_B}{S_B^2}(l_B + 2L_e). \tag{5.21}$$

We note that since the wet front is located beyond the junction at J, the quantities l_B and Δt_B necessarily depend on S_B but not on S_A. They do of course depend also on the ratio K_A/K_B through L_e.

The main features of these equations are illustrated in Figure 5.2, which shows the water absorption of the two-layer composite for typical values of hydraulic properties. We compute two examples, one in which $S_A < S_B$ and another in which $S_A > S_B$; and for these, we plot both $i(t^{1/2})$ and $j(\tau^{1/2})$. The behaviour is probably most easily understood from Eqns 5.10, 5.11 and 5.12. Both X and Y may have positive or negative values, depending on the magnitudes of the ratios S_A/S_B, K_A/K_B and f_A/f_B. If $S_A > S_B$ and $S_A/S_B < f_A K_A/(f_B K_B)$, we see that X is negative and Y positive. Then beyond the junction, $di/dt = \frac{1}{2}S_B(t - |L^2X|)^{-1/2} > \frac{1}{2}S_B t^{-1/2}$. At corresponding times t, the rate of absorption is greater in the composite than it would be in material B alone. This is because the equivalent length L_e is less than L. For the case $S_A < S_B$, $S_A/S_B > f_A K_A/(f_B K_B)$, X is positive, Y is negative and the rate of absorption is smaller in the composite than it would be in material B at time t. Here the equivalent length L_e is greater than L.

We see that there is greater sensitivity to the ratio K_A/K_B in the case $S_A < S_B$ – as is apparent from inspection of Eqn 5.10. Indeed, if the permeability contrast is large and the equivalent length L_e is much larger than L, the water absorption rate beyond the junction may initially be *lower* than before it, despite the higher sorptivity of B. We also see that at long times when $t \gg L^2 X$, the slope of the $i(t^{1/2})$ curve becomes equal to the sorptivity of B, S_B, but that this value is attained only slowly if there is a large contrast in K between the two materials. In all cases, the influence of the first layer diminishes with time.

Experimental evidence

We do not yet have comprehensive experimental data on capillary transport in layered media. Wilson [1313, 1325, 1326, 1319] carried out careful studies of water absorption into composite bars fabricated from gypsum plaster

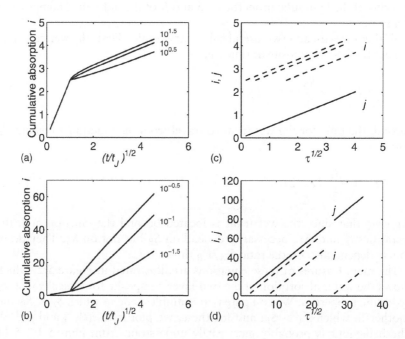

Figure 5.2 Absorption by a two-layer composite: Sharp Front model. (a) The cumulative absorption i versus $(t/t_J)^{1/2}$ calculated from Eqns 5.16 and 5.18, for the case $S_A > S_B$ using parameter values $S_A = 3$, $S_B = 0.5$, and $K_A/K_B = 10^{0.5}$, 10 and $10^{1.5}$; (b) i versus $(t/t_J)^{1/2}$ for the case $S_A < S_B$ with $S_A = 0.5$, $S_B = 3$, and $K_A/K_B = 10^{-1.5}$, 10^{-1}, and $10^{-0.5}$. (c) and (d) are corresponding plots of $i(\tau^{1/2})$ (dashed lines) and $j(\tau^{1/2})$ (solid lines). Throughout, the porosities f_A and f_B are 0.25 and the length L is 10.

mixes of different compositions. For these materials, the hydraulic properties of which were measured independently, the SF model described rather accurately the absorption of water into bars having $S_A > S_B$. We show some results in Figure 5.3. Here the contrast in hydraulic properties is not great; the permeabilities differ by a factor of about 6 and the sorptivities by about three. We see that once the wet front passes through the junction between the two materials, the rate of absorption soon approaches the value of the less sorptive material B. The validity of the simple equation $j = S_B \tau^{-1/2}$ in describing the water absorption after the wet front has passed the junction is demonstrated in Figure 5.4 by the way that the experimental curves $i(t^{1/2})$ collapse to a single straight line of slope S_B when plotted as $j(\tau^{1/2})$. Independently [1050], the imbibition of a silicone oil into a two-layer composite of glass beads of different sizes has been described by the same Darcian model that underpins the SF Eqns 5.16, 5.18.

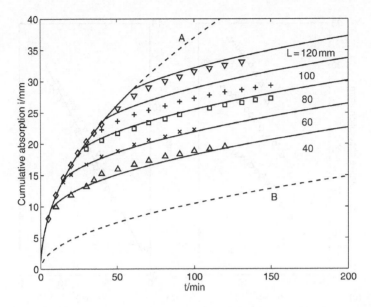

Figure 5.3 Absorption by a two-layer composite: experimental data on gypsum plaster composite bars [1313, 1319] for the case $S_A > S_B$. Solid lines are predicted water absorptions computed from Eqns 5.16 and 5.18; dashed lines show the absorptions of A and B individually.

For $S_A < S_B$, both model and experiment show that the water absorption beyond the junction is initially low, and is much slower to reflect the properties of layer B than in the case of $S_A > S_B$. This is because the presence of layer A imposes a large equivalent length L_e in series with B. If the permeability ratio $K_A/K_B \ll 1$, as it may commonly be, then $L_e = LK_B/K_A$ may be large and so the water absorption rate falls sharply after the wet front passes the junction. Capillary absorption is still strongly impeded by the low permeability of A but it is no longer promoted by its relatively high wet front capillary potential. It is only after the wet front has penetrated a considerable distance beyond the junction (several times L_e) that the effect of layer A diminishes and ultimately $i \to S_B t^{1/2}$.

While SF theory offers a good way to tackle such problems, it needs to be used judiciously. The Sharp Front (Green-Ampt) model is a rather simple way of representing unsaturated capillary flow, and there are several discussions of its physical validity in describing water transport in heterogeneous systems, particularly in gravity-assisted infiltration in layered systems ([242, 977, 843]). There is no doubt that as we move from the reservoir at $x = 0$ towards the wet front the saturation diminishes. At each interface we have a condition that the hydraulic potential is equal in the two materials. We know that except at $\theta_r = 1$ two different materials will in general have different water contents. We can say that the SF two-layer theory is at

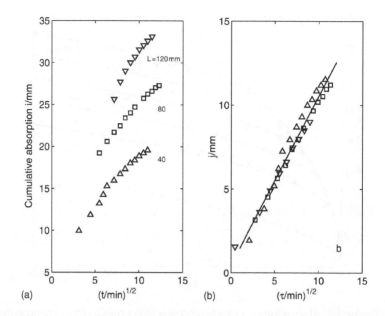

Figure 5.4 The two-layer composite: water absorption into gypsum plaster composite bars. (a) Absorption into the second layer $i(t^{1/2})$ (raw data as in Figure 5.3). (b) The same data transformed to $j(\tau^{1/2})$, using Eqns 5.14 and 5.15. The best-fit straight line has slope 1.01 mm/min$^{1/2}$, close to the independently measured value of S_B.

its most accurate when the wetted region is close to saturation, for example in materials of high porosity in good contact with the reservoir. Childs [243] made a stronger statement in placing strict limits on the validity of the approach. He considered that the Green-Ampt theory was well suited to infiltration into a composite in which the more permeable layer lies above a layer of lower hydraulic conductivity. 'When on the other hand, the layer of lower conductivity rests on that of the higher conductivity, ...the lower layer needs to have a moisture content short of saturation to accept the relatively low rate of percolation transmitted to it by the upper layer. This is contrary to the Green-Ampt concept, which therefore has no relevance to it.' Philip's view ([974, 977]) that SF descriptions are unsuited to heterogeneous media seems overstated. The admittedly limited experimental data of [487, 1050] on imbibition into layered and graded materials support their use for engineering purposes. The application to the case $S_A < S_B$ requires further validation but when the model is viewed as an effective one-component analysis, using the equivalent length concept, its general application can perhaps be accepted more easily.

Interfacial contact resistance

The question of whether there is an interfacial contact resistance has been raised many times, notably in several early analyses [454, 583, 177]. That there can be such a contact resistance is now clear, but what controls it is less clear. We have so far assumed that there is *perfect hydraulic contact* between the two layers. This means that the hydraulic potential Ψ is continuous across the junction (Figure 5.5) and has a well-defined value $\Psi_A(x = x_J) = \Psi_B(x = x_J) = \Psi_J$. Since in general $\theta_A(\Psi_J) \neq \theta_B(\Psi_J)$, the water content is not continuous across the interface. We note that of course the flow velocity is also continuous, so that $u_A(x = x_J) = u_B(x = x_J) = K_A \nabla \Psi_A = K_B \nabla \Psi_B$. For *imperfect hydraulic contact*, where there is a finite contact resistance, Ψ is no longer continuous across the interface, although u is. The contact resistance can be considered to arise from the existence of a thin interfacial zone with a distinct permeability, which therefore provides an impedance in series with the two principal layers. We usually know neither the thickness L_I nor the permeability K_I of the interfacial zone but in SF models we can represent the contact resistance as a lumped quantity R_J notionally equal to $L_I/K_I = (\Delta\Psi)_J/u$ where $\Psi_J = \Psi_{IB} - \Psi_{IA}$.[2] This of course is a 'saturated' view of interfacial transfer. It is likely that, strictly speaking, the interfacial impedance is not constant but varies with water content, although such a refinement far outruns our present understanding. The hydraulic contact resistance is analogous to the heat transfer coefficient used in the modelling of thermal phenomena at a surface of contact.

Pel [937, 180] and then Brocken [181, 178, 177], using NMR imaging, have provided evidence for the existence of imperfect hydraulic contact at the brick/mortar interface in several experimental specimens. A contact resistance was detected by Derluyn *et al.* [309, 308] who used a microfocus X-ray method to image water absorption in brick/mortar/brick stacks. De Freitas *et al.* [389] mapped water content distributions by gamma-ray attenuation

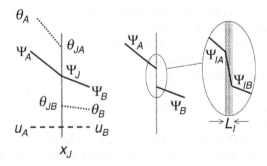

Figure 5.5 Transfer of water through the interface between two materials A and B. *Left*: Perfect hydraulic contact, Ψ continuous. *Right*: Imperfect contact, Ψ discontinuous, represented as an interfacial zone with contact resistance R_J.

during water absorption into clay brick and aerated autoclaved concrete materials forced into mechanical contact. Contact resistance is expected to arise whenever the pore networks of A and B are not well connected across the junction AB. For example, when brick/mortar junctions are formed in masonry construction we may expect the suction of the brick to draw fine particles from the wet mortar into the surface pores and occlude them. Further occlusion may occur as solid cement hydrate material forms in the surface pores during setting. A rather different form of interfacial resistance may develop when shrinkage stress causes the brick/mortar bond to delaminate, leaving a 'capillary break' of low suction at the joint. Similar capillary breaks no doubt arise when flat but microscopically rough surfaces of rigid porous materials are placed in contact. Effective capillary contact may occur only through touching asperities.

The formulation of the two-layer problem given here allows such a contact resistance R_J to be included easily. We simply add a term $K_B R_J$ to the equivalent hydraulic length in the calculation of L_e. We show how this is done on p 191.

5.1.2   Multiple layers

The approach we have used for two layers in contact can be extended in what might be called a bootstrapping algorithm to provide a solution for the n-layer problem [487]. We have seen that as the wet-front passes the first junction and enters the second layer, the effect of the fully wetted first layer is to provide an impedance which may just as well be expressed as an equivalent length of the second material. For the n-layer material, we can carry out this same procedure as the wet front passes each junction in turn. Mathematically, we can do this as many times as we wish. We may also add an interfacial or contact impedance at any or all of the junctions.

This method turns out to be computationally simple, especially if we are content to calculate just the times, t_{Ji}, when the wet front reaches each junction. For an n-layer composite which has more than say 4 or 5 layers these t_{Ji} define the overall cumulative absorption adequately.

In our Sharp Front analysis of absorption into the two-layer composite (Section 5.1.1), we showed that the kinetics of liquid absorption into the second layer is described by Eqn 5.13 $j = S_B \tau^{1/2}$, where $j = i - L_A(f_A - f_B K_B / K_A)$ and $\tau = t + L_A^2 X$ with $X = f_B^2 K_B^2 / (K_A^2 S_B^2) - f_A^2 / S_A^2$. Here f denotes the volume fraction porosity, S the sorptivity, K the permeability and L_A the length of element A.

As Wilson [1313] first noted, this equation implies that once the wet front has passed the junction $(t > t_J)$ the composite behaves as though it were composed solely of material B, the A layer of length L being replaced by a fictional length L_e of B, where as we have seen $L_e = L_A K_B / K_A$. Thus we replace length L_A of A by a length of B having the same hydraulic resistance – the equivalent (hydraulic) length. Absorption into the second layer can then be described solely in terms of the properties of material B. The properties of material A however determine the time variable τ and the equivalent length L_e. (Note in passing that these are independent, since L_e depends only on the permeability ratio but τ depends also on the sorptivity/porosity property of the two materials.)

This line of argument suggests a solution to the n-layer problem, which in essence involves replacing all wetted layers by their equivalent lengths. Thus for water absorption in layer j (in the time interval in which the wet front passes through layer j), we replace layers $1 \ldots j-1$ by their hydraulic equivalent length $L_{e(j-1)}$ of the material of layer j. Thereafter we proceed as for the two layer composite. The equivalent length $L_{e(j-1)} = K_j \sum_{i=1}^{j-1} L_i/K_i$. The time variable τ expresses a shift in the time origin and can always be written $\tau_j = t + \delta_j$ where δ_j is a time offset.

An essential result is the time at which the wet front reaches junction j:

$$t_{Jj} = \sum_{i=1}^{j} \frac{f_i^2}{S_i^2} L_i^2 \left(1 + 2\frac{L_{e(i-1)}}{L_i}\right) \tag{5.22}$$

with $L_{e0} = 0$. This equation allows the time interval during which each layer is being wetted to be calculated. Then for each such time interval (and thus for each corresponding layer), we apply the equation $j_j = S_j\tau_j^{1/2}$, with

$$\delta_j = \left(\frac{f_j L_{e(j-1)}}{S_j}\right)^2 - \sum_{i=1}^{j-1} \frac{f_i^2}{S_i^2} L_i^2 \left(1 + 2\frac{L_{e(i-1)}}{L_i}\right). \tag{5.23}$$

The total cumulative absorption is given by

$$i = S_w \tau_w^{\frac{1}{2}} - f_w L_{e(w-1)} + \sum_{i=1}^{w-1} f_i L_i, \tag{5.24}$$

where the subscript w denotes the junction at which the wet front is located.

The analysis given here is an *exact* solution of the one-dimensional SF problem for n layers having arbitrary properties and thicknesses. It contains no mathematical approximations but of course, as we have already noted, the SF model is a fairly severe physical simplification of unsaturated flow theory.

Streamlined calculation

For composites consisting of more than just a few layers (say $n \geq 5$), the absorption history is well described just by $i(t_J)$, that is, by calculating the times at which the wet front reaches each successive junction. To calculate these times requires the use of Eqns 5.22 and 5.24 only. We note also that Eqn 5.22 can be written in the form

$$t_{Ji} = t_{J(j-1)} + \frac{f_j^2}{S_j^2} L_j^2 \left(1 + 2\frac{L_{e(j-1)}}{L_j}\right),$$ (5.25)

with $t_{J0} = 0$ and $L_{e0} = 0$. This form is easy to compute. Likewise the cumulative absorption at each t_J is also easy to calculate since it is just the sum of the fully wetted fluid contents of all preceding layers. Thus Eqn 5.24 is replaced by the much simpler

$$i(t_{Ji}) = \sum_1^j f_j L_j,$$ (5.26)

avoiding the need to calculate δ_j and τ_j. Therefore, to calculate the absorption – time history: calculate for each junction (1) the equivalent length L_e; (2) the time t_J; and (3) the cumulative absorption $i(t_J)$. This can be computed with no more than a few lines of code.

As an illustration of this Figure 5.6 shows a calculation for the case of 10 layers. We also show how including a contact resistance affects the cumulative absorption in this case.

Alternating layers: quasi-masonry

Of several particular cases of the n-layer composite, the many-layer alternating case (ABAB...) is worth examining further because it is a fair model of a masonry structure (brickwork for example), at least for in-plane capillary transport. (We call this 'quasi-masonry' because it represents the masonry as a one-dimensional chain of alternating units but neglects the parallel connections.) For the case ABAB..., we find a useful asymptotic result. For large n

$$t_{Jn} \simeq \frac{n^2}{4}(1 + K_r^{-1}) \left(\frac{K_r f_A^2 L_A^2}{S_A^2} + \frac{f_B^2 L_B^2}{S_B^2}\right),$$ (5.27)

where $K_r = K_A L_B / K_B L_A$ is the ratio of the hydraulic resistances of the B and A layers. We define an effective sorptivity $S_{eff} = i(t_{Jn})/t_{Jn}^{1/2}$ as $n \to \infty$. For large n, we have $i(t_J) \simeq n(f_A L_A + f_B L_B)/2$ and so

$$S_{eff} = (f_A L_A + f_B L_B)\left[\frac{K_r}{1 + K_r}\right]^{1/2} \Big/ \left[\frac{K_r f_A^2 L_A^2}{S_A^2} + \frac{f_B^2 L_B^2}{S_B^2}\right]^{1/2}.$$ (5.28)

This is an immediately useful result for engineering calculations, for example to estimate capillary rise rates in masonry structures [463].

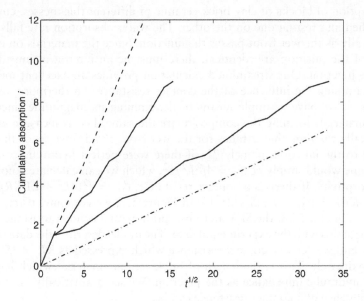

Figure 5.6 Absorption by a 10-layer ABAB... composite [487]: the cumulative absorption i versus $t^{1/2}$. $L_A = 5$, $L_B = 1$; $K_A/K_B = 10$; $f_A = f_B = 0.3$; $S_A = 1$, $S_B = 0.2$. Solid lines show the absorption of the composite: *upper*, $R_J = 0$ (without contact resistance) and *lower* $R_J = 30$ (with contact resistance). The dashed lines show the absorption of the materials A and B individually.

We find by evaluating Eqns 5.25, 5.26 and 5.28 over a large range of parameters that Eqn 5.28 is an excellent representation of the absorption behaviour even for quite a small number of layers, say 7 and more. The difference between S_{eff} and the slope of the regression line to calculated $i(t_j^{1/2})$ is rarely more than 2 per cent and often much less.

Provided that the contrast in hydraulic resistance between layers is not large (K_r in the range 0.1–10, say), S_{eff} lies between S_A and S_B. However, a strong contrast in hydraulic resistance greatly reduces S_{eff}. For the particular case of equal layer thickness, $S_{eff} \simeq 2S_h(K_l/K_h)^{1/2}$ as $K_r \to \infty$ or $\to 0$, where S_h denotes the sorptivity of the high permeability layer and K_h and K_l the higher and lower permeabilities. Thus the effective sorptivity tends to some small fraction of the sorptivity of the higher permeability layer. This result immediately suggests the practical value of introducing hydraulic resistance contrast into masonry structures as a means of retarding capillary transport.

Determining the contact resistance

In the elegant experiment already mentioned de Freitas *et al.* [389] provide a clear demonstration of a contact resistance in measurements of the water absorption of blocks of clay brick ceramic of different thicknesses, cut and polished and resting one on the other. The water absorption rate falls dramatically as the wet front passes the junction. Since the materials on either side of the junction are identical, there must be an interfacial impedance at the junction. Our streamlined calculation provides an excellent method of examining the influence of the contact resistance. Furthermore, in this instance, we have a simple means of determining its magnitude since the two materials forming the composite are the same. Let us measure experimentally the time that it takes for the wet front to advance twice the distance to the junction, namely $2L$. If there were perfect hydraulic contact, this time would simply be $t_{2L} = 4f^2L^2/S^2$, which we can calculate, knowing the sorptivity. If there is a contact resistance, $t'_{2L} = f^2(4L^2 + 2LKR_J)/S^2$. Thus $KR_J = (t'_{2L} - t_{2L})S^2/(2f^2L)$. In Figure 5.7, we compute, using Eqns 5.25, 5.26 and 5.28, the SF water absorption with a contact resistance and compare this with the experimental data. The model describes the data excellently and we derive a contact resistance which expressed as $KR_J = 350$ mm approximately. This is the length of brick ceramic material which has the same hydraulic impedance as the junction. We see dramatically how great the influence of a contact resistance can be.

Experimental data on multi-layer composites

Tests of water transport in multi-layer composites are sparse. Green [441, 487] describes work on water absorption into composite bars composed of several alternating layers of different plaster mixes. Beck [98] gives experimental results on an ABA system with $S_A > S_B$.

In Figure 5.8 we show experimental $i(t)$ data from [487] for ABAB... plaster bars and the theoretical curves calculated from Eqns 5.25 and 5.26. The estimates of $i(t)$ during absorption are mostly good to within a few per cent, although the experimental data do not show the discontinuities of slope that are seen in the calculated curves. This is expected since the SF model represents the diffuse wet front as a step. The calculated effective sorptivity for the combination of materials and thicknesses used in these specimens is about 2.66 mm/min$^{1/2}$. The experimental value for the sample with the largest number of layers, Figure 5.8c, is about 2.61 mm/min$^{1/2}$.

These experimental data can be modelled by the equations given, but it requires further experimental investigation to establish how well the SF model represents real multilayer structures over larger ranges of parameters; and how well the K_i values of the model (which always appear as ratios) can be estimated from measured permeabilities.

Graded layers

The layers which we employ do not have to be physically distinct or separate but may be notional elements used for the purposes of modelling. Consider,

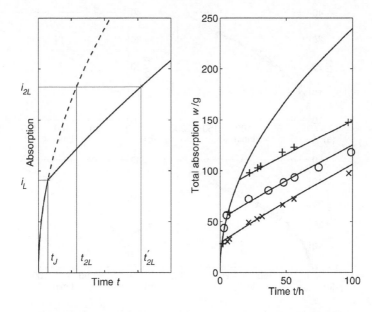

Figure 5.7 Left: The effect of a contact resistance on water absorption through an AA composite formed of two layers of the same material. Dashed curve: no contact resistance. Solid line: with contact resistance. The magnitude of the contact resistance can be obtained from the quantity $t_{2L} - t'_{2L}$. *Right*: Data from de Freitas *et al.* [389] on clay brick ceramic AA composites, with $L = 20$ (×), 50 (○) and 70 mm (+). The solid lines are computed from the *n*-layer Sharp Front model, using 300 layers, a contact resistance $KR_J = 350$ mm and material property data $S = 7.7$ mm h$^{-1/2}$ and $f = 0.28$.

for instance, a concrete slab which has a graded variation of properties from the surface inwards. We may choose to represent this by 5 or 10 or even 50 layers with progressively varying properties. Let us take as an example the common case of a concrete with a more sorptive and more permeable surface layer, the properties of which gradually approach those of the bulk material over a depth of, say, 20 mm. We represent the surface layer as 20 graded sublayers each 1 mm thick. Eqn 5.25 predicts the water absorption which would be measured in a sorptivity test as a function of time. We show the results for illustrative values of the material properties in Figure 5.9a. While the wet front passes through the property-varying surface layer, the cumulative absorption deviates markedly from $t^{1/2}$ behaviour and falls rapidly. At sufficiently long times, a linear dependence on $t^{1/2}$ is established and the slope of $i(t^{1/2})$ eventually becomes equal to the sorptivity of the bulk material. The effect of the highly sorptive surface layer is to produce a large positive

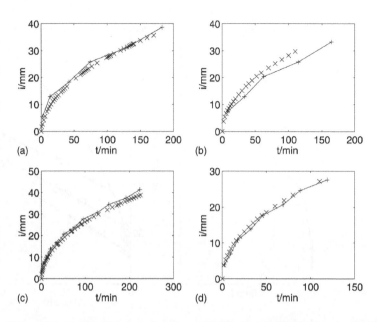

Figure 5.8 Comparison of experimental data ($\times$) and calculated cumulative absorption $i(t)$ ($+$ and solid lines) for absorption into a multi-layer composite. (a) ABAB..., 6 layers, $L_A = 18$ mm, $L_B = 25$ mm; (b) BABA..., 5 layers $L_A = 25$ mm, $L_B = 18$ mm; (c) ABAB..., 12 layers, $L_A = 10$ mm, $L_B = 13$ mm; (d) BABA..., 8 layers, $L_A = 13$ mm, $L_B = 10$ mm. Values of t_J ($+$) were calculated from Eqns 5.25 and 5.26 using the physical property data $S_A = 3.90$ mm min$^{-1/2}$, $S_B = 2.53$ mm min$^{-1/2}$, $K_A = 0.0159$ mm min^{-1}, $K_B = 0.0037$ mm min^{-1}, and $f_A = f_B = 0.30$.

i-offset. This offset is a measure of the difference in water capacity of the surface layer compared with the bulk. Of course, the surface layer may also be of lower sorptivity and lower permeability than the bulk. In that case, as is shown in Figure 5.9b, the water absorption once again fails to show $t^{1/2}$ behaviour at early times as the wet front passes through the surface zone. The 'tight' surface produces a negative intercept when the linear long-term absorption is extrapolated back to $t = 0$.

The surfaces of porous materials may often differ somewhat from the bulk. Causes are numerous: differences in firing temperatures in brick [792] and other heavy clay materials; effects of trowelling, bleeding and contact with formwork in concretes [695, 319, 756, 757, 811, 212]; dewatering by contact with porous substrates in mortars, screeds and plasters. Of special importance is the *cover zone* in reinforced concrete and a large research effort is devoted to understanding its role in concrete deterioration [90, 923, 924, 808, 816]. A difference between surface and bulk is no doubt one common cause of intercepts and offsets which are often found in i versus

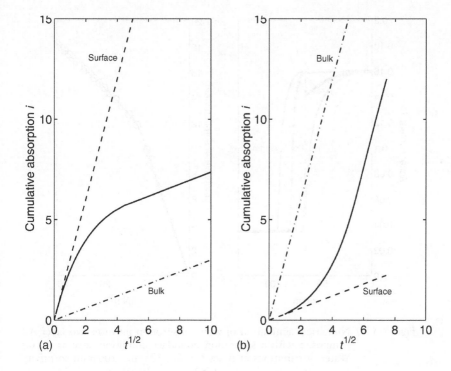

Figure 5.9 Capillary absorption through a surface layer of continuously varying hydraulic properties. (a) The surface is modelled as 20 sublayers,
with sorptivity varying linearly from 3 at the surface to 0.3 in the
bulk, and permeability linearly from 10 to 1. (b) Surface sorptivity
varies from 0.3 to 3 and permeability from 1 to 10. The porosity
is 0.3 throughout and the sublayers are of equal thickness. Dashed
and dot-dash lines show the surface and bulk absorptions.

$t^{1/2}$ water absorption plots. Our analysis here shows that as water absorption proceeds the influence of the surface layer diminishes and the absorption
rate eventually attains the bulk value. This reflects a general rule of capillary
flows that at long times, the influence of the impedance of the inflow surface
on the absorption rate tends to disappear. This will be encountered again in
Chapter 6 in connection with the Massaris' problem.

We discuss the topic of transport in nonuniform materials with continuous variation of properties more comprehensively later in this chapter, Section 5.2.

5.1.3 Diffusivity analysis of layered composites

Our analysis of layered materials has been in the language of the Sharp Front
model. The advantage of this approach is that it can provide explicit and

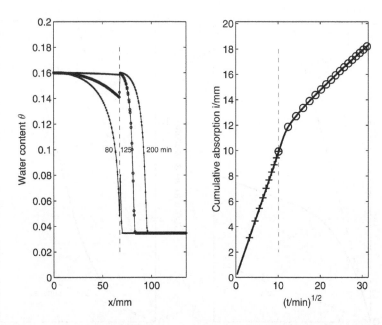

Figure 5.10 Numerical simulation of water absorption into the two layer AB composite with a saturation boundary condition at $x = 0$. (a) Water distributions at times $t = 80$, 125 and 200 min; sorptivity $S_A = 1.0 \, \text{mm/min}^{1/2}$; $S_B = 0.3 \, \text{mm/min}^{1/2}$. (b) Cumulative water absorption (solid line) compared with the SF two-layer model (+, ○), Eqns 5.16 and 5.18, using the same values of S_A and S_B. The SF permeability ratio K_A/K_B is set equal to K_{sA}/K_{sB}, the ratio of the hydraulic conductivities at saturation.

relatively simple equations for describing the water transfer process. SF theory predicts the location of the wet front but does not of course provide any information about the moisture distribution within the wetted region. As an alternative, we can of course resort to fully numerical simulations of the transfer process, using the complete Buckingham-Richards description of unsaturated flow. This has the virtue of modelling the complete moisture distribution as a function of time, but at the price of requiring complete hydraulic property function data on the materials. Several studies of this kind have been reported on layered soils [533, 1044, 1180]; Wang *et al.* [1293] have measured water-distribution profiles in two-layer gypsum composites, while Pel [937] and Brocken [177] have published simulations of one-dimensional absorption into brick/mortar/brick composites in the studies of contact resistance mentioned earlier. Roels discusses the $S_A > S_B$ two-layer case [1074]. We can illustrate this approach by applying it to the layered composites that we have already discussed. In Figure 5.10, we show the full numerical solution of the absorption into the two-layer AB composite for which we gave an SF analysis in Section 5.1.1. We use hydraulic parameters such that A is a low suction, high permeability material, while B is a high suction, low permeability material. We see clearly in Figure 5.10 the discontinuity in water content at the interface and the comparatively slow rate of advance of the steep wet front beyond the junction. The higher suction of B means that as the wet front moves through the vicinity of the junction, the water content in B is markedly higher than in A. In Figure 5.10, we compare the cumulative absorption obtained numerically with the predictions of the simple SF equations. We see that they are in excellent agreement.

5.1.4 Flow parallel to interfaces

Our discussion of capillary flow in layered structures has dealt mainly with flow *normal* to the layering. This reflects the importance of layers and interfaces as barriers and impedances in composite construction, but flow *parallel* to a conductive interface between two dissimilar porous materials, as drawn in Figure 5.11, merits a mention. We ask how capillary absorption proceeds in such a simple composite if liquid is supplied at the end face AOB

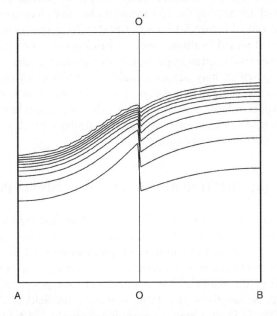

Figure 5.11 Numerical unsaturated flow solution for two parallel layers in hydraulic contact. A saturation boundary condition is applied at the face AOB (length 300 mm) and capillary absorption proceeds from bottom to top. The sorptivity ratio of the layers S_f/S_s is 1.4 and $S_f = 1.0$ mm min$^{1/2}$. The water content distribution (10 equally spaced isohygral contours) is shown at $t = 1000$ min.

($x = 0$). If the interface is nonconducting (or if there is a large hydraulic contact resistance along OO'), the two parts of the composite absorb water independently at rates determined by their individual sorptivities S_A and S_B. However, hydraulic contact along OO' means that the more sorptive material can supply water to the less sorptive, so that there is flow across the interface and the problem becomes fully two-dimensional. Straddling the interface is a zone of disturbance where the capillary absorption rate deviates from the far-field values. We have no simple solution to the SF problem in this composite. A numerical solution to the unsaturated flow problem is shown in Figure 5.11. The flow net suggests that the disturbed region is more prominent on the dry side of the interface. Water moves across the interface from wet to dry but the perturbation in the wet region is slight, because the higher hydraulic conductivity allows high water contents to be maintained.[3] The capillary potential is continuous across the interface but there is a corresponding discontinuity in water content. The lateral extent of the interfacial zone, say l_w, increases as $t^{1/2}$: l_w/l_{ff} varies roughly as $(1 - S_s f_f / S_f f_s)$ where l_{ff} is the location of the faster moving front and S_s, S_f and f_s, f_f the sorptivities and porosities of the slower and faster materials. A consequence of this is that a thin low sorptivity layer sandwiched between two higher sorptivity layers behaves as though it has an effective sorptivity (estimated for example from the rate of advance of the wet front) higher than its true sorptivity.

The simulations of Figure 5.11 assume perfect hydraulic contact along the interface. In real-world examples such as brick-mortar or render-substrate composites, the bond is often imperfect. Poor adhesion or debonding creates a capillary gap which may act as a high conductivity pathway for water absorption, for example of rain falling on brickwork. This is in contrast to the case of capillary flow at right angles to the interface where, as we have mentioned on p 188, such a gap may act as a capillary break and contribute to an interfacial contact resistance.

5.2   MATERIALS WITH NONUNIFORM TRANSPORT PROPERTIES

We have already (p 192) introduced the topic of graded layers where transport properties vary smoothly from one location to another within a material. Our earlier discussion of multiple layers (Section 5.1.2), in particular of the n-layer model, enables us now to deal in a more general way with situations where the material has nonuniform transport properties along the flow path. While there is a large literature on field heterogeneity in soils ([977, 978, 175], and more recently for example, [249, 660]) the topic of imbibition into nonuniform porous materials on the laboratory scale has received surprisingly little attention. But fired-clay bricks may be laminated as result of extrusion during manufacture, building stones often have pronounced bedding planes, and surface segregation of sand and aggregates may occur in concretes.[4] All of these types of heterogeneity give rise to nonuniform transport properties, typically on a millimetre/centimetre length-scale. The n-layer model provides a computationally simple procedure for calculating the kinetics of 1-D imbibition into a material composed of n-layers with arbitrary thicknesses and material properties. This model embodies a Sharp Front description in which the sorptivity plays a leading role. It therefore provides a way to analyze capillary imbibition in materials with spatially varying sorptivity.

Sorptivity as a local property

Porosity and pore-size distribution may vary spatially within a porous material, and as a result the permeability, the capillary potential, and the sorptivity may also vary. In modelling water transport in porous construction materials and building elements, fundamental unsaturated flow parameters such as water retention and hydraulic conductivity are rarely available, and many of our models rely on SF descriptions. SF analyses treat systems as composed of Green-Ampt materials, characterized by the wet front capillary potential Ψ_f, and the permeability K of the wetted zone. While K and Ψ_f are rarely known separately, the sorptivity $S = (2f_e K |\Psi_f|)^{1/2}$ is the main accessible capillary-transport material property.

The sorptivity S is almost always measured on uniform bench-scale specimens (for example, on prisms of rock, brick, or concrete), but there is in principle no difficulty in defining the sorptivity of a small volume element. This follows since each of the three quantities f, K, and Ψ_f on which S depends can be defined locally. The sorptivity $S = (2f_e K |\Psi_f|)^{1/2}$ can therefore also be defined locally within a nonuniform material, and a spatially varying sorptivity can be used to describe capillary transport in such a nonuniform medium [451].

The model of SF capillary imbibition into a material with uniform properties has been discussed fully in Chapter 4. where the defining Eqns 4.36, 4.37 can be found on p 134. For nonuniform materials, in which the properties f_e, K, Ψ_f and S vary along the flow path, the SF equations for one-dimensional imbibition become

$$\frac{dl}{dt} = \frac{1}{f_e(l)} |\Psi_f(l)| / \int_0^l \frac{dx}{K(x)}, \tag{5.29}$$

or

$$dt = \left[\int_0^l \frac{dx}{K(x)} \right] \cdot \frac{2f_e(l)^2 K(l)}{S(l)^2} dl \tag{5.30}$$

with $l = 0$ at $t = 0$. The cumulative absorption i and the position of the wet front l are related by

$$i = \int_0^l f_e(x)dx. \tag{5.31}$$

An alternative and equivalent approach is to represent the nonuniform 1-D system as a composite of a (large) number of n layers with progressively changing material properties S_j, f_j, and K_j. We have already discussed this at length earlier in the chapter and applied the n-layer model to composite materials with physically distinct layers. But now we extend this to nonuniform materials where the variation of material properties is continuous. In such cases, the n-layer algorithms of Eqns 5.25 and 5.26 can be seen as discretizations of the continuum Eqns 5.30, 5.31 [486]. We show below that the two representations give identical results.

Some examples

- First, we calculate the capillary imbibition behaviour of a material in which the sorptivity S and the permeability K vary linearly along the flow path, with the porosity f held constant. Results for cases where these quantities increase or decrease with increasing x, shown in Figure 5.12, are compared with the baseline case of constant properties, where the cumulative absorption i varies linearly with $t^{1/2}$. The direct numerical solution of Eqns 5.30 and 5.31 coincides with the results using the n-layer algorithm of Eqns 5.25 and 5.26. The variation of S and K along the flow path produces strong curvature in $i(t^{1/2})$. Curves (b) and (c) describe imbibition along the same flow path but in opposite directions. For the parameter values of Figure 5.12, it takes about three times as long to fill the length L when sorptivity and permeability increase along the flow path as when the flow is in the reverse direction.

- In a second example (Figure 5.13), we calculate the imbibition kinetics of a liquid absorbed by an ABAB... system of alternating layers. We have already given the n-layer solution for this case, which we called quasi-masonry. The cumulative imbibition i climbs a staircase when plotted against $t^{1/2}$, such that the slope $di/dt^{1/2}$ averaged over several layers rapidly approaches a constant value. This is the effective sorptivity [487], which from Eqn 5.28 for equal layer thicknesses is

$$S_{\text{eff}} = (f_A + f_B)\left[\frac{K_r}{1 + K_r}\right]^{1/2} \Bigg/ \left[\frac{K_r f_A^2}{S_A^2} + \frac{f_B^2}{S_B^2}\right]^{1/2}. \tag{5.32}$$

In Figure 5.14, we show the imbibition for both ABAB ...and BABA ....
These lie symmetrically about the $i(t^{1/2})$ line with slope S_{eff}, which of

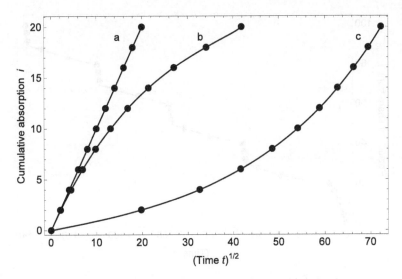

Figure 5.12 Comparison of SF cumulative absorption i vs $t^{1/2}$ calculated from Eqns 5.30, 5.31 (solid lines), and from Eqns 5.25, 5.26 with $n = 300$ (points). (*a*): Constant material properties, $S = 1$, $K = 1$, $f = 0.2$. (*b*): Linearly decreasing sorptivity and permeability; (*c*): linearly increasing sorptivity and permeability, $S_{max} = 1$, $S_{min} = 0.1$, $K_{max}/K_{min} = 100$ and $f = 0.2$. For all cases, the length $L = 100$. Here and in Figs 5.13, 5.14, 5.15 parameter values are given without units, and are assumed to be dimensionally consistent (S [$LT^{-1/2}$], K [LT^{-1}], Ψ [L]).

course is the same for ABAB... and BABA.... Here, $S_{eff} = 0.162$, lower than both S_A and S_B, as can be seen in the early-time behaviour. This illustrates the feature of alternating-layer systems ([487]) that a strong contrast in permeability, say $K_r > 10$, strongly reduces the effective sorptivity of the system. In turn, this is an example of the general tendency, noted by Philip [977], for the effective sorptivity to be greatly reduced by heterogeneities, particularly if there is a strong contrast in capillary properties, and especially in one-dimensional flows.

- As a third example, we calculate the imbibition into an n-layer material in which the properties vary randomly from layer to layer along the flow path (Figure 5.15). If we allow each of f, K and S to have uniformly-distributed random values within prescribed ranges, the advance of the wet front l shows erratic behaviour which is roughly linear in $t^{1/2}$. The overall slope of this line is less than that a uniform material having the mean parameter values, and decreases as the variance of S and K increases. When $K_r = 10^3$, the long-term slope appears to depend on the random

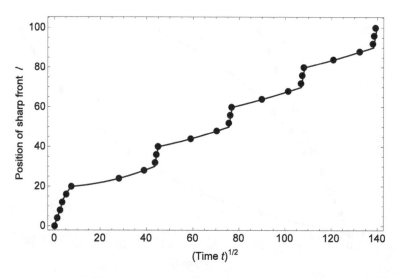

Figure 5.13 Imbibition into a system of 10 equal-thickness alternating layers (ABAB ...), total length $L = 100$, and $S_A = 1$, $S_B = 0.3$, $K_A/K_B = 100$, $f_A = 0.3$, $f_B = 0.2$. Position of sharp front l vs $t^{1/2}$ calculated from Eqn 5.30 (solid line), and from Eqn 5.25 (points).

values of K at early times, which of course vary from one simulation run to another.

• In composite materials built of layers of different materials there is no reason to expect any relationship between the properties K, S, and f in adjacent layers. But in graded materials, and no doubt in other cases, these quantities may be more or less strongly correlated. For example, both the permeability K and the capillary potential Ψ_f (and hence the sorptivity S) may be controlled by an underlying pore size (or particle size), say $r(x)$, that varies along the flow path. In such 'scale-heterogeneous' systems ([973]), it is common to assume, as in a Miller soil ([836]), that $K \sim r^2$ (Poiseuille), $\Psi_f \sim r^{-1}$ (Young-Laplace), and therefore that $S \sim r^{1/2}$ ([502]). Accordingly, if we set $K = K_0(r/r_0)^2$, $\Psi_f = \Psi_0 r_0/r$, and $S = S_0(r/r_0)^{1/2}$ where r_0 is the value of r at $x = 0$, then Eqn 5.30 becomes

$$dt = \frac{2f^2}{S_0^2} \cdot \left[\int_0^l \frac{dx}{(r/r_0)^2}\right] \cdot \frac{r}{r_0} dl \qquad (5.33)$$

where $S_0 = (2fK_0|\Psi_0|)^{1/2}$.

In the case where r varies linearly with x, so that $r/r_0 = (1 + ax)$, with constant a, and where the porosity f is constant throughout, we see from Eqn 5.33 that $l = (S_0/f)t^{1/2}$. The position of the wet front l advances as

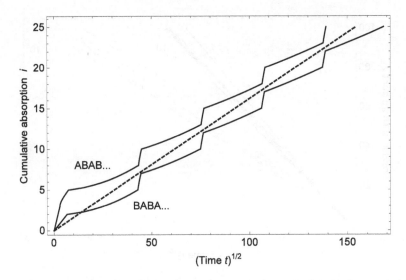

Figure 5.14 Imbibition into ABAB ... and BABA ... systems of 10 alternating layers of equal thickness, with material properties S, K, f as in Figure 5.13, and total length $L = 100$. Cumulative absorption i vs $t^{1/2}$ from Eqns 5.25, 5.26, $n = 100$ (solid lines). The dashed line shows the imbibition into a uniform material having the effective sorptivity $S_{eff} = 0.162$, evaluated from Eqn 5.32.

$t^{1/2}$ along the entire flow path. Since f is constant, the cumulative absorption $i = fl = S_0 t^{1/2}$, so that there is a constant composite sorptivity S_0, independent of a. Although the local sorptivity $S(x) = S_0(1+ax)^{1/2}$ varies along the flow path, the composite sorptivity of the system as a whole remains constant. Since S_0 is independent of a, it can be identified with the sorptivity of the first layer, S at $x = 0$. This remarkable result (noted earlier by [175]) arises because, for a linear variation in r, the variation in the integrated Darcy impedance per unit length of the wetted zone exactly compensates for the variation in the capillary potential at the wet front. This is true whether the local sorptivity increases or decreases along the flow path, and irrespective of how much the sorptivity changes. We show this behaviour in Figure 5.16, where we compare $i(t^{1/2})$ for a material in which the sorptivity $S(x) = S_0(1+ax)^m$ for $m = 0.25, 0.5$, and 0.75. Only the value of $m = 0.5$ gives linear behaviour. In this restrictive case, where the porous medium is geometrically similar along the entire flow path but has a linear variation of length-scale, a single imbibition history $i(t)$ provides no information about how the sorptivity and permeability vary with x. On the other hand, from two tests on the same specimen with flow in opposite directions we obtain two values of the apparent sorptivity S_0 and

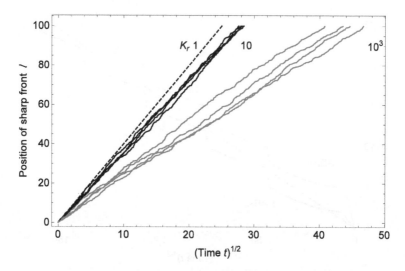

Figure 5.15 Advance of the wet front into a material with uniformly-
distributed randomly-varying properties. The solid black lines
show four simulations (Eqn 5.25), total length $L = 100$, $n = 1000$,
with porosity f randomly varying in the range 0.1–0.3, permeability K 0.2–1.8 (permeability ratio $K_r = 10$), and sorptivity S 0.5–
1.5. The solid grey lines show four further simulations with a larger
permeability range K 0.002–2.0 (permeability ratio $K_r = 10^3$),
and other properties as before. The dashed line shows the imbibition into a uniform material with sorptivity $S = 1.0$ and porosity
$f = 0.2$.

S_0' such that $a = (S_0'^2 - S_0^2)/(LS_0^2)$. The parameter a describes the linear
variation of length-scale and material properties $S(x)$ and $K(x)$.

Reyssat [1050] has analyzed a related case where the permeability
K varies linearly with x rather than with x^2, and the capillary potential
varies as $x^{-1/2}$ (rather than as x^{-1}). The sorptivity consequently varies as
$x^{1/4}$, rather than as $x^{1/2}$. The position of the wet front, l, then increases
as $t^{1/2}$ only at early times, while at long times $l^{3/2} \ln(l) \sim t$. Experimental
data on graded bead-packs confirm the analysis.

Variable sorptivity in shale bricks

We can apply a variable-sorptivity model to interpret imbibition data which
deviate from the standard linear $t^{1/2}$ behaviour of a uniform material, as we
demonstrate with data on fired-clay shale brick[5] taken from an 80-year-old
structure [451]. In standard water-imbibition tests to measure sorptivity, the
cumulative absorption i shows strong curvature when plotted against $t^{1/2}$.
Tests were carried out on cylindrical cores, taken from individual bricks by

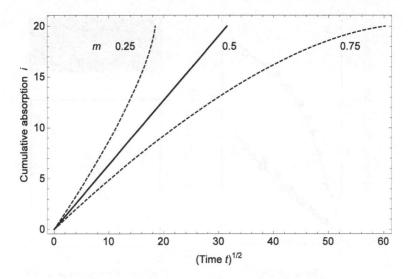

Figure 5.16 Imbibition into a material with permeability ratio $K_r = (1 + ax)^2$ varying along the flow path x, and sorptivity $S(x) = S_0(1 + ax)^m$ for $m = 0.5$ (solid line), $m = 0.25, 0.75$ (dashed lines). The total length $L = 100$, curves calculated from Eqns 5.25, 5.26.

drilling through one face, so that the flow path was at right angles to the surface. The idea that the fired bricks may have a surface skin suggests that we can represent their imbibition behaviour as capillary absorption through a succession of layers parallel to the surface. The imbibition curves in Figure 5.17a resemble those of Figure 5.12, and indicate that the sorptivity is lowest at the brick surface and increases towards the interior. Trial-and-error fits show that the cumulative absorption curve A can be modelled as three segments of linearly decreasing sorptivity, with minor changes only in porosity and permeability. The maximum penetration of the front is 22 mm. In the tests with flow in the reverse direction, curve B, the maximum distance of penetration is 42 mm, and the data can be represented by two segments of linearly increasing sorptivity. Since the core length is 55 mm, there is some overlap in the flow paths. We expect to see consistent values of local sorptivity from tests with flow in different directions, and this is what we find, as shown in Figure 5.17c. There is a marked variation in sorptivity along the core. S increases from about $0.30\,\text{mm/min}^{1/2}$ at the surface to about $1.80\,\text{mm/min}^{1/2}$ in the centre of the brick, with an abrupt change about 25 mm below the brick surface. The permeability is lower at the surface than in the interior, the permeability ratio K_r increasing from 1 at the surface to about 6 at the centre. There is only a small increase in effective porosity f, which rises from 0.20 at the surface to 0.22 at the centre.

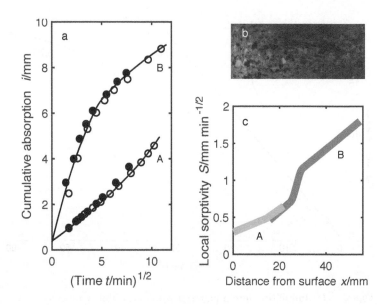

Figure 5.17 (a): Cumulative water absorption i vs $t^{1/2}$ into a bed-face core of shale brick (length 55.1 mm × 24.4 mm diameter). The brick ceramic has a bulk density of 1790 ± 20 kg/m³, and a volume-fraction porosity (by vacuum saturation with water) of 0.262 ± 0.005. Solid curves are fits to n-layer model with $n = 100$. A: Flow from the brick surface towards the interior (repeat tests, ○, ●); B: Flow towards the brick surface (repeat tests, ○, ●); (b): Core from shale brick, with the surface face on the left. (c): Variation of the local sorptivity S along the core.

5.3 MATERIALS WITH INCLUSIONS

We have dealt at length with various kinds of layered composites. Common and important as these are, there are many composite materials which cannot be represented in this way. We consider next how the hydraulic properties of a homogeneous porous material are expected to change when regions, or *inclusions*, having different properties are dispersed within it. These constitute another major class of composite materials. We shall consider separately the cases of nonsorptive and sorptive inclusions. We assume that such inclusions, of either kind, can be embedded in the material without modifying the matrix in any way: we imagine that small regions of the original material are simply replaced by a different material. In practice, when mineral particles are mixed into a cement or gypsum slurry, it may be difficult to avoid incorporating air and hence additional porosity into the mix. In some cases, the microstructure of the matrix may be somewhat modified near interfaces.[6] If the inclusion is highly sorptive (as some synthetic lightweight aggregate particles are) and is added dry to the wet slurry, then it is probable that fine particles may be drawn into the surface pores, giving rise to an interfacial hydraulic impedance (as discussed earlier). However, the theory we describe here provides a basis for simple models of capillary behaviour in the absence of such complications [510].

5.3.1 Nonsorptive inclusions

We assume the inclusions are approximately spherical, well dispersed and uniformly distributed so that each experiences a modified average and isotropic environment. There is no restriction on particle size or its distribution provided that all particles are large compared with the pore size of the homogeneous matrix. Any hydraulic properties must be defined or measured on volumes large compared with individual inclusions. Such a set of requirements would probably be well satisfied by a cement paste or gypsum paste to which up to 20 per cent by volume of coarse sand was added, and on which measurements are made on specimens of dimensions of several centimetres. Likewise concrete cubes containing 10–20 per cent by volume of coarse mineral aggregate would also be satisfactory, provided that properties are averaged over volumes of at least 0.001 m^3.

The inclusions themselves are assumed to have no connected porosity and so are necessarily nonsorptive. We define the volume fraction of inclusions $\alpha = $ (volume of inclusions/bulk volume). It follows that

$$f' = (1 - \alpha)f \tag{5.34}$$

where the primed quantity denotes the material with inclusions and the unprimed, the material in the absence of inclusions. Wet and dry states for the material with inclusions are

$$\theta'_s = (1 - \alpha)\theta_s, \quad \theta'_0 = (1 - \alpha)\theta_0. \tag{5.35}$$

It is tidier to use the dimensionless water content $\theta_r = (\theta - \theta_0)/(\theta_s - \theta_0)$ as the independent variable. It then follows that the condition $\theta'_r = \theta_r$ is equivalent to $\theta' = (1 - \alpha)\theta$.

The hydraulic potential of the matrix material is unchanged by the presence of inclusions, provided that account is taken of the rescaling of the water content axis. That is to say,

$$\Psi'(\theta') = \Psi(\theta) \text{ for } \theta' = (1 - \alpha)\theta \tag{5.36}$$

and hence $\Psi'(\theta_r) = \Psi(\theta_r)$.

This of course states the condition for hydraulic equilibrium between the materials with and without inclusions. Capillary equilibrium exists when the water content in the sorptive matrix of the material with inclusions is the same as the water content of the material without inclusions.

The effect of impermeable inclusions is to reduce the hydraulic conductivity at saturation K_s, so that we write $K'_s = \gamma_0(\alpha)K_s$, where K_s is an effective water permeability defined for steady Darcian flow by $u = -K_s \nabla P$, where u is the flow velocity and the potential $P = p/\rho g$, with fluid pressure p and density ρ. The important step is that the factor $\gamma_0(\alpha)$ may be written down from the theory of electrical or thermal conduction in random suspensions. The classical Maxwell formula for *insulating* spheres, $\gamma_0 = 1 - 3\alpha/(2 + \alpha)$, exact only to first order in α, has been extended to second order by Jeffrey [642]. Using Jeffrey's result, we obtain

$$K'_s = K_s(1 - 3\alpha/2 + 0.588\alpha^2). \tag{5.37}$$

In passing we note a result for a high concentration of inclusions obtained by Sangani and Acrivos [1110], who find $\gamma_0 = 0.27$ for close-packed spheres of equal size, for which $\alpha = 0.62$.

We now extend Darcy's equation to unsaturated flow [510]. The factor $\gamma_0(\alpha)$ does not depend on θ_r, so that the hydraulic conductivity in the presence of inclusions

$$K'(\theta_r) = \gamma_0 K(\theta_r). \tag{5.38}$$

By definition,

$$D(\theta) = K(\theta)\frac{d\Psi(\theta)}{d\theta} \tag{5.39}$$

and so

$$D(\theta_r) = \frac{K(\theta_r)}{\theta_s - \theta_0}\frac{d\Psi(\theta_r)}{d\theta_r}. \tag{5.40}$$

It follows that for the material with inclusions,

$$\begin{aligned} D'(\theta_r) &= \frac{K'(\theta_r)}{\theta'_s - \theta'_0}\frac{d\Psi'(\theta_r)}{d\theta_r} \\ &= \frac{\gamma_0 K(\theta_r)}{(1-\alpha)(\theta_s - \theta_0)}\frac{d\Psi(\theta_r)}{d\theta_r}. \end{aligned} \tag{5.41}$$

If $\phi' = x[\gamma_0 t/(1 - \alpha)]^{-1/2}$, then by substitution in Eqn 3.19 we have

$$i = \left(\frac{\gamma_0}{1-\alpha}\right)^{1/2}(\theta'_s - \theta'_0)t^{1/2}\int_0^1 \phi' d\theta_r = S't^{1/2} \tag{5.42}$$

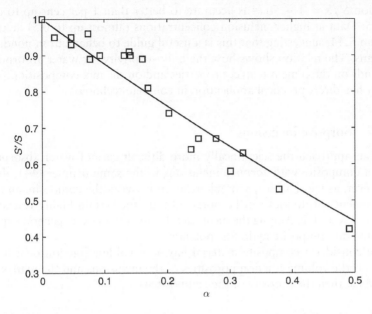

Figure 5.18 Gypsum plaster with sand inclusions: the normalized sorptivity S'/S versus volume fraction of sand α. Solid curve: Eqn 5.44. The least-squares straight line through the data points has the equation $S'/S = 1.01 - 1.24\alpha$ (not shown).

and thus by comparison with Eqn 4.11

$$\frac{S}{S'} = [\gamma_0(1-\alpha)]^{1/2}. \tag{5.43}$$

Using Jeffrey's expression for γ_0 we have to a good approximation

$$\frac{S}{S'} = 1 - 1.25\alpha + 0.263\alpha^2. \tag{5.44}$$

In Figure 5.18 we show some experimental data which were obtained [510] in an attempt to verify this result. The materials used were gypsum plaster slurries which have the property that they can be easily mixed with sand fillers and set rapidly without sedimentation. It appears that within the accuracy of this rather limited experiment, there is a good agreement with the predicted dependence of S on α. When the concentration of sand is low, the fractional reduction in S is proportional to the volume fraction of added sand. The inclusions reduce the cross section available to flow in all planes normal to the flow in direct proportion to their volume. The factor 5/4 evidently reflects the bending of the flow around the inclusions. The simple relation $S'/S = 1 - 5\alpha/4$ is accurate to better than 1 per cent up to $\alpha = 0.175$. Data at higher inclusion concentrations (almost up to 0.5) lie close to Eqn 5.44, suggesting that this is a useful guide to behaviour in nondilute systems. The relation shows how the bulk sorptivity (or water absorption) depends on the cement matrix properties and on the mix composition. This result has direct practical application in concrete technology.

5.3.2   Sorptive inclusions

We can approach the scientifically more difficult case of water absorption into a composite with *sorptive* inclusions in the same manner [441, 443]. However, as we shall see, a simple relation between the composite and the component sorptivities can be obtained only for certain highly restrictive forms of K and Ψ. Among the most useful results is an exact general expression for the composite hydraulic potential.

We consider a composite material having a volume fraction α of inclusions. If the volume-fraction porosities of the inclusions and the matrix are f_i and f_m, then the porosity of the composite is

$$f_c = (1 - \alpha)f_m + \alpha f_i. \tag{5.45}$$

Let the porosity ratio of the components $f_i/f_m = r$. Then

$$\frac{f_c}{f_m} = 1 - \alpha(1 - r) \tag{5.46}$$

and

$$\frac{f_c}{f_i} = [1 - \alpha(1 - r)]/r. \tag{5.47}$$

Likewise we have a relationship between the water content of the components θ_i and θ_m and of the composite θ_c:

$$\theta_c = (1 - \alpha)\theta_m + \alpha\theta_i. \tag{5.48}$$

At saturation, $\theta_{cs} = f_c$, $\theta_{is} = f_i$ and $\theta_{ms} = f_m$ of course. Let us define reduced water contents $\theta_{cr} = \theta_c/f_c$, $\theta_{ir} = \theta_i/f_i$ and $\theta_{mr} = \theta_m/f_m$. We then have

$$\theta_{cr} = (1 - \alpha)\frac{f_m}{f_c}\theta_{mr} + \alpha\frac{f_i}{f_c}\theta_{ir}. \tag{5.49}$$

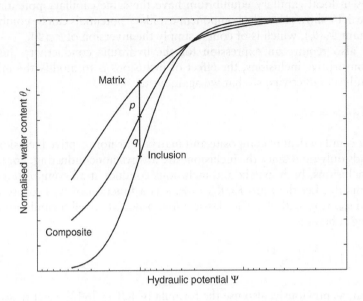

Figure 5.19 Schematic showing the relation between the hydraulic potential of a sorptive matrix and a sorptive inclusion, and the composite potential at different water contents. The ratio $p/q = \alpha r/(1 - \alpha)$.

Using Eqns 5.46 and 5.47, we obtain a general relation between the reduced water contents and the quantities α and r that define the composition:

$$\theta_{cr} = \frac{1 - \alpha}{1 - \alpha(1 - r)}\theta_{mr} + \frac{\alpha r}{1 - \alpha(1 - r)}\theta_{ir}. \tag{5.50}$$

Next, we consider the hydraulic or capillary potential. Let us take a small volume element of the composite which is nevertheless large enough to have the bulk composition (that is, it contains a volume fraction f_i of inclusions). In the unsaturated state, the reduced water content of the composite θ_{cr} is related to θ_{ir} and θ_{mr} by Eqn 5.50. In this volume element, the capillary potential of the matrix is $\Psi(\theta_{mr})$ and of the inclusions is $\Psi(\theta_{ir})$. But for local capillary equilibrium we have $\Psi_i = \Psi_m = \Psi_c$. Therefore at any hydraulic potential Ψ, Eqn 5.50 holds, so that we have

$$\theta_{cr}(\Psi) = \frac{1 - \alpha}{1 - \alpha(1 - r)}\theta_{mr}(\Psi) + \frac{\alpha r}{1 - \alpha(1 - r)}\theta_{ir}(\Psi). \tag{5.51}$$

This is the general equation for the hydraulic potential of the composite of inclusions i in a matrix m. $\theta_{ir}(\Psi)$ and $\theta_{mr}(\Psi)$ are the water characteristics of the inclusions and matrix. Normally, $\theta_{ir}(\Psi)$ and $\theta_{mr}(\Psi)$ – or equivalently $\Psi_i(\theta_r)$ and $\Psi_m(\theta_r)$ – are known independently. Eqn 5.51 recognizes that all phases in local capillary equilibrium have the same capillary potential Ψ. Figure 5.19 shows how the component capillary potentials can be combined to obtain $\Psi_c(\theta_r)$, which is of course simply the inversion of $\theta_{cr}(\Psi)$.

We also require an expression for the hydraulic conductivity. Just as for nonsorptive inclusions, the effect of inclusions is to modify the matrix hydraulic conductivity, so that we again write

$$K_c(\theta_{cr}) = \gamma K_m \tag{5.52}$$

where c and m denote composite and matrix. For nonsorptive inclusions, γ depends only on α since the inclusions are always nonconducting. For sorptive inclusions, both matrix and inclusions conduct at all composite water contents θ_{cr}. Let the ratio $K_i/K_m = \kappa$. κ is a function of θ_{cr} because both θ_{ir} and θ_{mr} vary with θ_{cr}. The classical first order Maxwell formula for *conducting* spheres is

$$\gamma = 1 + \frac{3\alpha(\kappa - 1)}{\kappa + 2}. \tag{5.53}$$

We can, as previously, also use the formula of Jeffrey [642] exact to second order. Whichever expression we use, we see that for sorptive inclusions γ is a function of θ_{cr} since both inclusions and matrix contribute to the composite hydraulic conductivity. However, provided that the component hydraulic conductivity functions $K_i(\theta_{ir})$ and $K_m(\theta_{mr})$ are known, this presents no difficulty. $K_{cr}(\theta_{cr})$, the complete hydraulic conductivity function of the composite, can be calculated using the chosen effective medium formula for γ and setting $\kappa = K(\theta_{ir})/K(\theta_{mr})$ at each θ_{cr}.

We have now obtained expressions for the water content, the hydraulic potential and the hydraulic conductivity of the composite in terms of the corresponding properties of the components. We can finally derive an expression for the composite hydraulic diffusivity. $D_c(\theta_c) = K_c d\Psi_c/d\theta_c$, but $\theta_c = f_c\theta_{cr}$ so that

$$D(\theta_{cr}) = \frac{K_c}{f_c}\frac{d\Psi_c}{d\theta_{cr}}. \tag{5.54}$$

Applying the general equation for the hydraulic potential, Eqn 5.51, we have

$$D_c(\theta_{cr}) = \frac{K_c}{f_c}\left(A_1\frac{d\theta_{mr}}{d\Psi} + A_2\frac{d\theta_{ir}}{d\Psi}\right)^{-1}, \tag{5.55}$$

with $A_1 = (1-\alpha)/[1-\alpha(1-r)]$ and $A_2 = \alpha r/[1-\alpha(1-r)]$. Now substituting for K_c we obtain a general expression for the composite diffusivity

$$D_c(\theta_{cr}) = \frac{\gamma(\theta_{cr})K_m(\theta_{mr})}{f_c}\left(A_1\frac{d\theta_{mr}}{d\Psi} + A_2\frac{d\theta_{ir}}{d\Psi}\right)^{-1}. \tag{5.56}$$

Eqns 5.49, 5.50 and 5.56 are exact relationships for unsaturated composite materials.

For nonsorptive inclusions, we were able to find a general relation for the composite sorptivity S' in terms of the matrix sorptivity S and the concentration of inclusions α. No such general relation exists for a composite containing sorptive inclusions. Only by imposing some severe restrictions on the forms both of the hydraulic potential functions Ψ_i and Ψ_m and of the conductivity functions K_i and K_m can we proceed further.

It may be that matrix and inclusions are composed of similar materials, with similar hydraulic properties. For example, if Ψ_i and Ψ_m are such that $\theta_{ir}(\Psi) = p_1\theta_{mr}(\Psi)+p_2$, where p_1 and p_2 are constants; and if $K_i(\Psi)/K_m(\Psi) = \kappa_1$ where κ_1 is also a constant, then Eqn 5.56 can be simplified. Since $\kappa = \kappa_1$ then, for any particular value of α, γ is also a constant, say γ_1, independent of water content. Thus

$$D(\theta_{cr}) = CK_m\frac{d\Psi}{d\theta_{mr}} = CD(\theta_{mr}),\tag{5.57}$$

in which $C = \gamma_1/[(A_1 + A_2p_1r)]$ is a constant, and $D(\theta_{mr})$ denotes the hydraulic diffusivity of the matrix. We have shown in Chapter 3 that if two materials have diffusivities of the same functional form their sorptivities scale as $fD^{1/2} = f^{1/2}D_r^{1/2}$, where $D = Kd\Psi/d\theta$ and $D_r = Kd\Psi/d\theta_r$. Therefore in this case, we find that the sorptivity of composite and matrix are related by the following equation

$$S_c = C^{1/2}S_m\tag{5.58}$$

where

$$C^{1/2} = \left[\frac{\gamma_1f_c}{[f_m(A_1 + A_2p_1r)]}\right]^{1/2} = \frac{\gamma_1^{1/2}[1 - \alpha(1 - r)]}{[1 - \alpha(1 - p_1r^2)]^{1/2}}.\tag{5.59}$$

This result is valid only for a composite in which matrix and inclusions are made of *hydraulically similar* materials. However, in the limit that $r \to 0$, we recover the exact and general result already obtained for nonsorptive inclusions, namely that $S_c/S_m = [\gamma_0(1 - \alpha)]^{1/2}$ (Eqn 5.43).

To validate these equations, and especially Eqns 5.56 and 5.58, sets an experimental challenge for the future. Green [441] has measured the permeabilities and sorptivities of composites containing spherical particles of gypsum plaster embedded in a gypsum plaster matrix of different composition and of plaster and mortar composites containing a commercial sintered flyash aggregate. The normalized sorptivity S_c/S_m as α varies is shown in Figure 5.20 for several of these composites. The relative sorptivities of materials in which the inclusions were less sorptive than the matrix fall close to the limiting values expected for nonsorptive inclusions. For the materials

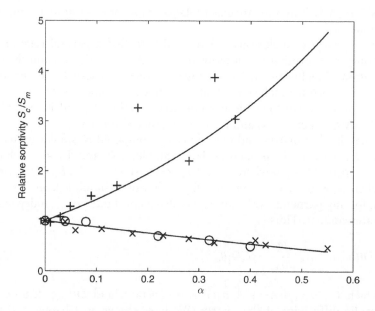

Figure 5.20 Experimental data on sorptivity of composites containing sorptive inclusions [441]. Data are for gypsum plaster inclusions in a gypsum plaster matrix of different composition (○), and sintered pfa aggregate in mortar (+) and gypsum plaster (×) matrices. The lower line shows the prediction of Eqn 5.43 for nonsorptive inclusions. The upper line represents Eqn 5.59 with $\kappa = 100, p_1 = 0.01$ and $r = 3$ to illustrate the extreme case of a coarse-pored aggregate in a fine-pored matrix.

containing inclusions of higher permeability and sorptivity, the composite sorptivity increases with α. However, there is no simple limit for comparison. The value of γ for perfectly conducting inclusions is $1 + 3\alpha$, but the relative sorptivity is sensitive also to the values of the porosity ratio r and the constant p_1 (the ratio of the water contents of inclusion and matrix at corresponding hydraulic potentials). In the extreme case when $p_1 \ll 1$ and when $\kappa \gg 1$, S_c/S_m varies approximately as $1 + \alpha r$. Such conditions apply when the inclusion has a much lower suction and a much higher permeability than the matrix, for example a coarse-pored aggregate in a fine-pored matrix. In the case of the data shown in Figure 5.20, p_1 is not known and indeed it is not known if they are strictly hydraulically similar according to our definition. Valuable as these results are, they do not allow a full test of the theory of unsaturated flow in the sorptive inclusion composite. For the time being, we have no simple validated formula for such materials which can be used in materials design.

5.4   OTHER COMPOSITE MATERIALS

This chapter has dealt in some detail with two of the main classes of composite porous materials: layered materials and materials with dispersed inclusions. In Chapter 8 we shall consider another inhomogeneous composite system when we ask how water moves from a wet slurry such as a mortar or plaster into a dry sorptive material such as a brick.

Our treatment here takes us some way towards a theory of water transport in composite construction materials. An omission is the analysis of materials in which the presence of conductive elements can strongly enhance the bulk transport properties even at small volume fractions. In inorganic porous materials such as concrete and stone (just as in rocks and soils), this commonly happens when the matrix is cracked and fractured. If our interest is in the barrier properties of concrete, the matrix permeability and sorptivity may have little relevance if the material is extensively cracked and fluid transport (liquid and vapour) can occur efficiently by routes which bypass the smaller scale pore structure. On the other hand, if chemical deterioration within the material is our interest, we shall be concerned with the composite behaviour of the crack system and the matrix. In this context, a percolating network of fractures forms a transport system within the material which may have a small volume but may be highly effective in distributing fluids within the bulk. Transport in cracked and fractured construction materials is still not yet a well explored topic.[7] We note nevertheless considerable recent work on effects of cracking and damage on the saturated (or gas) permeability of concrete [547, 418, 171, 420, 16, 550, 641, 245, 592, 987, 990, 315], some of which draws on the better developed field of transport in fractured rock [77, 983, 1103], and some also on salt diffusion in cracked, saturated brick [1006, 1007, 1005]. The influence of cracks on the phenomena of *unsaturated* flow such as water absorption and the sorptivity property has been investigated in only a few studies [1258, 1082, 224, 1104, 1333, 1118].

NOTES

1 For the two-layer composite, we can recast Eqn 5.10 using nondimensional variables [1050, 484]. With $\mathsf{L} = l/L = i/(f_A L)$ and $\mathsf{T} = t/t_J$, we obtain $2(\mathsf{L} - 1) + a(\mathsf{L} - 1)^2 = b(\mathsf{T} - 1)$, where $a = K_A/K_B$ and $b = a[S_B f_A/(S_A f_B)]^2$. The wet front passes the junction at position $\mathsf{L} = 1$ at time $\mathsf{T} = 1$, and for short times after that $u = \mathrm{d}\mathsf{L}/\mathrm{d}\mathsf{T} \approx b/2$, so that the imbibition rate is then roughly constant.

2 We assume here that flow through the interface is Darcian: that is, that the flow rate is proportional to the pressure drop across it. If we work in terms of capillary pressure potential Ψ with dimension [L] and volume flow rate u with dimension $[\mathrm{LT}^{-1}]$, then $R_J = \Delta\Psi/u$ has dimension [T]. If flow is formulated in terms of capillary pressure p_c with dimension $[\mathrm{ML}^{-1}\mathrm{T}^{-2}]$ and mass flow rate u_m with dimension $[\mathrm{ML}^{-2}\mathrm{T}^{-1}]$, then $R'_J = \Delta p_c/u_m$ has dimension $[\mathrm{LT}^{-1}]$ [352, 308, 213], with $R'_J = gR_J$.

3 Capillary flow parallel to an interface has been only rarely studied experimentally [102, 47]. However, the general features of the numerical simulation shown in Figure 5.11 are apparent in a sketch by Massari and Massari [795] of the position of the wet front in a simple capillary rise water absorption test through the header face of a brick rendered on its bed face with mortar.

4 The surfaces of porous materials often differ somewhat from the bulk. Causes are numerous: differences in firing temperatures in brick [792] and other heavy clay materials; effects of trowelling, bleeding and contact with formwork in concretes [695, 319, 756, 757, 811, 212]; dewatering by contact with porous substrates in mortars, screeds and plasters. Of special importance is the *cover zone* in reinforced concrete and a large research effort is devoted to understanding its role in concrete deterioration [90, 923, 924, 808, 816]. These skin effects are often related to manufacture and, in the case of concrete, to effects in placement and curing. Much less attention has been given to the development of surface layers as a result of weathering and long-term alteration, an effect which applies to many types of materials. Surface porosity frequently increases with time by leaching, but sometimes surface porosity may be reduced, for example by pore-filling deposition of salts. Precise measurements of capillary absorption rates can reveal the presence of such altered surface layers, as in [99]. In cases where pores are blocked by water-soluble salts the capillary absorption behaviour can be probed using nonaqueous liquids such as *n*-decane [497, 355].

5 These bricks were manufactured in the 1940s from colliery-waste shale. Such shale bricks were widely used in southern Scotland from the mid-nineteenth century until the 1970s [328].

6 It is widely recognized (see for example [1142]) that there is an *interfacial transition zone* about 50 micron thick at the surface of aggregate particles. This zone is thought to have properties considerably different from those of the rest of the hardened cement paste forming the matrix within which the aggregate particles are bonded.

7 The need for a general theory of transport which provides for the effects of fractures is especially urgent in relation to durability. Innumerable processes acting on materials during their performance lifetime produce damage [1330, 223] in the form of cracking on many length scales. We can list drying shrinkage in cement-based materials, chemical dissolution in concrete and stones, fatigue accompanying freeze-thaw episodes and chemomechanical action in salt crystallization. In all cases, there is a strong coupling between damage mechanisms and transport processes.

6 Unsaturated flow in building physics

In Chapters 3 and 4, we have set out the fundamental ideas of unsaturated flow theory as they have been developed from the Richards equation. We have shown that there are material properties which can be precisely defined and for which methods of measurement have been established. Given data on these properties, then we can predict the water transport processes in the materials we are interested in. In Chapter 4, we discussed in some detail how this is done for rather simple one-dimensional cases. In this chapter, we start to take a broader look at the application of these ideas to more complicated situations; in particular to two- and three-dimensional flows, which are of course extremely common in practice.

6.1 METHODS OF CALCULATION AND ANALYSIS

Problems in unsaturated flow have much in common with those of heat transfer and diffusion, with additional difficulties which arise from the strong dependence of the fundamental hydraulic properties Ψ, K and D on the water content θ. This introduces a strong nonlinearity into the Buckingham flux law and all that follows from it. Further complications arise from the hysteresis found in material properties. As a result, only steady flows and time-dependent flows in the simplest of geometries in homogeneous domains can be solved directly. Two approaches are available: first, we can simplify the transport equations by judicious approximations, retaining some at least of the essential physics of unsaturated flow, so as to obtain analytical solutions to some straightforward boundary value problems; and second, we can apply fully numerical methods to solve the Richards equation. In the rest of this book, we shall mix these approaches, while preferring the first. We especially exploit Sharp Front models for their flexibility and simplicity. Apart from the value of analytical results in providing insight and clarity, such results provide the theoretical framework for experimental studies, for test methods and the rigorous definition of material properties.

6.1.1 Two-dimensional steady flows

We have already seen that steady *saturated* flows are obtained by solving Laplace's equation. The streamlines and the pressure distribution are independent of permeability which controls only the flow rate. For *unsaturated* flows, we can use the Kirchhoff potential already defined in Eqn 4.3 to transform the unsaturated flow equation to the Laplace equation. In Figure 6.1 we compare steady flow in a rectangle in saturated and unsaturated systems.

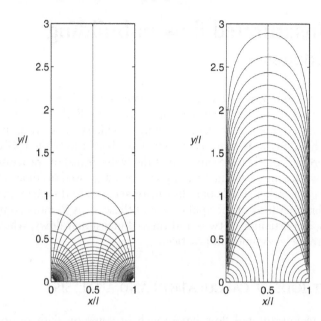

Figure 6.1 Steady flow in a rectangle: comparison of saturated and unsaturated flow. *Left*: Saturated flow, constant pressure difference maintained between face $y = 0$ and faces $x = 0$, $x = 1$. Figure shows flow grid of 20 equi-spaced streamlines and equipotentials. *Right*: Unsaturated flow, constant capillary potential difference maintained between face $y = 0$ and faces $x = 0$, $x = 1$, with exponential diffusivity function $D = D_0 \exp(6\theta_r)$. Figure shows flow grid of 20 equi-spaced streamlines and isohygrals (lines of equal water content).

In both cases, adjacent boundaries are maintained at different potentials. In the saturated case, the potential is a pressure potential and we have a difference in hydrostatic pressure between the adjacent faces. In the unsaturated case, the faces are maintained at different capillary potentials, Ψ_1 at $y = 0$ and Ψ_0 along faces at $x = 0$ and at $x = 1$. If we set $\Psi_1 = 0$, the face at $y = 0$ is saturated and $\theta_r = 1$ (the free water boundary condition). The adjacent faces are 'dry' boundaries on which θ_0 corresponds to the capillary potential Ψ_0. The equipotentials are given [231, 473, 477] by $\pi^{-1} \tan[(\sin \pi x)/(\sinh \pi x)] = $ constant, and the streamlines by $\pi^{-1}(\cos \pi x + \cosh \pi y)/(-\cos \pi x + \cosh \pi y) = $ constant. The contours of the Kirchhoff potential are the same as the equipotentials in the saturated case, but the contours of water content distribution, the *isohygrals*, are not. We can see from Figure 6.1 that the water penetrates far from the inflow face and that there are steep water content gradients near the dry faces. This reflects directly the low values of the capillary diffusivity in the drier parts of the rectangle. Water transport is efficient in the wetter regions and inefficient in the drier regions.

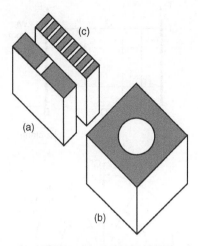

Figure 6.2 (a) Strip source. (b) Circular (patch) source. (c) Multi-stripe or leaky seal.

6.1.2 Finite sources

Figure 6.2 shows various simple two- and three-dimensional absorption geometries. An example of two-dimensional absorption is provided by the strip source [474]. Such a source is formed on the inflow face of a semi-infinite slice of absorbent material if the inflow face is sealed except for a finite length AB which acts as the strip source. As water is absorbed through this strip it advances perpendicular to AB and also sideways to produce a curved wet front. To analyze this problem we use the SF approximation noting that Laplace's equation holds. The solution Ψ as a function of space coordinates gives the shape of the wet front and the flow lines may be obtained as the conjugate harmonic function of Ψ in the wetted region. Analysis of the problem is made mathematically tractable using the method of conformal mapping. Conformal mapping is a powerful technique for solving certain boundary value problems by the use of geometrical transformations in the complex plane [251, 94, 868]. It is especially useful in finding solutions to Laplace's equation in two dimensions, since solutions remain solutions under conformal mapping. A suitable transformation can therefore be used to map a known solution in a simple geometry (such as a rectangle) to another geometry of interest. A large number of such analytical transformations is known: a useful set is given by Churchill [251].

We first consider the case of one-dimensional absorption into a slice of solid, Figure 6.3. Water enters through the surface AB which is maintained in contact with free water so that $\Psi = 0$. We assume that the boundaries ADE and BCF are impermeable so that on these lines $d\Psi/dx = 0$. At time t the wet front ($\Phi = \Psi_f$) lies on the line $y = l$. The cumulative absorption per

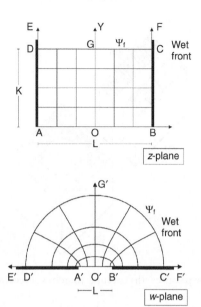

Figure 6.3 Conformal mapping of flow from a strip source.

unit area is given by $i = (2f_e K_e |\Psi_f|)^{1/2} t^{1/2}$, Eqn 4.37. The equipotential lines are defined by $\Phi = \Psi_f y/l = $ constant. The velocity potential is defined as $\zeta = K_e \Psi_f y/l$, and the stream function $\eta = K_e \Psi_f x/l$. Hence $\zeta + i\eta$ is the complex potential of the flow. The boundaries $x = \pm L/2$ coincide with streamlines and the total flow between them is $\eta(L/2) - \eta(-L/2) = K_e \Psi_f L/l = uL$ where u is the inflow velocity.

We can relate this analysis to the case of two-dimensional absorption through a finite strip source of length L by the conformal transformation $w = (L/2)\sin(\pi z/L)$ which maps the rectangle ABCD in the z plane on to the semi-ellipse A′B′C′G′D′ in the w plane with A′ and B′ as foci. The boundary conditions are unchanged so that $\Phi = 0$ on A′B′, $d\Phi/dv = 0$ on the rest of the line $v = 0$, and $\Phi = \Psi_f$ on C′G′D′.

Now since $w = u + iv = (L/2)\sin(\pi z/L) = (L/2)[\sin(\pi x/L)\cosh(\pi y/L) + i\cos(\pi x/L)\sinh(\pi y/L)]$ the equipotential line $\Phi = \Psi_f$ defining the wet front maps on to the semi-ellipse

$$u^2 \left(\frac{L^2}{4}\cosh^2\frac{\pi l}{L}\right)^{-1} + v^2 \left(\frac{L^2}{4}\sinh^2\frac{\pi l}{L}\right)^{-1} = 1, \ v \geq 0. \qquad (6.1)$$

The streamlines $\eta = $ constant are confocal hyperbolae. The boundary streamlines $x = \pm L/2$ in the z-plane become the boundary streamlines along A′D′ and B′C′ in the w-plane. The total flow between corresponding streamlines is unchanged and in the w-plane $\eta(L/2) - \eta(-L/2) = uL = K_e \Psi_f L/l$, where u is now the mean flow velocity across A'B'. The semi-minor axis b of the ellipse is given by $b = (L/2)\sinh(\pi l/L)$, so that $l = (L/\pi)\sinh^{-1}(2b/L)$. Therefore $u = \pi K_e \Psi_f/(L\sinh^{-1}(2b/L))$ and $b = (L/2)\sinh(\pi K_e \Psi_f/uL)$.

The area of the semi-ellipse is $\pi ab/2$ and therefore the cumulative absorbed volume per unit source area

$$i = \pi abf_e/2L = \frac{\pi f_e L}{8} \sinh\left(\frac{\pi K_e \Psi_f}{uL}\right) \cosh\left(\frac{\pi K_e \Psi_f}{uL}\right). \tag{6.2}$$

Further development of the analysis is simplified by using the dimensionless variables I, U, and T. In this case these are defined as $I = 2i/f_e L$, $U = uL/\pi K_e \Psi_f = 2uLf_e/\pi S^2$ and $T = 2\pi K_e \Psi_f t/f_e L^2 = \pi S^2 t/f_e^2 L^2$. Thus we obtain the results

$$I = \frac{\pi}{8} \sinh \frac{2}{U} \tag{6.3}$$

and

$$T = \frac{\pi}{16}\left\{\frac{8I}{\pi}\sinh^{-1}\left(\frac{8I}{\pi}\right) - \left[1 + \left(\frac{8I}{\pi}\right)^2\right]^{1/2} + 1\right\} \tag{6.4}$$

and

$$T = \frac{\pi}{16}\left[\frac{2}{U}\sinh\left(\frac{2}{U}\right) - \cosh\left(\frac{2}{U}\right) + 1\right]. \tag{6.5}$$

At short times $I = (\pi T/2)^{1/2}$ so that $i = (\pi/2\sqrt{2})St^{1/2} \approx 1.11St^{1/2}$. This result therefore differs by a factor of 1.11 from the standard result $i = St^{1/2}$ for the one-dimensional case.

The solutions given above are exact in the long-time limit. At long times the wet front becomes approximately circular so that Eqn 6.4 reduces to

$$T = \frac{I}{2}\left(\ln\frac{8I}{\pi} - 1\right) \tag{6.6}$$

and Eqn 6.5 to

$$U = \frac{2}{\ln T}. \tag{6.7}$$

The cylindrical source

A cylindrical cavity is formed in a porous solid of finite thickness by drilling a circular hole (radius r_0) right through the solid and sealing one end of the

222 Unsaturated flow in building physics

hole with an impervious plate. If this cavity is maintained completely full of water the absorption process will produce an advancing cylindrical wet front (radius r).

The radial flow of water from a cylindrical cavity has been analyzed by Philip [971, 974, 275] and Wilson et al. [1323] have developed an SF model to describe the radial absorption process.

As we noted in Chapter 4 Laplace's equation holds generally in SF problems. In cylindrical coordinates this equation is

$$\nabla^2 \Psi = \frac{1}{r} \frac{\partial}{\partial r} \left(r \frac{\partial \Psi}{\partial r} \right) = 0 \tag{6.8}$$

which, on first integration gives $r \partial \Psi / \partial r = A$ and on second integration gives $\Psi = A \ln r + B$. The values of the constants A and B are defined by the values of Ψ at the wet front (Ψ_f) and at the supply surface (0).

The inflow velocity of water v_0 through the surface of the cavity is defined by Darcy's law

$$v_0 = -K_e \left(\frac{\partial \Psi}{\partial r} \right)_{r=r_0} \tag{6.9}$$

which combined with the results of integration of the Laplace equation gives

$$v_0 = -\frac{K_e}{r} \left(\frac{\Psi_f}{\ln(r/r_0)} \right). \tag{6.10}$$

The cumulative absorbed volume of water per unit area of cylindrical supply surface is $i = f_e(r^2 - r_0^2)/2r_0$ so that

$$v_0 = -\frac{2K_e \Psi_f}{r_0 \ln(2i/f_e r_0 + 1)} = \frac{di}{dt}. \tag{6.11}$$

Further development of the analysis is simplified by defining the dimensionless variables $I = i/f_e r_0$, $V = v_0 r_0 / K_e \Psi_f$ and $T = K_e \Psi_f t / f r_0^2$.

Integrating Eqn 6.11 and expressing the results in terms of these dimensionless variables leads to the equations

$$T = \frac{1}{4} \left[(2I + 1) \ln(2I + 1) - 2I \right] \tag{6.12}$$

and

$$T = \frac{1}{4} \left[\left(\frac{2}{V} - 1 \right) \exp \left(\frac{2}{V} \right) + 1 \right]. \tag{6.13}$$

For small values of T, $I = (2T)^{1/2}$, and thus $i = St^{1/2}$ as for simple one-dimensional absorption. However, the times over which one-dimensional behaviour may be assumed are short – typically less than 3 min – for most construction materials when the cavity radius $r_0 \approx 10$ mm.

Expansion of Eqn 6.13 leads to the result that at long times

$$V = \frac{2}{\ln T}. \tag{6.14}$$

This is identical to the result of Eqn 6.7, $U = 2/(\ln T)$, for absorption from a strip source at long times since the length L of absorbing surface in the strip source is equivalent to the length πr_0 of the absorbing surface of a semi-cylindrical source.

A useful result, which can readily be applied to the analysis of experimental data, is obtained by expanding the logarithm in Eqn 6.12 and retaining terms up to I^2 to give

$$I = (2T)^{1/2} \left(1 - \frac{2\sqrt{2}}{3} T^{1/2} \right)^{-1/2}. \tag{6.15}$$

Further expansion, substituting for I and t and retaining the first two terms gives

$$i = St^{1/2} + \frac{1}{3} \frac{S^2}{f_e r_0} t \ldots \tag{6.16}$$

There is close agreement between this approximate solution and the full SF solution given by Eqn 6.12.

The hemispherical source

Absorption from a water-filled hemispherical cavity in a porous solid is the most straightforward three-dimensional absorption process to analyze [971, 906, 907, 909, 750, 1324]. Starting with the Laplace equation in spherical polar coordinates we can develop an SF model following an exactly similar procedure to that adopted for a cylindrical source. The relationship between inflow velocity and cumulative volume of water absorbed is obtained in terms of the dimensionless variables V and I to give

$$V = [1 - (3I + 1)^{-1/3}]^{-1}. \tag{6.17}$$

The relationship between the dimensionless variables T and I is

$$T = I - \frac{1}{2}[(3I + 1)^{2/3} - 1]. \tag{6.18}$$

From these two equations we can obtain the equation relating T and V

$$T = \frac{1}{6}\left[2\left(\frac{V-1}{V}\right)^{-3} - 3\left(\frac{V-1}{V}\right)^{-2} + 1\right]. \tag{6.19}$$

At short times $V = (2T)^{-1/2}$ or, in terms of v_0 and t, $v_0 = St^{-1/2}/2$, which is identical to the result for one-dimensional absorption. Once again, the time over which the one-dimensional result is valid is extremely short being an order of magnitude shorter than in the case of absorption from a cylindrical cavity.

At long times $V \to 1$. However, this is a difficult result to confirm experimentally since some days are needed to attain this constant rate of absorption from a relatively small cavity in a typical porous construction material.

The most useful result is obtained by expanding Eqn 6.18 and retaining the first two terms. The resulting equation expressed in terms of i and t is

$$i = St^{1/2} + \frac{2}{3}\frac{S^2}{f_e r_0}t. \tag{6.20}$$

There is good agreement between this two-term approximate solution and the exact SF solution given by Eqn 6.18.

The circular source

We have shown that an SF analysis of capillary absorption from a line source produces a wetting front which is semi-elliptical in shape. If we imagine a circular source as being produced by rotation of a line source, then it is clear that the wetting front from such a circular source will form a hemi-ellipsoid. As a first approximation this suggests that a simple rotation of the semi-ellipse produced by conformal mapping of the line source would define the amount of water absorbed from a circular source. However, as far as the physics of absorption is concerned this does not take into account all the flow lines that are possible in the three-dimensional case. Taking the two-dimensional solution (the line source) to determine the volume of the hemi-ellipsoid wetted in the three-dimensional case effectively assumes that the hemi-ellipsoid is built up of semi-elliptical slices to which the flow lines are confined. Clearly there must also be lateral spreading perpendicular to these slices. Nevertheless such an approximation has been shown to be accurate enough for practical purposes over a reasonable time range [1328].

A rigorous analysis of capillary absorption from a circular source is a relatively complex problem which is covered by a series of papers in the literature of soil science [543, 1253, 1169]. The appropriate result for capillary absorption from a circular source for all practical times is

$$i = St^{1/2} + \frac{gS^2 t}{f_e r} \tag{6.21}$$

where g is a function of time which increases slowly from 0.6 at short times to about 0.8 for long times.

Radially symmetrical sources in general

Simple inspection of the results given in the previous sections suggests a unified approach to the mathematical description of capillary absorption from a range of sources having different, but radially symmetrical, geometries [754, 1321]. Summarizing the relevant equations we have

$$i = St^{1/2} + \frac{1}{3} \frac{S^2 t}{f_e r_0} \tag{6.22}$$

for a cylindrical source;

$$i = St^{1/2} + \frac{2}{3} \frac{S^2 t}{f_e r_0} \tag{6.23}$$

for a hemispherical source; and

$$i = St^{1/2} + g \frac{S^2 t}{f_e r_0} \tag{6.24}$$

for a circular source. We note that Eqns 6.23 and 6.24 are identical if $g = 2/3$. At long times the absorption rate from a hemispherical source becomes constant. A similar result is found for a circular source. It is clear that at long times absorption rates from a circular source and from a hemispherical source of equal radii will tend to become identical since both may be regarded as point sources in these circumstances. In both cases the wetted region becomes a hemisphere provided that the effects of gravity can be neglected.

We can also combine the analyses of absorption from cylindrical and hemispherical cavities to derive an equation defining absorption from a drilled hole with a hemispherical end [1318]. The resulting equation is

$$i = St^{1/2} + \frac{1}{3} \frac{S^2 t}{f_e r_0} \left(\frac{\alpha + 2}{\alpha + 1} \right) \tag{6.25}$$

where $\alpha = h/r_0$, h being the depth of the cylindrical part of the drilled hole.

Combining all of these results suggests that absorption from any radially symmetrical source may be described by an equation of the form

$$i = St^{1/2} + GS^2 t \tag{6.26}$$

where G is a geometrical factor.

Experimental considerations

The results of careful experiments have been reported [1323, 1313, 1324, 1318, 1314] which confirm the general validity of the analyses we have summarized in the preceding sections. The practical value of fitting experimentally-determined absorption data to Eqn 6.26 is that the sorptivity is given by the coefficient of the $t^{1/2}$ term.

In applying the analysis in practice it must be noted that the rate of absorption is very high at short times ($v_0 \rightarrow \infty$ as $t \rightarrow 0$). This can lead to significant intercepts in the $i(t)$ data at $t = 0$, particularly in the case of drilled cavities for which the time of filling is significant. This does not present a problem for the analysis of experimental data provided that the relevant equation is modified by the addition of a constant term. In practice therefore experimental data are fitted to an equation of the form

$$i = a + St^{1/2} + GS^2 t. \tag{6.27}$$

6.1.3 Field test methods

The results we have derived in the preceding sections provide a basis for interpreting the results from the empirical test procedures that are used to assess the water transport properties of concrete materials in building and civil engineering structures (see for example [475, 84, 86]). The processes which affect the durability of concretes include leaching, chemical attack, mineralogical instability and steel reinforcement corrosion. All of these processes are mediated by water and it is generally recognized that a dense concrete of low permeability will prove to be the most durable. Thus the two hydraulic transport properties that are of particular interest are the sorptivity and the hydraulic conductivity. In fact the saturated hydraulic conductivity is difficult to measure except under laboratory conditions.[1] However, in most practical situations the forces of suction dominate any movement of water (or salt solutions) into the concrete material, and the field test methods that are widely used have been designed to obtain some measure of the capillary suction properties. These tests fall into two broad types: those which monitor the absorption of water from a water-filled cavity drilled into the concrete, and those which monitor the absorption of water from a water-filled cap fixed to the surface of the concrete.

Tests that measure absorption from drilled cavities

Two examples of such tests are the Figg test [377, 378] and the covercrete absorption test (CAT) [320]. These were developed as empirical methods to provide data which enable comparisons to be made between different concretes. Neither test was designed to measure a fundamental hydraulic property of the absorbing solid. However, our SF analyses of absorption from drilled cavities enable us to evaluate these tests and suggest how the data may be analyzed to allow the sorptivity to be calculated from the absorption data.

The Figg test uses a cavity 5.5 mm in diameter and 10 mm deep. (A modification of this test arrangement for determining an empirical measure of air permeability uses a cavity 10 mm in diameter and 40 mm deep.) A water-filled capillary tube is connected to the cavity through a silicone rubber seal which is cast in the top of the drilled hole. Water is forced into the cavity using a hypodermic syringe. One minute after filling the cavity with water the time taken for the meniscus in the cavity to travel 50 mm is recorded.

The CAT is similar to the Figg test, but uses a hole 13 mm in diameter and 50 mm deep. This hole is filled with water and a head of 200 mm of water is maintained to exert a small positive pressure on the water in the cavity. This water is connected by a gasketted cap to a water-filled capillary tube. In the CAT the movement of the meniscus in the capillary is measured between the tenth and eleventh minutes after filling the cavity.

Thus both the Figg and covercrete absorption tests express the water absorption properties of a concrete in terms of the time to absorb a fixed volume of water albeit at different stages of the absorption process. Clearly more useful information would be obtained if the absorption were monitored continuously to provide a set of $i(t)$ data over an extended period of time. Both the Figg test and the CAT are geometrically somewhat more complex than the cases we have analyzed in the previous sections. In both cases the drilled holes normally have conical ends, and in the Figg apparatus the top of the cylindrical part of the hole is blocked with sealant. Although these absorption geometries are intractable to analyze directly, inspection of the relevant $i(t)$ equations for other radially symmetrical geometries suggests that appropriate $i(t)$ data from either the Figg test or the CAT could be fitted to Eqns 6.26 and 6.27 to enable the sorptivity to be calculated.

Tests which measure absorption from a surface cap

We consider two essentially similar tests which fall into this category. The initial surface absorption test (ISAT) (see below) is a British Standard Test [735, 736, 193] and is used to give an empirical measure of the water absorption properties of concretes *in situ*. The Autoclam test [83, 87, 85, 88, 89] was designed with the objective of providing *in situ* measurements of the sorptivity and permeability of concretes.

The ISAT uses a circular or square cap having an area of 5000 mm². A small pressure head of 200 mm of water is maintained and the absorption of water is monitored by measuring the movement of a meniscus in a water-filled capillary connected to the cap. The absorption rate is determined at 10, 30, 60 and 120 min after the start of the test by measuring the movement of the capillary meniscus over a time interval of one minute. The results are expressed in mL/m²s.

If a circular cap is used then it is possible to determine the sorptivity directly from a set of $i(t)$ data obtained using the ISAT by fitting these data to Eqn 6.24 (or to Eqn 6.26 in the form of 6.27) which is accurate for all practical times.[2] This is a much better way of interpreting ISAT data than using the data for empirical comparisons, which can be misleading as discussed by Wilson *et al.* [1328].

The Autoclam apparatus uses a circular cap of 50 mm radius, and the amount of water absorbed is measured by monitoring the movement of a piston in a hydraulic cylinder attached to the surface cap. As with the ISAT a small positive pressure – in this case 0.01 bar (≈ 100 mm water) – is maintained in the water held in the cap during the sorptivity measurements. The $i(t)$ data are plotted as graphs of i versus $t^{1/2}$ and the slope of a straight line fitted to these data between the 10th and 20th minute is taken to define the sorptivity. As would be expected from Eqns 6.24 and 6.26 the published data from Autoclam tests are not exactly linear but show a small upward curvature. To obtain strictly accurate values of sorptivity the data should be fitted to Eqn 6.26 or Eqn 6.27.

When the Autoclam apparatus is used to assess the permeability of a concrete the procedure used is identical to that adopted for sorptivity measurement except that the water in the cap is maintained at a pressure of 1.5 bar. The results are expressed in the same unit as sorptivity. In fact what is being measured is the sorptivity under pressure. We discussed effects of pressure head on sorptivity in Section 4.6 and obtained the result $S_h = [S_0^2 + 2hK_s f]^{1/2}$ where S_h is the sorptivity under an applied head h. This provides a method of obtaining K_s from Autoclam data. Normally f will not be known, but if S_h is measured for two values of h then in principle K_s can be determined.

General comments on field tests

It is unfortunate that the field tests we have described have been designed without reference to unsaturated flow theory. As empirical tests the results must be viewed with caution. In comparing absorption rates in different materials at identical times different parts of the absorption versus time curves are being compared, so that detailed comparisons on this basis can lead to erroneous judgements. Nevertheless we have shown that correct analysis of experimental data from these tests can, in principle, allow the fundamental characterizing parameter of absorption, the sorptivity, to be determined [1314]. For example, Wilson *et al.* [1328, 754] have published the results of such analysis of ISAT data and shown that accurate values of sorptivity can be obtained. In principle it is possible to determine the permeability from Autoclam test data using the correct analysis, but this has not yet been carried out and no independent confirmation of the accuracy of the approach we suggest has been obtained.

In order that reliable absorption data are obtained it is essential that certain conditions are satisfied. The surface area of the source must be sufficiently large to represent the average microstructure of the material. In the case of concrete materials having aggregate particles up to ≈20 mm in size this clearly implies a surface area much larger than that of the aggregate particles (a requirement not met by several established test methods). Also, if we are to apply unsaturated flow theory to the analysis of water absorption data, the material through which the wet front passes must be of uniform water content. It does not need to be dry although that is usually the easiest condition to obtain in the laboratory; the variation of sorptivity with uniform water content is well-defined [508], as we have explained in Section 4.2. Apart from oven-drying, which is clearly not possible in site tests, it is difficult to achieve a uniform water content in cement-based materials. Often the surface layers are dry while the inner layers have a much higher water content. (This is less of a problem in brick ceramic and natural stone. In these materials the water content versus distance profiles on drying tend to be relatively flat [997].)

An additional characteristic of concrete materials, which is widely recognized, is that the surface layers of the concrete often contain an excess of fine constituents. In principle we can analyze the surface water absorption characteristics of such a concrete by treating it as a two-layer absorption problem (Chapter 5).

The foregoing comments are helpful in evaluating the detailed design of the tests discussed in Section 6.1.3. The drilled cavities have the advantage that the absorbing surface is a cut surface typical of the concrete and is essentially unaffected by any thin surface layer. Nevertheless it is clear that the drilled hole used in the Figg test has too small a surface area to represent the average microstructure of most structural concretes. The cavity used in the CAT is probably of the minimum size that is acceptable. The ISAT and Autoclam test both have an adequate cap size. For the ISAT a circular cap must be used if the data are to be analyzed to derive a sorptivity. The absorption from a square cap (as permitted in the British Standard) cannot be analyzed in this way.

At first sight the surface absorption tests (ISAT and Autoclam) might be expected to give unreliable data in respect of the absorption properties of the main body of the concrete because of the effects of the fine surface layer. However, the two-layer analysis would indicate that provided absorption is carried out for long enough this need not be a problem. Once the wet front has passed through the surface layer it is the capillary suction properties of the concrete that determine the absorption characteristics.

6.2   FLOW IN OTHER GEOMETRIES

Leaky seals

This result on the strip source provides a basis for looking at an important practical problem, which we can call the case of the *leaky seal*. Let us imagine that we have a porous material which is sealed on the inflow surface, for example with a coating of bituminous paint. When the coating is free of defects and completely impermeable, no water can be absorbed through the surface. However, let us represent an imperfectly sealed surface by a series of stripes of paint applied to the inflow surface, Figure 6.2c. Let the width of stripe be l_s and the space between the stripes be αl_s. The fraction of the surface sealed is therefore $\beta = 1/(1 + \alpha)$. The unsealed region between each stripe acts as a strip source and at early times water is absorbed independently through each, according to the equations we have just given. The absorption is two-dimensional as the streamlines diverge to supply water to the dry material behind each sealed part of the surface; and of course the cumulative absorption during this period increases more rapidly than $t^{1/2}$. When the wet fronts have penetrated a distance $l_s/2$ parallel to the surface behind each stripe, the wet fronts from adjacent sources begin to meet up. After passing through a transitional phase, where the wet front has a complicated shape, the wet front advance eventually becomes increasingly flat and the absorption process takes on a more and more one-dimensional character. It is clear that the transitional zone in which the streamlines are disturbed by the presence of the impermeable stripes on the inflow surface depends on l_s and must in fact be several times l_s in thickness.

We can develop an SF model for this case too. We cannot simply superimpose the profiles we have already obtained for the single strip source because this does not adequately describe the way in which the streamlines are swept upwards as the fronts from adjacent regions meet. Even so, we can represent the flow by means of another conformal mapping, this time however a numerical one. We can consider our material with its array of stripes as composed of semi-infinite regions like ABCDEF in Figure 6.4. CD is the unsealed surface through which water can be absorbed and therefore with a saturation water content boundary condition $\theta_r = 1$. It is situated between a pair of impermeable stripes, half of each of which is represented by BC and DE. By symmetry the streamlines can never cross the lines BA and EF, so that we have a no-flux boundary condition on these lines, as of course also on BC and DE. A solution to flow in this region is obtained by finding numerically the mapping of the polygon ABCDEF on to a simple rectangle using the Schwarz-Christoffel method.[3] We show the solution in Figure 6.4.

It is certainly useful to be able to calculate the shape of the wetting front and to map the streamlines, from which we obtain a clear impression of what occurs physically and spatially during the absorption process. However, to calculate the rates of absorption and the cumulative absorption as a function

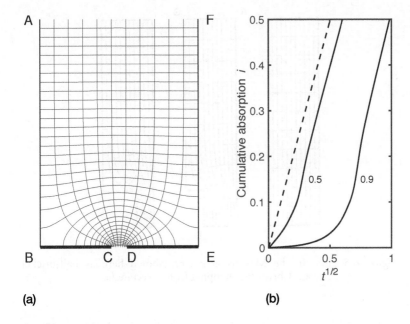

Figure 6.4 The leaky seal problem. (a): Water is supplied on the face BCDE; BC and
DE are impermeable stripes and CD is a leak. The fraction of the surface which is sealed $\beta = 0.9$. (b): The cumulative absorption i is plotted
against $t^{1/2}$ for $\beta = 0.5$ and 0.9. The dashed line shows the absorption
for the unsealed surface.

of time, we need to proceed as we did in the case of the simple strip source.
We obtain the cumulative absorption i by calculating the area of the wetted region and we obtain the flow rate across the inflow surface CD either
numerically from the flow mesh ($u = d\zeta/dy$ at $y = 0$) or else by noting that
the total flow between two streamlines is the same in the physical domain
as in the rectangle to which we have mapped it. In Figure 6.4 we show the
results for two different values of β, the sealed fraction and compare this
with the value for the unsealed surface. We see that the presence of the seal
is shortlived. Even a small leak ($\beta = 0.9$) allows the *rate* of absorption to
become much the same as for the completely unsealed surface.

The Massaris' problem

In their wide-ranging practical book *Damp Buildings* [795] G and I Massari
ask how the water absorption of a porous material is diminished by reducing
the area of the base in contact with the source of moisture. They illustrated
this by comparing rates of capillary absorption into three bricks, two of

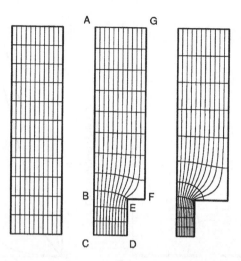

Figure 6.5 Flow in the Massari geometry (shown here as half-bricks) by Schwarz-Christoffel mapping from a rectangle.

which have been cut to reduce the areas of their header faces. We show the Massaris' problem schematically in Figure 6.5. Absorption into such a geometry has much in common with the case we have just discussed. It is also a two-dimensional flow which eventually becomes approximately one-dimensional. But we now have a new length (BC here) which has a strong influence on the way that the wetting profiles develop. Massaris' problem is also amenable to solution by the Schwarz-Christoffel mapping and we show the result in Figure 6.5. Of course the whole of the progress of the wet front up the leg BCDE is strictly and simply one-dimensional. When the front reaches the height BE the streamlines swing sharply towards FG and we have a locally elliptical front near the corner E. At higher levels, the front again becomes more or less horizontal and the streamlines arrange themselves once again parallel to BA and FG.

We can also use the Massaris' problem to illustrate the use of a full unsaturated flow analysis using purely numerical methods. We show the results of a finite element simulation[4] in Figure 6.6. The graph in Figure 6.6 makes it clear that at long times the three *i* curves become parallel. This means that the *rates* of water absorption ultimately become the same and the effects of the reduced area of inflow surface disappear. At early times, we have a simple $t^{1/2}$ process in all three cases and the rates of absorption are in proportion to the surface areas, in these examples 14:9:5. The Massaris' claim that the 'speed of moisture invasion is reduced to one-seventh' by reducing the area of contact to one-third is roughly true in the particular sense that it takes about seven times as long to wet the brick on the right as that on the left.

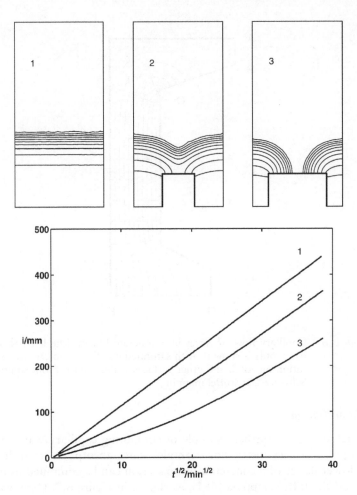

Figure 6.6 Advance of the wetting front into the Massaris' geometry; finite element solution of the Richards equation. The lower figure shows the cumulative absorption versus $t^{1/2}$ for the three cases.

However, this result is tempered by a second conclusion: namely, that the rate of absorption when the wet front approaches the top of the brick is similar in all three cases. The absorption rates are in the ratio 1:0.89:0.70.[5] As the height of rise increases, so the absorption rates converge towards a common value. The higher the wet front travels, the smaller the influence of the hydraulic impedance imposed by the small inflow surface. In most damp buildings, we have a slow, steady (or roughly steady) flow from a source of moisture to a drying surface, and in such cases it is the hydraulic impedance of the entire path, not the local characteristics of the source, that determines the flow. For a more detailed discussion of the Massaris' problem, see [481].

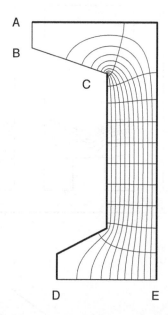

Figure 6.7 Capillary flow of water in a concrete I-beam (the left half of the beam only is shown), with saturated conditions on DE, free evaporation on ABC, and other surfaces sealed: Sharp Front solution by Schwarz-Christoffel mapping.

Flow in an I-beam

We conclude with a further example of computing capillary water migration in polygonal geometry. For example, water absorption from the face of the lower flange of a concrete I-beam section can be computed using the Schwarz-Christoffel mapping [481], as shown in Figure 6.7. Here water is supplied on face DE and we impose a constant hydraulic potential $|\Psi| > 0$ at the faces AB and BC (representing for instance an evaporation boundary condition). The flow is traced by the mesh mapped from the Schwarz-Christoffel rectangle. This flow mesh is of course the same as the saturated flow in the same geometry (for example, if there were an external pressure head on DE and a lower pressure on ABC).

6.3   FLOW IN TEMPERATURE GRADIENTS

In this and earlier chapters we have taken an isothermal view of water transport, that is to say we have not considered the direct effect of temperature gradients on flow. For most purposes in building physics this is justified, because gradients of temperature are usually small and changes of temperature are slow. Of course, we have often drawn attention to how the properties of water (and other liquids) vary with temperature, and how those variations influence properties like the permeability and the sorptivity. Consequently, isothermal flows *at different temperatures* occur at significantly different rates. Now we go further, to the case of flow in an unsaturated porous material in the presence of a *gradient* of temperature.

As the hydraulic potential Ψ is a function both of water (or more generally liquid) content θ and of temperature T we have

$$d\Psi = \frac{\partial \Psi}{\partial T} dT + \frac{\partial \Psi}{\partial \theta} d\theta. \tag{6.28}$$

The extended Darcy equation given in Eqn 3.9 then becomes

$$\mathbf{u} = -K(\theta, T)[\frac{\partial \Psi}{\partial \theta} \nabla \theta + \frac{\partial \Psi}{\partial T} \nabla T]. \tag{6.29}$$

Likewise, the Richards equation given in Eqn 3.10 becomes

$$\frac{\partial \theta}{\partial t} = \nabla \cdot [K \frac{\partial \Psi}{\partial \theta} \nabla \theta + K \frac{\partial \Psi}{\partial T} \nabla T] \tag{6.30}$$

or

$$\frac{\partial \theta}{\partial t} = \nabla \cdot [D \nabla \theta + D_T \nabla T], \tag{6.31}$$

where $D = K(d\Psi/d\theta)$ is the hydraulic diffusivity function as previously defined on p 93 for isothermal flow, and $D_T = K(d\Psi/dT)$ is a thermal diffusivity function for unsaturated flow.[6]

From Eqn 6.31, a case of particular interest is that where $\partial \theta/\partial t = 0$. Let us apply this to the system shown in Figure 6.8, where a bar of porous material containing some liquid, but unsaturated ($\theta < f$), is sealed on all faces. A temperature gradient is established by maintaining the end faces at AA' and BB' at constant but different temperatures $T_0 < T_1$. The system is therefore open to heat transfer but closed to mass transfer. At mass-transfer equilibrium there are no internal flows and $d\Psi/dx = 0$. Then from Eqn 6.31 we have

$$\frac{d\theta}{dx} = -(\frac{\partial \Psi}{\partial T} / \frac{\partial \Psi}{\partial \theta}) \cdot \frac{dT}{dx}. \tag{6.32}$$

It follows from our definitions of the diffusivities D and D_T that

$$\frac{d\theta}{dx} = \frac{D_T}{D} \cdot \frac{dT}{dx}. \tag{6.33}$$

Thus the distribution of liquid content along the bar provides [768] direct

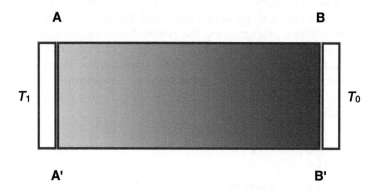

Figure 6.8 Non-uniform water content in a sealed bar of porous material subject to a temperature gradient.

information about the ratio D_T/D, here denoted δ. These diffusivities of
course reflect mass transfer in both liquid and vapour states. Some values of
δ obtained in this way are given by Luikov [767]. A study by van der Kooi
[686] provides data on an AAC material (bulk density ρ_b 700 kg/m^3, porosity
f 0.7), for which δ varies strongly with water content and has a maximum
value of about 0.015 K^{-1} at a water content $\theta_r \approx 0.2$. The value of δ cannot
be taken directly as a measure of the relative importance of gradients of
moisture content and of temperature in driving unsaturated flow without
considering the magnitude of the gradients themselves.

The thermal diffusivity D_T combines contributions to flow from both liquid and vapour transfer [980, 767, 768, 318, 290]. Vapour transfer occurs
predominantly at low water contents and is largely suppressed at higher
water contents. Liquid transfer is favoured at higher water contents but necessarily falls to zero at saturation. The underlying mechanisms are briefly as
follows. For liquid transfer, we assume that the hydraulic potential is con-
trolled by capillarity, so that $\Psi \approx \Psi_c$. We saw on p 52 that $\Psi_c \sim \sigma_L/\rho_L$, and
therefore (neglecting the small variation of density ρ_L with temperature) we
have

$$\partial \Psi/\partial T = \frac{\Psi}{\sigma_L} \cdot \frac{d\sigma_L}{dT} = -\Psi \frac{d\ln \sigma_L}{dT}. \tag{6.34}$$

The variation of liquid surface tension σ_L with temperature T is generally
known (see p 352 for water and [1346] for other liquids). For all liquids
σ_L decreases as temperature T increases, so that $|\Psi|$ decreases in magnitude
as T increases. We conclude that with rising temperature, water (or other
liquid) in an unsaturated material tends to move from the warmer region to
the cooler.

For vapour transfer, the thermal diffusivity is controlled by the variation of water vapour pressure with temperature [980, 70]. Then since $p_w/p_{w0} = h$, the relative humidity, we have

$$\frac{\mathrm{d}p_w}{\mathrm{d}x} = h\frac{\partial p_{w0}}{\partial T} \cdot \frac{\mathrm{d}T}{\mathrm{d}x} \tag{6.35}$$

and from Eqn 3.28 and Eqn 6.29 we obtain

$$u = \frac{j_m}{\rho_L} = -\frac{D_w \rho_v}{\rho_L p_{w0}} \frac{\partial p_{w0}}{\partial T} \cdot \frac{\mathrm{d}T}{\mathrm{d}x}. \tag{6.36}$$

The thermal diffusivity for vapour transport is then [980, 769, 318]

$$D_T = \frac{D_w \rho_v}{\rho_L p_{w0}} \frac{\partial p_{w0}}{\partial T}. \tag{6.37}$$

In deriving this expression for D_T it is assumed that the relative humidity h at any moisture content θ is rather insensitive to changes of temperature [980]. This is equivalent to assuming that the fractional variation of p_w and of p_{w0} with temperature are the same or similar. For molecular multilayers of adsorbed water this is true. The vapour pressure of pure water p_{w0} increases rapidly with temperature in the range of interest, say 0–40 °C. Values and interpolating equations are given in Appendix B. At 25 °C, the rate of increase is about 150 Pa/K or about 6 per cent/K.

6.4 HYGROTHERMAL SIMULATION TOOLS

Taken together, the contents of this chapter and Chapter 5 show that – at least in principle – it is possible to describe water transport in composite structures of elaborate geometry. In complicated cases of this kind, even with Sharp Front models, there are no analytical solutions to represent unsaturated flows, and fully numerical methods are required. Several such numerical simulation tools now exist [303, 559], with applications both in research and in design.[7]

Whatever individual features they may have, all simulation tools combine a module for representing and discretizing the geometry and structure of the system, a module to define initial and boundary conditions, a source of values of material properties, and a solver to find solutions of the underlying flow equations. The solver invariably operates within a finite-element numerical framework. In the main, available simulation tools use the flow equations which have been developed in earlier chapters of this book, but often formulated in terms of mass flow rates [559, 560]. These tools provide a vehicle for translational HAM engineering, although important relationships between controlling variables and parameters may be obscured. Using simulations as numerical experiments in combination with metamodelling [1231] may allow simple models of hygrothermal behaviour to be recovered. In all cases, empty (or false) precision is to be avoided in transferring results to real buildings.

Dependable simulations require not only adequate modelling of the interior flows, but equally require ways to represent boundary conditions. These define the exchanges between a structure and its environment, internal and external. Boundary conditions are usually time-varying. We discuss some processes which control the boundary exchanges in Chapters 7 and 9.

NOTES

1 The pressure-decay *air probe permeameter* has been used to make site measurements of permeability in building stones [822, 804]. While not accurate, it is useful as a rapid survey method.

2 The deviations from linear $i(t^{1/2})$ behaviour in cap-type devices arise from the lateral spreading of the wetting front, as we have shown. One practical means of reducing this effect is through the use of a cap which incorporates a guard ring [475, 1019].

3 Many of the problems in unsaturated flow that arise in building structures involve water absorption into elements defined by straight boundaries in rectilinear or polygonal shapes [481]. The Schwarz-Christoffel formula provides a general conformal mapping algorithm for transforming polygonal regions of arbitrary shape into simple forms such as the unit disc, strip or rectangle. The formula is difficult to use analytically for anything but the simplest shapes, but thanks to developments in numerical methods [1246, 333, 334] it is now possible to compute easily the Schwarz-Christoffel solution to problems in most polygonal geometries.

4 This and other numerical solutions of the Richards equation in this book have been obtained using the HYDRUS2D/3D code developed by van Genuchten and collaborators at the US Salinity Laboratory [1163, 1276, 1164, 1035, 1162]. HYDRUS uses the K–Ψ formulation of unsaturated flow. We use K, Ψ parameter values typical of brick ceramic.

5 The rates of absorption are inversely proportional to the *conformal moduli* of the Schwarz-Christoffel rectangles.

6 For a $K(\Psi)$ formulation of unsaturated flow in a temperature gradient, see [1224].

7 Water-transport simulation tools have emerged from several different fields. The Hydrus suite has its origin in soil physics and vadose-zone hydrology (see Note 4 above). We have used this several times in this book as it embodies a representation of unsaturated flow that is closely aligned with our own. The WUFI [Wärme und Feuchte Instationär] codes [667] evolved from research on moisture transport in building physics [705], as did the Delphin codes [877, 453]. The ESP-r suite has been developed from energy-performance models for buildings but now has water-transfer capabilities [256]. Other codes for hygrothermal application are noted in [303]. For research purposes, generic numerical modelling tools such as COMSOL Multiphysics [683, 684] are sometimes used. Certain needs may be met by more limited codes such as FLoW1D [209] and HAM-Tools [250].

7 Evaporation and drying

There are several ways in which water can enter the fabric of a building but there is only one important way in which water can leave it and that is by evaporation. Therefore evaporation has a central place in the description of water transport in brick, stone and concrete. By *evaporation* we mean the transfer of a substance (usually but not always water) from the liquid state to the vapour state and the associated transport of the vapour. If the rate of evaporation of water from a porous material exceeds the rate at which it is replaced by an absorption process, then the water content of the material falls and we speak of 'drying'. However, quite apart from drying, evaporation plays a strong role in determining water distributions within structures or limiting wetting processes such as rising damp. It is the physics of evaporation which usually controls the behaviour of water at the boundary between a material and its immediate environment. There are therefore many water transport problems in which we need to apply an *evaporation boundary condition*. To put the point more strongly, it is the evaporation of water at building surfaces that drives the flow of moisture through building structures [501, 496].

It is through evaporation that salts crystallize on and within porous materials. It was with this in mind that Schaffer [1119] in his classic study of the weathering of building stones wrote: 'For a porous solid of appreciable thickness to dry completely, ...water must travel in one form or another from the interior to the surface before it can escape as vapour into the surrounding air. The water lost from the surface by evaporation may be replaced by water flowing under the action of capillary forces from the interior to the surface, or the evaporating surface may fall below the surface of the solid, and water vapour must then traverse a certain length of pore space before it can escape at the surface.' Unsaturated flow theory now provides the means to represent the processes which Schaffer describes so clearly.

7.1 PHYSICS OF EVAPORATION

Before we bring into play a porous material, we consider first the evaporation of water (or any other simple liquid) from an open dish [172]. At the water surface, the partial pressure of water vapour is fixed by the saturated vapour pressure of water, so $p_w = p_{w0}$. The air in direct contact with the water is saturated with water vapour and the local relative humidity at the water surface is 100 per cent. If the relative humidity of the air well away from the surface is below 100 per cent, water vapour moves outwards from the surface and an evaporation flux is established. The rate of evaporation, which we denote e, is equal to the water vapour flux away from the surface. We can write this formally in terms of Fick's law, as already given in Eqns 3.27 and 3.28. We usually express the evaporation rate in terms of the *volume* of liquid which evaporates per unit area, thus as a volume flux (or velocity) with dimension $[L\ T^{-1}]$. Therefore we have

$$e = \rho_w j_w = -\rho_w D_w \frac{dc_w}{dx} = -\rho_w D_v \frac{dp_w}{dx}, \qquad (7.1)$$

where ρ_w is the density of *liquid* water, c_w is the water vapour concentration, D_w is the molecular diffusivity of water in air, and we recall from Chapter 3 that $D_v = D_w M/(RT)$. For clarity, let us separate the factors which depend simply on the physicochemical properties of water from environmental factors by writing

$$e = -\frac{p_{w0} D_w \rho_w M}{RT} \frac{dH}{dx} \qquad (7.2)$$

where $H = p_w/p_{w0}$ is the fractional relative humidity (RH/100). The dependence of e on physicochemical properties is straightforward enough. Under constant environmental conditions, we expect the evaporation rate to depend on the vapour pressure and the vapour phase molecular diffusivity of the evaporating substance. We note in passing that p_{w0} dominates the temperature dependence of e. As we see from data in Appendix B, the vapour pressure of water p_{w0} rises rapidly with increasing temperature, increasing threefold between 10–30 °C.[1]

Most of the complexity of evaporation theory lies in the second factor in Eqn 7.2, since the gradient of the humidity (or vapour pressure) at the surface which drives the evaporation flux depends on circumstances. Broadly speaking there are two approaches. The first is to attempt to model the structure and composition of the layer of air in immediate contact with the liquid surface and to express the formal surface gradient in terms of environmental parameters [951, 191, 172, 205]. For example, if the evaporating liquid is placed at the bottom of a long tube of length L containing still air, then (dp_w/dx) may be taken to be equal to $(p_{w0} - p_{w*})/L$ where p_{w*} is the vapour pressure outside the tube, which may be kept constant. Such an arrangement provides a direct and effective method for measuring the molecular diffusivity in air of the vapours of volatile liquids [766] by means of Eqn 7.1. As we shall see this approach is useful for some well-defined practical situations, for example involving the steady laminar flow of air across liquid surfaces or surfaces of saturated or unsaturated porous materials. The case of the greatest general practical importance is that of transfer into a turbulent air stream above the surface. Models of this kind seek to predict how natural evaporation rates from the surface of a liquid pool depend on the pool size and the wind speed across it [172]. Empirically and theoretically, e varies roughly as $W^{1/2}$ where W is the wind speed and depends only weakly on the pool radius. Evaporation is accompanied by a heat change. Heat flows from the surroundings into the vaporizing liquid such that $Q_e = H_{lv} j_w$ where Q_e is the evaporative heat flux and H_{lv} is the enthalpy of vaporization. For water, H_{lv} is 2.44×10^3 kJ/kg at 25 °C.

Potential evaporation

The other approach is to take an empirical and practical view of evaporation and to measure evaporation rates directly under particular environmental conditions. Such an approach is the basis of meteorological estimates of *potential evaporation (PE)* based on total water loss from open pans under standard conditions of exposure [582, 714, 562]. In the United Kingdom, the PE is about 400–600 mm/y, corresponding to an average evaporation rate of 1.4 mm/day over a full year [496]. The midsummer values are higher: about 85 mm/month for June and July, giving an average evaporation rate for these two months of about 2.8 mm/day. Under winter conditions the potential evaporation falls to low values, around 0.2–0.3 mm/day. Laboratory experiments at air speeds of several m/s and normal indoor temperatures and humidities show that evaporation rates as high as 0.5–1.0 mm/h may occur. Overall, there is good reason to expect large spatial and temporal (daily and seasonal) variations in the potential evaporation within a microenvironment.

Since direct PE measurements are not widely made, the PE is commonly calculated from other more accessible meteorological data. Of the many calculation methods proposed, the best established is the Penman-Monteith equation [852, 24, 46, 1207], a variant of the original Penman equation [952]. This estimates PE from air temperature, wind speed, humidity and solar radiation (sunshine) data.[2] Several simpler calculation methods are available which require less input data (see for example [672]).

7.2 DRYING OF POROUS MATERIALS

By *drying* we mean the transfer of a liquid (normally water) from the pores of a solid material to the surrounding air. The process generally includes: unsaturated flow of liquid within the porous solid; vapour flow within the porous solid; the liquid-vapour phase change; and convective-diffusive transfer of vapour from the surface of the solid to the surroundings. The first two of

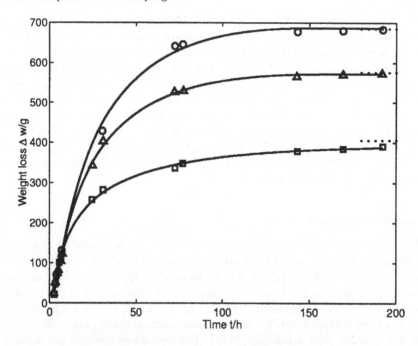

Figure 7.1 Drying of three types of clay brick at 23.5 °C dry bulb temperature and 55 per cent relative humidity [505]. Weight loss Δw from bricks initially vacuum saturated with water drying through all faces. The total saturation water content in each case is shown at the right as a dotted line.

these sub-processes may be described in terms of the concepts of unsaturated flow theory which we have discussed previously.

Figure 7.1 shows typical drying curves for three clay bricks of different porosities obtained in laboratory tests [505]. The timescale for drying individual whole bricks is 100–200 h. The rate of drying is greatest at the beginning and falls with time. Under constant drying conditions, the drying rate at early times is roughly constant, does not depend on the nature of the porous material and is found to be about the same as the rate of evaporation from a free water surface exposed to the same conditions [505].

The idea that drying under constant external conditions occurs in two distinct stages, often called the constant drying rate period (stage I) and the falling drying rate period (stage II), is well-established in the scientific literature (see for example [1123]), and for building materials can be traced back at least to Cooling's 1930 paper on the drying of brick [278]. Stage I behaviour is apparent in Figure 7.1 and also in Figure 7.2 where we plot the drying rate against time from another laboratory drying experiment on another brick material [997]. Here we see that, under the particular test conditions which were used, the stage I drying rate is about 0.55 mm/h and is maintained for the first 10 h of drying, after which the drying rate falls

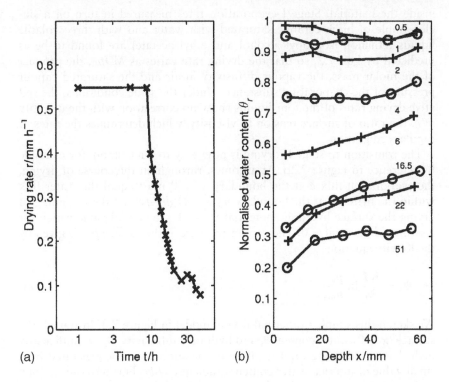

Figure 7.2 Drying of common clay brick ceramic specimens (10 × 10 × 60 mm) from one end face at 25 °C, 55 per cent relative humidity and 1.5 m/s crossflow air speed [997]. (a) Drying rates by weight loss. (b) Drying profiles by destructive sampling at various times *t*/h.

sharply and progressively. In Figure 7.2b we show the moisture distribution behind the drying surface face. During stage I, the water distribution does not show steep internal gradients. The switch to stage II drying occurs at about 10 h, after which the surface water content falls rapidly and steeper gradients of water content develop behind the drying surface. Higher resolution water content distributions in single-sided drying experiments such as this have since been obtained by neutron radiography for clay brick [942] and by NMR for clay brick, sand-lime brick and gypsum plaster [937, 944, 945], and for concrete [1145, 1146, 122]. These show similar features: flat water content distributions at early time and steeper gradients near the surface in the later stages.

Stage I behaviour occurs when the rate of evaporation is limited or controlled by the external conditions rather than by the rate of transport within the material.[3] The evidence for stage I behaviour in the drying of many kinds of porous materials has been discussed at length by van Brakel [1257]. In the case of brick materials, there are experimental data to show unambiguously that stage I behaviour is independent of capillary processes inside the material. Stage I evaporation rates measured in turn on a single sample of brick ceramic saturated with water and with three volatile liquids (ethanol, isopropyl alcohol and ethyl acetate) are found to be as predicted by Eqn 7.2, so that the drying rate varies as MDp_0, the product of the molar mass, the vapour diffusivity in air and the saturated vapour pressure of the evaporating substance. Under the same conditions, the relative drying rates of the four liquids show no correlation with the quantity σ/η, the ratio of surface tension to viscosity, which determines the rates of capillary migration.

The transition to stage II drying is now easy to understand, for example by reference to Figure 7.2b. At all times, throughout the course of drying, the evaporation flux e at the boundary $x = 0$ must equal the water flux within the material at the boundary $u_0 = -D(d\theta/dx)$. At the beginning of drying the surface hydraulic potential $\Psi_s \approx \Psi_i$, the initial value which for a saturated material ≈ 0. The vapour pressure at the surface p_{ws} is given by the Kelvin equation

$$\Psi_s = \frac{RT}{M} \ln \frac{p_{ws}}{p_{w0}}. \tag{7.3}$$

We sketch this simple isothermal drying model in Figure 7.3. In stage I, the surface ($x = 0$) water content θ_s and hydraulic diffusivity D_s are sufficiently high that an adequate capillary flow to the surface can be generated by a small value of internal water content gradient $d\theta/dx$. Furthermore, so long as $\Psi_s \ll RT/M$, p_{ws} remains almost equal to p_{w0}, the saturated vapour pressure. Thus the surface acts as a source of almost constant vapour pressure. If we disregard transient effects we may use Fick's law, Eqn 7.1, and write the stage I drying rate

$$r_1 = -\rho_w D_v \left(\frac{dp}{dx}\right)_s = -\rho_w \frac{MD_w}{RT} \left(\frac{dp}{dx}\right)_s. \tag{7.4}$$

We assume that the diffusion of vapour occurs through a boundary layer adjacent to the solid surface. We shall assume further that p varies linearly across the boundary layer which is of thickness δ so that from Eqn 7.4 we have

$$r_1 = \rho_w \frac{MD_w}{RT} \frac{p_s - p_\star}{\delta} \tag{7.5}$$

where $p_\star$ is the vapour pressure outside the boundary layer. Finally writing, for water, $p_s = p_0$ and $p_\star = p_0 H$ gives

$$r_1 = \rho_w \frac{MD_w}{RT} \frac{p_0 H'}{\delta} \tag{7.6}$$

where $H' = (1 - RH/100)$ is a humidity factor.

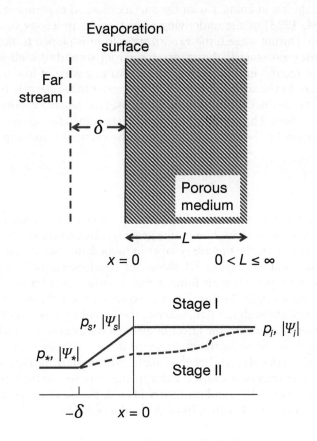

Figure 7.3 A two-stage isothermal drying model.

As drying proceeds further, both the surface and the mean water contents fall, and the corresponding values of the hydraulic diffusivity D likewise fall. The water content distributions become steeper towards the surface to support the demands of the evaporation flux. As the surface hydraulic potential Ψ_s falls and the condition $\Psi_s \ll RT/M$ is no longer satisfied, p_s also shifts away from p_{w0} and the vapour flux through the boundary layer then diminishes. Eventually the surface water content falls to the value θ_0 such that $\Psi(\theta_0)$ is in hygral equilibrium with the environment and at this point it can fall no further. Unsaturated capillary flow can no longer supply water at the surface at a rate sufficient to maintain the evaporation flux at its previous value. At this point, we enter the stage II drying régime. Unsaturated flow within the porous material now controls the rate of drying. The flux boundary condition of stage I is replaced by a constant concentration boundary condition, namely $\theta = \theta_0$ and $\Psi = \Psi_0$ at $x = 0$, where Ψ_0 is the value of the hydraulic potential measured on the drying branch which is in equilibrium with the air in contact with the surface. Several experimental studies [1156, 894, 1223] of the underlying mass transfer processes confirm this description. During stage I, the vaporization front is pinned to the surface. At the crossover to stage II, the vaporization front abruptly detaches from the surface and recedes into the interior. This creates a zone of low water content adjacent to the surface, through which water moves largely by vapour diffusion. As the thickness of this zone increases the rate of evaporation necessarily decreases. The stage II evaporation rate is therefore controlled (and limited) largely by the zone thickness and the external water vapour pressure.

Air flow

The air flow above the surface has a strong influence on r_1 since it determines dp_w/dx. As we have hinted, the general relation between the air flow and the structure of the boundary layer in immediate contact with the surface may be complex. Figure 7.4 shows the development of a simple laminar boundary layer when air flows across a surface of a slab of length L, here from left to right. In Eqn 7.5, we expressed the influence of air flow on drying rate through the parameter δ, the boundary layer thickness. We would prefer to represent the effect of air flow on quantities which we can measure such as the mainstream air speed u_* or a Reynolds number: that is, $(dp/dx)_s = f(p_0, \mathrm{Re} \ldots)$. For the simple case we show in Figure 7.4, the boundary layer thickness δ varies with x, rising from zero at the leading edge $x = 0$. Evaluating f by standard theory [1165], the mean evaporation rate per unit length over a length L from the leading edge is

$$\bar{r_1} = \frac{MD_w}{RT} p_0 H \frac{0.65 \mathrm{Sc}^{1/3} \mathrm{Re}^{1/2}}{L^{1/2}} \tag{7.7}$$

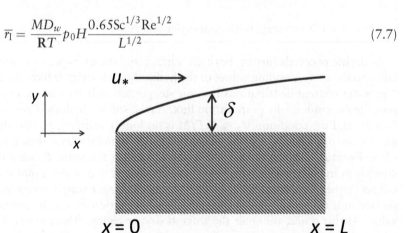

Figure 7.4 Development of a laminar boundary layer.

where the Reynolds number Re $= \rho_a u_* L / \eta_a$, the Schmidt number Sc $= \eta_a / \rho_a D_w$ and η_a, ρ_a are the viscosity and density of air.[4] Thus

$$\bar{r_1} = A \frac{u_*^{1/2} p_0 H}{L^{1/2}} \tag{7.8}$$

where

$$A = \frac{M D_w^{2/3}}{RT} \frac{0.65 \rho_a^{1/6}}{\eta_a^{1/6}}. \tag{7.9}$$

Eqn 7.9 shows the dependence of the stage I drying rate on the main environmental factors u_* and H for one particular laminar flow geometry.

The quantities D_w, p_0, ρ_a, and η_a which appear in Eqn 7.9 all change appreciably with temperature. However, for the purpose of finding $d r_1 / dT$ we can neglect the small contribution arising from $(\rho_a / \eta_a)^{1/6}$ and consider only D_w and p_0. Let us assume[5] that the diffusivity varies as $T^{3/2}$ and that the vapour pressure p_{w0} obeys the Clapeyron-Clausius law so that $p_{w0} = b \exp(-C/T)$. Then combining Eqns 7.8 and 7.9 gives

$$\ln(\bar{r_1}/H) = \ln \frac{A}{L^{1/2}} - \frac{C}{T} + \frac{1}{2} \ln u_*. \tag{7.10}$$

This shows clearly how r_1 depends on temperature and air flow velocity. It is derived from Eqn 7.7 which assumes a particular laminar air flow geometry and of course is not generally valid. The temperature dependent term $-C/T$ is independent of these geometrical and aerodynamic assumptions but the last term $\ln u_*/2$ arises from an $Re^{1/2}$ dependence of the boundary layer thickness and may need to be established empirically for air flows typical of those which occur around buildings. Nonetheless with all these caveats this model provides useful guidance on the way that stage I drying rates depend on the two main factors, air speed and temperature. In Figure 7.5 we depict graphically the relation between r_1/H and T and u_* expressed in Eqn 7.10. The figure shows lines of constant r_1/H (drying rate normalized for the effects of humidity) on a $\ln u_*$–$\ln T$ field. In constructing this figure we have used a value of r_1 determined empirically for a particular specimen geometry.

Heat flow in drying

We have assumed tacitly in the model of drying we have described that mass flow and heat flow are uncoupled.[6] This is clearly not rigorously true, since the enthalpy of vaporization must be supplied to the evaporating water, and this entails the development of temperature gradients within the drying solid. However in marked contrast to industrial and process drying, in

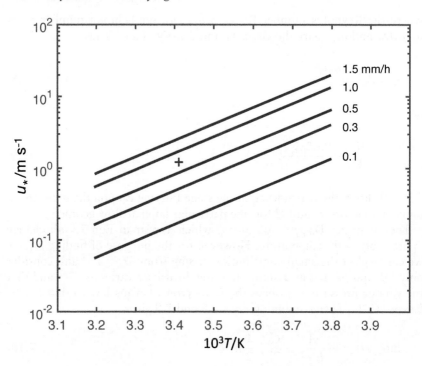

Figure 7.5 Effect of air speed u_* and temperature T on the humidity-corrected first stage drying rate r_1/H. The position of the family of lines of constant r_1/H (0.1–1.5 mm/h) is fixed by a single experimental point for clay brick in laminar air flow [505].

which the drying rate is determined principally by the rate of heat input, the surface temperature in evaporation of water from porous building materials generally does not fall significantly below the ambient value. For cases where heat inputs are greater, fully coupled heat and mass transfer drying models have been developed [116, 470, 240, 163, 1307, 956]. These incorporate unsaturated and vapour flow and account for the main features of two-stage drying.

Modelling drying: the evaporation boundary condition

The process of desorption by evaporation is not simply a reversal of the capillary absorption process. There is no liquid/vapour phase change in simple absorption but evaporation inescapably involves such a phase change. It is for this reason that the *evaporation boundary condition* is unavoidably more complex than the free water reservoir condition which we usually employ for absorption processes. The surroundings serve as a 'free-vapour reservoir' but the movement of liquid water within the porous material is coupled to this reservoir only through a phase change which occurs either at the surface or below the surface, within the porous material. For modelling purposes, we need a special boundary condition which can encompass both stage I and stage II behaviour. This is most simply achieved by recognizing that in stage I drying the material responds to a constant flux boundary condition, the flux being set by the evaporative capacity of the environment. In stage II drying the surface hydraulic potential approaches hygral equilibrium with the surroundings and further water transport in the material occurs under the action of a constant $\Psi(\theta)$ condition at the boundary $x = 0$. We can express the composite evaporation boundary condition as

$$u_0 = -D\frac{d\theta}{dx} = e_{\max}, \quad x = 0, \ t \geq 0 \tag{7.11}$$

$$\Psi \leq \Psi_*, \quad x = 0, \ u_0 \leq e_{\max}. \tag{7.12}$$

Here Ψ_* is the critical value of the hydraulic potential at which stage I behaviour gives way to stage II behaviour. In soil physics, where this evapo-ration (or *atmospheric*) boundary condition is widely used, Ψ_* is often taken to correspond to the hydraulic potential equivalent to the humidity of the immediate environment [368].

We illustrate the use of an evaporation boundary condition by looking again at a two-dimensional unsaturated flow problem which we discussed in Chapter 6. In Figure 6.1 we showed the results of the steady-state calcula-tion with a constant hydraulic potential boundary condition applied along both long sides of the rectangle. A more realistic way to represent the migra-tion of water under drying conditions is to apply an evaporation boundary condition. This we do in Figure 7.6, which shows water distributions in a similar rectangle at two times. We have imposed an evaporation boundary condition along one long edge. The material is initially dry. A free water reservoir is then applied at AA′ and the system evolves towards a steady-state in which water flows from the inflow face to evaporate from the edge AB. The water content distribution reflects the existence of flux-limited stage I behaviour on the lower part of the edge AB where the water content is high. The water content on this part of AB is high and stabilizes rapidly (see Figure 7.6c). On the upper part of AB the water content and evaporation flux are much lower (and the hydraulic potential much more negative). Stage II dry-ing applies here. Water continues to migrate slowly upwards, as the advance of the water content distribution along A′B′ reveals.

Comment on desorptivity and drying diffusivity

The evaporation boundary condition can be established under laboratory conditions so that well-defined experimental studies of drying in brick, stone and concrete are feasible. However, the evaporation boundary condition

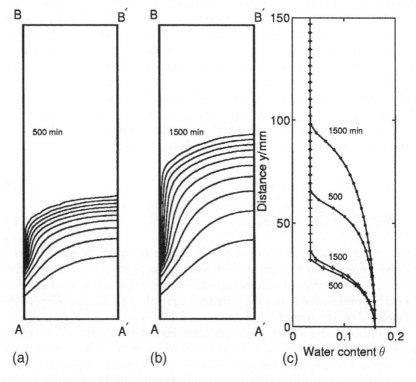

Figure 7.6 Two-dimensional steady unsaturated flow in a rectangle 50 × 150 mm with an evaporation boundary condition along on AB, a free water condition along AA' and no flux across A'B'. The evaporation rate is 0.6 mm/h, the sorptivity 0.3 mm min$^{1/2}$. (a) and (b) show the water content contours at 500 and 1500 min (ten equally spaced isohygrals). (c) shows the water content along the boundaries AB (+) and A'B' (•) at 500 and 1500 min.

does not provide a good basis for procedures for measuring transport properties such as the desorptivity and the hydraulic diffusivity. The desorption analogue of the simple one-dimensional sorptivity test is a procedure in which a water content (or hydraulic potential) boundary condition is imposed on an initially saturated semi-infinite specimen at the inflow surface at $x = 0$ and time $t = 0$. The cumulative desorption $i_d = Rt^{1/2}$ under the same conditions, where R is the desorptivity [918, 749]. Water content profiles $x(\theta, t)$ under these conditions scale as $t^{1/2}$ so that a drying diffusivity $D(\theta)$ can in principle be obtained. In practice, *experimentally* it is difficult if not impossible to impose a 'dry' boundary instantaneously in this way. If an evaporation boundary condition is applied, then stage I drying occurs at the outset, which is tantamount to a constant flux condition. When the system moves into the stage II régime and a constant hydraulic potential is

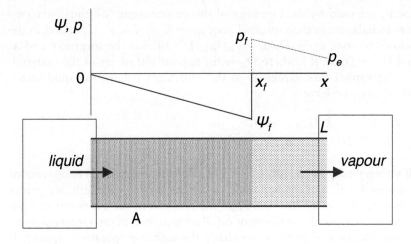

Figure 7.7 Sharp Front model of one-dimensional wick action [482]. Water is moving at a steady rate from the liquid reservoir on the left to a drying environment on the right.

established at the boundary the water content distribution within the material is no longer uniform. To determine the desorptivity and the drying diffusivity experimentally [678] is therefore much more difficult than to measure the sorptivity and the wetting diffusivity.

7.3   WICK ACTION

Wicking describes the migration of a liquid from a source by capillary flow through a highly sorptive medium, for example to an evaporating surface. The term is often applied to a steady process in which the capillary flow rate of the liquid is equal to the evaporation rate [433, 198, 1030]. As such, the steady migration of water through a concrete element such as a tunnel lining is sometimes represented as an example of wick action.

An elementary one-dimensional Sharp Front model [482] is represented in Figure 7.7. Here the saturated zone is of length l and the unsaturated zone of length $L - l$. In this highly idealized description, the transport in the unsaturated zone is by vapour diffusion alone. We assume that the capillary potential at the Sharp Front is Ψ_f. This of course is the routine SF assumption but it is the first time we have applied it in a steady-state process. The other novelty is that we now fix the water vapour pressure at x_f by the local equilibrium condition $p_f = p_0 \exp(-|\Psi_f|/\mathbf{R}T)$. Since $\Psi_f \ll \mathbf{R}T$ for materials of interest, the water vapour pressure p_f is close to the saturated vapour pressure p_0. The vapour pressure at the boundary at L is set at a constant value p_e imposed by the humidity of the environment. We thus have two fluxes in balance: in the saturated zone $u_1 = K_s \Psi_f / l = S^2/(2fl)$, and in the unsaturated zone $u_2 = D_v(p_f - p_e)/[\rho_w(L - l)]$. S is the sorptivity and as usual $D_v = D_w M/\mathbf{R}T$ where D_w is the vapour diffusivity of the material. u_2 is the vapour flux expressed as the equivalent volume of liquid water. With $u_1 = u_2$ we have

$$\frac{L - l}{L} = \frac{2fD_v(p_f - p_e)}{2fD_v(p_f - p_e) + \rho_w S^2}. \tag{7.13}$$

If we vary only the length L, the length of the unsaturated zone remains a constant fraction of the whole. If, on a sample of fixed length, we reduce the external humidity (lowering p_e), the position of the evaporation front retreats to increase the gradient of capillary potential in the saturated zone. This establishes a higher flow to satisfy the higher evaporative capacity at the boundary L. Equation 7.13 tells us that unless the two terms in the denominator are of similar magnitude the evaporation front will lie near one or other of the boundaries.

The wick-action test is a useful arrangement for exploring transport behaviour, since it establishes a one-dimensional flow with constant boundary conditions. Unless material properties change with time a steady-state is eventually established. Conversely, the flow is an indicator of changes or differences in transport properties, as shown in a study of the effect of initial moisture content on wick-action flow through concrete [17].

7.4 CAPILLARY RISE WITH EVAPORATION: A SHARP FRONT ANALYSIS

We can also couple evaporation into the simple capillary absorption and capillary rise Sharp Front models which we described in Chapter 4. As in these earlier cases (which we designated CR and CRG), we consider water absorption through the end of a uniform bar or slab of unlimited length, but as we show in Figure 7.8 we now add lateral evaporation (for the original analysis, see [501, 496]).[7] At sufficiently long times the total absorption rate and the total evaporation rate come into balance and a steady-state is established. We designate these cases CREG and CRE (capillary rise with evaporation, with and without gravity effects). CRE in particular has wide application to water transport processes in many building situations. It provides of course a description of the moisture dynamics of rising damp, as we see in Chapter 9.

As in all Sharp Front models, we have well-defined wet and dry zones. It is natural therefore to assume that we have free (stage I) evaporation from all surfaces in the wetted zone, while from surfaces in the dry zone there is

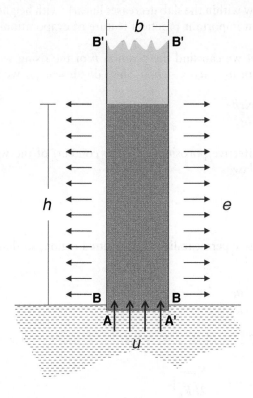

Figure 7.8 One-dimensional water absorption into a porous material with lateral evaporation: Sharp Front model.

no evaporation. In the simplest case, we shall assume constant environmental conditions (constant potential evaporation PE) and therefore a constant evaporation flux e on the wetted surface. We shall see that the CREG and CRE models can accommodate time-variable boundary conditions also.

We consider the case of water absorbed at the base of a slab from a free water reservoir at $z = 0$, and rising upwards against gravity (z positive). The slab is of thickness b and unlimited length. We assume as usual a constant capillary potential Ψ_f at the wet front. We denote by $h(t)$ the position of the wet front. Therefore the total evaporation flow $E = Neh$, where we set $N = 1$ if evaporation occurs on one side of the slab, $N = 2$ for two-sided evaporation. The total capillary absorption at $z = 0$ is $U_0 = bu_0$ where u_0 is the inflow velocity. The upward flow in the slab is $U(z,t)$ and by volume balance we have $dU/dz = -Ne$ throughout the wetted region, so that for $z \le h$

$$U(z) = U_0 - Nez. \qquad (7.14)$$

Thus the total flow within the slab decreases linearly with height and is greatest at the base (an important practical feature of evaporation-pumped systems).

From Eqn 7.14 we can find the position h of the rising wet front from $U_h - U_0 = -eh$, or $u_h - u_0 = -eh/b$. Since $dh/dt = u_h/f_e$ we have

$$\frac{dh}{dt} = \frac{u_0}{f_e} - \frac{Neh}{bf_e},$$

(7.15)

where f_e is the effective porosity (or water content) of the wetted region. Now by Darcy's law

$$u = -K_e \frac{d\Phi}{dz},$$

(7.16)

with K_e the effective permeability of the wetted region, so that by substitution into Eqn 7.14

$$\frac{d\Phi}{dz} = \frac{Nez}{bK_e} - \frac{u_0}{K_e}.$$

(7.17)

Integrating Eqn 7.17 with $\Phi = \Psi_f + h$ at $z = h$, and $\Phi = 0$ at $z = 0$ we find

$$u_0 = \frac{K_e}{h}[-\Psi_f - h + \frac{Neh^2}{2bK_e}].$$

(7.18)

Next, to express u_0 in terms of the sorptivity S, we use the standard relations $S = (2f_e K_e|\Psi_f|)^{1/2}$ (Eqn 4.38) and $|\Psi_f| = h_\infty$ (Eqn 4.92), where h_∞ is the ultimate equilibrium height of rise in the absence of evaporation. We obtain

$$u_0 = \frac{S^2}{2f_e}[\frac{1}{h} - \frac{1}{h_\infty}] + \frac{Neh}{2b}$$

(7.19)

or

$$h\frac{dh}{dt} = c[1 - \frac{h}{h_\infty}] - a'h^2$$

(7.20)

where $c = S^2/(2f_e^2)$ and $a' = Ne/(2bf_e)$. This is the differential equation for the CREG height of rise $h(t)$. If we use the dimensionless variables $H = h/h_\infty$ and $T = (S^2/2f_e^2 h_\infty^2)t$ we have

$$H\frac{dH}{dT} = 1 - H - \alpha'H^2$$

(7.21)

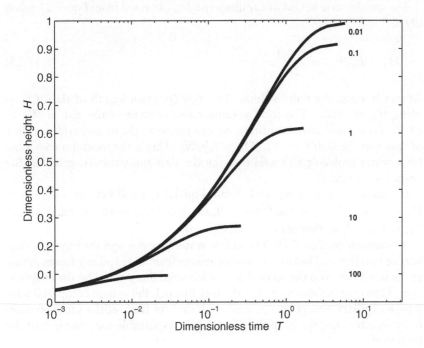

Figure 7.9 The approach to steady-state $H(T)$ in the CREG model for various
values of the parameter α', Eqn 7.21 [501].

where $\alpha' = (a'/c)b_\infty^2 = f_e Neb_\infty^2/bS^2$.

The complete solution of Eqn 7.21 for initial conditions $H = 0$, $T = 0$ is
[501]

$$-T = \frac{1}{2\alpha'} \ln|\alpha'H^2 + H - 1| + \frac{1}{2\alpha'\beta} \ln\left|\frac{(2\alpha'H + 1 + \beta)(1 - \beta)}{(2\alpha'H + 1 - \beta)(1 + \beta)}\right| \quad (7.22)$$

where $\beta = (1 + 4\alpha')^{1/2}$.

Equation 7.22 describes the entire process of capillary rise with both
evaporation and gravitational effects included. The sole parameter α' is a
dimensionless group that can however take a wide range of values (strictly,
$0 \leq \alpha' \leq \infty$). In Figure 7.9 the influence of the parameter α' on the capillary rise dynamics is shown graphically. Since $\alpha' = f_e Neb_\infty^2/bS^2$, we see
large values of α' correspond to high evaporation rate e, and small values of
α' to low e.

The steady-state height of capillary rise H_{ss} obtained from Eqn 7.21 when $dH/dT = 0$ is

$$H_{ss} = h_{ss}/h_\infty = \frac{\beta - 1}{2\alpha'}. \tag{7.23}$$

At steady-state, the finite volume flow rate (per unit length of slab) $Q_{ss} = Neh_\infty H_{ss} = Neh_{ss}$. The total volume water content of the slab is $W_{ss} = f_e b h_{ss}$. From these two quantities, we can calculate the *mean residence time* of water in the slab $t_r = W_{ss}/Q_{ss} = f_e b/Ne$. This is the mean journey time for a water molecule to travel through the slab and varies inversely as the evaporation rate e.

H_{ss} must lie in the range 0–1. From Eqn 7.23, it follows that as $\alpha' \to 0$, $H_{ss} \sim 1 - \alpha' + 2\alpha'^2$, so that for $\alpha' = 0$, $H_{ss} = 1$. On the other hand, $\alpha' \to \infty$, $H_{ss} \sim 1/\alpha'^{1/2}$, so that for $\alpha' = \infty$, $H_{ss} = 0$.

A comment on Eqn 7.19. The inflow water flux through the base, u_0, consists of two terms. The first is the flux arising from the capillary forces acting at the wet front, and the second is an additional flux caused by the evaporation. Thus evaporation *increases* the flux through the system compared with a pure capillary absorption process with the wet front at the same position h. At steady-state, the evaporative pump is responsible for exactly half the total flow.

Switching off the effects of gravity: the CRE case

For many materials and for many situations, the heights of rise h of interest are far smaller than the ultimate equilibrium height of rise h_∞ which would be achieved in the absence of evaporation. In such cases, the effects of gravity can be ignored, and this simplifies considerably the mathematical results. As we have seen, this behaviour is associated with large values of α'. We therefore neglect the second term H in Eqn 7.21 to obtain

$$H\frac{dH}{dt} = 1 - \alpha'H^2. \tag{7.24}$$

By substituting for α', H and T we obtain the equivalent differential equation in $h(t)$

$$h\frac{dh}{dt} = -a'h^2 + c \tag{7.25}$$

where $a' = Ne/(2f_e b)$ and $c = S^2/2f_e^2$. Equation 7.25 may be obtained directly from Eqn 7.20 by taking $h/h_\infty \ll 1$ and omitting the second term.

These equations describe the case where gravity effects are negligible. This occurs when the capillary forces are strong, so that h_∞ is large, and the evaporation rate e is appreciable. For $h = 0, t = 0$, Eqn 7.25 has the solution

$$h^2 = \frac{c}{a'}[1 - \exp(-2a't)]. \tag{7.26}$$

At long times, the system reaches a capillary rise steady-state H_{ss}, with a finite flow rate Q_{ss}. As we have already seen, $H_{ss} = (\alpha')^{-1/2}$ and, explicitly,

$$h_{ss} = S(b/Nef_e)^{1/2}. \tag{7.27}$$

This result is of the greatest importance. It shows that the height of rise is proportional to the sorptivity S and increases as $b^{1/2}$. On the other hand it is inversely proportional to $e^{1/2}$.[8] From an initial dry state, the steady-state is reached in a time $t \approx 3bf_e/2Ne$. We shall consider the CRE model as the basis of a practical analysis of moisture dynamics in walls in Chapter 9.

Switching off evaporation: the CRG case

In the other limit, if $\alpha' \ll 1$ Eqn 7.21 reduces to the expression

$$H\frac{dH}{dt} = 1 - H, \tag{7.28}$$

equivalent to Eqn 4.93 derived earlier for simple capillary rise equilibrium with gravity (Chapter 4). This case is most easily obtained by switching off the evaporation, so that $e = 0$ and $\alpha' = 0$. At long times, the system reaches a true equilibrium $H(\infty) = 1$, where the flow rate $Q(\infty) = 0$.

Synopsis

The complete CREG case (of capillary rise with both evaporation and gravitational effects) is the most comprehensive Sharp Front model for moisture dynamics in brick, stone and concrete. By switching off evaporation we recover the CRG case; by switching off gravitational effects, we recover the CRE case; and by switching off both evaporation and gravity the equations reduce to those of simple capillary absorption, CR.[9] We summarize these relationships in Table 7.1. We have assumed tacitly that the evaporation rate e is constant with time, but we note that these differential equations apply equally to situations in which the potential evaporation PE of the microenvironment varies with time, so that the evaporation flux $e(t)$ is likewise time-dependent. However, in these cases the differential equations generally require numerical solution [496].

Table 7.1 Synopsis of Sharp Front CREG equations

CREG	$H\dfrac{dH}{dt} = 1 - H - \alpha'H^2$	$b\dfrac{db}{dt} = c\left(1 - \dfrac{b}{b_\infty}\right) - a'b^2$
CRE	$H\dfrac{dH}{dt} = 1 - \alpha'H^2$	$b\dfrac{db}{dt} = c - a'b^2$
CRG	$H\dfrac{dH}{dt} = 1 - H$	$b\dfrac{db}{dt} = c\left(1 - \dfrac{b}{b_\infty}\right)$
CR	$H\dfrac{dH}{dt} = 1$	$b\dfrac{db}{dt} = c$

Slabs, pillars and columns

In our analysis, we have used the parameter N to allow us to distinguish between systems subject to one-sided and two-sided evaporation. It can be seen that N always appears in the combination Ne/b, so that a two-sided system of thickness b is equivalent to a one-sided system of thickness $b/2$; or to a one-sided system with evaporation flux $2e$. Thus the results are applicable to walls and other practical structures which can be represented as simple slabs. We note that the quantity N/b is the ratio (evaporating perimeter)/(cross-section area), say γ. This suggests that we can apply our results to structures of other geometries by replacing N/b by the appropriate value of γ. Thus for a square column $b \times b$ with evaporation from all four faces, $\gamma = 4/b$. For a circular column of radius r, $\gamma = 2/r$.

7.5   SALT CRYSTALLIZATION AND EFFLORESCENCE

Crystals of salts such as potassium and sodium sulphate are a common sight on walls, especially in the summer months. Such deposits are a certain sign of evaporation processes at work. Many bricks contain soluble salts from the clays of which they are made, and absorbed ground water may provide more. Water can exist and migrate both as liquid and as vapour, but waterborne salts can move only as dissolved substances. When water evaporates, any dissolved salts remain behind. Unless the evaporating water is replaced, the salt concentration in the residual water rises, perhaps to levels that exceed the solubility of the salt. Mineral surfaces provide ideal situations for the nucleation and growth of crystals from supersaturated solutions. The efflorescent salts which form mark the position of evaporation fronts, which may be on the surface of porous materials or just as often below the surface within the pores themselves.

Let us start by considering how our simple Sharp Front model of steady-state evaporation will change if the water is replaced by an aqueous salt solution. The liquid phase transport is unaltered, apart from the unimportant effect caused by the small change in viscosity η. (We can allow for this if we wish to by noting that the sorptivity $S = S_0(\eta_0/\eta)^{1/2}$.) However, the changes at the evaporation front are much more far reaching and, strictly speaking, destroy the steady-state process altogether. Imagine that we first set up the steady evaporation front with pure water. Then we replace the water at the inflow surface by a salt solution, of concentration c. While Ψ_f is scarcely changed (the effect of dissolved salts on surface tension is very small: see Appendix B), the effect on p_f may be far greater. Therefore the vapour pressure gradient driving vapour diffusion in Figure 7.7 may be much reduced, or even changed in sign. This causes the evaporation front to advance towards the surface in order to find a new position at which the liquid and vapour fluxes balance. The increase in l and the reduced vapour pressure gradient $(p_f - p_e)/(L - l)$ both show that the evaporation rate will be lower for the salt solution than for pure water. (How much of course depends on the salt and its concentration.) There is also a second effect: as the evaporation proceeds, the liquid flux continues to feed more and more dissolved salt to the front, where it can migrate no further and accumulates. The salt concentration in solution rises. If we neglect for the moment the possibility of back-diffusion of salt against the capillary flux, then the salt concentration at the front rises as uc. Sooner or later, the solubility limit is exceeded and the salt starts to deposit from solution. At this point, the local salt solution at the front is *saturated* (in the solubility sense). For highly soluble salts such as sodium chloride and potassium sulphate the saturated solutions are concentrated and the corresponding values of p_f low. Consequently, evaporation and vapour diffusion are both retarded. Indeed p_f may actually fall below p_e so that water condenses on the surface of the material even at relative humidities in the normal ambient range (*hygroscopicity*). The build-up of salts may also act to block transport both of solution and of water vapour at the evaporation front [1149, 804]. These effects are progressive and inevitably superimpose a slow time-dependence on the steady evaporation process which we originally established with pure water.

As soon as the dissolved salt reaches the evaporation front, a variation of salt concentration begins to develop in the wetted zone. In the Sharp Front model, there is a discontinuity of salt concentration at the evaporation front. This is unphysical and is eliminated by a diffusive flux away from the front. At sufficiently small values of the total evaporative flux u, the diffusive back-flow may appreciably reduce the salt concentration at the evaporation front. At sufficiently small values of the Péclet number $\mathrm{Pe} = ul/fD_l$ (where D_l is the molecular diffusivity of the salt in the porous medium), the evaporating solution may be unable to attain supersaturation [603, 459]. In that case, there is a critical Péclet number for salt crystallization.

Unsaturated flow theory for solutions

The Sharp Front model we have just described is perhaps too simple to be an adequate description of the complicated processes which occur in the evaporation of salt solutions in porous materials. However, it has the considerable virtue of providing a clear description of the main physical ingredients. While the capillary flow can be expressed in the language of the Richards equation, there is at present little experimental evidence for the mechanisms of ion transport in unsaturated media.

NOTES

1 There are many more or less accurate interpolation equations for calculating the vapour pressure of water at a given temperature $p_{w0}(T)$ [862, 598]. Several of the most widely used [18] are of the form $p_{w0}/\text{kPa} = a \exp[bT/(T+c)]$ proposed long ago by Magnus [774]. With values $a = 0.61082$, $b = 17.324$ and $c = 238.02\,°\text{C}$, we can calculate the water vapour pressure for temperature T from 0 to 40 °C (as given to greater accuracy in Appendix B) to within 0.02 per cent standard error. Such a Magnus equation has been used for many years in estimating the drying rates of freshly placed concrete slabs in order to avoid shrinkage cracking [595].

2 Meteorological information on potential evaporation PE, whether directly measured or estimated, for example from the Penman equation, is available as rather coarse averages over large areas, perhaps on a 5 km grid. For application in building physics, we need ultimately to understand the fine-scale variation of PE in the immediate microenvironment of structures such as walls and monuments. The study of evaporation rates within and close to buildings is in its infancy. It is possible to use porous plug evaporimeters (or atmometers) [185, 450], but these are not well suited to measurements on building surfaces. Measuring the rates of drying of small water-saturated stone blocks [523, 575] can provide local PE data but is laborious. A more practical prototype device has been described in which the drying of a sintered-glass disc is monitored remotely via a humidity sensor [494]. However, little is yet known about microenvironmental features of evaporation because local mapping of PE is almost never undertaken.

3 To call Stage I *constant rate* drying is misleading. The characteristic of stage I behaviour is that the rate of drying is controlled by external conditions. In laboratory tests, which are usually conducted under constant drying conditions, this leads of course to constant stage I drying rates. If drying conditions are varied with time, for example by changing the humidity or air flow, then the stage I drying rate varies correspondingly. Similarly, the essence of stage II drying is that the rate is determined primarily by the unsaturated flow properties of the porous material, not on the external conditions. If the evaporation process is steady (as in Figure 7.6) then the stage II régime proceeds of course at a constant rate.

4 Asano and Fujita [45] have shown in an experimental study that the evaporation rate depends on $\text{Sc}^{1/2}\text{Re}^{2/3}$ rather than $\text{Sc}^{1/3}\text{Re}^{1/2}$ as predicted by simple theory.

5 We noted in Chapter 4 that the vapour diffusivity varies as $T^{1.81}$ where T is the absolute temperature. The effect of this on the predicted drying rates is negligible.

6 Penman [951] asks Aristotle's question: 'Is wind or sun more important in promoting natural evaporation?' There is no doubt that at the drying rates which typically occur on the surfaces of buildings evaporation occurs without much local cooling [505, 413]. The heat flows are weak and rarely exert much influence on the evaporation rate. This is the justification for the isothermal assumption [968].

However, the temperature at which stage I drying takes place is a strong factor through the influence which it has on the vapour pressure of water. Stage II drying is promoted less strongly by increasing temperature, since the drying rate scales as η/σ, the ratio of liquid viscosity to surface tension (see Appendix B for values for water). Stage II drying rates are of course almost independent of air flow across the surface.

7 The CREG model we describe here incorporates *distributed* evaporation: that is, evaporation occurs uniformly over the wetted surface. Briefly in [500] and fully in [501], we described a simpler Sharp Front CREG model in which the water content of the system was calculated from a simple integral (lumped) mass balance. We obtained a differential equation for the position of the wet front $h(t)$ from the relation $dh/dt = (U - E)/bf_e$ by setting the inflow $U = bS^2/(2f_e h)$ and the outflow $E = eh$. U was taken to be a constant throughout the wetted region. In the distributed case, we require that U varies linearly from the inflow boundary at height $z = 0$ to the wet front at height $z = h$, such that $U - U_0 = -ez, 0 \leq z \leq h$. This ensures that water is lost uniformly from the wetted region. It follows then that the capillary pressure potential varies nonlinearly from the inflow face to the wet front. In the distributed-evaporation model, as we have seen, the total flow through the inflow boundary $U_0 = bS^2/(2f_e h) + eh/2$. At steady-state, $U(h) = 0$, so that the steady-state height of rise is $h_{ss} = S(b/ef_e)^{1/2}$ (Eqn 7.27). This differs from the result for the lumped case by a factor $1/\sqrt{2}$ only.

8 These important scalings emerge also from a nonlinear diffusion analysis of the distributed CRE problem [755].

9 The CREG result gives a solution to the Lucas-Washburn problem with distributed evaporation and gravity [335, 15, 391, 1260].

8 Topics in materials behaviour

Earlier chapters have shown how the moisture state of brick, stone and concrete can be characterized, primarily through the water content, the hydraulic potential and the porosity. These quantities appear as essential variables in the analysis of water transport. However the moisture state of these materials also underlies other materials processes and phenomena, several of which we discuss in this chapter.

8.1 AIR TRAPPING IN WATER ABSORPTION

When water is absorbed into a dry porous material by capillary forces, there is no doubt that some air is trapped in the process, as we have seen in our earlier discussion of the Hirschwald coefficient (p 162). Much of the air is displaced ahead of the advancing wet front and is expelled. However, a fraction (and not always a small fraction) of the air originally present throughout the pore network becomes disconnected and isolated [362]. This happens when water invades blind pores from which the air cannot escape, when small regions of the pore network become encircled by invading water and when thickening liquid films on the pore walls jump together in a process known as *snap-off* [149]. We depict these occurrences schematically in Figure 8.1. The pressure inside a pocket of trapped air is determined by the radius of curvature r_a of the trapping meniscus, so that $p_a = 2\sigma/r_a$, where σ is the surface tension. The pocket adjusts its shape until it finds an equilibrium configuration in which the meniscus curvature and the contact angle are matched to the pore geometry. While local mechanical equilibrium is established in this way, we do not have equilibrium in respect of diffusion of gas. For all pockets, p_a is greater than the air pressure at the external surface of the material. Since the solubility of a gas increases in direct proportion to its pressure (Henry's law), the local solubility at the pocket is greater than at the external surface. As a result, there exists a gradient in the concentration of dissolved gas in the pore network between trapped gas pockets and the boundary. It is this gradient that drives a long-term (and long-range) diffusion that causes

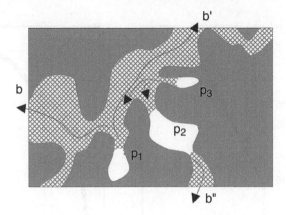

Figure 8.1 Cartoon of air trapped in pockets in blind pores and branches in a porous material. Air is trapped in blind pores, by encirclement and by snap-off. The trapped air has pressure $p_1, p_2 \ldots$ greater than the boundary pressure and is initially different from pocket to pocket. There is a rapid local equilibration by diffusion of dissolved gas through the liquid phase from neighbouring pockets; and a much slower general diffusion to the boundaries $b, b' \ldots$.

the pockets to shrink and eventually to disappear. We should also note that there is no reason for every pocket of trapped air to have the same internal pressure when it is created, since the pressure of each depends on accidents of pore geometry and of the microscopic motion of the wet front. Therefore, at first pockets are no doubt at different pressures, so that gas migrates by *local* diffusion paths between pockets in close proximity, equalizing the pressure of all the trapped air. The diffusion to the external surfaces of the material is a much slower long-term process which is superimposed on the local equilibration. We may assume that in a representative volume of the material, the trapped air comes rapidly to a uniform pressure, which we can take as a characteristic of the material, p_a.

Gummerson's experiment

There is a remarkable experiment of R. J. Gummerson [463] which reveals much about the physics of air-trapping. Gummerson's experiment was simple and consisted of measuring the water absorption of a common clay brick, standing on a header face in a shallow tray of water, set on a laboratory bench, just as for a standard water absorption test. Free evaporation was allowed on all non-immersed faces. The weight of the brick was measured from time to time for a period of nearly two years. We show the data in Figure 8.2. It takes a little over one day for the wet front to reach the top surface of the brick and during this stage the water absorption shows exact $t^{1/2}$ behaviour. The mean water content of the brick is then about $0.87f$, where

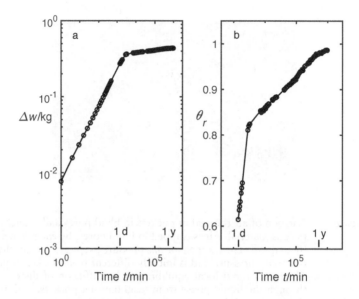

Figure 8.2 Gummerson's experiment [463]: long-term data on capillary rise water absorption by a single common clay brick. The brick used had dry mass 2.737 kg, dry bulk density ρ 1910 kg/m^3 and volume fraction open porosity f 0.31 determined by vacuum saturation. (a): Δw, the gain in mass, plotted against elapsed time t on log axes. (b): Data plotted as $\theta_r = \theta/f$ vs t (log axis).

f is the open porosity measured on the same brick by vacuum saturation. This is the Hirschwald state that we have defined in Chapter 4 (p 163), and so the fractional Hirschwald coefficient h = 0.87. Thereafter, we see a slow progressive increase in mass which continues for nearly two years throughout the rest of the experiment. The long-term mass gain is seen more clearly in Figure 8.2b. The water content at the end of the experiment is close to the independently measured vacuum saturation porosity, when $\theta_r = \theta_s/f = 1$.

We can account for the kinetics of the long-term process by means of a model of diffusion of trapped air to the surface of the brick. The most important parameter is the trapped gas pressure p_a. We shall assume that all air pockets come rapidly to a common pressure by means of the local diffusion processes we have described. We shall also assume for simplicity that p_a remains constant as the volume of a pocket decreases: this is what would happen if all pockets were cylindrical in shape. Then we can use Henry's law to calculate the concentration of dissolved air within the material. We see that initially since the trapped air is distributed throughout the material, the dissolved gas concentration is uniform everywhere when averaged over volumes larger than the pore scale. Thus initially, we can imagine the brick with a constant dissolved gas concentration throughout except at the boundary, where the value is lower since the water here is in equilibrium with air at atmospheric pressure p_0. Dissolved gas then diffuses to the boundary and a *saturation front* characterized by a higher water content moves inwards as the air pockets shrink and are filled with water. In fact this description applies equally to each of the two main components of air, nitrogen and oxygen. They should be considered separately as they diffuse independently, and have different Henry's law solubilities and molecular diffusivities in water.

In the particular case of a whole brick, of dimensions $A \times B \times C = V$ and porosity f, we have a total open pore volume fV. After initial water absorption, the volume of trapped air $V_a = \lambda_0 fV$ at pressure p_a, so λ_0 is the fraction of the open porosity which is air-filled. Applying the ideal gas law $nRT = p_aV_a$ to both nitrogen and oxygen we have $n_o + n_n = (\epsilon_o + \epsilon_n)p_aV_a/RT$, where n_o and n_n are the amounts of oxygen and nitrogen and $\epsilon_o p_a$ and $\epsilon_n p_a$ are the partial pressures of oxygen and nitrogen in the trapped gas. In air $\epsilon_o = 0.21$ and $\epsilon_n = 0.79$. Therefore the amount of trapped oxygen is

$$n_o = \frac{\epsilon_o P_a \lambda_0 fV}{RT} \tag{8.1}$$

and likewise for nitrogen. Henry's law[1] tells us that the concentration c of a gas in solution is proportional to the pressure p of the gas in contact with the solvent, that is

$$c = Hp. \tag{8.2}$$

(We give values of the Henry's law solubility constant H for oxygen and nitrogen in water in Appendix E.) With these preliminaries, we can now consider the situation depicted in Figure 8.3, where we show a total saturation front moving from the surface inwards to the centre of the brick. The flux of dissolved gas (in air there is a separate flux of oxygen and of nitrogen) is described by Fick's law, so that

$$j = -D'\frac{dc}{dx} = -D'(c_a - c_0)/x_f, \tag{8.3}$$

where D' is the diffusivity of the dissolved gas in the water-saturated brick. The diffusivity D' is smaller than the diffusivity D_0 of the dissolved gas in water at the same temperature because of the restrictions imposed by the pore structure of the brick. Thus $D' = D_0/\tau$ where τ is a tortuosity factor. (As we have mentioned in Chapter 1, the experimental formation factor provides a way of determining the tortuosity for ion diffusion. We have no comparable direct method for the diffusion of gas molecules but it is likely the tortuosity is similar.) The rate of advance of the saturation front then depends on the concentration of dissolved gas at the front

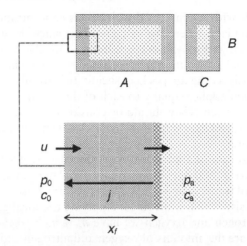

Figure 8.3 Schematic of the development of a zone of total saturation as air
trapped at pressure p_a dissolves at concentration c_a and diffuses to
the surface. In a whole brick of dimensions $A \times B \times C$, the saturation
zone moves inwards parallel to all faces. The rate of inward water
absorption u is coupled to the outward flux of dissolved air, j. The
saturation front is located at a distance x_f from the surface, where
the air pressure is p_0 and dissolved gas concentration is c_0.

$c_a = Hp_a$ and on the amount of trapped gas to be replaced by water, so that
$u = di/dt = \lambda_0 f dx_f/dt = j dn/dx$. Thus

$$x_f \frac{dx_f}{dt} = -\frac{D_0(c_a - c_0)RT}{\tau p_a \lambda_0 f}, \tag{8.4}$$

so that

$$x_f = A't^{1/2} \tag{8.5}$$

where

$$A' = \left(\frac{2D_0 H \Delta p RT}{\tau \lambda_0 f p_a} \right)^{1/2}. \tag{8.6}$$

We note that $RT/p_a = \rho_g$, the density of the trapped gas. Air is lost from
a whole brick by diffusion towards all faces, so the zone of total saturation
moves inwards parallel to all faces (Figure 8.3). The total volume of the
saturated zone $V_s = Fx_f - Ex_f^2 + x_f^3$ with the total area of all faces $F =
2(AB + BC + CA)$ and the length of edges $E = 4(A + B + C)$. The mass gain
is therefore $\Delta w = f\lambda_0 \rho_w V_s$. Since $x_f = A't^{1/2}$, we find that

$$\Delta w = f\lambda_0 \rho_w (FA't^{1/2} - EA'^2 t + A'^3 t^{3/2}). \tag{8.7}$$

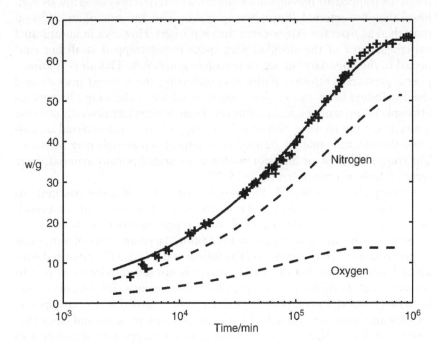

Figure 8.4 The long-term water absorption data of Figure 8.2 compared with the air diffusion model. The dashed lines are calculated from Eqn 8.7, with $D_0 = 1.95 \times 10^{-9}$ m^2 s^{-1} for oxygen and $D_0 = 1.80 \times 10^{-9}$ m^2 s^{-1} for nitrogen at temperature $T = 20\,°$C and $r_p = 0.099$. The solid line is the total water absorption from the separate processes of oxygen and nitrogen elimination.

The saturation process is complete when $x_f = C/2$, where C is the smallest of the three dimensions of the brick. In A', we know D_0, H, λ and f, but we do not know the value of the group of quantities $r_p = \Delta p/p_a \tau$. In Figure 8.4 we show the best fit of Eqn 8.7 to the experimental data [463], with a single disposable parameter r_p. We find for this case that $r_p = 0.099$. If we assume that $\tau \approx 4$, then p_a is about 1.7 atm. For water at 25 °C, this pressure tells us that the air is trapped in pores by water/air menisci with a radius of curvature of about 2 μm. In Figure 8.4 we also show the individual contributions of the nitrogen and oxygen flux and see that the oxygen diffuses somewhat more rapidly than the nitrogen.

This line of argument applies only to materials which are at or close to saturation, so that the capillary potential Ψ is zero or close to zero. In unsaturated materials, the pressure of trapped air p_a is still greater than the liquid phase pressure at the meniscus by an amount $2\sigma/r$, but this liquid phase pressure is in turn lower than atmospheric pressure by an amount Ψ. As a result the trapped air pressure in unsaturated materials may be as low or even lower than the external atmospheric pressure. The direction of air diffusion must then be *from* the exterior *into* the air pockets. However, in unsaturated materials, most of the air-filled pore space is not trapped at all but connected to the boundary through a percolating network. This air is at atmospheric pressure. Diffusion pathways connecting the trapped pockets and the distributed network are short and trapped air pockets rapidly come to atmospheric pressure by local diffusion. There is therefore no concentration gradient serving to drive diffusion from trapped air to the external boundaries. We conclude that air trapped in unsaturated materials may be stable. The complexities of air diffusion within unsaturated porous materials have received little attention (but see [935, 775]).

Air may also be removed efficiently by convection if water continues to flow through the material after it is first wetted, most commonly as a result of evaporation. Provided a source of water is present from which water lost by evaporation can be replaced by imbibition, large amounts of water can be pumped through the material. The inflow water is usually saturated with air at 1 atm pressure but this means that it is not saturated with respect to trapped air at the higher pressure p_a, which consequently dissolves into it and is carried towards the evaporating surface to be returned to the atmosphere. 1 L of water dissolves about 11.5 mg of air at 1 atm pressure and twice that amount at 2 atm. If, for sake of illustration, the trapped air is assumed to be at a pressure of 2 atm, we see that all the air trapped in Gummerson's experiment, about 73 mL (or 47 mg at 2 atm), can be removed by passing about 4 L of water through the brick. This is about ten times the total open pore volume, and at reasonable evaporation rates – say 1 mm/day on the exposed surface – this would take no more than a few months.

Comment

We see that given sufficient time for trapped air to be eliminated by diffusion or convection, materials in contact with a source of water tend to reach a saturated state in which the open porosity is completely water-filled. This leads us to conclude that brick and stone masonry materials that have prolonged access to a source of water (for example in persistently damp ground) reach a moisture state of saturation given sufficient time. This is significant for both rising damp and frost damage. A traditional test for durability in stone and brick is the measurement of the saturation coefficient, defined as we have seen (p 176) as the percentage of the open pore space filled in a 24 or 48 h total immersion soak. It is sometimes considered that this is the maximum water content that is likely to be achieved in practice. The Gummerson experiment and the analysis of air diffusion show that this is not the case.

There have been many studies of the trapping of air during water absorption in soils and porous media, notably those of Corey and his collaborators [4, 825] (whose analysis of air diffusion in ceramics and sandstones the preceding model resembles), Peck [1355, 933, 934], Gras [437], Parlange [915], Touma [1243], Culligan [282] and Geistlinger [414]. Most of these deal with the effects of air on absorption and infiltration kinetics, a matter which deserves more attention in connection with brick, stone and concrete than it has yet received.

Water and nonaqueous liquids compared

We have often noted in earlier chapters that to compare the behaviour of water and nonaqueous liquids in transport processes can be illuminating. The case of the release of trapped air confirms us in that view. We show in Figure 8.5a that secondary imbibition leading to saturation occurs much more rapidly with *n*-dodecane and isopropyl alcohol than with water. This

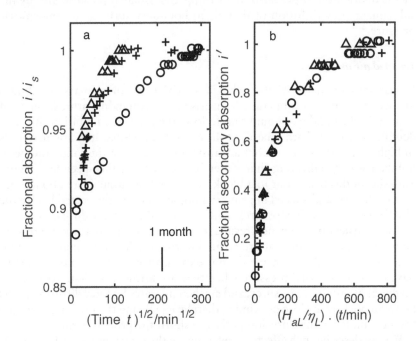

Figure 8.5 Cumulative secondary imbibition of △ *n*-dodecane (h 0.92), + isopropyl alcohol (h 0.91), and ○ water (h 0.90) by an Ancaster limestone block (50 mm cube, $f = 0.161$) [472]. (a) Secondary imbibition curves i/i_s vs $t^{1/2}$. (b) Secondary imbibition $i' = (i - i_h/(i_s - i_h)$ vs $H_{aL}t/\eta_L$. Values of H_{aL}/η_L: for dodecane, 0.045; isopropyl alcohol, 0.034; water, 0.0087 mol/(m³ Pa² s). All tests at 25 °C.

is chiefly because air is more soluble in these nonaqueous liquids than in water. We may expect, at any given temperature T and certainly to a good first approximation, that the rate of secondary imbibition scales as $H_{aL}D_L$ where H_{aL} is the Henry's law solubility constant of air in the liquid and D_L is the diffusivity of air in that liquid. We also know from the Stokes-Einstein law that, at any T, $D_L \sim \eta_L^{-1}$ (where η_L is the liquid viscosity) so that the rate of imbibition $\sim H_{aL}/\eta_L$, or alternatively the time to saturation $t_s \sim \eta_L/H_{aL}$. The factor H_{aL}/η_L is five times greater for n-dodecane than for water at 25 °C. In Figure 8.5b we see that using the scaled time variable $H_{aL}t/\eta_L$ collapses the three individual imbibition curves of the Ancaster limestone, and so confirms our simple scaling. We note that for this Ancaster limestone the Hirschwald coefficient h is similar for all three liquids, a result found as well for several other limestones [513], so that there is apparently little or no influence of the liquid surface tension on the timescale of secondary imbibition. The imbibition of nonaqueous liquids into brick, stone and concrete is no doubt of modest interest in itself, but these results are of great scientific value in confirming that the secondary process is indeed controlled by the dissolution of pressurized air trapped in isolated pockets, and by the subsequent slow diffusion of that air to boundary surfaces at atmospheric pressure.[2]

Trapped air as a foam

Precise measurements of the behaviour at the end of primary imbibition uncover a number of subtleties. A surprising but common feature is the brief plateau in the uptake of liquid that follows the primary imbibition. It is evident in the case of Bath limestone shown in Figure 8.6a. In a few materials of high sorptivity, there is even a transient reduction in the total volume of imbibed water, indicating that water is ejected from the specimen. Figure 8.6b shows this behaviour in a block of Ketton limestone. Here about 6 per cent of the water absorbed in primary imbibition is briefly ejected before the block continues its slow progress to saturation through air diffusion.

This transient phenomenon results from the local equilibration of pressure between pockets of air that are created during the initial (primary) imbibition. As we noted earlier, we do not expect all pockets of trapped air to have the same internal pressure when they are formed. At first, pockets are no doubt at different pressures, and air then migrates by *local* diffusion paths between pockets in close proximity, thereby equalizing the pressure of all the trapped air. Since the diffusion paths are short, the process is rapid.

We can describe such effects by reference to the sketch model in Figure 8.7. Here two adjacent pockets contain trapped air at different pressures, p_1, p_2, related to the different pore diameters. The initial pressure of the liquid water $p_w = p_0$, the ambient pressure, while the excess pressure in each pocket equals the Young-Laplace pressure created at its meniscus. While the configuration shown is at mechanical equilibrium, it is not at mass-transfer equilibrium, since the higher pressure in pocket 1 ensures that the dissolved-air

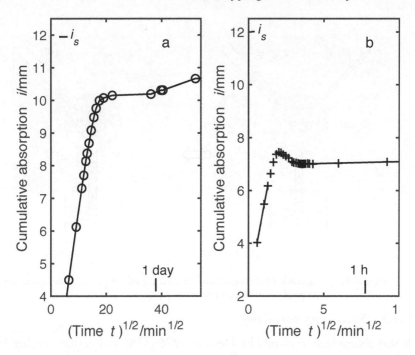

Figure 8.6 Cumulative absorption in late stages of the primary imbibition of water in two 50 mm limestone cubes: (a) Bath ($S = 0.606$ mm/min$^{1/2}$, $f = 0.242$); (b) Ketton ($S = 3.03$ mm/min$^{1/2}$, $f = 0.241$). i_s marks water saturation; tests at 25 °C [472].

concentration at its meniscus is greater than that at the meniscus of pocket 2. Consequently, there is a flux of dissolved air from 1 to 2. If the system is closed (with valve A shut), the system volume $V_1 + V_2 + V_w$ is fixed. The water is incompressible and so $V_1 + V_2$ is constant. At diffusion equilibrium, all air is in pocket 2, which therefore has air volume $V_2' = V_1 + V_2$, and air pressure $p_2' = (p_1 V_1 + p_2 V_2)/(V_1 + V_2)$, the volume-weighted mean initial pressure.

If we now open the system (by opening valve A), water is ejected until p_w falls to atmospheric pressure, and the final pressure of the trapped air $p_2'' = p_2$. The final volume of trapped air $V_2'' = (p_1 V_1 + p_2 V_2)/p_2$. The volume of water ejected $\Delta V_w = V_2'' - V_2' = V_1(p_1 - p_2)/p_2$. This is the state of an open system when local pressure equalization is attained.

Similar processes occur in foams and bubbly liquids and cause the bubble structure to evolve after a foam is formed [1305]. This similarity suggests that we can consider the liquid and the trapped air within it in a porous material as a *supported foam*, having much in common with foams and bubbly liquids, but supported (or constrained) by the framework of the solid matrix.[3]

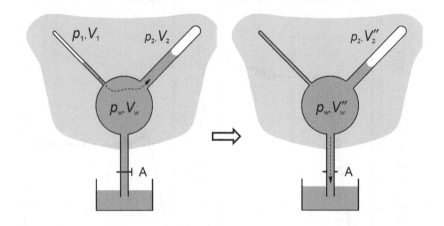

Figure 8.7 Schematic of the equalization of trapped air pressure between adjacent pockets at initial pressures p_1, p_2.

8.1.1   Secondary sorptivity

It was recognized, certainly by Hens in 1976 [558] and perhaps earlier by others, that after primary imbibition is complete, water continues to be slowly absorbed, That observation led to the two-tangent method of determining w_{cap} (p 176), although the secondary imbibition was not studied in detail. No significance was attached to the *rate* of the secondary imbibition, and there was until recently little interest in its theoretical interpretation. The capillary moisture content (or the closely related saturation coefficient) has been used over many years as a guide to durability, especially in relation to freeze-thaw damage in building stone [565, 1119]. Long-term water absorption and associated air-diffusion have also been studied in relation to freeze-thaw damage in air-entrained concretes [362].

Definition and terminology

In 2004, ASTM C1585 [55], a standard concerned mostly with the primary sorptivity of concretes, first described a longer-term test in which the imbibition is extended well beyond the primary stage, typically for up to 7 days. This standard defined for the first time a *secondary rate of water absorption*, obtained from the slope of the second-stage Δw vs $t^{1/2}$ plot. This quantity is defined by the equation

$$i = S_2 t^{1/2} + \text{const} \tag{8.8}$$

where $i = \Delta w/(\rho_w A)$ with A the area of the immersed face, and t the elapsed time from the beginning of the test. The quantity S_2 so defined has dimension $[L\ T^{-1/2}]$, just as the sorptivity S, and the same unit, commonly mm/min$^{1/2}$. In technical publications, S_2 is now often called the secondary sorptivity [557, 739, 422, 709, 747, 1304]. While the primary sorptivity is rigorously defined and has a clear theoretical basis, the secondary sorptivity has only recently been placed on a firmer footing [493] and its value as material property has yet to be established.

One distinction between primary and secondary sorptivity not reflected in Eqn 8.8 lies in the relation of imbibed volumes to the size and shape of the test specimen. In measuring the (primary) sorptivity the imbibed volume ΔV_1 is invariably scaled by the area of the inflow face A to yield a value of S that does not depend on the dimensions of the test piece. However, in secondary imbibition, the imbibed volume ΔV_2 depends not on A but on F, the total area of all surfaces at which air can escape. This total surface area includes all unsealed faces, whether immersed or not. So while the correct experimental quantity for calculating the primary sorptivity is $\Delta V_1/A$, that for the secondary sorptivity is $\Delta V_2/F$. To obtain a true secondary sorptivity it is then logical to use the scaled quantity $i_2 = \Delta V_2/F$ in Eqn 8.8. Limited data on test specimens of different shape support this view [493]. More broadly, we note that it is far from certain that the secondary imbibition consistently scales as $t^{1/2}$, as required by Eqn 8.8. The effects of pressure equalization shown in Figure 8.6 make clear that there can be strong deviations from $t^{1/2}$-behaviour in the early stages of secondary imbibition; and both theory and experiment show deviations in long-term behaviour as the test specimen approaches saturation, as we see for instance in Figures 8.2 and 8.8.

Significance of the secondary sorptivity

Although the water-transport mechanisms at work in primary and secondary imbibition are different, both depend on capillarity to fill open porosity. There can therefore be no objection to using the term sorptivity to describe both. In primary imbibition, capillary forces act to draw water (or other liquid) into the material at a rate which is controlled by the strength of these forces and by the resistance of the material to viscous flow. It is assumed (implicitly) that no resistance arises from the viscous flow of the displaced air. This conforms to the accepted definition of spontaneous imbibition [15]. In contrast, the rate of secondary imbibition is controlled by the resistance of the saturated material to the molecular diffusion of air in water. This depends on the properties of air and water, and on certain properties of the material, although the material properties involved are not the same as those controlling primary imbibition. The secondary sorptivity is determined by the rate of change of the trapped-air volume. Secondary imbibition is a particular case of forced imbibition, in which the saturation front is close to mechanical equilibrium at all times. The strength of the capillary forces and the viscous impedance do not directly influence the rate of movement of the front. Because the rate of primary imbibition is usually much greater than that of secondary imbibition, the two processes may be treated as though they are sequential. In summary, the secondary sorptivity characterizes the tendency of a porous material to release trapped or entrained air by molecular diffusion. Defined in this way, the secondary sorptivity excludes any contribution to the release of air by advection in pore water.

Our earlier theoretical analysis of trapped-air diffusion has uncovered some complexities in the mechanism. However, broadly speaking, in secondary imbibition the timescale for reaching saturation depends primarily (and simply) on the initial volume fraction of trapped air, $\lambda_a f = (1 - h)f$. There seems no reason to expect a strong dependence on pore-size. Neither do we expect much dependence on the trapped-air pressure. The mass of air in a given volume of trapped air is proportional to the pressure, but by Henry's law the mass of air that dissolves is also proportional to the pressure, thus largely cancelling the influence of pressure. As yet there are no systematic tests of the underlying theory, but we see at least qualitative agreement with this explanatory model in Figure 8.8. Here the time to reach saturation is about 160 d for Ancaster stone and about 440 d for Clipsham stone, a ratio of about 2.8, in more or less the same ratio as their $\lambda_a f$ values.

8.2   SOME PHYSICAL EFFECTS OF MOISTURE

A detailed discussion of the dimensional changes which accompany wetting and drying in porous materials is outside the scope of this book, although these changes are often closely coupled to water transport. In this section we mention briefly a few topics which are of practical significance.

8.2.1   Shrinkage and expansion in cements and binders

The dimensional changes that occur in cementitious materials as a result of wetting and drying have been extensively studied and comprehensively reviewed (see for example [114, 872, 112]). In construction applications it is the drying shrinkage that occurs in cement-based materials that is of the greater practical importance. As the solid dries the loss of free water has little effect, but further drying, resulting in loss of adsorbed water from the gel particles, causes significant shrinkage. This drying shrinkage is not fully reversible on wetting. In concretes approximately half of the drying shrinkage is irreversible. Typically cyclic moisture movement produces a reversible strain of order 10^{-4} in concretes and mortars. The amount of reversible moisture movement depends to some extent on the degree of hydration with better cured materials showing smaller reversible strains.

We have already discussed in Chapter 4 the effect of the swelling reactions on the water absorption properties of initially dry cementitious specimens.

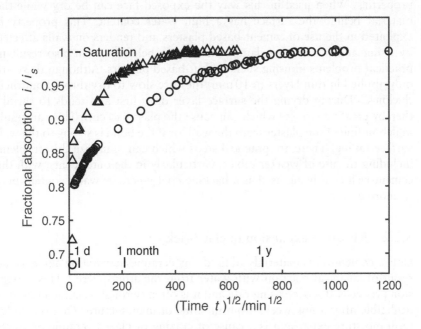

Figure 8.8 Long-term imbibition of water in two 50 mm limestone cubes at 25 °C [472]: △ Ancaster limestone, $f = 0.143$, $\lambda_a = 0.11$; ○ Clipsham limestone, $f = 0.214$, $\lambda_a = 0.21$.

The linear expansion follows a $t^{1/2}$ relationship as water is absorbed by capillarity. The water sorptivities of these materials are anomalously low [509]. Significantly, there are also further reductions in water absorption rates in the long term (as we saw in Figure 4.23). Consistent with these results, the hydraulic permeability of cementitious materials is also anomalously low [1221], as noted in Chapter 3. These effects clearly modify the hydraulic barrier properties of concretes and mortars; and generally they must be beneficial in reducing the rate of ingress of water and salt solutions.

In practical engineering design we can detail buildings and structures to accommodate the overall changes in dimensions that must occur as cement-based solids dry. However, the water transport processes during drying can result in practical problems. We have seen that cement-based materials dry slowly. The surface layers dry first but the flow of water from the inner regions of the solid to the drying surface is slow, producing a low and decreasing rate of stage II drying. In this respect the kinetics of drying of cement-based solids are quite different from those observed in clay brick and stone materials, in which stage I drying is more prolonged and redistribution of water is relatively rapid during stage II. The unusual drying characteristics of cement-based materials give them valuable hydraulic properties. When used in this way the exposed face can be dry while the material behind the surface has a high water content. This property is exploited in the use of cement-based plasters and renders on walls affected by rising and penetrating damp. The drying behaviour can also result in practical problems in using such cement-based plasters. Although these are only applied in thin layers ($\approx$10 mm) they are slow to dry throughout their thickness. During drying the surface layer dries first and tends to shrink, thereby creating stresses which can cause the plaster to curl. This can result in debonding of the plaster from the wall, or if the bond is strong to the wall surface failing. There are practical steps which can minimize this problem, including the use of weaker mixes, particularly in the outer coats, with the cement-rich coat being used as a backing coat where its water content may be more uniform.

8.2.2   Moisture expansion in clay brick

Unlike cementitious materials all fired clay ceramics *expand* on aging as the result of chemical reaction with water from the atmosphere.[4] This expansion proceeds at a decreasing rate and it is often (wrongly) claimed that it is negligible after a few weeks from the time of manufacture. That this long-term moisture expansion is a cause of crazing of glazed ceramic products was first suggested by Schurecht [1140]. It was not until some 20 years later that moisture expansion was recognized as a cause of cracking in brickwork [803], perhaps because earlier brick masonry had used soft lime mortars that accommodated some structural movement. It is generally found that the long-term expansion of clay brick and tile is about 0.1–0.4 per cent linear strain [593, 594, 1168, 824, 1182, 516, 503].

The expansion is caused by a slow chemical rehydration reaction between water and some components of the fired ceramic [529]. The amount of water needed to sustain the expansive reaction is extremely small, and can be supplied by transport through the pore system of the brick even at low humidities. The rate of reaction is controlled by diffusion of water within the solid phases of the ceramic matrix rather than by mass transport within the pores.

Bricks fired at higher temperatures and those made from lime-bearing clays show less expansion, while compositions richer in alkalis tend to show larger expansions [1351, 1182, 503]. Cole [265] was the first to make the ultimately fruitful link between moisture expansion and mass gain, showing that the expansion was accompanied by an increase in mass, and that roughly but not exactly the two were proportional. Later work [1327] shows that the mass gain can be measured more accurately than the expansion strain itself. The expansion process is accelerated by high-temperature steaming in an autoclave. Normal prolonged wetting by storage under water or in a high humidity atmosphere does not produce significantly faster expansion than normal exposure in ambient atmospheric conditions.

Power-law description of expansion

Various logarithmic relationships describing the expansion versus time have been suggested [264, 268, 267]. Subsequent work [821, 1327, 516, 503] has led to the alternative conclusion that both the expansion and the associated mass gain increase as $t^{1/4}$, where t is the elapsed time since firing, that is to say

$$\epsilon = at^{1/4} + b \qquad\qquad (8.9)$$

where ϵ is the moisture-expansion strain. The constant b describes a rapid transient expansion which occurs immediately after firing and which stabilizes in (at most) several days. The first term, $at^{1/4}$, describes the long-term expansion gain which arises from the chemical combination of the ceramic with environmental moisture. Here a, a constant which we call the *moisture expansivity* [502], is a material property which describes the magnitude of the progressive long-term moisture expansion. The transient process (associated with b) and the long-term process (associated with a) are mechanistically and kinetically distinct. The transient expansion is reversible and its magnitude is humidity dependent. The long-term expansion is reversible only by re-firing to about 500 °C. As the rehydroxylation reaction which underlies the long-term moisture expansion is extremely slow, sufficient environmental moisture is generally available to feed the reaction, and for all practical purposes the long-term process is insensitive to the ambient humidity.

In Figure 8.9, we show published expansion strain data ϵ replotted against $t^{1/4}$, indicating excellent agreement with Eqn 8.9 over many years of measurement. The duration of these experiments is remarkable, extending over several decades and in the case of the wall at the National Physical Laboratory over 64 years. Evidently there must be a time after which no further chemical recombination is possible because the capacity of the material for reaction is exhausted, but this time appears to be extremely long, perhaps thousands of years. Indeed steam autoclaving experiments on Roman brick [1327] have shown that there is considerable reactivity after 2000 y.[5] The unusual $t^{1/4}$ power law of moisture expansion indicates that the underlying diffusion of water in the matrix is anomalous, but a satisfactory explanation is still to be found.

Construction aspects

The $t^{1/4}$ law provides guidance [503] for estimating expansion effects in brick masonry or in fired-clay ceramic tiling. In masonry design, it is usually assumed that expansive effects are unimportant provided that bricks are not used until some days or perhaps weeks after firing. In fact, the $t^{1/4}$ dependence of Eqn 8.9 shows that equal amounts of expansion occur after 1, 16,

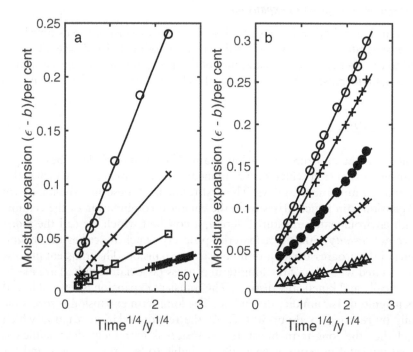

Figure 8.9 Moisture expansion in fired-clay brick fitted to the $t^{1/4}$ power law, Eqn 8.9. (a) Data of Smith [1182] extending over 28 years: ○ Devonian shale brick fired at 1025 °C, × Keuper marl fired at 950 °C, □ Keuper marl fired at 1025 °C; + data over 64 y from test wall at the National Physical Laboratory [266, 1181, 516]. (b) Data on natural moisture expansion of groups of Australian bricks over 35 y [1374]: bricks grouped by steam-autoclave expansion, ○ 0.075 per cent, + 0.045 per cent, ● 0.025 per cent, × 0.015 per cent, △ 0.005 per cent.

81, 256 ... units of time. Building structures are designed for long lifetimes and the cumulative expansion continues indefinitely, albeit at a diminishing rate. It is perhaps surprising that in modern structures using hard cement-based mortars that we have not seen more problems caused by moisture expansion.[6] Unrestrained expansion strains are large, and in such stiff materials [478] rehydroxylation may lead to large stresses in restrained structures [495]. Creep in mortar joints perhaps reduces these long-term effects, but that the expansion process continues over the long term is certain. We remark also that the moisture expansivity increases markedly with increasing temperature. This points to the more severe effects of moisture expansion in warmer climates noted by McNeilly [824], or in any situation where high lifetime temperatures are experienced.

8.2.3 Chemical action in water transport

Chemical action is so strongly coupled to the process of water transport in building materials that it is an almost universal feature of it. All inorganic materials are composed of minerals and all minerals are to some extent soluble.[7] Water migration also carries atmospheric pollutants, salts and other contaminants into the fabric from the environment. Whether the chemical action is a minor secondary aspect or a primary feature depends on the case, but there are many situations where the chemical action is the primary process and the water transport the means of delivering it. The various forms of chemical action, which include chemical reaction, dissolution (leaching) and deposition, are frequently the principal cause of mechanical damage in building materials. It is these complex interactions which set limits to the durability of brick, stone and concrete [428]. Many effects of chemical transport are deleterious and involve chemical reactions or chemo-mechanical action such as crystallization stress. Such effects underlie various kinds of long-term deterioration in masonry structures, in concrete and in stone weathering. There is a close relation between these processes in brick, stone and concrete [586, 865, 31, 48, 130, 1359, 276, 277, 25, 1133] and salt weathering effects in rocks [434]. It is outside the scope of this book to discuss coupling of water transport and chemical action in detail.

8.3 SLURRIES: WATER RETENTION AND TRANSFER

Mortars and plasters are a distinctive group of construction materials that are processed in the soft state and then set and harden over time. Good workability, adhesion, strength and durability require fine control of water content not only in the wet mixes themselves but also after they are applied, often as thin coatings, to absorbent backgrounds such as brick or stone or block. The water retention and water transfer properties of wet plaster mixes and bricklaying mortars have received surprisingly little scientific attention and deserve more.[8] The main matter of engineering significance is how to represent their hydraulic properties, especially those which control the desorption of water. We shall show that the physics of desorption can be described in much the same language as unsaturated flow in hardened materials. In fact the dewatering of soft wet materials can be represented by models which closely resemble either the Sharp Front model of unsaturated flow or the nonlinear diffusion formulation of Buckingham-Richards theory, both of which of course we discuss at length in this book. These approaches have been developed primarily in connection with the filtration and sedimentation of granular slurries used in mineral processing and oilfield engineering. They can be adopted also for wet mix construction materials such as mortars and plasters and provide a firm basis for materials specification and testing.

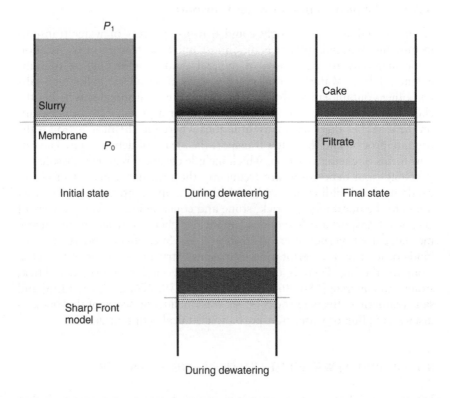

Figure 8.10 Pressure dewatering of a slurry.

Using a common language and theoretical framework for water transfer in wet (soft) mixes and in unsaturated (hard) materials is valuable because it allows us to treat cases where both kinds of material are present. In particular, we shall analyze the important *composite* case of water transfer from a wet mix into a dry substrate by capillary suction.

Figure 8.10 shows the stages in the dewatering of a slurry on a thin filter membrane which is permeable to water but not to solid particles. The driving force for the desorption of water is a pressure difference $\Delta P = P_1 - P_0$ acting across the slurry. Here ΔP is produced by a compressed gas or a piston but it may also be generated by capillary suction as we shall see later. During desorption, water and particles move towards the membrane but because of the filtering action the water also moves relative to the particles. The motion of the water relative to the particles is described by Darcy's law $u = -kdP/dz$ (that is, there is a viscous flow pressure gradient at every point, which is described by Darcy's law). In the general case, there is a gradient of particle concentration ϕ_s from top to bottom of the slurry and the Darcy permeability k (strictly a hydraulic conductivity) varies with particle concentration. The equilibrium particle concentration at any pressure depends on interparticle forces: the pressure-concentration curve maps out the hydraulic potential of the water in the slurry and is a material property. Combining the concentration-dependent form of Darcy's law with material balances yields equations which describe the entire slurry filtration/consolidation process.

In the constant pressure, one-dimensional case shown in Figure 8.10, the cumulative volume of water expressed increases as the square root of the time, $t^{1/2}$, thus $i = Rt^{1/2}$. The desorptivity $R(P)$ is a material property of the slurry and depends strongly on the applied pressure. The concentration-distance profiles during desorption vary with time as $t^{1/2}$ and analysis of these can be used to obtain the hydraulic diffusivity D of the slurry, in the same way that the hydraulic diffusivity for unsaturated flow is obtained from water content profiles. If the slurry has a compressive yield stress then no filtration occurs and no water is expressed until the pressure exceeds this [837].

This approach to slurry filtration has its origin in a paper by Smiles [1170] who showed that the filtration of a suspension can be described by the same nonlinear diffusion equation as used for unsaturated flow. It has been developed in many later publications by Smiles [1171, 1172, 981, 1177, 1175] and others. The theory has been applied to a series of problems in oil-field engineering, in particular the fluid loss of clay and cement slurries, by Meeten and his collaborators [830, 1151]. We shall have more to say about this approach later in Section 8.3.5.

8.3.1 Sharp Front analysis of slurry dewatering

We can simplify the full analysis by using a Sharp Front approximation in which we assume that during dewatering a distinct filtercake is formed which has a well-defined solids content: in other words that the cake is a compact porous material of definite and uniform porosity. Let us consider a simple one-dimensional pressure-driven filtration process (Figure 8.10) in which a length L of slurry is dewatered. At the beginning of the process, the slurry has volume fraction ϕ_{si} of solids which is uniform. The initial volume fraction of water in the slurry of course is $\phi_{wi} = 1 - \phi_{si}$. As dewatering proceeds, a cake is formed which has a solids content ϕ_{sc}, also uniform. The length L of slurry produces a cake of thickness $L_c = L\phi_{si}/\phi_{sc} = L\beta$. The amount of desorbed or expelled water (the cumulative desorption) is

$$i = L(\phi_{wi} - \phi_{si}\phi_{wc}/\phi_{sc}) = L\alpha \tag{8.10}$$

where ϕ_{wc} is the volume fraction of water in the cake. Clearly $L_c + i = L$, $i = L_c\alpha/\beta$ and $\alpha + \beta = 1$. Throughout the dewatering process, the cake thickness builds up in proportion to the amount of water desorbed and at a rate which is controlled by the permeability K_c of the cake.[9] Therefore by Darcy's law

$$\frac{di}{dt} = -K_c \frac{\Delta P}{L_c} = -K_c \frac{\alpha}{\beta} \frac{\Delta P}{i}. \tag{8.11}$$

Hence

$$i = \left(\frac{2K_c \Delta P \alpha}{\beta}\right)^{1/2} t^{1/2} = Rt^{1/2}. \tag{8.12}$$

We therefore have a desorption process in which the cumulative volume of expressed water increases as $t^{1/2}$ and the desorptivity

$$R = (2K_c \Delta P \alpha / \beta)^{1/2}. \tag{8.13}$$

This simple description of dewatering is appropriate for slurries which contain hard particles which pack to form a more or less incompressible cake. Equation 8.13 shows us that the desorptivity depends on the applied pressure and increases as $\Delta P^{1/2}$. R also depends on solids content of both slurry and cake through the factor $(\alpha/\beta)^{1/2} = (\phi_{sc}/\phi_{si} - 1)^{1/2}$. If we take the cake solids content to be a material property independent of P, we see that the desorptivity increases as the solids content of the slurry falls, and varies as $\phi_{si}^{-1/2}$ in the dilute limit $\phi_{si} \ll \phi_{sc}$.

The desorption of water from a simple uniform slurry by the action of a pressure difference leads to the formation of a cake of slurry on the filtering surface. At the point that all the slurry solids are incorporated into the cake, there is a sharp change in the nature of the flow. If no further fluid is available (for example if the pressure is applied by a piston), water flow ceases abruptly. On the other hand if air can enter the system the saturated flow process is succeeded by an unsaturated flow process. This second phase of desorption can of course be represented by the models already described. The cake comes to a residual water content which is determined by its capillary potential and the applied air pressure.

We have described the desorption process in rather simple Sharp Front terms, neglecting the fact that the cake may be compressible and that the boundary between cake and slurry may be diffuse rather than sharp. These complexities are treated in the full mathematical theory [1170, 981, 830].

8.3.2   Measuring slurry hydraulic properties

The theory allows us to replace qualitative and vague notions such as suction and water retention with precisely defined physical properties such as hydraulic potential, desorptivity and hydraulic conductivity. The theory also shows us how such properties may be measured. For example, we may

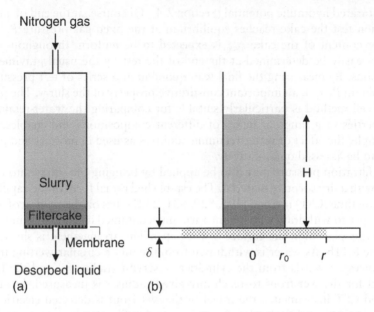

Nitrogen gas

Slurry

Filtercake

Membrane

Desorbed liquid

(a)

H

δ   0 r_0 r

(b)

Figure 8.11 (a) Schematic of pressure filtration cell for slurries. (b) Schematic of capillary suction time test.

determine the desorptivity by one of two methods used by Meeten and his collaborators [829, 831]. The theory predicts that the dewatering of a slurry at constant filtration pressure proceeds as the square root of the elapsed time and varies with applied pressure in a way which depends on the compressibility of the cake.

The pressure filtration method uses gas pressure to cause water to desorb from the slurry. The American Petroleum Institute filtration cell [27], illustrated schematically in Figure 8.11a, is ideal for this purpose. A filter membrane with appropriate particle retention properties is placed at the outflow and a constant gas pressure (typically a few bar) applied to a known volume of wet mix placed in the cell. The rate of desorption is determined by measuring the volume of filtrate as a function of time. As we have seen, at constant pressure the cumulative volume of water desorbed per unit membrane area $i = Rt^{1/2}$, where R is the desorptivity. By carrying out measurements at different pressures, the dependence of the desorptivity on pressure is obtained [1170, 442, 232]. This simple model of the test assumes that neither the membrane itself nor the membrane/cake interface contribute appreciably to the overall resistance to flow, for example by clogging the membrane as the slurry dewaters. Filter membrane effects have been investigated by theory and experiment [1177, 828] and can be detected and allowed for in careful experimental work. We note the similarity between this filter cell for use with slurries and the pressure membrane method of determining the unsaturated hydraulic potential (Section 2.4). Of course, at the end of a desorption test the cake reaches equilibrium at the fixed gas pressure P. The water content of the cake ϕ_{wc} is expected to be uniform throughout and it can easily be determined at the end of the test by the usual gravimetric methods. By measuring the final water content at a series of test pressures, we obtain $P(\phi_{wc})$, an important constitutive property of the slurry. The pressure cell method is particularly suitable for comparing the water-retaining properties of a range of mixes of different compositions and enables, for example, the effect of water-retaining additives as used in mortars and plasters to be assessed quantitatively.

A filtration pressure may also be applied by bringing the slurry into contact with a dry sorptive material. The established radial form of the capillary suction time (CST) method [395, 829, 831, 232] relies on the suction of a filter paper to withdraw water from a wet mix contained in a small cylindrical reservoir placed on the surface of the paper. The arrangement is shown in Figure 8.11b. As water is withdrawn from the mix a circular wetting front advances outwards from the cylindrical reservoir (radius r_0) and the time taken for the wet front to reach any given radius r is measured. In automated CST instruments, the travel of the wet front is detected electrically [91]. The CST is thus the time for a given area of filter paper to be wetted by capillary suction acting on the slurry. Provided that the process is controlled by the hydraulic permeability of the filter cake rather than that of the filter paper, the time of travel of the wet front is given (using a radial flow Sharp Front approximation) by

$$ t = \left(\frac{\pi f_f \delta}{RA} \right)^2 (r^4 - r_0^4) \tag{8.14} $$

where f_f is the porosity of the filter paper, δ its thickness and A is the cross-section area of the reservoir. The porosity of the filter paper is probably best determined by measuring the decrease in volume of slurry in the reservoir as the filtrate spreads outwards between two fixed radii [831]. The desorptivity R can be found from the gradient of a plot of $(r^4 - r_0^4)^{1/2}$ versus $t^{1/2}$. The desorptivity which is measured in the CST test is that which corresponds to the particular suction pressure exerted by the filter paper, plus the pressure arising from the height H of the material in the reservoir. Clearly measurements can be made at different values of H, although in practice this provides only a small range of pressure variation. The capillary suction pressure Ψ_f of the filter paper has been found by measuring the rise of a wetting front in a vertical strip of filter paper with its lower end in a water reservoir [829, 1173]. This is the capillary rise process we have described before (4.5). Although the capillary rise experiment is not a practical way to determine the wet front capillary potential of most building materials (the capillary forces are too strong and the capillary rise timescale too long), the situation is more favourable for filter paper. Here we can apply the simple Sharp Front result for the height of wet front $h(t)$:

$$h = \left(\frac{A^2}{B}\frac{dh}{dt} + A\right)^{-1} \tag{8.15}$$

where $A = \rho g/\Psi_f$, $B = K_e\rho g^2/f_f\Psi_f$, K_e is the effective permeability of the filter paper and ρ is the liquid density. The largest capillary pressures that can be achieved using the CST method are typically an order of magnitude less than the capillary pressures associated with clay brick ceramic. To obtain desorptivity data over a larger pressure range, which reflects the practical situation of mortars or plasters applied to masonry materials, it is necessary to use pressure filtration.

Determining the hydraulic conductivity, diffusivity and potential is more complicated and depends on being able to measure the variation of solids content (or porosity) throughout the cake as a function of time at a series of applied pressures. Destructive methods for doing this are laborious and difficult. Tomographic methods are probably to be preferred. Both have been used to determine the properties of clay suspensions [591, 830, 1176]; and recently to cement mortars [556].

The pressure filtration of cement pastes and grouts has been investigated in several studies [827, 156, 823, 442, 233, 271, 615, 614]. All these reports confirm that desorption at constant pressure is a $t^{1/2}$ process. Green *et al.* [442] measured the desorptivities of a series of cement mortars with and without lime at pressures from 0.03–0.5 MPa (Figure 8.12). The desorptivity R is proportional to ΔP^n with n in the narrow range 0.51–0.68, close to the theoretical value of 0.5 for a stiff, non-compactible material. The 1:3 lime:sand mortar has desorptivity about half that of the cement-based mortars. The addition of water-retaining carboxymethylcellulose additives strongly reduces the desorptivity, demonstrating that the desorptivity is an extremely useful measure of the resistance to dewatering of wet mixes.

8.3.3 Dewatering in controlled permeability formwork

Controlled permeability formwork (CPF) is used to allow deliberate dewatering of the surface layers of cast in situ concrete [1018]. The concrete is placed against forms covered with textile liners. The liners act as filtration membranes and allow water to be expressed from the concrete under the hydrostatic pressure of the wet mix (Figure 8.13). A surface layer of high solids content develops in contact with the formwork, which produces benefits in properties such as permeability and sorptivity [756, 757, 212, 43].

The dewatering process in CPF is a simple application of the process of slurry desorption which we have just described. The textile membrane is freely draining and so maintains an atmospheric pressure boundary condition on the surface of the freshly placed concrete. The wet concrete loses

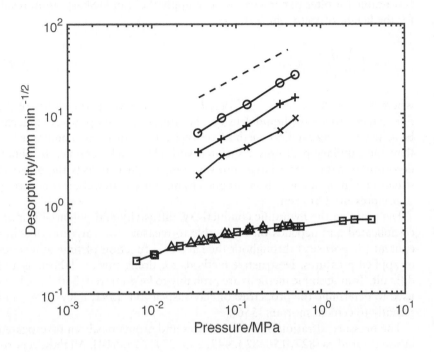

Figure 8.12 Desorptivity of mortars: dependence on filtration pressure. Mortars [442]: ○ 1:5 cement/sand; + 1:3 cement:sand; × 1:3 lime/sand. Bentonite clay: □ [1151]; △ [1176]. Dashed line shows the theoretical slope for an incompressible cake.

water and forms a dense cake which grows inwards. The cake thickness $L_c = i\beta/\alpha = (2K_c\alpha P/\beta)^{1/2}t^{1/2}$ where P is the hydrostatic pressure exerted by the wet concrete, which for a vertical surface is roughly 0.02 MPa/m depth. A rough calculation based on a desorptivity of $5P^{1/2}$ mm/(min MPa)$^{1/2}$ (a figure based on data for mortars [442] reduced by a factor to allow for coarse aggregate) suggests that the dense surface layer against the formwork at 1 m vertical depth below the top of the placed concrete may be about 10 mm thick after 5 h. This thickness increases as (depth)$^{1/2}$. Once the concrete starts to develop strength, the hydrostatic pressure of the pore fluid falls sharply and no more water is expelled.

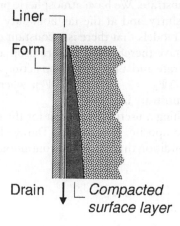

Figure 8.13 Controlled permeability formwork: an application of slurry desorption.

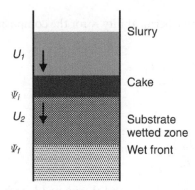

Figure 8.14 Water transfer from a slurry to a dry substrate by capillary action: one-dimensional Sharp Front model.

8.3.4 Wet mixes and dry backgrounds

We have described a Sharp Front theory of simple water desorption from a slurry. The real technical interest lies in using this to describe what happens when a slurry such as a mortar is applied to a dry (or at least less than saturated) substrate such as a brick and is dewatered by capillary suction.

A Sharp Front analysis of the transfer of water from a wet mix to a dry substrate can be developed as follows. We refer to Figure 8.14. The movement of water from the slurry to the substrate is driven by the capillary suction of the substrate. We have atmospheric pressure P_0 both at the upper surface of the slurry and at the far boundary of the substrate. We assume as usual in SF models that there is a constant capillary potential Ψ_f at the wet front. We have therefore a pressure drop acting across the wetted region of the substrate and a pressure drop acting across the cake. Thus $\Delta\Psi = \Psi_f = \Delta\Psi_1 + \Delta\Psi_2 = -\Psi_i + (\Psi_i - \Psi_f)$, where Ψ_i is the hydraulic potential at the cake/substrate interface.

We start by establishing a useful expression for the effective permeability of the cake/substrate composite. We can apply Darcy's law separately to each part and impose the condition that the flux is continuous across the interface, so that

$$\Delta\Psi = -\frac{u_1 L_c}{K_c} - \frac{u_2 L_w}{K_w}. \tag{8.16}$$

where u_1 and u_2 are the flow rates out of the cake and into the substrate. But $u_1 = u_2 = u$, so that

$$\Delta\Psi = -u\left(\frac{L_c}{K_c} + \frac{L_w}{K_w}\right). \tag{8.17}$$

Let us define an effective permeability $\overline{K}$ for the composite system by writing $u = -\overline{K}\Delta\Psi/L$. Then

$$\frac{L_c}{K_c} + \frac{L_w}{K_w} = \frac{L}{\overline{K}} = \frac{L_c + L_w}{\overline{K}} \tag{8.18}$$

so that

$$\overline{K} = \frac{K_c K_w (L_c + L_w)}{L_c K_w + L_w K_c}. \tag{8.19}$$

But the thickness of the cake L_c and the wetted length of the substrate L_w grow in proportion to one another so that $L_c/L_w = r$ where r is a constant. Therefore

$$\overline{K} = \frac{K_c K_w (r + 1)}{K_c + r K_w}. \tag{8.20}$$

Now we have already shown that $i/L_c = \alpha/\beta$ and since $L_w = i/f$, where f is the porosity of the substrate, we see that $r = f\beta/\alpha$. Thus we find that in the one-dimensional capillary suction of water from a wet mix, we can derive an effective permeability $\overline{K}$ which depends only on material properties. Equation 8.19 tells us that when the cake is thin $\overline{K} \to K_w$, and when the cake is thick $\overline{K} \to K_c$.

The existence of an effective permeability which depends only on material properties and does not change with time allows us to obtain some simple results for the complete transfer process. We first apply Darcy's law to the whole system:

$$u = -\overline{K}\frac{\Psi_f}{L_w + L_c}. \tag{8.21}$$

But $i = L\alpha$, $L_w = L\alpha/f$, $L_c = L\beta$ and $r = f\beta/\alpha$. Therefore $L_w + L_c = i(r+1)/f$ and from Eqn 8.21

$$\frac{di}{dt} = -\overline{K}\frac{f\Psi_f}{i(r+1)} \tag{8.22}$$

and

$$i = \left(2\overline{K}\frac{f|\Psi_f|}{r+1}\right)^{1/2} t^{1/2} = At^{1/2}. \tag{8.23}$$

The cumulative transfer i increases as $t^{1/2}$ up to the point at which all the slurry present at $t = 0$ has been dewatered and converted to cake. We call the constant A with dimension $[LT^{-1/2}]$ the *transfer sorptivity*. It is also easy to show that the hydraulic potential at the cake/substrate interface is constant throughout the water transfer process. Since the rates of flow out of the cake and into the substrate are the same we have

$$\frac{K_c\Psi_i}{L_c} = \frac{K_w(\Psi_f - \Psi_i)}{L_w} \tag{8.24}$$

so that

$$\frac{\Psi_f}{\Psi_i} = \frac{K_cL_w}{K_wL_c} + 1. \tag{8.25}$$

But $L_c/L_w = \alpha/f\beta$ which is a constant of the materials. Therefore the hydraulic potential at the interface

$$\Psi_i = \Psi_f\left(\frac{f\beta K_c}{\alpha K_w} + 1\right)^{-1}, \tag{8.26}$$

and does not change during the desorption. This important feature of the process was described by Smiles and Kirby [1176] in their study of dewatering of a bentonite clay slurry using a dry plaster-of-Paris mould.

We take one more step to show how the properties of the slurry and of the substrate control the rate of the water transfer. Since the hydraulic potential at the interface Ψ_i is constant both the growth of the cake and the absorption of water by the substrate are $t^{1/2}$ processes. In effect, Ψ_i settles at a value which makes the desorptivity of the slurry and the sorptivity of the substrate equal to each other [1176, 1173], and both of course are also equal to the transfer sorptivity. We show this graphically in Figure 8.15.

First let us find Ψ_i in terms of material properties. We have seen in Eqn 8.13 that the slurry desorptivity R varies as $\Delta P^{1/2}$. Here the hydraulic potential across the cake must lie between 0 and Ψ_f. Therefore let us write

$$R^2 = R_s^2 \frac{\Psi_i}{\Psi_f} \tag{8.27}$$

where R_s is the slurry desorptivity which matches the substrate suction, that is when $\Delta P = \Psi_f$. Likewise, we have shown in Chapter 4, Eqn 4.40 that the sorptivity of a porous material, here the substrate, varies with the hydraulic potential at the inflow face in such a way that we can write

$$S^2 = S_s^2 \left(1 - \frac{\Psi_i}{\Psi_f}\right) \tag{8.28}$$

where S_s is the standard sorptivity of the substrate with $\Psi_i = 0$. If we put $R = S$, we find that

$$\Psi_i = \Psi_f \frac{S_s^2}{R_s^2 + S_s^2}. \tag{8.29}$$

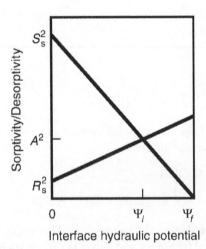

Figure 8.15 Water transfer from a slurry to a dry substrate: The transfer sorptivity A is fixed by the intersection of the slurry desorptivity R and the substrate sorptivity S at the interface hydraulic potential Ψ_i.

and hence

$$R = S = \left(\frac{R_s S_s}{R_s^2 + S_s^2}\right)^{1/2} = A. \tag{8.30}$$

Second, let us express the sorptivities in terms of primary material properties, so that

$$S_s = (2|\Psi_f|)^{1/2}(fK_w)^{1/2} \tag{8.31}$$

and

$$R_s = (2|\Psi_f|)^{1/2}\left(\frac{K_c\alpha}{\beta}\right)^{1/2}. \tag{8.32}$$

From Eqn 8.23 we have for the transfer sorptivity

$$A = (2|\Psi_f|)^{1/2}\left(\frac{fK}{r+1}\right)^{1/2} \tag{8.33}$$

or using Eqn 8.20 with $r = f\beta/\alpha$

$$A = (2|\Psi_f|)^{1/2}\left(\frac{f\alpha K_c K_w}{\alpha K_c + f\beta K_w)}\right)^{1/2}. \tag{8.34}$$

Eqns 8.31, 8.32 and 8.34 lead us to the important headline result that

$$\frac{1}{A^2} = \frac{1}{R_s^2} + \frac{1}{S_s^2}. \tag{8.35}$$

When $R \gg S$ the transfer rate is dominated by the substrate; and when $R \ll S$, it is controlled by the slurry properties.

The Sharp Front model we describe provides the theoretical framework for several experimental studies of water transfer between wet mortars and clay bricks [271, 616, 310]. It was found that the cumulative transfer of water across the brick-mortar interface increases as $t^{1/2}$ as predicted, enabling a transfer sorptivity A to be measured. The mortar desorptivity R and the sorptivity S of the brick substrate were measured independently, and this allowed the relation between these quantities given in Eqn 8.35 to be confirmed. The estimated value of the interface capillary pressure Ψ_i was found to be in the range 0.005–0.020 MPa, depending on the mortar mix composition.

For thin mortar joints, a dry substrate is usually capable of dewatering the wet mortar to an equilibrium water content at which the capillary potential of substrate and mortar become equal. The *time for dewatering* t_{dw} is then an interesting property of the system [616]. For a mortar joint of initial thickness L, we have shown that $i = L\alpha$ and since $i = At^{1/2}$ also, we have $t_{dw} = (L\alpha/A)^2$. Clearly t_{dw} increases as the bed or joint thickness increases and also as the transfer desorptivity decreases. Particularly striking is the dependence of t_{dw} on the mix composition through the parameter α, a result which is useful for optimizing mix design for water retention.

8.3.5   Diffusivity model

The Sharp Front model is a useful approximation to the complete Smiles theory [1170, 981], which is closely analogous to Buckingham-Richards theory for unsaturated flow. The thermodynamic state of the water in the suspension is described by means of a hydraulic or extended Buckingham potential which depends on the solids content of the suspension, often expressed as the void ratio e: thus $\Psi(e)$. An extended form of Darcy's law is used to describe the motion of water relative to particles: $u = -k(e)d\Psi(e)/dx$ where flow is assumed to be driven by the gradient of the potential $\Psi(e)$. This may be generalized to combine the potential arising from particle-liquid interactions with external forces into a total potential $\Phi = \Psi + P$ where P includes hydrostatic and applied pressures. By an equation of continuity we obtain a Richards equation for the time evolution of the water content

$$\frac{\partial e}{\partial t} = \frac{\partial}{\partial m}\left[D(e)\frac{\partial e}{\partial m}\right]. \tag{8.36}$$

Here $m = \int_0^z (1+e)^{-1}dz$ is a coordinate variable based on the distribution of material in the system. Smiles' original formulation of pressure filtration was strongly influenced by earlier work on unsaturated flow in swelling soils, where questions also arise about the coordinate frame in which to set the analysis.

The full machinery of the Smiles theory is needed for suspensions which are strongly colloidal in nature, in which the cakes formed in filtration are progressively consolidated with increasing pressure. In the case of mortars and plasters, the evidence which we have is that the cakes are almost incompressible. Water may move relatively freely in the wet mix and the hydraulic potential is close to zero since there are at most only weak colloidal forces acting. The slurry may be dewatered at comparatively low pressures up to the point where a dense cake is formed. Further dewatering only occurs at much larger pressures to consolidate the cake further. In forming a dense cake, the particles come into something resembling a random close packing, with direct particle-particle contacts. At this point there is a marked reduction in permeability. It is in this sense that the 'two-state' Sharp Front model appears to be appropriate. The water retention of the slurry is largely or entirely kinetic (that is, controlled by the hydraulic conductivity of the cake) up to the point that all the available slurry is dewatered. Further desorption then entails entry of air into the pore system and capillary forces come into play [556].

8.3.6 Plastering and bond

The trade practices of bricklaying and plastering involve water flow from soft solid (mortar or plaster) to substrate (brick or block material). The flow results from a difference in hydraulic potential between the soft solid and substrate, and the tension forces which produce the capillary flow act on the soft solid to draw it into intimate contact with the surface. The practical consequences are particularly evident in plastering. The capillary suction which the substrate exerts on water held in the soft plaster mix pulls the plaster against the vertical or horizontal surface to which it is applied. The greater the rate of water transfer, the greater is the viscous drag on the particles of the wet mix pulling them into contact with the surface of the substrate. Dewatering also consolidates the wet mix, increasing its solids volume fraction ϕ_s and enhancing its stiffness.[10]

On walls and ceilings, the substrate suction must also overcome the effects of the gravitational forces acting on the wet mix which would otherwise cause the freshly placed plaster layer to flow and sag, and water within it to drain downwards. Let us call this additional contribution to the total potential Φ_g. At first, the entire weight of the wet layer is probably carried by the capillary water and opposes the capillary tension generated by absorption into the substrate. At this stage $\Phi_g \approx \rho g L$, where ρ is the slurry density and L the thickness of the layer. Water is withdrawn from the wet mix until the condition is reached when $\Psi_{\text{substrate}} = \Psi_{\text{plaster}} + \Phi_g$, although as the slurry consolidates as it dewaters the weight of the plaster layer is increasingly carried by the solid part of the cake, so that Φ_g falls. Eventually when the plaster sets, $\Psi_{\text{substrate}} = \Psi_{\text{plaster}}$, the usual condition of hydraulic equilibrium between unsaturated materials in hydraulic contact. The adhesive bond, part mechanical and part chemical, develops when the hydrate crystals of the plaster lock into the microscopic roughness and pores of the substrate surface.

If the sorptivity of the substrate is low as for example in the case of a wall of dense concrete or of clay engineering bricks, then the substrate may be unable to generate sufficient capillary tension to support the weight of the wet layer, so that $\Psi_{\text{substrate}} < \Psi_{\text{plaster}} + \Phi_g$. It may be impossible to carry out plastering satisfactorily without taking additional steps to improve adhesion. These include using adhesive bonding agents and roughening the substrate surface to improve the microscopic keying of the plaster to the wall in the hardened state. Scratching, abrading or hacking the surface may also increase the capillary suction forces acting on the wet mix by removing a low sorptivity surface layer from the substrate. In concrete there is often a dense surface layer of low sorptivity and some engineering bricks have a vitrified surface which is less sorptive than the interior of the brick.

On the other hand if the sorptivity of the substrate is high, water is withdrawn rapidly from the soft plaster. A thin plaster layer can provide only a small amount of water before it is entirely converted into a compact cake. If the substrate suction is high, the cake itself rapidly loses more water and becomes unsaturated. When water transfer equilibrium is reached the water content of the plaster layer may be below the air-entry value. In consequence liquid continuity breaks down at the interface and with it the continuity of capillary tension. Excessive dewatering of the plaster layer also reduces the water available for chemical hydration. Both effects increase the risk of poor bonding.

It is interesting to analyze the practical steps that are normally taken to attempt to overcome the disadvantages of high sorptivity substrates. Pre-wetting of high suction surfaces prior to plastering has long been employed, and high sorptivity bricks are routinely pre-wetted in bricklaying [454]. We noted Thoreau's comment at the beginning of Chapter 2. At first sight it might be thought that the effect of pre-wetting is to reduce the sorptivity of the substrate. In Chapter 4, we discussed the variation of sorptivity with uniform water content. Following that analysis we see that to reduce clay brick sorptivity by a factor of two the water content of the brick needs to be increased to ≈ 70 per cent of saturation. To achieve a uniform water content as high as this requires prolonged soaking of individual bricks or sustained wetting of a wall. This is both impractical and undesirable for other reasons. Surface wetting, as carried out in practice by brief immersion or flooding, will not cause a significant reduction in sorptivity of high sorptivity materials. In support of this conclusion, Gummerson *et al.* [462] showed that the total *amount* of water withdrawn in 30 min from a soft mortar mix placed on a clay brick was unaffected by pre-wetting the bricks unless long (half-hour) soaking times were used.

However, pre-wetting does have an important effect. The rate of absorption of free water by a porous solid of sorptivity S is $u = \frac{1}{2}St^{-1/2} = \frac{1}{2}S^2/i$, and the initial rate of absorption is very high ($u \to \infty$ as $t \to 0$ and $i \to 0$). A brief pre-wetting satisfies this high initial rate of absorption before the wet mix is applied. If a mortar or plaster is then quickly placed in contact with the substrate the initial rate of withdrawal of water is much slower than it would be had the surface not been pre-wetted. Effectively the dewatering of the wet mix commences well after the overall absorption process itself (Figure 8.16), when the cumulative absorption i_0 equals the amount of water supplied in pre-wetting. A slower initial rate of absorption u_0 allows the opportunity for an even distribution of water in the wet layer so that there is less likelihood of a breakdown of hydraulic continuity at the interface. This leads us to conclude that pre-wetting high sorptivity substrates can only be effective if carried out immediately before the mortar or plaster is applied. The value of pre-wetting is much reduced if there is a delay in applying the wet mix. NMR methods have provided valuable experimental

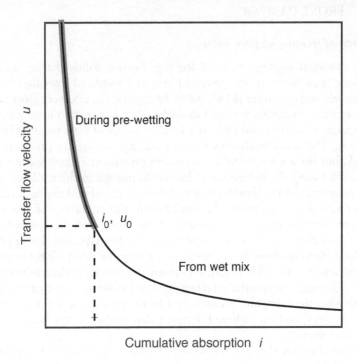

During pre-wetting

i_0, u_0

From wet mix

Transfer flow velocity u

Cumulative absorption i

Figure 8.16 Water transfer from a plaster coat to a sorptive substrate. The solid curve shows how the rate of absorption u varies with the cumulative absorption i. u_0 is the initial rate of absorption from a wet mix applied immediately after a brief pre-wetting in which a quantity i_0 is absorbed.

data on water distributions on water transfer at the mortar-brick interface [182, 184].

An alternative to pre-wetting is to use water-retaining additives such as carboxymethylcelluloses in mortars or plasters. These produce mixes of low desorptivity [442] with the result that high sorptivity backgrounds do not withdraw water from them so rapidly. It is likely that water soluble polymers reduce the desorptivity and the transfer sorptivity mainly by increasing the viscosity of the desorbed liquid (thereby decreasing the effective permeability of the wetted region K_e). Water retaining additives are sometimes recommended for use with autoclaved aerated concretes which are often considered to be high suction materials. In fact many AACs have lower sorptivities than many clay bricks.

8.4   FROST DAMAGE

Effects of freezing on pore water

The practical consequences of freezing porous solids that contain water include frost heave of the ground [953] and localized fracture of masonry materials and concretes [1148, 989]. To explain the effects of frost action on any of these materials we must describe what happens to pore water as the temperature of the solid falls to a level at which at least some of this water freezes. The solid mechanics of frost damage is outside the scope of this book, but the associated water transport phenomena merit some attention.

In discussing the behaviour of liquids in porous media we have seen that the properties of the liquid–gas interface are critical in defining water movement and water retention. At equilibrium, the curvature of this interface is controlled by the surface tension of the liquid and the contact angle of the liquid at the walls of the capillary pores. In extending this approach to include freezing phenomena, we consider now the interface between ice and liquid water [544, 545, 1125]. As before, the curvature determines the pressure difference across the interface and as before the contact angle which establishes the curvature is controlled by the balance of interfacial tensions, here σ_{IS}, σ_{IL}, and σ_{SL}, where I, L and S denote the ice, the liquid water and the pore surface.

If we consider the freezing of water held in a cylindrical capillary pore there will be an excess pressure in the ice phase because the ice–water interface is curved. This excess pressure is $2\sigma_{IL}/r$, where σ_{IL} is the surface tension of the ice phase and r is the radius of the capillary (assuming that the contact angle is zero). Because the ice phase is under an excess pressure its freezing point is depressed. If we consider as an example water held in capillaries of radius 10^{-8} m, the excess pressure in the ice phase is about 47 atm and the freezing point is depressed by approximately 5 K. To depress the freezing point of bulk water by 5 K requires a pressure on both phases of approximately 650 atm (see Appendix B, Table B.4).

In many practical situations solids which are subject to freezing are unsaturated so that the analysis has to take account of the presence of solid, liquid and gas phases. The extension of the capillary theory to three phase systems has also been considered by Haynes [544, 545].

In an alternative approach the Kelvin equation (p 49)

$$\ln \frac{p_w}{p_{w0}} = -\frac{2M_w\sigma_w}{RT\rho_w r} \tag{8.37}$$

has been used to predict the freezing point depression of capillary water. Here p_w is the vapour pressure over the meniscus, p_{w0} is the saturation vapour pressure of the bulk liquid and M_w the molar mass of water. Thus the water in a partially filled capillary is under a reduced vapour pressure due to the curvature of the air–water interface. Once the temperature falls below 0 °C any bulk water external to the capillary will freeze, and as it is cooled further the vapour pressure of the bulk ice falls. A temperature is eventually reached at which the vapour pressure of the capillary water is greater than that of the bulk ice. For water held in a cylindrical capillary of radius 10^{-8} m, this temperature is about 260 K, suggesting a freezing point depression of ≈ 14 K rather than 5 K as calculated from the Haynes analysis. It can be argued that at this temperature the capillary water is under a thermodynamic force to desorb from the capillary to the bulk ice, external to the capillary, where it will freeze.

The approach based on the Haynes analysis and the approach based on the Kelvin equation are both founded on the same fundamental principles. The difference in freezing point depression calculated from these two approaches are associated with the use of different values of surface tension. If the liquid water is to freeze in the capillary the important interface is that between the growing ice crystal and the water. When the Kelvin equation is used the relevant interface is that between liquid and vapour.

In summary these thermodynamic analyses suggest that pressures are developed due to the curvature of the ice-water interface as water freezes in a capillary and that stresses may arise due to rapid desorption of water via the vapour phase once the temperature falls below 0 °C. In addition there is clearly a potential source of damaging stress due to the 9 per cent increase in volume that occurs when water freezes. It is on the basis of these various potential sources of stress that the main theories of frost action have been developed.

Theories of damage caused by freezing

Everett [356] developed a thermodynamic (or capillary) theory of frost action that can be explained by reference to the diagram shown in Figure 8.17. Heat is withdrawn from the top of the system shown so that bulk ice forms in the large open region at the top. In this model it is assumed

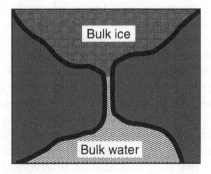

Figure 8.17 Everett's capillary theory of frost action.

that there is room to accommodate the volume change on freezing and that the system allows the pressures in bulk ice and bulk water to remain equal. Under these circumstances, once the freezing front reaches the capillary, ice cannot grow into the capillary because this would require the formation of a curved ice–water interface and the generation of excess pressure in the ice phase. But at any temperature just below 0 °C, the chemical potential of bulk ice is less than that of the bulk water, and so the water in the reservoir will migrate through the capillary to the bulk ice where it then freezes. This process results in the growth of an ice lens at the top of the system. This is the process which causes frost heave in soils. The formation of ice lenses was described as long ago as 1765 by Runeberg, and quoted by Everett.

More generally the excess pressure which can be built up in a coarse pore of radius R connected to a supply of water by a capillary of radius r is proportional to $(1/r - 1/R)$. In soils, provided this excess pressure exceeds the pressure due to the overburden, water will flow up into the freezing zone to form ice lenses which in turn lift the overburden. Consistent with this theory is the empirical Casagrande criterion which suggests that frost heave is less the more uniform the particle size of the soil. The introduction of fine material into a uniform, coarse particle sized soil increases $(1/r - 1/R)$ and leads to increased frost heave.

In rigid porous solids, including clay brick and building stones, it is suggested that the excess pressure in the ice phase can lead to damaging stresses sufficient to cause fracture. This argument is supported by the observation that building stones which show good frost resistance tend to have a coarse-pored structure without microporous regions, so that $(1/r - 1/R)$ is small.

Of course, in a rigid solid a bulk ice lens cannot grow. However, the ice phase still has to be under the excess pressure $2\sigma_{SL}/r$ before the ice can grow into a capillary. Should the solid develop a crack before this pressure is reached then an ice lens will grow. Garden [402] has observed such lenses in frost-damaged masonry.

This thermodynamic or capillary theory of frost action has been further developed by Everett and Haynes [357], who have considered freezing in various geometrical situations including solids made up of close-packed spheres. This approach is successful in modelling soils, but it is arguable as to whether a masonry material can be satisfactorily represented in this manner. A similar derivation of thermodynamic theory has been developed by Beruto *et al.* [119], who also acknowledge that the 9 per cent increase in volume on freezing may be a major contributor to frost damage. The application of the thermodynamic theory has been investigated by Blachere and Young [134, 135, 136] and their results are broadly supported by the earlier work of Watson [1302]. Their experimental data show that capillary theory cannot provide the sole explanation of frost damage in ceramics. It should be noted also that their tests used omnidirectional freezing rather the unidirectional freezing that generally occurs in practice.

An alternative approach to explain frost damage, which is also based on thermodynamic theory, has been developed by Litvan and investigated experimentally in a series of papers [743, 744, 745, 746]. In essence this theory is based on the fact that the freezing point depression of capillary water results in it having a higher vapour pressure than bulk ice on the surface of a porous solid. As we have discussed the resultant thermodynamic force will encourage this water to be desorbed through the vapour phase to the surface of the specimen where it will freeze. Frost damage is exacerbated by any hindrance to desorption. Such factors as low permeability, high water content and rapid freezing will all hinder desorption and increase the risk of damage. An important point is made [744] concerning any voids within a specimen that are large enough for water contained within them to be regarded as bulk liquid. During the desorption process they will become full of water and the 9 per cent increase in volume on freezing will cause potentially disruptive forces to build up.

It is clear that the theories of frost action we have outlined have support from experimental observations. The formation of ice lenses during frost heave in the ground is clear evidence of the flow of liquid into the freezing zone. On the other hand vapour transfer and subsequent freezing is indicated by the formation of ice droplets on the outer surfaces of specimens after freezing. It is also clear that the expansion of water on freezing will develop additional forces within a porous solid. If we consider unidirectional freezing, which is normal in most practical construction situations, water must flow away from the freezing zone to accommodate the volume increase or must expand into unfilled pore space in the case of partially-saturated solids. A hydraulic theory to explain frost damage in terms of hydraulic pressures resulting from these flows was first developed by Powers [1008, 1009], but was later [1015, 1012] revised. His analysis was based on frost action in concretes rather than in brick ceramic or stone. As we have noted earlier, concrete materials generally have a much lower permeability than these other materials and consequently higher stresses can be developed by the resistance to capillary water flow.

It has also been noted [694] that the permeability will itself change as the water in pores solidifies and in turn this will increase the hydraulic stresses that are developed.

In practice it is well-established that the freeze-thaw durability of concrete is enhanced by air entrainment. This observation supports the theory that frost damage is due to the build up of hydraulic pressures in these materials. The air entrainment pores are much larger than the capillary pores and so do not readily fill with water by suction. They thus provide space into which water may flow during freezing. The freeze-thaw durability of concrete is affected by the separation of these pores [362] and also by whether or not the concrete is operating in conditions under which these pores may become filled with water.

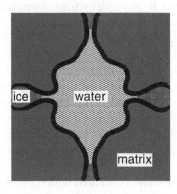

Figure 8.18 Schematic of entrapment of unfrozen water.

Prout's experiments

Evidence for another source of damaging stresses during freeze-thaw cycling is found in the work of Prout [1026, 1027], who carried out unidirectional freezing of saturated clay brick and stone materials down to −15 °C. Results suggest that even at this temperature a significant amount of water remains unfrozen in a 'fully-frozen' specimen. The thermodynamic analysis shows that only water held in pores of radius less than 3×10^{-9} m will remain unfrozen at this temperature. The total volume of pores of this size in brick and stone materials is much less than the volume of unfrozen water suggested by the results of these workers, and so the only explanation for the presence of unfrozen water is that it is trapped under pressure. Such entrapment can occur even in unidirectional freezing because of the order in which water-filled pores freeze. As the temperature falls ice will nucleate in the outer pores and subsequently in those which have at least one end at a node in which there is ice present. Because the depression of the freezing point of water held in a capillary pore is greatest in the finest pores, in general the larger pores freeze first. Figure 8.18 is a schematic diagram of a two-dimensional pore network in which freezing leads to entrapment of unfrozen water. In this network the outer medium-sized pores freeze first. The water in the inner larger pore cannot freeze because its freezing temperature is controlled by the narrow pores between it and the medium-sized pores. Once the outer pores have frozen then the water in both the small and the large pores is trapped and any advance of the ice phase into these pores increases the pressure on this trapped water and further depresses its freezing point. That significant amounts of water can be entrapped in this way can be shown by an analysis of the unidirectional freezing of two-dimensional pore networks derived from mercury intrusion porosimetry data [1026].

The pressure necessary for water to remain unfrozen at −15 °C is about 150 MPa, which is considerably greater than the tensile strength of a typical brick ceramic, although the presence of ice probably has a reinforcing effect on the brick material. In contrast the stresses predicted from the thermo-dynamic theory and those predicted from the resistance to water flow are both approximately a factor of 10 lower than brick ceramic tensile strength. Taken together with the experimental evidence for unfrozen water this gives confidence in the view that entrapment is a major contributing source of freeze-thaw damage.

That entrapment of unfrozen water can generate high stresses is seen in omnidirectional freezing. In these circumstances the freezing front advances from all surfaces towards the centre of the specimen being frozen. The expansion associated with the water–ice phase change causes large pressures to build up in the trapped water in the centre of the specimen and this can lead to a characteristic explosive failure of the solid. A similar effect is seen in the omnidirectional freezing of bulk water. Above a critical volume the ice rup-tures. This process has been analyzed by Chatterji [239] who reports water pressures of over 500 atm during refreezing of Antarctic ice.

Omnidirectional freezing, although used in some fundamental labora-tory studies, is unusual in most construction situations. Test procedures to produce the types of freeze-thaw damage that are likely to occur in practice use unidirectional freezing. Several methods are used to assess the extent of freeze-thaw damage during testing. These include simple visual observations, measurement of the dynamic Young's modulus and measurement of strain [1026]. It is well-established that water saturated porous solids expand on freezing and contract on thawing, and it has been shown [1026] that strain measurements provide a particularly sensitive indication of damage. Non-reversible expansion occurs even when no visible damage is apparent. One interesting result [1026, 1027] is that straining is a minimum at the surface which freezes first and is a maximum on the surface which freezes last. This is associated with the observation in laboratory studies that damage also tends to initiate on the face which freezes last – a disturbing finding which suggests that the unexposed faces of construction materials may be suffering damage.

Perhaps the most important aspect of any test procedure is the choice of the initial water content of the test specimens. Lower water contents (<90 per cent saturation) result in less damage. For engineers and others respon-sible for assessing potential damage, there is a need to estimate the probable maximum water contents that will occur in practice. We have seen that brick masonry below damp-proof course (dpc) can reach a fully saturated state. It may also be expected that brick pavers and some retaining walls can also reach saturation. On the other hand, the air entrainment pores in concrete are only likely to fill after being submerged for significant periods of time and the testing of vacuum-saturated specimens might be unreasonable. It is nevertheless clear that the initial water content associated with any test must be defined.

Comment

Each of the theories of frost action has support from experimental observations [953, 305]. The formation of ice lenses during frost heave in the ground is clear evidence of the flow of liquid into the freezing zone. On the other hand vapour transfer and subsequent freezing are indicated by the formation of ice droplets on the outer surfaces of specimens after freezing. That hydraulic pressures build up as a result of the volume expansion on freezing is self-evident, and the effectiveness of air entrainment in improving the freeze-thaw durability of concrete adds weight to the hydraulic theory. Entrapment of unfrozen water can produce high stresses which are fully sufficient to account for observed damage and this theory is supported by experimental data and a thermodynamic analysis of the sequence in which pores freeze.

A common feature of the various theoretical models is that they all suggest that the frost resistance of porous construction materials depends in some way on the pore size distribution and the nature of the pore networks present. The complexity of the problem is seen in the observations of frost damage in clay bricks. Those bricks of high strength and low porosity (engineering bricks) generally suffer little damage on freeze-thaw cycling – although significantly some may be damaged in the more extreme laboratory tests in which vacuum saturated bricks are used. On the other hand low strength, high porosity bricks often show poor frost resistance. The interesting observation is that some low strength, high porosity hand-made bricks show quite exceptional frost resistance even in severe laboratory tests. It is significant that these bricks tend to have rather coarser pore sizes than the others.

NOTES

1 We follow [1107] in using the symbol H for the Henry's law solubility coefficient. As defined in Eqn 8.2, H has SI unit $mol/(m^3\ Pa)$, but is often expressed in the unit $mol/(L\ atm)$.

2 Of course, the atmospheric pressure at boundary surfaces varies about its mean value from day to day, typically in the range $\pm\ 0$–2.5 per cent. Close inspection of secondary imbibition curves such as those in Figure 8.8 shows that the volume of imbibed water deviates erratically from the trend line by small amounts that are nonetheless outside the measurement uncertainty. These deviations are caused by changes in atmospheric pressure. When the pressure rises, the trapped air is compressed and water is imbibed by capillarity to make up the decrease in volume; when the atmospheric pressure falls, trapped air expands and water is ejected. The size of these effects diminishes as the water content approaches saturation. Such phenomena are mentioned briefly by Adam [4], and analyzed rather more fully for soils by Norum and Luthin [890].

3 At the end of primary imbibition the unsaturated material with trapped air is in the Hirschwald state, with $\theta = \theta_h$. The analogy between the Hirschwald state and foams is illuminating, as the same phenomena may be expected to occur in both. The evolution of bubble size and pressure in foams, called *coarsening*

or *Ostwald ripening,* has been much studied both theoretically and experimentally [396, 1105, 1196, 993]. Another effect well-established in foams made with mixed gases (such as air) is the gradual change in the composition of the trapped gas [1022], a process known to occur also in soils [584].

4 These chemomechanical changes occur in heavy clay ceramics as the result of the rehydration (strictly, rehydroxylation) of partially reacted material produced during the original firing of the raw clay [489, 529]. During firing, the green clay first loses weakly bound molecular water and then at temperatures in the range 450–900 °C water is lost from the octahedral sheets by chemical dehydroxylation. At higher temperatures further reactions occur to form anhydrous minerals such as spinels, mullite and wollastonite [1072, 818, 1245]. In heavy clay ceramics these reactions are evidently incomplete [284, 92]. After cooling, slow rehydroxylation of partially reacted material occurs [265, 555, 1158]. We have mentioned the early work of Washburn and Foottit on rehydration in Chapter 1, pp 12, 34.

5 The precision of the $t^{1/4}$ power law over long times has been demonstrated in its application to the dating of archaeological ceramics [1315]. This technique relies on the fact that fired clay ceramics can be returned to their original as-fired condition by heating for about 4 h at 500 °C and reweighed to determine the mass gain over the specimen's lifetime. Immediately after heating, the mass gain of the specimen is measured over several days to determine the gradient of the $t^{1/4}$ plot for that particular ceramic. Extrapolating these data to the point at which as the mass lost on heating is regained gives the age of the ceramic. That this extrapolation over several orders of magnitude in time gives excellent results demonstrates how precisely the chemical recombination reaction with water follows the $t^{1/4}$ law.

6 In Britain, there are many road bridges over 100 years old built of brick masonry. These bridges now carry much increased traffic loads but investigations have shown them to be surprisingly strong [292, 293]. It is possible that continuing moisture expansion of the brick has a useful strengthening effect in such structures. It will tend to press together ever more firmly the brickwork forming the arch ring and reduce effects of mortar shrinkage, so enhancing the integrity of the arch. Even so, the effects of moisture expansion in brick masonry structures can often be damaging, see for example [495].

7 The water solubilities of all cement minerals are now established [760]. Such data can be used with chemical reaction modelling tools such as PHREEQC, which in turn (or in principle) can be coupled with water-transport simulation tools. Such combined reaction-transport simulations are now carried out in hydrology [1162], but not yet in construction.

8 We emphasize mortars and plasters here because water retention is of particular significance in masonry construction. Controlled permeability formwork for concrete construction is discussed in Section 8.3.

9 The filter membrane may itself have an appreciable resistance to flow, and then the rate at which the cake builds up is controlled at least in the beginning by the filter resistance. See Meeten [828] for theory and experiment and a review of previous work.

10 Both the hydraulic conductivity and the mechanical properties of the slurry vary strongly with the solid volume fraction ϕ. For granular (hard-sphere) suspensions like cements, the viscosity η is generally well described by the Krieger-Dougherty equation $\eta/\eta_w = (1 - \phi/\phi_m)^{-n\phi_m}$, where η_w is the viscosity of the suspending liquid (here water), ϕ_m is the maximum (close packed) solids loading (as measured for example in the consolidated filtration cake) and n is a constant ≈ 2.5 [1201, 781, 737].

9 Topics in moisture dynamics

In the fabric of buildings the internal processes of water transport that we have described in detail in the earlier parts of this book are almost always coupled to external conditions. The migration and storage of water then respond dynamically to changes in those conditions. In this final chapter, we discuss several examples of problems in moisture dynamics, and point to some practical implications of the water-transport models we use.

9.1 RAIN ABSORPTION ON BUILDING SURFACES

When rain falls on *sorptive* building surfaces much of it is absorbed. The absorbed water is captured, to be released later by evaporation. On non-sorptive building surfaces all rain water is free to flow. Thus the capillary absorption of most brick, stone and concrete surfaces greatly reduces the amount of water which buildings must shed in rain. Construction in sorptive materials requires less attention to the sealing of joints and to drainage details such as drips and gulleys. On the other hand, impermeable facings such as glazed tile, glass and painted timber cladding shed large amounts of water during rain, placing heavy demands on joints and seals. Severe leakage of rainwater can occur through defective joints between glazed ceramic cladding tiles fixed to a vertical external wall and adjacent sills and soffits. Glazed tiles are chosen no doubt to provide a weathertight impermeable facing, but inevitably in rain the wall surface is flooded with water which penetrates freely into any capillary channels opened up at joints by minor differential movements in the wall structure. This design is intolerant of imperfections in construction. As a basis for good design, it is useful to set out the fundamentals of water absorption by porous building surfaces exposed to rain. In particular, we ask how long it takes for a sorptive material to become saturated in rain and how this depends on hydraulic properties such as the sorptivity.

In most of the systems we have discussed, water is available freely at the surface of the material. We then have a *saturation* boundary condition $\theta_r = 1$

at the wetted surface. We know that if this condition is applied to an initially dry material of sorptivity S at some time $t = 0$, the initial rate of water absorption is indefinitely large, since $u = \frac{1}{2}St^{-1/2} \to \infty$ as $t \to 0$. In rain the rate of supply is limited by the rainfall rate. However great this is, there will always be a period of time for which the rate of absorption by the sorptive surface is supply-limited and is less than the rate at which the material would absorb water if it were freely available. Therefore, in modelling the effects of rain, we consider capillary water absorption under a *constant flux* boundary condition rather than a saturation boundary condition. For a one-dimensional semi-infinite homogeneous material, Figure 9.1, the constant flux condition is $u_0 = -Kd\Psi/dx = -Dd\theta/dx = \text{constant}$ at $x = 0$ where K, D and Ψ are the hydraulic conductivity, diffusivity and capillary potential and θ the water content. The one-dimensional Richards equation subject to a constant flux boundary condition, which has been studied extensively in soil physics [1353, 958], can be solved by several approximate methods such as that of Parlange [910] or we can easily obtain a numerical solution for any appropriate values of the hydraulic properties of the material.[1] Figure 9.2 shows the results of such a numerical simulation. The surface is clearly unsaturated for a period of time and the surface water content rises progressively. Eventually, at a well-defined time t_s, the surface becomes saturated. At times $t > t_s$, the flux exceeds the rate at which the material can absorb water and the water which falls on the surface now divides into two components: a part which is absorbed u_0 and a part $r = V_0 - u_0$ which is in excess. The fraction which is absorbed diminishes with time. The fate of the excess depends on circumstances. On horizontal surfaces, it may accumu-

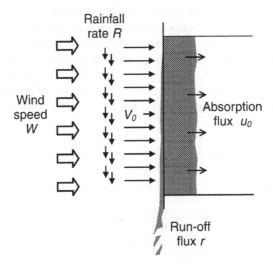

Figure 9.1 Water absorption and run-off at a building surface exposed to driving rain.

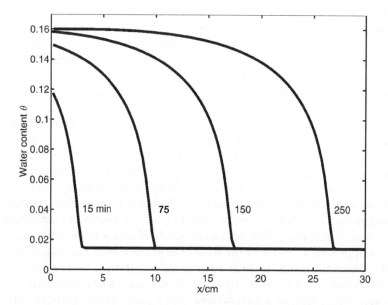

Figure 9.2 Constant flux water absorption: numerical simulation. Water content distributions at elapsed times $t = 15$, 75, 150 and 250 min. Sorptivity $S = 3.0$ mm/min$^{1/2}$ and rain flux $V_0 = 10$ mm/h; $\theta_s = 0.160$ and $\theta_0 = 0.014$.

late as ponding. On inclined surfaces, it drains either as a film over a large surface area or it may be channelled as a controlled run-off [348, 144].

For design purposes, the main matter of interest is how the time to reach surface saturation t_s depends on the rainfall rate and on the hydraulic properties of the material forming the exposed surface. Our attention lies principally in the water contents at and near the surface. We therefore use the $D(\theta_r)$ form of the Richards equation. For constant flux, we write

$$\frac{\partial \theta_r}{\partial t_r} = \frac{\partial}{\partial x}\left(D(\theta_r)\frac{\partial \theta_r}{\partial x}\right) \tag{9.1}$$

subject to the following boundary and initial conditions

$$\theta_r = 0, \quad t_r = 0, \quad x \geq 0 \tag{9.2}$$

$$D(\theta_r)\frac{\partial \theta_r}{\partial x} = -V_0, \quad t_r \geq 0, \quad x = 0 \tag{9.3}$$

$$\frac{\partial \theta_r}{\partial x} = 0, \quad t_r > 0, \quad x = L. \tag{9.4}$$

Here $\theta_r = (\theta - \theta_0)/(\theta_s - \theta_0)$ is the normalized water content, $t_r = t/(\theta_s - \theta_0)$, x is the horizontal space variable, $D(\theta_r)$ the hydraulic diffusivity, V_0 the constant applied flux and L the length of the medium considered. The flux may be identified with the rate at which rain is received per unit area of surface. Lacy [714] has proposed the expression for the driving rain flux V_0 on a vertical surface

$$V_0/\mathrm{mm\,h^{-1}} = 0.22 (W/\mathrm{m\,s^{-1}})\,(R/\mathrm{mm\,h^{-1}})^{0.88} \qquad (9.5)$$

where W is the wind speed (strictly the component of the wind velocity normal to the vertical surface), and R is the rainfall rate.[2] The unit of V_0, mm/h, is of course the same as $L/(\mathrm{m^2\,h})$.

Let us recast these equations in terms of the new variables $X_1 = V_0 x$ and $T_1 = V_0^2 t_r$ so that Eqns 9.1 and conditions 9.2, 9.3 and 9.4 become

$$\frac{\partial \theta_r}{\partial T_1} = \frac{\partial}{\partial X_1}\left(D(\theta_r)\frac{\partial \theta_r}{\partial X_1}\right) \qquad (9.6)$$

subject to

$$\theta_r = 0, \quad T_1 = 0, \quad X_1 > 0 \qquad (9.7)$$

$$D(\theta_r)\frac{\partial \theta_r}{\partial X_1} = -1, \quad T_1 \geq 0, \quad X_1 = 0 \qquad (9.8)$$

$$\frac{\partial \theta_r}{\partial X_1} = 0, \quad T_1 > 0, \quad X_1 = LV_0. \qquad (9.9)$$

We see that if the reduced variables T_1 and X_1 are used the process of one-dimensional constant-flux capillary absorption into a porous material with a uniform initial water content produces the same time history regardless of the flux V_0. This tells us that the time evolution of the profiles (and hence the surface water content) scales with $1/V_0^2$: if we double the rain flux at the surface, we reduce by a factor of four the time taken to attain surface saturation.

As for the influence of the sorptive surface, let us consider hydraulically similar materials which have diffusivity $D = D_1 f(\theta_r)$, where the function $f(\theta_r)$ is common to all members of the class and only $D_1 = S^2/(\theta_s - \theta_0)$ varies from material. If we use the dimensionless variables

$$X_2 = \frac{V_0 x}{D_1} = \frac{V_0 x(\theta_s - \theta_0)}{S^2} \qquad (9.10)$$

and

$$T_2 = \frac{V_0^2 t_r}{D_1} = \frac{V_0^2 t}{S^2}, \qquad (9.11)$$

Eqn 9.1 reduces to

$$\frac{\partial \theta_r}{\partial T_2} = \frac{\partial}{\partial X_2}\left(f(\theta_r)\frac{\partial \theta_r}{\partial X_2}\right)$$

(9.12)

subject to conditions

$$\theta_r = 0, \quad T_2 = 0, \quad X_2 > 0$$

(9.13)

$$f(\theta_r)\frac{\partial \theta_r}{\partial X_2} = -1, \quad T_2 \geq 0, \quad X_2 = 0$$

(9.14)

$$\frac{\partial \theta_r}{\partial X_2} = 0, \quad T_2 > 0, \quad X_2 = \frac{LV_0}{D_1}.$$

(9.15)

Eqns 9.12, 9.13, 9.14 and 9.15 tell us that for any group of hydraulically similar porous materials, the time-history of the water content distribution for any value of the flux V_0 and sorptivity S can be obtained from a single set of experimental or computed profiles $X(\theta_r, T_2)$. In particular, surface saturation occurs at the same dimensionless time $T_2 = T_s$ for all members of a class of hydraulically similar materials. We know experimentally that many brick, stone and concrete materials have hydraulic diffusivities of the form $D = D_1 \exp[B_r(\theta_r - 1)]$ with $B_r \approx 7$. For such materials, numerical simulations [511, 664, 663, 512] show that $T_s \approx 0.64$,[3] that is to say

$$t_s = 0.64\frac{S^2}{V_0^2}.$$

(9.16)

If we take 5 mm/h as typical of moderate rain flux, we see from Eqn 9.16 that a material of sorptivity $S = 3$ mm/min$^{1/2}$ takes some 13 h to become saturated at its surface. Until that time, all rain striking the surface is absorbed. If the sorptivity is reduced to 0.3 mm/min$^{1/2}$, the time to reach surface saturation falls to some 8 min. There is a similar analysis by Descamps [312], who calculates surface saturation times for AAC, fired clay and calcium silicate brick materials of particular sorptivities.

The problem of surface saturation in rain can also be attacked using Sharp Front methods, and as usual this brings some simple insights. Our starting point is to remember that SF theory is a limiting form of nonlinear diffusion theory in which the diffusivity has a non-zero value only at saturation. Under driving rain conditions, water can advance into the sorptive material only if saturation can be maintained behind the wetting front. With a constant flux condition at the surface, this cannot happen until $u_0 \leq V_0$. In fact we can take $u_0 = V_0$ as the condition for the time to attain surface saturation, t_s. Thus at $t = t_s$, $u_0 = V_0$. In SF models $u_0 = S^2/2i$ where i is the cumulative absorption; but for a surface subject to constant flux $i = V_0 t_s$ at $t = t_s$. Therefore

$$u_0 = \frac{S^2}{2V_0 t_s} \tag{9.17}$$

and so

$$t_s = \frac{S^2}{2V_0^2}. \tag{9.18}$$

This is the same as Eqn 9.16 apart from small difference in the numerical factor.

The SF model also represents the behaviour at $t > t_s$, after the surface has become saturated. Since SF water content profiles are always rectangular, the state of the system at t_s is identical with that which would be obtained if the surface had been put in contact with a free water reservoir (as in a sorptivity test) at some earlier time τ. Now at t_s, $i_s = V_0 t_s = S^2/2V_0$ and $u_{0s} = S^2/2i_s = S^2/2V_0 t_s$, where we denote the values of i and u_0 at $t = t_s$ by i_s and u_{0s}. But we can write $i = S\tau^{1/2}$, so that at $t = t_s$

$$\tau = \frac{1}{4}\frac{S^2}{V_0^2} = \frac{1}{2}t_s. \tag{9.19}$$

The origin of the τ timescale in the SF model lies halfway between $t = 0$ and t_s, the time at which the surface reaches saturation. In summary we have for $t \le t_s$

$$u = V_0 \tag{9.20}$$
$$i = V_0 t \tag{9.21}$$

and for $t > t_s$

$$u = \frac{1}{2}S\tau^{-1/2} \tag{9.22}$$
$$i = S\tau^{1/2} \tag{9.23}$$

with

$$\tau = t - \frac{1}{4}\frac{S^2}{V_0^2}. \tag{9.24}$$

In Figure 9.3 we illustrate the behaviour of the SF rain absorption model. We take three typical sorptivities and two typical rainfall rates. On the left, we plot the absorption rate against $\tau^{-1/2}$. In this diagram, clock time

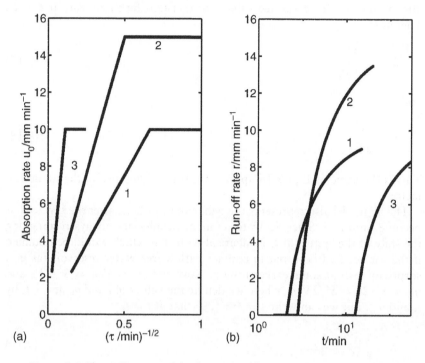

Figure 9.3 Sharp Front model of constant flux rain absorption. (a) Rate of absorption u_0 plotted against time variable $\tau^{-1/2}$, for (1) sorptivity $S = 0.5$ mm/min$^{1/2}$ and rain flux $V_0 = 10$ mm/h; (2) $S = 1.0$ mm/min$^{1/2}$, $V_0 = 15$ mm/h; and (3) $S = 3.0$ mm/min$^{1/2}$, $V_0 = 10$ mm/h. (b) Dependence of run-off flux r on elapsed time t (note log scale).

increases from right to left. The entire surface flux is absorbed until the surface reaches saturation, after which the absorption rate falls. For a given flux V_0, the time to surface saturation increases with sorptivity S. For a given S, the time to surface saturation decreases with increasing flux. The decline in absorption rate after saturation $du_0/d\tau^{-1/2}$ is proportional to S. For the cases we plot, in which fluxes V_0 are typical of moderate to heavy rain and the sorptivities are typical of clay brick and stone, the surfaces reach saturation in times between ranging from 4.5 to 162 min, the large range reflecting the dependence of t_s on $(S/V_0)^2$. Figure 9.3b shows how the corresponding run-off rates vary with time, from which it is evident that a large fraction of the incident rain flux continues to be absorbed long after the surface reaches saturation.

Experimental studies of flux-limited absorption in brick, stone and concrete are extreme rarities. As laboratory tests of Eqn 9.16 and 9.18, we know only of the experiments of Kalimeris [663], who used a spray to supply water

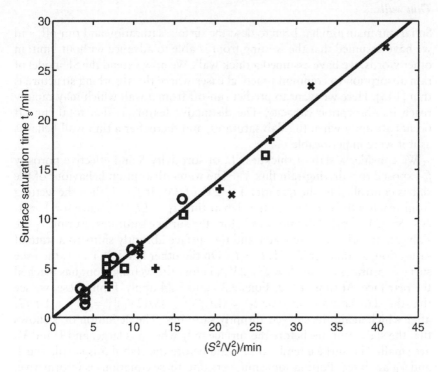

Figure 9.4 Surface saturation times: constant flux absorption by fired clay
brick [663]. Different symbols denote four different wirecut clay
brick materials. S is the independently measured sorptivity and V_0
the water flux. The solid line is the least squares fit to the data
$t_s = 0.68 \, S^2/V_0^2$.

at rates from 11–24 mm/h to the surfaces of four clay brick materials of
different sorptivity. The surface saturation time t_s is estimated from the first
appearance of visible run-off. How t_s varies with sorptivity and flux is shown
in Figure 9.4. The results confirm that t_s depends on S^2/V_0^2 as predicted by
theory and that T_s is about 0.68. The validity of these scalings and the utility
of the SF model receive support also from large-scale field tests [1268].

Seasonal differences. We recall from p 175 that the sorptivity increases
with temperature, and so we expect times to surface saturation to be shorter
in winter than in summer. A wall that reaches surface saturation in time t_s
at 35 °C does so in half the time, $t_s/2$, at 5 °C. For any wall under the same
conditions of rain exposure the run-off is greater in winter than in summer,
and less water is absorbed.

Thin walls

So far our main aim has been to describe surface saturation and run-off, and we have assumed that the wetting front is able to advance without limit: in other words, we have assumed a thick wall. We now extend the SF model of rain absorption to common practical cases where the absorbing structure is thin [143]. Here we want to predict run-off from a wall which may rapidly reach its absorption capacity. The distinctive feature is that total run-off occurs abruptly when the slab saturates, and thereafter a thin wall behaves as if it were impermeable.

We consider a slab of thickness L, of sorptivity S and effective porosity f_e exposed to a driving-rain flux V_0. The water absorption behaviour of the slab is controlled by the quantity $\mathsf{T} = 2V_0Lf_e/S^2$. If $\mathsf{T} < 1$, then the wetting front reaches the rear face of the slab at time $t_1 = Lf_e/V_0$. Since for $\mathsf{T} < 1$, $t_1 < S^2/(2V_0^2)$, the slab saturates before the surface saturates. At time t_1 the slab can absorb no more water and the surface abruptly shifts to a state of saturation, so that for $\mathsf{T} < 1$, $t_s = t_1$. On the other hand, if $\mathsf{T} > 1$, then the surface saturates at time $t_s = S^2/(2V_0^2)$, before the wetting front has reached the rear face. At times $t > t_s$ Eqns 9.23 and 9.24 apply. From these, we see that the slab saturates in time $t_1 = (Lf_e/S)^2 + [S/(2V_0)]^2 = (\mathsf{T}^2 + 1)t_s/2$, after which again the surface abruptly saturates. The definition of T shows that the slab saturates before the surface only when S is large, and L and V_0 are small. The surface tends to saturate before the slab if S is small, and L and V_0 are large. Putting some numbers into these equations is informative. We consider as an example a stone veneer on a building façade, initially dry, with $L = 50$ mm, $f_e = 0.15$ and $S = 1.6$ mm/min$^{1/2}$, exposed to rain flux $V_0 = 10$ mm/h. Then $\mathsf{T} = 1$. The slab saturates at $t_1 = 45$ min, after which all incident rain becomes run-off.

There is a sharp contrast between the run-off behaviour of thick and thin sorptive structures. A thick masonry structure can absorb large amounts of driving rain – in the case of massive stone masonry perhaps most or all of it. Even if run-off occurs at long times, it takes away only a part of the incident rain flux. In thin brick and veneer structures, through-saturation may often occur, after which run-off is total.

In traditional ashlar construction a thin surface layer of stone is in hydraulic contact with a clay-brick or stone backing layer. On wetting from prolonged driving rain (or equally from façade cleaning) the backing may also become wet. On drying the absorbed water moves back to the surface and evaporates (with the risk of crystallization damage from any salts in the backing). For this situation, the SF thin-wall analysis can easily be extended to incorporate our two-layer composite model of water absorption (p 179). The outer leaf of a cavity wall (p 336) is another common instance of a thin structure that may reach through-saturation in a short time under conditions of severe exposure

Comment

Our constant flux models of rain absorption are useful above all to show the role of the sorptivity in controlling the time to reach surface saturation. Rain of course is intermittent: building surfaces experience alternating episodes of wetting and drying. A good deal is known about the statistics of rain [582, 1023, 1306, 896]. From what we have said, it appears that many traditional building materials, especially brick and stone masonry, are able to absorb a high proportion of the water which they receive as driving rain throughout their lifetimes. This means that the cumulative lifetime absorption approximately equals (or is not much less than) the long-term driving rain load.[4] The mean lifetime water content is therefore set by the balance between the driving rain load and the evaporative loss. We develop the idea of water balances further in section 9.2.5 later in this chapter. The extent to which the water content shows short-term variation (daily or seasonal) clearly depends on the hydraulic properties of the materials. It is an important matter which has received almost no scientific attention. For those interested in chemical durability, the cumulative rain absorption is an important component in any overall mass balance analysis of long-term chemical change within the material, see for example [218, 1043, 219]. On the other hand, to analyze in detail the response of a porous building element to an episode of driving rain over a period of say a few hours or days requires a more precise simulation in which the absorption is controlled by a time-variable rain flux boundary condition. Hamilton *et al.* [525] have shown how environmental rainfall data may be used to drive a full unsaturated flow numerical model to study the moisture dynamics of limestone slabs. However, the full complexity of the rain dynamics of brick, stone and concrete structures has not yet been explored.

9.2 MOISTURE DYNAMICS

In Chapter 7 we gave a full analysis of coupled capillary rise and evaporation (the CREG and CRE models). We now use these models as the basis for a discussion of moisture dynamics[5] in walls and other structures of brick, stone and concrete. We shall generally assume in what follows that the flux $e(t)$ at wetted surfaces is equal to the local potential evaporation PE, which we denote $\epsilon(t)$. In many practical situations, the evaporation is subject to daily, seasonal and long-term variation, and the analysis of moisture dynamics takes this into account through the evaporation boundary condition which must include a time-variable evaporation flux $e(t)$. As we noted earlier, the differential equations of the CREG and CRE models remain fully applicable when a time-variable flux $e(t)$ is used, although analytical solutions can no longer be obtained. In what follows, we use both constant and time-variable evaporation conditions.

9.2.1   Rising damp

Rising damp is the common term for the slow upward movement of water in the low parts of walls and other ground-supported structures. Analysis of these phenomena follows naturally from the treatments of capillary rise given in Chapter 4 and of evaporation and drying in Chapter 7. In Chapter 4 we mentioned the experimental evidence, from measurements of hydraulic potential, that in most masonry materials capillary forces are great enough to cause water to rise to heights of many metres. Here we consider the practical causes of rising damp in which both capillary flow and evaporative drying produce a dynamically varying water content.

For most masonry walls (or indeed for other masonry structures such as columns and monoliths) the foundation is normally well below ground level, usually at a depth of 1 m or more. As a result the lowest part of the wall is generally in contact with ground that has a high water content. The water content of the wall materials is defined by the condition $\Psi_{wall} \approx \Psi_{soil}$. Masonry materials are usually finer-pored than the soils and can draw water from them to attain relatively high water contents, higher than the ground itself. In Figure 9.5 we show the wetting hydraulic-potential curves of a clay brick ceramic and a 1:3 mortar, together with the corresponding curves of several soils. The comparison shows the higher water contents that are attained by the brick material and mortar materials in hydraulic equilibrium with these soils. If the lowest levels of ground in which the wall has its foundation are saturated or even of reasonably high water content then the wall material must become saturated at this level. Water rises up the wall from the wettest part under the action of capillary forces. Because there is little or no evaporation below ground level the wall fabric is saturated or close to saturation right up to ground level. Only at the lowest water contents can the clay soil compete in suction with the clay brick. In any wall which lacks a dpc, typically a polymer membrane, or in which the dpc has become defective, water continues to rise above ground by capillarity. If there is no evaporative loss of water from the wall a state of capillary rise equilibrium is eventually reached in which the variation of water content with height is defined by the wetting branch of the water retention (hydraulic potential) curve. In such an equilibrium state, the flow through the wall is zero. The curve for the clay brick shown in Figure 9.5 defines such a state of capillary rise equilibrium for a wall built of this particular material. Strictly, the water content of the masonry units (brick or stone) follows the wetting curve of the masonry material and the water content of the mortar joints follows the wetting curve of the mortar material [463]. However, in most situations evaporative drying holds in check the capillary rise process, and the extent of rising damp in walls is then determined by the balance between the upward flow of water from the ground and the evaporation of water from the wall surfaces. When the upward capillary inflow and evaporation outflow are in balance, the total water content of the wall is constant ('steady'). Nonetheless, even

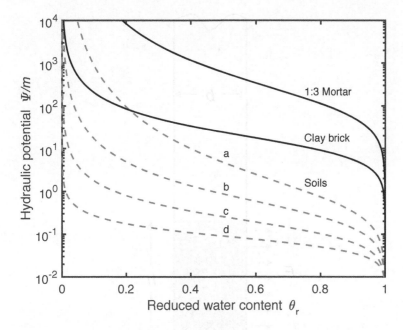

Figure 9.5 Water retention curves of fired-clay brick, 1:3 cement/sand mortar and typical soils, calculated from van Genuchten parameters of Table 2.4: (a) clay; (b) clay loam; (c) loam; (d) sandy loam.

though the wall is in steady-state, there is a continuous flow of water through it. These continuous evaporation-driven flows, though largely invisible, are of the greatest importance for long-term performance and durability.

Sharp Front model of rising damp: constant evaporation

We consider the physical view of rising damp given in Figure 9.6 where we have a wall structure (or equally a monolith) in hydraulic contact with the ground and of unlimited height. The structure is of constant thickness b, of unlimited length, and composed of a porous material. Water enters the structure at the base, where water is considered to be freely available, and rises under the action of capillary forces. In a Sharp Front model, the height of rise $h(t)$ is well-defined as the position of the boundary of demarcation between wetted and dry zones. Evaporation occurs from the wetted vertical surface (here $N = 1$ for a wall subject to evaporation from one face and $N = 2$ for two-sided evaporation). Evaporation per unit area of the wetted region occurs at a rate equal to the potential evaporation of the immediate environment, $e = \epsilon$. For this analysis, the only material properties that we need to know are the sorptivity S and the effective porosity of the wetted

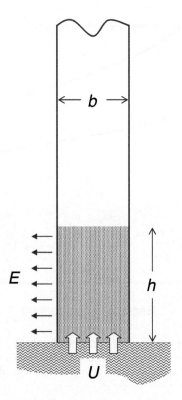

Figure 9.6 Schematic of Sharp Front model of rising damp in walls.

region f_e. If the structure is composed of several materials then an average or composite sorptivity is used (see Chapter 5).

Rising damp results from the competition between the capillary absorption of water from the base of the wall and evaporative loss of water along the exposed surface or surfaces. In Chapter 7 we described a Sharp Front model of capillary rise with distributed evaporation (CRE). We derived a differential equation for the height of rise $h(t)$, Eqn 7.25,

$$h\frac{\mathrm{d}h}{\mathrm{d}t} = c - a'h^2 \tag{9.25}$$

where $c = S^2/2f_e^2$ and $a' = Ne/2bf_e$, and e is the evaporation flux from the wall surfaces, f_e the water content of the wetted region and N is the number of faces subject to evaporation (1 or 2 for a wall).

At rising damp steady state, $dh/dt = 0$ and h_{ss}, the CRE steady-state height of rise, is given by

$$c = a'h_{ss}^2, \tag{9.26}$$

that is,

$$h_{ss} = S\left(\frac{b}{Nef_e}\right)^{1/2}. \tag{9.27}$$

This simple but important formula tells us that the steady-state height of rise varies as $b^{1/2}$, the square root of the wall thickness, and inversely as $e^{1/2}$, the square root of the microenvironmental evaporation rate.

As we noted in Chapter 7 three additional and important quantities follow immediately from this result. At steady-state, the total volume of water per unit length of wall $W_{ss} = f_e b h_{ss}$. Second, the steady-state flow of water through the wall $Q_{ss} = Neh_{ss}$. Third, the mean residence time for the movement of water through the wall, $t_r = W_{ss}/Q_{ss} = f_e b/Ne$.

In the situation in which the absorption inflow and the evaporative loss are not in balance, we can solve Eqn 9.25 for constant evaporation rate e and initial conditions $h = 0$, $t = 0$ as in Eqn 7.26 to obtain

$$h^2 = \frac{c}{a'}[1 - \exp(-2a't)]. \tag{9.28}$$

At long times, $t \to \infty$ and $h \to h_{ss} = (c/a')^{1/2}$ as in Eqn 9.26. From an initial dry state the system reaches $h = 0.95h_{ss}$ at a time $t_{95} \approx 3f_e b/Ne$ which we take as the timescale for reaching rising damp steady-state.[6]

For completeness we also consider the effects of gravitational forces acting on water in the wall. In Chapter 7 we showed that the CREG differential equation for $h(t)$, Eqn 7.20 is

$$h\frac{dh}{dt} = c[1 - \frac{h}{h_\infty}] - a'h^2 \tag{9.29}$$

where h_∞ is the ultimate height of capillary rise in the absence of evaporation. Using this equation capillary rise steady state is defined by

$$c(1 - \frac{h_{ssg}}{h_\infty}) = a'h_{ssg}^2 \tag{9.30}$$

where h_{ssg} is the height of capillary rise allowing for gravitational effects. For many masonry materials $h_{ssg} \ll h_\infty$ so that $h_{ssg} \approx h_{ss}$. However, Eqn 9.30 also shows that the effect of gravity is weak even for somewhat larger values of h_{ssg}. For example, even if $h_{ssg} = 0.2h_\infty$, $h_{ssg} \approx 0.9h_{ss}$.

Table 9.1 Steady-state heights of rise and associated quantities

Thickness b	N	Potential evaporation ϵ	Height of rise h_{ss}	t_{95}	Stored water W_{ss}	Total flow Q_{ss}	
mm		mm/day	mm	day	L	L/day	L/y
					per m length of wall		
150[a]	1	1.44[b]	865	62	26	1.3	460
	2	1.44	610	31	18	1.8	640
215	1	1.44	1040	90	45	1.5	550
	2	1.44	730	45	31	2.1	765
1000	1	1.44	2240	415	450	3.2	1170
	2	1.44	1580	210	315	4.6	1660
4000	1	1.44	4470	1670	3580	6.5	2350
	2	1.44	3160	835	2530	9.1	3320
150	1	0.36	1730	250	52	0.62	225
	2	0.36	1225	125	36	0.88	320

Notes
a Benchmark case.
b 1.44 mm/day = 0.001 mm/min.
All quantities calculated for $S = 0.3$ mm/min$^{1/2}$, $f_e = 0.2$.

First we consider the calculation of steady-state heights of rise from Eqn 9.27. Critical in these calculations is the evaporation rate e. We have shown in Chapter 7 that the rate of evaporation of water from most porous materials is determined solely by the environmental conditions over a wide range of water contents from saturated to fairly dry. For example, in the case of clay brick the range of stage I drying (constant evaporation rate under constant environmental conditions) extends from saturation to about one-third saturation. We know that e is influenced by temperature, air humidity and air flow speed in a complex way. Ideally a direct site measurement of e is desirable. For practical purposes we use the potential evaporation PE, ϵ, and set the evaporation rate of the wetted surface $e = \epsilon$.

In Table 9.1 we give some values of the heights of rise calculated from Eqn 9.27 for various wall thicknesses. For most of these examples, an evaporation rate of 0.001 mm/min has been chosen. This corresponds to the UK potential evaporation averaged over the whole year. When we look at published survey data on older buildings, our estimated heights of rise are in good agreement with practical observations. For example, there is the common observation [200] that in UK houses built without a damp-proof course rising damp forms a band of saturated wall typically to a height of 0.5–1 m. In [795] Massari and Massari describe their observations of capillary rise in buildings in Rome, noting the importance of wall thickness and evaporating geometry on the height of rise. From visual surveys of walls and pillars, they define a quantity which in our notation is h_{ss}/b, and which they call the *climb index*. They conclude from their long experience that this quantity lies in fairly narrow ranges for walls and for pillars exposed to interior or exterior conditions. This is equivalent to proposing a simple scaling of $h_{ss} \propto b$. Thus for walls, they suggest that h_{ss}/b lies in the range 1.5–5. Using values from Table 9.1 for walls 0.15–4.0 m thick drying from one side, the CRE model gives h_{ss}/b in the range 1.1–5.8. Of course, uncertainties in sorptivity and evaporation rate introduce some corresponding uncertainties into these estimates but there is a valuable general conclusion. This is that the SF CRE model explains the dependence of the height of rise on wall thickness and gives numerical results in good overall agreement with the Massaris' field observations. That the height of rise depends on thickness is shown also by other later results on stone test walls [1242].

Especially notable in these results are the high flow rates of ground-sourced water through the masonry materials at rising damp steady-state. Such high flows are the cause of considerable damage to the wall fabric and to finishes, as we discuss later in this chapter.

Sharp Front model: variable evaporation

The dynamic rising damp equilibrium and the flow of water through the porous fabric depend on the evaporation rate e at the wall surface. Thus far we have used a constant value of e based on a yearly average potential evaporation. This is a satisfactory approach for estimating average and approximate values of capillary rise and flow in masonry walls and monoliths, but in practice there are substantial seasonal variations in potential evaporation. We shall see how this leads to characteristic patterns of damage to walls. Of course, rough estimates of the seasonal differences in heights of rise can be obtained from Eqn 9.27 by using appropriate values of e for each season. However, recognizing that the potential evaporation ϵ is subject to daily, seasonal and secular variations, a more thorough approach is to apply realistic time-dependent evaporation boundary conditions to the SF model [496]. The SF differential equation for the height of rise (Eqn 9.25) cannot be integrated analytically for $e = \epsilon(t)$ so the equation is solved numerically.

In [496], potential evaporation data from two locations are used: one in southern England (Silwood Park, Berkshire, UK) [1340] and the other in Greece (Helliniko Station, Athens) [692]. We refer to these below as the London and Athens datasets. Figure 9.7 shows how the PE varies at these two sites. The PE datasets provide an interesting view of regional differences.[7] In both cases the PE is calculated using the Penman equation (or variants of it); and in both cases Fourier regression equations are used to represent the variation of the mean daily potential evaporation over a calendar year. The London data extend over a period of 5 years (1989–1994); the Athens

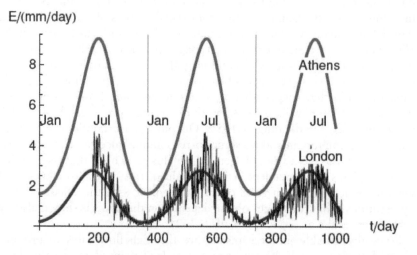

Figure 9.7 Daily potential evaporation [496]. *Lower*: raw daily data from Silwood Park, Berkshire UK (London) with regression curve (superimposed solid line). *Upper*: regression curve for data from Helliniko
Station, Athens.

data over a 9 year period (1977–1985). Figure 9.7 shows smoothed daily
London and Athens PE data over three years calculated from the regression
equations. For London, we show also the raw daily data. The total PE over
a full year at the Athens site is 1750 mm; and at the London site is 485 mm.
The winter minimum daily PE for London is extremely low, 0.21 mm/day.
The ratio of winter minimum to summer maximum is 0.175 in Athens; but
only 0.075 in London. The winter minimum occurs about 14 days later in
Athens than in London; and the summer maximum about 20 days later.

We solve Eqn 9.25 with the dry-wall initial condition $h = 0$, $t = 0$ and
with a time-dependent evaporation rate $e(t)$ equal to the mean daily potential
evaporation $\epsilon(t)$ for each location. The results for the *benchmark case* of a
wall 150 mm thick, with sorptivity $S = 1$ mm/min$^{1/2}$, $f_e = 0.2$ and $N = 1$ are
shown in Figure 9.8. For both London and Athens there is a strong seasonal
variation of h. In London the summer minimum height of rise is 630 mm,
the winter maximum is 1660 mm and the annual mean is 1080 mm. We note
that the height of rise for constant evaporation set at the London annual
mean PE is 905 mm. The difference arises because h varies as $e^{-1/2}$ not e^{-1}
so that the low PE (and high height of rise) in winter months contributes
disproportionately to the mean annual height of rise. The results are given
in Table 9.2. In Athens conditions, the total annual flows are roughly double
those in London (Table 9.2). Thus, although the total stored water is less in
Athens, the higher PE draws water more rapidly through the wetted part of

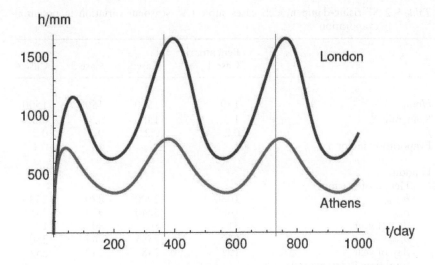

Figure 9.8 The benchmark case with London and Athens evaporation boundary conditions [496]. SF height of rise h against elapsed time t. Vertical lines mark 1, 2 y. Computed curves start with an initially dry
system, $h = 0$ at $t(0)$ at 1 January.

the wall. Taken over the entire year, the cumulative flux (flow per unit wetted
wall area) is about 3.6 times greater than in London (this of course is equal
to the ratio of the mean annual evaporation rate).

In the benchmark case, the wall is thin and the sorptivity high. The thin-
ness of the wall means that the stored water is correspondingly small (over
the course of the year under London conditions, it lies in the range 19–68
L per m length of wall). This together with the high sorptivity of the material means that the height of rise h responds both quickly and strongly to
the seasonal changes in potential evaporation. However, when the wall is
thicker and the sorptivity lower, the response of the wall is more sluggish,
and the system dynamics damped. We show the effects of wall thickness and
sorptivity on the height of rise in London PE conditions in Figure 9.9. SF
results are given in Table 9.2. Increasing the wall thickness by a factor 10 to
1500 mm (case 2) causes water to rise much higher (by a factor of roughly
$\sqrt{10}$). The large amount of stored water produces sizeable lags. For example, under London conditions the maximum height of rise is reached 46 days
after the minimum in the potential evaporation. Reducing the sorptivity to
0.3 mm min$^{-1/2}$ (case 3) largely cancels the effect on h of the increased wall
thickness, but the peak-to-trough changes in h are considerably smaller compared with the benchmark case 1. Another example, case 4, shows the effect
of reducing the evaporation rate by a factor $\gamma = e/\epsilon = 0.1$ to represent the

Table 9.2 SF rising-damp model: cases subject to seasonal variation in potential evaporation

	Benchmark Case 1	Case 2	Case 3	Case 4
b/mm	150	1500	1500	1500
S mm min$^{-1/2}$	1.0	1.0	0.3	0.3
f_e	0.2	0.2	0.2	0.2
Evaporation factor γ	1	1	1	0.1
London				
Height of rise mm				
h_{mean}	1080	2900	870	2530
h_{max}	1660	3240	970	2555
day of year	31	80	80	102
h_{min}	630	2545	765	2505
day of year	192	248	248	252
total flow L/day per m length				
Q_{mean}	1.13	3.74	1.12	0.33
Q_{max}	1.78	7.79	2.34	0.70
Q_{min}	0.52	2.13	0.64	0.21
Athens				
Height of rise mm				
h_{mean}	545	1585	475	1425
h_{max}	800	1985	595	1475
day of year	15	66	66	96
h_{min}	340	1160	350	1370
day of year	203	233	233	259
total flow L/day per m length				
Q_{mean}	2.17	7.03	2.11	0.68
Q_{max}	3.17	12.11	3.63	1.31
Q_{min}	1.26	2.85	0.85	0.23

effect of poor ventilation. The behaviour of $h(t)$ changes markedly as the lower flux causes the system to respond more slowly to seasonal variations in potential evaporation.

Unsaturated flow analysis

The SF model is a simple representation of the full nonlinear diffusion model of UF built on the Buckingham-Richards equation. In [496], the rising damp process is also analyzed using the numerical UF simulation. Using UF methods provides a valuable test of the simpler SF models. For UF simulations, we need a more comprehensive description of material properties than the sorptivity and porosity alone. We require information also on the unsaturated

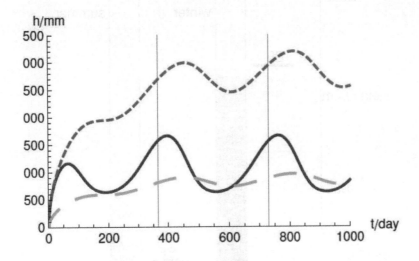

Figure 9.9 Height of rise calculated from the SF model subject to London
        evaporation conditions: the effect of changes in wall thickness and
        sorptivity. Solid line, benchmark case 1; short dashes, case 2; long
        dashes, case 3.

hydraulic conductivity and water retention (capillary potential) behaviour,
for example from the van-Genuchten-Mualem parameters.

In Figure 9.10 are the results of such a UF analysis for winter and summer
London conditions for the benchmark case. The water content distributions
support the use of the SF model. The UF simulations show only low volume
fraction water contents above the wet front. It is clear that the level of the wet
front provides a good measure of limit of the wetted region, and its seasonal
movement. The flows calculated using the full UF simulations are also in
good agreement with the SF model. For the benchmark case, SF and UF
models are in excellent agreement [496]. For constant potential evaporation
with $e = 0.001$ mm/min, UF and SF stored water, inflow and outflow are
similar. The UF equivalent steady-state height of rise is 800 mm, compared
with the SF value of 865 mm.

Practical consequences of rising damp

We have shown that rising damp is the result of a dynamic interplay between
upward flow of water within a ground-supported structure and evaporative
loss of water from the exposed surfaces of that structure. Most significantly,
the analysis shows that the quantities of water flowing under the action of

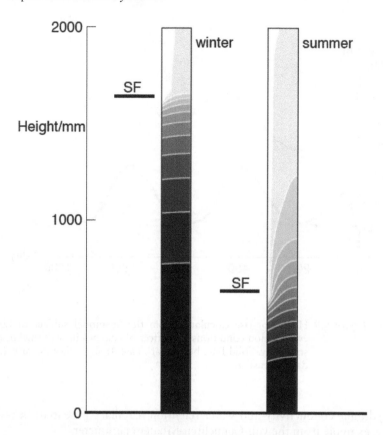

Figure 9.10 (a) Winter and (b) summer water distributions for one-sided benchmark problem (London conditions) computed using the UF model
[496]. Water content contours are at 11 intervals in the range
0.01–0.20 volume fraction. The corresponding SF heights of rise
are shown. The winter distribution is calculated at the mid-winter
evaporation minimum, day 350; the summer distribution at the
summer evaporation maximum, day 180. Van Genuchten-Mualem
parameter values: $\alpha = 8.6 \times 10^{-4}$ cm^{-1}; $K_s = 7.6 \times 10^{-5}$ cm/min;
$n = 1.80$.

capillarity and evaporation are prodigious. These flows largely control the
rates of processes causing decay [524]. For example, in London conditions
the water flow is sufficient to dissolve 2 kg of calcitic limestone per m length
of structure in 100 y. In 100 y groundwater containing as little as 100 ppm
of dissolved salts transports 4.2 kg salt into each m length of wall. These
estimates are dramatic and show clearly why rising damp can be so harmful
to masonry structures.

The fact that the height of rising damp varies with seasonal changes in
evaporation conditions also has a controlling influence on damage patterns,

Figure 9.11 A part of the SE façade of the El Merdani Mosque (Mosque of Alt-inbugha al-Maridani), Cairo, Egypt, showing severe stone decay in the region of the wall bounded by the estimated minimum and maximum heights of rise. The staff is 3 m long. Photograph by Bernd Fitzner.

especially in stone masonry which is susceptible to salt crystallization damage. Thus the variation in h_{ss} produces a zone at the capillary fringe which becomes wet in the winter and dries out in summer. For example, in the London benchmark problem this zone lies roughly in the range 630–1660 mm above ground level. It is only in this zone where the wall dries out in summer that evaporation occurs beneath the surface, and so it is in this zone that salts accumulate and crystallize deep within the porous fabric (*cryptoflorescence*), causing damage. In the lower parts of walls, salts within the fabric generally remain in solution and no salt crystallization occurs. This effect is clearly observed in the example shown in Figure 9.11 of the south-east façade of the El Merdani Mosque in Cairo. Here Fitzner *et al.* [382] found that the decay of stone was most severe at elevations of 1.2–2.8 m where there is band of intense damage. The wall thickness is 1.67 m, the annual PE for Cairo [859] is about 1170 mm. The winter PE is about 0.79 mm/d and the summer PE about 5.7 mm/d (averages over 3 months). Using $S = 1.0$ mm/min$^{1/2}$ and $f_e = 0.2$, the calculated height of rise varies with the season in the range 1.2–2.8 m for two-sided evaporation. Thus it appears that the severe damage is to the part of the wall that is subject to the rise and fall of the wet front as we see vividly in Figure 9.11. Such a distribution of stone damage in a broad band well above ground level, with comparatively undamaged stone below, is found widely on the walls of the El Merdani Mosque and indeed extensively in many historic buildings in Cairo. Similar patterns of decay are observed in stone buildings in other climates.[8]

9.2.2   Flow and damage at the base of masonry walls

In our discussion of the Sharp Front CREG/CRE models in Chapter 7 we pointed out that in systems with distributed lateral evaporation the maximum flux occurs at the inflow surface. This means that in a wall the greatest flux occurs at its base. In addition, even though the height of rise is subject to seasonal variation, the base is generally wet throughout the year. Therefore we expect that damage processes are likely to be particularly active at the base of walls.

The analysis is as follows. We consider first a masonry wall, for example of brickwork, without a damp-proof course. We can use the formulae of the CRE model. At steady-state, the total flow at the inflow face (per unit length of wall) is

$$Q_{ss} = Neh_{ss} = S\left(\frac{Neb}{f_e}\right)^{1/2}. \tag{9.31}$$

The flux (flow per unit area) $u_0 = Q_{ss}/b = S(Ne/f_e b)^{1/2}$, or in terms of the parameters $a = Ne/2f_e b$ and $c = S^2/2f_e^2$

$$u_0 = 2f_e(ac)^{1/2}. \tag{9.32}$$

A quantity of considerable practical interest is u_0/Ne, the ratio of the inflow flux through the base to the evaporative flux through the sides of the wall. Since $h_{ss} = (c/a)^{1/2}$, we have $u_0/Ne = h_{ss}/b$. This result is intuitively obvious since the total flow through the base bu_0 and the sides $h_{ss}Ne$ must be equal at steady-state, but nonetheless it is striking. In the case of thin walls, it shows that the evaporative pump amplifies the flux (or flow intensity) through the base of the wall by a factor h_{ss}/b.

To illustrate this analysis, we apply it to the benchmark case which we have used earlier, with $b = 150$ mm, $N = 1$, $S = 1.0$ mm min$^{-1/2}$, $f_e = 0.2$, and $e = 0.001$ mm/min. We find that $u_0 = 5.8 \times 10^{-3}$ mm/min. This corresponds to a total flow of 1.3 L/day per m length of wall. Furthermore we have $u_0/Ne = 5.8$: in this case there is a strong intensification of flux through the base of the wall.

Figure 9.12 An example of long-term damage at the foot of a brick masonry wall.

If the wall has a damp-proof course this is usually located about two courses above ground level (h_{dpc} = 150 mm approximately). The height of rise is capped by the dpc, no capillary forces act at the level of the dpc, and the entire flow is evaporation-driven. The total flow is reduced compared with the case without dpc by a factor h_{dpc}/h_{ss}, but nonetheless the upward flux through the brickwork is considerable.

These simple results provide an explanation for the damage which is often seen at the base of masonry walls, Figure 9.12. The continuous upward flow of water, driven by the largely invisible process of evaporation, has several deleterious effects. First, it progressively alters the mortar joints by leaching soluble components which are carried upwards. It is likely that mortar joints are slowly degraded and rendered more permeable by these mineralogical changes.[9] Second, the upward flow brings into the wall soluble components of groundwater such as salts which may contribute to crystallization damage or to sulphate attack on portland cement mortars. Third, the upward flow probably brings about a gradual loss of trapped air and a corresponding increase in water content by means of the Gummerson effect described in Chapter 8.[10] This makes the wall materials increasingly vulnerable to freeze-thaw damage. The effects of such processes are frequently

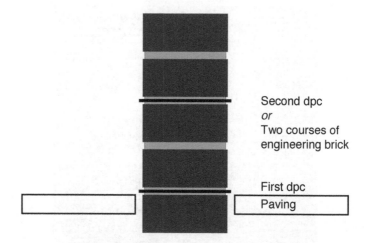

Figure 9.13 The optimal position of a damp-proof course in a masonry wall.

visible on old walls. The bottom courses just above ground level, particularly but not invariably without dpcs, show loss of mortar from the lowest joints. This is no doubt the result of loss of binder or chemical attack (or both). The calculated flows are greater for walls without dpcs than for those with. Nonetheless, even with a dpc, the water flows that we calculate are sizeable and capable of causing severe long-term damage to the exposed joints below dpc level.

Construction practice

Since the end of the nineteenth century impermeable damp proof courses of polymer, slate, metal or engineering brick have been installed in walls about 150 mm above ground level.[11] The question that arises from our analysis of moisture dynamics is whether the modern dpc is in the best position in the wall. The base of a wall constructed in the traditional way exposes the materials below 150 mm to substantial evaporation-driven flows of water, and therefore to long-term damage from deterioration of the mortar joints and from frost attack (perhaps partially mitigated by specifying bricks of good frost resistance).

In terms of the fundamentals of moisture dynamics the best position for a dpc is exactly at ground level (Figure 9.13). All of the wall above ground level is then protected from upward flows of water. All of the wall below ground level is also protected from flows because there is no evaporation here, and the wall remains in a stable saturated no-flow condition. In practice a 'ground level' location for the dpc can be defined by placing hard paving against the wall. A further protection against damp problems arising by bridging of the dpc or water splash is to use engineering bricks for the two courses of brickwork above dpc, or indeed to use a second dpc at the normal height. It may be thought that the common practice of having two courses of engineering brick above ground but below dpc would work just as well. However, although the engineering bricks themselves usually perform satisfactorily, the mortar joints are vulnerable to damaging capillary flows of water from the ground.

9.2.3 Remedial treatments: methods

We can use our theoretical model of rising damp and our understanding of capillary water movement as a basis for best practice in diagnosis and treatment. Practical experience over the years has suggested similar approaches (for example, [200, 201]).

Surveying and diagnosis

In site testing of walls for rising damp, it is the water content of the masonry units (clay bricks or natural stone) that must be measured since these generally have a higher water content than the mortar and in any case make up the greater part of the wall structure. Gravimetric analysis of drillings – or even of whole brick or other masonry units taken from the wall – is a reliable method of determining water content (see Section 2.2.3). The carbide moisture meters also provide an accurate method of water content determination. Electrical resistance measurements, using simple meters, while convenient and widely used, cannot give a reliable diagnosis because the conductivity of the wall material is affected not only by the amount of water in the pore structure but also by the presence of soluble salts. The use of impulse radar also shows promise in the surveying of rising damp (see Section 2.2.3).

In the previous section we discussed the movement of soluble salts to the top of the wet zone and some problems that salt movements can cause. In brick masonry, salts carried to the top of the wet zone produce a tidemark of efflorescence on the surface of wall rather than the damage caused by the sub-surface cryptoflorescence that we noted in stonework, Figure 9.11. Some of these salts may be hygroscopic and as a consequence may contribute to the damp problem, but in general this is probably a minor effect when compared with the action of the normal capillary forces.[12]

Treatments

In order to solve a rising damp problem, it is necessary to impede the capillary rise process. The most reliable method of stopping capillary rise is to install a traditional damp proof membrane of polymer or metal in the affected wall. Several techniques are available to do this [873]. Care is needed to prevent structural movement and cracking during the installation. A general principle also follows from our earlier analysis of the leaky seal and of the Massaris' problem (pp 230–231). We showed that even a small source can supply sufficient water to maintain large-scale flows, since the diverging wetting front creates steep suction gradients near the source. These in turn generate strong local flows at the source. Therefore, remedial treatments should aim if possible to create impermeable barriers.

An alternative to fitting a traditional damp proof course is to inject the base of the wall with a solution of a substance which dries or cures to form a water repellent barrier [1150]. Methods include high pressure injection of repellents (for example aluminium stearate dissolved in a nonaqueous solvent) and low pressure infusion of repellents (such as sodium methyl-siliconate dissolved in water). The water repellency conferred by various substances and procedures can be seen directly by comparing the sorptivity of the masonry material before and after treatment [465]. Two important results have emerged from analysis of the physical processes involved in chemical injection damp-proofing [608, 609]. First, injection must be continued for a sufficiently long time to give a continuous treated layer throughout the wall cross-section; there is evidence that once the pumping or infusion process stops the solutions do not spread out in the wall. Second, it may take some time for the treatment to become fully effective.

What are the optimum treatment times for injection and infusion processes? An analysis of treatment times has been proposed [609] which is based on the miscible or immiscible displacement of the pore water by the invading solution. The times of injection which this analysis indicates are relatively long. In typical clay bricks optimum high pressure injection times are in the range 5–20 min per injection hole; the equivalent low pressure infusion times are in the range 8–44 h. The calculated equivalent high pressure injection times are consistent with results reported in simple laboratory tests [465]. Calculating optimum times for low pressure infusion is of less practical importance because the volume of fluid entering the masonry is known and the quantity required for satisfactory treatment may be calculated from the porosity of the masonry material. If the infusion time needed is much less than the calculated value it is likely that fluid is being lost through leakage.

The time taken for the treatment to become effective is related to the fact that the compounds used are pore-lining water repellents. These hydrophobic compounds prevent water being drawn by capillarity into the pores by changing the wettability (assessed for example by measuring the change in the wetting index of the material on treatment). If the pores are completely filled with water so that there is no air/water interface in the pores then water can pass through the material unimpeded. There is experimental evidence [607] that if the wall above and below the treated region is more or less completely saturated – typical in a true case of rising damp – then the treated region becomes saturated by capillary condensation as the solvent evaporates following injection. In these circumstances the capillary rise process will continue. Strong drying conditions, including removing plaster from the wall, help to change this situation, and allow the repellent treatment to begin to work and the wall to become (and remain) dry. It is likely that it is this aspect of water repellent chemical injection treatments that leads to the suggestion that long periods of time (around two years) are needed for walls to dry out. It may well be that in practice in some situations the strong drying conditions of certain seasons are essential in order for the water repellent treatments to become fully effective. There is no doubt that the chemical injection systems are the most convincing of the non-traditional methods of curing rising damp in walls, but care is needed if these systems are to work effectively.

Other alternative remedial methods include the use of electroosmosis and of Knapen siphons. Two electroosmotic techniques are used – active and passive. In active electroosmosis, electrodes are embedded both in the wall and in the ground and an electrical potential difference is applied between them. There is no doubt that water migration can be produced in a porous medium in response to an electric field; whether such an effect is sufficient to cause drying in a masonry wall is doubtful [118]. The passive electroosmotic systems do not use an impressed voltage, but consist simply in connecting the wall electrodes to ground electrodes. The initial difference in potential which can be measured between wall and ground electrodes is due to their different electrochemical environments. The mechanism by which such a system might operate is not clear.[13]

Knapen siphons [795] are porous ceramic tubes fitted into damp affected walls. It is claimed that the ceramic material has a high suction and draws water from the wall fabric – water which is then lost by evaporation from the inner surfaces of the tubes. Even if the presence of the tubes produces localized drying around each tube the regions between the tubes provide paths for rising damp. The situation is similar to that which we have in the Massaris' problem discussed in Chapter 6. There is undoubtedly a need for a rigorous theoretical analysis of both the electroosmotic and the Knapen siphon systems based on unsaturated flow theory. There is also a lack of clear experimental evidence in respect of their efficiency and effectiveness.

There are other commercial systems that apparently rely on increasing drying of walls by including special elements to increase ventilation at or around the traditional dpc level. In discussing Eqn 9.27, we noted that the equilibrium height of rise varies inversely as $e^{1/2}$. So to reduce the height of rise by, say, a factor 10, requires a 100-fold increase in the evaporation rate. This shows that extremely large increases in evaporation rate are necessary to combat established rising damp.

Whatever the remedial method, it is essential to allow adequate time for drying out of damp affected walls. When a traditional damp proof course is installed drying is relatively rapid although the rate clearly depends on the wall thickness. Drying is always much faster if the wall is left unplastered for at least a few days. An indication of drying times can be gained from Figure 7.1 in Chapter 7. While the final stages of drying are slow, in practice a wall should reach a reasonable state of dryness within a few weeks if the damp proof course is a perfect barrier. For the reasons we have discussed, chemical injection damp proof courses may take longer to become fully effective and this is probably the reason for the trade view that walls may take one or two years to dry. When a chemical injection damp proof course is installed it is better to remove the plaster in the damp affected region and encourage good drying by ventilation both before and after injection. In this way the damp proof course is likely to work much more quickly. The suggestion that the old plaster should be left on the wall to absorb soluble salts during drying has little merit when compared with the need to encourage drying.

The presence of capillary moisture below the surface can be masked by replastering the damp-affected region with a water resistant plaster (typically a Portland cement-based undercoat plaster). It is normal practice to do this as part of many processes of remediation. The risk is that the wall may appear dry even if the system used to inhibit capillary rise is not working. Eventually damp reappears as it rises above the region covered by the new plaster (where evaporation is reduced), but the failure may take a long time, perhaps years, to manifest itself.

We can analyze the effects of replastering the lower part of the wall with a water-resistant plaster by using the SF model. Consider, for example, a wall of thickness 215 mm having a composite sorptivity of 0.3 mm/min$^{1/2}$, f_e 0.2 and $N = 2$ subject to rising damp. Setting $e = 1 \times 10^{-4}$ mm/min, typical of drying conditions in a poorly ventilated space, we calculate the height of rise at steady-state $h_{ss} = 695$ mm. If we now apply a water-resistant plaster to a height of 1.25 m we reduce the evaporation rate from the wall surface to, say, $0.1e = 1 \times 10^{-5}$ mm/min. Water will now rise further up the wall and we calculate that the wet front takes about 425 days to reach the top of the plastered zone. Thereafter a band of dampness will appear on the wall above 1.25 m.

This suggests that the wall should also be surveyed at some appropriate time after the installation of a remedial treatment to ensure that the interior is indeed drying and that the treatment is effective.

9.2.4   Remedial treatments: requirements

The problems posed in many countries in the temperate zone by damp-affected buildings are perennial and often intractable.[14] They arise in many contexts: the maintenance and rehabilitation of housing and the management and conservation of historic buildings are two of the most obvious. Whatever the context, there is a need, largely unmet today, to set *performance requirements* for the design of remedial systems. A complete treatment of this is outside our scope in these few pages. Here we wish simply to suggest how the ideas of unsaturated flow theory, and particularly the concept of hydraulic potential, may be useful in specifying performance targets.

Today, the specification of remedial treatments for damp-affected buildings rarely contains objective measures of the target performance. For example, in treating the fabric, it is usual to seek 'best efforts' in bringing about improvements, usually in qualitative terms. Survey is almost invariably carried out by visual inspection, backed up by some attempt to sample the water content by simple tests; and the improvements achieved are assessed on the same basis. Can we do better?

As we have pointed out several times earlier, the condition for equilibrium between wet materials of different composition and also for equilibrium between wet materials and the atmosphere to which they are exposed is that the *hydraulic potentials* should be equal. We have argued [498] that it is therefore more logical to set up a *performance criterion* based on the hydraulic potential than on the water content.

Performance requirements of walls

Putting it simply, the four main purposes in damp-proofing treatments for walls are:

1   to improve the thermal performance of exterior walls,
2   to eliminate an interior source of water vapour,
3   to eliminate the degradation and decay of building materials,
4   to eliminate visible dampness.

Thermal performance. There is much evidence that the *thermal* resistance of a wall can be strongly degraded by the presence of capillary water. Long ago Jakob [636] discussed the influence of water content on the thermal conductivity of porous building materials and subsequent work has confirmed a strong dependence [42, 327]. The mechanism of heat conduction in damp materials is complicated [161] and the effect perhaps deserves continuing study, but the facts are clear enough. Dry brick of bulk density 2400 kg m^{-3} has a thermal conductivity of about 1.2 W m^{-1} K^{-1}. However the thermal conductivity rises sharply with increasing water content, by about 60 per cent at 0.03 volume fraction water content and by about 135 per cent at 0.15 volume fraction water content. It follows that improving the thermal performance may often be one of the main reasons for carrying out remedial damp-proofing work on exterior masonry walls. A target performance expressed in terms of thermal resistance may therefore be translated directly into a target water content or hydraulic potential.

Interior humidity. The effect of water content on water migration within walls and on water exchange with the inside atmosphere of a dwelling is

Table 9.3 Equilibrium volume-fraction water content θ and corresponding hydraulic potential Ψ for several building materials at given relative humidity *RH* at 20 °C

Relative humidity RH/per cent	50	70	90	95
Hydraulic potential Ψ/MPa	93.8	48.2	14.3	6.93
	Volume fraction water content θ			
Brick: density 1910 kg/m³	–	0.002	–	0.023
Cement sand mortar	0.051	0.061	0.092	0.102
Gypsum plaster	–	<0.002	0.009	0.013
Wood: sitka spruce	0.035	0.050	0.081	0.092

more complex, since we are dealing with unsaturated flow in a composite material. In - damp-affected buildings the role of the damp wall surface as an unwanted source of water vapour in the dwelling is of overriding importance. The comfort of the interior of a dwelling is not strongly influenced by the humidity and there is evidence that most people can tolerate a wide humidity variation [364]. Nevertheless, it is usually considered desirable that the mean relative humidity should lie in the range 40–60 per cent. At equilibrium with such an atmosphere building materials attain a characteristic water content, which as we have seen is different for different materials and which depends on material composition and microstructure. A relative humidity of 60 per cent at 20 °C is equivalent to a water suction or hydraulic potential Ψ of 69.1 MPa (or alternately expressed a tension head of about 7000 m). This in turn corresponds to a Kelvin equation radius of 0.002 μm. In the case of clay brick, the equilibrium water content at 60 per cent relative humidity is very low (generally less than 1 per cent by volume) because there are few fine pores in brick ceramic. For timber and cementitious materials, the corresponding water content is considerably higher (see Table 9.3). If the water content is higher than the equilibrium value the wall will of course release water to the atmosphere by evaporation. The important questions are: what is the rate of evaporation from the interior surface of a damp wall to the atmosphere within the building; and what is the capacity of the atmosphere to take up such water without becoming excessively humid?

The fractional increase in humidity $F = \Delta H/H$ (where $H = RH/100$) caused by the continuous release of water vapour from a damp wall of area A in a room of volume V may easily be calculated: $F = eA/(aVH\rho_{w0})$, where e is the evaporation rate/unit area of wall surface, a is the air change rate and ρ_{w0} is the saturated vapour density at the ambient temperature T. For illustration, if we take $e = 0.02$ mm/h, $A/V = 0.2$ m^{-1}, $H = 0.6$, $T = 20$ °C (so that $\rho_{w0} = 0.017$ kg m^{-3}) and $a = 3$ h^{-1}, then $F = 0.15$. This simple calculation of course assumes perfect mixing of the air; near stagnation points in the air flow (in corners of rooms and behind furniture) the effective value of *a* may be considerably less.

We may reverse the calculation to obtain the maximum rate of water evaporation which may be tolerated from the damp wall without an unacceptable rise in room humidity. It is reasonable to take a value of, say, $F = 0.1$. In damp affected buildings remedial treatment should reduce the water flow through the wall to such an extent that the evaporation rate is brought well below the calculated maximum. Our earlier calculation suggests that it may often be necessary to bring down the rate of evaporation from wall surfaces well to below 0.01 mm/h in order to maintain acceptable humidity.

The difficulty in exploiting this relation is in measuring the evaporation rate *e* and in understanding the factors which control it. *e* depends in a complicated way both on the hydraulic properties and water contents of the materials and on air movement and on humidity itself. We have seen that when the wall surface is very wet *e* is determined largely by environmental factors: temperature, humidity and air speed. At lower water contents material transport properties become dominant. It would be possible to lay down for the wall a performance requirement related to humidity and the rate of release of water vapour; and thence a performance criterion based on the maximum evaporation rate under specified interior conditions. However, this is not readily measured and there is no way in which the evaporation rate can be linked solely and simply to the water content of the wall as this is only one of the several factors upon which it depends. It is probable that under normal conditions evaporation rates as low as 0.01 kg m^{-2} h^{-1} can only be achieved at relatively high hydraulic potentials. We do not yet have sufficient data on evaporation rates from porous wall materials at very low air velocities to firmly establish an appropriate value of the hydraulic potential.[15]

Decay and deterioration. The requirements placed on the structural performance of exterior walls have no direct short-term implications for permissible water contents. Of course, the expectation that walls should maintain their performance indefinitely is essentially a durability target, and durability and water content are strongly linked for most materials. In traditional construction, timber (and paper), plaster and metals are the materials whose integrity is most seriously threatened by prolonged exposure to dampness. Electrochemical corrosion of metals generally ceases below a characteristic humidity, which for iron is about 70 per cent *RH* ($\Psi = 48.2$ MPa). Timber decay likewise ceases below definite water contents, somewhat dependent on species, but generally about 20–30 per cent by weight [449], corresponding to a humidity of about 85–95 per cent ($|\Psi| = 7$–22 MPa). The critical humidity for mould growth on interior surfaces is similar [436, 1335], the RH range 79–95 per cent covering most species at typical building temperatures. The decay of plaster has been less studied. It seems reasonable to require that the water content of walls should be sufficiently low that all constructional materials in hydraulic contact with the wall fabric should retain their integrity indefinitely; and that metallic corrosion, timber decay and degradation of plaster should not occur. It seems that a performance criterion based on hydraulic potential has the greatest generality.

Appearance. Severe cases of capillary dampness manifest themselves visually, as darkening or staining of moist regions of wall surface. Long before timber decay is apparent (and certainly before any reduction in thermal performance could be suspected) the change in appearance may be obvious. How porous materials change in appearance as the water content is progressively increased depends mainly on the effect of pore water on the absorption and scattering of light, as described in Chapter 2. The effects depend critically on pore size distribution and the main changes in reflectance are expected when the pores comparable in size with the wavelength of visible light (say 0.5 μm) become filled. Thus materials quite generally may be expected to appear essentially dry at suctions of about 1 MPa and higher.

Comment. The analysis we have given suggests that direct measurement of the hydraulic potential and of the evaporation rate would be of value in assessing the performance of damp-proofing treatments. In particular it appears that performance criteria could be established on the basis of hydraulic potential *which are broadly independent of materials*. We have suggested [498] that damp-proofing treatments should bring the potential of the fabric to about 30 MPa or higher.

9.2.5   Moisture state of a cavity wall

A common element of construction (both traditional and modern) is the two-leaf cavity wall [561, 1266]. We now use our analyses of rain absorption and evaporation to make some estimates of the moisture state of the outer leaf. We take this to be formed of brick masonry of thickness $L = 100$ mm. The cavity between outer and inner leaves is commonly 50 mm wide.

We consider first a single driving rain event and use Eqns 9.18 and 9.24. For illustration we take mid-range values for the driving rain flux $V_0 = 10$ mm/h, the brick sorptivity $S = 1.5$ mm/min$^{1/2}$ and its effective porosity $f_e = 0.15$. We assume that the wall is initially dry. Then the time to surface saturation $t_s = 40$ min. We calculate that the wetting front reaches the inner surface of the outer leaf at time $t_1 = t_s/2 + (Lf_e/S)^2 = 120$ min. Here $(Lf_e/S)^2 = \tau_1 = 100$ min. The cumulative absorption is then (in the notation of Figure 4.19) $i_h = Lf_e = 15$ mm. Over 120 min the total rain deposited on the wall is 20 mm, of which three-quarters is absorbed and one-quarter is shed as run-off. At time t_1, the inner surface of the outer leaf reaches its maximum imbibition water content $f_e = \theta_h$, that is, the Hirschwald water content. This inner surface establishes a relative humidity of 100 per cent in the air in immediate contact with it.

We have assumed that the rainfall event lasts long enough (at least for duration t_1, here 120 min) for the wetting front to penetrate to the back of the outer leaf. However, even in the course of a brief spell of rain lasting for only 45 min $(t_s/2 + \tau_1/4)$, the wetting front reaches halfway through the outer leaf. When rain then ceases, the water already absorbed continues to redistribute from the wetted region to the adjacent dry zone under the action of capillary forces. The water content of the inner surface eventually rises to about $\theta_h/2$, sufficient again to establish a high humidity. Of course, if the wall is not initially dry, then its capacity to absorb driving rain is correspondingly reduced, and the time to surface saturation t_s decreases. The higher initial water content entails a lower effective sorptivity (see p 129), and hence from Eqn 9.18 a shorter time to surface saturation t_s. We remark that the initial water content has a strong influence on t_s, a matter to consider in calculating water absorption during sequences of closely spaced rain events (as are common [897]).

Next, we consider what happens after the rain stops. The wall tends slowly to lose water by evaporation. On the exterior face, the moisture state responds to the potential evaporation PE of the environment. The PE depends strongly on the climatic conditions, and varies from season to season (as we see on p 320). A summer value may be as high as 4 mm/day (London) or 8 mm/day (Athens), while a winter value may be close to zero. In this example, the water absorbed during the rainfall event is 15 mm. In summer this is lost by evaporation in a few days, while in winter this may take several weeks or more to be lost.

The conditions inside the cavity play an important role. If the cavity is itself well-ventilated water can be lost by evaporation from both faces of the outer leaf; of course, if the cavity is poorly ventilated (if for example the cavity is filled with thermal insulant and air movement is impeded), little evaporation occurs on the inner face, and high humidity is maintained in the cavity with potential for transfer by condensation. The rate of evaporative water loss from the wall is then only (or mostly) by a single-sided external process, and is necessarily less than if there is a contribution also from evaporation within the cavity.

Long-term water balances in building elements

Our particular discussion of the moisture state of a cavity wall points towards a general statement about the long-term relation between water absorption and evaporation in built structures of all kinds. This follows by considering the overall balance which must exist between water absorption, evaporation and stored water in any building element. Broadly speaking, in circumstances in which the total (potential) evaporation exceeds the total water absorption, the stored water in the fabric averaged over the long term remains low. Conversely, if the situation favours water absorption over evaporation, then the stored water in the fabric must necessarily reach a high level.

We can state this balance for a time interval Δt as $E = I - \Delta W$ where E is the total cumulative evaporation, I the total cumulative water absorption, and ΔW is the change in total stored water over Δt. All quantities E, I and W are per unit area of surface, so have dimension [L]. If, over the long term ($\Delta t > 1\,\mathrm{y}$ say), $I > E$ then the water content of the structure increases. We now ask: when is this likely to be the case? Assuming that, as often holds, the only significant source of absorbed water is driving rain, I is limited by and cannot exceed $I_A \Delta t$ where I_A is the annual driving rain load [633, 897]. The driving rain may be entirely absorbed or else part may be absorbed and part shed as run-off. Here we are interested only in the absorbed fraction. The factors which favour prolonged or total absorption are (as shown on p 308) high material sorptivity S, low driving-rain flux V_0, driving-rain events of short duration, and large material thickness L. Then for an initially dry structure we can set $I \approx I_A \Delta t$. On the other hand, the total evaporation E is controlled by the local potential evaporation (denoted previously as e) over the interval Δt, such that E can equal but cannot exceed $e\Delta t$. It follows that high stored water contents are to be expected in the long term if $I_A / e > 1$. We expect that this condition is met in thick-walled structures of high sorptivity in locations of low potential evaporation and high driving-rain exposure. This corresponds to the moisture state of 'deep wetting' described in [1178].

Ultimately, water absorption is self-limiting. As the stored water increases, the ability to absorb further water is reduced. In driving rain, the time to surface saturation decreases as the initial water content rises. Over the long term the change in stored water $\Delta W \rightarrow 0$, and $I \rightarrow E$. Since the stored water content is high, $E \approx e\Delta t$ and $I \rightarrow e\Delta t$. In other words, the stored water tends to rise to a level which is determined by the local potential evaporation. In contrast, in sheltered locations with only moderate exposure to driving rain and with adequate evaporation, stored water is low. Then the total cumulative evaporation over the long term is less than the potential evaporation PE because in a structure that is dry over the long term E is limited by the low amount of stored water.

Finally, we note that such water balances are much influenced by geography. Potential evaporation PE varies greatly from place to place, as we have already seen in comparing annual PE in Athens, Cairo and London (pp 319, 325). The driving rain load also depends on geography but topography and orientation contribute marked local variations as well. We can see this in Figure 9.14, where driving rain indices I_A and potential evaporation PE are plotted for sites in three countries. Sites lying above the line of equality are liable to experience high stored water in the long term, while those below the line largely avoid that risk. While undoubtedly simplified such a water-balance analysis does provide a way to assess the likelihood of long-term material damage.[16] At minimum, it draws attention to the role of evaporation in moisture dynamics. We have often noted (for example [494]) that while driving rain events are clear to see evaporation remains invisible.

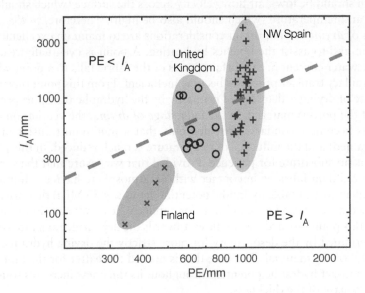

Figure 9.14 Driving rain index I_A (at orientation of maximum exposure) vs potential evaporation PE (annual total) for sites in three European countries. DRI data: NW Spain [954], United Kingdom [1098, 896], Finland [902]; all PE values calculated from TerraClimate gridded data for the year 2017 (Penman-Monteith method) [1]; dashed line of equality I_A = PE.

Yet over the long term the evaporation is of the same magnitude as the water absorption, and equally powerful in driving water migration in the building fabric.

9.3 DRYING OF BUILDINGS

Buildings can become thoroughly wet [199]. We can reasonably ask: does a scientific analysis of the physics of drying allow us to offer any guidance in drying buildings? We have earlier described in detail what laboratory studies tell us about how water is lost by evaporation from building materials such as brick and aerated concrete. In the last section, we also proposed a performance criterion based on hydraulic potential which can be used to set a target for a practical remedial drying treatment.

Research studies of drying in porous building materials – and incidentally many other kinds of porous materials – show conclusively that at high water contents the rate of drying depends entirely on the transfer of moisture from the surface to the atmosphere (see Chapter 7). This depends on the efficiency of aerodynamic processes, and is affected primarily by the humidity (which should be low), air flow velocity across the surface (which should be high) and temperature (which should also be high). Therefore, *in the early stages of drying* the important considerations are to maintain excellent ventilation and to assist the kinetics by heating. A point is eventually reached where water content in the surface layers of the fabric falls to a point where the capillary transfer processes become inefficient. From this point onwards, the rate of drying is determined primarily by the hydraulic transport properties of the porous material. In the *later stage of drying*, the ventilation conditions become secondary (provided only that a minimum transfer rate is maintained) and the influence of temperature is much reduced. In this phase there is no substitute for patience. Provided that we ensure that the surface of the building fabric is in contact with an atmosphere having a humidity equivalent to a suitable hydraulic potential (let us say 70 MPa) then we have imposed a dry boundary condition for capillary flow. We can do no more. From this point onwards, water flows towards the dry surface at a rate which is determined by the desorptivity (or more strictly the drying hydraulic diffusivity) of the material. The time that is needed thereafter for the fabric to reach a target hydraulic potential throughout its thickness increases roughly as the square of the thickness.

We described the two stages of drying earlier, on p 243. We may now ask whether in drying buildings it is an advantage to prolong the time spent in stage I and to defer the crossover to stage II. A simple SF analysis suggests that the duration of stage I, say t_1, varies inversely as the square of the drying rate e^2. The result, not by any means exact, is that $t_1 = (R/e)^2$ where R is the desorptivity of the material. Because the rate of evaporation is at its greatest in stage I, there are advantages in prolonging stage I drying. To take an extreme case, if a high stage I drying rate is encouraged by heating, fast air flows and low humidities, the surface dries rapidly and the transition to stage II drying occurs early. On the other hand, a slower drying process prolongs stage I. By reducing the drying rate in stage I there is more time for water to flow from the interior of the wall to the evaporating surface and overall we expect that the time to dry the entire thickness of the wall is reduced. Our simple analysis says that if we halve the stage I drying rate, we maintain stage I drying for four times as long, the effect being to double the cumulative evaporation achieved in the stage I process. This is a complex problem[17] but our simple argument does suggest that in drying damp-affected buildings it is probably more efficient to eschew aggressive drying, and to rely on good ventilation only to avoid accumulating stagnant, humid air. Dehumidifiers are needed in sealed rooms; but in most circumstances natural ventilation suffices. There are, of course, other good reasons to avoid forced drying, particularly in new buildings and remedial work. High rates of drying can encourage surface shrinkage of cement-based plasters causing them to crack and to detach from the backing.

NOTES

1 There are exact analytical solutions of the constant flux infiltration problem only for certain restricted forms of the diffusivity and conductivity functions [176, 1108, 751]. The extended Heaslet-Alksne method (see Chapter 4) now provides an approximate method for one-dimensional absorption with a surface flux boundary condition [916].

2 Lacy's formula provides a simple way to use weather data to predict rain loadings on buildings [715, 713, 714], and to relate exposure to climate. It was derived from studies of the sizes and rates of fall of raindrops by others [720, 120]. Eqn 9.5 as originally stated implies more precision than is warranted. It is now commonly written (for instance in [633, 141]) as $V_0 = (2/9)WR^{8/9}$. In either form it is often combined with a simple cosine formula [896] to allow for wind direction, although this is of limited accuracy [141]. In practice, how much rain is deposited on a given building surface depends in a complicated way on local air flows [397] and the amounts of rain, and indeed their droplet size distribution. More recent work on the topic makes extensive use of numerical modelling of air flow around buildings to estimate driving rain rates as a function of time and position [137, 138, 139, 145].

3 The value 0.64 for T_s has been obtained from numerical simulations for diffusivity functions representative of brick and stone materials. Kalimeris showed [662] that T_s varies only weakly with the parameter B. In the case that the diffusivity is constant (and hence $B = 0$), for which there is an analytical solution [231], T_s has the exact value $\pi^2/16 = 0.62$.

4 The Lacy equation combined with the cosine formula approximately describes the short-term rain loading on a vertical surface. Lacy and others saw the need also for a metric to describe the long-term exposure of buildings to driving rain at any particular location (see [140] for a review of early work). The first such *driving rain index* DRI was obtained simply by calculating the product of mean wind speed and total rainfall over a complete year [715]. It is a measure of the rain deposited on a notional vertical surface always facing the wind and in the far field of all obstructions. As an annual index it is generally expressed in unit m^2/s (although strictly it is per year). Several refinements followed, mainly to find indices able to predict driving rain loads on true building surfaces. The cosine formula was incorporated to allow for the influences of wind direction and wall orientation; and the quantity WR was calculated from hourly data and summed over a complete year to form the annual index [1023]. In the now established method of calculation [633, 896], the simple WR product is also replaced by Lacy's Eqn 9.5, as written in Note 2 above, to give an annual index $I_A = (2/9N)\Sigma[WR^{8/9}\cos(D - \Theta)]$, summed over hourly data for N years to give an N-year annual average. Here D is the wind direction and Θ is the direction of the normal to the wall, both measured clockwise from north. Since I_A incorporates the Lacy equation, its unit is now mm, or more usually, the equivalent L/m^2. So computed, I_A provides a reasonable estimate of the annual driving rain load arising from wind of direction D on a wall at orientation Θ at a specified location. How to best estimate the exposure to short intense rain events remains a long unsettled question [715, 142, 897, 895].

5 We use the term *moisture dynamics* to emphasize that the water in building elements is generally in flux – the water moves. A sorptive building element is an open system, subject to continuous exchanges of water with its immediate environment, and to the associated internal flows. This is true even at steady state. Our emphasis is a corrective to the rather static view of the moisture state often suggested in building physics.

6 The long t_{95} timescales for reaching steady-state mean that rising damp can be slow to develop from an initially dry condition in laboratory experiments and tests. Nevertheless useful experiments can be undertaken using brick stacks [882, 581, 499, 883, 1066, 204, 1111, 387]. The analysis of absorption into multi-layer composites shows that it is helpful to select an appropriately sorptive mortar if capillary rise is to occur efficiently throughout a bonded stack [881]. Cement-based mortars tend to be of low sorptivity and to impede the capillary rise process. Lime mortars are better for use in capillary rise experiments, but replacing mortar joints with porous paper pads can be an even more effective alternative.

7 Climate change models commonly predict future potential evaporation, and therefore our models allow us to estimate the effects of climate change on moisture regimes directly [496]. For the UK, published work from various sources agrees in predicting that PE will rise substantially in future decades. For example, estimates [343] of monthly average PE for the period 2070–2100 for NW England based on a Penman-Monteith calculation suggest that PE over a full year increases by about 55 per cent as a result of higher temperatures and lower summer rainfall. The increase in PE is considerably greater in summer than in winter. It is easy to apply these monthly factors in calculating the capillary flux (either by SF or UF methods). In our benchmark problem (a wall of 150 mm exposed to single-sided evaporation), the mean height of rise is reduced by about 15 per cent. The total annual flow through the wall increases by about 22 per cent, but there is a much larger rise in the evaporative flow during the summer months. The results of SF and UF simulations are in close agreement. At the summer maximum, the rate of evaporation per unit area increases by 55–60 per cent, from 2.8 mm/day to 4.4 mm/day. As a result of this, we anticipate a consequent marked increase in the rate of material damage. For the Netherlands, see [884].

8 We note several important field studies of rising damp in historic buildings. Working in the framework of the SF CRE model, D'Agostino [286] measured local evaporation rates in the cathedral of Lecce, and used a simplified form of the Penman equation to calculate PE from meteorological data. Vogel [1275] used a UF simulation in a study of the Church of All Saints at Heřmánkovice and showed the value of making water-content measurements in both soil and building fabric. Comprehensive data of this quality open the way to refined models of moisture dynamics, and ultimately to improved conservation practice [742]. Both D'Agostino's work at Lecce and that of Falchi [363] on historic masonry buildings in Venice also made use of salt analysis to explore long-term processes at play in rising damp.

9 It seems inevitable that evaporatively pumped water flow through the lower courses of ground-supported brick and other masonry structures must eventually degrade the mortar joints. The groundwater entering the base of the wall is not generally lime-saturated and so the lowest courses experience greater chemical stress than the courses higher in the wall. Flows of the magnitude we estimate are sufficient to dissolve all of the calcite from a fully carbonated 10 mm mortar joint in about 100 y. Such effects, which can be observed widely in walls, have only occasionally been mentioned in technical publications [832, 1065].

10 Another important consequence of the gradual flushing of trapped air at the base of the wall is to increase the sorptivity. Both the CRE height of rise and the total water flow are proportional to the sorptivity. The magnitude of the change in sorptivity may be appreciable. Direct measurement of the sorptivity of Portland stone under vacuum, where air-trapping cannot occur, shows that sorptivity is about 1.8–2.5 times the sorptivity measured in air [1029].

11 It was towards the end of the nineteenth century as a result of public health

concerns that the inclusion of damp proof courses [dpcs] in walls became a legal requirement in the United Kingdom [329]. Before dpcs were used other attempts were made to counteract the problem of rising damp, notably by using 'air drains' [1350]. These were ventilated trenches or slots, perhaps 1 m deep, around the perimeters of buildings. The SF CRE analysis shows that for a typical solid wall of that time, 340 mm thick, with evaporation from both sides, it is necessary to have an evaporation rate e of about 6 mm/day to limit the height of rise to about 0.5 m. This rate of drying is difficult to achieve by natural ventilation within the restricted space of an air drain (and indeed within the subfloor space inside the building). Forced ventilation at the base of damp-affected structures is proposed (and used) as a means of reducing rising damp [1241, 460, 461, 1222]. While high evaporation rates may be achieved, the enhanced water flow through the base of the structure may cause long-term deterioration.

12 We have not included in our analysis the effects of the upward transfer of salts in rising damp [14, 800, 1360]. This occurs as a result of the wick action which we have discussed separately in Chapter 7. The effects of salt can be severe in localities with saline ground waters, where the term *salt damp* is employed [1106, 1350, 759].

13 Electroosmosis is the flow of an aqueous electrolyte solution in a capillary system (a porous medium or a capillary tube) under the action of an electric field. The phenomenon is well understood, at least for dilute solutions: the flow arises from the action which the electric field exerts on the electrical double layer at the interface between the solution and the solid surface [337, 734, 1232]. The result is a steady shear flow. The flow rate is proportional to the electric field and depends on the *zeta potential*, the potential difference between the fixed charges on the solid surface and the viscous shear plane in the solution. The zeta potential depends both on the chemical nature of the solid surface and on the composition of the electrolyte solution. Thus for electroosmotic flow in a porous material we have $u_{eo} = K_{eo} \nabla V$, where ∇V is electrical potential gradient and K_{eo} is a transport property of the material. For dilute solutions, theory shows that K_{eo} does not depend on pore size. The application of active electroosmosis to dewatering of soils is also adequately understood [234, 214]. However, the use of passive systems for controlling water migration in masonry is not. Scientific investigations and clear conclusions are few [109, 1311]. It has been established [488, 472] that in a laboratory brick stack a small electrical potential difference exists between a copper electrode embedded in a cement mortar joint and a similar electrode in a soil bed in hydraulic contact with the stack. The potential difference is at most about 300 mV (soil electrode positive) and is due principally to differences in the solution composition, and especially the pH, in the environment of the two electrodes. The associated electric field is the *gradient* of the potential difference and is therefore extremely weak. Complementary measurements on electroosmosis in small brick plugs [472, 448] suggest that the flow produced by an electric field of this magnitude is generally insignificant compared with the upward flux produced in capillary rise. Furthermore electroosmosis is strongly suppressed in the presence of salts (see [899] for experimental confirmation in brick) and is likely to be unpredictable in masonry structures. In spite of a long history of use, no satisfactory scientific study of passive electroosmosis in masonry has yet been published. A number of explanations have been proposed but these have been descriptive rather than quantitative, and some indeed are quite unscientific.

14 In the United Kingdom, there are large stocks of housing in both public and private ownership built in brick and stone masonry without physical damp-proof membranes [498]. These houses (most of which were constructed before 1890) usually have walls of solid construction, nominally 225 mm thick. There

344 Topics in moisture dynamics

are also many other dwellings with various kinds of solid and cavity walls in which the damp-proof course has become ineffective since construction. Such walls are not resistant to the upward movement of water from the ground and often show signs of local or general dampness. Those engaged in the rehabilitation of older dwellings often and rightly consider that dampness in the fabric of the building is undesirable and should be eliminated. Public authorities may require the installation of an 'approved damp-course' before awarding an improvement grant. There are several remedial methods which aim to isolate the building structure from direct hydraulic contact with the ground and suppress or at least impede capillary rise. Undoubtedly some of these methods may succeed in reducing dampness but in precise technical terms it is often unclear what is required of such work. After installation it is similarly unclear what has been achieved. There are no generally accepted criteria of performance laid down in specification or available in cases of dispute. Indeed there may have been little objective evidence of the need for any remedial treatment in the first place. Nevertheless many thousands of such systems are installed every year.

15 We have suggested elsewhere [462] that the measurement of the sorptivity provides a simple means of assessing the water repellency achieved in chemical injection damp-proofing treatments. It is interesting to ask if the sorptivity S may be directly linked to the evaporation rate e. It is reasonable to expect that a reduction in S should cause a reduction in e, by the following argument. Here θ represents the water content. Consider a porous material of sorptivity S and hydraulic diffusivity $D(\theta)$. As we have already discussed, analysis of diffusivity data for a number of porous materials shows that $D(\theta) = D_0 \exp(B\theta)$ where B is roughly constant. If after chemical treatment the sorptivity is reduced to S' then the diffusivity after treatment $D'(\theta) = D'_0 \exp(B\theta) = D_0(S'/S)^2 \exp(B\theta)$. Now we may assume that a steady-state water distribution exists in the damp wall so that the flow rate u is equal to the evaporation rate e at the surface. But $u = l^{-1} \int_{\theta_1}^{\theta_0} D d\theta$ where l is the length of the flow path and θ_1 and θ_0 are the water contents of the wet and dry material. It follows that $u/u' = (S/S')^2$. Thus in order to reduce the evaporation rate from e to e', we need to reduce the sorptivity from S to $S(e'/e)^{1/2}$. Despite the numerous simplifications, this analysis does emphasize the delicate balance between water absorption and evaporation in relation to building dampness.

16 Water balance is a long established concept in groundwater hydrology [41, 817], where it is expressed as precipitation = evaporation + streamflow. To develop a similar framework for the water cycle in building physics may help to integrate the moisture dynamics of buildings into the developing field of urban hydrology [452, 703].

17 It is a matter with a long history in soil physics. In his preface to Buckingham's 1907 USDA bulletin [195] Cameron wrote of 'the apparently contradictory facts ...that the soils of arid regions, at depths a little below the surface, are generally wetter and hold their moisture for much longer periods than do the soils of humid areas in dry seasons.' This phenomenon was later called the *Buckingham effect* by Covey [280], who found that '...a rapid initial drying of a moist soil, under the influence of a condition of high evaporativity, builds into the soil a greater resistance to future water loss than would the same total water loss at a slower rate under lower evaporativity.' For evaporativity, read PE.

Appendix A: symbols and acronyms

A	area
A	moisture (buffering) effusivity
A_s	surface area
A_w	CIB water absorption coefficient
B, B_r	constant in exponential form of hydraulic diffusivity
B_w	CIB water penetration coefficient
Br	Brenner number
Ca	capillary number
C	compression index
d	pore size length scale
D	capillary or hydraulic diffusivity
D	wind direction
$\mathcal{D}$	scaled capillary or hydraulic diffusivity
D_d	dispersion coefficient
D_l	molecular diffusivity, liquid phase
D_l'	apparent molecular diffusivity, liquid phase
D_r	hydraulic diffusivity defined in terms of θ_r
D_v	molecular diffusivity, vapour phase
e	void ratio
e	evaporation rate (flux)
E	total evaporation rate
f	volume-fraction porosity
f_c	closed porosity
f_e	wetted-zone water content (Sharp Front theory)
f_o	open porosity
f_p	total porosity at the percolation threshold
f_r	residence time density
F	formation factor
F	total face area of test specimen
F'	shape factor
g	gravitational acceleration
h	hydrostatic head

h	height of rise
h_{ss}	steady-state height of rise
h	fractional Hirschwald coefficient
H	fractional relative humidity, RH/100
H	diimensionless height
H	Henry's law solubility constant
H	Hirschwald coefficient
i	cumulative absorption, volume basis
i_e	cumulative evaporation
i_h	cumulative absorption at Hirschwald water content
i_m	cumulative absorption, mass basis
I	cumulative absorbed volume
I	dimensionless cumulative absorption
I	X-ray intensity
I	imbibition parameter
I_A	annual driving rain index
j	cumulative absorption in two-layer composite
j_m	diffusion mass flux
k	Darcy permeability
k'	intrinsic permeability
k_m	mass-flow permeability
k_r	relative permeability
K	capillary or hydraulic conductivity
K	bulk elastic modulus
$\mathcal{K}$	scaled capillary or hydraulic conductivity
K_e	wetted zone effective permeability (Sharp Front theory)
K_{eo}	electroosmotic transport parameter
K_r	permeability ratio
K_s	permeability
l	wetted zone length (Sharp Front theory)
l	lengthscale
l_c	characteristic length in MIP
L	length
L_e	1/e stopping distance for X-rays, gamma rays and neutrons
m	Archie exponent
M	molar mass
p, p_f	fluid pressure
p_c	capillary pressure
p_{cr}	critical percolation pressure in MIP
p_w	vapour pressure of water
p_{w0}	saturated vapour pressure of water
P	fluid pressure potential
P'	gauge or differential pressure
P_c	capillary (pressure) potential
Pe	Péclet number

Q	total volume flow rate
r	rate of water run-off
r_c	radius of curvature of liquid interface
r_I	stage I drying rate
R	rainfall rate
$\mathbf{R}$	gas constant [8.31446 J/(mol K)]
R_J	hydraulic contact resistance
Re	Reynold's number
Re_k	permeability Reynold's number
RH	relative humidity
S	sorptivity
S_h	hybrid sorptivity
$\mathbb{S}$	intrinsic sorptivity
S	spreading parameter
Sc	Schmidt number
t	elapsed time
t_c	contact time
t_r	mean residence time
T	dimensionless elapsed time
T	temperature
T_f	ice-point temperature
u	scalar volume flow rate
u	moisture content, mass by mass
u_m	scalar mass flow rate
$\mathbf{u}$	vector flow velocity
U	total volume flow rate
V	volume
V_0	driving rain flux
V_b	bulk volume of a porous material
V_p	pore volume
V_s	solid volume of a porous material
w	weight
w	moisture content, mass by volume
w	weight-fraction water (or liquid) content
w_A	Archimedes weight
W	washout function
W	wind speed
WA	water absorption, weight/weight
x_f	location of SF or other front
x_p	penetration depth in moisture buffering
α	volume fraction of dispersed material or inclusion
α	Biot coefficient
α	mass-attenuation coefficient
α_t	thermal expansivity
β	parameter of exponential diffusivity function

348   *Appendix A: symbols and acronyms*

β	wettability coefficient
γ	contact angle
δ	thermal diffusivity/hydraulic diffusivity ratio
ΔH	enthalpy
ϵ	local potential evaporation
ζ	parameter of SF immiscible displacement model
η	dynamic viscosity
θ	volume-fraction liquid content
θ_d	volume-fraction liquid content in nominal dry state
θ_h	volume-fraction liquid content at Hirschwald state
θ_m	mass-fraction liquid content
θ_r	reduced or normalized volume-fraction liquid content
θ_s	volume-fraction liquid content at saturation
θ_1	volume-fraction water content at monolayer coverage
Θ	orientation of normal to wall
κ	dielectric constant
λ	mean free path in a gas
λ_a	fraction of porosity occupied by air
λ_c	capillary length
Λ_A	volume/(surface area) of pores
ν	liquid (or moisture) ratio
ξ	moisture (differential) capacity
ρ	density
ρ_b	bulk density
ρ_s	solid density
ρ_w	density of liquid water
ρ_{wv}	density of water vapour
ρ_{wv0}	saturated water vapour density
σ	surface tension
σ	electrical conductivity
τ	tortuosity
ϕ	Boltzmann variable $xt^{-1/2}$
ϕ_s	volume-fraction of solids
Φ	total potential
χ	parameter of SF immiscible displacement model
Ψ	capillary or hydraulic potential
Ψ_f	front capillary potential (Sharp Front theory)

Subscripts

a, A	air
A	Archimedes
ad	adsorbed/adsorption
b	bulk

d	dry state
f	Sharp Front or wet front
h	Hirschwald water content
i	ith part or component
I	ice
l, L	liquid state
m	mass
r	relative
s	saturated state
s	surface
ss	steady-state
S	solid state
v	vapour
w	water
y	year

Note: We follow the conventions of quantity calculus in expressing equations, formulae and data [634]. Symbols, as above, represent physical quantities. Equations relating different physical quantities generally do not depend on the choice of units. The value A of a physical quantity is the product of a number $\{A\}_U$ and a unit U, so that $A = \{A\}_U U$. It is numerical values $\{A\}_U = A/U$ that are shown in tables and graphs. Sometimes formulae contain numerical parameters that do depend on the units used for physical quantities. The formulae can then be expressed explicitly in terms of A/U: that is, as relations between numerical values rather than physical quantities. SI units used include $10^{\pm 3}$ multiples and submultiples, and time units min, h, d (and occasionally y).

Dimensional analysis

[L]	length
[M]	mass
[T]	time

Mathematical symbols

$\sim$	varies as, scales as
$\approx$	approximately equals

Acronyms

AAC	autoclaved aerated concrete
BET	Brunauer-Emmett-Teller adsorption function
CMD	composite mineral density
CREG	capillary rise, evaporation and gravity model
dpc	damp-proof course
DRI	driving rain index
GAB	Guggenheim-Anderson-de Boer adsorption function
HAM	heat, air and moisture (or mass) transfer
hcp	hardened cement paste
MIP	mercury intrusion porosimetry
MRI	magnetic resonance imaging
NMR	nuclear magnetic resonance
OPC	ordinary portland cement
PE	potential evaporation
PET	positron emission tomography
RH	relative humidity
SD	standard deviation
SEM	scanning electron microscope
SF	sharp front
TDR	time-domain reflectometry
UF	unsaturated flow
WDR	wind-driven rain
WR	water retention function
XCT	X-ray computerized tomography
XRD	X-ray diffraction

Appendix B: properties of water

- Density, viscosity, surface tension and vapour pressure of liquid water over the temperature range 0 to +60 °C.
- Interpolating equations.
- Supercooled liquid water: density, viscosity, surface tension and vapour pressure from 0 to −30 °C.
- Water vapour diffusivity from −40 to +60 °C.
- Ice: density, vapour pressure and melting pressure from −40 to 0 °C.
- Liquid water at 25 °C: molar mass, compressibility, thermal expansivity, thermal conductivity, heat capacity, enthalpy and entropy of vaporization, enthalpy and entropy of fusion.

Table B.1 Physical properties of liquid water from 0 to 60 °C

Temperature $T/°C$	Density $\rho_w/\text{kg m}^{-3}$	Viscosity $\eta_w/\text{mPa s}$	Surface tension $\sigma_w/\text{mN m}^{-1}$	Vapour pressure p_{w0}/kPa
0	999.84	1.792	75.65	0.611
5	999.96	1.518	74.94	0.873
10	999.70	1.306	74.22	1.23
15	999.10	1.138	73.49	1.71
20	998.20	1.002	72.74	2.34
25	997.04	0.8900	71.97	3.17
30	995.65	0.7972	71.19	4.25
35	994.03	0.7191	70.40	5.63
40	992.21	0.6527	69.60	7.39
45	990.21	0.5958	68.78	9.60
50	988.03	0.5465	67.94	12.35
55	985.69	0.5036	67.10	15.76
60	983.20	0.4660	66.24	19.95

Notes
Water density in equilibrium with air at 1 atm pressure: from 0–40°C, calculated CIPM values [1216]; for >40°C, calculated IAPWS-95 values [612, 1290, 928]; for all, small correction for dissolved air applied [540]. Other quantities are calculated from recommended equations of the International Association for the Properties of Water and Steam: viscosity [613, 928, 600]; surface tension [610]; and vapour pressure [611]. The viscosity of water at 1 atm and 20 °C $\eta_{w,20}$ is an important calibration standard, for which the accepted value is 1.0016 mPa s [49].

Interpolating equations

The following provide accurate estimates of the properties of liquid water in the temperature range 0–40 °C.

- *Density* [1216]

$$\rho_w = a_5[1 - \frac{(T + a_1)^2(T + a_2)}{a_3(T + a_4)}],$$ (B.1)

  with T in °C, and with $a_1 = -3.9830\,°C$, $a_2 = 301.80\,°C$, $a_3 = 5.2253 \times 10^5 (°C)^2$, $a_4 = 69.349\,°C$, $a_5 = 999.97\,kg/m^3$.

- *Viscosity* [677]

$$\ln \frac{\eta_w(T)}{\eta_{w,20}} = c_1[1 + c_2 \Delta T + c_3(\Delta T)^2] \frac{\Delta T}{T + 96.0},$$ (B.2)

  with T in °C, $\Delta T = (20.0 - T)$, and $c_1 = 1.2364$, $c_2 = -1.1081 \times 10^{-3} (°C)^{-1}$, $c_3 = 4.6102 \times 10^{-6} (°C)^{-1}$, $\eta_{w,20} = 1.0016\,mPa\,s$.

- *Surface tension*   Simplified form of IAPWS equation [610].

$$\sigma_w(T) = \sigma_{w,20}(1 + b_1 \Delta T + b_2 \Delta T^2 + b_3 \Delta T^3)$$ (B.3)

  with T in °C, $\Delta T = (20.0 - T)$, and with $b_1 = 2.0810 \times 10^{-3}$, $b_2 = -3.9244 \times 10^{-6}$, $b_3 = -2.7825 \times 10^{-9}$, $\sigma_{w,20} = 72.736\,mN\,m^{-1}$.

- *Vapour pressure*   See p 260 for the Magnus equation. The variation of water vapour pressure p_{w0} (kPa) with temperature T (°C) in terms of the Magnus parameters b, c is

$$\frac{dp_{w0}}{dT} = p_{w0} \cdot \frac{bc}{(T + c)^2}.$$ (B.4)

  The factor $bc/(T + c)^2 \approx \Delta H_{vap}/(RT^2)$ where ΔH_{vap} is the enthalpy of vaporization of water (Table B.5).

- *(Surface tension / viscosity)*$^{1/2}$ See p 175.

Table B.2 Physical properties of supercooled liquid water from 0 to $-30\,^{\circ}$C

Temperature $T/^{\circ}$C	Density $\rho_w/$kg m^{-3}	Viscosity $\eta_w/$mPa s	Surface tension $\sigma_w/$mN m^{-1}	Vapour pressure $p_{w0}/$Pa
0	999.8	1.792	75.6	611.2
-5	999.3	2.15	76.3	421.8
-10	998.2	2.65	77.0	286.5
-15	996.3	3.35	77.7	191.4
-20	993.5	4.39	78.3	125.6
-25	989.5	6.45	79.0	80.9
-30	983.9	10.2	79.6	51.0

Notes
Density from [537]; viscosity from [34, 600]; surface tension from [610, 596]; vapour pressure from [611].

Table B.3 Water vapour diffusivity in air from -40 to 60° C [797]

Temperature $T/^{\circ}$C	Diffusivity $10^5 D_w/$ m^2 s^{-1}
-40	1.64
-20	1.90
0	2.18
5	2.25
10	2.32
15	2.40
20	2.48
25	2.55
30	2.63
35	2.71
40	2.79
50	2.95
60	3.12

Table B.4 Properties of ice from 0 to −40 °C [1291]

Temperature $T/^\circ$C	Density $\rho_w/\text{kg m}^{-3}$	Vapour pressure p_{w0}/Pa	Melting pressure MPa
0	916.7	611.66	0
−10	918.7	260.13	111.2
−20	920.3	103.36	194.6
−30	921.6	38.05	270.3
−40	922.8	12.85	349.2

Table B.5 Other physical properties of water at 25 °C

Molar mass	18.0150×10^{-3} kg/mol
Ice-point temperature	273.15 K
Triple-point temperature	273.16 K
Isothermal compressibility	0.4524 GPa^{-1}
Volume thermal expansivity	0.2573×10^{-3} K^{-1}
Thermal conductivity	0.6065 W/(m K)
Heat capacity at constant pressure	4.1813 kJ/(kg K)
Enthalpy of vaporization	43.99 kJ/mol
Entropy of vaporization	118.826 J/(mol K)
Enthalpy of fusion (0 °C)	6.0095 kJ/mol
Entropy of fusion (0 °C)	22.01 J/(mol K)

Notes
Compressibility and expansivity from [674]; heat capacity from [730]; thermal conductivity from [1039, 601]; enthalpies and entropies from Gmelin [429]; ice-point temperature T_f is melting point of ice at 1 atm pressure; kelvin–°Celsius conversion, $T/\text{K} = T/^\circ\text{C} + T_f/\text{K}$.

Appendix C: minerals, salts and solutions

Soluble inorganic salts and minerals are often present in construction materials. The physical properties of water are changed by the presence of dissolved material. We give here some data on the solubility of common salts and minerals, and on the properties of their aqueous solutions:

1 Calcium carbonate *calcite*
2 Calcium chloride
3 Calcium hydroxide *portlandite*
4 Calcium sulphate *gypsum*
5 Magnesium calcium carbonate *dolomite*
6 Potassium chloride *sylvite*
7 Potassium sulphate *arcanite*
8 Sodium chloride *halite*
9 Sodium sulphate *mirabilite, thenardite*

- Data on mineral and salt solubility in water at 0–35 °C.
- Data on density, viscosity, surface tension and vapour pressure of salt solutions. For vapour pressures and relative humidities of other aqueous solutions, see Greenspan [446].

Table C.1 Solubility of minerals, g/kg water

Temperature $T/^\circ C$	Calcite	Dolomite	Gypsum	Portlandite
0	0.0104	0.0157	2.288	1.712
5	0.0107	0.0157	2.392	1.684
10	0.0111	0.0147	2.486	1.648
15	0.0115	0.0145	2.568	1.605
20	0.0119	0.0143	2.637	1.556
25	0.0123	0.0143	2.692	1.504
30	0.0127	0.0144	2.735	1.451
35	0.0132	0.0146	2.764	1.396

Notes
Calcite, dolomite and gypsum computed using PHREEQC [903] from thermodynamic data in the Wateq4f tabulation [72]; portlandite interpolated from [719]. Tabulated values are for solubility in pure water in a closed system. Solubilities of calcite and dolomite are increased in the presence of CO_2: for a typical atmospheric CO_2 concentration of 390 ppm, solubilities at 25 °C are 0.0530 g/kg water (calcite) and 0.0593 g/kg water (dolomite). In the presence of CO_2, portlandite is converted to calcium carbonate.

Table C.2 Solubility of salts, g/kg water

Temperature $T/^\circ C$	Calcium chloride $CaCl_2$	Potassium chloride KCl	Potassium sulphate K_2SO_4	Sodium chloride $NaCl$	Sodium sulphate Na_2SO_4
0	589.4	280.4	73.3	356.3	46.7
5	616.3	296.7	82.8	356.7	64.6
10	651.8	312.7	93.6	357.2	92.7
15	697.0	328.4	102.8	357.8	132.2
20	753.4	343.8	111.9	358.7	192.6
25	823.0	353.8	121.0	359.8	279.6
30	974.3	373.6	130.0	360.9	405.9
35	1038.1	388.0	139.0	362.2	490.3

Notes
Sodium chloride from [262]; sodium sulphate (solubility of decahydrate *mirabilite* [$Na_2SO_4.10H_2O$], 0–30 °C and anhydride *thenardite* [Na_2SO_4], 35 °C), from [563, 429]; potassium chloride, potassium sulphate (0–5 °C), calcium chloride (solubility of hexahydrate [$CaCl_2.6H_2O$], 0–25 °C and α-tetrahydrate [$CaCl_2.4H_2O$], 30–35 °C), all from [429]; potassium sulphate, 10–35 °C, from [864]. Sodium sulphate readily forms a metastable *heptahydrate* from aqueous solution around 10 °C [528].

Table C.3 Properties of sodium chloride solutions at 25 °C

Concentration g/kg water	Density ρ/kg m^{-3}	Viscosity η/mPa s	Surface tension σ/mN m^{-1}	Vapour pressure p_w/kPa
50	1030.7	0.9610	73.56	3.077
100	1062.1	1.042	74.98	2.984
150	1091.5	1.137	76.39	2.884
200	1119.2	1.253	77.82	2.774
250	1145.3	1.389	79.29	2.654
300	1170.2	1.544	80.75	2.532
350	1193.8	1.730	82.16	2.400
359.8	1198.3	1.771	82.42	2.373

Note
From [429, 262].

Table C.4 Properties of sodium sulphate solutions at 25 °C

Concentration g/kg water	Density ρ/kg m^{-3}	Viscosity η/mPa s	Surface tension σ/mN m^{-1}	Vapour pressure p_w/kPa
14.20	1009.7	0.9288	72.24	3.153
28.41	1021.9	0.9676	72.51	3.142
56.82	1045.7	1.0513	73.03	3.119
85.23	1068.6	1.1460	73.56	3.097
113.6	1090.8	1.2491	74.08	3.076
142.0	1112.3	1.3759	74.61	3.057
213.1	1163.4	1.7201	–	3.008
278.4	1207.4	2.1741	–	2.965

Notes
Data sources: densities and water vapour pressures from [932]; viscosities interpolated from [1197]; surface tension estimated from [429, 68].

Appendix D: other liquids

- Physical properties of some nonaqueous liquids.

Table D.1 Physical properties of selected nonaqueous liquids at 25 °C

	Viscosity η/mPa s	Surface tension σ/mN m^{-1}	Density ρ/kg m^{-3}	Vapour pressure p_{v0}/kPa	Vapour diffusivity $10^{-5}D_v$/m^{2}s^{-1}
Water-miscible					
Methanol	0.545	22.1	787	16.7	1.66
Ethanol	1.082	22.0	785	8.7	1.29
n-Propyl alcohol	1.939	23.3	800	3.3	0.99
Isopropyl alcohol	2.023	20.9	781	6.9	1.04
Isobutyl alcohol	3.269	22.6	797	1.37	-
Ethylene glycol	16.61	48.4	1110	0.01	1.00
Ethyl acetate	0.426	23.2	894	12.8	0.88
Acetone	0.308	23.0	785	30.4	1.07
Tetrahydrofuran	0.465	26.7	882	22.5	1.01
Dimethyl sulfoxide	1.997	42.9	1096	0.08	1.01
Water-immiscible					
n-Hexane	0.296	17.9	656	19.7	0.78
n-Decane	0.863	23.4	728	0.21	0.58
n-Dodecane	1.390	24.9	745	0.02	0.49
Dichloromethane	0.417	27.8	1317	58.0	1.04
Toluene	0.553	27.9	865	3.9	0.88
Fuel oil	650	20–30	950	low	-
Diesel fuel	25	20–30	870	low	-
Kerosene	2.0	20–30	800	1	-
Motor gasoline	1.2	20–30	730	70	-

Note
Viscosities [1344], except methanol, ethanol, ethyl acetate [431], ethylene glycol [1034], dimethyl sulfoxide [435]; surface tensions [1346]; densities [1345], except ethanol [431], *n*-propyl alcohol, isopropyl alcohol [790], tetrahydrofuran [241], dimethyl sulfoxide [435]; vapour pressures calculated from Antoine equation [1343]; vapour diffusivities [1217], except tetrahydrofuran [1212], dimethyl sulfoxide (calculated) [392], dichloromethane [766].

Appendix E: other data

- Density and viscosity of air.
- Solubility of air in water.
- Diffusivity of air in water.

Table E.1 Density and viscosity of dry air

Temperature $T/°C$	Density $\rho/\mathrm{kg\ m}^{-3}$	Viscosity $10^{-6}\eta/\mathrm{Pa\ s}$
−25	1.424	15.96
0	1.293	17.24
25	1.184	18.48
50	1.092	19.67

Notes
The density is calculated from the CIPM-81/91 equation [297]. The viscosity is calculated from equations of Kadoya *et al.* [661].

Table E.2 Solubility of air in water

Temperature T/°C	Henry's law constant $10^3 H$/mol L^{-1} atm^{-1}		Dissolved gas concentration at 1 atm air pressure c/mg L^{-1}		
	Nitrogen	Oxygen	Nitrogen	Oxygen	Air
−5	1.08	2.31	23.6	15.5	39.1
0	0.99	2.09	21.6	14.0	35.5
5	0.90	1.89	19.8	12.7	32.4
10	0.83	1.72	18.2	11.5	29.7
15	0.77	1.57	16.8	10.5	27.3
20	0.71	1.44	15.5	9.6	25.1
25	0.66	1.32	14.4	8.8	23.2
30	0.61	1.21	13.4	8.1	21.5
35	0.57	1.12	12.5	7.5	20.0

Notes
The Henry's law constant H is defined in Eqn 8.2. The values at 25 °C are taken from Sander [1107] and values at other temperatures calculated using $\ln(H/H^\ominus) = A(1/T - 1/T^\ominus)$, with $T^\ominus = 25$ °C, $A = 1300$ K for nitrogen and $A = 1500$ K for oxygen [1107]. Dry air at 1 atm pressure has 0.78 atm nitrogen and 0.21 atm oxygen partial pressures.

Table E.3 Diffusivity of air in water

Temperature T/°C	Diffusivity $10^9 D$/m^2 s^{-1}	
	Nitrogen	Oxygen
10	1.29	1.54
25	2.10	2.20
40	2.83	3.33

Note
Nitrogen [376], oxygen [531].

Bibliography

[1] Abatzoglou J.T., Dobrowski S. Z., Parks S. A. and Hegewisch K. C. (2018) TerraClimate, a high-resolution global dataset of monthly climate and climatic water balance from 1958–2015. *Scientific Data*, **5**, 170191.

[2] Abbas A., Carcasses M. and Ollivier J.-P. (1999) Gas permeability of concrete in relation to its degree of saturation. *Materials and Structures*, **32**, 3–8.

[3] Abell A. B., Willis K. L. and Lange D. A. (1999) Mercury porosimetry and image analysis of cement-based materials. *Journal of Colloid and Interface Science*, **211**, 39–44.

[4] Adam K. M., Bloomsburg G. L. and Corey A. T. (1969) Diffusion of trapped gas from porous media. *Water Resources Research*, **5**, 840–849.

[5] Adan O. C. G. (1995) Determination of moisture diffusivities in gypsum renders. *Heron*, **40**, 201–215.

[6] AFPC-AFREM. (1998) Essai de perméabilité aux gaz du béton durci. Mode opératoire recommandé. *Compte-rendu des journées techniques AFPC-AFREM, Durabilité des bétons*, LMDC Toulouse, France, pp 125–134.

[7] Agliata R., Bogaard T. A., Greco R., Mollo L., Slob E. C. and Steele-Dunne S. C. (2018) Non-invasive estimation of moisture content in tuff bricks by GPR. *Construction and Building Materials*, **160**, 698–706.

[8] Agliata R., Greco R. and Mollo L. (2018) Moisture measurements in heritage masonries: A review of current techniques. *Materials Evaluation*, November, pp 1468–1477.

[9] Agliata R., Mollo L. and Greco R. (2017) Use of TDR to compare rising damp in three tuff walls made with different mortars. *Journal of Materials in Civil Engineering*, **29**, 04016262.

[10] Aharonov E., Rothman D. H. and Thompson A. H. (1997) Transport properties and diagenesis in sedimentary rocks: the role of micro-scale geometry. *Geology*, **25**, 547–550.

[11] Ahlgren L. (1972) *Moisture fixation in porous building materials*, Report 36, Division of Building Materials, Lund Institute of Technology.

[12] Ahmad A. (2020) Investigation of marble deterioration and development of a classification system for condition assessment using non-destructive ultrasonic technique. *Mediterranean Archaeology and Archaeometry*, **20**, 75–89.

[13] Ai H., Young J. F. and Scherer G. W. (2001) Thermal expansion kinetics: Method to measure permeability of cementitious materials: II, Application to hardened cement pastes. *Journal of the American Ceramic Society*, **84**, 385–391.

[14] Akiner S., Cooke R. U. and French R. A. (1992) Salt damage to Islamic monuments in Uzbekistan. *The Geographical Journal*, **158**, 257–272.

[15] Alava M., Dubé M. and Rost M. (2004) Imbibition in disordered media. *Advances in Physics*, **53**, 83–175.

[16] Aldea C.-M., Shah S. P. and Karr A. (1999) Permeability of cracked concrete. *Materials and Structures*, **32**, 370–376.

[17] Aldred J. M., Rangan B. V. and Buenfeld N. R. (2004) Effect of initial moisture content on wick action through concrete. *Cement and Concrete Research*, **34**, 907–912.

[18] Alduchov O. A. and Eskridge R. E. (1996) Improved Magnus form approximation of saturation vapor pressure. *Journal of Applied Meteorology*, **35**, 601–609.

[19] Aligizaki K. K. (2006) *Pore structure of cement-based materials*, Taylor and Francis, London.

[20] Al-Khafaf S. and Hanks R. J. (1974) Evaluation of the filter paper method for estimating soil water potential. *Soil Science*, **117**, 194–199.

[21] Al-Naddaf M. (2018) A new automatic method for continuous measurement of the capillary water absorption of building materials. *Construction and Building Materials*, **160**, 639–643.

[22] Allen A. J. (1991) Time-resolved phenomena in cements, clays and porous rocks. *Journal of Applied Crystallography*, **24**, 624–634.

[23] Allen A. J., Windsor C. G., Rainey V., Pearson D., Double D. D. and Alford N. M. (1982) A small-angle neutron-scattering study of cement porosities. *Journal of Physics D – Applied Physics*, **15**, 1817–1833.

[24] Allen R. G., Pereira L. S., Raes D. and Smith M. (1998) Crop evapotranspiration: Guidelines for computing crop water requirements. *FAO Irrigation and Drainage Paper*, no 56, Food and Agriculture Organization of the United Nations, Rome.

[25] Alves C., Sequeira Braga M. A. and Hammecker C. (1996) Water transfer and decay of granitic stones in monuments. *Comptes Rendus de l'Académie des Sciences Paris* sér IIa, **397**, 397–402.

[26] Alyafei N. and Blunt M. J. (2018) Estimation of relative permeability and capillary pressure from mass imbibition experiments. *Advances in Water Resources*, **115**, 88–94.

[27] American Petroleum Institute. (2005) *Recommended practice for testing well cements*, API RP 10B-2/ISO 10426-2:2003, Dallas, TX.

[28] American Petroleum Institute. (1998) *Recommended practices for core analysis*, API RP 40, 2nd edn, Dallas, TX.

[29] Amin M. H. G., Chorley R. J., Richards K. S., Hall L. D., Carpenter T. A., Cislerova M. and Vogel T. (1997) Study of infiltration into a heterogeneous soil using magnetic resonance imaging. *Hydrological Processes*, **11**, 471–483.

[30] Amin M. H. G., Hall L. D., Chorley R. J. and Richards K. S. (1998) Infiltration into soils, with particular reference to its visualization and measurement by magnetic resonance imaging (MRI). *Progress in Physical Geography*, **22**, 135–166.

[31] Amoroso G. G. and Fassina V. (1983) *Stone decay and conservation*, Elsevier, Amsterdam, The Netherlands.

[32] Andraski B. J. and Scanlon B. R. (2002) Thermocouple psychrometry. In J. H. Dane and G. Topp (eds), *Methods of soil analysis: Part 4 Physical methods*, Soil Science Society of America, Madison, WI, pp 609–642.

[33] Andreasen M., Jensen K. H., Desilets D., Franz T. E., Zreda M., Bogena H. R. and Looms M. C. (2017) Status and perspectives on the cosmic-ray neutron method for soil moisture estimation and other environmental science applications. *Vadose Zone Journal* 16, 1–11.

[34] Angell C. A. (1982) Supercooled water. In F. Franks (ed.), *Water: a comprehensive treatise*, vol. 7, Springer, Boston, MA, pp 1–81.

[35] Anovitz L. M. and Cole D. R. (2015) Characterization and analysis of porosity and pore structures. *Reviews in Mineralogy and Geochemistry*, 80, 61–164.

[36] Antón C., Climent M. A., de Vera G., Sánchez I. and Andrade C. (2013) An improved procedure for obtaining and maintaining well characterized partial water saturation states on concrete samples to be used for mass transport tests. *Materials and Structures*, 46, 1389–1400.

[37] Archie G. E. (1942) The electrical resistivity log as an aid in determining some reservoir characteristics. *Transactions of the American Institute of Mining and Metallurgical Engineers*, 146, 54–61.

[38] Arfvidsson J. (1998) *Moisture transport in porous media: modelling based on Kirchhoff potentials*, PhD thesis, Lund University; Report TVBH-1010, Dept of Building Physics, Lund.

[39] Arfvidsson J. and Claesson J. (2000) Isothermal moisture flow in building materials: modelling, measurements and calculations based in Kirchhoff's potential. *Building and Environment*, 35, 519–536.

[40] Arfvidsson J. and Cunningham M. J. (2000) A transient technique for determining diffusion coefficients in hygroscopic materials. *Building and Environment*, 35, 239–249.

[41] Arnell N. W. (1999) A simple water balance model for the simulation of streamflow over a large geographic domain. *Journal of Hydrology*, 217, 314–335.

[42] Arnold P. J. (1969) Thermal conductivity of masonry materials. *Journal of the Institute of Heating and Ventilating Engineers*, 37, 101–108, 117.

[43] Arslan M. (2001) The effects of permeable formworks with sucker liners on the physical properties of concrete surfaces. *Construction and Building Materials*, 15, 149–156.

[44] Arthur E., Tuller M., Moldrup P., Greve M. H., Knadel M. and de Jonge L. W. (2018) Applicability of the Guggenheim–Anderson–Boer water vapour sorption model for estimation of soil specific surface area. *European Journal of Soil Science*, 69, 245–255.

[45] Asano K. and Fujita S. (1971) Mass transfer for a wide range of driving force. Evaporation of pure liquids. *Chemical Engineering Science*, 26, 1187–1194.

[46] ASCE Environmental and Water Resources Institute. (2002) *The ASCE standarized reference evapotranspiration equation*, revised, ASCE.

[47] Ashraf S. and Phirani J. (2019) A generalized model for spontaneous imbibition in a horizontal, multi-layered porous medium. *Chemical Engineering Science*, 209, 115175.

[48] Ashurst J. and Dimes F. G. (1990) *Conservation of building and decorative stone*, Butterworth-Heinemann, Oxford.

[49] Assael M. J., Bekou E., Giakoumakis D., Friend D. G., Killeeen M. A., Millat J. and Nagashima A. (2000) Experimental data for the viscosity and thermal conductivity of water and steam. *Journal of Physical and Chemical Reference Data*, 29, 141–166.

[50] ASTM. C20-00. *Standard test methods for apparent porosity, water absorption, apparent specific gravity, and bulk density of burned refractory brick and shapes by boiling water.*

[51] ASTM. C67-19. *Standard test methods for sampling and testing brick and structural clay tile.*

[52] ASTM. C373-18. *Standard test methods for determination of water absorption and associated properties by vacuum method for pressed ceramic tiles and glass tiles and boil method for extruded ceramic tiles and non-tile fired ceramic whiteware products.*

[53] ASTM. C457-10a. *Standard test method for microscopical determination of parameters of the air-void system in hardened concrete.*

[54] ASTM. C642-13. *Standard test method for density, absorption, and voids in hardened concrete.*

[55] ASTM. C1585-20. *Standard test method for measurement of rate of absorption of water by hydraulic-cement concretes.*

[56] ASTM. C1699-09. *Standard test method for moisture retention curves of porous building materials using pressure plates.*

[57] ASTM. D2325-68. *Standard test method for capillary-moisture relationships for coarse- and medium-textured soils by porous-plate apparatus.*

[58] ASTM. D3152-72. *Standard test method for capillary-moisture relationships for fine-textured soils by pressure-membrane apparatus.*

[59] ASTM. D4404-18. *Standard test method for determination of pore volume and pore volume distribution of soil and rock by mercury intrusion porosimetry.*

[60] ASTM. D4525-13. *Standard test method for permeability of rocks by flowing air.*

[61] ASTM. D5298-16. *Standard test method for measurement of soil potential (suction) using filter paper.*

[62] ASTM. D6836-16. *Standard test methods for determination of the soil water characteristic curve for desorption using a hanging column, pressure extractor, chilled mirror hygrometer, and/or centrifuge.*

[63] ASTM. E104-02. *Standard practice for maintaining constant relative humidity by means of aqueous solutions.*

[64] Aufrecht M. and Reinhardt H.-W. (1991) Concrete as a second surrounding system against hazardous organic fluids. *Otto Graf Journal*, 2, 37–49.

[65] Auroy M., Poyet S., Le Bescop P., Torrenti J. M., Charpentier T., Moskura M. and Bourbon X. (2015) Impact of carbonation on unsaturated water transport properties of cement-based materials. *Cement and Concrete Research*, 74, 44–58.

[66] Austin J. B. (1936) The use of penetrating radiation in the measurement of porosity of refractory brick. *Journal of the American Ceramic Society*, 19, 29–36.

[67] Auzerais F. M., Dunsmuir J., Ferreol B. B., Martys N., Olson J., Ramakrishnan T. S., Rothman D. H. and Schwartz L. M. (1996) Transport in sandstone: a study based on three dimensional microtomography. *Geophysical Research Letters*, 23, 705–708.

[68] Aveyard R. and Saleem S. M. (1976) Interfacial tensions at alkane-aqueous electrolyte interfaces. *Journal of the Chemical Society: Faraday Transactions I*, 1609–1617.

[69] Bahadur J., Medina C. R., He L., Melnichenko Y. B., Rupp J. A., Blach T. P. and Mildner D. F. (2016) Determination of closed porosity in rocks by small-angle neutron scattering. *Journal of Applied Crystallography*, 49, 2021–2030.

[70] Baker P. H., Galbraith G. H. and McLean R. C. (2009) Temperature gradient effects on moisture transport in porous building materials. *Building Services Engineering Research and Technology*, 30, 37–48.

[71] Baldanza A., Gioncada A. and Lezzerini, M. (2012) Historical building stones of the western Tuscany (Italy): the Acquabona Limestones from Mts. Livornesi. *Periodico di Mineralogia*, 81, 1–17.

[72] Ball J. W. and Nordstrom D. K. (1991) *WATEQ4F – User's manual with revised thermodynamic data base and test cases for calculating speciation of major, trace and redox elements in natural waters*, US Geological Survey Open File Report 90–129, USGS Denver CO.

[73] Balonis M. and Glasser F. P. (2009) The density of cement phases. *Cement and Concrete Research*, 39, 733–739.

[74] Bamforth P. B. (1987) The relationship between permeability coefficients for concrete obtained using liquid and gas. *Magazine of Concrete Research*, 39, 3–11.

[75] Bamforth P. B. (1991) The water permeability of concrete and its relationship with strength. *Magazine of Concrete Research*, 43, 233–241.

[76] Banthia N. and Mindess S. (1989) Water permeability of cement paste. *Cement and Concrete Research*, 19, 727–736.

[77] Barenblatt G. I., Entov V. M. and Ryzhik V. V. (1990) *Theory of fluid flows through natural rocks*, Kluwer, Dordrecht, The Netherlands.

[78] Baroghel-Bouny V. (2007) Water vapour sorption experiments on hardened cementitious materials. Part I: Essential tool for analysis of hygral behaviour and its relation to pore structure. *Cement and Concrete Research*, 37, 414–437.

[79] Baroghel-Bouny V. (2007) Water vapour sorption experiments on hardened cementitious materials. Part II: Essential tool for assessment of transport properties and for durability prediction. *Cement and Concrete Research*, 37, 438–454.

[80] Baroghel-Bouny V., Mainguy M., Lassabatere T. and Coussy O. (1999) Characterization and identification of equilibrium and transfer moisture properties for ordinary and high-performance cementitious materials. *Cement and Concrete Research*, 29, 1225–1238.

[81] Baroghel-Bouny V., Mainguy M. and Coussy O. (2001) Isothermal drying process in weakly permeable cementitious materials – Assessment of water permeability. In R. D. Hooton, M. D. A. Thomas, J. Marchand and J. J. Beaudoin (eds), *Ion and mass transport in cement-based materials*, *Materials science of concrete*, Special Volume, American Ceramic Society, Westerville, OH, pp 59–80.

[82] Barry D. A., Parlange J.-Y., Sander G. C. and Sivaplan M. (1993) A class of exact solutions for Richards' equation. *Journal of Hydrology*, 142, 29–46.

[83] Basheer P. A. M. (1991) *'Clam' tests for assessing the durability of concrete*, PhD thesis, Queen's University, Belfast.

[84] Basheer P. A. M. (1993) A brief review of methods for measuring the permeation properties of concrete in situ. *Proceedings of the Institution of Civil Engineers: Structures and Buildings*, 99, 74–83.

[85] Basheer L., Cleland D. J., Basheer M. and Long A. E. (1993) An in-situ method for assessing surface treated concrete. In R. K. Dhir and M. R. Jones (eds), *Concrete 2000*, Spon, London, 1, pp 805–814.

[86] Basheer P. A. M., Gonçalves A. F. and Torrent R. (2007) Non-destructive methods to measure water transport. In *Non-destructive evaluation of the penetrability and thickness of the concrete cover*, RILEM TC 189-NEC: State-of-the-Art Report.

[87] Basheer P. A. M., Long A. E. and Montgomery F. R. (1992) The 'Autoclam' for measuring the surface absorption and permeability of concrete on site. In V. M. Malhotra (ed.), *Proceedings of CANMET/ACI international conference on advances in concrete technology*, Athens, Greece, pp 107–132.

[88] Basheer P. A. M., Long A. E. and Montgomery F. R. (1994) The Autoclam – a new test for permeability. *Concrete* July–August, pp 27–29.

[89] Basheer P. A. M., Montgomery F. R. and Long A. E. (1995) 'Clam' tests for measuring in-situ permeation properties of concrete. *Nondestructive Testing and Evaluation*, 12, 53–73.

[90] Basheer P. A. M., Montgomery F. R., Long A. E. and Batayneh M. (1990) Durability of surface treated concrete. In R. K. Dhir and J. W. Green (eds), *Protection of concrete: proceedings of international conference*, Dundee, September, Spon, 1990.

[91] Baskerville R. C. and Gale R. S. (1968) A simple automatic instrument for determining the filtrability of sewage sludges. *Journal of the Institute of Water Pollution and Control*, 2, 3–11.

[92] Bauluz B., Mayayo M. J., Yuste A., Fernandez-Nieto C. and Gonzalez Lopez J. M. (2004) TEM study of mineral transformations in fired carbonated clays: relevance to brick making. *Clay Minerals*, 39, 333–344.

[93] Bazant M. Z. and Bažant Z. P. (2012) Theory of sorption hysteresis in nanoporous solids: Part II Molecular condensation. *Journal of the Mechanics and Physics of Solids*, 60, 1660–1675.

[94] Bear J. (1972) *Dynamics of fluids in porous media*, Elsevier, New York.

[95] Bear J. (1996) Modeling transport phenomena in porous media. In M. F. Wheeler (ed.) *Environmental studies: mathematical, computational, and statistical analysis*, IMA Volumes in Mathematics and Its Applications, vol. 79, Springer, pp 27–64, New York.

[96] Bear J. and Bachmat Y. (1991) *Introduction to modeling of transport phenomena in porous media*, Kluwer, Dordrecht, The Netherlands.

[97] Bear J. and Nitao J. J. (1995) On equilibrium and primary variables in transport in porous media. *Transport in Porous Media*, 18, 151–184.

[98] Beck K. (2006) *Étude des propriétés hydriques et des mécanismes d'altération de pierres calcaires à forte porosité*, PhD thesis, L'Université d'Orléans.

[99] Beck K. and Al-Mukhtar M. (2010) Weathering effects in an urban environment: a case study of tuffeau, a French porous limestone. In B. J. Smith, M. Gomez-Heras, H. A. Viles and J. Cassar (eds), *Limestone in the built environment: present-day challenges for the preservation of the past*, Geological Society, London, Special Publications, 331, 103–111.

[100] Beck K., Al-Mukhtar M., Rozenbaum O. and Rautureau M. (2003) Characterization, water transfer properties and deterioration in tuffeau: building material in the Loire valley–France. *Building and Environment*, 38, 1151–1162.

[101] Bednarik M., Moshammer B., Heinrich M., Holzer R., Laho M., Rabeder J., Uhlir C. and Unterwurzacher M. (2014) Engineering geological properties of Leitha Limestone from historical quarries in Burgenland and Styria, Austria. *Engineering Geology*, 176, 66–78.

[102] Belghaug Knarud J. I., Kvande T. and Geving S. (2016) Experimental investigation of capillary absorption along mortar-brick interface plane. In *Central European Symposium on Building Physics, BauSIM 2016*, Dresden, Germany, 1, 117–124.

[103] Beltrán V., Barba A., Jarque J. C. and Escardino A. (1991) Liquid suction by porous ceramic materials: 3 – Influence of the nature of the composition and the preparation method of the pressing powder. *British Ceramic Transactions and Journal*, 90, 77–80.

[104] Beltrán V., Escardino A., Feliu C. and Rodrigo Ma D. (1988) Liquid suction by porous ceramic materials. *British Ceramic Transactions and Journal*, 87, 64–69.

[105] Beltrán V., Ferrer C., Bagán V., Sanchez E., Garcia J. and Mestre S. (1996) Influence of pressing powder characteristics and firing temperature on the porous microstructure and stain resistance of porcelain tile. *Ceramica Acta*, 8, 37–51.

[106] Benavente D., Martínez-Martínez J., Cueto N. and García-del-Cura M. (2007) Salt weathering in dual-porosity building dolostones. *Engineering Geology*, 94, 215–226.

[107] Benavente D., Pla C., Cueto N., Galvañ S., Martínez-Martínez J., García-del-Cura M. A. and Ordóñez S. (2015) Predicting water permeability in sedimentary rocks from capillary imbibition and pore structure. *Engineering Geology*, 195, 301–311.

[108] Benson T. B., McDonald P. J., Mulheron M. and Nwaubani S. O. (1998) The use of magnetic resonance imaging techniques in assessing the uptake of surface treatments and water movement through stone faces. *Materials and Structures*, 31, 423–427.

[109] Benster N. A. (1968) *An investigation into rising damp and associated problems in buildings and the application of electro-osmotic techniques*, MSc thesis, UMIST, Manchester.

[110] Bentz D. P. (2007) Virtual pervious concrete: microstructure, percolation and permeability. *ACI Materials Journal*, 105, 297–301.

[111] Bentz D. P. (2007) Cement hydration: building bridges and dams at the microstructure level. *Materials and Structures*, 40, 397–404.

[112] Bentz D. P. (2008) A review of early-age properties of cement-based materials. *Cement and Concrete Research*, 38, 196–204.

[113] Bentz D. P. and Martys N. S. (1994) Hydraulic radius and transport in reconstructed model 3-dimensional porous-media. *Transport in Porous Media*, 17, 221–238.

[114] Bentz D. P., Quénard D. A., Baroghel-Bouny V., Garboczi E. J. and Jennings H. M. (1995) Modelling drying shrinkage of cement paste and mortar. Part 1. Structural models from nanometres to millimetres. *Materials and Structures*, 28, 450–458.

[115] Bentz D. P., Quenard D. A., Kunzel H. M., Baruchel J., Peyrin F., Martys N. S. and Garboczi E. J. (2000) Microstructure and transport properties of porous building materials. II: Three-dimensional X-ray tomographic studies. *Materials and Structures*, 33, 147–153.

[116] Berger D. and Pei D. C. T. (1973) Drying of hygroscopic, capillary porous solids – a theoretical approach. *International Journal of Heat and Mass Transfer*, **16**, 293–302.

[117] Berodier E., Bizzozero J. and Muller A. C. A. (2016) Mercury intrusion porosimetry. In K. L. Scrivener, R. Snellings and B. Lothenbach (eds), *A practical guide to microstructural analysis of cementitious materials*, CRC Press, Boca Raton, FL, pp 419–444.

[118] Bertolini L., Coppola L., Gastaldi M. and Redaelli E. (2009) Electroosmotic transport in porous construction materials and dehumidification of masonry. *Construction and Building Materials*, **23**, 254–263.

[119] Beruto D., Giordini M. and Turriziani R. (1985) Frost-resistance and related structural and chemical material properties. *Materials Chemistry and Physics*, **12**, 407–418.

[120] Best A. C. (1950) The size distribution of raindrops. *Quarterly Journal of the Royal Meteorological Society*, **76**, 16–36.

[121] Beyea S. D., Balcom B. J., Bremner T. W., Prado P. J., Cross A. R., Armstrong R. L. and Grattan-Bellew P. E. (1998) The influence of shrinkage-cracking on the drying behaviour of white portland cement using single-point imaging (SPI). *Solid State Nuclear Magnetic Resonance*, **13**, 93–100.

[122] Beyea S. D., Balcom B. J., Bremner T. W., Prado P. J., Green D. P., Armstrong R. L. and Grattan-Bellew P. E. (1998) Magnetic resonance imaging and moisture content profiles of drying concrete. *Cement and Concrete Research*, **28**, 453–463.

[123] Beyea S. D., Balcom B. J., Prado P. J., Cross A. R., Kennedy C. B., Armstrong R. L. and Bremner T. W. (1998) Relaxation time mapping of short T_2^* nuclei with single-point imaging (SPI) methods. *Journal of Magnetic Resonance*, **135**, 156–164.

[124] Beyea S. D., Bremner T. W., Prado P. J. and Balcom B. J. (1997) Magnetic resonance imaging (MRI) of moisture distribution in concrete. In *Annual conference of the Canadian Society for Civil Engineering*, Montreal, Canada, 7, 61–70.

[125] Bico J. and Queré D. (2000) Liquid trains in a tube. *Europhysics Letters*, **51**, 546–550.

[126] Bico J. and Queré D. (2002) Self-propelling slugs. *Journal of Fluid Mechanics*, **467**, 101–127.

[127] Bikerman J. J. (1975) Theories of capillary attraction. *Centaurus* **19**, 182–206.

[128] Bikerman J. J. (1978) Capillarity before Laplace: Clairaut, Segner, Monge, Young. *Archive for History of the Exact Sciences*, **18**, 103–122.

[129] Binda L. (1996) RILEM TC127-MS: Tests for masonry materials and structures. *Materials and Structures*, **29**, 459–475.

[130] Binda L., Baronio G. and Squarcina T. (1992) Evaluation of the durability of bricks and stones and of preservation treatments. In J. Delgado Rodrigues, F. Henriques and F. Telmo Jeremisa (eds), *7th international congress on deterioration and conservation of stone*, Lisbon, Portugal, vol. 2, pp 753–761.

[131] Binda L., Colla C. and Forde M. C. (1994) Identification of moisture capillarity in masonry using digital impulse radar. *Construction and Building Materials*, **8**, 101–107.

[132] Binda L., Squarcina T. and van Hees R. (1996) Determination of moisture content in masonry materials: calibration of some direct methods. In J. Riederer (ed.), *8th international congress on the deterioration and conservation of stone*, Berlin, Germany, 1, 423–436.

[133] Bisaillon A. and Malhotra V. M. (1988) Permeability of concrete using a uni-axial water-flow method. In D. Whiting and A. Walitt (eds), *Permeability of concrete*, ACI SP-108, American Concrete Institute, Detroit, MI, pp 175–193.

[134] Blachere J. R. and Young J. E. (1972) Freezing point of water in porous glass. *Journal of the American Ceramic Society*, 55, 306–308.

[135] Blachere J. R. and Young J. E. (1974) Failure of capillary theory of frost damage as applied to ceramics. *Journal of the American Ceramic Society*, 57, 212–216.

[136] Blachere J. R. and Young J. E. (1975) Freezing and thawing tests and theories of frost damage. *Journal of Testing and Evaluation*, 3, 273–277.

[137] Blocken B. and Carmeliet J. (2000) Driving rain on building envelopes – I. Numerical estimation and full-scale experimental verification. *Journal of Thermal Environment and Building Science*, 24, 61–85.

[138] Blocken B. and Carmeliet J. (2000) Driving rain on building envelopes – I. Representative experimental data for driving rain estimation. *Journal of Thermal Environment and Building Science*, 24, 89–110.

[139] Blocken B. and Carmeliet J. (2002) Spatial and temporal distribution of driving rain on a low-rise building. *Wind and Structures*, 5, 441–462.

[140] Blocken B. and Carmeliet J. (2004) A review of wind-driven rain research in building science. *Journal of Wind Engineering and Industrial Aerodynamics*, 92, 1079–1130.

[141] Blocken B. and Carmeliet J. (2006) On the validity of the cosine projection in wind-driven rain calculations on buildings. *Building and Environment*, 41, 1182–1189.

[142] Blocken B. and Carmeliet J. (2007) On the errors associated with the use of hourly data in wind-driven rain calculations on building facades. *Atmospheric Environment*, 41, 2335–2343.

[143] Blocken B. and Carmeliet J. (2012) A simplified numerical model for rainwater runoff on building facades: Possibilities and limitations. *Building and Environment*, 53, 59–73.

[144] Blocken B., Derome D. and Carmeliet J. (2013) Rainwater runoff from building facades: A review. *Building and Environment*, 60, 339–361.

[145] Blocken B., Roels S. and Carmeliet J. (2007) A combined CFD–HAM approach for wind-driven rain on building facades. *Journal of Wind Engineering and Industrial Aerodynamics*, 95, 585–607.

[146] Bloxam T. (1857) The analysis of Craigleith sandstone. *Proceedings of the Royal Society of Edinburgh*, 3, 390–395.

[147] Bloxam T. (1862) On the composition of the building sandstones of Craigleith, Binnie, Gifnock and Partick Bridge. *Proceedings of the Royal Society of Edinburgh*, 4, 42–50.

[148] Blunt, M. J. (2017) *Multiphase flow in permeable media: A pore-scale perspective*, Cambridge University Press.

[149] Blunt M. J. and Scher, H. (1995) Pore-level modeling of wetting. *Physical Review E*, 52, 6387.

[150] Bodwadkar S. V. and Reis J. C. (1994) Porosity measurements of core samples using gamma-ray attenuation. *Nuclear Geophysics*, 8, 61–78.

[151] Bogahawatta V. T. L. and Poole A. B. (1991) Strength-porosity-mullite content relationships for kaolinitic clay bodies containg lime additive. *British Ceramic Transactions and Journal*, 90, 184–189.

[152] Bogdan M., Balcom B. J., Bremner T. W. and Armstrong R. L. (1995) Single-point imaging of partially-dried hydrated white Portland cement. *Journal of Magnetic Resonance* Series A, **116**, 266–269.

[153] Bohris A. J., McDonald P. J. and Mulheron M. (1996) The visualization of water transport through hydrophobic polymer coatings applied to building sandstones by broad line magnetic resonance imaging. *Journal of Materials Science*, **31**, 5859–5864.

[154] Bohris A. J., Newling B., McDonald P. J., Raoof A. and Tran N. L. (1998) A broad-line nuclear magnetic resonance study of water absorption and transport in fibrous cement roofing tiles. *Journal of Materials Science*, **33**, 859–867.

[155] Bolt G. H., Iwata S., Peck A. J., Raats P. A. C., Rode A. A., Vachaud G. and Voronin A. D. (1976) Soil physics terminology. *Bulletin of the International Society of Soil Science*, **49**, 26–36.

[156] Bolton M. D. and McKinley J. D. (1997) Geotechnical properties of fresh cement grout – pressure filtration and consolidation tests. *Géotechnique*, **47**, 347–352.

[157] Bomberg M. (1971) *Water flow through porous materials: Part 1*, Report no. 19, Lund Institute of Technology, Division of Building Technology, Lund Institute of Technology, Lund, Sweden.

[158] Bomberg M. (1971) *Water flow through porous materials: Part 2*, Report no. 20, Lund Institute of Technology, Division of Building Technology, Lund Institute of Technology, Lund, Sweden.

[159] Bomberg M. (1972) *Water flow through porous materials: Part 3*, Report no. 21, Lund Institute of Technology, Division of Building Technology, Lund Institute of Technology, Lund, Sweden.

[160] Bomberg M. (1974) *Moisture flow through porous building materials*, Report no. 52, Division of Building Technology, Lund Institute of Technology, Lund, Sweden.

[161] Bomberg M. and Shirtliffe C. J. (1978) Influence of moisture and moisture gradients on heat transfer through porous building materials. In *Thermal transmission measurements of insulation*, STP 660, ASTM, pp 211–233.

[162] Bonn D., Eggers J., Indekeu J., Meunier J. and Rolley E. (2009) Wetting and spreading. *Reviews of Modern Physics*, **81**, 739–805.

[163] Bories S. A. (1991) Fundamentals of drying of capillary-porous bodies. In S. Katac *et al.* (eds), *Convective heat and mass transfer in porous media*, NATO ASI Series, Series E, Applied Sciences, vol. 196, Kluwer Academic, Dordrecht, The Netherlands, pp 391–434.

[164] Bower C. A. (1972) In recognition of L. A. Richards on the occasion of his 68th birthday. *Soil Science*, **113**, 229–231.

[165] Brace W. F., Walsh J. B. and Frangos W. T. (1968) Permeability of granite under high pressure. *Journal of Geophysical Research*, **73**, 2225–2236.

[166] Bradley H. B. (ed.) (1987) *Petroleum engineering handbook*, Society of Petroleum Engineers, Richardson, TX.

[167] Bravo M. C. (2007) Effect of transition from slip to free molecular flow on gas transport in porous media. *Journal of Applied Physics*, **102**, 074905.

[168] Brenner A. M., Adkins B. D., Spooner S. and Davis B. H. (1995) Porosity by small-angle X-ray-scattering (SAXS) – comparison with results from mercury penetration and nitrogen adsorption. *Journal of Non-Crystalline Solids*, **185**, 73–77.

[169] Brew D. R. M., de Beer F. C., Radebe M. J., Nshimirimana R., McGlinn P. J., Aldridge L. P. and Payne T. E. (2009) Water transport through cement-based barriers – A preliminary study using neutron radiography and tomography. *Nuclear Instruments and Methods in Physics Research A*, 605, 163–166.

[170] Breysse D. and Gérard B. (1997) Modelling of permeability in cement-based materials: Part 1 – Uncracked medium. *Cement and Concrete Research*, 27, 761–775.

[171] Breysse D. and Gérard B. (1997) Transport of fluids in cracked media. In H.-W. Reinhardt (ed.), *Penetration and permeability of concrete: barriers to organic and contaminating liquids*, RILEM Report no. 16, Spon, London, pp 123–153.

[172] Brighton P. W. M. (1985) Evaporation from a plane liquid surface into a turbulent boundary layer. *Journal of Fluid Mechanics*, 159, 323–345.

[173] Brinker C. J. and Scherer G. W. (1990) *Sol-gel science: the physics and chemistry of sol-gel processing*, Academic Press, Boston, MA.

[174] Brinkworth B. J. (1971) On the theory of reflection by scattering and absorbing media. *Journal of Physics D: Applied Physics*, 4, 1105–1106.

[175] Broadbridge P. (1987) Integrable flow equations that incorporate spatial heterogeneity. *Transport in Porous Media*, 2, 129–144.

[176] Broadbridge P. and White I. (1988) Constant rate rainfall infiltration: a versatile nonlinear model. 1. Analytical solution. *Water Resources Research*, 24, 145–154.

[177] Brocken H. J. P. (1998) *Moisture transport in brick masonry: the grey area between bricks*, PhD thesis, Eindhoven University of Technology.

[178] Brocken H. J. P., Adan O. C. G. and Pel L. (1997) Moisture transport properties of mortar and mortar joint: a NMR study. *Heron*, 42, 55–69.

[179] Brocken H. J. P. and Hendriks N. A. (1998) *Retention curves measured using a pressure membrane apparatus: Results for an interlaboratory comparison*, FAGO Report 98.03M, Eindhoven University of Technology.

[180] Brocken H. J. P. and Pel L. (1995) Moisture transport over the brick/mortar interface. *International symposium on moisture problems in building walls*, Porto, 11–13 September, p10.

[181] Brocken H. J. P. and Pel L. (1997) Moisture transport over the brick-mortar interface: water absorption and drying. *Proceedings of 11th international brick/block masonry conference*, October, Shanghai, China, pp 826–835.

[182] Brocken H., Pel L. and Kopinga K. (1998) Water extraction out of mortar during brick laying: A NMR study. In P. Colombet, A.-R. Grimmer, H. Zanni and P. Sozzani (eds), *Nuclear magnetic resonance spectroscopy of cement-based materials*, Proceedings of the second international conference, Bergamo 1996, Springer Verlag, Berlin/Heidelberg, Germany, pp 387–395.

[183] Brocken H. J. P., Pel L. and Kopinga K. (1998) Moisture transport over the brick/mortar interface. In P. Colombet, A.-R. Grimmer, H. Zanni and P. Sozzani (eds), *Nuclear magnetic resonance spectroscopy of cement-based materials*, Proceedings of the second international conference, Bergamo 1996, Springer Verlag, Berlin/Heidelberg, Germany, pp 397–402.

[184] Brocken H. J. P., Spiekman M. E., Pel L., Kopinga K. and Larbi J. A. (1998) Water extraction out of mortar during brick laying: A NMR study. *Materials and Structures*, 31, 49–57.

[185] Broner I. and Law R. A. P. (1991) Evaluation of a modified atmometer for estimating reference ET. *Irrigation Science*, 12, 21–26.

[186] Brooks R. H. and Corey A. T. (1964) *Hydraulic properties of porous media*, Hydrology Papers no. 3, Colorado State University, Fort Collins, Colorado 27pp.

[187] Bruce R. R. and Klute A. (1956) The measurement of soil moisture diffusivity. *Soil Science Society America Proceedings*, 20, 458–462.

[188] Brun M., Lallemand A., Quinson J. F. and Eyraud C. (1977) A new method for the simultaneous determination of the size and the shape of pores: the thermoporometry. *Thermochimica Acta*, 21, 59–88.

[189] Brutsaert W. (1976) The concise formulation of diffusive sorption of water in a dry soil. *Water Resources Research*, 12, 1118–1124.

[190] Brutsaert W. (1979) Universal constants for scaling the exponential soil water diffusivity? *Water Resources Research*, 15, 481–483.

[191] Brutsaert W. (1982) *Evaporation into the atmosphere: theory, history and applications*, Reidel, Dordrecht.

[192] BS 1881–124:2015 *Testing concrete – Part 124: Methods for analysis of hardened concrete.*

[193] BS 1881–208:1996. *Testing concrete – Part 208: Recommendations for the determination of the initial surface absorption of concrete.*

[194] BS 3921:1985. *Specification for clay bricks.*

[195] Buckingham E. (1907) *Studies on the movement of soil moisture*, Bulletin no. 38, Bureau of Soils, US Department of Agriculture, Washington, DC.

[196] Buckley S. E. and Leverett M. C. (1942) Mechanism of fluid displacement in sands. *American Institute of Mining and Metallurgical Engineers (Petroleum Development and Technology)*, 146, 107–116.

[197] Budd C. J. and Stockie J. M. (2016) Multilayer asymptotic solution for wetting fronts in porous media with exponential moisture diffusivity. *Studies in Applied Mathematics*, 136, 424–458.

[198] Buenfeld N. R., Shurafa-Daoudi M.-T. and McLoughlin I. M. (1997) Chloride transport due to wick action in concrete. In L. O. Nilsson and J. P. Ollivier (eds), *Chloride penetration into concrete*, RILEM, Paris.

[199] Building Research Establishment. (1974) Drying out buildings, *Building Research Establishment Digest* 163, HMSO, London.

[200] Building Research Establishment. (1989) Rising damp in walls: diagnosis and treatment, *Building Research Establishment Digest* 245, HMSO, London.

[201] Building Research Establishment. (1997) Treating rising damp in houses, *Building Research Establishment Good Repair Guide* no. 6, CRC, London.

[202] Bullard J. W., Jennings H. M., Livingston R. A., Nonat A., Scherer G. W., Schweitzer J. S., Scrivener K. L. and Thomas J. J. (2010) Mechanisms of cement hydration. *Cement and Concrete Research*, 41, 1208–1223.

[203] Burch D. M., Thomas W. C. and Fanney A. H. (1992) Water vapour permeability measurements of common building materials. *ASHRAE Transactions*, 98, 486–494.

[204] Burkinshaw R. (2010) The rising damp tests of Camberwell Pier: Potential height of moisture rise in brickwork and the effectiveness of a modern chemical injection cream damp coursing application. *Journal of Building Appraisal*, 6, 5–19.

[205] Burman R. D. and Pochop L. O. (1994) *Evaporation, evapotranspiration and climatic data*, Developments in Atmospheric Science no. 22, Elsevier, Amsterdam.

[206] Butterworth B. (1947) The rate of absorption of water by partly saturated bricks. *Transactions British Ceramic Society*, **46**, 72–76.

[207] Butterworth B. (1948) *Clay building bricks. Their manufacture, properties and testing with notes on the efficiency of brickwork*, National Building Studies, Bulletin no. 1, London.

[208] Cabrera J. G. and Lynsdale C. J. (1988) A new gas permeameter for measuring the permeability of mortar and concrete. *Magazine of Concrete Research*, **40**, 177–182.

[209] Cabrera V., López-Vizcaíno R., Yustres Á., Ruiz M. Á., Torrero E. and Navarro V. (2020) A user-friendly tool to characterize the moisture transfer in porous building materials: FLoW1D. *Applied Sciences*, **10**, 5090.

[210] Cacciotti R. (2020) Brick masonry response to wind driven rain. *Engineering Structures*, **204**, 110080.

[211] Cai J., Wei W., Hu X. and Wood D. A. (2017) Electrical conductivity models in saturated porous media: A review. *Earth-Science Reviews*, **171**, 419–433.

[212] Cairns J. (1999) Enhancements in surface quality of concrete through the use of controlled permeability formwork liners. *Magazine of Concrete Research*, **51**, 73–86.

[213] Calle K., De Kock T., Cnudde V. and Van den Bossche N. (2019) Liquid moisture transport in combined ceramic brick and natural hydraulic lime mortar samples: Does the hygric interface resistance dominate the moisture transport? *Journal of Building Physics*, **43**, 208–228.

[214] Cambefort H. and Caron C. (1961) Electro-osmose et consolidation electrochimique des argiles. *Géotechnique*, **11**, 203–223.

[215] Cammerer W. F. (1954) Properties of the most important building materials in the presence of water and water vapour. *Tonindustrie-Zeitung*, **78**, 199–204.

[216] Cammerer W. F. (1963) Capillary motion of moisture in porous solids. *VDI Forschungsheft* 500, VDI-Forschung, Dusseldorf, Germany.

[217] Cammerer W. F. (1974) The capillary motion of moisture in building materials. *Proceedings of the second international CIB/RILEM symposium on moisture problems in buildings*, September, Rotterdam, The Netherlands, Paper 2.1.2.

[218] Camuffo D., Del Monte M., Sabbioni C. and Vittori O. (1982) Wetting, deterioration and visual features of stone surfaces in an urban area. *Atmospheric Environment*, **16**, 2253–2259.

[219] Caneva G., Gori E. and Danin A. (1992) Incident rainfall in Rome and its relation to biodeterioration of buildings. *Atmospheric Environment*, **26B**, 255–259.

[220] Capitani D., Proietti N., Gobbino M., Soroldoni L., Casellato U., Valentini M. and Rosina E. (2009) An integrated study for mapping the moisture distribution in an ancient damaged wall painting. *Analytical and Bioanalytical Chemistry*, **395**, 2245–2253.

[221] Carcassès M., Abbas A., Ollivier J.-P. and Verdier J. (2002) An optimised preconditioning procedure for gas permeability measurement. *Materials and Structures*, **35**, 22–27.

[222] Carman P. C. (1956) *Flow of gases through porous media*. Butterworths, London.

[223] Carmeliet J. (2001) Coupling of damage and fluid-solid interactions in quasi-brittle unsaturated porous materials. *IUTAM symposium on theoreti-*

cal and numerical methods in continuum mechanics of porous materials: Solid mechanics and its applications, vol. 87, Kluwer, Boston, MA, pp 307–312.

[224] Carmeliet J., Delerue J.-F., Vandersteen K. and Roels S. (2004) Three-dimensional liquid transport in concrete cracks. *International Journal for Numerical and Analytical Methods in Geomechanics*, 28, 671–687.

[225] Carmeliet J., Descamps F. and Houvenaghel G. (1999) A multiscale network model for simulating moisture transfer properties of porous media. *Transport in Porous Media*, 35, 67–88.

[226] Carmeliet J., Hens H., Roels S., Adan O., Brocken H., Cerny R., Pavlik Z., Hall C. and Kumaran K. (2004) Determination of the liquid water diffusivity from transient moisture transfer experiments. *Journal of Thermal Envelope and Building Science*, 27, 277–305.

[227] Carmeliet J. and Roels S. (2000) Determination of the isothermal moisture transport properties of porous building materials. *Journal of Thermal Envelope and Building Science*, 24, 183–210.

[228] Carmeliet J. and Roels S. (2002) Determination of the moisture capacity of porous building materials. *Journal of Thermal Envelope and Building Science*, 25, 209–237.

[229] Carpenter T. A., Davies E. S., Hall C., Hall L. D., Hoff W. D. and Wilson M. A. (1993) Capillary water migration in rock: process and material properties examined by NMR imaging. *Materials and Structures*, 26, 286–292.

[230] Carsel R. F. and Parrish R. S. (1988) Developing joint probability distributions of soil water retention characteristics. *Water Resources Research*, 24, 755–769.

[231] Carslaw H. S. and Jaeger J. C. (1959) *Conduction of heat in solids*, 2nd edn, Clarendon, Oxford.

[232] Carter M. A., Green K. M., Wilson M. A. and Hoff W. D. (2001) Measurement of water retentivity of cement mortars. *Proceedings of 11th annual BCA/Concrete Society communication conference*, pp 85–92.

[233] Carter M. A., Green K. M., Wilson M. A. and Hoff W. D. (2003) Measurement of water retentivity of cement mortars. *Advances in Cement Research*, 15, 155–159.

[234] Casagrande L. (1949) Electro-osmosis in soils. *Géotechnique*, 1, 159–177.

[235] Cataldo A. De Benedetto E., Cannazza G., Monti G. and Piuzzi E. (2017) TDR-based monitoring of rising damp through the embedding of wire-like sensing elements in building structures. *Measurement*, 98, 355–360.

[236] Černý R. (2009) Time-domain reflectometry method and its application for measuring moisture content in porous materials: A review. *Measurement*, 42, 329–336.

[237] Chandler R. J. and Gutierrez C. I. (1986) The filter-paper method of suction measurement. *Géotechnique*, 36, 265–269.

[238] Chapwanya M., Stockie J. M. and Liu W. (2009) A model for reactive porous transport during re-wetting of hardened concrete. *Journal of Engineering Mathematics*, 65, 53–73.

[239] Chatterji S. (1999) Aspects of the freezing process in a porous material-water system. *Cement and Concrete Research*, 29, 627–630.

[240] Chen P. and Pei D. C. T. (1989) A mathematical model of drying processes. *International Journal of Heat and Mass Transfer*, 32, 297–310.

[241] Chen F., Yang Z., Chen Z., Hu J., Chen C. and Cai J. (2015) Density, viscosity, speed of sound, excess property and bulk modulus of binary mixtures of

γ-butyrolactone with acetonitrile, dimethyl carbonate, and tetrahydrofuran at temperatures (293.15 to 333.15) K, *Journal of Molecular Liquids*, **209**, 683–692.

[242] Childs E. C. (1969) *An introduction to the physical basis of soil-water phenomena*, Wiley Interscience, London.

[243] Childs E. C. and Bybordi M. (1969) The vertical movement of water in a stratified porous material. 1. Infiltration. *Water Resources Research*, **5**, 446–451.

[244] Childs E. C. and Collis-George N. (1950) The permeability of porous materials. *Proceedings of the Royal Society*, **201A**, 392–405.

[245] Choinska M., Khelidj A., Chatzigeorgiou G. and Pijaudier-Cabot G. (2007) Effects and interactions of temperature and stress-level related damage on permeability of concrete. *Cement and Concrete Research*, **37**, 79–88.

[246] Christensen B. J., Coverdale R. T., Olson R. A., Ford S. J., Garboczi E. J., Jennings H. M. and Mason T. O. (1994) Impedance spectroscopy of hydrating cement-based materials: measurement, interpretation and application. *Journal of the American Ceramic Society*, **77**, 2789–2804.

[247] Christensen B. J., Mason T. O. and Jennings H. M. (1996) Comparison of the measured and calculated permeabilities for hardened cement pastes. *Cement and Concrete Research*, **26**, 1325–1334.

[248] Christensen G. and Hansen M. H. (2005) Measurement of moisture content in basement brick walls – a comparison of different methods. In *Seventh symposium on building physics in the Nordic countries*, Reykjavik, Iceland, June 2005, paper 36.

[249] Chu X. and Mariño M. A. (2005) Determination of ponding condition and infiltration into layered soils under unsteady rainfall. *Journal of Hydrology*, **313**, 195–207.

[250] Chung D., Wen J. and Lo L. J. (2019) Development and verification of the open source platform, HAM-Tools, for hygrothermal performance simulation of buildings using a stochastic approach. In *Building simulation*, Tsinghua University Press, Tsinghua, China, pp 1–18.

[251] Churchill R. V. *Complex variables and applications*, 2nd edn, McGraw-Hill, New York 1960; Brown J. W. and Churchill R. V, 8th edn, 2009.

[252] Ciardullo J. P., Sweeney D. J. and Scherer G. W. (2005) Thermal expansion kinetics: Method to measure permeability of cementitious materials, IV. Effect of thermal gradients and viscoelasticity. *Journal of the American Ceramic Society*, **88**, 1213–1221.

[253] CIB (1977) *Quantities, symbols and units for the description of heat and moisture transfer in buildings; conversion factors*, Report no. 37, Rotterdam, The Netherlands.

[254] CIB (2012) *Heat, air and moisture transfer terminology: Concepts and parameters*, CIB-W040, V. P. de Freitas and E. Barreira (eds), FEUP Edições, Portugal.

[255] Claesson J. (1993) *A few remarks on moisture flow potentials*, Report TVBH-7163, Division of Building Physics, Lund Institute of Technology.

[256] Clarke J. (2013) Moisture flow modelling within the ESP-r integrated building performance simulation system. *Journal of Building Performance Simulation*, **6**, 385–399.

[257] Clennell M. B. (1997) Tortuosity: A guide through the maze. In M. A. Lovell and P. K. Harvey (eds), *Developments in Petrophysics*, Geological Society, London, Special Publications, **122**, 299–344.

[258] Cnudde V. (2005) *Exploring the potential of X-ray tomography as a new non-destructive research tool in conservation studies of natural building stones.* PhD thesis, Ghent University.

[259] Cnudde V., Dierick M., Vlassenbroeck J., Masschaele B., Lehmann E., Jacobs P. and Van Hoorebeke L. (2007) Determination of the impregnation depth of siloxanes and ethylsilicates in porous material by neutron radiography. *Journal of Cultural Heritage*, **8**, 331–338.

[260] Cnudde V., Cwirzen A., Masschaele B. and Jacobs P. J. S. (2009) Porosity and microstructure characterization of building stones and concretes. *Engineering Geology*, **103**, 76–83.

[261] Coble R. L. and Kingery W. D. (1956) Effect of porosity on physical properties of sintered alumina. *Journal of the American Ceramic Society*, **39**, 377–385.

[262] Cohen-Adad R. and Lorimer J. W. (eds) (1991) *Alkali metal and ammonium chlorides in water and heavy water*, Solubility Data Series vol. 47, IUPAC, Pergamon, Oxford.

[263] Colantuono A., Dal Vecchio S., Mascolo G., Ferone C., Marino O. and Vitale A. (1997) Measuring capillary absorption coefficient of porous materials. *American Ceramic Society Bulletin*, **76**, 67–70.

[264] Cole W. F. (1961) Moisture expansion relationships for a fired kaolinite-hydrous mica-quartz clay. *Nature*, **192**, 737–739.

[265] Cole W. F. (1962) Possible significance of linear plots of moisture expansion against log a time function. *Nature*, **196**, 431–433.

[266] Cole W. F. (1967) Changes in a 50 m mural tape standardizing base. *The Engineer*, **223**, 769–770.

[267] Cole W. F. (1988) On the prediction of long-term natural moisture expansion of fired-clay bricks. *Journal of the Australian Ceramic Society*, **24**, 81–88.

[268] Cole W. F. and Birtwistle R. (1969) Kinetics of moisture expansion of ceramic bodies. *Ceramic Bulletin*, **48**, 1128–1132.

[269] Coleman J. D. and Marsh A. D. (1961) An investigation of the pressure-membrane method for measuring the suction properties of soil. *Journal of Soil Science*, **12**, 343–362.

[270] Collier N. C., Sharp J. H., Milestone N. B., Hill J. and Godfrey I. H. (2008) The influence of water removal techniques on the composition and microstructure of hardened cement pastes. *Cement and Concrete Research*, **38**, 737–744.

[271] Collier N. C., Wilson M. A., Carter M. A., Hoff W. D., Hall C., Ball R. J., El-Turki A. and Allen G. C. (2007) Theoretical development and validation of a Sharp Front model of the dewatering of a slurry by an absorbent substrate. *Journal of Physics D: Applied Physics*, **40**, 4049–4054.

[272] Comité Européen du Béton. (1992) *Durable concrete structures*, Telford, London.

[273] Concrete Society. (1985) *Permeability of concrete and its control*, conference, London December 1985, Concrete Society, London.

[274] Concrete Society. (1988) *Permeability testing of site concrete: a review of methods and experience*, Technical report no. 31.

[275] Conrath M., Fries N., Zhang M. and Dreyer M. E. (2010) Radial capillary transport from an infinite reservoir. *Transport in Porous Media*, **84**, 109–132.

[276] Cooke R. U. and Gibbs G. B. (1994) Crumbling heritage? *Atmospheric Environment*, **28**, 1355–1356.

[277] Cooke, R. U. and Gibbs G. B. (1995) *Crumbling heritage?: Studies of stone weathering in polluted atmospheres*, a report of research on atmospheric pollution and stone decay for the Joint Working Party between the Cathedrals Fabric Commission for England and the Joint Environmental Programme of National Power plc and PowerGen plc, National Power, Swindon.

[278] Cooling L. F. (1930) The evaporation of water from brick. *Transactions of the Ceramic Society*, **29**, 39–54.

[279] Copeland L. E. and Hayes J. C. (1953) Determination of nonevaporable water in hardened cement paste. *ASTM Bulletin*, **194**, 70–74.

[280] Covey W. G. Jr (1965) *Studies on the drying of bare ground*, PhD thesis, Texas A&M University.

[281] Croney D., Coleman J. D. and Bridge P. M. (1952) *Suction of moisture held in soil and other porous materials*, Road Research Technical Paper no. 24, HMSO, London.

[282] Culligan P. J., Barry D. A., Parlange J.-Y., Steenhuis T. S. and Haverkamp R. (2000) Infiltration with controlled air escape. *Water Resources Research*, **36**, 781–785.

[283] Cultrone G., De La Torre M. J., Sebastian E. M., Cazalla O. and Rodriguez-Navarro C. (2000) Behaviour of brick samples in aggressive environments. *Water, Air and Soil Pollution*, **119**, 191–207.

[284] Cultrone G., Rodriguez-Navarro C., Sebastian E., Cazalla O. and De La Torre M. J. (2001) Carbonate and silicate phase reactions during ceramic firing. *European Journal of Mineralogy*, **13**, 621–634.

[285] Cultrone G., Sebastian E., Elert K., De La Torre M. J., Cazalla O. and Rodriguez-Navarro C. (2004) Influence of mineralogy and firing temperature on the porosity of bricks. *Journal of the European Ceramic Society*, **24**, 547–564.

[286] D'Agostino D. (2013) Moisture dynamics in an historical masonry structure: The Cathedral of Lecce (South Italy). *Building and Environment*, **63**, 122–133.

[287] Daïan J.-F. (1988) Condensation and isothermal water transfer in cement mortar: Part I – Pore size distribution, equilibrium water condensation and imbibition. *Transport in Porous Media*, **3**, 563–589.

[288] Daïan J.-F. (1989) Condensation and isothermal water transfer in cement mortar: Part II – Transient condensation of water vapour. *Transport in Porous Media*, **4**, 1–16.

[289] Daïan J.-F. and Bellini de Cunha J. A. (1992) Experimental determination of AAC moisture transport coefficients under temperature gradients. In F. H. Wittmann (ed.), *Advances in autoclaved aerated concrete*: 3rd international symposium on autoclaved aerated Concrete, Zurich, Balkema, Rotterdam, pp 105–111.

[290] Daïan J.-F. (2014) *Equilibrium and transfer in porous media 3: Applications, isothermal transport and coupled transfers*, ISTE, London.

[291] Dautriat J., Gland N., Guelard J., Dimanov A. and Raphanel J. L. (2009) Axial and radial permeability evolutions of compressed sandstones: end effects and shear-band induced permeability anisotropy. *Pure and Applied Geophysics*, **166**, 1037–1061.

[292] Davey N. (1953) *Tests on road bridges*, National Building Studies Research Paper **116**, HMSO, London.

[293] Davey N. (1959) Research on the strength of highway bridges. *New Scientist*, 5, 748–751.

[294] Davidson S., Perkin M. and Buckley B. (2004) The measurement of mass and weight. *Measurement Good Practice Guide 71*, National Physical Laboratory, London.

[295] Davies M., Tirovic M., Ye Z. and Baker P. H. (2004) A low cost, accurate instrument to measure the moisture content of building envelopes in situ: a modelling study. *Building Services Engineering Research and Technology*, 25, 295–304.

[296] Davies M. and Ye Z. (2009) A 'pad' sensor for measuring the moisture content of building materials. *Building Services Engineering Research and Technology*, 30, 263–270.

[297] Davis R. S. (1992) Equation for the determination of the density of moist air. *Metrologia*, 29, 67–70.

[298] Davis R. S. (2011) Measurement of mass and density. In *Encyclopedia of Applied Physics*, Wiley-VCH.

[299] Davis R. S. and Koch W. F. (1992) Mass and density determinations. In B. W. Rossiter and R. C. Baetzold (eds), *Physical methods of chemistry*, 2nd edn, vol. 6, *Determination of thermodynamic properties*, Wiley, New York, pp 1–99.

[300] Dawei M., Chaozong Z., Zhiping G., Yisi L., Fulin A. and Quitian M. (1986) The application of neutron radiography to the measurement of the water permeability of concrete. In *Proceedings of the second world conference on neutron radiography*, Paris, June, pp 255–262.

[301] Deka R. N., Wairiu M., Mtakwa P. W., Mullins C. E., Veenendaal E. M. and Townend J. (1995) Use and accuracy of the filter-paper technique for measurement of soil matric potential. *European Journal of Soil Science*, 46, 233–238.

[302] De Kock T., Dewanckele J., Boone M., De Schutter G., Jacobs P. and Cnudde V. (2014) Replacement stones for Lede stone in Belgian historical monuments. In: J. Cassar, M. G. Winter, B. R. Marker, N. R. G. Entwistle, E. N. Bromhead and J. W. N. Smith (eds) *Stone in historical buildings: characterization and performance*, Geological Society, London, Special Publications, 391, 31–46.

[303] Delgado J. M. P. Q., Ramos N. M., Barreira E. and De Freitas V. P. (2010) A critical review of hygrothermal models used in porous building materials. *Journal of Porous Media*, 13, 221–234.

[304] Delker T., Pengra D. B. and Wong P.-Z. (1996) Interface pinning and the dynamics of capillary rise in porous media. *Physical Review Letters*, 76, 2902–2907.

[305] Deprez M., De Kock T., De Schutter G. and Cnudde V. (2020). A review on freeze-thaw action and weathering of rocks. *Earth-Science Reviews*, 203, 103143.

[306] Derluyn H. (2012) *Salt transport and crystallization in porous limestone: neutron-X-ray imaging and poromechanical modeling*, PhD thesis, ETH Zurich.

[307] Derluyn H., Dewanckele J., Boone M. N., Cnudde V., Derome D. and Carmeliet J. (2014) Crystallization of hydrated and anhydrous salts in porous limestone resolved by synchrotron X-ray microtomography. *Nuclear Instruments and Methods in Physics Research Section B*, 324, 102–112.

[308] Derluyn H., Janssen H. and Carmeliet J. (2011) Influence of the nature of interfaces on the capillary transport in layered materials. *Construction and Building Materials*, 25, 3685–3693.

[309] Derluyn H., Janssen H., Moonen P. and Carmeliet J. (2008) Moisture transfer across the interface between brick and mortar joint. *Eighth symposium on building physics in the Nordic countries*, Copenhagen, Denmark, June 16–18, pp 865–872.

[310] Derogar S. (2017) Effect of zeolite on dewatering, mechanical properties and durability of cement mortar. *Advances in Cement Research*, 29, 174–182.

[311] Descamps F. (1990) *Moisture content measurement using gamma ray attenuation*, Research Report, Laboratorium Bouwfysica, Katholieke Universiteit Leuven.

[312] Descamps F. (1997) *Continuum and discrete modelling of isothermal water and air transfer in porous media*, PhD thesis, Katholieke Universiteit Leuven.

[313] Desmettre C. and Charron J. P. (2011) Novel water permeability device for reinforced concrete under load. *Materials and Structures*, 44, 1713–1723.

[314] Desmettre C. and Charron J. P. (2012) Water permeability of reinforced concrete with and without fiber subjected to static and constant tensile loading. *Cement and Concrete Research*, 42, 945–952.

[315] Desmettre C. and Charron J. P. (2013) Water permeability of reinforced concrete subjected to cyclic tensile loading. *ACI Materials Journal*, 110, 79–88.

[316] DeSouza S. J., Hooton R. D. and Bickley J. A. (1997) Evaluation of laboratory drying procedures relevant to field conditions for concrete sorptivity measurements. *Cement and Concrete Aggregates*, 19, 59–63.

[317] Detournay E. and Cheng H. D. (1993) Fundamentals of poroelasticity. In J. A. Hudson (ed.) *Comprehensive rock engineering*, Pergamon, Oxford, 2, Ch. 5.

[318] De Vries D. A. (1987) The theory of heat and moisture transfer in porous media revisited. *International Journal of Heat and Mass Transfer*, 30, 1343–1350.

[319] Dhir R. K., Chan Y. N. and Hewlett P. C. (1986) Near surface characteristics and durability of concrete: an initial appraisal. *Magazine of Concrete Research*, 38, 54–56.

[320] Dhir R. K., Hewlett P. C. and Chan Y. N. (1987) Near-surface characteristics of concrete: assessment and development of in situ test methods. *Magazine of Concrete Research*, 39, 183–195.

[321] Dhir R. K., Hewlett P. C. and Chan Y. N. (1989) Near surface characteristics of concrete: intrinsic permeability. *Magazine of Concrete Research*, 41, 87–97.

[322] Diamond S. (1999) Aspects of concrete porosity revisited. *Cement and Concrete Research*, 29, 1181–1188.

[323] Diamond S. (2000) Mercury porosimetry – An inappropriate method for the measurement of pore size distributions in cement-based materials. *Cement and Concrete Research*, 30, 1517–1525.

[324] Dias W. P. S. (2000) Reduction of sorptivity with age through carbonation. *Cement and Concrete Research*, 30, 1255–1261.

[325] Dondi M., Marsigli M. and Venturi I. (1999) Microstructure and mechanical properties of clay bricks: comparison between fast firing and traditional firing. *British Ceramic Transactions*, 98, 12–18.

[326] Dondi M., Principi P., Raimondo M. and Zavarini G. (2000) The thermal conductivity of bricks produced with Italian clays. *L'Industria dei Laterizi*, 65, 309–320.

[327] Dos Santos W. N. (2000) Experimental investigation of the effect of moisture on thermal conductivity and specific heat of porous ceramic materials. *Journal of Materials Science*, 35, 3977–3982.

[328] Douglas G. J. and Oglethorpe M. K. (1993) *Brick, tile and fireclay industries in Scotland*, Royal Commission on the Ancient and Historical Monuments of Scotland, Edinburgh.

[329] Douglas J. (1998) The development of ground floor constructions: Part III (damp proofing materials). *Structural Survey*, 16, 18–22.

[330] Drchalová J., Pavlik Z. and Černý R. (2002) A comparison of various techniques for determination of moisture diffusivity from moisture profiles. In *Sixth Symposium on Building Physics in the Nordic Countries*, Norwegian University of Science and Technology, Trondheim, Norway, 1, 135–142.

[331] Dreesen R. and Dusar M. (2004) Historical building stones in the province of Limburg (NE Belgium): role of petrography in provenance and durability assessment. *Materials Characterization*, 53, 273–287.

[332] Drelich J. W., Boinovich L., Chibowski E., Della Volpe C., Hołysz L., Marmur A. and Siboni S. (2019) Contact angles: history of over 200 years of open questions. *Surface Innovations*, 8, 3–27.

[333] Driscoll T. A. (1996) A Matlab toolbox for Schwarz-Christoffel mapping. *ACM Transactions on Mathematical Software*, 22, 168–186.

[334] Driscoll T. A. and Trefethen L. N. (2002) *Schwarz-Christoffel mapping*, Cambridge University Press.

[335] Dubé M., Rost M. and Alava M. (2000) Conserved dynamics and interface roughening in spontaneous imbibition: A critical overview. *European Physical Journal B*, 15, 691–699.

[336] Dubelaar C. W., Engering S., van Hees R. P. J., Koch R. and Lorenz H.-G. (2003) Lithofacies and petrophysical properties of Portland Base Bed and Portland Whit Bed limestone as related to durability. *Heron*, 48, 221–229.

[337] Dukhin S. S. and Djeraguin B. V. (1974) Equilibrium double-layer and electrokinetic phenomena. *Surface and Colloid Science*, 7, 49–272.

[338] Dullien F. A. L. (1992) *Porous media: fluid transport and pore structure*, 2nd edn, Academic Press, San Diego.

[339] Dunham A. C. (1992) Developments in industrial mineralogy: I. The mineralogy of brick-making. *Proceedings of the Yorkshire Geological Society*, 49, 95–104.

[340] Dunham A. C., McKnight A. S. and Warren I. (2001) Mineral assemblages formed in Oxford Clay fired under different time–temperature conditions with reference to brick manufacture. *Proceedings of the Yorkshire Geological Society*, 53, 221–230.

[341] Edlefsen N. E. and Anderson A. B. C. (1943) The thermodynamics of soil moisture. *Hilgardia*, 15, 31–299.

[342] Edmunds F. H. and Schaffer R. J. (1932) Portland stone: its geology and properties as a building stone. *Proceedings of the Geologists' Association*, 43, 225–240.

[343] Ekström M., Jones P. D., Fowler H. J., Lenderink G., Buishand T. A. and Conway D. 2007 Regional climate model data used within the SWURVE project 1: projected changes in seasonal patterns and estimation of PET. *Hydrology and Earth System Science*, 11, 1069–1083.

[344] El-Dieb A. S. and Hooton R. D. (1994) Evaluation of the Katz-Thompson model for estimating the water permeability of cement-based materials from mercury intrusion porosimetry. *Cement and Concrete Research*, 24, 443–455.

[345] El-Dieb A. S. and Hooton R. D. (1994) A high-pressure triaxial cell with improved measurement sensitivity for saturated water permeability of high performance concrete. *Cement and Concrete Research*, 24, 854–862.

[346] El-Dieb A. S. and Hooton R. D. (1995) Water permeability measurement of high performance concrete using a high-pressure triaxial cell. *Cement and Concrete Research*, 25, 1199–1208.

[347] Eley D. D. and Pepper D. C. (1946) The dynamical determination of adhesion tension. *Transactions of the Faraday Society*, 42, 697–702.

[348] El-Shimi M., White R. and Fazio P. (1980) Influence of façade geometry on weathering. *Canadian Journal of Civil Engineering*, 7, 597–613.

[349] Emerson M. (1990) Mechanisms of water absorption by concrete. In R. K. Dhir and J. W. Green (eds), *Protection of concrete*, Proceedings of international conference, Dundee, September 1990, Spon, London, pp 689–700.

[350] EN 1925:1999. *Natural stone test methods. Determination of water absorption coefficient by capillarity.*

[351] EN 12390–7:2019. *Testing hardened concrete. Part 7: Density of hardened concrete.*

[352] EN 15026:2007 *Hygrothermal performance of building components and building elements – Assessment of moisture transfer by numerical simulation.*

[353] Escardino A., Beltrán V., Barba A. and Sánchez E. (1999) Liquid suction by porous ceramic materials 4: Influence of firing conditions. *British Ceramic Transactions*, 98, 225–229.

[354] Eslami J., Walbert C., Beaucour A.-L., Bourges A. and Noumowe A. (2018) Influence of physical and mechanical properties on the durability of limestone subjected to freeze-thaw cycles. *Construction and Building Materials*, 162, 420–429.

[355] Espinosa-Marzal R. M. and Scherer G. W. (2010) Mechanisms of damage by salt. In B. J. Smith, M. Gomez-Heras, H. A. Viles and J. Cassar (eds), *Limestone in the built environment: present-day challenges for the preservation of the past*, Geological Society, London, Special Publications, 331, 61–77.

[356] Everett D. H. (1961) The dynamics of frost damage to porous solids. *Transactions of the Faraday Society*, 57, 1541–1551.

[357] Everett D. H. and Haynes J. M. (1965) Capillary properties of some model pore systems with special reference to porous solids. *Matériaux et Constructions*, 27, 31–36.

[358] Ewing R. P. and Hunt A. G. (2006) Dependence of the electrical conductivity on saturation in real porous media. *Vadose Zone Journal*, 5, 731–741.

[359] Exner H. E. (1994) Quantitative description of microstructures by image analysis. In E. Lifshin (ed.), *Materials science and technology: a comprehensive treatment*, vol. 2B, Part II, *Characterization of materials*, VCH, Weinheim, Germany, pp 282–350.

[360] Fagerlund G (1973) Determination of pore size distribution by suction porosimetry. *Materials and Structures*, 6, 191–201.

[361] Fagerlund G. (1973) Determination of specific surface by the BET method. *Materials and Structures*, 6, 239–245.

[362] Fagerlund G. (1993) *The long time water absorption in the air-pore structure of concrete*, Report TVBM-3051, Division of Building Materials, Lund Institute of Technology.

[363] Falchi L., Slanzi D., Balliana E., Driussi G. and Zendri E. (2018) Rising damp in historical buildings: A Venetian perspective. *Building and Environment*, 131, 117–127.

[364] Fanger P. (1973) Thermal environments preferred by man. *Build International*, 6, 127–141.

[365] Fanney A. H., Thomas W. C., Burch D. M. and Mathena L. R. Jr. (1991) Measurements of moisture diffusion in building materials. *ASHRAE Transactions*, 97, 99–113.

[366] Fatt I. (1958) The compressibility of sandstones at low to moderate pressure. *Bulletin of the American Association of Petroleum Geologists*, 42, 1924–1957.

[367] Fatt I. (1959) The Biot-Willis elastic coefficients for a sandstone. *Journal of Applied Mechanics*, 26, 296–297.

[368] Feddes R. A., Kabat P., van Bakel P. J. T., Bronswijk J. J. B. and Halbertsma J. (1988) Modelling soil water dynamics in the unsaturated zone – state of the art. *Journal of Hydrology*, 100, 69–111.

[369] Fehlhaber T., Reinhardt H.-W., Drawer O., Sosoro M. and Krumpe A. (1991) *Transportphänomene organischer, wasserlöslicher Flüssigkeiten in Beton*, Research report 691/4-1, Darmstadt and Stuttgart.

[370] Feldman R. F. (1986) Pore structure, permeability and diffusivity as related to durability. *8th International congress on the chemistry of cement*, Rio de Janeiro, 1, 336–356.

[371] Feldman R. F. (1987) Diffusion measurements in cement paste by water replacement using 2-propanol. *Cement and Concrete Research*, 17, 602–612.

[372] Feng C., Guimarães A. S., Ramos N., Sun L., Gawin D., Konca P., Hall C., Zhao J., Hirsch H., Grunewald J., Fredriksson M., Hansen K. K., Pavlik Z., Hamilton A. and Janssen H. (2020) Hygric properties of porous building materials (VI): A round robin campaign. *Building and Environment*, 185, 107242.

[373] Feng C. and Janssen H. (2016) Hygric properties of porous building materials (II): Analysis of temperature influence. *Building and Environment*, 99, 107–118.

[374] Feng C. and Janssen H. (2018) Hygric properties of porous building materials (III): Impact factors and data processing methods of the capillary absorption test. *Building and Environment*, 134, 21–34.

[375] Feng C. and Janssen H. (2019) Hygric properties of porous building materials (IV): Semi-permeable membrane and psychrometer methods for measuring moisture storage curves. *Building and Environment*, 152, 39–49.

[376] Ferrell R. T. and Himmelbau D. M. (1967) Diffusion coefficients of nitrogen and oxygen in water. *Journal of Chemical and Engineering Data*, 12, 111–115.

[377] Figg J. W. (1973) Methods of measuring air and water permeability of concrete. *Magazine of Concrete Research*, 25, 213–219.

[378] Figg J. W. (1989) Concrete surface permeability: measurement and meaning. *Chemistry and Industry*, November, pp 714–719.

[379] Figg J. W. and Bowden S. R. (1971) *The analysis of concretes*, HMSO, London.

[380] Finn R. (1986) *Equilibrium capillary surfaces*, Springer, Berlin, Germany.

[381] Fisher L. R., Gamble R. A. and Middlehurst J. (1981) The Kelvin equation and the capillary condensation of water. *Nature*, 290, 575–576.

[382] Fitzner B., Heinrichs K. and La Bouchardière D. (2002) Limestone weathering of historical monuments in Cairo, Egypt. In S. Siegesmund, T. Weiss and A. Vollbrecht (eds), *Natural stone, weathering phenomena, conservation strategies and case studies*, Geological Society, London, Special Publications, 205, 217–239.

[383] Forchheimer P. (1901) Wasserbewegung durch Boden. *Zeitschrift des Vereines Deutscher Ingenieure*, 45, 1736–1741, 1781–1788.

[384] Fordham E. J., Roberts T. P. L., Carpenter T. A., Hall L. D., Maitland G. C. and Hall C. (1991) Nuclear magnetic resonance imaging of simulated voids in cement slurries. *AIChE Journal*, 37, 1895–1899.

[385] Fordham E. J. and Sharpe M. R. Unpublished data.

[386] Franzen C. and Mirwald P. W. (2004) Moisture content of natural stone: static and dynamic equilibrium with atmospheric humidity. *Environmental Geology*, 46, 391–401.

[387] Franzoni E., Rirsch E. and Paselli Y. (2020) Which methods are suitable to assess the effectiveness of chemical injection treatments in the laboratory? *Journal of Building Engineering*, 29, 101131.

[388] Freeze R. A. (1994) Henry Darcy and the fountains of Dijon. *Ground Water*, 32, 23–30.

[389] Freitas V. P. de, Abrantes V. and Crausse P. (1996) Moisture migration in building walls – Analysis of the interface problem. *Building and Environment*, 31, 99–108.

[390] Fries N. and Dreyer M. (2008) An analytic solution of capillary rise restrained by gravity. *Journal of Colloid and Interface Science*, 320, 259–263.

[391] Fries N., Odic K., Conrath M. and Dreyer M. (2008) The effect of evaporation on the wicking of liquids into a metallic weave. *Journal of Colloid and Interface Science*, 321, 118–129.

[392] Fuller E. N., Schettler P. D. and Giddings J. C. (1966) New method for prediction of binary gas-phase diffusion coefficients. *Industrial and Engineering Chemistry*, 58, 18–27.

[393] Galbraith G. H. and McLean R. C. (1998) Moisture permeability data: mathematical presentation. *Building Services Engineering Research and Technology*, 19, 31–36.

[394] Galbraith G. H., McLean R. C., Tao Z. and Kang N. (1992) The comparability of water vapour permeability measurements. *Building Research and Information*, 20, 364–372.

[395] Gale R. S. and Baskerville R. C. (1967) Capillary suction method for determination of the filtration properties of a solid/liquid suspension. *Chemistry and Industry*, 9, 355–356.

[396] Gandolfo F. G. and Rosano H. L. (1997) Interbubble gas diffusion and the stability of foams. *Journal of Colloid and Interface Science*, 194, 31–36.

[397] Gao G., Zhao L., Wang C., Grunewald J. and Li L. (2017) Wind-driven rain on a building façade in urban environment. *Procedia Engineering*, 205, 1678–1684.

[398] Garbalińska H., Bochenek M., Malorny W. and von Werder J. (2017) Comparative analysis of the dynamic vapor sorption (DVS) technique and the traditional method for sorption isotherms determination – Exemplified by autoclaved aerated concrete samples of four density classes. *Cement and Concrete Research*, 91, 97–105.

[399] Garboczi E. J. (1990) Permeability, diffusivity and microstructural parameters: a critical review. *Cement and Concrete Research*, 20, 591–601.

[400] Garboczi E. J. (1991) Mercury porosimetry and effective networks for permeability calculations in porous materials. *Powder Technology*, 67, 121–125.

[401] Garboczi E. J., Bentz D. P., Snyder K. A., Martys N. S., Stutzman P. E., Ferraris C. F. and Bullard J. W. (2010) *Modeling and measuring the structure and*

properties of cement-based materials, Electronic monograph, NIST, Gaithersburg, MD.

[402] Garden G. K. (1965) Damage to masonry constructions by the ice lensing mechanism. In *Proceedings of the RILEM/CIB conference on moisture problems in building*, Helsinki, Finland, vol. 1, section 2, paper 6.

[403] Gardner D. R., Jefferson A. D. and Lark R. J. (2008) An experimental, numerical and analytical investigation of gas flow characteristics in concrete. *Cement and Concrete Research*, **38**, 360–367.

[404] Gardner W. R. (1956) Calculation of capillary conductivity from pressure plate outflow data. *Soil Science Society of America Proceedings*, **20**, 317–320.

[405] Gardner W. R. (1972) The impact of L. A. Richards upon the field of soil water physics. *Soil Science*, **113**, 232–237.

[406] Gardner W. R. (2005) Lorenzo A. Richards. In D. Hillel (ed.), *Encyclopedia of soils in the environment*, Elsevier Academic Press, Amsterdam, The Netherlands, **3**, pp 407–411.

[407] Gardner W. R. and Mayhugh M. S. (1958) Solutions and tests of the diffusion equation for the movement of water in soil. *Soil Science Society America Proceedings*, **22**, 197–201.

[408] Garnier P., Angulo-Jaramillo R., DiCarlo D. A., Bauters T. W. J., Darnault C. J. G., Steenhuis T. S., Parlange J.-Y. and Baveye P. (1998) Dual-energy synchrotron X-ray measurements of rapid soil density and water content changes in swelling soils during infiltration. *Water Resources Research*, **34**, 2837–2842.

[409] Garofalini S. H., Mahadevan T. S., Xu S. and Scherer G. W. (2008) Molecular mechanisms causing anomalously high thermal expansion of nanoconfined water. *ChemPhysChem*, **9**, 1997–2001.

[410] Garrecht H. H. and Hackner G. (1997) *Alterung von Baustoffen: Bauwerksschäden durch Einwerkung von Feuchte*, Institut für Massivbau und Baustofftechnologie, University of Karlsruhe.

[411] Gate L. F. (1971) The determination of light absorption in diffusing materials by a photon diffusion model. *Journal of Phyics D: Applied Physics*, **4**, 1049–1056.

[412] Gate L. F. (1974) Comparison of the photon diffusion model and Kubelka-Munk equation with the exact solution of the radiative transport equation. *Applied Optics*, **13**, 236–238.

[413] Gayo E., De Frutos J., Palamo A. and Massa S. (1996) A mathematical model simulating the evaporation processes in building materials: experimental checking through infrared thermography. *Building and Environment*, **31**, 469–475.

[414] Geistlinger H. and Mohammadian S. (2015) Capillary trapping mechanism in strongly water wet systems: Comparison between experiment and percolation theory. *Advances in Water Resources*, **79**, 35–50.

[415] de Gennes P.-G. (1976) Percolation: un concept unificateur. *La Recherche*, **7**, 919–927.

[416] de Gennes P.-G. (1985) Wetting: statics and dynamics. *Reviews of Modern Physics*, **57**, 827–86 3.

[417] de Gennes P.-G. (1997) *Soft interfaces: The 1994 Dirac memorial lecture*, Cambridge University Press.

[418] Gérard B. (1996) *Contribution des couplages mécanique-chimie-transfert dans la tenue à long terme des ouvrages de stockage de déchets radioactifs*, PhD thesis, Laval and ENS Cachan.

[419] Gérard B., Breysse D., Ammouche A., Houdusse O. and Didry O. (1996) Cracking and permeability of concrete under tension. *Materials and Structures*, **29**, 141–151.

[420] Gérard B., Reinhardt H.-W and Breysse D. (1997) Measured transport in cracked concrete. In H.-W. Reinhardt (ed.), *Penetration and permeability of concrete: barriers to organic and contaminating liquids*, RILEM Report no. 16, Spon, London, pp 265–324.

[421] Ghanbarian B., Hunt A. G., Ewing R. P. and Sahimi M. (2013) Tortuosity in porous media: a critical review. *Soil Science Society of America Journal*, **77**, 1461–1477.

[422] Ghasemzadeh F. and Pour-Ghaz M. (2015) Effect of damage on moisture transport in concrete. *Journal of Materials in Civil Engineering*, **27**, 04014242.

[423] Glanville W. H. (1931) The permeability of Portland cement concrete. *Building Research Technical Paper*, no. 3, HMSO, London.

[424] Glaser H. (1958) Wärmeleitung und Feuchtigkeitsdurchgang durch Kühlraumisolierungen. *Kältetechnik*, no. 3, 86–91.

[425] Glaser H. (1958) Temperatur- und dampfdruckverlauf in einer homogener Wand bein Feuchtigkeitsaussscheidung. *Kältetechnik*, no. 6, 174–181.

[426] Glaser H. (1959) Grafischer Verfahren zur Untersuchung von Diffusionsvorgänge. *Kältetechnik*, no. 10, 345–349.

[427] Glaser H. (1959) Vereinfachte Berechnung der Dampfdiffusion durch geschichtete Wände bei Feuchteausscheidung. *Kältetechnik*, no. 11, 358–364; no. 12, 586–590.

[428] Glasser F. P., Marchand J. and Samson E. (2008) Durability of concrete – degradation phenomena involving detrimental chemical reactions. *Cement and Concrete Research*, **38**, 226–246.

[429] *Gmelins Handbuch der anorganischen Chemie*, 8th edn, Verlag Chemie, Weinheim.

[430] Goethals P., Volkaert A., Jacobs P., Roels S. and Carmeliet J. (2009) Comparison of positron emission tomography and X-ray radiography for studies of physical processes in sandstone. *Engineering Geology*, **103**, 134–138.

[431] González, B., Calvar, N., Gómez, E., and Domínguez Á. (2007) Density, dynamic viscosity, and derived properties of binary mixtures of methanol or ethanol with water, ethyl acetate, and methyl acetate at $T = (293.15, 298.15,$ and $303.15)$ K. *Journal of Chemical Thermodynamics*, **39**, 1578–1588.

[432] Good R. J. (1984) The contact angle of mercury on the internal surfaces of porous bodies. *Surface and Colloid Science*, **13**, 283–287.

[433] Goudie A. S. (1986) Laboratory simulation of 'the wick effect' in salt weathering of rock. *Earth Surface Processes and Landforms*, **11**, 275–285.

[434] Goudie A. S. and Viles H. A. (1997) *Salt weathering hazards*, Wiley, Chichester, UK.

[435] Grande M. del C., Juliá J. A., Garíca M. and Marschoff C. M. (2007) On the density and viscosity of (water + dimethylsulphoxide) binary mixtures. *Journal of Chemical Thermodynamics*, **39**, 1049–1056.

[436] Grant C., Hunter C. A., Flannigan B. and Bravery A. F. (1989) The moisture requirements of moulds isolated from domestic dwellings. *International Biodeterioration*, 25, 259–284.

[437] Gras R. (1974) L'emprisonnement d'air lors de l'humectation des corps poreux. *Bulletin de l'association française pour l'étude du sol*, 1, 49–59.

[438] Grasley Z. C, Scherer G. W., Lange D. A. and Valenza II J. J. (2007), Dynamic pressurization method for measuring permeability and modulus: II. Cementitious materials. *Materials and Structures*, 40 711–721.

[439] Grasley Z. C., Valenza II, J. J., Scherer G. W. and Lange D. A. (2005) Measuring permeability and bulk modulus of cementitious materials. In G. Pijaudier-Cabot, B. Gérard and P. Acker (eds), *Creep, shrinkage and durability of concrete and concrete structures*, Hermes, London, pp 213–218.

[440] Greacen E. L., Walker G. R. and Cook P. G. (1989) *Procedure for filter paper method of measuring soil water suction*, CSIRO Division of Soils, Divisional Report no. 108.

[441] Green K. M. (1998) *A study of water movement in composite porous materials*, PhD thesis, UMIST, Manchester.

[442] Green K. M., Carter M. A., Hoff W. D. and Wilson M. A. (1999) The effect of lime and admixtures on the water-retaining properties of cement mortars. *Cement and Concrete Research*, 29, 1743–1747.

[443] Green K. M., Hall C., Hoff W. D. and Wilson M. A. Unpublished material.

[444] Green K. M., Hoff W. D., Carter M. A., Wilson M. A. and Hyatt J. P. (1999) A high pressure permeameter for the measurement of liquid conductivity of porous construction materials. *Review of Scientific Instruments*, 70, 3397–3401.

[445] Green W. H. and Ampt G. A. (1911) Studies on soil physics. Part 1 – The flow of air and water through soils. *Journal of Agricultural Science*, 4, 1–24.

[446] Greenspan L. (1977) Humidity fixed points of binary saturated aqueous solutions. *Journal of Research of the National Bureau of Standards*, 81A, 89–96.

[447] Gregg S. J. and Sing K. S. W. (1982) *Adsorption, surface area and porosity*, 2nd edn, Academic Press, London.

[448] Gribanova E. V. and Grigorov O. N. (1969) Influence of countercurrent electroosmosis on capillary rise of water in brick ceramics. *Journal of Applied Chemistry USSR*, 42, 2365–2369.

[449] Griffin D. M. (1977) Water potential and wood-decay fungi. *Annual Review of Phytopathology*, 15, 319–329.

[450] Griffin I. M. (2013) *Deterioration mechanisms of historic cement renders and concrete*, PhD thesis, University of Edinburgh.

[451] Griffin I. M., Hall C. and Hamilton A. (2014) Unusual water transport properties of some traditional Scottish shale bricks. *Materials and Structures*, 47, 1761–1771.

[452] Grimmond C. S. B., Oke T. R. and Steyn D. G. (1986) Urban water balance: 1. A model for daily totals. *Water Resources Research*, 22, 1397–1403.

[453] Grint N., Marincioni V. and Elwell C. A. (2020) Sensitivity and uncertainty analyses on a DELPHIN model: The impact of material properties on moisture in a solid brick wall. *E3S Web of Conferences*, 172, 04006.

[454] Groot C. J. W. P. (1993) *Effect of water on brick-mortar bond*, PhD thesis, Delft University of Technology.

[455] Groot C. J. W. P., Verkerk P., van Tricht J. B. and van der Ende P. (1989) Study of water distribution in joints and bricks using neutron radiography. *Proceedings of the 5th Canadian masonry symposium*, Vancouver, Canada, pp 477–485.

[456] Gross J. and Scherer G. W. (2003) Dynamic pressurization: novel method for measuring fluid permeability. *Journal of Non-Crystalline Solids*, 325, 34–47.

[457] Gualtieri A. F., Riva V., Bresciani A., Maretti S., Tamburini M., and Viani A. (2014) Accuracy in quantitative phase analysis of mixtures with large amorphous contents. The case of stoneware ceramics and bricks. *Journal of Applied Crystallography*, 47, 835–846.

[458] Gueguen Y., Chelidze T. and LeRavalec M. (1997) Microstructures, percolation thresholds and rock physical properties. *Tectonophysics*, 279, 23–35.

[459] Guglielmini L., Gontcharov A., Aldykiewicz A. J. Jr, and Stone H. A. (2008) Drying of salt solutions in porous materials: Intermediate-time dynamics and efflorescence. *Physics of Fluids*, 20, 077101.

[460] Guimarães A. S., Delgado J. M. P. Q. and de Freitas V. P. (2010) Mathematical analysis of the evaporative process of a new technological treatment of rising damp in historic buildings. *Building and Environment*, 45, 2410–2414.

[461] Guimarães A. S. and Teixeira M. J. (2016) Project design abacus for wall base ventilation drying systems to control dampness. *Drying Technology*, 34, 1380–1396.

[462] Gummerson R. J., Hall C. and Hoff W. D. (1980) Water movement in porous building materials – II. Hydraulic suction and sorptivity of brick and other masonry materials. *Building and Environment*, 15, 101–108.

[463] Gummerson R. J., Hall C. and Hoff W. D. (1980) Capillary water transport in masonry structures: building construction applications of Darcy's law. *Construction Papers*, 1, 17–27.

[464] Gummerson R. J., Hall C. and Hoff W. D. (1981) The suction rate and the sorptivity of brick. *Transactions and Journal of the British Ceramic Society*, 80, 150–152.

[465] Gummerson R. J., Hall C. and Hoff W. D. (1981) Water transport in porous building materials – III. A sorptivity test procedure for chemical injection damp-proofing. *Building and Environment*, 16, 193–199.

[466] Gummerson R. J., Hall C., Hoff W. D., Hawkes R., Holland G. N. and Moore W. S. (1979) Unsaturated water flow within porous materials observed by NMR imaging. *Nature*, 281, 56–57.

[467] Guz Ł., Majerek D., Sobczuk H., Guz E. and Połednik B. (2017) Comparison of interpretation methods of thermocouple psychrometer readouts. *AIP Conference Proceedings*, 1866, 040013.

[468] Guz Ł., Sobczuk H., Połednik B. and Guz E. (2016) Calibration of thermocouple psychrometers and moisture measurements in porous materials. *AIP Conference Proceedings*, 1752, 040007.

[469] Hadley D. W., Dolch W. L. and Diamond S. (2000) On the occurrence of hollow-shell grains in hydrated cement paste. *Cement and Concrete Research*, 30, 1–6.

[470] Hadley R. H. (1982) Theoretical treatment of evaporation front drying. *International Journal of Heat and Mass Transfer*, 25, 1511–1522.

[471] Hagymassy Jr J., Odler I., Yudenfreund M., Skalny J. and Brunauer S. (1972) Pore structure analysis by water vapor adsorption. III. Analysis of hydrated

calcium silicates and portland cements. *Journal of Colloid and Interface Science*, 38, 20–34.

[472] Hall C. Unpublished material.

[473] Hall C. (1977) Water movement in porous building materials – I. Unsaturated flow theory and its application. *Building and Environment*, 12, 117–125.

[474] Hall C. (1981) Water movement in porous building materials – IV. The initial surface absorption and the sorptivity. *Building and Environment*, 16, 201–207.

[475] Hall C. (1989) The water sorptivity of mortars and concretes: a review. *Magazine of Concrete Research*, 41, 51–61.

[476] Hall C. (1990) Reply to discussion contribution by B. Marchese and F. D'Amore. *Magazine of Concrete Research*, 42, 105–109.

[477] Hall C. (1994) Barrier performance of concrete: a review of fluid transport theory. *Materials and Structures*, 27, 291–306.

[478] Hall C. (1996) Clay brick. In N. Jackson and R. Dhir (ed.), *Civil engineering materials*, Macmillan Press, London, 5th edn, Ch 31.

[479] Hall C. (1997) Concrete chromatography: miscible displacement in cementitious materials. In H.-W. Reinhardt (ed.), *Penetration and permeability of concrete: Barriers to organic and contaminating liquids*, RILEM Report no. 16, Spon, London, pp 94–106.

[480] Hall C. (1998) Amendment to 'Barrier performance of concrete: a review of fluid transport theory' by Christopher Hall. *Materials and Structures*, 31, 216.

[481] Hall C. (1999) Capillary flows in building elements: Sharp Front theory and conformal mapping. In R. Eligehausen (ed.), *Festschrift for Hans-Wolf Reinhardt*, University of Stuttgart, Stuttgart, Germany, pp 323–340.

[482] Hall C. (2001) Unsaturated flow. In R. D. Hooton, M. D. A. Thomas, J. Marchand and J. J. Beaudoin (eds), *Ion and mass transport in cement-based materials*, Materials Science of Concrete, Special Volume, American Ceramic Society, Westerville, OH, pp 29–57.

[483] Hall C. (2006) Anomalous diffusion in unsaturated flow – fact or fiction? *Cement and Concrete Research*, 37, 378–385.

[484] Hall C. (2012) Comment on "Imbibition in layered systems of packed beads" by Reyssat M. et al. *Europhysics Letters*, 98, 56003.

[485] Hall C. (2018) Capillary water absorption by a porous cylinder. *Journal of Building Physics*, 42, 120–124.

[486] Hall, C. (2019) Capillary imbibition in cement-based materials with time-dependent permeability. *Cement and Concrete Research*, 124, 105835.

[487] Hall C., Green K., Hoff W. D. and Wilson M. A. (1996) A sharp wet front analysis of capillary absorption into the *n*-layer composite. *Journal of Physics D: Applied Physics*, 29, 2947–2950.

[488] Hall C. and Gummerson R. J. (1978) Electrical phenomena associated with the movement of water in masonry structures. *Heat and moisture transfer in buildings*, CIB Working Commission W-40, May 22–26, Trondheim, Norway.

[489] Hall C. and Hamilton A. (2011) Rehydroxylation in fired-clay ceramics. Unpublished ms.

[490] Hall C. and Hamilton A. (2015) Porosity–density relations in stone and brick materials. *Materials and Structures*, 48, 1265–1271.

[491] Hall C. and Hamilton A. (2016) Porosities of building limestones: using the solid density to assess data quality. *Materials and Structures*, 49, 3969–3979.

[492] Hall, C. and Hamilton A. (2016) Discussion of 'Predicting water permeability in sedimentary rocks from capillary imbibition and pore structure by D. Benavente et al., Engineering Geology 2015'. *Engineering Geology*, **204**, 121–122.

[493] Hall C. and Hamilton A. (2018) Beyond the sorptivity: definition, measurement and properties of the secondary sorptivity. *Journal of Materials in Civil Engineering*, **30**, 04018049.

[494] Hall C. and Hamilton A. (2020) A device for the local measurement of water evaporation rate. *Measurement Science and Technology*, **31**, 127001.

[495] Hall C., Hoff W. D. and Hamilton A. (2014) Discussion of "Learning from failure of a long curved veneer wall: Structural analysis and repair" by Paulo B. Lourenço and Pedro Medeiros. *Journal of Performance of Constructed Facilities*, **28**, 629.

[496] Hall C., Hamilton A., Hoff W. D., Viles H. A. and Eklund J. E. (2011) Moisture dynamics of walls: Response to microenvironment and climate change. *Proceedings of the Royal Society A*, **467**, 194–211.

[497] Hall C and Hoff W. D. Unpublished material.

[498] Hall C. and Hoff W. D. (1982) Dampness in dwellings: performance requirements for remedial treatments. *Proceedings of 3rd ASTM/CIB/RILEM symposium on the performance concept in building*, Lisbon.

[499] Hall C. and Hoff W. D. (1992) Capillary rise in brick stacks. *American Ceramic Society Bulletin*, **71**, 767–769.

[500] Hall C. and Hoff W. D. (2002) *Water transport in brick, stone and concrete*, 1st edn, Spon Press, London.

[501] Hall C. and Hoff W. D. (2007) Rising damp: capillary rise dynamics in walls. *Proceedings of the Royal Society A*, **463**, 1871–1884.

[502] Hall C. and Hoff W. D. (2012) *Water transport in brick, stone and concrete*, 2nd edn, Spon Press, London.

[503] Hall C. and Hoff W. D. (2012) Moisture expansivity of fired-clay ceramics. *Journal of the American Ceramic Society*, **95**, 1204–1207.

[504] Hall C, Hoff W. D. and Gummerson R. J. (1978) Water transport in porous building materials: application of soil physics theory. *Heat and moisture transfer in buildings*, CIB Working Commission W-40, May 22–26, Trondheim.

[505] Hall C., Hoff W. D. and Nixon M. R. (1984) Water movement in porous building materials – VI. Evaporation and drying in brick and block materials. *Building and Environment*, **19**, 13–20.

[506] Hall C., Hoff W. D. and Prout W. (1992) Sorptivity-porosity relations in clay brick ceramic. *American Ceramic Society Bulletin*, **71**, 1112–1116.

[507] Hall C., Hoff W. D., Reinhardt H.-W., Pfingstner A., Wilson M. A. and Serino L. (2007) Sequential imbibition of two immiscible liquids into concrete. *Journal of Physics D: Applied Physics*, **40**, 4642–4646.

[508] Hall C., Hoff W. D. and Skeldon M.(1983) The sorptivity of brick: dependence on initial water content. *Journal of Physics D: Applied Physics*, **16**, 1875–1880.

[509] Hall C., Hoff W. D., Taylor S. C., Wilson M. A., Beom-Gi Yoon, Reinhardt H.-W., Sosoro M., Meredith P. and Donald A. M. (1995) Water anomaly in capillary liquid absorption by cement-based materials. *Journal of Materials Science Letters* **14**, 1178–1181.

[510] Hall C., Hoff W. D. and Wilson M. A. (1993) Effect of non-sorptive inclusions on capillary absorption by a porous material. *Journal of Physics D: Applied Physics*, **26**, 31–34.

[511] Hall C. and Kalimeris A. N. (1982) Water movement in porous building materials. – V. Absorption and shedding of rain by building surfaces. *Building and Environment*, **19**, 13–20.

[512] Hall C. and Kalimeris A. N. (1984) Rain absorption and run-off on porous building surfaces. *Canadian Journal of Civil Engineering*, **11**, 108–111.

[513] Hall C. and Pugsley V. A. (2020) Spontaneous capillary imbibition of water and nonaqueous liquids into dry quarry limestones. *Transport in Porous Media*, **135**, 619–631.

[514] Hall C. and Tse T. K.-M. (1986) Water movement in porous building materials – VII. The sorptivity of mortars. *Building and Environment*, **21**, 113–118.

[515] Hall C. and Wilson M. A. (2020) Water vapour adsorption in some fired-clay ceramics. Unpublished ms.

[516] Hall C., Wilson M. A. and Hoff W. D. (2011) Kinetics of long-term moisture expansion in fired-clay brick. *Journal of the American Ceramic Society*, **94**, 3651–3654.

[517] Hall C. and Yau M. H. R. (1987) Water movement in porous building materials – IX. The water absorption and sorptivity of concretes. *Building and Environment*, **22**, 77–82.

[518] Hall L. D., Rajanayagam V. and Hall C. (1986) Chemical-shift imaging of water and *n*-dodecane in sedimentary rocks. *Journal of Magnetic Resonance*, **68**, 185–188.

[519] Hall M. and Allinson D. (2009) Analysis of the hygrothermal functional properties of stabilised rammed earth materials. *Building and Environment*, **44**, 1935–1942.

[520] Hall M. and Allinson D. (2009) Influence of cementitious binder content on moisture transport in stabilised earth materials analysed using 1-dimensional sharp wet front theory. *Building and Environment*, **44**, 688–693.

[521] Hall M. and Djerbib Y. (2006) Moisture ingress in rammed earth: Part 3 – Sorptivity, surface receptiveness and surface inflow velocity. *Construction and Building Materials*, **20**, 384–395.

[522] Hamblin A. P. (1981) Filter paper method for routine measurement of field water potential. *Journal of Hydrology*, **53**, 355–360.

[523] Hamilton A. Unpublished results.

[524] Hamilton A. (2005) *Sodium sulphate crystallization, water transport and stone decay*. PhD thesis, University of Edinburgh.

[525] Hamilton A., Eklund J. and Viles H. A. Private communication.

[526] Hamilton A. and Hall C. (2005) Physicochemical characterization of a hydrated calcium silicate board material. *Journal of Building Physics*, **29**, 9–19.

[527] Hamilton A. and Hall C. (2007) A note on the density of a calcium silicate hydrate board material. *Journal of Building Physics*, **31**, 69–71.

[528] Hamilton A. and Hall C.(2008) Sodium sulfate heptahydrate: a synchrotron energy-dispersive diffraction study of an elusive metastable hydrated salt. *Journal of Analytical Atomic Spectrometry*, **23**, 840–844.

[529] Hamilton A. and Hall C. (2012) A review of rehydroxylation in fired-clay ceramics. *Journal of the American Ceramic Society*, **95**, 2673–2678.

[530] Hamilton A. and Hall C. (2013) The mechanics of moisture-expansion cracking in fired-clay ceramics. *Journal of Physics D: Applied Physics*, 46, 092003.

[531] Han P. and Bartels D. M. (1996) Temperature dependence of oxygen diffusion in H_2O and D_2O. *Journal of Physical Chemistry*, 100, 5597–5602.

[532] Handy L. L. (1960) Determination of effective capillary pressures for porous media from imbibition data. *Transactions of the AIME*, 219, 75–80.

[533] Hanks R. J. and Bowers S. A. (1962) Numerical solution of the moisture flow equation for infiltration into layered soils. *Soil Science Society of America Proceedings*, 26, 530–534.

[534] Hansen K. K. (1986) *Sorption isotherms: a catalogue*, Technical University of Denmark, Building Materials Laboratory, Technical Report 162/86.

[535] Hansen K. K., Jensen S. K., Gerward L. and Singh K. (1999) Dual-energy X-ray absorptiometry for the simultaneous determination of density and moisture content in porous structural materials. In *Fifth symposium on building physics in the Nordic countries*, Gothenburg, Sweden, August 24–26.

[536] Hansen M. H. (1998) *Retention curves measured using the pressure plate and pressure membrane apparatus: Description of method and interlaboratory comparison*, Nordtest technical report 367 (SBI report 295), Danish Building Research Institute, Hørsholm, Denmark.

[537] Hare D. E. and Sorensen C. M. (1987) The density of supercooled water, II, Bulk samples cooled to the homogeneous nucleation limit. *Journal of Chemical Physics*, 87, 4840–4845.

[538] Hart, Diane. (1988) *The building magnesian limestones of the British Isles*, Report no. 134, Building Research Establishment, Garston.

[539] Hart, Diane. (1991) *The building slates of the British Isles*, Report no. 195, Building Research Establishment, Garston.

[540] Harvey A. H., Kaplan S. G. and Burnett J. H. (2005) Effect of dissolved air on the density and refractive index of water. *International Journal of Thermophysics*, 26, 1495–1514.

[541] Hassanein R., Meyer H. O., Carminati A., Estermann M., Lehmann E. and Vontobel P. (2006) Investigation of water imbibition in porous stone by thermal neutron radiography. *Journal of Physics D: Applied Physics*, 39, 4284–4291.

[542] Häupl, P. and Fechner H. (2003) Hygric material properties of porous building materials. *Journal of Thermal Envelope and Building Science*, 26, 259–284.

[543] Haverkamp R., Ross P. J., Smettem K. R. J. and Parlange J.-Y. (1994) Three-dimensional analysis of infiltration from the disk infiltrometer. 2. Physically based infiltration equation. *Water Resources Research*, 30, 2931–2935.

[544] Haynes J. M. (1964) Frost action as a capillary effect. *Transactions of the British Ceramic Society*, 63, 697–703.

[545] Haynes J. M. (1968) Thermodynamics of freezing in porous solids. In J. Hawthorn and E. J. Rolfe (eds), *Low temperature biology of foodstuffs*, Pergamon, Oxford, pp 79–104.

[546] Hearn N. (1990) A recording permeameter for measuring time-sensitive permeability of concrete. In S. Mindess (ed.), *Advances in cementitious materials*, Proceedings of the conference on advances in cementitious materials, Gaithersburg, MD, July, American Ceramic Society, Westerville, OH, pp 463–475.

[547] Hearn N. (1993) *Saturated permeability of concrete as influenced by cracking and self-sealing*, PhD thesis, University of Cambridge.

[548] Hearn N. (1996) Comparison of water and propan-2-ol permeability in mortar specimens. *Advances in Cement Research*, **8**, 81–86.

[549] Hearn N. (1998) Self-sealing, autogenous healing and continued hydration: What is the difference? *Materials and Structures*, **31**, 563–567.

[550] Hearn N. (1999) Effect of shrinkage and load-induced cracking on water permeability of concrete. *American Concrete Institute Materials Journal*, **96**, 234–241.

[551] Hearn N. and Hooton R. D. (1992) Sample mass and dimension effects on mercury intrusion porosimetry results. *Cement and Concrete Research*, **22**, 970–980.

[552] Hearn N., Hooton R. D. and Nokken M. R. (2006) Pore structure, permeability and penetration resistance characteristics of concrete. In J. F. Lamond and J. H. Pielert (eds), *Significance of tests and properties of concrete and concrete-making materials*, ASTM STP 169D, Ch. 26.

[553] Hearn N. and Morley C. T. (1997) Self-sealing property of concrete – experimental evidence. *Materials and Structures*, **30**, 404–411.

[554] Heaslet M. A. and Alksne A. (1961) Diffusion from a fixed surface with a concentration-dependent coefficient. *Journal of the Society for Industrial and Applied Mathematics*, **9**, 584–596.

[555] Heller L., Farmer V. C., Mackenzie R. C., Mitchell B. D. and Taylor H. F. W. (1962) The dehydroxylation and rehydroxylation of triphormic dioctahedral clay minerals. *Clay Minerals Bulletin*, **5**, 56–72.

[556] Hendrickx R., Roels S. and van Balen K. (2010) Measuring the water capacity and transfer properties of fresh mortar. *Cement and Concrete Research*, **40**, 1650–1655.

[557] Henkensiefken R., Castro J., Bentz D., Nantung T. and Weiss J. (2009) Water absorption in internally cured mortar made with water-filled lightweight aggregate. *Cement and Concrete Research*, **39** , 883–892.

[558] Hens H. (1976) Die hygrischen Eigenschaften von Ziegel. *Proceedings of the 4th International Brick Masonry Conference*, Bruges, Belgium.

[559] Hens H. S. L. C. (2015) Combined heat, air, moisture modelling: a look back, how, of help? *Building and Environment*, **91**, 138–151.

[560] Hens H. S. L. (2017) *Building physics – heat, air and moisture: Fundamentals and engineering methods with examples and exercises*, 3rd edn, Ernst & Sohn, Berlin.

[561] Hens H., Janssens A., Depraetere W., Carmeliet J. and Lecompte J. (2007) Brick cavity walls: a performance analysis based on measurements and simulations. *Journal of Building Physics*, **31**, 95–124.

[562] Hess T. M. (1996) Evapotranspiration estimates for water balance scheduling in the UK. *Irrigation News*, **25**, 31–36.

[563] Hill A. E. and Wills J. H. (1938) Ternary systems. XXIV. Calcium sulfate, sodium sulfate and water. *Journal of the American Chemical Society*, **60**, 1647–1655.

[564] Hilsdorf H. and Kropp J. (eds) (1995) *Performance criteria for concrete durability*, Spon, London.

[565] Hirschwald J. (1912) *Handbuch der bautechnischen Gesteinsprüfung*. Bornträger, Berlin.

[566] Ho D. W. S. (1998) Quantifying the quality of concrete. In V. M. Malhotra (ed.) *Recent advances in concrete technology*, Proceedings of the 4th CAN-

MET/ACI/JCI international conference, Tokushima, Japan 1998, ACI SP-179, American Concrete Institute, Farmington Hills, MI, pp 15–25.

[567] Ho D. W. S. and Chirgwin G. J. (1996) A performance specification for durable concrete. *Construction and Building Materials*, **10**, 375–379.

[568] Ho D. W. S., Chirgwin G. J. and Mak S. L. (1997) Water sorptivity of heat-cured concrete for bridge structures. In V. M. Malhotra (ed.), *Advances in concrete technology*, 3rd CANMET/ACI international conference, Auckland, New Zealand, ACI SP-171, pp 97–108.

[569] Ho D. W. S., Cui Q. Y. and Ritchie D. J. (1989) The influence of humidity and curing time on the quality of concrete. *Cement and Concrete Research*, **19**, 457–464.

[570] Ho D. W. S., Hinczak I., Conroy I. J. and Lewis R. K. (1986) Influence of slag cement on the water sorptivity of concrete. *Fly ash, silica fume, slag and natural pozzolans in concrete*, SP-91, American Concrete Institute, Detroit, pp 1463–1473.

[571] Ho D. W. S. and Lewis R. K. (1984) Concrete quality as measured by water sorptivity. *Civil Engineering Transactions, Institution of Engineers, Australia*, **CE26**, 306–313.

[572] Ho D. W. S. and Lewis R. K. (1987) Concrete quality after one year of outdoor exposure. *Durability of Building Materials*, **5**, 1–11.

[573] Ho D. W. S. and Lewis R. K. (1987) The water sorptivity of concretes: the influence of constituents under continuous curing. *Durability of Building Materials*, **4**, 241–252.

[574] Ho D. W. S. and Lewis R. K. (1987) The assessment of concrete quality and the implication of code requirements for durability. In *4th international conference on durability of building materials and components*, Singapore, pp 508–515.

[575] Hoff W. D. Unpublished material.

[576] Hoff W. D., Taylor S. C., Wilson M. A., Hawkesworth M. R. and Dale K. (1996) The use of neutron radiography to monitor water content distributions in porous construction materials. In *Proceedings of the 5th world conference on neutron radiography*, Berlin, Germany, pp 594–601.

[577] Hoff W. D. and Wilson M. A. (1995) Discussion on 'Neutron radiography: An excellent method of measuring water penetration and moisture distribution in cementitious materials, by H. Justnes, K. Bryhn-Ingebrigtsen and G. O. Rosvold'. *Advances in Cement Research*, **7**, 135–137.

[578] Hoff W. D., Wilson M. A., Benton D. M., Hawkesworth M. R., Parker D. and Fowles P. (1996) The use of positron emission tomography to monitor unsaturated water flow within porous construction materials. *Journal of Materials Science Letters*, **15**, 1101–1104.

[579] Hoff W. D., Wilson M. A. and Sosoro M. (1997) Transport in composite media. In H.-W. Reinhardt (ed.) *Penetration and permeability of concrete: barriers to organic and contaminating liquids*, RILEM Report no. 16, Spon, London, pp 107–122.

[580] Hoffmann D. and Niesel K. (1988) Quantifying capillary rise in columns of porous material. *American Ceramic Society Bulletin*, **67**, 1418.

[581] Hoffmann D., Niesel K. and Wagner A. (1990) Capillary rise and the subsequent evaporation process measured on columns of porous material. *Ceramic Bulletin*, **69**, 392, 394, 396.

[582] Holland D. J. (1961) Rain intensity frequency relationships in Britain. *British Rainfall* Part III, HMSO, London, pp 43–51.

[583] Holm A., Krus M. and Künzel H. M. (1996) Feuchtetransport über Materialgrenzen im Mauerwerk. *Internationale Zeitschrift für Bauinstandsetzen*, 2, 375–396.

[584] Holocher J., Peeters F., Aeschbach-Hertig W., Kinzelbach W. and Kipfer R. (2003) Kinetic model of gas bubble dissolution in groundwater and its implications for the dissolved gas composition. *Environmental Science and Technology*, 37, 1337–1343.

[585] Honeyborne D. B. (1982) *The building limestones of France*, HMSO, London.

[586] Honeyborne D. B. and Harris P. B. (1958) The structure of porous building stone and its relation to weathering behaviour. In D. H. Everett and F. S. Stone (eds), *Proceedings of 10th symposium of the Colston Research Society*, Butterworths, London, pp 343–365.

[587] Hooton R. D. (1988) Problems inherent in permeability measurement. In E. Gartner (ed.), *Advances in cement manufacture and use*, Engineering Foundation, New York.

[588] Hooton R. D. (1993) High strength concrete as a by-product of design for low permeability. In R. K. Dhir and M. R. Jones (eds) *Concrete 2000*, Spon, London, pp 1627–1637.

[589] Hooton R. D., Mesic T. and Beal D. L. (1993) Sorptivity testing of concrete as an indicator of concrete durability and curing efficiency. In *3rd Canadian symposium on cement and concrete*, Ottawa, Canada.

[590] Hope B. B. and Malhotra V. M. (1984) The measurement of concrete permeability. *Canadian Journal of Civil Engineering*, 11, 287–292.

[591] Horsfield M. A., Fordham E. J., Hall C. and Hall L. D. (1989) ^{1}H NMR imaging studies of filtration in colloidal suspensions. *Journal of Magnetic Resonance*, 81, 593–596.

[592] Hoseini M., Bindiganavile V. and Banthia N. (2009) The effect of mechanical stress on permeability of concrete: A review. *Cement and Concrete Composites*, 31, 213–220.

[593] Hosking J. S. and Hueber H. V. (1958) Permanent moisture expansion of clay products on autoclaving. *Nature*, 182, 1142–1144.

[594] Hosking J. S. and Hueber H. V. (1959) Permanent moisture expansion of clay products on natural exposure. *Nature*, 184, 1373–1375.

[595] Hover K. C. (2006) Evaporation of water from concrete surfaces. *ACI Materials Journal*, 103, 384–389.

[596] Hrubý J., Vinš V., Mareš R., Hykl J. and Kalová J. (2014) Surface tension of supercooled water: no inflection point down to $-25\,°C$. *Journal of Physical Chemistry Letters*, 5, 425–428.

[597] Hsieh P. A., Tracy J. V., Neuzil C. E., Bredehoeft J. D. and Silliman S. E. (1981) A transient laboratory method for determining the hydraulic properties of 'tight' rocks – I. Theory. *International Journal of Rock Mechanics, Mining Sciences and Geomechanics Abstracts*, 18, 245–252.

[598] Huang J. (2018) A simple accurate formula for calculating saturation vapor pressure of water and ice. *Journal of Applied Meteorology and Climatology*, 57, 1265–1272.

[599] Hubbell J. H. and Seltzer S. M. (1996) *Tables of X-ray mass attenuation coefficients and mass energy-absorption coefficients*, National Institute of Standards and Technology, Gaithersburg, MD.

[600] Huber M. L., Perkins R. A., Laesecke A., Friend D. G., Sengers J. V., Assael M. J., Metaxa I. N., Vogel E., Mareš R. and Miyagawa K. (2009) New international formulation for the viscosity of H_2O. *Journal of Physical and Chemical Reference Data*, **38**, 101–125.

[601] Huber M. L., Perkins R. A., Friend D. G., Sengers J. V., Assael M. J., Metaxa I. N., Miyagawa K., Hellmann R. and Vogel E. (2012) New international formulation for the thermal conductivity of H_2O. *Journal of Physical and Chemical Reference Data*, **41**, 033102.

[602] Hughes S. W. (2005) Archimedes revisited: A faster, better, cheaper method of accurately measuring the volume of small objects. *Physics Education*, **40**, 468–474.

[603] Huinink H. P., Pel L. and Michels M. A. J. (2002) How ions distribute in a drying porous medium: A simple model. *Physics of Fluids*, **14**, 1389–1395.

[604] Hunt A. G. (2004) Continuum percolation and Archie's law. *Geophysical Research Letters*, **31**, L19503.

[605] Hunt A. G. (2004a) Comparing van Genuchten and percolation theoretical formulations of the hydraulic properties of unsaturated media. *Vadose Zone Journal*, **3**, 1483–1488.

[606] Hunt A. G., Ewing R. P. and Ghanbarian B. (2014) *Percolation theory for flow in porous media*, 3rd edn, Lecture Notes in Physics **880**, Springer, Heidelberg, Germany.

[607] I'Anson S. J. (1985) *Physical aspects of chemical injection damp-proof courses*, PhD thesis, Manchester.

[608] I'Anson S. J. and Hoff W. D. (1988) Chemical injection remedial treatments for rising damp – I. The interaction of damp-proofing materials with porous building materials. *Building and Environment*, **23**, 171–178.

[609] I'Anson S. J. and Hoff W. D. (1990) Chemical injection remedial treatments for rising damp – II. Calculation of injection times. *Building and Environment*, **25**, 63–70.

[610] International Association for the Properties of Water and Steam. (2014) *Revised release on surface tension of ordinary water substance*, IAPWS, Moscow.

[611] International Association for the Properties of Water and Steam. (1992) *Supplementary release on saturation properties of ordinary water substance*, IAPWS, St. Petersburg.

[612] International Association for the Properties of Water and Steam. (2018) *Revised release on the IAPWS formulation 1995 for the thermodynamic properties of ordinary water substance for general and scientific use*, IAPWS, Prague.

[613] International Association for the Properties of Water and Steam. (2008) *Release on the IAPWS formulation 2008 for the viscosity of ordinary water substance*, IAPWS, Berlin.

[614] Ince C., Carter M. A. and Wilson M. A. (2015) The water retaining characteristics of lime mortar. *Materials and Structures*, **48**, 1177–1185.

[615] Ince C., Carter M. A., Wilson M. A., Collier N. C., El-Turki A., Ball R. J. and Allen G. C. (2011) Factors affecting the water retaining characteristics of lime and cement mortars in the freshly-mixed state. *Materials and Structures*, **44**, 509–516.

[616] Ince C., Carter M. A., Wilson M. A., El-Turki E., Ball R. J., Allen G. C. and Collier N. C. (2010) Analysis of the abstraction of water from freshly mixed

jointing mortars in masonry construction. *Materials and Structures*, **43**, 985–992.

[617] Ioannou I., Andreou A., Tsikouras B. and Hatzipanagiotou K. (2009) Application of the Sharp Front Model to capillary absorption in a vuggy limestone. *Engineering Geology*, **105**, 20–23.

[618] Ioannou I., Charalambous C. and Hall C. (2017) The temperature variation of the water sorptivity of construction materials. *Materials and Structures*, **50**, 208.

[619] Ioannou I., Hall C. and Hamilton A. (2008) Application of the Sharp Front model to capillary absorption in concrete materials with bimodal pore size distribution. In *Proceedings of the international RILEM symposium on concrete modelling*, Delft, pp 521–525.

[620] Ioannou I., Hall C., Wilson M. A., Hoff W. D. and Carter M. A. (2003) Direct measurement of the wetting front capillary pressure in a clay brick ceramic. *Journal of Physics D: Applied Physics*, **36**, 3176–3182.

[621] Ioannou I., Hamilton A. and Hall C. (2008) Capillary absorption of water and *n*-decane by autoclaved aerated concrete. *Cement and Concrete Research*, **38**, 766–771.

[622] Ioannou I., Hoff W. D. and Hall C. (2004) On the role of organic adlayers in the anomalous water sorptivity of Lépine limestone. *Journal of Colloid and Interface Science*, **279**, 228–234.

[623] ISO 760:1978. *Determination of water – Karl Fischer method (general method).*

[624] ISO 9346:2007. *Hygrothermal performance of buildings and building materials – Physical quantities for mass transfer – Vocabulary.*

[625] ISO 11274:2019. *Soil quality – Determination of the water-retention characteristic – Laboratory methods.*

[626] ISO 12570:2000. *Hygrothermal performance of building materials – Determination of moisture content by drying at elevated temperature.*

[627] ISO 12571:2013. *Hygrothermal performance of building materials – Determination of hygroscopic sorption properties.*

[628] ISO 12572:2016. *Hygrothermal performance of building materials and products – Determination of water vapour transmission properties – Cup method.*

[629] ISO 15148:2002/A1:2016 *Hygrothermal performance of building materials and products – Determination of water absorption coefficient by partial immersion.*

[630] ISO 15901-1:2016. *Pore size distribution and porosity of solid materials by mercury porosimetry and gas adsorption – Part 1: Mercury porosimetry.*

[631] ISO 15901-2:2006. *Pore size distribution and porosity of solid materials by mercury porosimetry and gas adsorption – Part 2: Analysis of mesopores and macropores by gas adsorption.*

[632] ISO 15901-3:2007. *Pore size distribution and porosity of solid materials by mercury porosimetry and gas adsorption – Part 3: Analysis of micropores by gas adsorption.*

[633] ISO 15927-3:2009. *Hygrothermal performance of buildings – Calculation and presentation of climatic data. Part 3: Calculation of a driving rain index for vertical surfaces from hourly wind and rain data.*

[634] IUPAC. (2007) *Quantities, units and symbols in physical chemistry*, 3rd edn, IUPAC and RSC Publishing, Cambridge.

[635] Jacobs F. and Mayer G. (1992) Porosity and permeability of autoclaved aerated concrete. In F. H. Wittmann (ed.), *Advances in autoclaved aerated concrete: 3rd RILEM international symposium on autoclaved aerated concrete*, Zurich, Balkema, Rotterdam, pp 71–75.

[636] Jakob M. (1949) *Heat transfer*, Chapman and Hall, London.

[637] Jamtveit B. and Hammer Ø. (2012) Sculpting of rocks by reactive fluids. *Geochemical Perspectives*, 1, 341–480.

[638] Janz M. (1995) A test method for the moisture diffusivity at very high moisture levels. In *Moisture problems in building walls*, international symposium, Porto, pp 168–177.

[639] Janz M. (1997) *Methods of measuring the moisture diffusivity at high moisture levels*, Licentiate thesis, Lund.

[640] Janz M. (2001) Technique for measuring moisture storage capacity at high moisture levels. *Journal of Materials in Civil Engineering*, 13, 364–370.

[641] Jason L., Pijaudier-Cabot G., Ghavamian S. and Huerta A. (2007) Hydraulic behaviour of a representative structural volume for containment buildings. *Nuclear Engineering and Design*, 237, 1259–1274.

[642] Jeffrey D. J. (1973) Conduction through a random suspension of spheres. *Proceedings of the Royal Society A*, 335, 355–367.

[643] Jennings H. M. (2008) Refinements to colloid model of C-S-H in cement: CM-II. *Cement and Concrete Research*, 38, 275–289.

[644] Jennings H. M., Hsieh J., Srinivasan R., Jaiswal S., Garci M., Sohn D., Hinners C., Heppner S. and Neubauer C. (1996) Modelling and materials science of cement-based materials – Part I: An overview. In H. M. Jennings, J. Kropp and K. Scrivener (eds), *The modelling of microstructure and its potential for studying transport and durability*, NATO ASI Series E Applied Sciences vol. 304, Kluwer, Dordrecht, The Netherlands, pp 29–62.

[645] Jennings H. M., Kropp J. and Scrivener K. (eds) (1996) *The modelling of microstructure and its potential for studying transport and durability*, NATO ASI Series E Applied Sciences vol. 304, Kluwer, Dordrecht, The Netherlands.

[646] Jennings H. M. and Tennis P. D. (1994) Model for the developing microstructure in portland cement pastes. *Journal of the American Ceramic Society*, 77, 3161–3172.

[647] Jennings H. M., Thomas J. J., Gevrenov J. S., Constantinides G. and Ulm F.-J. (2007) A multi-technique investigation of the nanoporosity of cement paste. *Cement and Concrete Research*, 37, 329–336.

[648] Jennings H. M., Thomas J. J., Rothstein D. and Chen J. J. (2008) Cements as porous materials. In F. Schüth, K. S. W. Sing and J. Weitkamp (eds), *Handbook of porous solids*, Wiley-VCH, Weinheim, Germany, vol 6, pp 2971–3028.

[649] Jiménez-González I., Rodriguez-Navarro C. and Scherer G. W. (2008) Role of clay minerals in the physicomechanical deterioration of sandstone. *Journal of Geophysical Research*, 113, F02021.

[650] Jiménez González I. and Scherer G. W. (2006) Evaluating the potential damage to stones from wetting and drying cycles. In M. S. Konsta-Gdoutos (ed.), *Measuring, monitoring and modeling concrete properties*, Springer, Dordrecht, The Netherlands, pp 685–693.

[651] Johannesson B. and Janz M. (2002) Test of four different experimental methods to determine sorption isotherms. *Journal of Materials in Civil Engineering*, 14, 471–477.

[652] Johansson P. S. (2005) *Water absorption in two-layer masonry systems*, PhD thesis, Lund University.

[653] Johansson P. S. and Nilsson L.-O. (2008) Water absorption in two-layer masonry systems. Moisture fixation measured over the complete moisture range. In *Eighth symposium on building physics in the Nordic countries*, Copenhagen, Denmark, June 16–18, pp 857–864.

[654] Jones S. C. (1994) A technique for faster pulse-decay permeametry in tight rocks. *SPE Formation Evaluation*, **9**, 193–199.

[655] Jones C. A. and Grasley Z. C. (2009) Novel and flexible dual permeability measurement device for cementitious materials. *ACI Materials Journal*, **106**, 192–197.

[656] Jones C. A. and Grasley Z. C. (2009) Correlation of radial flow-through and hollow cylinder dynamic pressurization test for measuring permeability. *Journal of Materials in Civil Engineering*, **21**, 594–600.

[657] Jones C. A. and Grasley Z. C. (2009) Correlation of hollow and solid cylinder dynamic pressurization tests for measuring permeability. *Cement and Concrete Research*, **39**, 345–352.

[658] Joshi D. C., Iden S. C., Peters A., Das B. S. and Durner W. (2019) Temperature dependence of soil hydraulic properties: Transient measurements and modeling. *Soil Science Society of America Journal*, **83**, 1628–1636.

[659] Justnes H., Bryhn-Ingebrigtsen K. and Rosvold G. O. (1994) Neutron radiography: an excellent method of measuring water penetration and moisture distribution in cementitious materials. *Advances in Cement Research*, **6**, 67–72.

[660] Kacimov A. R., Al-Ismaily S. and Al-Maktoumi A. (2010) Green-Ampt one-dimensional infiltration from a ponded surface into a heterogeneous soil. *ASCE Journal of Irrigation and Drainage Engineering*, **136**, 68–72.

[661] Kadoya K., Matsunaga N. and Nagashima A. (1985) Viscosity and thermal conductivity of dry air in the gaseous phase. *Journal of Chemical and Physical Reference Data*, **14**, 947–970.

[662] Kalimeris A. N. (1981) *Studies of water movement in building materials*, MSc thesis, Manchester.

[663] Kalimeris A. N. (1984) *Water flow processes in porous building materials*, PhD thesis, Manchester.

[664] Kalimeris A. N. and Hall C. (1983) Absorption and desorption of water by porous building materials. In F. H. Wittmann (ed.), *Materials science and restoration*, Edition Lack und Chemie, Stuttgart, Germany.

[665] Kam S., Zerbo L., Bathiebo J., Soro J., Naba S., Wenmenga U., Traoré K., Gomina M. and Blanchart P. (2009) Permeability to water of sintered clay ceramics. *Applied Clay Science*, **46**, 351–357.

[666] Karagiannis N., Karoglou M., Bakolas A. and Moropoulou A. (2016) Effect of temperature on water capillary rise coefficient of building materials. *Building and Environment*, **106**, 402–408.

[667] Karagiozis A., Künzel H. and Holm A. (2001) WUFI-ORNL/IBP – a North American hygrothermal model. *Performance of exterior envelopes of whole buildings*, **VIII**, pp 2–7.

[668] Katz A. J. and Thompson A. H. (1986) Quantitative prediction of permeability in porous rock. *Physical Review B*, **34**, 8179–8181.

[669] Katz A. J., Thompson A. H. and Krohn C. E. (1987) Microgeometry and transport properties of sedimentary rock. *Advances in Physics*, **36**, 625–694.

[670] Kaufmann J. and Studer W. (1995) One-dimensional water transport in covercrete – Application of non-destructive methods. *Materials and Structures*, **28**, 115–124.

[671] Kaufmann J., Studer W., Link J. and Schenker K. (1997) Study of water suction of concrete with magnetic resonance imaging methods. *Magazine of Concrete Research*, **49**, 157–166.

[672] Kay A. L. and Davies H. N. (2008) Calculating potential evaporation from climate model data: A source of uncertainty for hydrological climate change impacts. *Journal of Hydrology*, **358**, 221–229.

[673] Kelham S. (1988) A water absorption test for concrete. *Magazine of Concrete Research*, **40**, 106–110.

[674] Kell G. S. (1975) Density, thermal expansivity and compressibility of liquid water from 0 to 150 °C. *Journal of Chemical and Engineering Data*, **20**, 97–105.

[675] Kendall K., Howard A. J. and Birchall J. D. (1983) The relation between porosity, microstructure and strength, and the approach to advanced cement-based materials. *Philosophical Transactions of the Royal Society A*, **310**, 139–153.

[676] Kessler D. G. (2003) Building stones. In E. W. Washburn (ed.), *International critical tables of numerical data, physics, chemistry and technology, 1926–1930*, 1st electronic edn, Knovel, New York, NY, vol 2, pp 47–56.

[677] Kestin J., Sokolov M. and Wakeham W. A. (1978) Viscosity of liquid water in the range −8°C to 150°C . *Journal of Physical and Chemical Reference Data*, **7**, 941–948.

[678] Ketelaars A. A. J., Pel L., Coumans W. J. and Kerkhof P. J. A. M. (1995) Drying kinetics; a comparison of diffusion coefficients from moisture concentration profiles and drying curves. *Chemical Engineering Science*, **50**, 1187–1191.

[679] Kirkham D. and Powers W. L. (1972) *Advanced soil physics*, Wiley-Interscience, New York.

[680] Klinkenberg L. J. (1941) The permeability of porous media to liquids and gases. *Drilling and Production Practice*, 200–211.

[681] Klute A. (1952) A numerical method for solving the flow equation for water in unsaturated materials. *Soil Science*, **73**, 105–116.

[682] Klute A. (1952) Some theoretical aspects of the flow of water in unsaturated soils. *Soil Science Society America Proceedings*, **16**, 144–148.

[683] Knarud J. I. and Geving S. (2015) Implementation and benchmarking of a 3D hygrothermal model in the COMSOL Multiphysics software. *Energy Procedia*, **78**, 3440–3445.

[684] Knarud J. I. and Geving S. (2017) Comparative study of hygrothermal simulations of a masonry wall. *Energy Procedia*, **132**, 771–776.

[685] Kollek J. J. (1989) The determination of the permeability of concrete to oxygen by the Cembureau method – a recommendation. *Materials and Structures*, **22**, 225–230.

[686] Kooi van der J. (1971) *Moisture transport in cellular concrete roofs*. PhD thesis, Eindhoven University of Technology.

[687] Kopinga K. and Pel L. (1994) One dimensional scanning of moisture in porous materials with NMR. *Review of Scientific Instruments*, **65**, 3673–3681.

[688] Korb J.-P. (2009) NMR and nuclear spin relaxation of cement and concrete materials. *Current Opinion in Colloid and Interface Science*, **14**, 192–202.

[689] Koroth S. R., Fazio P. and Feldman D. (1998) Comparative study of durability indices for clay bricks. *Journal of Architectural Engineering* 4, 26–33.

[690] Koroth S. R., Feldman D. and Fazio P. (1998) Development of a new durability index for clay bricks. *Journal of Architectural Engineering*, 4, 87–93.

[691] Kostinski A. B. and Shaw R. A. (2009) Raindrops large and small. *Nature Physics*, 5, 624–625.

[692] Kotsopulos S. I. and Svehlik Z. J. (1989) Analysis and synthesis of seasonality and variability of daily potential evapotranspiration. *Water Resources Management*, 3, 259–269.

[693] Krakowiak K., Lourenço and Ulm F.-J. (2011) Multi-technique investigation of extruded clay brick microstructure. *Journal of the American Ceramic Society*, 94, 3012–3022.

[694] Krajl B. and Pande G. N. (1996) A stochastic model for the permeability characteristics of saturated cemented porous media. *Transport in Porous Media*, 22, 345–357.

[695] Kreijger P. C. (1984) The skin of concrete: composition and properties. *Materials and Structures* 17, 275–283.

[696] Krischer O. (1963) *Die wissenschaftlichen Grundlagen der Trocknungstechnik*, 2nd edn, Springer, Berlin, Germany.

[697] Krohn C. E. (1988) Fractal measurements of sandstones, shales and carbonates. *Journal of Geophysical Research*, 93, 3297–3305.

[698] Krohn C. E. and Thompson A. H. (1986) Fractal sandstone pores: Automated measurements using scanning-electron-microscope images. *Physical Review B*, 33, 6366–6374.

[699] Kropp J. and Hilsdorf H. K. (1995) *Performance criteria for concrete durability*, London, Spon.

[700] Krus M. (1996) *Moisture transport and storage coefficients of porous building materials: theoretical principles and new test methods*, PhD thesis, University of Stuttgart, Fraunhofer IRB, Stuttgart.

[701] Krus M., Hansen K. K. and Künzel H. M. (1997) Porosity and liquid absorption of cement paste. *Materials and Structures*, 30, 394–398.

[702] Krus M. and Kiessl K. (1998) Determination of the moisture storage characteristics of porous capillary active materials. *Materials and Structures*, 31, 522-529.

[703] Kubilay A., Derome D. and Carmeliet J. (2018) Coupling of physical phenomena in urban microclimate: A model integrating air flow, wind-driven rain, radiation and transport in building materials. *Urban Climate*, 24, 398–418.

[704] Kuczynski J., Lukjanik J. and Rojek W. (1979) Anwendung der Neutronenmethode zur Messung der Feuchtigkeit in dickem Mauerwerk. *Wissenschaftliche Berichte der Technischen Hochschule Leipzig*, 12, 79–86.

[705] Künzel H. M. (1995) *Simultaneous heat and moisture transport in building components: One- and two-dimensional calculation using simple parameters*, Fraunhofer IRB, Stuttgart.

[706] Kumar A. (2005) *Water flow and transport of chloride in unsaturated concrete*, MS thesis, University of Saskatchewan.

[707] Kumaran M. K. (1996) *Heat, air and moisture transfer in insulated envelope parts: Final report, Vol. 3, Task 3: Material properties*, International Energy Agency Annex 24, Laboratorium Bouwfysica, Katholieke Universiteit Leuven.

[708] Kumaran M. K. and Bomberg M. (1985) A gamma-spectrometer for determination of density distribution and moisture distribution in building materials. *Proceedings of the international symposium on moisture and humidity*, Washington DC, Instrument Society of America, April, pp 485–490.

[709] Kurtis K., Burris L. and Alapati P. (2016) Consider functional equivalence: a (faster) path to upscaling sustainable infrastructure materials compositions. In *Proceedings of 1st international conference on grand challenges in construction materials*, Los Angeles, pp 380–388.

[710] Kurz F. and Sgarz H. (2015) Measurement of moisture content in building materials using radar technology. In *International symposium on nondestructive testing in civil engineering (NDT-CE)*, Berlin, Germany.

[711] Kutílek M. and Valentová J. (1986) Sorptivity approximations. *Transport in Porous Media*, 1, 57–62.

[712] Kyritsis K., Hall C., Bentz D., Meller N. and Wilson M. A. (2009) Relationship between engineering properties, mineralogy, and microstructure in cement-based hydroceramic materials cured at 200°–350°C. *Journal of the American Ceramic Society*, 92, 694–701.

[713] Lacy R. E. (1976) *Driving-rain index*, BRE Report, HMSO, London.

[714] Lacy R. E. (1977) *Climate and building in Britain*, HMSO, London.

[715] Lacy R. E. and Shellard H. C. (1962) An index of driving rain. *Meteorological Magazine*, 91, 177–184.

[716] Lade P. V. and de Boer R. (1997) The concept of effective stress for soil, concrete and rock. *Géotechnique*, 47, 61–78.

[717] Lage J. L. (1998) The fundamental theory of flow through permeable media from Darcy to turbulence. In D. B. Ingham and I. Pop (eds), *Transport phenomena in porous media*, Elsevier, Oxford, pp 1–30.

[718] Lago M. and Araujo, M. (2001) Capillary rise in porous media. *Physica A: Statistical Mechanics and its Applications*, 289, 1–17.

[719] Lambert I. and Clever H. L. (1992) *Alkaline earth hydroxides in water and aqueous solutions*, Solubility Data Series vol. 52, IUPAC, Pergamon, Oxford.

[720] Laws J. O. and Parsons D. A. (1943) The relation of raindrop-size to intensity. *Eos, Transactions American Geophysical Union*, 24, 452–460.

[721] Lay J. (1998) Capillary porosity testing of concrete. *Concrete*, 32, p. 38.

[722] Leary E. (1984) *The building limestones of the British Isles*, HMSO, London.

[723] Leary E. (1986) *The building sandstones of the British Isles*, HMSO, London.

[724] Lee J. B., Radu A. I., Vontobel P., Derome D. and Carmeliet J. (2016) Absorption of impinging water droplet in porous stones. *Journal of Colloid and Interface Science*, 471, 59–70.

[725] Leech C. A. (2003) *Water movement in unsaturated concrete: Theory, experiments, models*, PhD thesis, University of Queensland.

[726] Leech C., Lockington D. and Hooton R. D. (2006) Estimation of water retention curve from mercury intrusion porosimetry and van Genuchten model. *ACI Structural Journal*, 103, 291–295.

[727] Leech C., Lockington D., Hooton R. D., Galloway G., Cowin G. and Dux P. (2008) Validation of Mualem's conductivity model and prediction of saturated permeability from sorptivity. *ACI Materials Journal*, 105, 44–51.

[728] Leij F. J., Alves W. J., van Genuchten M. Th. and Williams J. R. (1996) *The UNSODA unsaturated soil hydraulic database. User's manual, version 1.0*, Report EPA/600/R-96/095, National Risk Management Research Laboratory, USEPA, Cincinnati, OH.

[729] Leith S. D., Reddy M. M., Ramirez W. F. and Heymans M. J. (1996) Limestone characterization to model damage from acidic precipitation: Effects of pore structure on mass transfer. *Environmental Science and Technology*, **30**, 2202–2210.

[730] Lemmon E. W., McLinden M. O. and Friend D. G. (2001) Thermophysical properties of fluid systems. In P. J. Linstrom and W. G. Mallard (eds), *NIST chemistry webbook*, NIST Standard Reference Database Number 69, National Institute of Standards and Technology, Gaithersburg, MD.

[731] Leventis A., Verganelakis D. A., Halse M. R., Webber J. B. and Strange J. H. (2000) Capillary imbibition and characterisation in cement pastes. *Transport in Porous Media*, **39**, 143–157.

[732] Lever A. and Dawe R. A. (1984) Water-sensitivity and migration of fines in the Hopeman sandstone. *Journal of Petroleum Geology*, **7**, 97–108.

[733] Leverett M. (1941) Capillary behavior in porous solids. *Transactions of the AIME*, **142**, 152–169.

[734] Levine S., Marriott J. R, Neale G. and Epstein N. (1975) Theory of electrokinetic flow in fine cylindrical capillaries at high zeta-potentials. *Journal of Colloid and Interface Science*, **52**, 136–149.

[735] Levitt M. (1969) Non-destructive testing of concrete by the initial surface absorption method. *Proceedings of symposium on non-destructive testing of concrete and timber*, Institution of Civil Engineers, London, pp 23–36.

[736] Levitt M. (1971) The ISAT – a non-destructive test for the durability of concrete. *British Journal of Non-Destructive Testing*, **13**, 106–112.

[737] Lewis J. A. (2000) Colloidal processing of ceramics. *Journal of the American Ceramic Society*, **83**, 2341–2359.

[738] Li Q., Xu S. and Zeng Q. (2016) The effect of water saturation degree on the electrical properties of cement-based porous material. *Cement and Concrete Composites*, **70**, 35–47.

[739] Li W., Pour-Ghaz M., Castro J. and Weiss J. (2012) Water absorption and critical degree of saturation relating to freeze-thaw damage in concrete pavement joints. *Journal of Materials in Civil Engineering*, **24**, 299–307.

[740] Lin C., Pirie G. and Trimmer D. A. (1986) Low permeability rocks: laboratory measurements and three-dimensional microstructural analysis. *Journal of Geophysical Research*, **B91**, 2173–2181.

[741] Lin S. H. (1992) Water infiltration in porous materials. *Journal of the Franklin Institute*, **329**, 85–91.

[742] Little J., Ferraro C. and Arregi B. *Assessing risks in insulation retrofits using hygrothermal software tools: Heat and moisture transfer in internally insulated stone walls.* 2nd edn, Historic Environment Scotland technical paper 15, Edinburgh.

[743] Litvan G. G. (1972) Phase transitions of adsorbates. IV Mechanism of frost action in hardened cement paste. *Journal of the American Ceramic Society*, **55**, 38–42.

[744] Litvan G. G. (1973) Frost action in cement paste. *Matériaux et Constructions*, **6**, 293–298.

[745] Litvan G. G. (1975) Testing the frost susceptibility of bricks. In *Masonry: past and present*, ASTM STP 589, pp 123–132.

[746] Litvan G. G. (1980) Freeze thaw durability of porous building materials. In *Durability of building materials and components*, ASTM STP 691, pp 455–463.

[747] Liu Z. and Hansen W. (2016) A geometrical model for void saturation in air-entrained concrete under continuous water exposure. *Construction and Building Materials*, **124**, 475–484.

[748] Lockington D. (1993) Estimating the sorptivity for a wide range of diffusivity dependence on water content. *Transport in Porous Media*, **10**, 95–101.

[749] Lockington D. (1994) Falling rate evaporation and desorption estimates. *Water Resources Research*, **30**, 1071–1074.

[750] Lockington D., Hara M., Hogarth W. and Parlange J.-Y. (1989) Flow through porous media from a pressurised spherical cavity. *Water Resources Research*, **25**, 303–309.

[751] Lockington D. A. and Parlange J.-Y. (1995) Approximate formulae for the wetting front position and boundary water-content during horizontal infiltration. *Transport in Porous Media*, **18**, 95–105.

[752] Lockington D. A. and Parlange J.-Y. (2004) A new equation for macroscopic description of capillary rise in porous media. *Journal of Colloid and Interface Science*, **278**, 404–409.

[753] Lockington D. A., Parlange J.-Y. and Dux P. (1999) Sorptivity and the estimation of water penetration into unsaturated concrete. *Materials and Structures*, **32**, 342–347.

[754] Lockington D., Parlange J.-Y., Haverkamp R., Smettem K. R. J. and Ross P. J. (1999) Discussion on the paper: Wilson M. A., Taylor S. C. and Hoff W. D. 'The initial surface absorption test (ISAT): an analytical approach'. *Magazine of Concrete Research*, **51**, 449–451.

[755] Lockington D. A., Parlange J.-Y. and Lenkopane M. (2007) Capillary absorption in porous sheets and surfaces subject to evaporation. *Transport in Porous Media*, **68**, 29–36.

[756] Long A. E., Basheer M. and Callanan A. (1992) Controlled permeability formwork. *Construction Repair*, December, pp 36–40.

[757] Long A. E., Sha'at A. A. and Basheer P. A. M. (1995) The influence of controlled permeability formwork on the durability and transport propertis of near surface concrete. In V. M. Malhotra (ed.), *Advances in concrete technology*, Proceedings of the 2nd CANMET/ACI international conference, Las Vegas, NV, American Concrete Institute SP-154, Farmington Hills, MI, pp 41–54.

[758] Loosveldt H., Lafhaj Z. and Skoczylas F. (2002) Experimental study of gas and liquid permeability of a mortar. *Cement and Concrete Research*, **32**, 1357–1363.

[759] Lopez-Arce P., Doehne E., Greenshields J., Benavente D. and Young D. (2009) Treatment of rising damp and salt decay: the historic masonry buildings of Adelaide, South Australia. *Materials and Structures*, **42**, 827–848.

[760] Lothenbach B., Kulik D. A., Matschei T., Balonis M., Baquerizo L., Dilnesa B., Miron G. D. and Myers R. J. (2019) Cemdata18: A chemical thermodynamic database for hydrated Portland cements and alkali-activated materials. *Cement and Concrete Research*, **115**, 472–506.

[761] Lucero C. (2015) *Quantifying moisture transport in cementitious materials using neutron radiography*. PhD thesis, Purdue University.

[762] Lucero C. L., Spragg R. P., Bentz D. P., Hussey D. S., Jacobson D. L. and Weiss W. J. (2017) Neutron radiography measurement of salt solution absorption in mortar, *ACI Materials Journal*, **114**, 149–159.

[763] Ludirdja D. (1993) *Effect of early curing conditions on permeability of concrete*, PhD thesis, University of Illinois at Urbana-Champaign.

[764] Ludirdja D., Berger R. L. and Young J. F. (1989) Simple method for measuring water permeability of concrete. *ACI Materials Journal*, **86**, 433–439.

[765] Luffel D. L. and Howard W. E. (1988) Reliability of laboratory measurement of porosity in tight gas sands. *SPE Formation Evaluation*, **3**, 705–710.

[766] Lugg G. A. (1968) Diffusion coefficients of some organic and other vapours in air. *Analytical Chemistry*, **40**, 1072–1077.

[767] Luikov A. V. (1964) Heat and mass transfer in capillary-porous bodies. *Advances in Heat Transfer* **1**, 123–184.

[768] Luikov A. V. (1966) *Heat and mass transfer in capillary-porous bodies*, Pergamon, Oxford.

[769] Luikov A. V. (1975) Systems of differential equations of heat and mass transfer in capillary-porous bodies. *International Journal of Heat and Mass Transfer*, **18**, 1–14.

[770] Ma H. (2014) Mercury intrusion porosimetry in concrete technology: Tips in measurement, pore structure parameter acquisition and application. *Journal of Porous Materials*, **21**, 207–215.

[771] Madgwick E. (1932) Some properties of porous building materials. Part III. A theory of the absorption and transmission of water by porous bodies. *Philosophical Magazine*, **13**, 632–641.

[772] Madgwick E. (1932) Some properties of porous building materials. Part IV. A determination of the absorption constants of a homogeneous specimen. *Philosophical Magazine*, **13**, 641–650.

[773] Maekawa K., Chaube R. and Kishi T. (1999) *Modelling of concrete performance: hydration, microstructure formation and mass transport*, Spon, London.

[774] Magnus G. (1844) Versuche über die Spannkräfte des Wasserdampfs. *Annalen der Physik und Chemie*, **61**, 225–247

[775] Mainguy M., Coussy O. and Baroghel-Bouny V. (2001) Role of air pressure in drying of weakly permeable materials. *Journal of Engineering Mechanics – ASCE*, **127**, 582–592.

[776] Makhlouf N. N., Maskell D., Marsh A., Natarajan S., Dabaieh M. and Afify M. M. (2019) Hygrothermal performance of vernacular stone in a desert climate. *Construction and Building Materials*, **216**, 687–696.

[777] Mallidi S. R. (1996) Application of mercury intrusion porosimetry on clay bricks to assess freeze-thaw durability – a bibliography with abstracts. *Construction and Building Materials*, **10**, 461–465.

[778] Mallidi S. R. (1996) Regression analysis of initial rate of absorption of Canadian clay bricks. *International Journal of Housing Science*, **20**, 121–129.

[779] Mallidi S. R. (1998) Statistical analysis of certain physical properties of Canadian building bricks. *International Journal of Housing Science*, **22**, 67–76.

[780] Manger G. E. (1963) *Porosity and bulk density of sedimentary rocks*. Geological Survey Bulletin 1144-E, U. S. Government Printing Office, Washington.

[781] Mansoutre S., Colombet P. and van Damme H. (1999) Water retention and granular rheological behaviour of fresh C_3S paste as a function of concentration. *Cement and Concrete Research*, **29**, 1441–1453.

[782] Marchese B. and D'Amore F. (1993) Sorptivity and constitution of mature cementitious mortars. *Cemento*, **90**, 25–37.

[783] Marfisi E., Burgoyne C. J., Amin M. H. G. and Hall L. D. (2005) The use of MRI to observe the structure of concrete. *Magazine of Concrete Research*, 57, 101–109.

[784] Marica F., Chen Q., Hamilton A., Hall C., Al T. and Balcom B. J. (2006) Spatially resolved measurement of rock core porosity. *Journal of Magnetic Resonance*, 178, 136–141.

[785] Marinho F. A. M. and Oliveira O. M. (2006) The filter paper method revisited. *Geotechnical Testing Journal*, 29, 250–258.

[786] Marle C. M. (1981) *Multiphase flow in porous media*, Institut français du pétrole, Editions TECHNIP, Paris.

[787] Marrero T. R. and Mason E. A. (1972) Gaseous diffusion coefficients. *Journal of Physical and Chemical Reference Data*, 1, 3–118.

[788] Marshall T. J., Holmes J. W. and Rose C. W. (1996) *Soil physics*, 3rd edn, Cambridge University Press.

[789] Martín J., Mosquera M. J. and Merello R. (1996) New method for performing capillary absorption test. *American Ceramic Society Bulletin*, 75, 66–70.

[790] Martín Contreras S. (2001) Densities and viscosities of binary mixtures of 1, 4-dioxane with 1-propanol and 2-propanol at (25, 30, 35, and 40) °C. *Journal of Chemical and Engineering Data*, 46, 1149–1152.

[791] Martín-Márquez J., Rincón J. Ma. and Romero M. (2008) Effect of firing temperature on sintering of porcelain stoneware tiles. *Ceramics International*, 34, 1867–1873.

[792] Marusin S. L. (1985) Water absorption, interior fissures and microstructure of shale brick. *American Ceramic Society Bulletin*, 64, 674–678.

[793] Maskell D., Thomson A., Walker P. and Lemke M. (2018) Determination of optimal plaster thickness for moisture buffering of indoor air. *Building and Environment*, 130, 143–150.

[794] Masoodi R., Pillai K. M. and Varanasi P. P. (2007) Darcy's law-based models for liquid absorption in polymer wicks. *AIChE Journal*, 53, 2769–2782.

[795] Massari G. and Massari I. (1993) *Damp buildings, old and new*, ICCROM, Rome. [English translation of *Risanamento igienico dei locali humidi*, Ulrico Hoepli, Milan].

[796] Massey S. W. (1995) Discussion on paper by W. J. McCarter in *Advances in Cement Research* 1994, 6, 147–154. *Advances in Cement Research*, 7, 179–181.

[797] Massman W. J. (1998) A review of the molecular diffusivities of H_2O, CO_2, CH_4, CO, O_3, SO_2, NH_3, N_2O, NO and NO_2 in air, O_2 and N_2 near STP. *Atmospheric Environment*, 32, 1111–1127.

[798] Mastikhin I. V., Mullally H., MacMillan B and Balcom B. J. (2002) Water content profiles with a 1D centric SPRITE acquisition. *Journal of Magnetic Resonance*, 156, 122–130.

[799] Matano C. (1932–33) On the relation between the diffusion-coefficients and concentrations of solid metals (the nickel-copper system). *Japanese Journal of Physics*, 8, 109–113.

[800] Mayer G. and Wittmann F. H. (1996) Rising damp and salt transport in masonry. *Materials science and restoration* [Werkstoffwissenschaften und Bauinstandsetzen], 4th international colloquium, Esslingen, Aedificatio, Freiburg, pp 955–965.

[801] McBurney J. W. (1929) The water absorption and penetrability of brick. *ASTM Proceedings*, pp 711–734.

[802] McBurney J. W. (1936) Water absorption of building brick. *Proceedings ASTM*, 36, 260–271.

[803] McBurney J. W. (1954) Masonry cracking and damage caused by moisture expansion of structural clay tile. *Proceedings ASTM*, 54, 1219–1238.

[804] McCabe S., McKinley J. M., Gomez-Heras M. and Smith B. J. (2010) Dynamical instability in surface permeability characteristics of building sandstones in response to salt accumulation over time. *Geomorphology*, 130, 65–75.

[805] McCarter W. J. (1994) A parametric study of the impedance characteristics of cement-aggregate systems during early hydration. *Cement and Concrete Research*, 24, 1097–1110.

[806] McCarter W. J. (1994) The fractal surface of cementitious materials determined by impedance spectroscopy. *Advances in Cement Research*, 6, 147–154.

[807] McCarter W. J., Chrisp T. M., Butler A. and Basheer P. A. M. (2001) Near-surface sensors for condition monitoring of cover-zone concrete. *Construction and Building Materials* 15, 115–124.

[808] McCarter W. J., Chrisp T. M., Ezirim H. and Basheer P. A. M. (1996) In-situ evaluation of properties of concrete in the cover zone. In R. K. Dhir and M. R. Jones (eds), *Concrete repair, rehabilitation and protection*, Dundee, Spon, London, pp 113–124.

[809] McCarter W. J., Emerson M. and Ezirim H. (1995) Properties of concrete in the cover zone: developments in monitoring techniques. *Magazine of Concrete Research*, 47, 243–251.

[810] McCarter W. J. and Ezirim H. (1998) AC impedance profiling within cover zone concrete: influence of water and ionic ingress. *Advances in Cement Research*, 10, 57–66.

[811] McCarter W. J., Ezirim H. and Emerson M. (1996) Properties of concrete in the cover zone: water penetration, sorptivity and ionic ingress. *Magazine of Concrete Research*, 48, 149–156.

[812] McCarter W. J. and Garvin S. (1989) Dependence of electrical impedance of cement-based materials on their moisture condition. *Journal of Physics D: Applied Physics*, 22, 1773–1776.

[813] McCarter W. J., Garvin S. and Bouzid N. (1988) Impedance measurements on cement paste. *Journal of Materials Science Letters*, 7, 1056–1057.

[814] McCarter W. J., Starrs G. and Chrisp T. M. (2000) Electrical conductvity, diffusion and permeability of Portland cement concrete. *Cement and Concrete Research*, 30, 1395–1400.

[815] McCarter W. J., Starrs G. and Chrisp T. M. (2002) Electrical monitoring methods in cement science. In J. Bensted and P. Barnes (eds), *Structure and performance of cements*, 2nd edn, Taylor and Francis, London, pp 442–456.

[816] McCarter W. J., Watson D. W. and Chrisp T. M. (2001) Surface zone concrete: drying, absorption, and moisture distribution. *Journal of Materials in Civil Engineering*, 13, 49–57.

[817] McColl K. A., Alemohammad S. H., Akbar R., Konings A. G., Yueh S. and Entekhabi D. (2017) The global distribution and dynamics of surface soil moisture. *Nature Geoscience*, 10, 100–104.

[818] McConville C. J. and Lee W. E. (2005) Microstructural development on firing illite and smectite clays compared to that in kaolinite. *Journal of the American Ceramic Society*, 88, 2267–2276.

[819] McDonald P. J., Istok O., Janota M., Gajewicz-Jaromin A. M. and Faux D. A. (2020) Sorption, anomalous water transport and dynamic porosity in cement paste: A spatially localised ^{1}H NMR relaxation study and a proposed mechanism. *Cement and Concrete Research*, **133**, 106045.

[820] McGlinn P. J., De Beer F. C., Aldridge L. P., Radebe M. J., Nshimirimana R., Brew D. R., Payne T. E. and Olufson K. P. (2010) Appraisal of a cementitious material for waste disposal: Neutron imaging studies of pore structure and sorptivity. *Cement and Concrete Research*, **40**, 1320–1326.

[821] McKay B. (2000) *A study of moisture expansion in clay bricks*, MPhil thesis, UMIST, Manchester.

[822] McKinley J. M. and Warke P. A. (2007) Controls on permeability: implications for stone weathering. In R. Prikryl and B. J. Smith (eds), *Building stone decay: From diagnosis to conservation*, Geological Society, London, Special Publications **271**, 225–236.

[823] McKinley J. D. and Bolton M. D. (1999) A geotechnical description of fresh grout-filtration and consolidation behaviour. *Magazine of Concrete Research*, **30**, 295–307.

[824] McNeilly T. (1985) Moisture expansion of clay bricks: An appraisal of past experience and current knowledge. In *Proceedings of the seventh international brick masonry conference*, Melbourne, p13.

[825] McWhorter D. B., Corey A. T. and Adam K. M. (1973) The elimination of trapped gas from porous media by diffusion. *Soil Science*, **116**, 18–25.

[826] Meakin P. (1998) *Fractals, scaling and growth far from equilibrium*, Cambridge University Press.

[827] Meeten G. H. (1993) A dissection method for analysing filter cakes. *Chemical Engineering Science*, **48**, 2391–2398.

[828] Meeten G. H. (2000) Septum and filtration properties of rigid and deformable particle suspensions. *Chemical Engineering Science*, **55**, 1755–1767.

[829] Meeten G. H. and Lebreton C. (1993) A filtration model of the capillary suction time method. *Journal of Petroleum Science and Engineering*, **9**, 155–162.

[830] Meeten G. H. and Sherwood J. D. (1994) The hydraulic permeability of bentonite suspensions with granular inclusions. *Chemical Engineering Science*, **49**, 3249–3256.

[831] Meeten G. H. and Smeulders J. B. A. F. (1995) Interpretation of filterability measured by the capillary suction time method. *Chemical Engineering Science*, **50**, 1273–1279. [See also Comments by D. J. Lee and W. W. Lin (1996); and reply *ibid*, **51**, 1353–1356].

[832] Mellett J. S. and Smith S. E. (2010) Using ground-penetrating radar to investigate historic masonry buildings. *APT Bulletin: Journal of Preservation Technology*, **41**, 47–56.

[833] Merot P. and Widiatmaka. (1996) Mesure de sorptivité des sols par humectation per ascensum. *Comptes Rendus de l'Académie des Sciences Paris* sér IIa, **322**, 293–299.

[834] Merrill S. D. and Rawlins S. L. (1972) Field measurement of soil water potential with thermocouple psychrometers. *Soil Science*, **113**, 102–109.

[835] Merz S., Balcom B. J., Enjilela R., Vanderborght J., Rothfuss Y., Vereecken H. and Pohlmeier A. (2018) Magnetic resonance monitoring and numerical modeling of soil moisture during evaporation. *Vadose Zone Journal*, **17**, 1–15.

[836] Miller E. E. and Miller R. D. (1956) Physical theory for capillary flow phenomena, *Journal of Applied Physics*, 27, 324–332.

[837] Miller K. T., Melant R. M. and Zukoski C. F. (1996) Comparison of the compressive yield response of aggregated suspensions: Pressure filtration, centrifugation and osmotic consolidation. *Journal of the American Ceramic Society*, 79, 2545–2556.

[838] Mills E. O. (1933) The permeability to air and to water of some building bricks. *Transactions of the Ceramic Society*, 33, 200–212.

[839] Mills R. H. (1983) *The permeability of concrete for reactor containment vessels*, University of Toronto, Publication 84-01, July.

[840] Mills R. H. (1986) *Gas and water permeability of concrete for reactor buildings – small specimens*, Research report, Atomic Energy Control Board, Ottawa, March.

[841] Mills R. H. (1987) Mass transfer of gas and water through concrete. *American Concrete Institute SP-100*, 1, 621–644.

[842] Mills R. H. (1990) *Gas and water permeability tests of 25 year old concrete from the NPD nuclear generating station*, Research report, Atomic Energy Control Board, Ottawa, May.

[843] Milly P. C. D. (1985) Stability of the Green-Ampt profile in a delta function soil, *Water Resources Research*, 21, 399–402.

[844] Milly P. C. D. (1987) Estimation of Brooks-Corey parameters from water retention data. *Water Resources Research*, 23, 1085–1089.

[845] Mitchell J., Chandrasekera T. C., Holland D. J., Gladden L. F. and Fordham E. J. (2013) Magnetic resonance imaging in laboratory petrophysical core analysis. *Physics Reports*, 526, 165–225.

[846] Mitchell J. and Fordham E. J. (2014) Contributed review: Nuclear magnetic resonance core analysis at 0.3 T. *Review of Scientific Instruments*, 85, 111502.

[847] Mitchell J. Jr. and Smith D. M. (1948) *Aquametry: Application of the Karl Fischer reagent to quantitative analyses involving water*, Interscience, New York.

[848] Mitchell J., Webber J. B. W. and Strange J. H. (2008) Nuclear magnetic resonance cryoporometry. *Physics Reports*, 461, 1–36.

[849] Modestou S., Theodoridou M., Fournari R. and Ioannou I. (2016) Physicomechanical properties and durability performance of natural building and decorative carbonate stones from Cyprus. In R. Přikiryl, Á. Török, M. Gomez-Heras, K. Miskovsky and M. Theodoridou (eds), *Sustainable use of traditional geomaterials in construction practice*, Geological Society, London, Special Publications, 416, 145–162.

[850] Mollo L. and Greco R. (2011) Moisture measurements in masonry materials by time domain reflectometry. *Journal of Materials in Civil Engineering*, 23, 441–444.

[851] Monlouis-Bonnaire J. P., Verdier J. and Perrin B. (2004) Prediction of the relative permeability to gas flow of cement-based materials. *Cement and Concrete Research*, 34, 737–744.

[852] Monteith J. L. and Unsworth M. H. (2013) *Principles of environmental physics*, 4th edn, Academic Press, Oxford.

[853] Morriss C., Rossini D., Straley C., Tutunjian P. and Vinegar H. (1997) Core analysis by low-field NMR. *The Log Analyst*, 38, 83–94.

[854] Mosch S. (2008) *Optimierung der Exploration, Materialcharakterisierung von Naturwerkstein.* PhD thesis, Göttingen.

[855] Mosch S. and Siegesmund S. (2007) Statistisches Verhalten petrophysikalischer und technischer Eigenschaften von Naturwerkstein. *Zeitschrift der Deutschen Gesellschaft für Geowissenschaften*, **158**, 821–868.

[856] Mosquera M. J., Alcántara R. and Martín J. (1998) New procedure for performing moisture absorption tests. *American Ceramic Society Bulletin*, **77**, 76–81.

[857] Mossotti V. G. and Castanier L. M. (1990) The measurement of water transport in Salem limestone by X-ray compter-aided tomography. *18th International symposium on engineering geology of ancient works, monuments and historical sites: preservation and protection*, Athens, Greece 1988, pp 2079–2082.

[858] Mualem Y. (1976) A new model for predicting the hydraulic conductivity of unsaturated porous media. *Water Resources Research*, **12**, 513–522.

[859] Müller M. J. (1996) *Handbuch ausgewählter Klimastationen der Erde*, 5, Forschungsstelle Bodenerosion, University of Trier.

[860] Muller A. C. A. and Scrivener K. L. (2017) A reassessment of mercury intrusion porosimetry by comparison with ^{1}H NMR relaxometry. *Cement and Concrete Research*, **100**, 350–360.

[861] Muller A. C., Scrivener K. L. Gajewicz, A. M. and McDonald P. J. (2013) Densification of C–S–H measured by ^{1}H NMR relaxometry. *Journal of Physical Chemistry C*, **117**, 403–412.

[862] Murray F. W. (1967) On the computation of saturation vapor pressure. *Journal of Applied Meteorology*, **6**, 203–204.

[863] Muskat M. (1946) *The flow of homogeneous fluids through porous media*, Edwards, Ann Arbor, MI.

[864] Mydlarz J., Jones A. G. and Millan A. (1989) Solubility and density isotherms for potassium sulfate–water-2-propanol. *Journal of Chemical and Engineering Data*, **34**, 124–126.

[865] National Research Council. (1982) *Conservation of historic stone buildings and monuments*, Report of the Committee on Conservation of Historic Stone Buildings and Monuments, National Materials Advisory Board, Commission on Engineering and Technical Systems, National Academy Press, Washington, DC.

[866] Nauman E. B. and Buffham B. A. (1983) *Mixing in continuous flow systems*, Wiley, New York.

[867] Navarro V., Yustres Á, Cea L., Candel M., Juncosa R. and Delgado J. (2006) Characterization of the water flow through concrete based on parameter estimation from infiltration tests. *Cement and Concrete Research*, **36**, 1575–1582.

[868] Needham T. (1998) *Visual complex analysis*, Oxford.

[869] Nemec T., Rant J. and Apih V. (1999) Quantitative measurements of moisture transport in building materials by quasi-real-time neutron radiography. *Insight*, **41**, 449–452.

[870] Nemec T., Rant J., Apih V. and Glumac B. (1999) Study of building materials impregnation processes by quasi-real-time neutron radiography. *Nuclear Instruments and Methods in Physics Research Section A*, **424**, 242–247.

[871] Neuzil C. E., Cooley C., Silliman S. E., Bredehoeft J. D. and Hsieh P. A. (1981) A transient laboratory method for determining the hydraulic properties of

'tight' rocks. *International Journal of Rock Mechanics, Mining Sciences and Geomechanics Abstracts*, **18**, 253–258.

[872] Neville A. M. (2011) *Properties of concrete*, 5th edn, Pearson, London.

[873] Newman J. A. (1973) Protection of buildings against water from the ground. *BRE Current Paper* CP102/73, Building Research Establishment, Garston.

[874] Newman J. A. (1975) Improvement of the drilling method for the determination of moisture content in building materials. *BRE Current Paper* CP22/75, Building Research Establishment, Garston.

[875] Nguyen H. T., Rahimi-Aghdam S. and Bažant Z. P. (2019) Sorption isotherm restricted by multilayer hindered adsorption and its relation to nanopore size distribution. *Journal of the Mechanics and Physics of Solids*, **127**, 111–124.

[876] Nguyen H., Rahimi-Aghdam S. and Bažant Z. P. (2020) Unsaturated nanoporomechanics. *Proceedings of the National Academy of Sciences*, **117**, 3440–3445.

[877] Nicolai A., Scheffler G. A., Grunewald J. and Plagge R. (2009) An efficient numerical solution method and implementation for coupled heat, moisture and salt transport: The Delphin Simulation Program. In *Simulation of time dependent degradation of porous materials*, Cuvillier, The Netherlands, pp 85–100.

[878] Nielsen A. F. (1972) Gamma-ray-attenuation used for measuring the moisture content and homogeneity of porous concrete. *Building Science*, **7**, 257–263.

[879] Nielsen A. F. (1976) *Free water intake of cellular concrete and bricks measured by gamma ray attenuation*, Technical University of Denmark, Thermal Insulation Laboratory, Report no. 41, Copenhagen.

[880] Nielsen A. F. (1983) Gamma-ray attenuation used on free-water intake tests. In F. H. Wittmann (ed.), *Autoclaved aerated concrete, moisture and properties*, Elsevier, Amsterdam, The Netherlands, pp 43–53.

[881] Niesel K. (1989) Quelques aspects expérimentaux de l'étude du transfert d'humidité en maçonnerie. *Silicates Industriels*, **54**, 47–54.

[882] Niesel K. (1989) Migration d'humidité en maçonnerie de briques. *Revue des Archéologues et Historiens d'Art de Louvain*, no. 22, 99–106.

[883] Niesel K. (1992) Simple ways to obtain characteristic data on capillary liquid rise. *GIT Fachzeitschrift für das Laboratorium*, **36**, 347–349.

[884] Nijland T. G., Adan O. C. G., van Hees R. P. J. and van Etten B. D. (2009) Evaluation of the effects of expected climate change on the durability of building materials with suggestions for adaptation. *Heron*, **54**, 37–48.

[885] Nilsson L.-O. (ed.). (2018) *Methods of measuring moisture in building materials and structures*, RILEM State of the Art Report 26, Springer, Cham, Switzerland.

[886] Nitao J. J. and Bear J. (1996) Potentials and their role in transport in porous media. *Water Resources Research*, **32**, 225–250.

[887] Noborio K. (2001) Measurement of soil water content and electrical conductivity by time domain reflectometry: A review. *Computers and Electronics in Agriculture*, **31**, 213–237.

[888] Nokken M. R. and Hooton R. D. (2008) Using pore parameters to estimate peremability or conductivity of concrete. *Materials and Structures*, **41**, 1–16.

[889] Norling Mjörnell, K. (1994) *Self-desiccation in concrete*, Licentitiate thesis, Department of Building Materials, Chalmers University of Technology, Publication P-94:2, Göteborg.

[890] Norum D. I. and Luthin J. N. (1968) The effects of entrapped air and barometric fluctuations on the drainage of porous mediums. *Water Resources Research*, **4**, 417–424.

[891] Odler I., Hagymassy Jr J., Yudenfreund M., Hanna K. M. and Brunauer S. (1972) Pore structure analysis by water vapor adsorption. IV. Analysis of hydrated Portland cement pastes of low porosity. *Journal of Colloid and Interface Science*, **38**, 265–276.

[892] Olafuyi O. A., Cinar Y., Knackstedt M. A. and Pinczewski W. V. (2007) Spontaneous imbibition in small cores. Society of Petroleum Engineers, paper 109724.

[893] Olson R. A., Neubauer C. M. and Jennings H. M. (1997) Damage to the pore structure of hardened portland cement paste by mercury intrusion. *Journal of the American Ceramic Society*, **80**, 2454–2458.

[894] Or D., Lehmann P., Shahraeeni E. and Shokri N. (2013) Advances in soil evaporation physics – A review. *Vadose Zone Journal*, **12**, 1–16.

[895] Orr S. A. and Cassar M. (2020) Exposure indices of extreme wind-driven rain events for built heritage. *Atmosphere*, **11**, 163.

[896] Orr S. A. and Viles H. (2018) Characterisation of building exposure to wind-driven rain in the UK and evaluation of current standards. *Journal of Wind Engineering and Industrial Aerodynamics*, **180**, 88–97.

[897] Orr S. A., Young M., Stelfox D., Curran J. and Viles H. (2018) Wind-driven rain and future risk to built heritage in the United Kingdom: Novel metrics for characterising rain spells. *Science of the Total Environment*, **640**, 1098–1111.

[898] Ortín J. (2015) Non-equilibrium dynamics of fluids in disordered media. *Contributions to Science*, **11**, 189–198.

[899] Ottosen L. M. and Rörig-Dalgaard I. (2009) Desalination of a brick by application of an electric DC field. *Materials and Structures*, **42**, 961–971.

[900] Padday J. F. (ed.) (1975) *Wetting, spreading and adhesion*, Academic Press, New York.

[901] Page A. L. (ed.) (1982) *Methods of soil analysis*, 2nd edn, Pts 1 and 2, American Society of Agronomy and Soil Science Society of America, Madison, WI.

[902] Pakkala T. A., Lemberg A. M., Lahdensivu J. and Pentti M. (2016) Climate change effect on wind-driven rain on facades. *Nordic Concrete Research*, Nordic Concrete Federation, Oslo, Norway, no **54**, 31–49.

[903] Parkhurst D. L. and Appelo C. A. J. (1999) *User's guide to PHREEQC (version 2) – A computer program for speciation, batch-reaction, one-dimensional transport, and inverse geochemical calculations*, Water Resources Investigations Report 99-4259, US Geological Survey, Denver, CO.

[904] Parlange J.-Y. (1971) Theory of water-movement in soils: 1. One-dimensional absorption. *Soil Science*, **111**, 134–137.

[905] Parlange J.-Y. (1971) Theory of water movement in soils: 3. Two and three dimensional absorption. *Soil Science*, **112**, 313–317.

[906] Parlange J.-Y. (1972) Theory of water movement in soils: 4. Two and three dimensional steady infiltration. *Soil Science*, **113**, 96–101.

[907] Parlange J.-Y. (1972) Theory of water movement in soils: 5. Unsteady infiltration from spherical cavities. *Soil Science*, **113**, 156–161.

[908] Parlange J.-Y. (1972) Theory of water movement in soils: 6. Effect of water depth over soil. *Soil Science*, **113**, 308–312.

[909] Parlange J.-Y. (1972) Theory of water movement in soils: 7. Multidimensional cavities under pressure. *Soil Science*, **113**, 379–382.

[910] Parlange J.-Y. (1972) Theory of water-movement in soils: 8. One-dimensional infiltration with constant flux at the surface. *Soil Science*, 114, 1–4.

[911] Parlange J.-Y. (1975) Determination of soil water diffusivity by sorptivity measurements. *Soil Science Society of America Journal*, 39, 1011–1012.

[912] Parlange J.-Y. and Aylor D. (1972) Theory of water movement in soils: 9. The dynamics of capillary rise. *Soil Science*, 114, 79–81.

[913] Parlange J.-Y., Barry D. A., Parlange M-B. and Haverkamp R. (1992) Note on the sorptivity for mixed saturated-unsaturated flow. *Water Resources Research*, 28, 2529–2532.

[914] Parlange J.-Y., Barry D. A., Parlange M-B., Lockington D. A. and Haverkamp R. (1994) Sorptivity calculations for arbitrary diffusivity. *Transport in Porous Media*, 15, 197–208.

[915] Parlange J.-Y. and Hill D. E. (1979) Air and water movement in porous media: compressibility effects. *Soil Science*, 127, 257–263.

[916] Parlange J.-Y., Hogarth W. L., Parlange M-B., Haverkamp R., Barry D. A., Ross P. J. and Steenhuis T. S. (1998) Approximate analytical solution of the nonlinear diffusion equation for arbitrary boundary conditions. *Transport in Porous Media*, 30, 45–55.

[917] Parlange M. B., Prasad S. N., Parlange J.-Y. and Römkens M. J. M. (1992) Extension of the Heaslet-Alksne technique to arbitrary soil-water diffusivities. *Water Resources Research*, 28, 2793–2797.

[918] Parlange J.-Y., Vauclin M., Haverkamp R. and Lisle I. (1985) The relation between desorptivity and soil-water diffusivity. *Soil Science*, 139, 458–461.

[919] Parrott L. J. (1987) Measurements and modelling of moisture, microstructure and properties in drying concrete. *De la science des matériaux au génie des matériaux de construction. Vol. 1, Porosité et propriétés des matériaux*, Premier congrès international de la RILEM, Versailles, September, Chapman and Hall, London, pp 135–142.

[920] Parrott L. J. (1988) Moisture profiles in drying concrete. *Advances in Cement Research*, 1, 164–170.

[921] Parrott L. J. (1990) *A review of methods to determine the moisture conditions in concrete*, British Cement Association publication C/7, British Cement Association, Slough, UK.

[922] Parrott L. J. (1991) Factors influencing relative humidity in concrete. *Magazine of Concrete Research*, 43, 45–52.

[923] Parrott L. J. (1991) *Rate of weight loss during initial exposure as an indicator of cover concrete performance*, British Cement Association publication C/9, British Cement Association, Slough, UK.

[924] Parrott L. J. (1992) Variations of water absorption rate and porosity with depth from an exposed concrete surface: effects of exposure conditions and cement type. *Cement and Concrete Research*, 22, 1077–1088.

[925] Parrott L. J. (1994) Moisture conditioning and transport properties of concrete. *Materials and Structures*, 27, 460–468.

[926] Parrott L. J. (1995) Influence of cement type and curing on the drying and air permeability of cover concrete. *Magazine of Concrete Research*, 47, 103–111.

[927] Parrott L. J. and Hong C. Z. (1991) Some factors influencing air permeation measurements in cover concrete. *Materials and Structures*, 24, 403–408.

[928] Pátek J., Hrubý J., Klomfar J., Součková M. and Harvey A. H. (2009) Reference correlations for thermophysical properties of liquid water at 0.1 MPa. *Journal of Physical and Chemical Reference Data*, 38, 21–29.

[929] Pavlík Z., Jiřičková M., Černý, R., Sobczuk H. and Suchorab Z. (2006) Determination of moisture diffusivity using the time domain reflectometry (TDR) method. *Journal of Building Physics*, 30, 59–70.

[930] Pavlík Z., Žumár J., Medved I. and Černý R. (2012) Water vapor adsorption in porous building materials: experimental measurement and theoretical analysis. *Transport in Porous Media*, 91, 939–954.

[931] Peake F. and Ford R. W. (1982) A comparison of the vacuum and boiling methods for measuring the water absorption of bricks. *Transactions and Journal of the British Ceramic Society*, 81, 160–162.

[932] Pearce J. N. and Eckstrom H. C. (1937) Vapour pressures and partial molal volumes of aqueous solutions of the alkali sulfates at 25 °C. *Journal of the American Chemical Society*, 59, 2689–2691.

[933] Peck A. J. (1965) Moisture profile development and air compression during water uptake by bounded porous bodies: 2. Horizontal columns. *Soil Science*, 99, 327–334.

[934] Peck A. J. (1965) Moisture profile development and air compression during water uptake by bounded porous bodies: 3. Vertical columns. *Soil Science*, 100, 44–51.

[935] Peck A. J. (1969) Entrapment, stability and persistence of air bubbles in soil water. *Australian Journal of Soil Research*, 7, 79–90.

[936] Pel L. (1994) Moisture transport through masonry. *Proceedings of 10th international brick and block masonry conference*, Calgary, Canada, pp 803–810.

[937] Pel L. (1995) *Moisture transport in porous building materials*, PhD thesis, Eindhoven University of Technology.

[938] Pel L., Brocken H. and Kopinga K. (1996) Determination of moisture diffusivity in porous media using moisture concentration profiles. *International Journal of Heat and Mass Transfer*, 39, 1273–1280.

[939] Pel L., Brocken H. and Kopinga K. (1997) Moisture and salt transport in brick: a NMR study. *Proceedings of 11th international brick/block masonry conference*, October, Shanghai, China, pp 845–853.

[940] Pel L., Hazrati K., Kopinga K. and Marchand J. (1998) Water absorption in mortar determined by NMR. *Magnetic Resonance Imaging*, 16, 525–528.

[941] Pel L. and Huinink H. (2008) NMR imaging of moisture and ion transport in building materials. In S. L. Codd and J. D. Seymour (eds), *Magnetic resonance microscopy: spatially resolved NMR techniques and applications*, Wiley-VCH, Weinheim, Germany, pp 451–464.

[942] Pel L., Ketelaars A. A. J., Adan O. C. G. and van Well A. A. (1993) Determination of moisture diffusivity in porous media using scanning neutron radiography. *International Journal of Heat and Mass Transfer*, 36, 1261–1267.

[943] Pel L., Kopinga K., Bertram G. and Lang G. (1995) Water absorption in a fired-clay brick observed by NMR scanning. *Journal of Physics D: Applied Physics*, 28, 675–680.

[944] Pel L., Kopinga K. and Brocken H. (1995) Determination of moisture profiles in porous building materials by NMR. *International symposium on nondestructive testing in civil engineering (NDT-CE)*, 26–28 September, Berlin, Germany, pp 189–196.

[945] Pel L., Kopinga K. and Brocken H. (1996) Moisture transport in porous building materials. *Heron*, 41, 95–106.

[946] Pel L., Kopinga K. and Brocken H. (1996) Determination of moisture profiles in porous building materials by NMR. *Magnetic Resonance Imaging*, 14, 931–932.

[947] Pel L., Kopinga K. and Kaasschieter E. F. (2000) Saline absorption in calcium silicate brick observed by NMR scanning. *Journal of Physics D: Applied
Physics*, 33, 1380–1385.

[948] Pel L. and Landman K. A. (2004) A sharp drying front model. *Drying Technology*, 22, 637–647.

[949] Peng Z. and Tiejun Z. Neutron radiography. In L.-O. Nilsson (ed.), *Methods
of measuring moisture in building materials and structures*, RILEM State of
the Art Report 26, Springer, Cham, Switzerland, pp 141–155.

[950] Perfect E., Cheng C.-L., Kang M., Bilheux H. Z., Lamanna J. M., Gragg M. J.
and Wright D. M. (2014) Neutron imaging of hydrogen-rich fluids in geomaterials and engineered porous media: A review. *Earth-Science Reviews*, 129,
120–135.

[951] Penman H. L. (1946) Evaporation in nature. *Reports on Progress in Physics*,
11, 366–388.

[952] Penman H. L. 1948 Natural evaporation from open water, bare soil and grass.
Proceedings of the Royal Society A, 193, 120–145

[953] Peppin S. S. and Style R. W. (2013) The physics of frost heave and ice-lens
growth. *Vadose Zone Journal*, 12, 1–12.

[954] Pérez-Bella J. M., Domínguez-Hernández, J., Cano-Suñén, E., Martínez-
Martínez, J. E. and del Coz-Díaz J. J. (2020) Avoiding the need to directionally
determine the exposure to rainwater penetration for façade designs. *Building
and Environment*, 106850.

[955] Perkins T. K. Jr. and Johnson O. C. (1963) A review of diffusion and dispersion
in porous media. *Society of Petroleum Engineers Journal*, 3, 70–84.

[956] Perre P. and Turner I. W. (1999) A 3-D version of Transpore: a comprehensive heat and mass transfer computational model for simulating the drying of
porous media. *International Journal of Heat and Mass Transfer*, 42, 4501–
4521.

[957] Perrier E., Rieu M., Sposito G. and de Marsily G. (1996) Models of the water
retention curve for soils with a fractal pore size distribution. *Water Resources
Research*, 32, 3025–3031.

[958] Perroux K. M., Smiles D. E. and White I. (1981) Water movement in uniform
soils during constant-flux infiltration. *Soil Science Society of America Journal*,
45, 237–240.

[959] Peters T. and Jenni J.-P. (1973) Mineralogical studies of the firing behaviour
of brick clays. *Beiträge zur Geologie der Schweiz, Geotechnische Serie*, 50,
5–59.

[960] Petković J., Huinink H., Pel L., Kopinga K. and van Hees R. P. J. (2010) Moisture and salt transport in three-layer plaster/substrate systems. *Construction
and Building Materials*, 24, 118–127.

[961] Petrov O. V. and Furó I. (2009) I. NMR cryoporometry: Principles, applications and potential. *Progress in Nuclear Magnetic Resonance Spectroscopy*,
54, 97-122.

[962] Philip J. R. (1955) The concept of diffusion applied to soil water. *Proceedings
of the National Academy of Sciences, India*, 24, 93–104.

[963] Philip J. R. (1955) Numerical solution of equations of the diffusion type with
diffusivity concentration-dependent. *Transactions of the Faraday Society*, 51,
885–892.

[964] Philip J. R. (1957) Numerical solution of equations of the diffusion type with diffusivity concentration-dependent. II. *Australian Journal of Physics*, 10, 29–42.

[965] Philip J. R. (1957) The theory of infiltration: 1. The infiltration equation and its solution. *Soil Science*, 83, 345–357.

[966] Philip J. R. (1957) The theory of infiltration: 4. Sorptivity and algebraic infiltration equations. *Soil Science*, 84, 257–264.

[967] Philip J. R. (1957) The theory of infiltration: 5. The influence of initial moisture content. *Soil Science*, 84, 329–339.

[968] Philip J. R. (1957) Evaporation, and moisture and heat fields in the soil. *Journal of Meteorology*, 14, 354–366.

[969] Philip J. R. (1958) Theory of infiltration: 6. Effect of water depth over soil. *Soil Science*, 85, 278–286.

[970] Philip J. R. (1958) Theory of infiltration: 7. *Soil Science*, 85, 333–337.

[971] Philip J. R. (1966) Absorption and infiltration in two- and three-dimensional systems. *Unesco symposium on water in the unsaturated zone*, Wageningen, International Association for Scientific Hydrology, 1, 503–525.

[972] Philip J. R. (1966) The dynamics of capillary rise. *Unesco symposium on water in the unsaturated zone*, Wageningen, International Association for Scientific Hydrology, 2, 559–564.

[973] Philip J. R. (1967) Sorption and infiltration in heterogeneous media. *Australian Journal of Soil Research*, 5, 1–10.

[974] Philip J. R. (1969) Theory of infiltration. *Advances in Hydroscience*, 5, 215–296.

[975] Philip J. R. (1970) Flow in porous media. *Annual Review of Fluid Mechanics*, 2, 177–204.

[976] Philip J. R. (1973) Flow in porous media. In *Proceedings of 13th congress of theoretical and applied mechanics*, Moscow, August 1972, Springer-Verlag, Berlin, Germany, pp 279–294.

[977] Philip J. R. (1980) Field heterogeneity: Some basic issues. *Water Resources Research*, 16, 443–448.

[978] Philip J. R. (1986) Issues in flow and transport in heterogeneous porous media. *Transport in Porous Media*, 1, 319–338.

[979] Philip J. R. (1995) Desperately seeking Darcy in Dijon. *Soil Science Society of America Journal*, 59, 319–324.

[980] Philip J. R. and De Vries D. A. (1957) Moisture movement in porous materials under temperature gradients. *Eos, Transactions American Geophysical Union*, 38, 222–232.

[981] Philip J. R. and Smiles D. E. (1982) Macroscopic analysis of the behaviour of colloidal suspensions. *Advances in Colloid and Interface Science*, 17, 83–103.

[982] Phillips J. G. (1947) *The physical properties of Canadian building bricks*, Mines and Geology Branch, Report no. 816, Department of Mines and Resources, Ottawa.

[983] Phillips O. M. (1991) *Flow and reactions in permeable rocks*, Cambridge.

[984] Phillipson M. C., Baker P. H., Davies M., Ye Z., McNaughtan A., Galbraith G. H. and McLean R. C. (2007) Moisture measurement in building materials: an overview of current methods and new approaches. *Building Services Engineering Research and Technology*, 28, 303–316.

[985] Phillipson M. C., Baker P. H., Davies M., Ye Z., Galbraith G. H. and McLean R. C. (2007) Suitability of time domain reflectometry for monitoring moisture

in building materials. *Building Services Engineering Research and Technology*, 29, 261–272.

[986] Phung Q. T., Maes N., De Schutter G., Jacques D. and Ye G. (2013) Determination of water permeability of cementitious materials using a controlled constant flow method. *Construction and Building Materials*, 47, 1488–1496.

[987] Picandet V., Khelidj A. and Bellegou H. (2009) Crack effects on gas and water permeability of concretes. *Cement and Concrete Research*, 39, 537–547.

[988] Pihlajavaara S. E. and Vaisanen J. (1965) *Numerical solution of diffusion equation with diffusivity concentration dependent*, State Institute for Technical Research, Helsinki, Publication no. 87.

[989] Pigeon M. and Pleau R. (1995) *Durability of concrete in cold climates*, Taylor and Francis, London.

[990] Pijaudier-Cabot G., Dufour F. and Choinska M. (2009) Permeability due to the increase of damage in concrete: From diffuse to localized damage distributions. *Journal of Engineering Mechanics*, 135, 1022–1028.

[991] Pinchin S. E. (2008) Techniques for monitoring moisture in walls. *Reviews in Conservation*, 9, 33–45.

[992] Ping Gu, Zhongzi Xu, Ping Xie and Beaudoin J. J. (1993) Application of A.C. impedance techniques in studies of porous cementitious materials. *Cement and Concrete Research*, 23, 531–540.

[993] Pitois O. (2012) Foam ripening. In P. Stevenson (ed.), *Foam engineering: Fundamentals and applications*, Wiley-Blackwell, Oxford, pp 59–73.

[994] Plagge R. and Teutsch A. (2003) Water retention functions of ceramic bricks of the Dresden building stock. In J. Carmeliet, H. Hens and G. Vermeir (eds), *Research in building physics*, Proceedings of the 2nd international conference on building physics, pp 197–206.

[995] Plagge R., Scheffler G. and Grunewald J. (2005) Automatische Messung des Wasseraufnahmekoeffizienten und des kapillaren Wassergehaltes von porösen Baustoffen. *Bauphysik*, 27, 315–323.

[996] Plassais A., Pomiès M.-P., Lequeux N., Korb J.-P., Petit D., Barberon F. and Bresson B. (2005) Microstructure evolution of hydrated cement pastes. *Physical Review E*, 72, 041401.

[997] Platten A. K. (1985) *A study of evaporation and drying in porous building materials*, PhD thesis, UMIST, Manchester.

[998] Pleinert H. and Degueldre C. (1995) Neutron radiographic measurement of porosity of crystalline rock samples: a feasibility study. *Journal of Contaminant Hydrology*, 19, 29–46.

[999] Pleinert H., Sadouki H. and Wittmann F. H. (1997) Study of moisture transport by numerical modelling and neutron transmission analysis. *International Journal for Restoration of Buildings and Monuments*, 3, 355–370.

[1000] Pleinert H., Sadouki H. and Wittmann F. H. (1998) Determination of moisture distributions in porous building materials by neutron transmission analysis. *Materials and Structures*, 31, 218–224.

[1001] Poděbradská J., Maděra J., Tydlitát V., Rovnaníková P. and Černý R. (2000) Determination of moisture content in hydrating cement paste. *Ceramics-Silikaty*, 44, 35–38.

[1002] Poli T., Toniolo L., Valentini M., Bizzaro G., Melzi R., Tedoldi F. and Cannazza G. (2007) A portable NMR device for the evaluation of water presence in building materials. *Journal of Cultural Heritage*, 8, 134–140.

[1003] Pollio M. L., Kitic D. and Resnik S. L. (1996) Research note: A_w values of six saturated salt solutions at 25 °C. Re-examination for the purpose of maintaining a constant relative humidity in water sorption measurements. *LWT-Food Science and Technology*, **29**, 376–378.

[1004] Poole A. B., Sims I. and St John D. (2016) *Concrete petrography: A handbook of investigative techniques*, 2nd edn, Taylor and Francis, Boca Raton, FL.

[1005] Poupeleer A.S. (2007) *Transport and crystallization of dissolved salts in cracked porous building materials*, PhD thesis, Katholieke Universiteit Leuven.

[1006] Poupeleer A., Roels S., Carmeliet J. and Van Gemert D. (2006) Diffusion-Convection transport of salt solutions in cracked porous building materials Part 1: Parameters, model description and application to cracks. *International Journal for Restoration of Buildings and Monuments*, **12**, 187–204.

[1007] Poupeleer A., Roels S., Carmeliet J. and Van Gemert D. (2006) Diffusion-Convection transport of salt-solutions in cracked porous building materials. Part 2: Analysis of salt transport in cracked bricks and dead ending cracks. *International Journal for Restoration of Buildings and Monuments*, **12**, 205–218.

[1008] Powers T. C. (1945) A working hypothesis for further studies of frost resistance. *Proceedings of the American Concrete Institute*, **41**, 245–272.

[1009] Powers T. C. (1949) The air requirement of frost resistant concrete. *Highway Research Board Proceedings*, **29**, 184–211.

[1010] Powers T. C. (1959) Capillary continuity or discontinuity in cement pastes. *Journal of the PCA Research and Development Laboratories*, **1**, 38–48.

[1011] Powers T. C. (1964) The physical structure of Portland cement paste. In H. F. W. Taylor (ed.), *The chemistry of cements*, Academic Press, London, **1**, 391–416.

[1012] Powers T. C. (1975) Freezing effects in concrete. In *Durability of concrete*, American Concrete Institute SP47-1, pp 1–11.

[1013] Powers T. C. and Brownyard T. L. (1947) Studies of the physical properties of hardened cement paste. *Journal of the American Concrete Institute, Proceedings* **43**, pp 101–992. Reprinted as *Bulletin* 22, Portland Cement Association, Chicago 1948.

[1014] Powers T. C., Copeland L. E., Hayes J. C. and Mann H. M. (1954) Permeability of portland cement paste. *Proceedings of the American Concrete Institute*, **51**, 285–298.

[1015] Powers T. C. and Helmuth R. A. (1953) A theory of volume changes in hardened Portland cement paste during freezing. *Highway Research Board Proceedings*, **32**, 285–297.

[1016] Poyet S., Bary B. and Coppens E. (2019) Analysis of water transport in unsaturated conditions: Comparison between labcrete and fieldcrete. *Construction and Building Materials*, **205**, 443–455.

[1017] Pražák J., Tywoniak J., Peterka F. and Šlonc T. (1990) Description of transport of liquid in porous media – A study based on neutron radiography data. *International Journal of Heat and Mass Transfer*, **33**, 1105–1120.

[1018] Price W. F. (1998) Recent developments in the use of controlled permeability formwork. *Concrete*, **32**, 8–10.

[1019] Price W. F. and Bamforth P. B. (1993) Initial surface absorption of concrete: examination of modified test apparatus for obtaining uniaxial absorption. *Magazine of Concrete Research*, **45**, 17–24.

[1020] Prick A. (1997) Critical degree of saturation as a threshold moisture level in frost weathering of limestones. *Permafrost and Periglacial Processes*, **8**, 91–99.

[1021] Prim P. and Wittmann F. H. (1983) Structure and water absorption in aerated concrete. In F. H. Wittmann (ed.), *Autoclaved, aerated concrete: Moisture and properties*, Elsevier, Amsterdam, The Netherlands, pp 55–69.

[1022] Princen H. M. and Mason S. G. (1965) The permeability of soap films to gases. *Journal of Colloid Science*, **20**, 353–375.

[1023] Prior M. J. and Newman A. J. (1988) Driving rain – calculations and measurements for buildings. *Weather*, **43**, 146–155.

[1024] Proietti N., Capitani D. and Di Tullio V. (2018) Nuclear magnetic resonance, a powerful tool in cultural heritage. *Magnetochemistry*, **4**, 11.

[1025] Promentilla M. A. B., Sugiyama T., Hitomi T. and Takeda N. (2009) Quantification of tortuosity in hardened cement pastes using synchrotron-based X-ray computed microtomography. *Cement and Concrete Research*, **39**, 548–557.

[1026] Prout W. (1989) *Studies of frost damage in masonry*, PhD thesis, Manchester.

[1027] Prout W. and Hoff W. D. (1990) Fundamental studies of frost damage in clay bricks. In *Proceedings of the 5th international conference on the durability of building materials and components*, Spon, London, pp 39–51.

[1028] Prunty L. D., Bell J. S. and Zellis M. K. (1998) Soil water content by Karl Fischer titration. *Contaminated Soils*, **3**, 97–106.

[1029] Pugsley V. A. Unpublished results.

[1030] Puyate Y. T. and Lawrence C. J. (1999) Effect of solute parameters on wick action in concrete. *Chemical Engineering Science*, **54**, 4257–4265.

[1031] Quénard D and Sallée H. (1989) A gamma-ray spectrometer for measurement of the water diffusivity of cementitious materials. In L. R. Roberts and J. P. Skalny (eds), *Pore structure and permeability of cementitious materials*, MRS symposium series no. 137, Materials Research Society, Warrendale, PA.

[1032] Quénard D., Xu K., Künzel H. M., Bentz D. P. and Martys N. S. (1998) Microstructure and transport properties of porous building materials. *Materials and Structures*, **31**, 317–324.

[1033] Quéré D. (2002) Rough ideas on wetting. *Physica A: Statistical Mechanics and Its Applications*, **313**, 32–46.

[1034] Quijada-Maldonado E., Meindersma G. W. and de Haan A. B. (2013) Viscosity and density data for the ternary system water (1)–ethanol (2)–ethylene glycol (3) between 298.15 K and 328.15 K. *Journal of Chemical Thermodynamics*, **57**, 500–505.

[1035] Radcliffe D. E. and Simunek J. (2010) *Soil physics with HYDRUS: Modeling and applications*, CRC Press, Boca Raton, FL.

[1036] Radliński A. P., Radlińska E. Z., Agamalian M., Wignall G. D., Lindner P. and Randl O. G. (1999) Fractal geometry of rocks. *Physical Review Letters*, **82**, 3078.

[1037] Raimondo M., Dondi M., Gardini D., Guarini G. and Mazzanti F. (2009) Predicting the initial rate of water absorption in clay bricks. *Construction and Building Materials*, **23**, 2623–2630.

[1038] Ramakrishnan T. S. and Cappiello A. (1991) A new technique to measure static and dynamic properties of a partially saturated porous medium. *Chemical Engineering Science*, **46**, 1157–1163.

[1039] Ramires M. L., Nieto de Castro C. A., Nagasaka Y., Nagashima A., Assael M. J. and Wakeham W. A. (1995) Standard reference data for the thermal conductivity of water. *Journal of Physical and Chemical Reference Data*, **24**, 1377–1381.

[1040] Ramsay J. D. F. (1998) Surface and pore structure characterisation by neutron scattering techniques. *Advances in Colloid and Interface Science*, 77, 13–37.

[1041] Ramsay J. D. F. (2002) Scattering and diffraction methods. In F. Schüth, K. S. W. Sing and J. Weitkamp (eds), *Handbook of porous solids*, Wiley-VCH, Weinheim, Germany, vol 2, pp 135–181.

[1042] Raneri S., Barone G., Mazzoleni P. and Rabot E. (2016) Visualization and quantification of weathering effects on capillary water uptake of natural building stones by using neutron imaging. *Applied Physics A*, 122, 969.

[1043] Reddy M. M. (1988) Acid rain damage to carbonate stone: a quantitative assessment based on the aqueous geochemistry of rainfall runoff from stone. *Earth Surface Processes and Landforms*, 13, 335–354.

[1044] Reichardt K., Nielsen D. R. and Biggar J. W. (1972) Horizontal infiltration into layered soils. *Soil Science Society of America Proceedings*, 36, 858–863.

[1045] Reinhardt H.-W. (1992) Transport of chemicals through concrete. In J. Skalny (ed.), *Materials science of concrete III*, American Ceramic Society, Westerville, OH.

[1046] Reinhardt H.-W. (ed.) (1997) *Penetration and permeability of concrete: barriers to organic and contaminating liquids*, RILEM Report no. 16, Spon, London.

[1047] Reinhardt H.-W., Aufrecht M. and Sosoro M. (1993) The potential of concrete as a secondary barrier against hazardous organic fluids. *Concrete 2000*, Dundee, Spon, London, September.

[1048] Rescic S., Fratini F. and Tiano P. (2010) On-site evaluation of the 'mechanical' properties of Maastricht limestone and their relationship with the physical properties. In B. J. Smith, M. Gomez-Heras, H. A. Viles and J. Cassar (eds) *Limestone in the built environment: present-day challenges for the preservation of the past.* Geological Society, London, Special Publications, 331, 203–208.

[1049] Revil A., Kessouri P. and Torres-Verdín C. (2014) Electrical conductivity, induced polarization, and permeability of the Fontainebleau sandstone. *Geophysics*, 79, D301–D318.

[1050] Reyssat, M., Sangne L. Y., van Nierop E. A. and Stone H. A. (2009) Imbibition in layered systems of packed beads, *Europhysics Letters*, 86, 56002.

[1051] Riccardi M. P., Messiga B. and Duminuco P. (1999) An approach to the dynamics of clay firing. *Applied Clay Science*, 15, 393–409.

[1052] Richards L. A. (1931) Capillary conduction of liquids through porous mediums. *Physics*, 1, 318–333.

[1053] Richards L. A. (1941) A pressure-membrane extraction apparatus for soil solution. *Soil Science*, 51, 377–386.

[1054] Richards L. A. (1944) Pressure membrane extraction apparatus. U. S. Patent 2,353,760.

[1055] Richards L. A. (1947) Pressure membrane apparatus – construction and use. *Agricultural Engineering*, 28, 451–454, 460.

[1056] Richards L. A. (1949) Methods of measuring soil moisture tension. *Soil Science*, 68, 95–112.

[1057] Rieu M. and Sposito G. (1991) Fractal fragmentation, soil porosity and soil water properties: I. Theory. *Soil Science Society of America Journal*, 55, 1231–1238.

[1058] Rieu M. and Sposito G. (1991) Fractal fragmentation, soil porosity and soil water properties: II. Applications. *Soil Science Society of America Journal*, 55, 1239–1244.

[1059] RILEM. (2001) Non-destructive tests for masonry materials and structures. Recommendations of RILEM TC 127-MS: Tests for masonry materials and structures. *Materials and Structures*, **34**, 134–143.

[1060] RILEM. (2005) Determination of moisture distribution and level using radar in masonry built with regular units. Recommendations of TC 177-MDT: Masonry durability and on-site testing. *Materials and Structures*, **38**, 283–288.

[1061] RILEM. TC 25-PEM (1980) Recommended tests to measure the deterioration of stone and to assess the effectiveness of treatment methods. *Materials and Structures*, **13**, 175–253.

[1062] RILEM. CPC 11.3 (1984) Absorption of water by immersion under vacuum. *Materials and Structures*, **117**, 391–394.

[1063] RILEM. (1994) *RILEM technical recommendations for the testing and use of constructional materials*, Spon, London.

[1064] RILEM. (1999) Tests for gas permeability of concrete. Recommendations of RILEM TC 116-PCD: Permeability of concrete as a criterion of its durability. *Materials and Structures*, **32**, 174–179.

[1065] Rirsch E., MacMullen J. and Zhang Z. (2011) Evaluation of mortar samples obtained from UK houses treated for rising damp. *Construction and Building Materials*, **25**, 2845 –2850.

[1066] Rirsch E. and Zhang Z. (2010) Rising damp in masonry walls and the importance of mortar properties. *Construction and Building Materials*, **24**, 1815–1820.

[1067] Robert R. (2004) *Analytical characterization of porous geomaterials: reference assessment in some sedimentary rocks*. PhD thesis, Humboldt University, Berlin.

[1068] Roberts J. N. and Schwartz L. M. (1985) Grain consolidation and electrical conductivity in porous media. *Physical Review B*, **31**, 5990–5997.

[1069] Roberts L. R. and Skalny J. P. (eds) (1989) *Pore structure and permeability of cementitious materials*, Materials Research Society symposium no. 137, Materials Research Society, Pittsburgh, PA.

[1070] Robie R. A., Bethke P.M. and Beardsley K.M. (1967) *Selected X-ray crystallographic data, molar volumes, and densities of minerals and related substances*. Geological Survey Bulletin 1248, US Government Printing Office, Washington, DC.

[1071] Rode C., Peuhkuri R. H., Mortensen L. H., Hansen K. K., Time B., Gustavsen A., Ojanen T., Ahonen J., Svennberg K., Harderup L-E. and Arfvidsson J. (2005) *Moisture buffering of building materials*, Technical University of Denmark, Department of Civil Engineering. BYG Report R-127.

[1072] Rodriguez-Navarro C., Cultrone G., Sanchez-Navarro A. and Sebastian E. (2003) TEM study of mullite growth after muscovite breakdown. *American Mineralogist*, **88**, 713–724.

[1073] Roels S. Unpublished results.

[1074] Roels S. (2000) *Modelling unsaturated moisture transport in heterogeneous limestone*, PhD thesis, Katholieke Universiteit Leuven.

[1075] Roels S., van Besien T., Carmeliet J. and Wevers M. (2003) X-ray attenuation technique for the analysis of moisture flow in porous building materials. In J. Carmeliet, H. Hens and G. Vermeir (eds), *Research in building physics*, Proceedings of the 2nd international conference on building physics, pp 151–157.

[1076] Roels S. and Carmeliet J. (2006) Analysis of moisture flow in porous materials using microfocus X-ray radiography. *International Journal of Heat and Mass Transfer*, **49**, 4762–4772.

[1077] Roels S., Carmeliet J., Hens H., Adan O., Brocken H., Cerny R., Pavlik Z., Hall C., Kumaran K., Pel L. and Plagge R. (2004) Interlaboratory comparison of hygric properties of porous building materials. *Journal of Thermal Envelope and Building Science*, **27**, 307–325.

[1078] Roels S., Elsen J., Carmeliet J. and Hens H. (2001) Characterisation of pore structure by combining mercury porosimetry and micrography. *Materials and Structures*, **34**, 76–82.

[1079] Roels S., Carmeliet J., Hens H., Adan O., Brocken H., Cerny R., Pavlik Z., Ellis A. T., Hall C., Kumaran K, Pel L. and Plagge R. (2004) A comparison of different techniques to quantify moisture content profiles in porous building materials. *Journal of Thermal Envelope and Building Science*, **27**, 261–276.

[1080] Roels S. and Janssen H. (2006) A comparison of the Nordtest and Japanese test methods for the moisture buffering performance of building materials. *Journal of Building Physics*, **30**, 137–161.

[1081] Roels S., Sermijn J. and Carmeliet J. (2002) Modelling unsaturated moisture transport in autoclaved aerated concrete: a microstructural approach. In *Sixth symposium on building physics in the Nordic countries*, Norwegian University of Science and Technology, Trondheim, Norway, pp 167–174.

[1082] Roels S., Vandersteen K. and Carmeliet J. (2003) Measuring and simulating moisture uptake in a fractured porous medium. *Advances in Water Resources*, **26**, 237–246.

[1083] Rose D. A. (1963) Water movement in porous materials: Part 1 – Isothermal vapour transfer. *British Journal of Applied Physics*, **14**, 256–262.

[1084] Rose D. A. (1973) Some aspects of the hydrodynamic dispersion of solutes in porous materials. *Journal of Soil Science*, **24**, 284–293.

[1085] Rose D. A. (1977) Hydrodynamic dispersion in porous materials. *Soil Science*, **123**, 277–283.

[1086] Rose D. A. (1979) Soil water: quantities, units and symbols. *Journal of Soil Science*, **30**, 1–15.

[1087] Rose D. A. and Passioura J. B. (1971) The analysis of experiments on hydrodynamic dispersion. *Soil Science*, **111**, 252–257.

[1088] Ross K. D. and Butlin R. N. (1989) *Durability tests for building stone*, Building Research Establishment, Garston, report 141.

[1089] Rossi C. and Nimmo J. R. (1994) Modeling of soil water retention from saturation to oven dryness. *Water Resources Research*, **30**, 701–708.

[1090] Rougelot T., Skoczylas F. and Burlion N. (2009) Water desorption and shrinkage in mortars and cement pastes. Experimental study and poromechanical model. *Cement and Concrete Research*, **39**, 36–44.

[1091] Rowlinson J. S. and Widom B. (1982) *Molecular theory of capillarity*, Clarendon Press, Oxford.

[1092] Rucker-Gramm P. and Beddoe R. E. (2010) Effect of moisture content of concrete on water uptake. *Cement and Concrete Research*, **40**, 102–108.

[1093] Rudiyanto, Minasny B., Shah R. M., Setiawan B. I. and van Genuchten M. T. (2020) Simple functions for describing soil water retention and the unsaturated hydraulic conductivity from saturation to complete dryness. *Journal of Hydrology*, **588**, 125041.

[1094] Rudiyanto, Sakai M., van Genuchten M. T., Alazba A. A., Setiawan B. I. and Minasny B. (2015) A complete soil hydraulic model accounting for capillary and adsorptive water retention, capillary and film conductivity, and hysteresis. *Water Resources Research*, **51**, 8757–8772.

[1095] Ruiz de Argandoña V. G., Rodriguez-Rey A., Celorio C., Calleja L. and Suárez del Rio L. M. (2003) Characterization by X-ray computed tomography of water absorption in a limestone used as building stone in the Oviedo Cathedral (Spain). Geological Society, London, Special Publications, **215**, 127–134.

[1096] Rumer R. R. Jr. (1969) Resistance to flow through porous media. In R. J. M. de Wiest (ed.), *Flow through porous media*, Academic Press, New York.

[1097] Russ J. C. and Dehoff R. T. (2000) *Practical stereology*, 2nd edn, Kluwer Academic/Plenum, New York.

[1098] Rydock J. P. (2006) A look at driving rain intensities at five cities. *Building and Environment*, **41**, 1860–1866.

[1099] Sabir B. B., Wild S. and O'Farrell M. (1998) A water sorptivity test for mortar and concrete. *Materials and Structures*, **31**, 568–574.

[1100] Saenger E. H., Vialle S., Lebedev M., Uribe D., Osorno M., Duda M. and Steeb H. (2016) Digital carbonate rock physics. *Solid Earth*, **7**, 1185–1197.

[1101] Safiuddin M. and Hearn N. (2005) Comparison of ASTM saturation techniques for measuring the permeable porosity of concrete. *Cement and Concrete Research*, **35**, 1008–1013.

[1102] Sahimi M. (1994) *Applications of percolation theory*, Taylor and Francis, London.

[1103] Sahimi M. (1995) *Flow and transport in porous media and fractured rock*, VCH, Weinheim, Germany.

[1104] Şahmaran M. and Li V. C. (2009) Influence of microcracking on water absorption and sorptivity of ECC. *Materials and Structures*, **42**, 593–603.

[1105] Saint-Jalmes A. (2006) Physical chemistry in foam drainage and coarsening. *Soft Matter*, **2**, 836–849.

[1106] Salt Damp Research Committee. (1978) *2nd Report, incorporating the proceedings of the national conference on salt damp*, Adelaide.

[1107] Sander R. (1999) Compilation of Henry's law constants (version 4.0) for water as solvent. *Atmospheric Chemistry and Physics*, **15**, 4399–4981.

[1108] Sander G. C., Parlange J.-Y., Kühnel V., Hogarth W. L., Lockington D. and O'Kane J. P. J. (1988) Exact nonlinear solution for constant flux infiltration. *Journal of Hydrology*, **97**, 341–346.

[1109] Sandrolini F. and Franzoni E. (2006) An operative protocol for reliable measurements of moisture in porous materials of ancient buildings. *Building and Environment*, **41**, 1372–1380.

[1110] Sangani A. S. and Acrivos A. (1983) The effective conductivity of a periodic array of spheres. *Proceedings of the Royal Society A*, **386**, 263–275.

[1111] Sardella A., De Nuntiis P. and Bonazza A. (2018) Efficiency evaluation of treatments against rising damp by scale models and test *in situ. Journal of Cultural Heritage*, **31**, S30–S37.

[1112] Sass O. and Viles H. A. (2006) How wet are these walls? Testing a novel technique for measuring moisture in ruined walls. *Journal of Cultural Heritage*, **7**, 257–263.

[1113] Sass O. and Viles H. A. (2010) Wetting and drying of masonry walls: 2D-Resistivity monitoring of driving rain experiments on historic stonework in Oxford, UK. *Journal of Applied Geophysics*, **70**, 72–83.

[1114] Sass O. and Viles H. A. (2010) Two-dimensional resistivity surveys of the moisture content of historic limestone walls in Oxford, UK: Implications for understanding catastrophic stone deterioration. In B. J. Smith, M. Gomez-Heras, H. A. Viles and J. Cassar (eds), *Limestone in the built environment: present-day challenges for the preservation of the past*, Geological Society, London, Special Publications, **331**, 237–249.

[1115] Sato M., Panaghi K., Takada N. and Takeda M. (2019) Effect of bedding planes on the permeability and diffusivity anisotropies of Berea sandstone. *Transport in Porous Media*, **127**, 587–603.

[1116] Sattler H. (1997) The importance of porosity for the properties of hardened gypsum plaster products. *ZKG International*, **50**, 54–62.

[1117] Savage B. M. and Janssen D. J. (1997) Soil physics principles validated for use in predicting unsaturated moisture movement in Portland cement concrete. *ACI Materials Journal*, **94**, 63–70.

[1118] Šavija B., Luković, M. and Schlangen E. (2017) Influence of cracking on moisture uptake in strain-hardening cementitious composites. *Journal of Nanomechanics and Micromechanics*, **7**, 04016010.

[1119] Schaffer R. J. (1932) *The weathering of natural building stones*, HMSO, London.

[1120] Scheffler G. A. and Plagge R. (2010) A whole range hygric material model: Modelling liquid and vapour transport properties in porous media. *International Journal of Heat and Mass Transfer*, **53**, 286–296.

[1121] Scheidegger A. E. (1974) *The physics of flow through porous media*, 3rd edn, University of Toronto Press, Toronto, Canada.

[1122] Scherer G. W. (1989) Measurement of permeability I. Theory. *Journal of Non-Crystalline Solids*, **113**, 107–118.

[1123] Scherer G. W. (1990) Theory of drying. *Journal of the American Ceramic Society*, **73**, 3–14.

[1124] Scherer G. W. (1992) Bending of gel beams: Method for characterizing elastic properties and permeability. *Journal of Non-Crystalline Solids*, **142**, 18–35.

[1125] Scherer G. W. (1999) Crystallization in pores. *Cement and Concrete Research*, **29**, 1347–1358.

[1126] Scherer G. W. (2000) Thermal expansion kinetics: Method to measure permeability of cementitious materials: I, Theory. *Journal of the American Ceramic Society*, **83**, 2753–2761.

[1127] Scherer G. W. (2000) Measuring permeability of rigid materials by a beam-bending method: I, Theory. *Journal of the American Ceramic Society*, **83**, 2231–2239.

[1128] Scherer G. W. (2004) Thermal expansion kinetics – Method to measure permeability of cementitious materials: III, Effect of viscoelasticity. *Journal of the American Ceramic Society*, **87**, 1509–1516.

[1129] Scherer G. W. (2004) Measuring permeability of rigid materials by a beam-bending method: IV, Transversely isotropic plate. *Journal of the American Ceramic Society*, **87**, 1517–1524.

[1130] Scherer G. W. (2004) Characterization of saturated porous bodies. *Materials and Structures*, **37**, 21–30.

[1131] Scherer G. W. (2006) Dynamic pressurization method for measuring permeability and modulus. I. Theory. *Materials and Structures*, **39**, 1041–1057.

[1132] Scherer G. W. (2008) Poromechanics analysis of a flow-through permeameter with entrapped air. *Cement and Concrete Research*, 38, 368–378.

[1133] Scherer G. W., Flatt R. and Wheeler G. (2001) Materials science research for the conservation of sculpture and monuments. *Materials Research Society Bulletin*, 26, 44–50.

[1134] Scherer G. W., Hdach H. and Phalippou J. (1991) Thermal expansion of gels: A novel method for measuring permeability. *Journal of Non-Crystalline Solids*, 130, 157–170, 194, 326.

[1135] Scherer G. W. and Jimenez Gonzalez I. Characterization of swelling in clay-bearing stone. In A. V. Turkington (ed.), *Stone decay in the architectural environment*, Geological Society of America Special Paper, 390, 51–61.

[1136] Scherer G. W., Valenza II J. J. and Simmons G. (2007) New methods to measure liquid permeability in porous materials. *Cement and Concrete Research*, 37, 386–397.

[1137] Schirmer R. (1938) Die Diffusionzahl von Wasserdampf-Luft-Gemischen und die Verdampfungsgeschwindigkeit. *Zeitschrift des VDI, Beiheft Verfahrenstechnik*, 6, 170–177.

[1138] Schöffski K. and Strohm D. (2000) Karl Fischer moisture determination. In *Encyclopedia of analytical chemistry*, Wiley, Chichester, Chichester, UK, pp 13483–13495.

[1139] Schurecht H. G. (2003) Heavy clay products. In E. W. Washburn (ed.), *International critical tables of numerical data, physics, chemistry and technology, 1926–1930*, 1st electronic edn, Knovel, vol 2, New York, NY, pp 64–66.

[1140] Schurecht H. G. (1928) Methods of testing crazing of glazes caused by increases in size of ceramic bodies. *Journal of the American Ceramic Society*, 11, 271–277.

[1141] Schwartz L. M. and Kimminau S. (1987) Analysis of electrical conduction in the grain consolidation model. *Geophysics*, 52, 1402–1411.

[1142] Scrivener K. L., Crumbie A. K. and Laugesen P. (2004) The interfacial transition zone (ITZ) between cement paste and aggregate in concrete. *Interface Science*, 12, 411–421.

[1143] Sears V. F. (1992) Neutron scattering length and cross section. *Neutron News*, 3, 29–37.

[1144] Seeger A., Brickmann J. and Luft G. (2009) Penetration of organic liquids into dry portland cement mortar under ambient and high pressure. *Chemical Engineering and Technology*, 32, 891–902.

[1145] Selih J. and Bremner T. W. (1996) Drying of saturated lightweight concrete: an experimental investigation. *Materials and Structures*, 29, 401–405.

[1146] Selih J., Sousa A. C. M. and Bremner T. W. (1996) Moisture transport in initially fully saturated concrete during drying. *Transport in Porous Media*, 24, 81–106.

[1147] Senin S. F. and Hamid R. (2016) Ground penetrating radar wave attenuation models for estimation of moisture and chloride content in concrete slab. *Construction and Building Materials*, 106, 659–669.

[1148] Setzer M. J. and Auberg R. (eds) (1997). *Frost resistance of concrete: Proceedings of the international RILEM workshop on resistance of concrete to freezing and thawing with and without de-icing salts*, Spon, London.

[1149] Sghaier N and Prat M. (2009) Effect of efflorescence on drying kinetics of porous media. *Transport in Porous Media*, 80, 441–454.

[1150] Sharpe R. W. (1980) Injection systems for chemical damp proofing. *Building and Environment*, 15, 101–108.

[1151] Sherwood J. D. and Meeten G. H. (1997) The filtration properties of compressible mud filtercakes. *Journal of Petroleum Science and Engineering*, 18, 73–81.

[1152] Shikhmurzaev Y. D. and Sprittles J. E. (2012) Wetting front dynamics in an isotropic porous medium. *Journal of Fluid Mechanics*, 694, 399–407.

[1153] Shikhmurzaev Y. D. and Sprittles J. E. (2012) Anomalous dynamics of capillary rise in porous media. *Physical Review E*, 86, 016306.

[1154] Shokri N., Lehmann P. and Or D. (2010) Liquid-phase continuity and solute concentration dynamics during evaporation from porous media: Pore-scale processes near vaporization surface. *Physical Review E*, 81, 046308.

[1155] Shokri N., Lehmann P. and Or D. (2010) Evaporation from layered porous media. *Journal of Geophysical Research*, 115, B06204.

[1156] Shokri N. and Or D. (2011) What determines drying rates at the onset of diffusion controlled stage-2 evaporation from porous media? *Water Resources Research*, 47, W09513.

[1157] Shokri N., Lehmann P., Vontobel P. and Or D. (2008) Drying front and water content dynamics during evaporation from sand delineated by neutron radiography. *Water Resources Research*, 44, W06418.

[1158] Shoval S., Beck P., Kirsh Y., Levy D., Gaft M. and Yadin E. (1991) Rehydroxylation of clay minerals and hydration in ancient pottery from the 'Land of Geshur'. *Journal of Thermal Analysis*, 37, 1579–1592.

[1159] Siebold A., Walliser A., Nardin M., Oppliger M. and Schultz J. (1997) Capillary rise for thermodynamic characterization of solid particle surface. *Journal of Colloid and Interface Science*, 186, 60–70.

[1160] Siegesmund S. and Dürrast H. (2011) Physical and mechanical properties of rocks. In S. Siegesmund and R. Snethlage (eds) *Stone in Architecture*, Springer, Berlin, Germany.

[1161] Siegesmund S., Grimm W.-D., Dürrast H. and Ruedrich J. (2010) Limestones in Germany used as building stones. In B. J. Smith, M. Gomez-Heras, H. A. Viles and J. Cassar (eds), *Limestone in the built environment: present-day challenges for the preservation of the past*, Geological Society, London, Special Publications, 331, 37–59.

[1162] Šimůnek J., van Genuchten M. T. and Šejna M. (2016) Recent developments and applications of the HYDRUS computer software packages. *Vadose Zone Journal*, 15, 25pp.

[1163] Šimůnek J., Šejna M. and van Genuchten M. Th. (1996) *Hydrus2D: Simulating water flow and solute transport in two-dimensional variably saturated media*, International Ground Water Modeling Center, Golden, CO.

[1164] Šimůnek J., Šejna M. and van Genuchten M. Th. *The Hydrus2D software package for simulating the two-dimensional movement of water, heat and multiple solutes in variably saturated media*, Version 2.0, US Salinity Laboratory, Agricultural Research Service, US Department of Agriculture, Riverside, CA.

[1165] Skelland A. H. P. (1985) *Diffusional mass transfer*, 2nd edn, Krieger, Malabar, FL.

[1166] Skibsted J., Hall C. and Jakobsen H. J. (2002) Nuclear magnetic resonance spectroscopy and magnetic resonance imaging of cements and cement-based materials. In J. Bensted and P. Barnes (eds), *Structure and performance of cements*, 2nd edn, Taylor and Francis, London, pp 457–476.

[1167] Skinner L. M. and Sambles J. R. (1972) The Kelvin equation – a review. *Aerosol Science*, 3, 199–210.

[1168] Slyh J. A. (1984) Twenty-year moisture expansion on quarry tile. *American Ceramic Society Bulletin*, 63, 1495–1497.

[1169] Smettem K. R. J., Ross P. J., Haverkamp R. and Parlange J.-Y. (1995) Three-dimensional analysis of infiltration from the disk infiltrometer. 3. Parameter estimation using a double-disk tension infiltrometer. *Water Resources Research*, 31, 2491–2495.

[1170] Smiles D. E. (1970) A theory of constant pressure filtration. *Chemical Engineering Science*, 25, 985–996.

[1171] Smiles D. E. (1974) Aspects of self-weight filtration in consolidating slurries. *Soil Science*, 117, 288–294.

[1172] Smiles D. E. (1978) Constant rate filtration of bentonite. *Chemical Engineering Science*, 33, 1355–1361.

[1173] Smiles D. E. (1998) Water flow in filter paper and capillary suction time. *Chemical Engineering Science*, 53, 2211–2218.

[1174] Smiles D.E. (2000) Hydrology of swelling soils: a review. *Australian Journal of Soil Science*, 38, 501–521.

[1175] Smiles D. E and Kirby J. M. (1987) Aspects of one-dimensional filtration. *Separation Science and Technology*, 22, 1405–1423.

[1176] Smiles D. E. and Kirby J. M. (1994) Dewatering of sodium bentonite using a dry plaster-of-paris mould. *Chemical Engineering Science*, 49, 3711–3717.

[1177] Smiles D. E., Raats P. C. and Knight J. H. (1982) Constant pressure filtration: the effect of a filter membrane. *Chemical Engineering Science*, 37, 707–714.

[1178] Smith B. J., McCabe S., McAllister D., Adamson C., Viles H. A. and Curran J. M. (2011) A commentary on climate change, stone decay dynamics and the 'greening' of natural stone buildings: New perspectives on 'deep wetting'. *Environmental Earth Sciences*, 63, 1691–1700.

[1179] Smith K. A. and Mullins C. E. (1991) *Soil analysis: Physical methods*, Dekker, New York.

[1180] Smith R. E. (1990) Analysis of infiltration through a two-layer soil profile. *Soil Science Society of America Journal*, 54, 1219–1227.

[1181] Smith R. G. (1973) Moisture expansion of structural ceramics: Long term unrestrained expansion of test bricks. *Transactions and Journal of the British Ceramic Society*, 72, 1–5.

[1182] Smith R. G. (1993) Moisture expansion of structural ceramics. V: 28 Years of expansion. *British Ceramic Transactions*, 92, 233–238.

[1183] Smyl D. J. (2018) Relating unsaturated electrical and hydraulic conductivity of cement-based materials. *Australian Journal of Civil Engineering*, 16, 129–142.

[1184] Snyder K., Natesaiyer K. and Hover K. (2001) The stereological and statistical properties of entrained air voids: A mathematical basis for air void system characterization. In S. Mindess and J. Skalny (eds), *Materials science of concrete VI*, American Ceramic Society, Westerville, OH, pp 129–214.

[1185] Somorjai G. A. (1970) Surface chemistry. University of California, Berkeley, Lawrence Radiation Laboratory Preprint UCRL-20382.

[1186] Song C., Wang P. and Makse H. A. (2008) A phase diagram for jammed matter. *Nature*, 453, 629–632.

[1187] Song K. M., Mitchell J., Jaffel H. and Gladden L. F. (2011) Magnetic resonance imaging studies of spontaneous capillary water imbibition in aerated gypsum. *Journal of Physics D: Applied Physics*, **44**, 115403.

[1188] Sosoro M. (1994) *Modell zur Vorhersage des Eindringsverhaltnis von organischen Flüssigkeiten in Beton*, PhD thesis, Stuttgart.

[1189] Sosoro M. (1995) *Modell zur Vorhersage des Eindringsverhaltens von organischen Flüssigkeiten in Beton*. Deutscher Ausschuss für Stahlbeton, Heft 446, Berlin.

[1190] Sosoro M. (1998) Transport of organic fluids through concrete. *Materials and Structures*, **31**, 162–169.

[1191] Sosoro M., Hoff W. D. and Wilson M. A. (1997) Testing methods. In H.-W. Reinhardt (ed.) *Penetration and permeability of concrete: barriers to organic and contaminating liquids*, RILEM Report no. 16, Spon, London, pp 187–212.

[1192] Sposito G. (1986) The 'physics' of soil water physics. *Water Resources Research*, **22**, 83S–88S. [Reprinted with corrections in E. R. Landa and S. Ince (eds) (1987) *History of geophysics*, vol. 3, American Geophysical Union, Washington, DC, pp 93–98.]

[1193] Sposito G. (1990) Lie group invariance of the Richards equation. In J. H. Cushman (ed.), *Dynamics of fluids in hierarchical porous media*, Academic Press, London, pp 327–347.

[1194] Sposito G. and Jury W. A. (1990) Miller similitude and generalized scaling analysis. In D. Hillel and D. E. Elrick (eds), *Scaling in soil physics: Principles and applications*, Soil Science Society of America, Special Publication, **25**, Madison, WI, pp 13–22.

[1195] Stauffer D. and Aharony A. (1992) *Introduction to percolation theory*, 2nd edn, Taylor and Francis, London.

[1196] Stevenson P. (2010) Inter-bubble gas diffusion in liquid foam. *Current Opinion in Colloid and Interface Science*, **15**, 374–381.

[1197] Stokes R. H. and Mills R. (1965) *Viscosity of electrolytes and related properties*, Pergamon, Oxford.

[1198] Strange J. H., Rahman M. and Smith E. G. (1993) Characterization of porous solids by NMR. *Physical Review Letters*, **71**, 3589–3591.

[1199] Strange J. H. and Webber J. B. (1997) Multidimensional resolved pore size distributions. *Applied Magnetic Resonance*, **12**, 231–245.

[1200] Strange J. H., Webber J. B. and Schmidt S. D. (1996) Pore size distribution mapping. *Magnetic Resonance Imaging*, **14**, 803–805.

[1201] Struble L. and Sun G. K. (1995) Viscosity of portland-cement paste as a function of concentration. *Advanced Cement-Based Materials*, **2**, 62–69.

[1202] Stück H., Koch R. and Siegesmund S. (2013) Petrographical and petrophysical properties of sandstones: Statistical analysis as an approach to predict material behaviour and construction suitability. *Environmental Earth Sciences*, **69**, 1299–1332.

[1203] Stück H., Plagge R. and Siegesmund S. (2013) Numerical modeling of moisture transport in sandstone: The influence of pore space, fabric and clay content. *Environmental Earth Sciences*, **69**, 1161–1187.

[1204] Stück H. L., Platz T., Müller A. and Siegesmund S. (2018) Natural stones of the Saale–Unstrut Region (Germany): Petrography and weathering phenomena. *Environmental Earth Sciences*, **77**, 300.

[1205] Stück H., Siegesmund S. and Rüdrich J. (2011) Weathering behaviour and construction suitability of dimension stones from the Drei Gleichen area (Thuringia, Germany). *Environmental Earth Sciences*, 63, 1763–1786.

[1206] Stull R. T. and Johnson P. V. (1940) Some properties of the pore system in bricks and their relation to frost action. *United States Bureau of Standards Journal of Research*, 25, 711–730.

[1207] Suleiman A. A. and Hoogenboom G. (2009) A comparison of ASCE and FAO-56 reference evapotranspiration for a 15-min time step in humid climate conditions. *Journal of Hydrology*, 375, 326–333.

[1208] Suman R. and Ruth D. (1993) Formation factor and tortuosity of homogeneous porous media. *Transport in Porous Media*, 12, 185–206.

[1209] Sumanasooriya M. S., Bentz D. P. and Neithalath N. (2010) Planar image-based reconstruction of pervious concrete pore structure and permeability prediction. *ACI Materials Journal*, 107, 413–421.

[1210] Sun Z. and Scherer G. W. (2010) Pore size and shape in mortar by thermoporometry. *Cement and Concrete Research*, 40, 740–751.

[1211] Susha Lekshmi S. U., Singh D. N. and Baghini M. S. (2014) A critical review of soil moisture measurement. *Measurement*, 54, 92–105.

[1212] Suzuki T. and Ishida M. (1995) Neural network techniques applied to predict flammability limits of organic compounds. *Fire and Materials*, 19, 178–189.

[1213] Swartzendruber D. (1962) Modification of Darcy's law for the flow of water in soils. *Soil Science*, 93, 22–29.

[1214] Swartzendruber D. (1969) The flow of water in unsaturated soils. In R. J. M de Weist (ed.), *Flow through porous media*, Academic Press, New York, pp 215–292.

[1215] Tamari S. (2004) Optimum design of the constant-volume gas pycnometer for determining the volume of solid párticles. *Measurement Science and Technology*, 15, 549-558.

[1216] Tanaka M., Girard G., Davis R., Peuto A. and Bignell N. (2001) Recommended table for the density of water between 0 °C and 40 °C based on recent experimental reports. *Metrologia*, 38, 301–309.

[1217] Tang M. J., Shiraiwa M., Pöschl U., Cox R. A. and Kalberer M. (2015) Compilation and evaluation of gas phase diffusion coefficients of reactive trace gases in the atmosphere: Volume 2. Diffusivities of organic compounds, pressure-normalised mean free paths, and average Knudsen numbers for gas uptake calculations. *Atmospheric Chemistry and Physics*, 15, 5585–5598.

[1218] Tarara J. M. and Ham J. M. (1997) Measuring soil water content in the laboratory and field with dual-probe heat-capacity sensors. *Agronomy Journal*, 89, 535–542.

[1219] Taylor S. C. (1998) *A study of liquid transport properties of cement-based materials*, PhD thesis, UMIST, Manchester.

[1220] Taylor S. C., Hall C., Hoff W. D. and Wilson M. A. (2000) Partial wetting in capillary liquid absorption by limestones. *Journal of Colloid and Interface Science*, 224, 351–357.

[1221] Taylor S. C., Hoff W. D., Wilson M. A. and Green K. M. (1999) Anomalous water transport properties of Portland and blended cement-based materials. *Journal of Materials Science Letters*, 18, 1925–1928.

[1222] Tazky L. and Sedlakova A. (2016) Modeling of the airflow in the small-scale model of ventilated air channel. In M. Al Ali and P. Platko (eds), *Advances* and trends in engineering sciences and technologies II: proceedings of the 2nd international conference, Tatranské Matliare, Slovak Republic, CRC Press, pp 279–284.

[1223] Thiery J., Rodts S., Weitz D. A. and Coussot P. (2017) Drying regimes in homogeneous porous media from macro- to nanoscale. *Physical Review Fluids*, **2**, 074201.

[1224] Thomas H. R. and King S. D. (1991) Coupled temperature/capillary potential variations in unsaturated soil. *Journal of Engineering Mechanics*, **117**, 2475–2491.

[1225] Thomas J. J., Jennings H. M. and Allen A. J. (1999) The surface area of hardened cement paste as measured by various methods. *Concrete Science and Engineering*, **1**, 45–64.

[1226] Thomas J. J., Allen A. J. and Jennings H. M. (2008) Structural changes to the calcium-silicate-hydrate gel phase of hydrated cement with age, drying and resaturation. *Journal of the American Ceramic Society*, **91**, 3362–3369.

[1227] Thommes M., Kaneko K., Neimark A. V., Olivier J. P., Rodriguez-Reinoso F., Rouquerol J. and Sing K. S. (2015) Physisorption of gases, with special reference to the evaluation of surface area and pore size distribution (IUPAC Technical Report). *Pure and Applied Chemistry*, **87**, 1051–1069.

[1228] Thompson A. H. (1991) Fractals in rock physics. *Annual Reviews of Earth and Planetary Science*, **19**, 237–262.

[1229] Thoreau H. D. (1854) *Walden; or, life in the woods*, Ticknor and Fields, Boston.

[1230] Tibbetts C. M., Tao C., Paris J. M. and Ferraro C. C. (2020) Mercury intrusion porosimetry parameters for use in concrete penetrability qualification using the Katz-Thompson relationship. *Construction and Building Materials*, **263**, 119834.

[1231] Tijskens A., Roels S. and Janssen H. (2019) Neural networks for metamodelling the hygrothermal behaviour of building components. *Building and Environment*, **162**, 106282.

[1232] Tikhomolova K. P. (2000) *Electro-osmosis*, Ellis Horwood, Chichester.

[1233] Timmermann E. O. (1989) A BET-like three sorption stage isotherm. *Journal of the Chemical Society Faraday Transactions I*, **85**, 1631–1645.

[1234] Timmermann E. O. (2003) Multilayer sorption parameters: BET or GAB values? *Colloids and Surfaces A: Physicochemical and Engineering Aspects*, **220**, 235–260.

[1235] Tite M. S. and Maniatis Y. (1975) Examination of ancient pottery using the scanning electron microscope. *Nature*, **257**, 122–123.

[1236] Tite M. S. and Maniatis Y. (1975) Scanning electron microscopy of fired calcareous clays. *Transactions and Journal of the British Ceramic Society*, **74**, 19–22.

[1237] Torquato S. (2001) *Random heterogeneous materials: Microstructure and macroscopic properties*, Interdisciplinary Applied Mathematics **16**, Springer, New York.

[1238] Torquato S., Truskett T. M. and Debenedetti P. G. (2000) Is random close packing of spheres well defined? *Physical Review Letters*, **84**, 2064–2067.

[1239] Torquato S. and Stillinger F. H. (2010) Jammed hard-particle packings: From Kepler to Bernal and beyond. *Reviews of Modern Physics*, **82**, 2633–2672.

[1240] Torrent R. J. (1992) A two-chamber vacuum cell for measuring the coefficient of permeability to air of the concrete cover on site. *Materials and Structures*, 25, 358–365.

[1241] Torres M. I. M. and de Freitas V. P. (2007) Treatment of rising damp in historical buildings: Wall base ventilation. *Building and Environment*, 42, 424–435.

[1242] Torres M. I. M. and de Freitas V. P. (2010) The influence of the thickness of the walls and their properties on the treatment of rising damp in historic buildings. *Construction and Building Materials*, 24, 1331–1339.

[1243] Touma J. and Vauclin M. (1986) Experimental and numerical analysis of two-phase infiltration in a partially saturated soil. *Transport in Porous Media*, 1, 27–55.

[1244] Tracz T. (2016) Open porosity of cement pastes and their gas permeability. *Bulletin of the Polish Academy of Sciences: Technical Sciences*, 64, 775–783.

[1245] Traoré K., Gridi-Bennadji F. and Blanchart P. (2006) Significance of kinetic theories on the recrystallization of kaolinite. *Thermochimica Acta* 451 99–104.

[1246] Trefethen L. (1980) Numerical computation of the Schwarz-Christoffel transformation. *SIAM Journal of Statistics and Computation*, 1, 82–102.

[1247] Trimmer D. A. (1981) Design criteria for laboratory measurements of low permeability rocks. *Geophysical Research Letters*, 8, 973–975.

[1248] Trimmer D. (1982) Laboratory measurements of ultralow permeability of geologic materials. *Review of Scientific Instruments*, 53, 1246–1254.

[1249] Tuller M., Or D. and Dudley L. M. (1999) Adsorption and capillary condensation in porous media: Liquid retention and interfacial configurations in angular pores. *Water Resources Research*, 35, 1949–1964.

[1250] Tuller M., Or D. and Hillel D. (2004) Retention of water in soil and the soil water characteristic curve. In D. Hillel (ed.), *Encyclopedia of soils in the environment*, 4, pp 278–289.

[1251] Tumidajski P. J. and Lin B. (1998) On the validity of the Katz-Thompson equation for permeabilities in concrete. *Cement and Concrete Research*, 28, 643–647.

[1252] Tuominen E. and Vinha J. (2019) Calculation method to determine capillary properties of building materials with automatic free water intake test. 4th Central European Symposium on Building Physics (CESBP 2019). *MATEC Web of Conferences*, 282, 02037.

[1253] Turner N. C. and Parlange J.-Y. (1974) Lateral movement at the periphery of a one-dimensional flow of water. *Soil Science*, 118, 70–77.

[1254] Underwood E. E. (1970) *Quantitative stereology*, Addison-Wesley, Reading, MA.

[1255] Valdeon M., Esbert R. M. and Grossi C. M. (1993) Hydric properties of some Spanish building stones: A petrophysical interpretation. In P. B. Vandiver, J. R. Druzik, G. S. Wheeler and I. C. Freestone (eds), *Materials issues in art and archaeology*, MRS Proceedings vol 267, Materials Research Society, pp 911–916.

[1256] Valenza J. and Scherer G. W. (2004) Measuring permeability of rigid materials by a beam-bending method: V, Isotropic rectangular plates of cement paste. *Journal of the American Ceramic Society*, 87, 1927–1931.

[1257] van Brakel J. (1980) Mass transfer in convective drying. *Advances in Drying*, 1, 217–267.

[1258] Vandersteen K., Carmeliet J. and Feyen J. (2003) A network modeling approach to derive unsaturated hydraulic properties of a rough-walled fracture. *Transport in Porous Media*, 50, 197–221.

[1259] van Duynhoven J., Voda A., Witek M. and van As H. (2010) Time-domain NMR applied to food products. *Annual Reports on NMR Spectroscopy*, 69, 145–197.

[1260] Van Engeland C., Haut B., Spreutels L. and Sobac B. (2020) Evaporation versus imbibition in a porous medium. *Journal of Colloid and Interface Science*, 576, 280–290.

[1261] van Genuchten M. Th. (1980) A closed-form equation for predicting the hydraulic conductivity of unsaturated soils. *Soil Science Society of America Journal*, 44, 892–898.

[1262] van Genuchten M. Th., Leij F. J. and Yates S. R. (1991) *The RETC code for quantifying the hydraulic functions of unsaturated soils*, U S Salinity Laboratory, U S Department of Agriculture, Report EPA/600/2–91/065, Riverside CA.

[1263] van Genuchten M. Th. and Nielsen D. R. (1985) On describing and predicting the hydraulic properties of unsaturated soils. *Annales Geophysicae*, 3, 615–628.

[1264] van Hees R. P. and Nijland T. G. (2009) Assessment of the state of conservation of a Middle Neolithic flint mine in Maastricht limestone. *Heron*, 54, 227–250.

[1265] Vanorio T. and Mavko G. (2011) Laboratory measurements of the acoustic and transport properties of carbonate rocks and their link with the amount of microcrystalline matrix. *Geophysics* 76, E105–E115.

[1266] Vanpachtenbeke M., Langmans J., Van den Bulcke J., Van Acker J. and Roels S. (2020) Modelling moisture conditions behind brick veneer cladding: Verification of common approaches by field measurements. *Journal of Building Physics*, 44, 95–120.

[1267] Vázquez P., Alonso F. J., Carrizo L., Molina E., Cultrone G., Blanco M. and Zamora I. (2013) Evaluation of the petrophysical properties of sedimentary building stones in order to establish quality criteria. *Construction and Building Materials*, 41, 868–878.

[1268] Vega-Garcia P., Schwerd R., Scherer C., Schwitalla C. and Helmreich B. (2020) Development of a model for stormwater runoff prediction on vertical test panels coated with plaster and mortar. *Water*, 12, 2593.

[1269] Vejmelková E., Pavlíková M., Jerman M. and Černý R. (2009) Free water intake as means of material characterization. *Journal of Building Physics*, 33, 29–44.

[1270] Vichit-Vadakan W. and Scherer G. W. (2000) Measuring permeability of rigid materials by a beam-bending method: II, Porous glass. *Journal of the American Ceramic Society*, 83, 2240–2245.

[1271] Vichit-Vadakan W. and Scherer G. W. (2002) Measuring permeability of rigid materials by a beam-bending method: III, Cement paste. *Journal of the American Ceramic Society*, 85, 1537–1544.

[1272] Vichit-Vadakan W. and Scherer G. W. (2003) Measuring permeability and stress relaxation of young cement paste by beam bending. *Cement and Concrete Research*, 33, 1925–1932.

[1273] Villain G., Baroghel Bouny V., Kounkou C. and Hua C. (2001) Mesure de la perméabilité aux gaz en fonction du taux de saturation des bétons. *Revue Française de Génie Civil*, 5, 251-268.

[1274] Villmann B., Slowik V., Wittmann F. H., Vontobel P. and Hovind J. (2014) Time-dependent moisture distribution in drying cement mortars – results of neutron radiography and inverse analysis of drying tests. *Restoration of Buildings and Monuments*, 20, 49–62.

[1275] Vogel T., Dusek J., Dohnal M. and Snehota M. (2020) Moisture regime of historical sandstone masonry – A numerical study. *Journal of Cultural Heritage*, 42, 99–107.

[1276] Vogel T., Huang K., Zhang R. and van Genuchten M. Th. (1996) *The HYDRUS code for simulating one-dimensional water flow, solute transport, and heat movement in variably-saturated media: version 5.0*, U S Salinity Laboratory, U S Department of Agriculture, Riverside, CA, Report no. 140.

[1277] Vos B. H. (1965) *Determination of water content, water distribution and heat resistance of walls I*, Report SBR II:4, Institute TNO for Building Materials and Building Structures, Delft.

[1278] Vos B. H. (1967) *Moisture transport during drying of building materials: fundamental laws*, IBBC-TNO Report B II-19.

[1279] Vos B. H. (1967) Causes of moisture in building structures. *Colloquy on moisture in old buildings*, October, ICOMOS, Rome.

[1280] Vos B. H. (1967) *Condensation in structures*, Report BI-67-33, Institute TNO for Building Materials and Structures, Delft.

[1281] Vos B. H. (1975) Water absorption and drying of materials. In R. Rossi-Manaresi (ed.), *The conservation of stone*, vol. 1, Centro Conservazione Sculture all'Aperto, Bologna, Italy.

[1282] Vos B. H. (1978) Hydric methods for the determination of behaviour of stones. In *Proceedings of the UNESCO-RILEM international symposium on deterioration and protection of stone monuments*, Paris, CEBTB Paris, 1978, pp 1–10.

[1283] Vos B. H. *Suction of groundwater*, Institute TNO for Building Materials and Structure, Delft, undated.

[1284] Vos B. H. and Cruys G. W. (1967) *Measuring methods for evaluation of the liquid diffusivity coefficient*, IBBC-TNO Report BI-67-28, Delft.

[1285] Vos B. H. and van Minnen J. (1966) *Moisture transport in porous materials*, Report SBR II: 11, IBBC-TNO, Delft.

[1286] Vos B. H. and Tammes E. (1968) *Flow of water in the liquid phase*, Institute TNO for Building Materials and Building Structures, Report BI-68-38, Delft.

[1287] Vos B. H. and Tammes E. (1969) *Moisture and moisture transfer in porous materials*, Institute TNO for Building Materials and Structures, Report BI-69-96, Delft.

[1288] Vuorinen J. (1985) Applications of diffusion theory to permeability tests on concrete. Part I: Depth of water penetration into concrete and coefficient of permeability. *Magazine of Concrete Research*, 37, 145–152.

[1289] Wade J. B., Martin G. P. and Long D. F. (2015) An assessment of powder pycnometry as a means of determining granule porosity. *Pharmaceutical Development and Technology*, 20, 257–265.

[1290] Wagner W. and Pruss A. (2002) The IAPWS formulation 1995 for the thermodynamic properties of ordinary water substance for general and scientific use. *Journal of Physical and Chemical Reference Data*, 31, 387–535.

[1291] Wagner W., Saul A. and Pruss A. (1994) International equations for the pressure along the melting and along the sublimation curve of ordinary water substance. *Journal of Physical and Chemical Reference Data*, 23, 515–525.

[1292] Wang Y., Jin M. and Deng Z. (2018) Alternative model for predicting soil hydraulic conductivity over the complete moisture range. *Water Resources Research*, **54**, 6860–6876.

[1293] Wang Q. G., Ahmet K. and Yue Y. (2005) Research in moisture transport through one and two-layered porous composites. *International Journal of Automation and Computing*, **2**, 93–100.

[1294] Wang Y., Grove S. M. and Anderson M. G. (2008) A physical-chemical model for the static water retention characteristic of unsaturated porous media. *Advances in Water Resources*, **31**, 701–713.

[1295] Washburn E. W. (1921) The dynamics of capillary flow. *Physical Review*, **17**, 273–283.

[1296] Washburn E. W. (1921) Porosity: I. Purpose of the investigation. II. Porosity and the mechanism of absorption. *Journal of the American Ceramic Society*, **4**, 916–922.

[1297] Washburn E. W. (1921) Note on a method of determining the distribution of pore sizes in a porous material. *Proceedings of the National Academy of Sciences of the United States of America*, **7**, 115–116.

[1298] Washburn E. W. and Bunting E. N. (1922) Porosity: V. Recommended procedures for determining porosity by methods of absorption. *Journal of the American Ceramic Society*, **5**, 48–56.

[1299] Washburn E. W. and Bunting E. N. (1922) Porosity: VI. The determination of the porosity by the method of gas expansion. *Journal of the American Ceramic Society*, **5**, 112–129.

[1300] Washburn E. W. and Footitt F. F. (1921) Porosity: III. Water as an absorption liquid. *Journal of the American Ceramic Society*, **4**, 527–537.

[1301] Watkins C. M. and Butterworth B. (1933–34) The absorption of water by clay building bricks and some related properties. *Transactions of the Ceramic Society*, **33**, 444–478.

[1302] Watson A. (1964) Laboratory tests and the durability of bricks. VI The mechanism of frost action on bricks. *Transactions of the British Ceramic Society*, **63**, 665–680.

[1303] Webb P. A. and Orr C. (1997) *Analytical methods in fine particle technology*, Micromeritics Instrument Corporation, Norcross, GA.

[1304] Wei Z., Falzone G., Wang B., Thiele A., Puerta-Falla G., Pilon L., Neithalath N. and Sant G. (2017) The durability of cementitious composites containing microencapsulated phase change materials. *Cement and Concrete Composites*, **81**, 66–76.

[1305] Weaire D. and Hutzler S. (1999) *The physics of foams*, Clarendon Press, Oxford.

[1306] Wheater H. S., Isham V. S., Cox D. R., Chandler R. E., Kakou A., Northrop P. J., Oh L., Onof C. and Rodriguez-Iturbe I. (2000) Spatial-temporal rainfall fields: modelling and statistical aspects. *Hydrology and Earth Systems Sciences*, **4**, 581–601.

[1307] Whitaker S. (1998) Coupled transport in multiphase systems: a theory of drying. *Advances in Heat Transfer*, **31**, 1–104.

[1308] White E. L., Scheetz B. E., Roy D. M., Zimmerman K. G. and Grutzeck M. W. (1979) Permeability measurements on cementitious materials for nuclear waste isolation. In G. J. McCarthy (ed.), *Scientific basis for nuclear waste management*, Plenum Press, New York, **1**, 471–478.

[1309] Whiteley P., Russman H. D. and Bishop J. D. (1977) Porosity of building materials – a collection of published results. *Journal of Oil and Colour Chemists Association*, 60, 142–149.

[1310] Whittington H. W., McCarter (W.) J. and Forde M. C. (1981) The conduction of electricity through concrete. *Magazine of Concrete Research*, 33, 48–60.

[1311] Wieden P. (1965) *Das Entfeuchtung von Mauerwerk*, Ernst, Berlin, Germany.

[1312] Williams S. R. and Philipse A. P. (2003) Random packings of spheres and spherocylinders simulated by mechanical contraction. *Physical Review E*, 67, 051301.

[1313] Wilson M. A. (1992) *A study of water flow in porous construction materials*, PhD thesis, Manchester.

[1314] Wilson M. A. (2003) An analytical approach to water absorption based in situ test procedures for concrete. *Proceedings of the Institution of Mechanical Engineers, Part L, Journal of Materials: Design and Applications*, 217, 47–56.

[1315] Wilson M. A., Carter M. A., Hall C., Hoff W. D., Ince C., Savage S. D., McKay B. and Betts I. M. (2009) Dating fired-clay ceramics using long-term power law rehydroxylation kinetics. *Proceedings of the Royal Society A*, 465, 2407–2415.

[1316] Wilson M. A., Carter M. A. and Hoff W. D. (1999) British Standard and RILEM water absorption tests: a critical evaluation. *Materials and Structures*, 32, 571–578.

[1317] Wilson M. A. and Hall C. Unpublished results.

[1318] Wilson M. A. and Hoff W. D. (1994) Water movement in porous building materials – XII. Absorption from a drilled hole with a hemispherical end. *Building and Environment*, 29, 537–544.

[1319] Wilson M. A. and Hoff W. D. (1997) The absorption of water into a porous solid consisting of two dissimilar layers. *European Journal of Soil Science*, 48, 79–86.

[1320] Wilson M. A. and Hoff W. D. (1997) Discussion: Properties of concrete in the cover zone: developments in monitoring techniques by W. J. McCarter *et al.* *Magazine of Concrete Research*, 49, 149–152.

[1321] Wilson M. A. and Hoff W. D. (2001) Water absorption test methods for concrete: towards a unified approach. *Proceedings of the 11th annual BCA/Concrete Society communication conference*, pp 379–386.

[1322] Wilson M. A., Hoff W. D., Brown R. J. E. and Carter M. A. (2000) A falling head permeameter for the measurement of the hydraulic conductivty of granular solids. *Review of Scientific Instruments*, 71, 3942–3946.

[1323] Wilson M. A., Hoff W. D. and Hall C. (1991) Water movement in porous building materials – X. Absorption from a small cylindrical cavity. *Building and Environment*, 26, 143–152.

[1324] Wilson M. A., Hoff W. D. and Hall C. (1994) Water movement in porous building materials – XI. Capillary absorption from a hemispherical cavity. *Building and Environment*, 29, 99–104.

[1325] Wilson M. A., Hoff W. D. and Hall C. (1995) Water movement in porous building materials – XIII. Absorption into a two-layer composite. *Building and Environment*, 30, 209–219.

[1326] Wilson M. A., Hoff W. D. and Hall C. (1995) Water movement in porous building materials – XIV. Absorption into a two-layer composite ($S_A < S_B$). *Building and Environment*, 30, 221–227.

[1327] Wilson M. A., Hoff W. D., Hall C., McKay B. and Hiley A. (2003) Kinetics of moisture expansion in fired clay ceramics: a $(time)^{1/4}$ law. *Physical Review Letters*, **90**, 125503.

[1328] Wilson M. A., Taylor S. C. and Hoff W. D. (1998) The initial surface absorption test (ISAT): an analytical approach. *Magazine of Concrete Research*, **50**, 179–185.

[1329] Winslow D. N. (1984) Advances in experimental techniques for mercury intrusion porosimetry. *Surface and Colloid Science*, **13**, 259–282.

[1330] Wittmann F. H. (1995) Influence of drying induced damage on the hygral diffusion coefficient. In F. H. Wittmann (ed.), *Fracture mechanics of concrete structures (2nd international conference FRAMCOS-2)*, Zurich, Aedificatio, Freiburg, **2**, 1519–1528.

[1331] Wolter B. and Krus M. (2005) Moisture measuring with nuclear magnetic resonance (NMR). In K. Kupfer (ed.), *Electromagnetic aquametry*, Springer, Berlin, Germany, pp 491–515.

[1332] Wolter B., Netzelmann U., Dobmann G. and Bloem P. (1995) Investigation of moisture transport in concrete using a single-side nuclear magnetic resonance testing system. In G. Schickert and H. Wiggenhauser (eds), *Nondestructive testing in civil engineering*, British Institute of Nondestructive Testing; Bundesanstalt für Materialforschung und -prüfung -BAM-, Berlin; Deutsche Gesellschaft für Zerstörungsfreie Prüfung eV -DGZfP-, Berlin, Germany, **1**, pp 167–171.

[1333] Wong H. S., Zobel M., Buenfeld M. R. and Zimmerman R. W. (2009) Influence of the interfacial transition zone and microcracking on the diffusivity, permeability and sorptivity of cement-based materials after drying. *Magazine of Concrete Research*, **61**, 571–589.

[1334] Wong P.-Z., Koplik J. and Tomanic J. P. (1984) Conductivity and permeability of rocks. *Physical Review B*, **30**, 6606–6614.

[1335] World Health Organization. (2009) *WHO guidelines for indoor air quality: Dampness and mould*, WHO Regional Office for Europe, Copenhagen, Denmark.

[1336] Wormald R. and Britch A. L. (1969) Methods of measuring moisture content applicable to building materials. *Building Science*, **3**, 135–145.

[1337] Wu Y.-S., Preuss K. and Persoff P. (1998) Gas flow in porous media with Klinkenberg effects. *Transport in Porous Media*, **32**, 117–137.

[1338] Xi Y., Bažant Z. P. and Jennings H. M. (1994) Moisture diffusion in cementitious materials: adsorption isotherms. *Advanced Cement Based Materials*, **1**, 248–257.

[1339] Yamamuro J. A., Bopp P. A. and Lade P. V. (1996) One-dimensional compression of sands at high pressures. *Journal of Geotechnical Engineering*, **122**, 147–154.

[1340] Yang C., Chandler R. E., Isham V. S., Annoni C. and Wheater H. S. (2005) Simulation and downscaling models for potential evaporation. *Journal of Hydrology*, **302**, 239–254.

[1341] Yang K., Basheer, P. A. M., Magee B. and Bai Y. (2013) Investigation of moisture condition and Autoclam sensitivity on air permeability measurements for both normal concrete and high performance concrete. *Construction and Building Materials*, **48**, 306–314.

[1342] Yang K., Li M., Ling N. N., May E. F., Connolly P. R., Esteban L., Clennell M. B., Mahmoud M., El-Husseiny A., Adebayo A. R. and Elsayed M. M. (2019)

Quantitative tortuosity measurements of carbonate rocks using pulsed field gradient NMR. *Transport in Porous Media*, **130**, 847–865.

[1343] Yaws C. L. (2015) *The Yaws handbook of vapor pressure: Antoine coefficients*, 2nd edn, Gulf Professional, Amsterdam, The Netherlands.

[1344] Yaws C.L. and Lan L.X.D. (2009) Viscosity of liquid – Organic compounds. In C. L. Yaws (ed.), *Transport properties of chemicals and hydrocarbons*, William Andrew, Norwich, NY, Ch. 3, pp 101–193.

[1345] Yaws C. L. and Pike R.W. (2009) Density of liquid – Organic compounds. In C.L. Yaws (ed.), *Thermophysical properties of chemicals and hydrocarbons*, William Andrew, Norwich, NY, Ch. 3, pp 106–197.

[1346] Yaws C. L. and Richmond P. C. (2009) Surface tension – Organic compounds. In C.L. Yaws (ed.), *Thermophysical properties of chemicals and hydrocarbons*, William Andrew, Norwich, NY, Ch. 21, pp 686–781.

[1347] Ye Z., Tirovic M., Davies M., Baker P. H., Phillipson M., Galbraith G. H. and McLean R. C. (2007) The optimisation of a thermal dual probe instrument for the measurement of the moisture content of building envelopes. *Building Services Engineering Research and Technology*, **28**, 317–327.

[1348] Ye Z., Tirovic M., Davies M., Baker P. H., Phillipson M., Sanders C. H., Galbraith G. H. and McLean R. C. (2009) The testing of two methods for the moisture measurement of building fabrics via comparisons with data from an X-ray system. *Building and Environment*, **44**, 1409–1417.

[1349] Yoshimura Y., Mizuta M, Sunaga H., Otake Y., Kubo Y. and Hayashizaki N. (2019) Influence of ASR expansion on concrete deterioration observed with neutron imaging of water. In R. Caspeele, L. Taerwe and D. M. Frangopol (eds), *Life-cycle analysis and assessment in civil engineering*, Taylor & Francis, London.

[1350] Young D. (2008) *Salt attack and rising damp: A guide to salt damp in historic and older buildings*, Heritage Council of New South Wales, Adelaide.

[1351] Young J. E. and Brownell W. E. (1959) Moisture expansion of clay products. *Journal of the American Ceramic Society*, **42**, 571–581.

[1352] Youngs E. G. (1968) An estimation of sorptivity for infiltration studies from moisture moment considerations. *Soil Science*, **106**, 157–163.

[1353] Youngs E. G. (1972) An approximate evaluation of surface concentration during one-dimensional diffusion with surface flux a function of time for concentration-dependent diffusivity. *Journal of Physics D: Applied Physics*, **5**, 1592–1595.

[1354] Youngs E. G., Leeds-Harrison P. B. and Garnett R. S. (1994) Water uptake by aggregates. *European Journal of Soil Science*, **45**, 127–134.

[1355] Youngs E. G. and Peck A. J. (1964) Moisture profile development and air compression during water uptake by bounded porous bodies: 1. Theoretical introduction. *Soil Science*, **98**, 290–294.

[1356] Yssorche M.-P., Bigas J. P. and Ollivier J.-P. (1995) Mesure de la perméabilité à l'air des bétons au moyen d'un perméamètre à charge variable. *Materials and Structures*, **28**, 401–405.

[1357] Yu S. and Oguchi C. T. (2010) Role of pore size distribution in salt uptake, damage, and predicting salt susceptibility of eight types of Japanese building stones. *Engineering Geology*, **115**, 226–236.

[1358] Zanchetta L. M., Quattrone M., Aguilar R., Kahn H., Coelho A. C. and John V. M. (2020) Microstructures of building materials from Huaca De La Luna, Peru. *International Journal of Architectural Heritage*, **14**, 256–273.

[1359] Zehnder K. (1993) New aspects of decay caused by crystallization of gypsum. In M.-J. Thiel (ed.), *Conservation of stone and other materials*, Spon, London, pp 107–114.

[1360] Zehnder K. (1996) Gypsum efflorescence in the zone of rising damp. Monitoring of slow decay processes caused by crystallizing salts on wall paintings. In *Deterioration and conservation of stone*, 8th international congress, Berlin, Möller, Berlin, vol. 3, pp 1669–1678.

[1361] Zehnder K. and Arnold A. (1989) Crystal growth in salt efflorescence. *Journal of Crystal Growth*, **97**, 513–521.

[1362] Zellis M. K., Bell J. S. and Prunty L. (1998) Soil water content determination by Karl Fischer titration. *Soil Science Society of America Journal*, **62**, 257–262.

[1363] Zhang J. and Scherer G. W. (2011) Comparison of methods for arresting hydration of cement. *Cement and Concrete Research*, **41**, 1024–1036.

[1364] Zhang L. and Glasser F. P. (2000) Critical examination of drying damage to cement pastes. *Advances in Cement Research*, **12**, 79–88.

[1365] Zhang P., Wittmann F. H., Lura P., Müller H. S., Han S. and Zhao T. (2018) Application of neutron imaging to investigate fundamental aspects of durability of cement-based materials: A review. *Cement and Concrete Research*, **108**, 152–166.

[1366] Zhang P., Wittmann F. H., Zhao, T. J., Lehmann E. H. and Vontobel P. (2011) Neutron radiography, a powerful method to determine time-dependent moisture distributions in concrete. *Nuclear Engineering and Design*, **241**, 4758–4766.

[1367] Zhang Z. and Scherer G. W. (2017) Supercritical drying of cementitious materials. *Cement and Concrete Research*, **99**, 137–154.

[1368] Zhang Z. and Scherer G. (2018) Determination of water permeability for a moisture transport model with minimized batch effect. *Construction and Building Materials*, **191**, 193–205.

[1369] Zhang Z. and Scherer G. W. (2019) Evaluation of drying methods by nitrogen adsorption. *Cement and Concrete Research*, **120**, 13–26.

[1370] Zhou C., Ren F., Wang Z., Chen W. and Wang W. (2017) Why permeability to water is anomalously lower than that to many other fluids for cement-based material? *Cement and Concrete Research*, **100**, 373–384.

[1371] Zhou X., Desmarais G., Vontobel P., Carmeliet J. and Derome D. (2020) Masonry brick-cement mortar interface resistance to water transport determined with neutron radiography and numerical modeling. *Journal of Building Physics*, **44**, 251–271.

[1372] Zhu W. L., Evans B. and Bernabe Y. (1999) Densification and permeability reduction in hot-pressed calcite: a kinetic model. *Journal of Geophysical Research–Solid Earth*, **104**, 25501–25511.

[1373] Zinszner B. and Pellerin F. M. (2007) *A Geoscientist's Guide to Petrophysics*, Editions Technip, Paris.

[1374] Zsembery S., Waechter R. T. and McNeilly T. H. (2004) The expansion of clay bricks after 30 years and a method for its prediction. In *Proceedings of the seventh Australian masonry conference*, Newcastle, pp 182–191.

[1375] Zurmühl T. and Durner W. (1998) Determination of parameters for bimodal hydraulic functions by inverse modeling. *Soil Science Society of America Journal*, **62**, 874–880.

Index

Formation factor, 27–28, 34n20, 41,
113, 115n2, 265
Fourier regression equations, 319
Fractal objects, 27
Free water reservoir condition, 248–249
Freeze-thaw
cycling, 300, 302
damage, 272, 301, 327
durability of concrete, 299, 302
Freezing
damage due to, 277–279
omnidirectional, 301
effect on pore water, 296–297
Prout's experiments, 300–301
theories of damage by, 297–300
Frost damage, 296–302
caused by freezing, theories, 297–300
freezing on pore water, 296–297
Prout's experiments, 300–301
Fujita, S., 260n4

G

Gadolinium metal foil, 39
Galbraith, G. H., 106
Gamma-ray absorption, 98
Gamma-ray attenuation, 39, 187–188
Garden, G. K., 298
Gardner, D. R., 101
Gas; *see also* Diffusion
adsorption methods, 31
expansion pycnometry, 34n17
permeability measurements, 86–87
Gehlenite, 20
Geistlinger, H., 269
Gibbs function, 54–55
Giordini, M., 298
Glanville, W. H., 88, 90, 114
Glaser's method, 116n8
Glass fibre, 6
Grain consolidation model, 7
Gras, R., 269
Gravimetric analysis of drillings, 329
Gravimetric methods, 37
Gravitational effects on capillary rise,
151–155, 252–258
Gravitational potential, 55
Green, K. M., 192, 213, 285
Green, W. H., 114
Green-Ampt materials, 199
Green-Ampt model, of soil physics,
175n9
Green-Ampt soil, 176n16
Green-Ampt theory, 180, 186

Grossi, C. M., 24
Guggenheim-Anderson-de Boer (GAB)
function, 63–64, 73n25–74n25
Gulleys, 304
Gummerson, R. J., 59, 122, 166,
263–268, 294, 327
Gypsum, 25, 39, 106
blocks, 65
mineral dehydration in, 11
plaster, 213, 243
porosity in, 13, 25
slurry, 206

H

Hall, C., 294
Hamilton, A., 313
HAMSTAD project, 97, 98
HAM-Tools, 238n7
Handy, L. L., 175n10
Hanging column method, 59–60
Hart, D., 24
Hassler cell system, 80–85
Haynes, J. M., 296–297, 298
Hearn, N., 90–91
Heaslet, M. A., 120
Heaslet-Alksne method, 120–121, 156,
174n2, 341n1
Heat flow in drying, 247–248
Heavy-clay ceramics, 24
Height of rise
differential equation for, 316, 319
evaporating geometry on, 319
Sharp Front model, 315, 316, 317,
318, 319
steady-state, 317, 318, **318**
Heinrichs, K., 325
Helium pycnometry, 14–16
Hematite, 20, 21
Henry's law, 262, 264, 265, 270, 274,
302n1
Hens, H., 272
n-heptane, 125, 146
n-hexane, 39, 172
Hirschwald, J., 24–25, 114, 176n21,
176n22, 264, 270, 302n3
Hirschwald coefficient, 133, 162–163,
264, 270
Ho, D. W. S., 163
Hoff, W. D., 285, 294
Hollow shells, 33n4
Honeyborne, D. B., 24
Hooton, R. D., 88
Howard, W. E., *15*

For Product Safety Concerns and Information please contact our
EU representative GPSR@taylorandfrancis.com Taylor & Francis
Verlag GmbH, Kaufingerstraße 24, 80331 München, Germany